THE
DICTIONARY OF
CONTEMPORARY SLANG

With more than 5,000 racy and raffish colloquial
expressions — from America, Great Britain, Australia,
the Caribbean, and other English-speaking places

Tony Thorne

PANTHEON BOOKS 　 NEW YORK

For Lída and Saša

Copyright © 1990 by Tony Thorne

All rights reserved under International and Pan-American Copyright Conventions. Published in the United States by Pantheon Books, a division of Random House, Inc., New York. Originally published in Great Britain by Bloomsbury Publishing Ltd., London in 1990.

Library of Congress Cataloging-in-Publication Data
Thorne, Tony.
[Bloomsbury dictionary of contemporary slang]
The dictionary of contemporary slang: with more than 5000 racy and raffish colloquial expressions—from America, Great Britain, Australia, the Caribbean, and other English-speaking places / Tony Thorne.
p. cm.
Reprint. Originally published: Bloomsbury dictionary of contemporary slang. London: Bloomsbury Pub., 1990.
ISBN 0-679-73706-5
1. English language—Slang—Dictionaries. I. Title.
PE3721.T53 1991 427'.09—dc20 91-52645
CIP

Manufactured in the United States of America
First American Edition

1 3 5 7 9 B 8 6 4 2 0

Introduction

What is Slang?

The first problem confronting the compiler of a dictionary of slang is to define what slang does and does not include, firstly as an aid to compilation, and later for the benefit of the reader. Definitions chewed over in bar-room arguments or in learned debate may turn out to be red herrings; for example a symposium on slang held in France in 1989 broke up after several days without having arrived at a definition acceptable to even the majority of participants. Nevertheless, a multitude of possible definitions are available, ranging from 'illegitimate colloquial speech' and the language of 'low, illiterate or disreputable persons' to 'the plain man's poetry'. The American poet Carl Sandburg's memorable definition, ' . . . language that rolls up its sleeves, spits on its hands and goes to work . . . ', is often quoted, but is ultimately unhelpful, while the 1987 *Readers Digest Universal Dictionary* offers 'language peculiar to a group, argot or jargon'.

However, slang is not in fact jargon, a secret code, dialect, unacceptable usage or the idiom of everyday speech, although it may contain elements of all of these. To continue defining by exclusion, slang is *not* catchphrases, journalese, neologisms and buzzwords, or idiolect (the private language of an individual), although examples of all of these may be found within it. Looked at from a linguist's point of view, slang is a style category within the language, which occupies an extreme position on the spectrum of formality. Slang is at the end of the line; it lies beyond mere informality or colloquialism, where language is considered too racy, raffish, novel or unsavoury for use in conversation with strangers. Slang also includes forms of language through which speakers identify with or function within social sub-groups, ranging from surfers, schoolchildren and yuppies, to criminals, drinkers and fornicators.

All this may clarify the issue, but falls short of providing a universally applicable definition—one which can demonstrate beyond argument for instance that whereas in 1990 the adjective *sleazy* is a widespread and acceptable term, the noun **sleazeball** is slang and should (and does) appear in this dictionary. *Sleazy* itself was until recently considered to be a colloquialism by many speakers, and the borderline between what is considered to be colloquial and what is deemed to be slang is highly fluid, problematical and open to varied interpretation. The status of words varies in time: what was considered slang in the 1960s may by now have been assimilated into most people's vocabulary. It will vary according to the age, social background and the linguistic perceptions and prejudices of individual speakers, and, whatever linguists might say, most people think that they know what slang in general is, but their judgement about specific examples will differ.

In the pages that follow, the ultimate criterion for inclusion is the judgement of the compiler. Where there is doubt as to whether a term is true slang, or where the consensus on a particular term appears to have shifted, this is indicated in the text.

The lexicographer (characterized by Dr Johnson as a 'harmless drudge') is faced by other difficulties when working in the area of slang. An examination of the word 'slang' itself highlights some of these. Apart from the difficulty in defining the word as discussed above, the history and etymology of the term is uncertain, too—a feature shared by many of the expressions recorded in this book. When it was first used, 'slang' was probably a slang word itself, and as such may have existed for many years in the spoken language before becoming more widely known or being committed to paper. Its primary meaning when it first appeared in print in the mid 18th century seems to have been 'abuse'.

The origins of the word 'slang' are obscure and alternative derivations are on offer. This is likewise typical of the words in the following pages, and the lexicographer must beware of accepting too readily the explanations advanced by predecessors, however confidently they are expressed.

In the case of 'slang' the consensus is that it is related to the standard word 'sling' as used in picturesque archaic expressions such as 'to sling one's jaw', meaning 'to speak rowdily or insultingly' (itself perhaps inspired by cognate forms in other Germanic languages including *slenja kleften*, a synonymous phrase in Norwegian). A quite different theory is that the word is a corruption of the French word for language, *langue*, but this alteration goes against the normal sound patterns involved in anglicization.

I have noted in the text where I disagree with or doubt the standard etymologies for slang terms: in a few cases a new derivation is cautiously suggested.

Dictionaries of Slang

The first dictionary of English slang was Francis Grose's *Classical Dictionary of the Vulgar Tongue*, published in 1785. Since that date, several major works have been produced on the same subject, along with an increasing number of scholarly and popular glossaries and lexicons. Eric Partridge's monumental *Dictionary of Slang and Unconventional English* was last revised by Paul Beale in 1984; Robert L. Chapman's *New Dictionary of American Slang*, based on the earlier works by Wentworth and Flexner, appeared in Britain in 1987. Several interesting anthologies of new language have been published in the late 1980s, but these have treated slang only peripherally. Because of the frequently transitory nature of slang, there is a perennial need for updating such works.

As well as reflecting current speech accurately, the aim in compiling the *Bloomsbury Dictionary of Contemporary Slang* was to represent a fresh approach to the material itself. Previous compilers have been amateur enthusiasts, journalists or academics, each with their own idiosyncracies or preconceived opinions. Most of the existing dictionaries have a clear regional bias. Some have inappropriately excluded taboo items, others have drawn their examples mainly from fiction, the press and reference books and have excluded oral sources. Some have defined their headwords without further comment, a few have appeared distanced from, or disapproving of, the slang of certain social groups. The *Bloomsbury Dictionary of Contemporary Slang* will also inevitably reflect the obsessions and limitations of its originator, but I have attempted to combine the enthusiasms of a user and participator in the slang milieu with the more rigorous analysis demanded by the precepts of modern lexicography.

Having moved among mods, hippies and punks, and having observed **Sloane Rangers**, **preppies**, **Valley Girls** and **yuppies** at close quarters, I feel qualified to pass some comment on the peculiarities of their speech. Having some experience in branches of applied linguistics I am aware of the dangers of an entirely subjective approach (the risk of becoming, as a colleague damningly put it, 'self-authenticating').

Modern lexicography, the science, or rather, craft of dictionary-making, proceeds roughly as follows. One's choice of words to define should be based as far as possible on a survey of language in use, as well as the initial choices of the compiler. The terms chosen should be divided into different senses of meaning and each should be defined in natural, 'user-friendly' language. It is now thought preferable to go beyond the definition of a word or phrase and to look at how it 'behaves' in the language, in other words to comment on its overtones or nuances, to examine the unconscious associations and partly-perceived influences affecting the sound or meaning of the term. It is useful to read a term in its social context—who typically says it, in what circumstances and with what intention? Where possible, a history of the word and suggestions as to its origins should be given. The usage of the word should be illustrated by a quotation or example. Finally, when a word or phrase has been analysed in these ways, mention should be made of any interesting relationships with other words or groups of words.

The Bloomsbury Dictionary of Contemporary Slang

This dictionary aims to describe the core of English language slang in use between 1950 and 1990. These are the 5,000 or so terms and the 15,000 or so definitions most likely to be encountered by anyone reading modern fiction or journalism, listening to popular music, watching films and television or taking part in conversation. In a compendium of this size it is sometimes difficult to decide whether a particular item should be included or not. When all the criteria previously discussed have been applied, the final rule of thumb has been whether or not the word in question is inherently *interesting*. The words are here not only to help those wanting to 'de-code' difficult or unknown language or those hunting for colourful terms to use themselves, but also to amuse and distract the browser.

Although the collection has been assembled in Britain, I have made a conscious effort to include slang from the other anglophone areas. Whereas the most fertile source for many years was the United States, since the 1960s the often picturesque and sardonic idioms of Australia have been increasingly influential in Britain and North America. Disappointingly, speakers in the British Isles (with the possible exception of Northern Ireland and Eire) seem on the whole more reluctant to coin new and exciting forms than slang users in other parts of the English-speaking world. One theory is that as conscious or unconscious guardians of the 'parent tongue', they will prefer existing and orthodox patterns, even when expressing new ideas. American English has been influenced until very recently by the speech of people for whom it was not a first language, and by ethnic and regional variations. Australian speech has preserved and embellished earlier British and Irish eccentricities (notably dialect terms and rhyming slang), and **Jamaica talk** recycles even older forms.

In looking at English as a world language it is interesting too how the influence of the mass media in propagating slang has shifted subtly since the 1950s. At the time, American popular culture was dominant. Since the 1960s Britain has exported comedy and re-exported musical styles and youth cults to the USA. In the 1980s the Australian film and music industries have penetrated the US market, while Australian television series appear everyday in the UK. Rock, reggae, soul and disco music have spread American and Carribean slang worldwide.

Slang Today

Some general tendencies can be discerned in 20th-century English slang. The main categories of slang remain what they have always been, with one or two exceptions: the language of crime, or 'cant' as it used to be known, provides a large number of entries (**grass, snitch, squeal, banged-up**, etc.); sex, alcohol and drugs continue to feature strongly (witness the many euphemisms for sexual intercourse, the hundreds of synonyms for being drunk and the proliferation of alternative terms for illicit substances and the states of intoxication they produce); parts of the body (particularly the breasts and penis) and peculiarities of physique and personality are also popular sources. The argot of schools and colleges produces a wealth of slang terms, as do the youth cults of the last forty years. The slang of the workplace continues to be significant, although the workplace may now be a computer workstation or merchant bank rather than a factory, office, or farm. With the exceptions of the euphemisms of Vietnam and a few terms highlighted by the Falklands war, armed-services slang seems to have dwindled in relevance. The media and entertainment industry continue to contribute and promote novelty in language; a relatively new phenomenon is the free use of slang in the quality as well as the tabloid press (all types of newspaper and magazine were used in the preparation of citations for this dictionary).

Much slang is simply the substitution of more forceful, emotive or humorous forms for standard words—**pooch** or **mutt** for dog, **dogs** for feet, **rug** for wig or toupee, etc. In this context it is interesting to see how older slang expressions are often revived—in the money-conscious 1980s, many obsolescent synonyms such as **pelf, rhino, ackers, moolah, spondulicks** and **dosh** reappeared; in the drug world **dope** was replace during the 1950s by terms such as **charge, shit, gear**, etc and then resurfaced in the 1970s. Suceeding generations have their own terms of approbation—**fab** gives way to **groovy, brill** and **wicked**. In successive eras, slang reflects society's preoccupations (the 1960s were characterized by words of euphoria, sex, drugs and popular music; the later 1970s by epithets applied to misfits and unfortunates—**wally, nurd, wimp**, and the 1980s by references to money, work and consumerist sub-cultures). Who in the 1960s would have predicted that **serious** would become a fashionable buzzword twenty years later? On current evidence, adolescent slang in Britain seems to reflect a return to childish, schoolchildren's humour (**Desmond, love blobs**) and to native forms such

v

as rhyming slang (**Alans, porkies, farmers**), as opposed to the more worldly and cosmopolitian flavour of the 1970s. Fortunately, the use of wit by the anonymous coiners of slang is not dead—there are plenty of examples in the text, of which the archaic **love-in-a-punt** and the more recent **Archer** spring to mind.

Sources

To compile this dictionary I consulted both primary and secondary sources. The primary sources were the users of slang themselves who were interviewed, as were other informants such as teachers, colleagues and parents of slang users and 'connoisseurs' or collectors of slang. I also carried out 'fieldwork' which essentially consisted of eavesdropping on conversations, the contents of which the speakers were unlikely to recall accurately in an interview. A certain amount of first-hand information on earlier usage was supplied from my own notes and diaries, supplemented by similar extracts kindly made available by friends and acquaintances. A selective survey was made of written sources, including magazines, newspapers, comic books and novels. Films, television broadcasts and song lyrics were also consulted. Existing glossaries complied by researchers or journalists were inspected, but treated with caution: there has sometimes been a tendency for these authorities to be misled by their informants, just as language reported by the press (for example, the many post-yuppie acronyms) may be invented or embellished in the reporting, and slang occuring in fictional settings (the works of Raymond Chandler, Barry Humphries and Johnny Speight are examples) may not always be authentic. Finally, the data collected was checked against existing reference sources.

If one overall sense of a term is commonly subdivided into several slightly different meanings, these are indicated by LETTERS (in **bold** type: **a, b, c**, etc).

The headword, part of speech and regional label are followed by a DEFINITION (in roman typeface).

This in turn is followed by more information about the use and origin of the term (in roman typeface). In these explanations foreign words are placed in *italics* and slang terms found elsewhere in the dictionary are shown in **bold** (these act as cross references throughout the dictionary).

Many definitons are followed by an ILLUSTRATIVE PHRASE or sentence (in *italics*). If this example is an actual citation, its source follows in brackets.

Acknowledgements

For help in the preparation of the dictionary the following acknowledgements are due:
First and foremost, grateful thanks must go to Ray Granger who, during crucial stages of the project, performed the demanding role of amanuensis, editor and advisor, as well as allowing his extensive archives to be plundered. Also in the UK, particular thanks go to Kit Gleave, Jamie Morse, Stephanie Fayerman, Chip Granger, Gordon Lochhead, Gerald Miller, Bill Boyes, Terry Pizzey, Chris Pape and John Hackney; in Australia, Elizabeth and Chris Corbel, and Robyn Marsh; in the USA, Nick Harrison, Dan Rowe, Ellen Jo Schur and William Winship III; and at Bloomsbury, Kathy Rooney, Tracey Smith and Sian Facer.

Suggestions from Readers

This survey of English slang cannot be exhaustive; it is certain that many colourful and interesting expressions in use in many parts of the English-speaking community have so far escaped the collector's net. It is intended that this dictionary should be extended and updated and we would be very grateful for the help of readers in this task, Contributors, who will be acknowledged, should contact the publishers with slang terms or definitions, ideally adding details of where and when the word or phrase was used, and a direct quotation if possible. Comments or criticisms based on the current text would also be most welcome.

Tony Thorne
London May 1990

How to Use this Book

A typical entry in the dictionary will contain the components described below (with the typefaces explained in brackets):

The HEADWORDS are entered in alphabetical order (in **primary bold** face), together with any variant spellings or alternative forms.)

Next the PART OF SPEECH is given (in *italics*): these have been somewhat simplified so that an adjoctival phrase appears as an adjective, noun phrase as noun.

Unless a word is used in all parts of the English-speaking world, it is given a REGIONAL LABEL (in *italics*). This indicates the country of origin, or the country in which the term is most prevalent.

If a particular term has more that one quite separate meaning, these meanings are NUMBERED (in **bold** type).

A

aardvark *n British*
hard work, onerous tasks. A probably ephemeral pun heard among university students in the late 1980s.
- *'They're giving us too much bloody aardvark, that's the problem.'*
(Recorded, undergraduate, London University, 1988).

'abdabs *n pl British*
See **screaming (h)abdabs**.

Abdul *n*
a pejorative nickname for a Turk or other person of middle-eastern origin. The term is particularly prevalent in Australia where it is used to refer to immigrants.

abo *n Australian*
an Aboriginal. A standard shortening used by whites which is now considered condescending or abusive: it is often part of offensive comparisons, as in *'to smell like an abo's armpit/abo's jockstrap'*.

A.C.A.B. *phrase British*
an abbreviation of the catchphrase 'All coppers are bastards!' which appeared in graffiti, football and demonstration chants and on tattoos, leather jackets, etc., especially in the 1950s and 1960s.

Acapulco Gold *n*
a strain of marihuana or **grass** from the foothills above Acapulco in West-central Mexico. The golden leaves, imported into the USA in large quantities from the late 1960s, are sought after for their supposed potency and quality.

AC/DC *adj*
bisexual. From the label on electrical appliances indicating that they can be used with either alternating or direct current. The slang term originated in the USA and spread to Britain around 1960.

ace *n*
1 a best friend or good person. Used by males to other males, usually as a greeting or a term of endearment. In this sense the term probably spread from black American street-gangs in the 1950s to working-class whites in the USA, Australia and, to a lesser extent, Britain.
- *'Hey, ace!'*
2 *Australian* the anus. By association with **arse** and the black mark on a playing card.
3 a a single item or person, in the restricted jargon of many different trades. In street language, especially in the USA, the word is used to refer to an individual pill, banknote, etc.
   b *American* a one-dollar bill.

ace, ace out *vb*
1 to outmanoeuvre, outwit or defeat.
- *'I had it all figured, but those guys aced me!'*
(*The A Team*, US TV series, 1985).
2 *American* to succeed, win or score very highly.

1

- *'She aced out/aced the test.'*

ace, aces *adj*

excellent, first class. Used extensively since the late 1950s in the USA, since the mid-1960s in Australia, and by the 1970s, especially by teenagers, in Britain. The origin of the term is obviously in the highest value playing card, the meaning now extended from 'best' to 'smartest', 'cleverest', etc.

- *'An ace car/that film was really ace/she's aces!'*

ace in the hole *n*

an advantage held in reserve until it is needed. From American stud-poker terminology, an ace (the most valuable card) dealt face down and not revealed.

aces *n pl*

See **ace**.

acey-deucy *adj American*

both good and bad, of uncertain quality. The term is at least pre-World War II, but still heard occasionally, especially from middle-aged or elderly speakers. It comes from a card game similar to backgammon in which aces are high and deuces (twos) are low.

acher *n*

See **acre**.

acid *n*

1 LSD-25, the synthetic hallucinogenic drug. From the full name, Lysergic Acid Diethylamide. This has been the standard term by which users refer to the drug since its first popularity in California in 1965, in spite of the appearance of more picturesque but ephemeral alternatives. In the late 1980s, adherents of the **acid house** cult adopted the word as a slogan (usually a cry of *a-c-e-e-e-d!*) and to refer to LSD or **ecstasy**.

2 British sarcasm, snide comments, or cheeky exaggeration, especially in the expression *'come the old acid'*, popular in working-class usage in the 1950s and 60s and still heard. In such phrases as *'his acid comments'* the adjectival meaning is similar, but cannot be described as slang.

- *'Don't come the old acid with me!'*

3 Australian *'put the acid on'*, to demand money or information (from someone).

acid casualty *n*

a person supposedly suffering from impaired faculties, incoherence or derangement as a result of taking the drug LSD or other hallucinogens. The term was used particularly by young rock-journalists in the mid-to late 1970s when referring contemptuously to the remnants of the hippy movement.

acid flash *n*

a sudden recurrence of a much earlier experience of the drug LSD. Some users are disturbed months or years after taking the drug by sudden disorientation which lasts from seconds to hours and which may or may not be due to its effects.

acid head, acid freak *n*

a user, especially a heavy or habitual user, of the drug LSD. The terms are not pejorative, and were used from the late 1960s to the mid-1970s by takers of LSD or other hallucinogens about themselves and each other.

acid house *n*

a youth cult involving synthetic electronic dance-music (**house**) and the taking of euphoric hallucinogens such as **ecstasy** and LSD (**acid**). This fashion, celebrated in clubs and large impromptu parties, and with garish clothing and lighting effects, succeeded hip-hop, **rap** and other fads in 1988.

2

'*A-c-e-e-e-d!*' (an elongated version of **acid**) was a rallying cry of celebrants, shouted and written on walls.
- '*The redeeming features of last year's summer of Acid-House were that it generated energy and ideas for both the fashion and the music industry.*'
  (*Independent*, 11 July 1989).

acid rock n
guitar-based electric rock-music of the late 1960s and early 70s, supposedly influenced by, or trying to recreate, the effects of LSD. This is strictly speaking commercial jargon rather than a slang term, as it was probably coined, and certainly used, by the music industry rather than musicians or devotees.

acid test n
a party or informal ritual at which a group of people take food and/or drink laced with LSD. The expression and the practice were originated by Ken Kesey and the Merry Pranksters, a group of hedonistic travellers in the USA in the early 1960s who were successors to the beats and precursors of the hippies.
- '*The Electric Kool-Aid Acid Test.*'
  (Title of a book by Tom Wolfe, 1969).

acid trip n
a period under the influence of the drug LSD, or **acid** (which produces an altered state of awareness and, sometimes, hallucinations). The experience lasts 4–6 hours at an average dose.

ackers n British
money. The word, which has been in armed-forces and working-class use since the 1920s, has been revived, in common with synonyms such as **pelf**, rhino, etc., for jocular use in the 1980s by middle-class speakers. It comes

from the Egyptian word *akka*: a coin worth one *piastre*.

acre, acher n
1 buttock(s). In this sense the word is common in Australia, normally in the singular.
2 testicle(s). Usually in the plural, this sense of the word is typically used by British schoolboys.
  Both senses of both words stem from the simple play on the word 'ache' which has formed part of many different puns and dirty jokes, during the last forty years, involving sensitive parts of the (male) anatomy.
- '*I told the estate agent I couldn't afford any land, so he kicked me in the balls and said, "There's a couple of achers for you".*'
  (Schoolboy joke, London, 1965).

action n
something desirable or stimulating. Typically used as a euphemism for sex, profit, available drugs or fun and excitement. The word is often used in the phrase '*a piece of the action*', meaning a share in what is going on, or '(*let's go*) *where the action is*'; the most exciting place to be. This use of the word may derive from the military sense of 'to see action', meaning to be involved in fighting. Originally an Americanism, this usage was adopted in Britain in the late 1960s, and is now a widespread colloquialism.

action man n British
a devotee of military exercises or strenuous physical activities, or someone who makes a show of (relentless) energy. The term is applied derisively, originally by members of the armed forces to unpopular or excessively **gung-ho** colleagues, and now by extension to anyone who is showily or mindlessly **macho**. The satirical magazine *Private Eye* referred to Prince An-

3

drew by this name in 1986 and 1987. The origin of this piece of sarcasm is the 'Action Man' doll – a poseable commando scale model in full kit sold to children in Britain since the 1960s.

- 'Right little action man i'n' 'e? 'E simply wants to be prepared when the east wind blows 'ot.'

(Minder, British TV series, 1988).

actor n

a person who is good at playing a role, or bluffing, especially in order to deceive a victim or fool the authorities. In these specific senses the word is used typically by inmates of institutions or members of the underworld in the USA.

- 'We need an actor for this job.'
- 'I tell you, the guy's an actor.'

A.D. n

drug addict. From the first two letters of 'addict', or a reversal of the initials of 'drug addict' to avoid confusion with 'District Attorney'. The term was quite popular among addicts themselves and the police in the USA. (In Britain **D.A.** was the 1960s vogue version.)

adam n British

the drug MDA; methyl diamphetamine. Adam is an acronym from the initials, used by middle-class Londoners during the vogue for the drug since the mid-1980s. MDA is more commonly known to the press and non-users as **ecstasy**; to users it is also **E, X, xtc, Epsom salts**.

adam and eve vb British

to believe. Well-established rhyming slang which is still heard among working-class Londoners and middle-class imitators, usually in the expression of astonishment 'Would you adam 'n' eve it?'.

aerated adj

angrily over-excited or agitated. Perhaps originated by educated speakers who were familiar with the technical senses of aerate (to supply the blood with oxygen or to make effervescent), but usually used nowadays by less sophisticated speakers who may mispronounce it as 'aeriated'.

- 'Now, don't get all aerated.'

af, aff n South African

a black African. The shortening is normally used dismissively or pejoratively, and usually in the plural. The term was more widespread in the 1960s than today. It is less offensive than the synonymous **kaffir** or **munt**.

african lager n British

Guinness. A jocular London term of the 1970s, coined in the tradition of the earlier **african woodbine**. Lager has become the most popular beer served in southern English pubs; Guinness is of course black. The synonymous term 'Nigerian lager' has also been heard from the late 1980s.

african woodbine n British

a cigarette containing cannabis, a **joint** or **reefer**. Woodbines are a well-known and long-established brand of cheap cigarette, particularly popular in the 1950s and 1960s.

afro n

a hairstyle consisting of a mass of tight curls which was worn by Afro-Caribbeans and imitated (often by perming) by white **hippies**, particularly between 1967 and 1970.

afterbirth n

1 rhubarb (raw or stewed) in armed forces and school slang in Britain and America.

2 American excessive paperwork, **bumf**. A rare usage.

agate n

1 a marble (as used in children's games).

2 agates testicles. A usage which is archaic in Britain but which survives in Australian speech. (**Marbles** is a more common synonym.)

aggie n British

a marble (as used in children's games). An old term, usually for a striped marble, still heard in the 1950s. From agate, the banded stone from which marbles were originally made.
See **alley**.

aggravation n British

serious trouble, victimization or mutual harassment. A colloquial extension of the standard meaning of the word, used by police and the underworld. Aggravation is, like **bother** and **seeing-to**, a typical example of menacing understatement as practised in London working-class speech.

aggro n British and Australian

aggravation. Originally the slang term was a euphemism for threatened or actual violence, offered typically by skinheads, although it is not clear whether they or their (typically **hippy**) victims first adopted the shortened form at the end of the 1960s. (Whichever is the case, the word is a derivation of aggravation in its colloquial sense as used by police and criminals since the 1950s.) Aggro, like **bother**, is a typical example of the use of menacing understatement in British working-class slang. The word was soon taken up by other users and in informal English has now reverted to something like its original unspecific meaning of annoyance or trouble. In Australian usage aggro can be used as an adjective as in 'I guess I was a bit aggro last night'.

aggro adj American

wonderful, excellent. This probably ephemeral term was recorded among teenagers in New York and California in late 1987. It is probably based on a misunderstanding or deliberate shifting in the meaning of the earlier British term.

a-head n

a user of the drug amphetamine. An American term employed by those taking **speed** or **pep pills**, which was occasionally heard in Britain in the late 1960s and early 1970s. **Speedfreak** was a more popular alternative in both Britain and the USA.

a-hole n American

a euphemism for **asshole**, usually in the literal rather than metaphorical sense.

alm archie at the armitage vb Australian

(of a male) to urinate. A later version of the widely known **point percy at the porcelain**, popularized in Barry Humphries' Barry McKenzie cartoon series. ('Armitage Ware' is a brand name of toilet bowls.)

aimed adj American

identified, singled out, and/or victimized. A slang version of 'targeted' which probably originated in the argot of black street-gangs. It is now used in milder contexts by teenagers.

- 'There's no way we'll get out of this; we've been aimed . . .'

airball n American

a dim-witted, eccentric or unpleasant person. This mildly pejorative term of the 1980s is a combination of **airhead** and the more offensive **hairball**.

airbrained adj American

silly, frivolous, empty-headed. Slightly less derogatory than the noun **airhead**, this term has not been imported into Britain to any significant extent, perhaps because of possible confusion with 'hare-brained' which is still in widespread use.

- '*She's not just some airbrained bimbo, you know.*'

air-dance n

death by hanging. A sardonic euphemism in police and underworld use until the abolition of capital punishment in Britain in 1965.

airhead n

a fool; a silly, empty-headed person. An American teenager's term heard since the mid-1970s, used for instance by **Valley Girls**; it has been adopted by British teenagers in the 1980s.

- '*Debbie's a total airhead.*'
- '*The usual crowd of airheads, phonies, deadlegs, posers, bimbos, wallies, wannabees, hangers-on and gatecrashers . . .*'

(Christena Appleyard, *Daily Mirror*, 11 May 1989).

air hose n American

shoes, typically loafers (leather moccasins), worn without socks. A **preppie** term for a preppie sartorial convention, punning on the American sense of 'hose' meaning socks, stockings, etc. and the compressed air pipe at a filling station.

a.k.a., aka preposition, n

also known as, alias, in other words. Initials used by law enforcement agencies in the USA when giving suspect's aliases in official bulletins. The term was extended in America to a more general 'also' or 'alternatively' in writing and in speech (it is spoken as the three letters), and is sometimes used as

a noun as in '*what's his a.k.a.?*'. In Britain a.k.a. was picked up by rock music journalists in the 1970s but has not entered the spoken jargon.

à la adj British

pretentious, excessively refined or elegant. A term used typically by middle-aged and middle-class speakers in the 1950s and early 1960s, now colloquial but rare. It is usually said with envy or disapproval, or both, and derives from the French *à la*; in the style of, or *à la mode*; stylish, in fashion.

- '*They had a proper white wedding with a carriage and musicians; all very à la!*'

(Recorded, middle-aged woman, London, 1986).

Alan Whickers, Alans n pl British

knickers, panties. The terms are non-working-class rhyming slang, heard among young people, particularly students, in the 1970s and 1980s. The reference is to Alan Whicker, a well-known punctilious and dapper television interviewer.

- '*There was this huge pair of Alan Whickers hanging on the line.*'

alec, aleck n

a swindler's victim, dupe. This term from the early 20th century is still heard in the USA and Australia. It is not clear whether alec derives from 'smart alec' or vice versa. The word was used for instance in the film *House of Games* (1987, David Mamet), which dramatizes the world of small-time American gamblers.

aled, aled-up adj British

drunk. A mild and acceptable term which although short and to-the-point can be used in polite company or family newspapers. The expressions probably originated in the North of England

where ale has been and remains a common all-purpose word for beer.
- *'He's aled again.'*

alf n Australian

a common, foolish person. In the 1960s this term briefly vied with **ocker** as the generic term for uncouth manhood.

alfalfa n American

1 tobacco.
2 money.
3 marihuana. The plant alfalfa is widely used as cattle-feed in the USA. The slang term is typically heard in underworld and prison jargon.

alkie n

an alcoholic, especially one who lives rough or frequents the streets. The obvious term, which usually carries overtones of contempt, has been widespread in the USA at least since the Depression; it was adopted after World War II in Australia and since the 1960s has been in limited use in Britain.

alley, allie n British

a marble (as used in children's games). Like **aggie**, the word is approximately a hundred years old and refers to a pale or white marble. Although rarely heard today, these terms probably survive where the traditional game is still played. The most likely origin of the term is a shortening of 'alabaster', from which some Victorian marbles were made.

alley apple n American

a lump of horse manure. A less common version of the expression **road apple**, which is now an international English term.

alley cat n

a person who frequents the streets, particularly at night, a carouser, roisterer or promiscuous person. Those using this term, usually with disapproval, may have the cliché *'to have the morals of an alley cat'* in mind. Alley cat may be applied to either sex and, although heard in Britain and Australia since the 1960s, is originally pre-World-War II American.

alleycat vb

to prowl the streets, particularly late at night.
- *'There's Arthur Smith alleycatting around, trying to pick up chicks.'*
  (Kit Hollerbaoh, The 39,000 Steps, Channel 4 documentary on the Edinburgh Festival, July 1989).

alligator shoes/boots n pl

old footwear with the toes gaping open. A jocular play on (expensive and luxurious) alligator-skin shoes.

all mouth and trousers adj British

blustering and boastful, showing off without having the qualities to justify it. A commonly heard dismissive phrase, typically said by women about a loud or assertive man. There is a suggestion that this is a corruption of a more logical, but rarely heard expression, *'all mouth and no trousers'*, meaning full of talk but deficient in the sexual area. A less racy version is *'all talk and no action'*. There is an analogy with other colourful expressions, now mostly archaic, such as *'all my eye and Betty Martin'*, meaning nonsense, and more abusive versions such as **all piss and wind**.
- *'Oh him! He's all mouth and trousers, that one.'*

all over the shop/show/lot/ ballpark adj, adv

disorganized, in chaos or disarray. The first two versions are British, the

7

last two American. This is a more colourful extension into slang of the colloquial phrase '*all over the place*', and the first version at least dates from the 19th century. ('Shop' is a working-class catch-all for any workplace.)

all piss and wind *adj*

full of bluster and noise, but without real substance. This expression can have a similar meaning to **all mouth and trousers**, but can be applied for instance to a politician's speech or a theatrical performance, as well as to an individual. '*All piss and vinegar*' is a rarer synonym.

all right, awright *interjection*
American

an exclamation of recognition, greeting, approval or admiration. The 'right' is emphasized, high-pitched and elongated when shouted. Used in this way the phrase was originally black American; it was picked up by whites, especially hippies, in the late 1960s.

almond, almond rock *n*
British

penis. London working-class rhyming slang for **cock**, inspired by the almond rock cakes eaten in the early 20th century. The terms, like the sweetmeat, are now rarely encountered.

See also **almonds, almond rocks**.

almonds, almond rocks *n pl*
British

socks. A London rhyming-slang term which is still in use. (Almond rock cakes were a popular working-class treat early in the 20th century.)

amber fluid, amber nectar *n*

beer, Australian lager. A facetious euphemism used by Australians in the 1970s which was popularized in Britain first by Barry Humphries' *Barry*

McKenzie comic strip, then by TV advertisements featuring the actor Paul Hogan for Australian beer in the 1980s. The term was enthusiastically adopted by some middle-class British drinkers, themselves fond of mock-pompous coinages.

ambidextrous *adj*

bisexual, AC/DC. An obvious pun on the conventional meaning of ambidextrous, using the word as a sexual euphemism.

ambulance chaser *n*

a lawyer, literally one who specializes in claiming on behalf of accident victims. The phrase is also applied, facetiously or critically, to any lawyer who is known for sharp practice or unethical methods. This term was originally American (dating from the beginning of the century) but is now employed in other English-speaking areas.

- '*My daddy's a lawyer. Well, we often say he's an ambulance chaser.*'
  (Recorded, young woman, Chicago, 1983).

amp *n*

1 an ampoule (of a drug). An obvious shortening by drug users.

- '*I scored a couple of amps of meth*[edrine].'

2 an amplifier. A common shortening used by musicians and hi-fi enthusiasts since the 1960s.

- '*He rammed his guitar into the amp.*'

'ampsteads *n pl British*

teeth. Cockney rhyming slang referring to the London beauty spot Hampstead Heath. The term (which is still heard) is invariably used with the dropped aspirate.

8

- '*A lovely set of 'ampsteads/kicked in the 'ampsteads.*'

amscray *vb*
scram, go away. One of the few examples of backslang or pig Latin which is actually used in speech, albeit rarely. The word is a pre-World-War II Americanism which has been heard in Australia and in Britain since the 1950s.
- '*We'd better amscray before he gets back.*'

amyl *n*
amyl nitrite (sometimes called amyl nitrate), a very powerful stimulant drug inhaled from a broken phial, or **popper**. Amyl nitrite is prescribed for the treatment of angina pectoris; it has been taken for fun since the 1950s, and for its supposed sexually stimulating effects, especially by **gay** men, since the late 1970s.

anchors *n pl British*
brakes. Originally part of the jargon of pre-war professional drivers. The term was popular with some middle-class motorists throughout the 1950s and 1960s, usually in the phrase '*slam on the anchors*'; to brake suddenly. It now sounds rather dated.

the Andrew *n British*
the navy. A dated term which is a shortening of 'Andrew Miller' (or 'Andrew Millar'). The eponymous Andrew is said to have been a press-ganger whose name was taken as a nickname for a warship and later for the whole service.

'andsome *adj British*
See **handsome**.

angel *n British*
1 in theatrical parlance, a financial backer of a production.

2 a nurse, in colloquial usage.
3 a dot on a radar screen. The term was commonly used in this context until the late 1950s.

angel, angela, angelina *n*
a passive male homosexual. These are slang terms used by homosexuals themselves and (usually pejoratively) by heterosexuals. The words may originate as terms of affection, as feminine nicknames, or possibly from earlier slang usage denoting a (female) prostitute.

angel dust *n*
the drug **PCP**. A powdered (usually home-made) version of an animal tranquilizer which is smoked or sniffed through a tube and which produces in the user unpredictable and extreme physical and psychological effects. Users are capable of acts of violence, hallucinations and periods of imperviousness to pain and superhuman strength. PCP is easy to produce in home laboratories and became a severe social problem in US cities after 1975, principally among poorer teenagers. Fears of its spread to Britain and elsewhere were groundless. Its milieu is now largely given over to **crack**.
- '*For 15 years Washington has been struggling with abuse of PCP, also known as Angel Dust.*'
(*Independent*, 24 July 1989).

anglo *n American*
a person of (mainly) anglo-saxon ethnic origin. The term came into widespread use in the 1970s, especially among Hispanics. This was the first attempt by Americans from other ethnic backgrounds to categorize white anglo-saxons as a sub-group. (**WASP** was first coined by wasps themselves; **honky**, **pinkie**, etc. are terms of abuse.)
- '*They're mainly anglos out on Long Island these days.*'

9

(Recorded, suburban New Yorker, 1977).

• '"The Milagro Beanfield War" [is] based on John Nichol's novel about greedy Anglo developers encroaching on the land and water rights of New Mexican mountain men.'
(Observer Magazine, 3 April 1988).

animal n

a brutal or crude person, a person of disgusting habits or behaviour. Although this is an obvious term of disapproval, probably prompted by such phrases as 'animal instincts', it has only achieved relative popularity in Australia and Britain since the mid-1970s (perhaps because it is typically used of men and coincided with increasing criticism of male insensitivity). Since the 1950s in the USA (and more recently in Australia) 'animal' has typically been used with grudging admiration by men describing other men's excesses.

animal house n American

any dwelling, but especially a college fraternity house, whose occupants are excessively dirty and rowdy. This late 1950s campus term was revived by the film National Lampoon's Animal House, starring the late John Belushi in the role of a typical animal in 1978.

animal night/act n Australian

a planned or self-conscious bout of bad behaviour or excess. The term is typically used (by and about males) with pride or admiration rather than distaste.

ankle vb

to walk, stroll, saunter. A raffish expression heard in the USA and occasionally in Britain in the 1980s.

• 'Let's ankle down to the off-licence.'

ankle-biter n

a child, usually baby or a toddler. Commonly used with mock distaste by parents, sometimes with real distaste by others, ankle-biter was heard in all social classes in Britain and Australia in the late 1970s and 1980s. An alternative is leg-biter or rug rat.

annihilated adj

helplessly drunk, drugged or exhausted. A middle-class teenager's colloquial expression, popular in the 1970s and 1980s.

anorak n British

an unfashionable, studious or tedious person, usually a young male. A campus expression from the 1980s, based on the characteristic dress of these fellow-students. A sub-genre of jangling guitar pop music, supposedly beloved of such students, was dubbed 'anorak rock' in the music press in the mid-1980s.

• 'An anorak is one of those boring gits who sit at the front of every lecture with their Pringle jumpers asking the lecturer their clever questions.'
(Graffito in the toilets at King's College, London University, July 1988).

ante up vb

to pay one's contribution, put one's money in the common pot. This expression, not to be confused with 'up the ante', comes from the preliminary stage in a poker game when one or all of the players must put a stake in the pot. By extension ante up is sometimes used to mean settle accounts or (reluctantly) hand over something demanded.

• 'OK, you guys, it's time to ante up.'

antsy adj

a nervous, jumpy, agitated.

● 'She's been getting a little antsy lately – wants me to leave my wife.' (The Secret of my Success, US film, 1987).
b eager for sex.

Both senses of antsy are derived from the older, humorous colloquial expression 'to have ants in one's pants' (meaning to be restless or agitated). Antsy is a fairly common and inoffensive term in the USA and Australia, but rare in Britain.

ape n

a primitive, brutal person, invariably male. Used, for instance, by women to or about a clumsy, slow or aggressive man, the word may also refer to thugs or bodyguards.

ape(shit) adj, adv

out of control, berserk, used especially in the expression **go ape**; the image is of a person reduced to a primal state, either by infatuation, excitement or, especially, anger. An American teenagers' term from the late 1950s now in general currency.
● 'He's apeshit about her.'
● 'I go ape ev'ry time I see you smile.' ('I Go Ape', written and recorded by Neil Sedaka, 1960).
● 'After I'd left my last school, I pinched a wallet full of credit cards and went apeshit in about five different counties.' (Sunday Times magazine, Stephen Fry, August 1989).

ape-hangers n pl

extra-high handlebars for motorbikes or bicycles. The style was popularized by **bikers** in the USA in the 1950s, spreading to Britain where **rockers, greasers** and schoolchildren had adopted the style and the term by about 1959.

apparatchik n

a flunky, bureaucrat, 'yes-man'. An educated derogatory term adopted directly from Russian – in which it means a member of the party apparatus. The word is now colloquial.

apple-polisher n

a flatterer, someone who curries favour. The term comes from the image of the ingratiating pupil who polishes an apple carefully before presenting it to a teacher. The tradition of 'an apple for the teacher' was really practised in the rural USA before World War II, but the term is common in all English-speaking areas. It is sometimes in the form of a verb as in 'she's been apple-polishing again'; in Britain it is often shortened to **polisher**.
● 'I had few qualifications for Hollywood; I was immoderately slothful, had no facility for salesmanship or apple-polishing, and possessed a very low boiling point.' (S.J. Perelman, quoted in Groucho, Harpo, Chico & sometimes Zeppo, Joe Adamson, 1973).

apples n pl

1 breasts.
2 testicles.

Apples, like almost all other round fruits, have readily been used as euphemisms for these bodily parts. This type of metaphor may occur as a spontaneous coinage in any English-speaking community.

apples adj Australian

fine, perfect, OK. Often used in the expression 'she's apples', meaning 'everything is all right'. This use of the word may originate in 'apples and rice' or 'apples and spice', obsolete British and Australian rhyming slang for 'nice'.

apples and pears n pl British

stairs. One of the best known examples of Cockney rhyming slang which, although authentic, is rarely heard these days.

April fools n pl British

tools. Cockney rhyming slang still heard occasionally in workshops, garages and factories.

April showers n pl British

flowers. An item of London working-class rhyming slang which survives in market traders' jargon.

arab n

1 a wild or shiftless person. In Britain and Australia this is generally a derogatory term, although it can be used semi-affectionately, as by parents to unkempt children. This usage, no longer consciously racist, stems from the contempt felt by some members of the armed forces, stationed in colonies or protectorates, for 'street arabs', or from envious suspicion of the supposedly undisciplined lifestyle of the desert arabs.

2 a foreigner. A catch-all term generally used by uneducated speakers.

Archer n British

£2,000. A probably ephemeral invention by an anonymous wit in the tradition of a **monkey**, a pony, etc. It refers to the sum paid by the author and Tory politician Jeffrey Archer to Miss Monica Coughlan, a prostitute, to enable her to go abroad. Her return in 1987 resulted in Mr Archer bringing a libel case against the News of the World, which he won. (The synonym **Jeffrey** was also heard.)

● 'The usual two Archers in a plain envelope.'
(Weekending, BBC Radio 4, 9 March 1990).

argie n, adj British

(an) Argentinian. Although the abbreviation has an affectionate rather than abusive ring, it was the only epithet available to verbal attackers during the Anglo-Argentinian conflict over the Falkland Islands in 1982.

● 'Kill an Argie.'
(Headline in the Sun newspaper, 1982).

Aristotle, arry, arris n

1 a bottle. Rhyming slang, probably dating from the 19th century, but still occasionally heard in the London area and in Australia.

2 'arris (usually in the sense of 'courage, nerve').

arm n

1 British power, influence, coercion. A colloquial coinage on the lines of 'hold' or 'grip' or 'strong-arm'.

● 'This should give us some arm.'

2 a rare version of **short arm**.

armpit n

a very unpleasant place. The word usually forms part of the expression 'the armpit of the universe'; that is, the most unpleasant place in existence (a milder version of 'arsehole of the universe').

'arris n

1 backside, buttocks. A cockney elaboration of **arse** sometimes adopted by middle-class speakers who want to avoid the offensive term.

● 'A kick in the 'arris.'

2 courage, nerve (sense 3 of **arse**). A London working-class term.

● 'Loads of 'arris.'

Both senses derive from a double rhyme; 'arris from **Aristotle**, meaning bottle, while 'bottle and glass' gives **arse**.

12

arrows n pl British

darts; the game and the implements. This is the darts player's own term, although, since the game became a televised sport in the late 1980s, there are signs that the experts are abandoning the term to garrulous amateurs and returning to the simple reference 'darts'. This is a tendency in many areas of private language, once the mystique of the jargon has been breached.

● 'Can we have the arrows please, landlord?'

arse n British

1 backside, buttocks, anus. This word is not, strictly speaking, slang, but an ancient term ('aers' in Anglo Saxon, descended from Germanic nouns related to an Indo-European ancestor meaning tail) which since the 17th century has been considered too vulgar for polite conversation. Australia follows the British spelling, while in the USA and Canada the word is spelled **ass**

2 a foolish or contemptible person. A fairly mild term of exasperated contempt, popular in upper- and middle-class speech until the 1960s, now generally replaced by stronger or more colourful alternatives. 'Silly arse!' was a favourite British rebuke.

3 a courage, nerve or cheek. This has been a popular working-class usage in London and Australian slang. In Britain it has, since the 1960s, largely been supplanted by more colourful terms such as **'arris** or **bottle**, which are derived from it, or by synonyms such as **balls**.

b Australian good luck. This usage, which is more commonly expressed by the adjective **arsy**, probably derives from the previous sense, with the implication that the good fortune came as a result of daring or impudence.

4 the arse Australian a synonym for 'the heave-ho', the **elbow** or 'the boot', usually in the expression **give someone the arse**.

5 'My arse!' 'Nonsense!', 'I don't believe it!', or 'It's not true!' An exclamation of angry or impatient disbelief, dating at least from the 18th century. It is probably a shortening of a longer phrase such as the following.

6 'kiss my arse!' an exclamation of defiance or contempt.

7 'not to know one's arse from one's elbow/a hole in the ground' to be incapable or incompetent, stupid.

8 'the sun shines out of his/her arse' he or she is wonderful, perfect or the favourite. The expressions are used contemptuously or enviously of a person who, in their own opinion or that of others, can do no wrong.

arse about vb

to fool about, behave in an irresponsible or silly way. A favourite expression of many schoolmasters, especially in the 1950s and 1960s.

● 'Stop arsing about in there and get on with your work!'

arse about face adj, adv

back to front, the wrong way round or wrongly ordered or organized.

arse bandit n British

a male homosexual. The humorous but not affectionate term suggests an aggressive, predatory or desperate enemy. It is very much a term of jovial male abuse (there is no record of women saying it) in public schools, the army and the pub. Slightly less vulgar versions are bum bandit and **trouser bandit; chocolate bandit** is another synonym.

arse-end n

the end, back or bottom of anything. A common vulgarism also used in the phrase 'the arse-end of nowhere', a very remote and/or unpleasant place.

13

'*Arse-end Charlie*' is a more robust version of the colloquial 'tail-end Charlie', as applied to a straggler.

arsehole n British
1 anus. **asshole** in American English.

2 '*the arsehole of the universe/earth/world*' an extremely unpleasant place, especially one that is dirty, smelly and hot, but now by extension anywhere awful. The phrase was probably coined by troops stationed overseas, prompted by such captions as 'the pearl of the Orient' or 'the gateway to the Pacific'.

3 an extremely unpleasant person, especially one who combines offensiveness with stupidity. The term when used in Britain or Australia is stronger than the American equivalent **asshole**, and slightly different in emphasis. It shows real distaste and dislike rather than mild contempt.

arsehole vb
1 British to 'crawl', flatter or curry favour in a nauseating way. Typically used at work about a fellow employee, this is probably inspired by the now dated expressions **arsehole-crawler** or **arsehole-creep**.
- '*There he goes, arseholing again. It makes me sick.*'

2 *Australian* to throw someone out, to get rid of (an unwanted lover). The word is often used plaintively or resentfully by jilted teenagers.
- '*I can't understand it. Robyn arseholed me last night.*'

arsehole-crawler, arsehole-creep n British
a flatterer, sycophant. These synonyms of the more common **arse-licker** have been obsolete since the 1960s.

arseholed adj British
very drunk. A popular word among students, younger members of the armed forces and other heavy drinkers from the 1960s to the present. The image is of someone disgustingly or helplessly drunk, as in the expression '*pissed as an arsehole*'; but the term is neutral, not usually pejorative, and is used by all social classes.
- '*Once a month he gets completely arseholed and then comes home and asks me to forgive him.*'
(Recorded, housewife, Devon, 1986).

arseholes exclamation British
nonsense. A term expressing brusque dismissal or defiance which now seems to be falling into disuse. The singer Ian Dury included it in a stream of abuse featured on a 1978 record.

arsehole to breakfast time adj, adv British
1 completely disorganized, 'at sixes and sevens'. A picturesque if fundamentally meaningless expression sometimes heard in Britain, especially in the north of England.
- '*It's no good, it's all arsehole to breakfast time in that office at the moment.*'

2 thoroughly, constantly, or the full distance, as for instance in the expression '*he kicked him from arsehole to breakfast time*'. This may be an allusion to the complete digestive process (breakfast time referring to the mouth) but the origins of the phrase are obscure.

arse-licker n
a flatterer or toady, someone who is nauseatingly sycophantic. This ancient image and phrase is paralleled in many European languages (*Arschlechen* in German, *lèche-cul* in French).

arse-man n

1 a man whose favourite part of a woman's anatomy is the buttocks as opposed to a **leg-man** or **tit-man**.
2 a skilled or habitual seducer. An old-fashioned phrase.
3 a male homosexual. This usage is now confined mainly to public-school or armed-services slang.

arse over tip/tit adv

head over heels, upside down. The expression is typically cockney, but widespread in Britain and Australia. The American version is 'ass over tincups/teacups'.
● 'She tripped and fell arse over tit down the stairs.'
(Recorded, plumber, London, 1987).

arse up vb British

to make a mess of, mix up or spoil. A less common variation of **balls up** and the verb form of **cock-up**.
● 'He managed to completely arse up the whole job.'

arsy adj Australian

lucky. Usually said grudgingly or enviously about someone who has managed to get away with something. (**Arse** in Australian slang may signify luck as well as brazenness.)

arsy-versy adj British

1 back to front or upside down, topsy-turvy. This old and now fairly rare expression is an alteration of 'arse-versus' (a mock scholarly version of **arse about face**), influenced by vice-versa.
● 'He got it all arsy-versy.'
2 homosexual. The idea of 'inversion' contained in 1, plus the reference to **arse**, has given rise to this usage. This is now a word heard only among middle-class, middle-aged or elderly speakers, indicating quasi-hu-

morous disapproval and usually referring to males.

arthur, Arthur Rank n British

a bank. A rare working-class and underworld term rhyming on the name J. Arthur Rank, the cinema magnate. Not to be confused with **J Arthur**.

artic n British

a large lorry or truck. From 'articulated lorry'; the shortened form of the phrase has increased in popularity through the 1970s and 1980s while the full version, which was heard in the 1950s and 1960s, now sounds dated. An articulated lorry is so called because it is made up of two parts with a flexible connection between them; (the nearest American equivalent is **semi**).

artichoke n Australian

an elderly and/or unattractive (female) prostitute.

article n

a person, individual. Usually said quizzically or sarcastically to indicate that the person is peculiar or special in some (generally negative) way. This usage has continued from the 19th century.
● 'Who's this scruffy article?'
See also **the chilled article**.

artillery n

needles, hypodermic syringes and other paraphernalia used by heroin addicts. The image of an arsenal of deadly equipment is typical of addicts' own self-dramatizing slang (as in **shooting gallery**, **harpoon**, etc.).
● 'Have you got the artillery ready, man?'

artist, -artist n, suffix

an expert in, or devotee of, a particular activity. The word can be added to many others, but the most popular are bull(shit)-artist, **burn-artist**, con-artist, **piss-artist**, ripoff artist and sack artist.

This pattern entered modern British slang via the armed forces in the 1950s and 1960s, and separately via American **hippy** terminology of the late 1960s and early 1970s. The ultimate geographical origin of the usage is obscure; it may have come into use spontaneously in several English-speaking areas, perhaps prompted by the Edwardian habit of pompously applying 'artist' or 'artiste' to performers in various fields of expertise.

arty-farty, artsy-fartsy adj

pretentious, affected, more decorative than useful. A more vulgar parallel of the innocuous 'arty-crafty', which is Edwardian in origin and was usually applied to the pseudo-rustic, as in the Arts and Crafts design movement of the late 19th century.

arvo n Australian

afternoon. An example of the Australian tendency to abbreviate even the most mundane everyday words. The tendency is shared by nursery slang in general and, in Britain, especially the slang of Liverpool. (Arvo is, however, uniquely Australian.)

● 'There's no excuse for being in that state in the middle of the arvo!' (Recorded, Australian tourist, London, 1989).

asap, assap adv

immediately, as soon as possible. The spoken form of the commonly-used initials a.s.a.p. (sometimes also used in speech, pronounced letter by letter).

aspro n

a prostitute. This term is applied to male prostitutes, more often than fe-

male, being a play on the words **ass**, pro (as a shortening of prostitute) and the brand name of an aspirin preparation. The word is used in the USA and Australia.

ass n American

1 backside, buttocks, anus. The American spelling of the British **arse**.

2 sexual gratification. Usually used by men referring to women as anonymous sex objects.

● 'I'm going to grab me some ass/good ass.'

3 oneself, especially when thought of as an item to be manipulated.

● 'You gonna get yo' ass killed!'

4 'Your ass is mine!' You are in my power! A phrase used triumphantly, typically by representatives of authority to their victims.

5 'Your ass is grass' you are in very serious trouble. Usually said seriously as part of a threat, or ruefully by a victim.

● 'Get it right or your ass is grass!'

6 'have one's ass in a sling, ass on the line' to be in trouble, held responsible.

See also the entries following and **badass, candyass, chew ass, kick ass**.

assap adv

See **asap**.

asshole n American

1 anus. The American version of the British and Australian **arsehole**.

2 a very stupid person, someone who is pathetically or offensively foolish. This American word always implies contempt, but can also convey pity, unlike **arsehole**, which has overtones of real dislike. Since the 1960s, British and Australian speakers have adopted the American term in this sense, with its different spelling and pronunciation, for their own use. The word has become very widespread in the late 1970s and 1980s and has si-

16

multaneously become a vulgarism rather than a taboo term.

- *'It didn't take very long to realize that he wasn't a threat, just a total asshole.'*
  (Recorded, US executive, London, 1988).

3 a very unpleasant place.

- *'On top of a bleak, snow-swept hillside in Hermon, Maine, which, if not the asshole of the universe, is at least within farting distance of it.'*
  (Stephen King, *Sunday Times* magazine, 15 October 1989).

asshole buddy n American

a very close friend or ally, a 'bosom pal', a term that is used in both jocular and unfriendly contexts. It was coined by, and usually about, heterosexual men.

ass-kicker n American

an aggressive person, a disciplinari an; someone who kicks ass. An armed-forces term which has been adopted by students and school pupils, among others.

ass-kisser n American

a sycophant, flatterer or toady. The expression is based on kiss ass.

ass-licker n American

the American version of **arse-licker**.

ass over tincups/teacups
adv American

head over heels. A folksy American version of the British **arse over tip**.

ass-wipe n American

1 toilet paper. A working-class, blue-collar or armed-forces term.

2 a worthless, contemptible person. A term popular in the 1970s and 1980s.

at it vb British

1 having sex. A coy euphemism typically used by schoolchildren or the middle-aged.

2 committing a crime or crimes, or engaged in a confidence trick. A mild euphemism typically used by police or criminals themselves, from the common colloquialism 'at it again' referring to any repeated and troublesome activity.

attitude n American

bad attitude, antisocial behaviour, sullen hostility. This use of the word without 'an' or 'the' probably derives from the black American prisoners' shortening of the white authority figures' phrases *'bad/negative/antisocial attitude'* or their accusation, *'You've got an attitude problem'*.

Auntie n

1 the BBC in Britain or the ABC in Australia. A fairly affectionate term used by employees and implying a rather staid and stern benevolence. In use since the 1950s, the word Auntie was displaced in Britain by 'the Beeb' in the 1970s.

2 a middle-aged or elderly male homosexual. A term of mild derision, sometimes a nickname. The image is of a protective, perhaps fussy or fastidious person.

Aunt Jemima n American

a black woman who is suppliant or acquiescent in the face of racism. The female equivalent of **Uncle Tom**.

Aunt Nelly, Aunty Nelly n

belly. A rhyming-slang term in use in Britain and Australia, particularly in the 1950s when belly was a taboo word in many households.

Aunty

See **Auntie**.

17

Aussie adj
(an) Australian.

autograph n
a signature. Autograph is underworld argot, typically denoting a signature on a cheque or document, whether forged or genuine.

away-day n British
a single dose of LSD or another hallucinogenic drug. A pun on the notion of a **trip** and the name of a cheap excursion ticket on British Rail.

awesome adj
wonderful, excellent, very impressive. A popular teenage word, first used in the USA in the late 1970s and 1980s as part of the vocabulary of **Valley Girls**, **preppies** and hip-hop music enthusiasts, among others. This use of the adjective has been imported into Britain in the 1980s, especially by teenage skateboarders and **rap** music enthusiasts.

the awkward squad n British
inexperienced, clumsy or insubordinate people. Originally an informal army term for a group of inept or difficult recruits, now a middle-class civilian phrase used typically by authoritarian figures such as school teachers.

awol, A.W.O.L. adj
missing, not present when needed. The expression has been extended, especially by British middle-class speakers, from its original meaning in army jargon of 'absent without leave' to inexplicably absent, either with the implication of fleeing to avoid responsibilities, or wandering uncontrolled or running amok.
• '*Ollie's gone awol again; he

disappeared with a bottle and no one's seen him for days.*'
(Recorded, upper-class youth, London, 1985).

awright! interjection
an alternative spelling of **all right**. With drawn-out pronunciation, this forms an exclamatory expression of appreciation, agreement or solidarity in American English.

axe n
a guitar. The word in this sense was enthusiastically adopted by white rock musicians in the late 1960s. Black blues and jazz musicians had originally applied it to any instrument (such as a saxophone) that was held in both hands and 'wielded'. By the early 1970s the white use of the word, which had always had an element of self-consciousness, was mainly confined to rock music journalists or fans.

aya exclamation American
'*Oh, my gosh!*', an exclamation of amazement in vogue among teenagers in 1987 and 1988. The word may be a hearty cry or, more often, an affected shriek (possibly in imitation of Hispanic speech).

Aztec two-step, the Aztec two-step n
an attack of diarrhoea, particularly one suffered while travelling abroad. The image is of the agitation caused by impending diarrhoea, or more specifically the frantic and undignified clenched shuffle to the nearest toilet or bush. This parody of a dance title was coined by Americans who tend to suffer while on holiday in Mexico, and is a late 1970s alternative to **Montezuma's revenge** or the British **gyppy tummy** and **Delhi belly**.

18

B

B., b n British

a bastard, in the metaphorical rather than literal sense. An abbreviation mainly favoured by middle-class speakers, heard in Britain and Australia.

B.A. n American

a troublesome, violent or anti-social person. An abbreviation of **badass**, or 'bad attitude'. The letters were used as the initials of the surly black hero 'B.A. Baracas' played by Mr T in the US television series The A-Team in the 1980s.

babe, babes, baby n

sweetheart, lover. A usage imported from the USA into Britain via films, pop songs, etc. The word had begun to be used unselfconsciously in Britain in the late 1970s, particularly in the form **babes** and mainly by working-class speakers. It is used by both sexes, but when used by men to women it can be considered patronizing or offensive.

baby blues n pl

eyes. A humorous adult phrase from the clichéd, twee or amorous description, 'baby-blue eyes'.

Babylon n British

a racist white society, Britain. The term originates in the biblical imagery of the **rastas**, but has spread, largely via the medium of reggae music, to other black youth and disaffected whites.

b the Babylon the police force, as tokens of oppression or white racist authority. A specific usage of the more general term for society, now widely heard among white youth.

baby-sitting n

a accompanying someone engaged in taking illicit (especially hallucinogenic) drugs in order to instruct or reassure them.

b in the jargon of journalists, staying close to a source of information in order to protect them from the attention of other reporters.

baccy n British

tobacco. This now rather dated alteration of the standard term replaced the previous forms 'bacca' and 'bacco' early in the 20th century. (Cannabis was known jocularly in the 1960s and 70s as **wacky baccy**.)

backdoor vb

a to commit adultery (with).

● 'In Australia, you'd never get away with some of the things I've seen here because you'd get a punch in the mouth. We don't go in for backdooring someone else's woman.'

(Jamie Addicoat, fitness instructor, Observer, 30 April 1989).

b to act illicitly, covertly or deviously, to deceive or betray.

backdoor man n

a a secret lover, especially a married woman's lover. The term is originally black American slang dating from at least the 1950s.

● *'I'm your backdoor man ... the men don't know, but the little girls understand.'*
('Back Door Man', recorded by the Doors, 1968).
b a man who sodomizes. This usage is mainly applied to and by heterosexuals. The Australian 'backdoor merchant' means a homosexual.

backdoor work n
a euphemism for anal intercourse.

backfire vb
to **fart**. A term which is in use in Australia and has been heard occasionally in Britain, especially among schoolchildren, since the 1950s.

back garden, back way, backdoor n
the anus. Predictable euphemisms which are invariably used in a sexual context, usually by heterosexuals.

backhander n
1 a bribe. A colloquial term which has been widespread since before World War II.
2 a blow with the hand, a heavy cuff or slap. In this sense the word has been recorded since the mid-19th century.

the back of Bourke n
Australian
the 'back of beyond'. Bourke is a remote town in Northern New South Wales.

backslang n
backslang, in which a word or alteration of a word is reversed enjoyed some popularity in Britain, chiefly among members of the underworld, the subproletariat and certain trades such as meat portering. It is also sometimes

used by schoolchildren to disguise taboo conversations. Forms of backslang exist in other European languages, notably in the Parisian *verlan* which is still thriving. The only well-known 'mainstream' example of backslang is **yob** from boy.
Compare **pig Latin**.

back way n
See **back garden**.

bad adj
good. Originally from the terminology of the poorest black Americans, either as simple irony or based on the assumption that what is bad in the eyes of the white establishment is good for them; this usage spread via jazz musicians in the 1950s to teenagers in the 1970s. It is still primarily a black term, although occasionally used, rather self-consciously, by white teenagers in the USA and, under the influence of **rap** and hip-hop, in Britain since the early 1980s. This use of bad is normally distinguished from its opposite, literal meaning by a long drawn-out pronunciation. The superlative form is 'baddest'.
● *'In hip hop slang "That's bad" can mean "that's good", depending on the tone of voice.'*
(*Evening Standard*, 11 November 1987).

badass n, adj
(an) aggressive, antisocial or worthless (person). The word, first popular among black Americans, is almost always now used with an element of approval or admiration, albeit sometimes grudging. The 'ass' component simply signifies 'individual'. In the 1970s the term came into use among whites, but has not spread to Britain or Australia.
● *'Their badass biker style.'*
● *'He's been a badass since he was a kid.'*

20

bad egg n

a scoundrel, rogue or worthless person. If used today it is usually a light-hearted reference. Bad egg sounds dated in Britain (it originated at the end of the 19th century), but is still heard in Australia. The term is invariably used about a man rather than a woman.

badger game, the badger game n

a deception whereby a woman lures a victim into a compromising position, at which point her 'husband' catches him in flagrante. The couple then blackmail the 'lover'. This is an old North American term used by criminals and police, probably influenced by an older rural confidence trick, or possibly by the archaic use of 'badger' to mean prostitute or thief. The phrase's meaning is now sometimes stretched to encompass other forms of deception.

badmouth vb

to insult, denigrate or disparage. An Americanism, probably originating in black speech, which has been imported into British usage since the 1970s

bad news n

a person who is unwelcome or disliked, a bore or troublemaker. A usage that was imported to Britain from the USA at the end of the 1960s.

bag n

1 an unattractive and/or unpleasant woman. This usage originated in the early 20th century with the idea of a shapeless, heavy or burdensome female, previously expressed as 'baggage'.

2 one's special interest or current preoccupation, sphere of activity. This usage came into vogue in Britain among the **beatniks** and later **hippies** in the 1960s. It was derived from black

American jazz terminology, where it meant 'category' or 'style'. By the early 1980s the term had become distinctly dated.

- 'Papa's Got a Brand New Bag.'
  (Song title, James Brown, 1965).

3 American a package or some measured amount of marihuana or another drug. The custom of American street dealers of **grass** was, and is, to sell small amounts in paper envelopes or cellophane bags, typically **dime bags** or 'nickel bags'.

4 a condom.

5 the scrotum.

bag vb

1 a to arrest or catch. This sub-sense of the word is encountered in police usage, from the terminology of hunters.

b to have or take. In this sense the word is used as a synonym for 'grab' or 'cop' in such instances as 'let's bag some beers'. The usage also occurs in American adolescent argot which includes phrases such as **bag some z's/ rays.**

2 a American to conceal or suppress.

b to give up or abandon.

- 'Maybe I should bag this tugboat business and go into politics.'
  (Heywork US TV series, 1986)

c to dismiss, fire.

These usages, popular especially among teenagers, are all related by their suggestion of discarding someone or something with the trash. Similar meanings of bag were heard occasionally in Britain before 1950.

3 Australian to criticize. A **bagging** is a verbal attack or strong criticism.

4 American also **bag up**, to divide marihuana into small amounts and/or packages before selling it.

bagel-bender n

a Jew. A derogatory nickname, used principally in the USA, based on the name of the baked bread rings that are a jewish culinary delicacy.

Compare **spaghetti-bender** and **taco-bender**.

baggies n

long, wide shorts as worn by surfers since the 1960s.

- *'We'll be wearin' our baggies, huarache sandals, too.'*
  ('Surfin' USA', the Beach Boys, 1963).

bagging n

1 *British* a packed lunch, as carried by workers. A term heard especially in the north and midlands. **Snap** is an alternative.

2 *Australian* a criticism.

See to **bag 3**.

bag job n

a theft or burglary. An underworld term heard in Britain but more widespread in the USA; not to be confused with a **paper bag job**.

bag lady n

a female vagrant, specifically one who through obsession or necessity collects junk and carries it in bags. The term originated in the USA in the early 1970s; by the late 1980s it was occasionally also being used, there and elsewhere, to denote any excessively scruffy female.

bag man n

1 someone who collects, or looks after, money made illegally. An underworld and police term originating in the USA between the world wars and first applied to those sent by gangsters to collect extortion payments, illicit revenues or bribes.

- *'Before I got promoted I used to be a bag man for Kellom – just nickel and dime stuff.'*
  (The Big Easy, US film, 1986).

2 a (male) tramp or vagrant, specifically one who collects and carries garbage in bags.

bag one's face/head vb

American

to hide one's face or oneself. Invariably used as an imperative as in 'Go bag *your face!'*. This expression is popular among **Valley Girls** and other middle-class teenagers. It implies that the person in question is too hideous to contemplate and should put a bag over their head.

See also **bag someone's ass**.

bagpipe vb

to engage in sexual stimulation using the armpit rather than the usual orifices. A term whose rarity presumably corresponds to that of the practice.

bags n

1 trousers. The word has had this meaning since the mid-19th century and survives, usually in a humorous context.

2 *American* breasts.

bag someone's ass vb

American

to leave, go away, 'get lost'. The expression literally means to thrust into a garbage bag and throw away.

- *'She had no intention of having lunch with him and that was that ... Why couldn't she simply tell him to bag his ass?'*
  (Elmore Leonard, The Switch, 1978).

bag some z's vb American

an alternative version of **cop some z's**.

bagsy exclamation

a schoolchildren's term that indicates the speaker's choice of seat, cake, bed, etc.

• *'Bagsy the one with the chocolate icing!'*

bag up *vb American*

to divide marihuana into small amounts and/or packages, (typically nickel or dime **bags**), before selling it.

baidie *adj British*

bad-tempered, aggressive, provocative. An obscure term which is probably a dialect version of **batey**.

bail *vb American*

to leave (in a hurry). A teenagers' shortening of 'bail out'. The word has been fashionable among **Valley Girls** and others since the late 1970s.

bail/bale on someone *vb American*

to oppress, burden or trouble. The bail or bale in question may derive from cotton picking as in the words from 'Ole Man River'; *tote that barge, lift that bale, get a little drunk and you lands in jail*, or may refer to bailing as in dumping water (on). The expression is typically used by teenagers and students.

bait *n*

an attractive potential sexual partner. This term was used alone in the 1950s and 1960s or in compounds such as **bed-bait** and the surviving **jailbait**.

the baked bean *n British*

the Queen. An authentic item of rhyming slang.

baksheesh, bakshee *n*

a bribe, tip or payment. From the colonial era, the word is from Persian *bákshish*; something given.

bald *adj American*

terrible. A vogue term among American teenagers in 1987 and 1988. The origins of this kind of appropriation from standard English are unrecorded, but often begin in gang code or street jargon.

Bali belly *n Australian*

diarrhoea. The Australian traveller's equivalent of **Delhi belly**, **Montezuma's revenge**, **gyppy tummy**, etc.

ball *vb American*

1 to have sex. An American term which, apart from a brief vogue in the **hippy** era, has rarely been used in Britain or Australia. Originally an item of black argot, it gained wider popularity in the early 1960s and, as its anatomical origin suggests, is generally a male usage.

• *'Presley fired me because I balled his old lady.'*

(The singer P J Proby, interviewed in 1965).

2 to behave in a boisterous, fun-loving and uninhibited way; to 'have a ball'. The term usually implies dancing, but also a degree of Bacchanalian, even orgiastic revelry far beyond that signified by the standard English (hunt or charity) ball.

• *'Good golly, Miss Molly, you sure like to ball!'*

(Little Richard, [ambiguous] song lyrics, 1958).

3 to take in an illicit drug, for example amphetamines or cocaine, through the mucous membranes of the sex organs.

ball and chain *n*

a spouse, usually one's wife. This jocular and obvious phrase has been heard in English-speaking areas throughout the 20th century.

ball-breaker, ball-buster n

a a very aggressive, dominant or demanding woman.

b an excessively hard taskmaster or martinet.

c an exhausting, demanding task.

All these terms were adopted in Britain and Australia in the 1970s from American usage.

Compare **ball-tearer**.

ballocks n pl

testicles. An archaic spelling of **bollocks**.

balls n pl

1 testicles. A predictable use of the word, balls was first used as a euphemism in Renaissance England, later becoming a standard, if coarse synonym.

2 rubbish, nonsense. This use of the word, except perhaps as an exclamation, is surprisingly acceptable in middle-class speech (in such phrases as '*it's all balls*'), considering its derivation.

- '*He was awarded a campaign medal, "but I didn't go to get mine. I wasn't interested; I thought it was all balls".*'
  (Falklands war veteran quoted in *The Observer* review of *The Fight for the Malvinas* by Martin Middlebrook, 9 April 1989).

- '*Meyer? I think he's very lucky to get away with all that English gentleman balls.*'
  (Anonymous Tory minister quoted in the *Guardian*, 5 December 1989).

3 courage, nerve. In this sense the word may now be applied to women in spite of the anatomical inconsistency.

4 n a mess. This is a modern mainly middle-class shortening of **balls-up**, usually in the phrase to '*make a balls of it/something*'.

balls-ache n British

something or someone which is very tedious or trying.

balls-out adj

full-scale, full-tilt. A vulgar version of all-out, this fairly uncommon intensifying expression is normally used by males.

balls up vb

to make a mess of. In this mainly British expression, **balls** performs as a regular verb, (**ballsing up** and **ballsed up** being conjugated forms). To **ball up** is an American alternative.

balls-up n

a mess, mistake, disaster. This expression has been in use in Britain since the turn of the century.

ballsy n

courageous, spirited. A vulgar alternative to **gutsy**. The word can be applied to either sex.

ball-tearer n Australian

1 a very demanding or exhausting task.

2 something spectacular or sensationally impressive. These are versions of the international English **ball-breaker**.

ball-tearing adj Australian

1 very demanding or exhausting.

2 spectacular, sensationally impressive.

bally adj British

an outdated euphemism for **bloody**. The word, which is identified with the pre-World War II 'silly ass', is still employed by some middle-aged and elderly speakers.

Balt n *Australian*

an immigrant (to Australia), a 'new Australian'. Not all so-called Balts were in fact from the Baltic states, which was the origin of the term, commonly used in the early 1950s.

banana n

1 a foolish person. This childish term of mild abuse is now obsolescent in Britain, but predictably is still heard in post-colonial English in the Indian subcontinent, Malaysia, the Caribbean, etc. The 1950s **nana** was a shorter form.

2 penis. The mock nursery term **tummy banana** is more common.

3 *American* a light-skinned black woman. A term used by black men which is both appreciative and offensive.

banana-bender n *Australian*

a Queenslander. This pejorative nickname is a later version (on the lines of **spaghetti/bagel/taco-bender**) of the obsolete 'banana-lander', referring to a staple crop of the state in question.

bananas adj

crazy or berserk. This now common colloquialism originated either in the notion of 'softness' (in the head) or from the archaic 'banana oil', 'soft soap', or 'balderdash'.

banana truck n *American*

a crazy person. An expression which evokes a whole truck-full of bananas, hence an excess of 'softness' (in the head).

band n *Australian*

a prostitute. The word dates from before World War II, but its origin is obscure. The same word, perhaps coincidentally, was used in pre-war black American slang to mean a woman.

B and D n *British*

'bondage and discipline', sado-masochistic sex. A prostitutes' abbreviation, (one of the standard 'packages' of special services offered to clients), used in small ads and in conversation in Britain and Australia.

bandit n *British*

1 a homosexual. A dismissive or derisory term used by avowedly heterosexual males and deriving from longer expressions such as **trouser bandit**, **arse bandit**, **chocolate bandit**, etc.

2 -bandit. An ironic or jocular combining word, added to suggest a desperate or reprehensible character, or in police jargon, literally a criminal. In his *Field Manual for Police* (1977) David Powis cites '*milk bandit*' as an ironic term for penniless milk-bottle thieves; '*gas-meter bandit*' is self-explanatory.

band rat, band moll n

a groupie, girl who has sex with members of rock groups, especially one who follows or travels with them. Band rat is an American term from the mid-1900s, while band moll is Australian and from the early 1970s.

B and T n *British*

'bum and tit'. A schoolboy abbreviation, popular especially in public schools in the early 1970s. The phrase usually refers to a glimpse of, or brief contact with, the mentioned parts, but can mean sexual experience in general.

● '*He looks a bit tired; it's too much B and T.*'

bandy adj *British*

bow(or 'bandy')-legged as a result of sex. A working-class term used scornfully or jeeringly about a girl or woman by men. The term is not meant literally but the suggestion is that a girl has just

25

had sex or has sex constantly. 'She's bandy!' was shouted in the street by London **mods** and **skinheads** in the late 1960s.

bang vb

1 to have sex (with), **fuck**. The association with striking (as in the origin of the word 'fuck' itself) is said to suggest the masculine role in sex, but in practice the unaffectionate term can also apply to women, especially in Australian usage where it is more common than in America. In Britain bang in this sense has only been widely understood since the late 1960s. It was introduced via the phrase **gang bang** and the following expression.

- 'You're banging a major witness in a case you're trying?!'
(The Last Innocent Man, US film, 1987).

2 bang like a shithouse door (in a gale) to be a very energetic or enthusiastic sexual partner. An Australian expression, said by men of women and popularized in Britain by Barry Humphries' cartoon character, 'Barry McKenzie', in the 1960s.

3 American to be an active gang member. From the parlance of Los Angeles street gangs of the late 1980s, derived from the specific sense of **gangbanger**.

- 'He's been banging for two years now.'

bang n

1 a a sexual act. An unaffectionate term used more often by men. In this sense the word does not seem to be older than the 20th century.

- 'A quick bang.'
b a person rated as a sexual partner.
- 'A good bang.'

2 Australian a brothel. The word is now rather archaic, but is still heard among older speakers.

3 a an exciting experience, a thrill. In this sense the word goes in and out of vogue, particularly among schoolchildren in many parts of the English-speaking world.

b a great success, very popular person or thing.

c an injection of illicit drugs, especially heroin, morphine or amphetamines, or the resulting jolt of pleasure. From the lexicon of drug users and addicts, originating in the 1940s or earlier and related to the more recent verb **bang up**.

bang vb

to have sex (with).

banged-up adj British

imprisoned, shut away. From the second sense of the verb to **bang up**.

- 'A banged-up man's no good to me. I want to enjoy life, not spend it in prison waiting-rooms.'
(Recorded, drug-dealer's girlfriend, London, 1984).

banger n

1 a sausage. The word has been common in this sense since the 1940s. It derives of course from the explosion of the skin during frying.

2 an old and/or decrepit vehicle.

bangles n pl

a breasts.

b testicles. By association with the idea of adornment, as in **family jewels**, and with 'dangle'.

Both usages are most often heard among teenagers and schoolchildren all over the English-speaking world.

bang on vb British

to nag, harangue or talk incessantly and boringly. A popular term which has appeared in the 1980s in 'respectable' usage.

- 'She's been banging on about her bloody job all evening.'

bang/bash one's bishop vb

to masturbate. An old vulgarism once again in vogue among middle- and upper-class males in Britain in the 1980s.

bang to rights adj, adv British

red-handed, without hope of escape. This 19th-century expression (paralleled in American English by **dead to rights**) is usually heard in the form '*caught bang to rights*' or '*we've got him/her bang to rights*' (i.e. helpless, indefensible). Until the 1970s the term was part of the restricted codes of the police and underworld; since then the phrase has been given wider currency, particularly by the realist plays of G. F. Newman.

bang up vb

1 to inject oneself (with heroin or another hard drug). One of many drug-users' terms with overtones of bravado. Popular in Britain in the late 1960s and early 1970s.

2 British to imprison, shut away. A working class, police and prisoners' term.

● '*Being banged up's no joke, even in an open prison.*'
(Recorded, remand prisoner, 1986).

● '*It was now tea-time and we were banged up while the screws went off to have their own tea.*'
(Trevor Hercules, *Labelled a Black Villain*, 1989).

banjaxed adj Irish

defeated, overcome or overwhelmed. A humorous term from the early 20th century, often used ruefully by husbands floored or humiliated in a domestic dispute. This Irish word, probably formed by association with 'banged', 'bashed', 'smashed', has been popularized in Britain by the Irish broadcaster, Terry Wogan, who used it as the title of a book in 1980. It can now

be extended to mean stunned, flummoxed, amazed, drunk, etc.

banjo'd, banjoed adj British

a hopelessly drunk or under the influence of drugs. A jocular invention, perhaps influenced by **banjaxed** and sometimes heard among students and schoolchildren in the 1970s and the 1980s.

● '*... stupid how they strut, smoking Woodbines till they're banjoed smirking at the Swedish smut*'
(*Psycle Sluts*, poem by John Cooper Clarke, 1978).

b defeated, beaten. An armed-forces term of the late 1970s and 1980s. There may be a connection with **banjaxed** or with the archaic use of 'banjo' to mean a shovel or weapon.

bank n American

money. A (probably ephemeral) teenage vogue word of 1987 and 1988. The term was picked up by British **rap**, **hip hop** and **acid house** enthusiasts.

● '*Got any bank?*'

barb n

a barbiturate. A shortening employed by drug abusers since the late 1950s.

● '*We did a load of barbs and spent the rest of the day nailed to the floor.*'
(Recorded, student, Faversham, Kent, 1974).

barbie n Australian

a barbecue. A common term since the late 1960s, now spreading via Australian TV soap operas to Britain where it has been adopted by **yuppies** in particular.

● '*Australia was full of easy-going characters like Paul Hogan, who spent the day drinking Fosters and putting a shrimp on the barbie.*'

(Michael Parkinson, *Daily Mirror*, 17 April 1989).

Barbie Doll n

a vacuous passive and/or conformist young woman. Barbie is the trademark name of the well-known plastic doll originating in the USA.

barebum n *Australian*

a short jacket, especially a short dinner-jacket as worn by waiters. The British equivalent would probably be **bumfreezer**.

barf vb *American*

to vomit. A popular student term dating from the 1950s. The word is imitative in origin and is sometimes used as an exclamation of disgust.

barf bag n *American*

a a disgusting or very unpleasant person. A teenagers' slightly less offensive version of **scumbag**.

b an airsickness bag. The term is rarely used in this sense, which derives from the verb **barf**: to vomit.

● '*Word on the street is that you barf bags are giving the kids in the 7th grade a hard time.*'
(*Vice Versa*, US film, 1988).

barf city n, adj *American*

(a) disgusting, revolting (place). The expression from **barf** (to vomit) is usually used as an exclamation of revulsion, typically by schoolchildren and teenagers.

bar-fly n

a habitué of (cheap and seedy) bars. This pre-World War II Americanism applied to both sexes, was the title of a 1987 film scripted by Charles Bukowski.

barf (someone) out vb

American

to disgust, nauseate. A **Valley Girl** and teenagers' term, usually heard as an exclamation, as in '*It totally barfs me out!*'. It derives from **barf** meaning 'to vomit'.

bark vb *Australian*

to vomit. By extension from the earlier use of bark as a humorous synonym for 'cough'.

barking adj *British*

demented. A short form of '*barking mad*', evoking utter howling craziness, this expression is typically heard in upper- and middle-class speech, often preceded by 'absolutely'.

● '*A friend in the Business was hugely amused when told of a forthcoming interview with Carla Lane. "She's quite barking, you know," he warned cheerfully . . .*'
(*Sunday Times* magazine, 4 March 1990).

barm pot n *British*

a crazy, silly or eccentric person. A mild term of (often affectionate) abuse. Barm pot was on the way to becoming obsolete in the 1960s and 1970s but has enjoyed a revival in some circles in the 1980s. The phrase may either refer to a literal pot of barm (see **barmy**), or be an invention based on barmy, perhaps influenced by 'potty'.

barmy adj

crazy. Barm is the froth of yeast formed on fermenting drinks such as beer (the word itself is related to the 'ferm' of ferment). The image of frothing lightheadedness and relation to intoxication gave rise to the term which is now a common colloquialism.

barmy army n British

a wild or enthusiastic group of young people. The phrase has been adopted as a nickname by various loose aggregations of sport and music fans including the followers of the early 1980s **punk** group Serious Drinking.

barnet n British

hair, head of hair. A rhyming-slang term (from 'Barnet Fair'; both the event and the phrase in its full form were popular among Londoners in the second half of the 19th century) which is still widely used by working-class speakers and their imitators in and around London.

• *'I'm stayin' in tonight and washin' me barnet.'*
(Recorded, social worker, Willesden, London, 1987).

barney n British

an argument, fight or disturbance. Perhaps surprisingly the origin of this common term is obscure. It is assumed to derive from the male forename, but the connection between Barnaby and brawl or scuffle is unclear.

• *'I like a bit of a burney from time to time – it helps to clear the air.'*

baron n British

a prisoner enjoying a degree of power and influence over his fellow-inmates. The source of the power is usually economic, with the baron controlling trade in cigarettes (a 'tobacco baron'), drugs or other prison currency.

barren Joey, barrenjoey n

Australian

a prostitute. A **joey** is an orphaned kangaroo, but the connection is far from clear.

barsy, barzy adj British

mad, lunatic. A blend of barmy and

crazy favoured by some middle-class speakers since the mid-1970s.

bart n Australian

a girl or young woman, especially an immoral one. This word dates from the late 19th century when it was used as a more polite evasion of **tart**. It is now almost obsolete.

base n

crack. The term is a shortening of **freebase**, a system of smoking purified cocaine which pre-dated the use of the more refined and potent crack. The word base was in use among British users in 1989, together with many other nicknames.

basehead n American

a drug user who **freebases** cocaine or smokes **crack**. The term dates from the early 1980s, the practice from the 1970s.

basher n British

a shelter or shack made of cardboard, paper, plastic, etc. and lived in by a tramp or homeless person. The word is used by the 'gentlemen of the road' or **dossers** themselves.

• *'Their "bashers" (shacks) will be forcibly removed by police to make way for developers who want to "yuppify" the Charing Cross area.'*
(*Observer*, 16 August 1987).

basket n

1 bastard. A euphemism used in Britain and Australia, particularly in the 1950s and 1960s, and especially by middle-class speakers.
2 *American* the male genitals. A male homosexual term, heard in the late 1970s and early 1980s.

basket case n

a helpless invalid, a person who is mentally and/or physically incapacitated. Originally an Americanism, this expression (a variant of **cot-case**) has become widespread in recent years. It is now often used in journalists' jargon to refer to an irrevocably ruined enterprise.

bastard n

the standard term for an illegitimate person has been used as a term of abuse, disapproval, pity, or even affection (particularly in British and Australian usage) since the early years of the 20th century.

● 'Targets: banks, shops, DHSS, cop-shops, Job Centres, rich bastards.' (Observer, 3 April 1988).

bate n British

a rage, fury, bad temper or state of agitation. An upper-class schoolboy word still preserved in the public-school vocabulary. The earlier spelling was usually bait, which gives a clue as to the origin of the word; it is thought to be a back-formation from baited (in the sense of teased, harassed or provoked), and not as is sometimes claimed from 'debate'.

batey adj British

bad-tempered, irascible. A piece of dated but not yet archaic public-school slang deriving from the obsolescent use of **bate** to mean strife or argument.

bath bun n British

1 the sun. A less common alternative to **currant bun**.

● 'All this bleedin' rain. I've forgotten what the old bath bun looks like.' (Recorded, street trader, London, 1988).

2 son.

Both uses are London working-class rhyming slang from the sweet fruit bun originating in the city of Bath.

bath-dodger n British

an unwashed or habitually dirty individual. **Soap-dodger** is a synonym.

battle-cruiser n British

a **boozer**, the pub. This London rhyming-slang term originated, not surprisingly, in the 1940s, but is still heard, although **rub-a-dub** is probably more popular.

bazumas, bazungas n pl

female breasts. Supposedly humorous coinages (also rendered in other forms such as **gazungas, mazoomas**, etc.) which may have originated in an elaboration of 'bosom'.

beak n

1 nose. Beak has been used in this obvious sense since at least the beginning of the 19th century, although other terms, such as **hooter, bugle, conk** etc. are more popular.

2 a person in authority, especially a judge or schoolmaster. This old usage is now obsolete in American English but is retained in Britain in public-school slang and in the expression 'up before the beak' (appearing before a magistrate or someone else sitting in judgment). Attempts have been made to derive this meaning of beak from a Celtic term for judgment, but the more obvious derivation is from the intrusive beak (nose and/or mouth) of authority. The Tatler magazine reported in August 1989 that beak was still the standard Etonian slang for schoolmaster.

● 'Finally the beak turn his beetling brow to them and his xpression [sic] become suddenly soft, his stern eye mild.' (Geoffrey Willans and Ronald Searle, Back in the Jug Agane, 1959).

beamer n American

a BMW car. A **yuppie** nickname.

bean-bag n British

a mild term of abuse among younger schoolchildren. Bean bags were used in throwing games and sports.

beaner, bean, bean-eater n American

a Hispanic American, a Mexican or **Chicano**. A 1970s and 1980s term, highly offensive in the USA, which refers to poor Latin Americans' diet of frijoles or refried beans.

beans n pl American

dollars. A humorous synonym possibly influenced by the colloquialism 'a hill of beans' meaning something worth very little.

● 'At least we're sitting on around a hundred beans from my brilliant idea.'

(Planes, Trains and Automobiles, US film, 1987).

bear n American

a police officer, especially in the vocabulary of CB radio. This usage derives from the US Forest Services' fire-warning posters showing 'Smokey the Bear' in the uniform of a ranger. It was adopted by CB enthusiasts in the mid-1970s.

beard n

a male escort posing as a boyfriend, lover, husband, etc. The term (heard from the mid-1970s in showbiz and 'society' circles) may refer to a lesbian's 'official' partner, with whom she is seen in public.

beardie n British

a bearded **beatnik**. A mildly derogatory term, often coupled with **weirdie** in the 1960s.

beast n American

1 a girl or woman. The term, typically used by male college and high-school students, may be either pejorative or appreciative.

2 the beast heroin. A drug users' ironic nickname.

3 a sex offender, in prison slang. A more recent synonym for **nonce**.

● '20 prison officers in riot uniform were observed banging their shields in unison and chanting "Beast, beast, beast!".'

(Observer, 8 April 1990).

beastie n, adj American

a (a) disgusting, coarse or disreputable (person).

b (something or someone) impressive, powerful or enormous. This expression, used typically by female teenagers, was a vogue term among blacks and whites in the USA in the 1980s and was adopted ironically in the name of the white **rap** group the Beastie Boys.

beat n

someone who is a member of the 'beat generation' or aspires to its values. The term, coined by the influential American writer Jack Kerouac and first published by John Clellon Holmes in his novel Go is derived both from the notion of being beaten, downtrodden, or poor, and from the notion of beatitude, or holiness. The phrase 'the beat generation', coined in imitation of other literary groups such as the Lost Generation of the 1920s, originally applied to a relatively small group of writers, artists and bohemians in America immediately after World War II, whose activities and beliefs were minutely chronicled in autobiographical, mystical and experimental prose and poetry by Kerouac, Holmes, Gregory Corso, William Burroughs and Allen Ginsberg, among others.

31

The 1957 publication, and runaway success, of Kerouac's *On the Road* (a book about travelling back and forth across America in search of mystical truth), inspired teenagers to call themselves beats and adopt at least some of the trappings of the book's heroes, based on Kerouac and his friend Neal Cassady. The term **beatniks** (employing the Slavonic '-nik' suffix disparagingly) was applied to these and later followers by members of **straight** society, hostile to what they saw as the licentious, irreligious and communistic aspects of the beat lifestyle. In Britain the beats were a youth subculture of the early- to mid-1960s, which co-existed with **mods** and **rockers** and metamorphosed into **hippies**.

• '*The most beautifully executed, the clearest and most important utterance yet made by the generation Kerouac himself named years ago as "beat", and whose principal avatar he is.*'
(Gilbert Millstein, *New York Times*, 5 September 1957).

beat-box n
a ghettoblaster.

beatnik n
someone following a **beat** lifestyle or modes of dress. The term was coined by newspapermen to deride the self-styled members of the beat generation but was later adopted by beatniks themselves; the **-nik** suffix came from Russian and was meant to identify the beats with Godless Communism, (as well as being a derogatory word-ending in Yiddish terms such as **nudnik**). Aspects of the beatnik lifestyle included scruffy dress (often black), berets, modern jazz, coffee bars, a slightly more liberal attitude to sex than their contemporaries, at least a pretence at interest in modern arts and literature and a youth cult. Beatniks had passed

their peak by 1960, but many of them (who incidentally referred to themselves simply as **beats**) were absorbed into the **hippy** movement in the mid-1960s.

• '*A petition signed by 2,321 residents and holidaymakers at St Ives, Cornwall was handed to the Mayor, Ald. Archie Knight during the weekend. It calls for tighter vagrancy laws to rid the town of beatniks.*'
(*Daily Telegraph*, 21 July 1969).

beat off, beat one's meat vb
(of a male), to masturbate. The first expression is primarily American, the second international.

beaut adj Australian
excellent, first-rate. A well-known Australianism which, although dated, is still in use.

beaver n
1 a the female genitals. An American term meaning the pubic hair and vagina ('a beaver').
b an American term meaning a woman or women seen exclusively as sex objects ('beaver').
• '*Let's get some beaver!*'
These terms became known, though rarely used, outside the USA via pin-up magazines in the late 1960s.
2 a beard, especially a full or luxuriant one. A light-hearted 19th-century usage, still heard among adults.
• '*He's sporting a handsome beaver.*'

beaver shot n
a photo showing a woman's genitals, especially in close-up. An American term originally (in the late 1950s) from the jargon of pornographic magazine publishers and film makers. The expression was picked up by 'girlie' magazines in the USA and Britain in the

late 1960s, when this type of photograph became legally permissible.

bebop n
a fast syncopated style of modern jazz featuring lyrics made up of nonsense words. Also known as **bop**, bebop arose in the 1940s.

Bedfordshire n British
a bed or bedtime. A nursery joke-form of the standard words, from the parents' catchphrase 'up the wooden hill to Bedfordshire', meaning '(go) up the stairs to bed'. This usage is in fact 200-year-old peasant humour.

Beeb, the Beeb
See **Auntie**.

beef n
a complaint or grudge. This use of the word has occurred in American English since the early years of the 20th century, originating in the speech of criminals, pugilists and marginals, etc. Since the 1940s British speakers have also employed it. The relationship between this sense of the word and its literal meaning is not clear; the colloquial notion of 'brawn' may be involved.
● 'I just wanna tell you, I got no beef about last night.'
(Miami Vice, US TV series, 1987).

beef vb
to complain. In the 19th-century language of street sellers, and later in the theatre, beef was associated with shouting, yelling and hence complaining. By the early 20th century the word was in use in the USA in the sense of a grudge or complaint, but it is unclear whether the usages are related.

beef (someone) vb
to have sex with. A vulgarism in use all over the English-speaking world.

Beef has had sexual connotations, deriving from its use as a synonym for flesh, for hundreds of years. From the 1980s, as a verb **pork** is more common.

beef bayonet n
penis. A humorous euphemism on the lines of **mutton dagger**, etc. The phrase was first popularized in Britain by Barry Humphries' Barry McKenzie comic strip, in the satirical magazine Private Eye in the 1960s.

beef bugle n Australian
an obscure variant form of **beef bayonet**.

beef curtains n pl
breasts. A late 1980s vogue term among some male teenagers, particularly those affecting 'street credibility'.
● 'Man, look at the beef curtains. Yeah, the blonde one, know what I mean.'
(Recorded, youth, Baker Street station, London, 1985).

beefer n British
a male homosexual. This epithet has rarely been heard since the 1960s. It may derive from 'beef' as metaphor for penis, from the verb to beef, or conceivably from **b.f.**

beef up vb British
to intensify, make more substantial. Derived from the notion of fattening livestock for market.

beersucker n
a the mouth.
b a heavy drinker.

beer-tokens n pl British
one-pound coins or money in general, in the argot of students and other adolescents in the late 1980s. 'Beer-vouchers' is an alternative form.

bees 'n' honey n British
money. A piece of London rhyming slang which, while never being a popular term, is still heard occasionally.

bee-stings n pl
small female breasts. A jocular term employed by both sexes.

beetle vb British
to hurry. A dated colloquialism revived by **Sloane Rangers** in the early 1980s. It is inspired of course by the scuttling of the insects.
● *'I had to beetle along to Jonty's before lunch.'*

beetle-crushers n pl British
heavy work boots. A humorous phrase often extended to refer to heavy or large shoes or footwear in general.

beevo(s) n American
beer. A college students' term probably distantly related, via 'beverage', to the British **bevvy**. The fact that the Czech word for beer is *pivo* may be coincidental.

beggar vb, n
a euphemism for **bugger**, (except in the 'respectable' idioms 'beggar the imagination' or 'beggar description' when the meaning is to render impoverished or surpass).

beggar's velvet n American
another term for **dust bunny**.

bell vb, n British
(to make) a telephone call (to someone). A working-class usage which has become almost universal since the 1970s in the form *'give someone a bell'* or more racily, *'bell someone'*. It is also in Australian use.
● *'I got a bell from old Milward yesterday.'*

(Recorded, businessman, London, 1988).

Bells, the Bells n British
a nickname for Annabel's, the Berkeley Square nightclub frequented by the wealthy upper-class young.

bellyache vb
to complain or grumble continuously; it is unclear whether the term refers to the supposed source of the complaint or to the effects of the complaint on the listener.
● *'For Christ's sake stop bellyaching and get on with it!'*

bellyflop n
a a dive, landing stomach-first on water.
b an ignominious or total failure.

belter n
something wonderful, excellent or exciting. An expression of enthusiasm heard predominantly in the north of England which can be applied equally to a girlfriend, a car, party, etc. This noun derives from the colloquial senses of the verb 'to belt' denoting thrashing, speeding, etc.
● *'Just look at her. She's a right belter isn't she?'*

bender n
1 a bout of heavy drinking, a riotous spree. The term may have originated in North America in the mid-19th century when 'hell-bender' meant any event or spectacle which was outrageous, aggressive or exciting. An alternative derivation is from **bend the elbow**. In its narrower sense of unrestrained spree, the word was introduced in Britain at the end of the 19th century.
● *'When his marriage collapsed, Dick went on a four-day bender.'*

(Recorded, business executive, London, 1986).

2 *British* a homosexual. A term of contempt, originally for a passive male homosexual who supposedly **bends over**. The term is now probably heard less frequently than in the late 1960s and early 1970s.

• *'It's not every day that a man wakes up to find he's a screaming bender!'*
(*Blackadder II*, BBC TV comedy, 1988).

3 *British* a makeshift shelter. The word derives from the 'bender tents' used by gypsies or other travellers and made by stretching cloth or tarpaulin over bent-over saplings. It was brought into common currency by the women peace protesters camped outside the US base at Greenham Common in the mid-1980s.

bend over, bend down *vb*

a to submit to, or invite **buggery**. A euphemism popular among all social classes in Britain in the 1960s and early 1970s.

• *'He'd bend over on Blackfriars Bridge for ten bob.'*
(Recorded, public schoolboy, London, 1970).

b (by extension) to yield or submit to abuse or attack. A term popular among businessmen in the 1980s. This may be a shortening of the phrase *'bend over backwards'* and is a brusquer version of *'take it lying down'*.

• *'I'm certainly not going to bend over for them.'*
(Recorded, company director responding to take-over attempt, London, 1988).

bend the elbow *vb*

to drink alcohol. A hearty euphemism used by habitués of bars since the 19th century all over the English-speaking world.

bennie *n*

a tablet of Benzedrine, trade mark for a variety of amphetamine used and abused from the 1940s to the 1960s.

bent *adj*

1 a criminal, crooked, dishonest. This usage has been widespread in Britain at least since the beginning of the 20th century. It is still used by the police to refer to anyone who is not **straight**, and by criminals and others to refer to corrupt police officers (often by the cliché phrase 'a bent copper' – 'bent coppers' were damaged coins that could not be used in public lavatories in the 1950s and 1960s). A more colourful embroidery sometimes heard in Britain is *'bent as a butcher's hook'*.

• *'Remember, this happened in the 1960s when many detectives were bent.'*
(Former detective quoted in *Inside the Brotherhood*, Martin Short, 1989).
b stolen, forged.

• *'A bent motor.'*
2 sexually deviant, homosexual. A common term in Britain, mainly in working-class usage, since the 1940s. A London variant popular in the 1960s was *'as bent as a nine bob note'* (a non-existent, obviously forged denomination).

3 *American* drunk or under the influence of drugs. This usage is rather archaic, but the longer *'bent out of shape'* is still heard among college students and **preppies**.

4 *American* angry, furious. This seems to be an armed-forces term in origin. It is also more usual in the form *'bent out of shape'*.

beresk *adj*

berserk, out of control. A humorous corruption perhaps inspired by a genuinely mistaken pronunciation, perhaps by the influence of 'bereft'. An alternative is **besrek**. Both forms have been heard, mainly among middle-class speakers in Britain and Australia – students and rugby players are typical users – since the early 1970s.

berk n

a fool. This word, which has been widespread since the early 1960s, in Britain and Australia (where it was introduced via British TV comedies), is used as a form of mild derision by many speakers who would be shocked by its original meaning in rhyming slang. The origin is 'Berkeley hunt' or 'Berkshire hunt', meaning **cunt**, which in the late 19th and early 20th century was a Cockney synonym for fool.

- '*And how does he [Paul Thompson] see himself? Amiable berk? Complete nonentity? Heart-throb?*' (*Evening Standard*, 2 September 1988).
- '*Yet there's no doubting his commitment, it's just that [Stephen] Bayley's apt to sound like a complete berk in print – going on about how he finds throwing things away "absolutely thrilling".*' (John Preston, *Evening Standard* magazine, July 1989).

bertie n British

1 a male homosexual. The connection between the name and the subject is unclear.
- '*He looks a bit of a bertie to me.*'
2 See **do a bertie**.

besrek n

See **beresk**.

betty n. British

a girl, particularly a non-participant in sports such as skateboarding. A mildly derisory usage among some teenagers, possibly inspired by the character played by Michelle Dotrice

in the TV comedy series *Some Mothers do 'ave 'em*.

bevvied adj British

drunk. From the increasingly popular use of the noun and verb shortenings of 'beverage'.

bevvy, bevvie vb, n British

(to take) an alcoholic drink. A predominantly working-class abbreviation of 'beverage' in use since the 19th century, usually referring to beer. It seems to be gaining new popularity among students, etc. at the end of the 1980s.
- '*We had a few bevvies on the way here.*' (Recorded, workman, York, 1986).
- '*They've been bevvying since lunchtime.*'

B.F., b.f. n British

'bloody fool'. A pre-World War II, mainly middle-class euphemism, now sounding rather dated. The initials have sometimes been used with more vehemence, probably on the assumption that the 'f' in question stood for **fucker**.

B-52 n American

a beehive hairstyle (as worn in the early 1960s and occasionally revived). The nickname borrowed the designation of a bomber plane. A well-known avant-garde rock group from Macon, Georgia adopted the expression as their name in the late 1970s.

B-girl n American

a prostitute or woman of dubious morals who frequents bars.

bi- adj, n

bisexual.

bible n

See **Tijuana bible**.

bible-basher

an over-enthusiastic evangelist christian.

See also **jesus freak** and **god squad**.

biccy n

a biscuit. A nursery term, also used facetiously among themselves by adults.

bicycle n

See **town bike**.

biddy n

1 a woman, especially an old or middle-aged one. The word was originally applied as a term of endearment. It is an affectionate form of Bridget.

2 wine. Usually a short form of **red biddy**.

biffad n American

a male **preppie**. This comic but probably ephemeral coinage was recorded in use among American teenagers in 1987. It is a combination of two supposedly archetypal preppie nicknames as in the exchange:

'Say, Biff . . . '

'Yes Tad?'

the big A n Australian

Shortened form of the phrase 'the big arse', meaning the 'heave-ho' or giving someone 'the elbow'.

See **arse 4**.

the Big Apple n American

the nickname for New York City. It seems to have originated among jazz musicians, perhaps from the notion of 'a bite of the apple' meaning a chance of success.

big bamboo, the big bamboo n

penis. In Caribbean English (and joky white imitations thereof from America to Australia) this euphemism has featured since the 1950s.

Big Blue n

the nickname of IBM. The expression is inspired by the colour of the company's logo.

big brown eyes n pl

breasts. Usually used by men in the 'humorous' phrase 'a pair of big brown eyes'. A euphemism occasionally heard in Britain, America and Australia which manages to be coy, hearty, and presumably offensive to most women at the same time.

big E n

the **elbow**.

See also **arse 4**.

big enchilada n American

an important or self-important person, the boss. A humorous phrase from the 1970s. An enchilada is a Mexican filled pancake. The term is a later imitation of the pre-World War II colloquialisms, 'Big cheese/potato'.

big girl's blouse n British

a weak, ineffectual or pathetic male. A phrase usually heard in the north of England. It first came to prominence in the late 1960s.

● 'Naff ballet roles – the big girl's blouse in Les Sylphides.'
(The Complete Naff Guide, Bryson et al., 1983).

Big Green n American

The **preppies'** nickname for Dartmouth College, USA. It is one of the eight 'Ivy League' institutions.

the big house n American

a prison, especially federal prison. This underworld euphemism was publicized by its use as the title of an Oscar-winning film of 1930 starring Wallace Beery.

big jobs n British

excrement, defecation. A mainly middle-class nursery term, in use since the 1940s.

big man on campus n

American
See B.M.O.C.

big-note vb Australian

to boast or to praise. The term probably referred originally to large denomination bank notes.

● 'I big-noted myself.'
(Mel Gibson, Australian actor, 1987).

big-noter n Australian

a braggart, boastful person. From the verb form.

the big O n

orgasm, particularly female orgasm. A journalese catchphrase probably originating in therapy and feminist circles in the USA in the early 1970s.

Big Red n American

Cornell University, USA. The preppies' nickname.

the big spit n

an act of vomiting.

bike n

See town bike.

biker n

a motorcycle rider, a member of a motorcycle gang. This American usage was unknown in Britain until the late 1960s when biker style and hardware began to be imitated.

bikie n Australian

the Australian version of biker.

bikkie, bikky, biccy n

a biscuit. A nursery term also used by adults.

bilk vb

to cheat someone, especially by withholding due payment. This word was in use in the late 17th century, also having the meaning of frustrate. (It may therefore be related to balk and baulk.)

bill, the Bill, the Old Bill n

British
the police. A working-class London term which slowly entered common currency during the 1970s, partly owing to television police dramas. The term's origins are obscure. It seems to have passed from Bill or Old Bill, a mock affectionate name for individual policemen, via the Old Bill, a personification of the police force as a whole, to the Bill. It can also be used in expressions such as '(look out) (s)he's Bill!' – he or she is a police officer. Coincidentally or not, in 1917 the Metropolitan Police used Bruce Bairnsfather's famous cartoon figure 'Old Bill', (he of 'If you know of a better 'ole, go to it'), on a recruiting campaign. It may also be significant that when the Flying Squad was first motorized, all their licence plates had BYL registrations.

● 'A banner was draped from cell windows [at Wandsworth prison where police had taken over from striking warders] reading: support the screws – Old Bill out.'
(Guardian, 3 January 1989).

billiards n pl

See pocket billiards.

billies n pl American
money, dollar bills. A popular term
among **Valley Girls** and other teenagers in the early 1980s.

bimbette n
a silly, empty-headed young girl. A
jocular diminutive of **bimbo**, popular
in the mid-1980s, first in the USA and
then, via magazine articles, in Britain,
where it has been enthusiastically tak-
en up and over-used in the tabloid
press.

bimbo n
1 a silly, empty-headed or frivolous
woman. This is the sense of the word in
vogue in the late 1980s, imported to
Britain and Australia from the USA.
The origin is almost certainly a variant
of *bambino*, Italian for baby. In the early 1900s a bimbo, in American colloquial use, was a man, especially a big,
unintelligent and aggressive man or a
clumsy dupe. By the 1950s the word
was used as a nickname for boys in
England, perhaps inspired by a popular song of the time. By the 1920s
bimbo was being applied to women,
especially by popular crime-fiction
writers, and it is this use that has been
revived in the 1980s with the return to
fashion of glamorous but not over-cer-
ebral celebrities. In the late 1980s the
word has been applied again occasionally to males, although with less brutish and more frivolous overtones than
earlier.
● '*Darryl Hannah plays an interior
designer and Gekko's part-time
mistress who turns her attention to
Bud Fox's apartment and bed. She's
meant to be a rich man's bimbo.*'
(Oliver Stone, US film director,
Sunday Times magazine, February
1988).
● '*Charlotte Greig has a message for
fools such as I. Not all women in
pop are . . . brainless bimbos lured*

*into lurex by cynical rock business
shitheads . . .* '
(Ms London magazine, 4 September
1989).
● '*And only someone as sincerely
romantic as Wyman could have
chosen this occasion to appear
publicly, for the first time since
their engagement, with his bimbo-
to-be, Mandy Smith.*'
(Christena Appleyard, Daily Mirror,
11 May 1989).
2 British bottom, backside. A nursery and schoolchildren's word of the
1950s, now rarely heard.

bin vb British
to throw away, reject. A sharper or
more imperious version of 'chuck it' or
'dump it' is 'bin it', heard in the late
1980s, especially in offices and in a
broader business context.

the bin n British
a mental hospital or asylum. A shortening of **loony bin**.
● '*If she goes on like this she's going
to end up in the bin.*'
(Recorded, housewife, London,
1988)

bindle n American
a package of illicit drugs in the form
of a small bundle or packet. This item
of early 1960s drug-users' slang derives from bindle; a bundle of bedding
carried by a hobo, which in turn comes
from the German *Bundel*; bundle, (or
from the German pronunciation of the
standard English word).

bindlestiff n American
a migrant hobo. (For the origin of
bindle, see above.) This dated term is
still heard.

bingo n British
an arrest, a successful search. A customs officers' term employing the tri-

39

umphal cry from the popular game of chance.

• *'We got a bingo finally after three weeks.'*

bins n British
1 a glasses, spectacles. A Cockney shortening of binoculars, sometimes spelled **binns**. The term has been in use at least since the 1930s and is still heard.
b eyes. An extension of the previous usage.
2 a headphones. Part of the jargon of recording engineers and rock musicians in the late 1960s; the term was eagerly picked up by hi-fi enthusiasts and **musos** in the 1970s, although **cans** is more prevalent in this context.
b hi-fi or concert speakers. By extension from the above.

bint n British
a girl, (young) woman. *Bint* is Arabic for daughter or girl; the word was adopted by soldiers serving in Egypt and became widespread in Britain from the 1920s to the 1960s. In English the word nearly always had, and has, deprecatory overtones.
• *'I've got to keep him and that Russian bint one step ahead of the police.'*
(*Room at the Bottom*, TV comedy, 1987).

bird n British
1 a girl. A very common term in the late 1950s and 1960s, it is now somewhat dated and considered offensive or patronizing by most women. The word was first a 19th-century term of endearment, ultimately from Middle English, in which bird could be applied to young living things in general, not merely the feathered variety.
2 a prison sentence. From the rhyming slang 'birdlime'; time.
• *'He's doing bird in Wandsworth.'*

birdbath n British
a silly person. A humorous variant form of **birdbrain** typically used since the 1970s by parents and children.

birdbrain n
a stupid, inane or frivolous person. A common colloquial image which in the earlier form 'bird-witted' is at least 350 years old.
(For a sustained use of the term see Allen Ginsberg's 1980 song/poem of the same name, recorded with punk group the Gluons.)

bird droppings n British
an adolescent euphemism for **chickenshit** in the sense of something derisory or pitiful.

birding n British
chasing or trying to 'pick up' women. A northern English working-class term of the 1960s and 1970s, from the more widespread use of **bird**.

birf n British
a coy or jocular shortening of birthday, used typically by teenage-magazine journalists in the 1980s.

birl n
See **burl**.

Birmingham screwdriver n British
See **Brummagem screwdriver**.

bish-bash-bosh adv, adj British
quickly, efficiently, in quick succession. A vogue catchphrase in use among fashionable young professionals in London in the mid-1980s.
• *'It was bish-bash-bosh/a bish-bash-bosh job.'*

bishop n
See **bang/bash one's bishop**.

bit adj American

disappointed, resentful. A folksy version of 'bitter' or 'bitten' used by country people and poor blacks (in pre-war slang it usually meant 'cheated'); adopted as part of **preppie** language in the 1970s.

● *'She sure was bit when she found out she hadn't been chosen.'*

bit n

1 activity, scene, subject. In **hip** talk and the argot of **beatniks**, as in *'the whole religion bit'* or *'he did his mysticism bit'*.

2 A **bit** is used as a euphemism for sexual activity, as in *'a bit on the side'*.

bitch n

a a pejorative term for a woman which although not strictly speaking slang is normally highly offensive. As a term of denigration bitch, like its alternatives 'sow', 'vixen' etc. has been widespread since the Middle English period. In black American speech 'bitch' can be used with proprietorial or condescending overtones rather than with personalized malice.

● *'Ultimately, it [NWA's album]'s just another extension of the black underclass machismo which casts all women as "bitches".'*

(Independent, 8 September 1989).

b a spiteful or vindictive male homosexual.

c an infuriating or gruelling task.

d something impressive, admirable. This is another example of a negative term being employed in a contradictory sense (compare **bad**, **wicked**, etc.). It usually occurs in the appreciative phrase *'it's a bitch'* in American speech.

bitchin' adj American

excellent, first class. From the colloquial phrase *'it's a bitch!'*, expressing great enthusiasm.

bite n

an instance or act of coercion, taking money by force or guile. The word usually occurs in phrases such as **put the bite on** (someone).

biting n

selling a graffiti artist's pen name to another young person. Usually seen in this form rather than the verb 'bite'. It is a specialization of the sense of **bite** meaning coercion.

bit of fluff/stuff n British

a woman, seen as attractive but frivolous, or not to be taken seriously. A condescending male term from the early 1900s, still fairly widespread in the 1960s and not yet obsolete.

bit of rough n British

a lover, of either sex, who exhibits or feigns primitive, aggressive or socially inferior characteristics. A phrase often used jocularly in the 1980s, originally a variation of the prostitutes' and homosexual term **rough trade**.

● *'She's always preferred a bit of rough.'*

bitser, bitza n

a mongrel (usually a dog). A witticism based on the idea that the animal's pedigree is composed of 'bits of this and bits of that'. The expression, which probably originated in Australia, can also be applied to anything put together from disparate components.

bivvy vb British

to bivouac, make camp. A shortening used by scouts and the armed forces in the 1970s and 1980s.

bivvy n British

1 a a bivouac, camping place.

b a tent, especially a small tent. Both terms are, predictably, part of the vocabulary of soldiers, scouts, campers and ramblers, etc.

2 an alternative form of **bevvy**.

biz, the biz n

a the biz show business. A term used by the self-consciously theatrical, originating as 'show biz' in the style of journalese popularized by *Variety* magazine.

b any sphere of activity, such as the music biz, the public relations biz, etc., by extension from the first sense. It is often used ironically to add a sheen of cheap glamour to difficult or thoroughly mundane jobs. In the company of cognoscenti, any such group may be referred to as **the biz**.

c a term of approbation, as in '*this is the biz*' or '*he's the biz*'.

blab vb

to inform (on someone), to tell tales or reveal information. The term often has the sense of a garrulous or inadvertent revelation of a secret or confidence. Like blabber, the word has meant '(to engage in) voluble or indiscreet talk' since the 16th century.

blabber n Australian

a TV remote control. This item of domestic slang of the 1980s refers to the mute capability. No universal slang term for the remote control has yet emerged, though **zapper** is a recorded alternative.

black n

hashish from the Indian subcontinent or the Himalayas, from its characteristic dark colour. Black hashish has long been the most highly-prized by users and consequently the most highly-priced, with the result that in the 1980s lighter-coloured hashish from North Africa has been artificially darkened and sold as black Moroccan.

black and tan n British

1 a capsule of 'Durophet-M', a trademark amphetamine (known in a different packaging as 'black bomber') abused in the 1960s.

2 a drink mixing stout or porter with bitter or light ale. Both terms refer to the black and brown colours of the preparations in question, and are influenced by the nickname of the Irish auxiliary police force of the 1920s.

black bag job n American

a break-in or other covert operation carried out by a government agency. A piece of jargon from the time of the Watergate scandal.

black bombers n pl British

capsules of Durophet (a form of amphetamine popular among drug abusers in the 1960s), named from their colour and their powerful effects.

black box n British

a woman wearing a burka (a black garment covering the body to the ankles). Muslim women wear the burka to prevent lascivious glances from men, provoking the derisive comparison heard in British cities in the 1980s. (This in turn is no doubt influenced by the many press references to black-box flight recorders in reporting the air disasters of 1988–9.)

blackjacks n pl American

See **cosh boy**.

black maria n

a prison van or police car or van. The nickname originated in the USA in the mid-19th century. (Maria is probably an arbitrary borrowing of a female name as a familiarizing device).

42

black stuff n American

a a drug user's euphemism for opium.

b British tarmacadam.

black stump n Australian

the mythical starting point for the 'back of beyond'.

black tar n American

a potent dark-coloured refined form of heroin widespread in the USA in the 1980s and originating in Mexico.

black velvet n

black women seen as sexual partners or sex objects. An offensive term deriving from the material and in Britain reinforced by the name of a drink, a mixture of Guinness and champagne.

blade n

a knife, particularly when used for protective or offensive purposes.

blag n, vb British

a (to carry out) a robbery. This is the sense of the term familiar to most people since its use in TV shows of the 1970s giving a realistic perspective on criminal milieus.

b to scrounge, cadge, deceive or bamboozle, or the booty from such an activity. The word blag has been in widespread use in both senses in underworld and police circles since the early 1950s. It is presumed that it derives from the French blague; a joke or blunder, but the details of this etymology are unclear. There have been suggestions that it is more simply an elaboration of to **bag**.

blah n, adj

(something) dull, tedious, listless, inert. A pejorative term deriving from an exclamation of boredom or resigna-

tion. The word spread from the USA to Britain before World War II.

blank n American

extremely low-grade, diluted or imitation narcotic. From the lexicon of drug users and addicts of the 1950s.

blank (someone) vb British

to snub, refuse to speak to someone or acknowledge them. A mainly working-class expression becoming increasingly popular in London in the later 1980s. The past participle form 'blanked' in particular is a vogue term among schoolchildren.

- 'Donna went to see her and she totally blanked her.'
  (EastEnders, British TV drama series, March 1988).
- 'We walk past and they blank us, but we can't challenge them.'
  (British soldier serving in Northern Ireland, Families at War, BBC TV, 1989).

blast n

1 a a party or celebration.

b any enjoyable or exhilarating experience.

2 an inhalation of cannabis or another euphoric drug.

blatherskite, blatherskate, bletherskite n

a a boastful or bombastic person, a 'windbag'.

b a villainous or disreputable person.

This picturesque word is the American and Australian version of the Scottish dialect word 'bletherskate'. Although it is a fairly innocuous term of mild abuse it derives from 'blether' meaning a bladder or to blather, and 'skate', a dialect variant of **shit**. The image evoked is of someone who is 'full of shit'. During the War of Independence, Americans became familiar with the

43

word from the Scottish song, 'Maggie Lauder'.

bleeder n British

an individual, particularly an unfortunate or despicable person. This working-class term often conveys strong dislike or contempt. It dates from the 19th century, but has lost popularity since the 1960s.

bleeding adj British

an intensifying term, currently out of fashion, but widespread in the 1960s when it was significantly stronger than **bloody**. This usage probably dates from the 19th century in working-class speech.

Blighty n British

Britain. An anglicization of the Hindustani bilayati, meaning foreign. The word was originally used with some affection by the pre-World War I colonial army, but is now used only to suggest mock jingoism.

● 'I was blown through the door and put my hand to my head. It was covered in blood, but we had no thoughts of Blighty. We didn't want to go back, we'd only just come.'
(World War I veteran David Watson, Independent, 12 November 1988).

blikkeys n American

soap flakes masquerading as **crack**. A device employed by would-be drug dealers in American cities in 1989.

● 'He did it okay for us the next time, but then when I see him again he's cooking blikkeys.'
(Drug user, Guardian, 5 September 1989).

blim n British

a very small portion of a drug, usually hashish. A rare and obscure coinage, recorded among drug users and dealers in London in the late 1980s.

blimp n

1 British a pompous, old-fashioned, ineffectual person. The term was used to describe army officers of 'the old school' around 1939 and originated in Colonel Blimp, a character invented by the cartoonist David Low, probably inspired by blimp as the name of a small World War I barrage balloon. The word was commonly used in this sense in the 1950s.

● 'The Life and Death of Colonel Blimp.'
(Title of a British film by Powell and Pressburger, 1941).

2 a fat person. A favourite American college-student term of derision, also heard among British schoolchildren and others in the 1980s. From the name of the World War I barrage balloon.

● 'When I was playing tennis I was just a fat blimp waddling round the court.'
(Annabel Croft, Today, 7 February 1989).

blimp out vb American

to become sated and/or collapse from overeating. An elaboration of **blimp** in the sense of fat person.

blinder n British

an impressive or exciting action, thing or person. The word, which is often used for a sporting feat, commonly in the phrase to 'play a blinder', implies something 'visually stunning'.

blissed-out adj

ecstatic, euphoric or in a trance, specifically as a result of religious experience. The term is from the jargon of transcendent 'fringe' or alternative religious cults of the late 1960s.

blitzed adj

very drunk or **stoned**. The usage ultimately derives from the German Blitz (lightning) Krieg (war).

- *'Jesus, she was completely blitzed, absolutely out of her head.'*
  (Recorded, photographer, London, 1989).
- *'I see the Queen Mum's been reliving the blitz at the Blacksmith's Arms.'*
  'Good for her – I've been blitzed a few times in that place myself.'
  (Cartoon by Gray Jolliffe, *Evening Standard*, 22 July 1988).

blob n British

1 a corpse, road-accident victim. An unsympathetic term used by ambulance men, the police and tramps.

2 an ulcer, excrescence.

3 a bodily protruberance, a breast or a testicle.

The second and third senses of the word are recent mock-childish coinages in use particularly among school-children and students.

blob wagon n British

an ambulance. From the language of tramps and **dossers**.

- *'Being rescued by the "blob wagon" for hospital treatment.'*
  (*Observer*, August 1987).

block n British

1 head. Since the early 1950s this old term has only been used as part of phrases such as 'knock someone's *block off*' or '*do one's block*'.

2 **the block** solitary confinement. A prisoners' term which is a shortening of 'punishment block'. **Down the block** denotes being (sent) into solitary confinement.

block (in) vb British

to have sex (with). A working-class male vulgarism heard from the late 19th century until the 1960s. It may now be obsolete.

blocked adj British

under the influence of drugs, especially '**pep pills**' or amphetamines. This word was popular in the early 1960s among **mods**, who used it to refer to the state of intoxication caused by 'pep pills' or amphetamines, such as **purple hearts**, **blues**, **black bombers**, etc. The origin is probably in the idea that one's **block**, or head, was completely taken over, and partly incapacitated by the drug. This is reinforced by the fact that a side-effect of amphetamines is to make the user tongue-tied, so that communication is literally blocked.

- *'Does that mean you're blocked out of your mind on stage?.'*
- *'It means we're blocked out of our minds all the time.'*
  (Pete Townshend of The Who, interviewed on the television programme *A Whole Scene Going*, 1966).

block it vb British

to take illicit drugs, become stupefied by drugs. A fairly rare usage heard among drug users in the 1960s. The phrase is related to the adjective **blocked**.

bloke n

a man. The most widespread slang term in Britain and Australia from the 1950s, when it superseded 'chap' and 'fellow', to the 1970s, when 'guy' began to rival it in popularity among younger speakers. The exact origin of the word is mysterious. It seems to have entered working-class slang from vagrants' jargon; either from Shelta, the Irish travellers' secret language, or from Romany. Romany has a word *loke* which is derived from the Hindustani for man; in Dutch *blok* means a fool. Whatever its ultimate origin, bloke entered British usage early in the 19th century and is still thriving in colloquial speech.

- *'I went into the boozer the other day and there was this bloke I hadn't seen for 25 years.'*
(William Donaldson, Independent, 26 August 1989).

blood n American

a term of endearment or address used by black males to fellow males, it is a shortening of 'blood brother', or a version of 'young blood' as applied to tribal warriors.

bloodclat n Jamaican

1 a sanitary towel; a dialect form of blood-cloth, on the same lines as **raasclat**.

2 a despicable, worthless or unpleasant person. A strong term of abuse, used by men, invoking the taboo subject of menstruation. The word is also used as an exclamation of anger or distaste.

bloody adj British

an intensifying adjective which is now considered fairly mild, but which was held to be taboo in many circles until the later 1960s. The standard folk etymology is from the oath 'by our lady', but the word is more probably a simple extension of the literal meaning.

blooper n American

a mistake, blunder. A coinage influenced by bloomer.

- *'TV Censored Bloopers.'*
(US TV programme featuring humorous out-takes from films and TV series, 1988).

blot n Australian

one of many Australian vulgarisms for the anus.

blotto adj

drunk. The word appeared around 1905. It implies that the person in question had soaked up alcohol in the manner of blotting paper.

blow vb American

1 to leave, go. A shortening of 'blow away'.

- *'I better blow town before the cops come looking for me.'*
2 to perform fellatio (upon someone). In this sense the term may derive from **blow job** or may be the source of that expression.

- *'Who blew and were blown by those human seraphim, the sailors, caresses of Atlantic and Caribbean love.'*
(Howl, poem by Allen Ginsberg, 1956).
3 a to smoke. In this sense the verb is typically used by devotees of cannabis.

- *'Let's get together and blow a couple of numbers.'*
b to sniff, **snort**. A cocaine (and occasionally amphetamine) users' term for inhalation.

4 to be repellent; a rare synonym of to **suck**, heard among school and college students.

- *'Man, that study program really blows.'*
5 to play a musical instrument (not necessarily a wind instrument) in **hip** talk.

blow n

1 a cannabis for smoking (hashish or marihuana). A drug users' term.

b tobacco. A usage encountered especially in the speech of prison inmates.

Both instances are based on the use of the verb **blow** to mean to smoke.

2 cocaine. The use of blow to mean cocaine (from the slang use of the verb **blow** to mean both inhale and con-

46

sume) spread from the USA to Britain in the later 1970s.

blow (someone) away vb

to kill, especially by shooting. A widespread euphemism originally in American underworld and military usage.

the blower n British

a telephone. A slang term which was common by the 1940s and is still heard. It may originate in 'blow' as an archaic term meaning 'to talk', or from the habit of blowing into an old telephone mouthpiece before speaking.

• 'Get Nelson on the blower, will you.'

blowies n Australian

blowflies.

blow job n

an act of fellatio. This term, now widespread in English-speaking countries, spread from the USA in the 1960s. A puzzling misnomer to many, to **blow** in this context is probably a euphemism for ejaculate, a usage occasionally recorded in the 1950s. This may itself be influenced by the there (s)he blows of whaling cliché. An alternative and equally plausible derivation of blow job is from the black jazz musicians' **hip** talk expression **blow** meaning play (an instrument). This term probably caught on in Britain and Australia simply because there was no well-known alternative in existence.

blown away adj

1 killed. A cold-blooded euphemism on the same lines as **dusted**.

2 (pleasurably) surprised, 'transported', **gob-smacked**.

blown out adj

1 American tired, exhausted or hung over. A high-school and **preppie** term

probably adapted from the following sense.

2 American intoxicated or euphoric after taking drugs, **high**. This use is still heard, but less commonly than during the **hippy** era.

3 American ruined, failed. Used typically of an event or an opportunity.

4 full of food, gorged. From the verb to **blow out**.

5 rejected, cast aside, expelled. From the verb to **blow out**.

• 'Her past is littered with the corpses of blown out lovers.'

blow off vb

1 British to **fart**. A children's term of the 1950s revived in the 1980s.

• 'We were right in the middle of the restaurant and Kitty blew off in front of them all.'
(Recorded, father, London, 1986).

2 American to reject, get rid of. A less common variant of **blow out**.

• 'We had to blow off the trip after all.'

blow one's cookies/ doughnuts/groceries/lunch/ grits vb American

to vomit. Colourful euphemisms from the lexicon of high-school and college students.

blow one's mind vb

to be transported beyond a normal state of mental equilibrium, experience sudden euphoria or disorientation. A key term from the lexicon of drug users of the 1960s, this phrase was rapidly generalized to cover less momentous instances of surprise, awe, admiration, etc. Now dated, the expression is still in many people's passive vocabulary, allowing it to be used, for example, in advertizing copy as late as 1989.

• 'Happiness is hard to find   we just want peace to blow our minds.'

47

(Lyrics to *Revolution* by Tomorrow, 1967).

● '*She blew my nose and then she blew my mind.*'
(*Honky Tonk Woman*, Rolling Stones, 1971).

● '*The way she came on to me – it completely blew my mind.*'
(Recorded, student, London, 1976).

blow out vb

1 a to reject someone (especially a lover), or something. From the image of violently expelling something.

b to cancel, especially unexpectedly. In this sense the phrase applies typically to a pop group cancelling a tour or concert.

2 to over-eat as a matter of sensual indulgence. From the image of the stomach being blown out like a balloon.

blow-out n

an occasion of over-indulgence, particularly excessive eating and drinking.

● '*Have a blow-out at Les Trois Marches.*'
(*Mail on Sunday*, '*You*' magazine, March 1988).

blowser n British

a glue-sniffer. A rare vogue word from the early 1980s.

blowsing n British

glue-sniffing. This obscure term was used in the 1980s by young solvent abusers themselves. 'Blowsed-up' means under the influence of glue. The word is an invention, perhaps influenced by 'blow'.

blow someone's mind vb

a to give someone a hallucinogenic drug.

b to astound, transport, bamboozle or overwhelm someone, or in some other way to radically and rapidly alter

their mood or consciousness. An extension of the first sense. Both senses of the phrase were part of the **hippy** lexicon of the 1960s and are now dated. (The Beatles were castigated for their ambiguous use of '*I want to blow your mind*' in the lyrics of '*A day in the life*' in 1967).

● '*We're not out to blow people's minds however. We're out to get through to them.*'
(Pete Townshend, *Oz* magazine, June 1969).

● '*People had to sit down . . . We would blow their minds! . . . Their brains would dribble right out their nose.*'
(David Crosby, describing the effects of the music of the group, The Byrds, in *Long Time Gone*, 1989).

blow the gaff vb

to give away information, reveal a secret, inform on someone. This picturesque phrase was derived from the archaic 'gaff' meaning a trickster's strategy or paraphernalia. Although it dates from the early 19th century, and often evokes the world of **spivs** or gangsters, the expression is still used. Confusingly, blow the gaff could conceivably also now mean 'leave (**blow**) the premises (**gaff**)'.

blub vb British

to cry, weep. A middle-class children's and public-school term typically used derisively. It is a shortening of the colloquial 'blubber'.

● '*But the boiled egg made his gorge rise, and it was as much as he could do to stop himself blubbing over the toast and marmalade.*'
(*Scandal*, A. N. Wilson, 1983).

● '*Peelie [John Peel] blubbed throughout, the big jessie, and before long we all joined in.*'

(*Evening Standard*, 31 August 1989).

bludge vb *Australian*

to cadge, scrounge, shirk or loaf. Originally the word meant to bully and was a shortening of bludgeon. It later meant to live off immoral earnings. The word, which has given rise to the more common **bludger**, has been introduced to Britain via Australian TV soap operas in the late 1980s.

bludger n *Australian*

a cadger or scrounger, disreputable or despicable person. (A **dole-bludger** is the Australian equivalent of the British 'dole scrounger'.)

blue n

1 *Australian* a violent row or fight.
● '*They got into a blue – Kelly pushed Charlene into a gooseberry bush.*'
(*Neighbours*, Australian TV soap opera, 1987).
2 *British* an amphetamine tablet. A term from the 1960s when these tablets were light blue in colour and also known as **French blues** and **double-blues**. (Strictly speaking blues were tablets of drinamyl, a mixed amphetamine and barbiturate preparation, prescribed for slimmers.)
3 a police officer. A rare usage, but occasionally heard in all English-speaking countries; it is usually in the plural form.
4 *Australian* a red-headed man. A nickname mentioned in Rolf Harris's well known song 'Tie me kangaroo down, sport!'.

blue angel n *American*

a capsule or pill of Amytal, a strong barbiturate. From the lexicon of drug abusers and addicts of the late 1950s.

blue balls n

a condition of acute (male) sexual frustration, jocularly supposed to bring on a case of orchiditis, the testicles swelling to bursting point. This American expression of the 1950s, popular then among college students, has since spread to other English-speaking communities.

bluebottle n *British*

a police officer. A term popular in the 1950s and still heard. It has been used in Britain since the 16th century, well before policemen wore uniforms, and indeed existed in any organized form, which suggests that the original reference was to an annoying pestilential presence.
● '*Before you could turn round the place filled up with bluebottles.*'
(Recorded, pub habitué, London, 1987).

blue cheer n *American*

LSD (lysergic acid diethylamide). A term used in the late 1960s and early 1970s inspired probably by the colour of tablets in which the drug was sold or from the light blue tint of the LSD in liquid form. The expression either gave rise to, or was taken from the name of an American trio who were one of the first heavy rock groups.

blue foot n *British*

a prostitute. An ephemeral word of uncertain origin.
(Recorded by Deputy Assistant Commissioner David Powis in his *Field Manual for Police*, 1977).

blue lady n *American*

a form of synthetic heroin.
● '*I've been through pot, white lady and blue lady (forms of synthetic heroin) and I can't go through this much more.*'

49

(Jean Hobson, *Sunday Times*, 10 September 1989).

blue velvet *n American*
a mixture of paregoric (camphorated tincture of opium) and pyribenzamine (anti-histamine) as an injection. The term, the title of a popular song, is inspired by the supposed 'smoothness' of the effect. From the lexicon of drug abusers and addicts of the late 1950s.

bluie, bluey *n*
1 *British* a five-pound note; from its colour.
2 *Australian* a red-headed man. A common facetious nickname also rendered as **blue**.

B.M.O.C. *n American*
'big man on campus'; a **preppie** and student term for an influential fellow student.

boat (race) *n British*
face. A piece of London rhyming slang which is still heard in both the shortened and full form. (The Oxford and Cambridge boat race provided an annual excursion for many East Enders.)
● *'Nice legs, shame about the boat race.'*
(Sexist catchphrase from the 1970s).

bobby *n British*
a policeman. A widely known nickname, usually applied to constables or uniformed officers. Rarely heard except in jest since the 1960s, the word derived from the Christian name of Sir Robert Peel, who founded the Metropolitan Police in 1828.

bobbydazzler *n British*
something or someone impressive or dazzling. The word dates from the late 19th century.

bobby soxer *n American*
a teenage girl. The phrase referred to the short white socks worn as part of a standard ensemble in the 1930s and 1940s. The term itself survived until the 1960s.

Bob Hope *n British*
cannabis, **dope**. Rhyming slang from the name of the British-born American comedian. The term is usually said in full, as in *'We've run out of Bob Hope, let's call the man'*. The 'H' is often dropped, in self-conscious imitation of the appropriate accent (compare the self-conscious glottal stop in for example **bottle**). This is an example of rhyming slang used, and probably coined, by young middle-class soft-drug users in imitation of traditional working-class cockney rhyming slang. This tendency, noticeable in the 1980s, still seems to be confined to London and the south-east of England. For other examples of middle-class rhyming slang, see also **Uncle Mac**, **Sherman tank**, **merchant banker**, etc.

bod *n*
1 body. The short form is usually heard in American speech as in *'check out his great bod'*. In British middle-class speech it refers to an individual as in 'odd-bod'.
2 *British* a tedious, intrusive, pretentious or otherwise irritating person. A vogue term among the fashionable young in the later 1980s. The word may be a shortening of the synonymous 'wimp-bod'.
● *'We are going to create a club without bods . . . No bods. Bods being the sort of chaps who've got onto the scene and just stuck like glue.'*
(*Evening Standard*, 12 June 1989).

bodacious, boldacious *adj*
fearsome, enormous, impressive,

feisty. The word is now often used in black speech and by teenagers and has spread from American usage (where it originated) to the language of British teenagers. It appears to be a blend of bold and audacious, but Chapman's *New Dictionary of American Slang*, derives it from 'body-atiously'; bodily.

bodge n, vb British
(to do) a slapdash job, especially in constructing something. The term may be a back-formation from 'bodger', a rural craftsman who works out-of-doors in primitive conditions roughly shaping and turning chair-legs and spindles for example, or may be from the related standard verb, botch.

bodge-up n British
1 a makeshift repair, a ramshackle construction. The result of someone bodging a job.
2 a mess or disaster. A variant of **balls-up** or 'botch-up' influenced by meaning above.

bodgie n Australian
a male member of a youth cult, similar to the British **teddy boys** of the 1950s. (The female counterpart was a **widgie**.) In the 1930s bodgie was apparently used in American jive talk to denote a male jitterbug (dance) fanatic; some authorities dispute this and derive bodgie from the British and Australian verb to **bodge**.

bodgy adj British
inferior, malfunctioning or out of order. A late-1980s adolescent term based on **bodge-up**.
● '*Hey mate, your machine's bodgy!*'
(Recorded, video arcade habitué, 1989).

body n
a person, suspect, victim or 'arrestee'. A term used particularly by police

in counting up arrests or numbers of detainees. **To have a body** means to have a suspect in custody for a particular outstanding offence.
● '*The other frequently used term, "body", suggests detachment and indicates the appropriateness of behaviour that tends to deny or ... ignore the motivation and humanity that a detained person might reveal.*'
(*Inside the British Police Force*, Simon Holdaway, 1983).

bodyshop n
an employment or recruitment agency. The nickname may have originated in the USA among business people drawing a contrast with 'headhunters' (recruiters of senior personnel), and playing on the car repair workshop.
In Britain in the late 1980s the term has often been applied to Jobcentres, ironically recalling the name of a prominent chain of cosmetic retailers.

B.O.F., b.o.f. n British
a 'boring old fart'. An expression of derision institutionalized by rock music journalists in the mid- and late 1970s, usually applied by devotees of punk music to musicians of the hippy era who were entering middle age.
● '*Taking all my B.O.F. records and paperbacks down to [the] jumble sale ....*'
(*Sincerely yours, Biff*, Chris Garratt and Mick Kidd, 1986).

boff vb
1 to hit, to punch; a nursery variant of biff, occasionally used semi-facetiously by adults.
2 to have sex (with), **fuck**.
The term boff came to temporary prominence in Britain in 1974 when newspapers reported it as current among the upper-class set of which

51

Lord Lucan (fugitive and alleged murderer) was a member. This gentle-sounding word, with its suggestions of 'puff', 'buff' and 'buffer', next appeared as a convenient euphemism employed in US TV series, such as *Soap*, of the late 1970s and 1980s, where verisimilitude would demand a brusquer alternative. It is unclear whether the word is American or British in origin or a simultaneous coinage. It may derive from its nursery sense of 'to hit'.

● *'He's a logical choice.'*
  'So the fact he's boffing her has nothing to do with it?'
  (*Vice Versa*, US film, 1986).

boff n
  1 *British* the backside, buttocks.
● *'A kick up the boff.'*
  (*Only Fools and Horses*, British TV comedy series, 1989).
  2 a *American* a successful joke.
  b *American* a hearty laugh.
  Both senses of the word are part of the jargon of the entertainment industry and are probably imitative of an explosive chortle, or else like 'biff' denote a 'hit'.

boffo adj American
  excellent, first-rate. A piece of jargon from the entertainment world (derived by most experts from 'box-office') which has entered popular journalese.

boffola adj, n American
  an uproarious joke or laugh. The word is a form of **boff** with the Spanish '-ola' suffix denoting large-scale or extra.

bog n British
  a mess, disaster. The word occurs in the phrase 'make a bog of (something)', popular in the 1980s.

bog(s) n British
  a toilet. A widespread vulgar term, probably coined by students or servicemen in the 19th century in the form of 'boghouse' to describe foul communal lavatories. The term is used in Australia, too.
● *'"I ran into Shane", said Spider Stacey, "at a Ramones gig at the Roundhouse. He was standing on top of the bog, for some reason".'*
  (*Evening Standard*, 17 March 1988).

bog (up) vb British
  a to make a mess of, spoil. Usually heard in the form 'bog it' or 'bog it up'. A term especially popular in public schools and the armed forces.
  b to make the end of a cigarette or **joint** wet and mushy while smoking it.

bogart vb
  to monopolize or fail to pass on a **joint** or cigarette during communal smoking. This popular **hippy** term of the late 1960s was prompted by the actor Humphrey Bogart's habit in films of keeping a cigarette in his mouth for long periods. The verb originated in the USA and quickly spread to the other English-speaking areas.
● *'Don't Bogart that Joint.'*
  (Song title, The Holy Modal Rounders, featured on the soundtrack to the film *Easy Rider*, 1969).

bog-blocker n British
  something nauseating or grotesque. A vulgarism in use among adults, particularly in London in the 1980s. The image is of something blocking a toilet or causing the speaker to do so.
● *'That so-called funny story of his was a real bog-blocker.'*

bog-brush n British
  a nickname or term of abuse applied

by schoolchildren to a fellow pupil with cropped or spiky hair. ('Dunny-brush' is the Australian equivalent.)

bogey n
1 British a police officer. From the notion of the 'bogey man'.
2 an enemy aircraft or other enemy presence; a service term from the notion of the 'bogey man'.
• 'As they take evasive action, the "bogies", slang for the Libyan jets, continually come at them. "Bogies have jerked back at me again for the fifth time! They're on my nose now," one pilot says.'
(Evening Standard, 6 January 1989).
3 British a piece of mucus from the nose.

bogey team n British
in sports slang a team which usually manages to win against others in spite of seeming weaknesses. Bogey here has the sense of 'jinx' or 'charmed'. (In bingo a bogey call is a false or unlucky call.)

bog off vb British
go away. Nearly always used as an aggressive exclamation or instruction. A vulgar term that existed in armed-service use before becoming a vogue successor to **naff off** around 1980. In spite of the brusque nature, the phrase is not taboo and is used by women.
• 'If he's going to treat her like that he can just bog off.'
(Recorded, secretary, York, 1981).

bog-roll n British
a a toilet roll.
b paperwork or computer printout.

bog-standard adj British
totally unexceptional, normal and unremarkable. Bog is here used as an otherwise meaningless intensifier.

bog-trotter n British
an Irish person. A pejorative term heard since the 17th century. The alternative form 'bog-hopper' is sometimes used in the United States.

bogue n American
1 a state or period of drug withdrawal or deprivation.
2 a cigarette or **joint**.

bogue adj American
1 suffering from drug withdrawal. An obsolescent term of unknown origin from the jargon of narcotics addicts.
2 a worthless, counterfeit. From underworld usage.
b unpleasant, insincere. An adolescent term.
2a and 2b are probably derived from 'bogus'.

bog-up n British
a mess, a badly improvised job. A more vulgar form of botch up and bodge-up.

boho adj
bohemian, often in the sense of scruffy and/or irresponsible. This Americanism was fashionable from the late 1980s among London journalists.

bohunk n American
an East European immigrant. This old term deriving from Bohemian/Hungarian is offensive and occasionally still heard. It is synonymous with 'oaf'.

boiler n British
a woman. A contemptuous, derogatory term, implying a lack of both attractiveness and intelligence, commonly used by young working-class males. The phrase 'dodgy boiler' sug-

gests the extra possibility of sexually transmitted diseases. The word in this sense originated pre-World War II when it referred to an older woman with the dimensions and explosive attributes of the contraption. An alternative derivation is from boiler as used to denote a tough or scrawny chicken.

boink vb American

to have sex with, **fuck**. A 1980s variation of **bonk**, sufficiently inoffensive to be used in TV series such as *Moonlighting*.

bold adj British

flamboyant, daringly fashionable. A vogue word of the mid-1960s originating as a **camp** code word for a fashionable or overt **gay**. The word was adopted by **mods** as a term of approbation in 1965 and was used as the name of a chain of men's boutiques.

bollixed, bollixed-up adj

ruined, messed up. A derivation of **bollocks** which, in American English, is used as a less offensive version of 'ball(s)ed-up'.

bollock n British

a ball (in the sense of dance). A **Sloane Ranger** witticism said quite unselfconsciously by girls as well as boys, Hunt bollocks and Charity bollocks being regular features in the annual social calendar.

bollock vb British

to chastise, severely scold or dress down. The word has been used in this way since the early years of the 20th century.

bollocking n British

a severe telling-off, chastisement or dressing-down.

● '*If you are late for two days running*

on early turn you expect a bollocking from the skipper.' (*Inside the British Police*, Simon Holdaway, 1983).

● '*He was all set for giving me a bollocking for parking where I shouldn't.*' (*Guardian*, 12 December 1987).

bollock-naked adj British

completely nude. A more vehement version is 'stark bollock-naked'. In spite of its etymology, the expression may on occasion refer to women.

bollocks n pl

1 testicles. A version of this word has existed since Anglo-Saxon times; in Old English it was bealluc, a diminutive or familiar elaboration of bula; ball. For much of its existence the word, usually spelled 'ballocks' was standard (if coarse) English.

2 rubbish, nonsense. Often used as an exclamation or in expressing derision or dismissal such as '*a load of (old) bollocks*', this sense of the term has existed since the early 20th century. When the punk-rock group The Sex Pistols attempted to publicize their album whose title contained the word there was much agitation as to whether the term was still obscene or not.

● '*Never Mind the Bollocks, Here's the Sex Pistols.*' (Title of LP, 1977).

● '*That's a lot of bollocks. There aren't any styles, there's just good music and bad music, and that's ALL.*' (*Evening Standard*, 17 March 1988).
See also **bollock**.

bollocky adj

bollock-naked; a variant form from Australia.

bolt vb American

to leave, go away. A **Valley Girl** and teenager's expression usually denoting a leisurely departure.

bolted-up adj British

a synonym for **fitted up** or **framed**, in criminal jargon of the late 1980s.

- 'I've got about 30 previous – about half of those, I was bolted up.' (Recorded, bag snatcher, London, 1988).

bomb vb

to put one's **tag** (personal signature) on a building. From the jargon of graffiti 'artists'.

- 'Welcome to a freshly-bombed station.' (Graffito, East Putney underground station, London, 1988).

bombed adj

drunk or **stoned** on illicit drugs. 'Bombed out of one's mind/skull' is a common elaboration.

- 'Harvey decided his only real option was to get bombed out of his skull; some things never went out of style, thank God . . .' (The Serial, Cyra McFadden, 1976).
- 'Most of the troublemakers were bombed out of their skulls.' (Observer, 12 June 1988).

bomber n

1 a a pill or capsule of an illicit drug, especially amphetamines (see **black bomber**).

b a **joint**, especially a large or powerful one.

2 a graffiti artist. From the verb to **bomb**.

bombita n American

a pill, capsule or injection of amphetamines. From the drug-users' lexicon of the late 1950s. In Spanish, bombita means 'little bomb'.

bona adj, exclamation British

excellent, fine, the real thing. An all-purpose term of approbation increasingly heard among working-class Londoners in the 1980s, probably derived from bona fide or from the Spanish and Italian words for good (Buena and buona). In the 1960s bona was part of the **camp** lexicon (popularized in Kenneth Horne's radio comedy shows), originating in theatrical performers' and prostitutes' argot of the 19th century, in which it often meant 'beautiful'.

- 'A bona geezer.'

bonce n British

head. Bonce was a mid-19th-century dialect and schoolboy term for a big marble. The word was soon adapted to mean head, and in that sense remained popular in young people's usage until the 1960s. It now sounds old-fashioned or affectedly upper class, but may be due for revival, in common with other obsolescent but 'jolly' words.

bonehead n British

a a complete fool.

b a **skinhead** of unusually low intelligence and/or extremely right-wing views. The expression is used by skinheads themselves to characterize their more brutal fellows, who may also differentiate themselves by having almost completely shaven heads.

bone orchard n

a cemetery, graveyard. An alternative version of the more often heard **marble orchard** or **boneyard**.

boner n

1 a clumsy error, serious mistake. The origin of the term is not clear; it may be inspired by 'bone-headed' or by a 'bone-jarring' blow.

2 an erection. 'Bone', 'hambone' and

'jigging bone' are all archaic slang terms for the penis.

bones n pl

dice.

boneyard n

a cemetery.

bong, bhong n

a water-pipe for smoking cannabis, strictly one with a carburation hole so that the smoker can add air at will to the smoke. The typical bong is smaller than a hubble-bubble but larger than a pipe. A part of late 1960s drug paraphernalia.

bong, bong on vb Australian

to smoke cannabis in a water pipe (a **bong**).

bongo'd adj British

thoroughly intoxicated by an illicit drug or, less commonly, alcohol. A variant form of synonymous terms such as **bombed, banjo'd**.

bonk vb British

to have sex (with). A vogue word of the late 1980s; first heard in the late 1970s and quickly picked up by the media as a useful, vigorous, but printable euphemism for **fuck**. (The word was first broadcast in a British TV comedy series; at a later date, the tennis champion Boris Becker was dubbed 'Bonking Boris' by the gutter press.) It is a childish synonym for hit: the sexual sense may derive from the sound of energetic bouncing. Alternatively an extended correspondence in *Private Eye* magazine suggested that this had long been a schoolboy term meaning masturbate or ejaculate. It may also be significant that the immediately precedent vogue word for copulate among teenagers was **knob**, which in **backslang** would give bonk.

• *'They do call it bonking after all, which as everyone knows, is THE word used by promiscuous people who DON'T REALLY LIKE SEX.'* (Julie Burchill, *Elle* magazine, December 1987).

bonkers adj

crazy. A common colloquialism in Britain since the mid-1960s (it seems to have existed in restricted use since the 1920s), bonkers has more recently been adopted by American teenagers. The inspiration behind it is uncertain but may refer to a bang ('bonk') on the head.

bonzer adj Australian

excellent, great. A word sometimes adopted for humorous use by British speakers. It may derive from bonanza or from latinate words for 'good'.

boo n American

marihuana. A former blackslang word, adopted by **hippies** in the late 1970s. It is possibly a pre-World War II adoption of *jabooby*, an African term for fear, or else from the adjectival sense.

boo adj American

excellent, outstanding. A now obsolete piece of 1950s slang of obscure origin. It might possibly be based on 'beautiful'.

boob n

a a foolish, empty-headed person. A shortening of **booby**.

b a mistake or error, deriving from the verb sense. Neither sense of the word is particularly offensive, and may be used self-deprecatingly by the boob, or the perpetrator of the boob, themselves.

See also **boobs**.

boob, boo-boo vb
to blunder, commit a gaffe or error. The verb, based on the earlier nouns **booby** and **boob** in the sense of fool, has been in use since before World War II, the reduplicated form boo-boo since the 1960s.

boo-boo n
a blunder, error. A form of **boob**.

boobs n pl
breasts. The only slang word for breasts which is currently acceptable in 'polite circles'. (It is also used in the singular form, 'boob'.) It is a less brusque variant of the more vulgar **bubs** or **bubbies** which probably derive from the noises made by suckling babies. Boobs has been a fashionable term since the mid-1960s; bubbie since the 17th century.
- *'Gimme the good old days – when a pair of boobs was a couple of dumb guys.'*
  (Smokey and the Bandit III, US film, 1983).

booby n
a foolish person. An old and inoffensive colloquialism perhaps from the Spanish bobo; silly.

booby hatch n
a psychiatric hospital. A jocular term, originally from North America. The association with **boob** and **booby** is obvious; hutch or hatch is an archaic term for many different enclosures and containers.

booger n American
a piece of mucus from the nose, the American version of **bogey**.

boogie box n
a portable cassette player. The term, which originated in the 1970s, was first applied by young blacks in the USA to **ghettoblasters** and later sometimes to personal stereos. The expression spread to British teenagers and **Sloane Rangers** in the mid-1980s.
- *'I'm going on a train journey tomorrow, I mustn't forget my boogie box.'*
  (Recorded, secretary, London, 1987).

boom n
1 *American* a stereo cassette player, particularly one fitted in a car. A teenagers' term recorded in California in 1987.
2 a party. A teenagers' term in use in Britain and the USA since the early 1980s.

boomer n Australian
a particularly large kangaroo. Boom is an archaic term meaning to rush or move forcefully.

boondocks, the boondocks n American
an out-of-the-way place, a rural community, the back of beyond, **the sticks**. In Tagalog, a language spoken in the Philippines, bundok means mountain (area). The word was picked up by US service personnel in World War II.
- *'He comes from somewhere out in the boondocks.'*

boong n Australian
a coloured person. An offensive racist epithet based on an Aboriginal word, but used as a catch-all term regardless of nationality.

the boonies, booneys n pl
shorter forms of **boondocks**.

boost vb American
to steal. Originally from black slang, perhaps influenced by **lift**, **hoist** and **heist**, the term is now in general use

among young people. It usually refers to petty theft, often shoplifting.
- *'Some gals go in for boosting, or paper-pushing or lifting leathers. Others work the chloral hydrate.'* (Wild Town, Jim Thompson, 1957).

boot vb American
to vomit. This **preppie** expression is echoic or a blend of **barf** and 'hoot'.

booted adj American
expelled, 'booted out' (of school or college). A **preppie** term of the 1970s.

booze vb, n
(to drink) alcohol. 'On the booze' may mean habituated to alcohol or on a drinking binge. The word originated in Middle English as bousen, from Middle Dutch and Flemish busen; a word based on the root bus-; swelling.

boozer n British
a a public house.
b a heavy drinker.
Both meanings derive from **booze**, meaning to drink alcohol.
- *'I went into a boozer the other day and there was this bloke I hadn't seen for 25 years.'* (William Donaldson, Independent, 26 August 1989).

booze-up n
a drinking bout or drinks party.

bop vb
1 a to dance.
- *'Bop till you drop.'* (Record title, Ry Cooder, 1974).
b to move in a fast but relaxed way. This usage became popular in Britain in the late 1960s and is still heard.
- *'Why don't we bop down to the supermarket and grab some beers.'*
2 to hit or punch.
- *'Say that again and I'll bop you a good one.'*

bop n
1 a fast **cool** style of modern jazz introduced in the 1940s; also known as **bebop**. Bop was accompanied by rapid nonsense lyrics and dancing.
2 a dance. A word from America of the 1950s, revived in the 1970s and still popular in Britain, among teenagers and students in particular.
- *'Are you going to the art school bop?'*

bopper n
1 American a **cool** musician, dancer or devotee of **bop**.
2 a **teenybopper**. This shortened form of the word was especially popular in Britain in the 1970s to describe a vivacious, party-loving (usually small or child-like) young girl, a **raver**.

boracic, brassic(k) adj British
penniless, broke. The word is a shortening of the rhyming slang 'boracic lint': 'skint'. A genuine example of London working-class argot, this term was adopted into raffish speech in general in the early 1970s. (Boracic is an older name for boric acid used as a weak antiseptic impregnating bandages, etc.)

boss adj
excellent, first-rate, superlative. Currently a fashionable word among teenagers all over the English-speaking community, boss originated in American black street-jargon of the early 1960s. It was picked up by other speakers, but it remained an Americanism. (The music industry attempted to promote the 'Boss town sound' in order to establish Boston as the US equivalent of Liverpool in 1964; Duane Eddy had a 1960s hit with Boss Guitar.) In the 1970s and 1980s the usage spread through the language of disco, **funk** and **rap** to the young of Britain and Australia.

bot vb, n Australian

a (to behave as) an irritant or cadger. A shortening of bot-fly (a native parasite) or botulism.

b British shortened form of bottom, **arse**.

bother n Britain

trouble, violence, aggression. A typical example of menacing understatement as it occurs in London working-class speech (**spanking, seeing-to, have a word with (someone)** are other examples). The use of bother by police and thugs as a euphemism for violence reached public notice in the late 1960s when it became a **skinhead** rallying cry, usually rendered as **bovver**.

botheration n

minor annoyances or irritation. A colloquial back-formation from bother.

● 'Don't want your botheration, go away, don't bother me.'
(Too Much Monkey Business, Chuck Berry, 1957).

bottle n British

courage, bravery, 'nerve', especially in the phrases to 'have a lot of bottle', to **lose one's bottle**, 'his/her bottle's gone'. It derives from 'bottle and glass', rhyming slang for **arse**. Most users of **bottle** are ignorant of its derivation (compare the earlier **berk**). The word is long-established in the repertoire of south and east London rhyming slang, but surfaced in widespread usage only in the mid-1970s (probably via television renderings of police or criminal speech) to enjoy a vogue culminating in the adoption of the slogan 'Milk has gotta lotta bottle' for a nationwide advertising campaign in 1985. The word is pronounced with a medial glottal stop by cockneys and their imitators.

● 'If you've got an old PC trained twenty years ago and he's got no bottle, then you have to have somebody chase and get it [a stolen car].'
(Inside the British Police, Simon Holdaway, 1983).

bottle vb British

1 to hit with a bottle. A widespread brawler's tactic which seems to have become less widespread since the 1960s.

2 to collect money on behalf of a **busker** or other street entertainer.

bottle out vb British

to lose one's nerve. From **bottle** in the sense of courage.

bottom burp n British

a fart. An example of 'schoolboy humour' not confined solely to schoolchildren.

the bounce n

a the sack (from one's job) or a rejection (by a sweetheart). A later version of 'the boot'.

b one's fate, an inevitable result. Usually in expressions of resignation, such as 'that's the bounce'.

bounced (out) adj

fired from one's job, ejected, expelled or rejected. The image is one of forcible and speedy ejection resulting in one bouncing off one's backside on the floor or pavement.

bouncer n

a dud cheque, in debt collectors', underworld and police jargon all over the English-speaking world.

bounce-up n British

a fight, brawl. A short-lived synonym for 'punch-up' in the slang of **teddy boys** and toughs of the 1960s.

● 'A bounce-up in the Old Bailey –

*whatever next? You must control
yourselves.'*
(*Hancock's Half Hour*, British TV
comedy, 1959).

bouncy-bouncy n

sex. A coy or joking euphemism invented by adults in imitation of children's language. It is usually in the expression '*play bouncy-bouncy*'.

bounder n British

an unprincipled, dishonourable male. A now outdated term of disapproval. The word originally referred to someone who 'put themselves about' (expressed exaggeratedly as bounding) with unacceptable effrontery or showiness.

bounty bar n British

a black person who apes white manners or collaborates with white society, an **Uncle Tom**. The bounty bar, derived from the trademark name of a type of confectionery, like the synonym **coconut**, implies that such people are dark (like the chocolate) outside and white inside. The term is typically used by black or Asian teenagers.

bovver n British

trouble, **aggro**. A spelling, in imitation of a London accent, of **bother** in its menacing euphemistic sense of physical violence or extreme aggravation. '*You want bovver?*' was the standard challenge issued by **skinheads**.

bovver-boots n pl

heavy boots as worn as part of the **skinhead** uniform in the late 1960s. Skinheads first wore army surplus boots, later adopting 'Doc Martens' (DMs).

bovver-boy n

a a youth, particularly a **skinhead**, who enjoys fighting and conflict and is

always attempting to provoke trouble. A coinage based on the noun **bovver**, from the late 1960s.

b someone who is brought in to do a difficult job, a trouble-shooter. By humorous analogy with the above.

bowser n British

an ugly or unattractive woman. A male term of contempt coined on the basis of **dog** and the later **bow-wow**.

bow-wow n

a an unattractive woman.

b anything inferior, unappealing or worthless. Both senses of the nursery word are more recent synonyms for **dog** in its (originally American) slang sense. In city slang '**bow-wow** stocks' are poorly performing shares.

bow-wows n pl American

dogs in the sense of feet.

box n

1 a the anus. An old term popularized by male homosexuals in the 1970s.

b the male genitals. A term occasionally used by British schoolboys (influenced by 'cricket box', a protective shield for the genitals), and by male homosexuals.

c the vagina. An uncommon, but persistent, usage since the 1950s in all parts of the English-speaking world. The origin may be an unaffectionate reference to a 'container' or may derive from 'box of tricks'.

2 a a coffin.

● '*Be the first one on your block/to
have your boy come home in a box.*'
(Lyric to the anti-war song, 'Feel-
Like-I'm-Fixing-to-Die Rag',
Country Joe and the Fish, 1967).

b a safe. Used by criminals, among others, throughout the 20th century.

3 the box television. No longer really

slang, but a common colloquialism, especially in Britain.

4 a guitar. This usage was adopted by British rock musicians in the late 1960s from America, where it was originally used by black jazz and rock musicians in the 1950s.

5 American a portable cassette/radio player. A version of the longer **ghetto/ beat/rasta box**, heard in the later 1970s.

box of birds n British
a state of great elation or happiness. Usually in phrases such as 'like a box of birds' or 'as happy as a box of birds', this middle-class expression dates from the 1940s and is also heard in Australia.

boy racer n British
an irresponsible young car owner. A term of contempt applied to youths who characteristically decorate or customize cars and drive dangerously.

boystown n
the male homosexual scene, the gay milieu or part of town. A code term from the 1970s gay lexicon derived from the cult 1938 film Boys' Town, dealing sentimentally with juvenile delinquents.

bozo n
a buffoon, a clumsy or foolish person. A mild term of contempt which can sometimes sound almost affectionate. It has been widely applied to the former US president Ronald Reagan. Originally from the USA and Canada, and dating from at least the 1920s, the word is now in limited use in Britain and Australia. Before the 1960s it meant man or simple fellow; since then it has been adopted as a name for circus clowns for example. Attempts have been made to derive the word from Spanish origins such as vosotros,

(the familiar plural form of 'you') or a Mexican slang term for facial hair. In Italian, **bozo** means lump or bump.

● 'Capable of putting up with every bozo and meathead who comes his way.'
(Jonathan Keates reviewing Malcolm Bradbury's Unsent Letters, Observer, 5 June 1988).

brace vb American
to accost, **shake down**. A rather old-fashioned underworld term.

brackers adj British
broke, penniless. A word heard in the 1980s which is an invention based on **boracic** or a deformation of 'broke'.

bracket n British
the nose and mouth. A 'punch up the bracket' was a term used in the 1950s, introduced to middle-class audiences by the radio comedy Hancock's Half Hour. It is now almost never heard.

brahma, bramah, brammer n British
a a woman, particularly an attractive girl or girlfriend. A word adopted by **teddy boys** among others in the 1950s. The origin of the term may be in the Hindu deity (adored and decorated), the Brahman (sacred) cow, or the breed of large and colourful domestic fowls called brahmas.
b money, wealth or anything else attractive or desirable. Both senses of the word are now old-fashioned and rare.

Brahms (and Liszt) adj British
drunk. Rhyming slang for **pissed**. A fairly popular Cockney term since the 1930s, which was given wider currency by its use in television comedies of the early 1970s.

brainbox n British
an exceptionally intelligent person.

A term typically used derisively or enviously by children of, or to fellow pupils.

brass n British

1 money. Brass has been a obvious metaphor or euphemism as long as the metal has been used in coins. The word is currently more widespread in northern England.

2 a prostitute. Originally 'brass nail', this working-class usage is rhyming slang on **tail**, in the sexual sense.

3 a shorter form of **brass neck**.

brass adj British

broke, penniless. Pronounced to rhyme with 'gass', never southern English 'class', this is a short form of **boracic** or **brassick** heard among teenagers in 1990.

brassick adj British

broke, penniless. An alternative spelling of **boracic**.

brass-monkeys adj British

extremely cold. A shortening of 'brass-monkey time' or 'brass-monkey weather', this phrase refers to the widely known vulgar saying 'cold enough to freeze the balls off a brass monkey!'. A rather far-fetched explanation of the catchphrase is that a 'brass monkey' was a rack of cannonballs on board a warship.

brass neck n British

an intensive form of **neck** in the sense of 'cheek' or 'nerve'.

bread n

money. In the 1960s this usage supplanted the earlier **dough** in **hip** parlance; by the late 1970s the word was dated and in the 1980s has largely been replaced by a variety of colourful alternatives (in Britain, **dosh**, **rhino**, etc.).

• 'This year two chicks and I got enough bread together and flew to Eilat (Israel) to see what was happening out there.'
(Reader's letter in Oz magazine, February 1970).

breadbasket n

the abdomen. A pugilists' euphemism, first recorded in 1753.

breadhead n

someone who is motivated by money, a mercenary person. A term of disapproval from the **hippy** era, applied to those professing loyalty to the counterculture who openly or covertly sold out to commercialism or profit.

• 'Bob Geldof, then an impoverished photographer's assistant, sold him photos of Jagger and Pete Townshend which are still reproduced. Goldsmith, always an unrepentant "breadhead", parted with ten quid.'
(Sunday Times magazine, June 1989).

bread hooks n pl

hands or fingers. A jocular expression heard from cockneys and Canadians, among others.

breakfast n

See **dingo's breakfast**, **dog's breakfast**, **Mexican breakfast**.

brekkers, brekkie n

breakfast. The first form is British, the second American.

brew n

1 beer, or a beer. A word used by northern British drinkers (usually without the indefinite article) and by American college students (usually in the form 'a brew').

2 British tea. A term popular in institutions, especially in the 1950s.

brewer's, brewer's droop n
phrase

impotence, usually temporary, caused by drinking alcohol. The term is common in Britain, where it is now sometimes shortened to **brewer's**, and in Australia. (Brewers featured in many comic or ribald expressions from the 16th to the 19th centuries.)

brewski n American
a beer. An elaboration of **brew** popular with students.

Brian n British
a boring, vacuous person. Supposedly a typical name for an earnest and tedious working-class or lower-middle-class male. The term has been given humorous currency in the late 1970s and the 1980s by joking references to TV sports commentator Brian Johnson and a well-known sketch in the TV series Monty Python's Flying Circus concerning footballers. However, it was already heard among schoolboys in London in the late 1960s.

- 'Educating Brian.'
  (Title of an article on 'academic' footballers, You magazine, March 1988).

brick vb British
to castrate (an animal). This is probably a specialized use of a more general working-class slang sense of brick, meaning to destroy, ruin or thwart. The origin of the term is uncertain but may simply evoke hitting or crushing something with the object in question.

- 'He [a tom cat] was never the same once we had him bricked.'
  (Recorded, London, 1983).

brick it vb British
to be extremely nervous, overcome with fear. A recent usage derived from the vulgarism **shitting bricks**.

- 'Although I was bricking it, when the light came on on top of the camera, it was like this fifth gear'
  (Evening Standard, 2 September 1988).

brief n British
1 a lawyer. Derived from the briefs, or documents containing a resume of each case, with which the lawyer is prepared or 'briefed'. A working-class term used since before World War II by both police and criminals.

- 'One eight-year-old white boy brought in after being caught red-handed mugging in the area, astonished officers by refusing to say anything until he had seen "his brief".'
  (Observer, 22 May 1988).

2 a passport. A word from the lexicon of drug smugglers, among others.

- 'They picked him up with a suitcase full of cash and three false briefs.'
  (Recorded, convicted cocaine smuggler, London, 1987).

brill adj British
wonderful, exciting. A teenagers' shortening of brilliant, used as an all-purpose term of approval since the late 1970s.

- 'They are a wicked group and steam up the charts with brill singles in the US.'
  (Heavily ironic reader's letter, NME, 8 July 1989).
- 'I am having a completely utterly brill time ...'
  (Postcard from a 9 year-old, London, 1989).

bring down vb
to depress or disappoint. A black American and **beatnik** term, like the other phrasal verbs come down and **put down**, adopted in Britain in the

early 1960s by jazz enthusiasts among others. The phrase became one of the standard items in the **hippy** vocabulary. The past form brought down was also used in Britain to mean suddenly depressed, especially after an initial drug **high**.

- *'Don't Bring Me Down.'*
  (Title of song by the Pretty Things, 1964).

bringdown n

a a disappointment, a depressing experience. A black American and **beatnik** term popular among **hippies** in Britain. The word implies high expectations unfulfilled, or depression following elation.

- *'What a Bringdown.'*
  (Title of song recorded by Cream, 1969).

b a depressing or morose person.

- *'Don't invite John – he's a real bringdown since Sally dumped him.'*

briny, the briny n

the sea. Originally a literary or mock poetic euphemism (abbreviated from 'the briny wave' or 'the briny deep'), the word has been used humorously since the 19th century.

bristols n pl British

breasts. A common vulgarism, from the rhyming slang 'Bristol City'; **titty**. (Bristol City is the name of the city's chief football team.)

Brit n

a British person. The short form of the word British, first used by expatriates to refer to themselves, later by Australians and Americans, has only been in widespread use since the 1970s.

Brixton briefcase n British

a **ghettoblaster**. A late 1970s coinage, Brixton is a London district with a large black community.

bro' n American

a term of address used typically by black Americans to each other. It is a shortening of brother.

broad n American

a woman. A disparaging term in that it is exclusively used by men and implies a lack of respect for the woman in question. The origin of the word is not documented but is probably from 'broad-**ass**' or something similar, denoting an accommodating woman. (Immorality is not an integral part of the meaning in modern usage.)

- *'We've got Dustin Hoffman fighting Meryl Streep for a four-year-old in "Kramer vs Kramer" . . . Thirty years ago, the Duke would have slapped the broad around and shipped the kid off to military school.'*
  (*Real Men Don't Eat Quiche*, Bruce Feirstein, 1982).

Bronx cheer n American

a **farting** noise made with the lips and tongue, a **raspberry**. The Bronx is a mainly working-class borough of New York City.

broom-broom n British

a car. A nursery word sometimes used facetiously by adults.

- *'He's got himself a new broom-broom.'*

broomhead n

a dunce, stupid person. A homely term of (usually mild) abuse, used typically by parents and children.

- *'You broomhead! Why didn't you tell me?'*
  (*Degrassi Junior High*, Canadian TV series, 1987).

broom off vb British

to get rid of (something annoying).

● 'Some unscrupulous drivers resort to "brooming off", sweeping away the work they don't consider to be worth their while. One trick is to place a coin beneath one of the rear hubcaps.'

(Observer, Section 5, 9 April 1989).

brothel creepers n pl British

shoes with thick crepe soles, fashionable among **teddy boys** and others in the 1950s ('brothel stompers' is an American version). Brothel creepers has sometimes also denoted suede shoes or 'desert boots'.

● 'Red tiger-stripe brothel-creepers are all the rage.'

(Tatler, March 1987).

brown bread adj British

dead. A rhyming-slang expression which probably originated in the 1960s and which is still in working-class use in London.

brown eye n

the anus. An Australianism also heard in Britain, not to be confused with big brown eyes.

brown hatter n

a male homosexual. A derogatory term from the 1950s, still occasionally heard. The term refers both to the idea of contact between the head of the penis and excrement and to the archaic upper-class notion that the wearing of brown hats on certain formal occasions marked out a man as socially unacceptable.

brownie n British

a Scotch, drink of whiskey. A word used by middle-class and usually middle-aged drinkers.

brownie-hound n

a male homosexual. One of several 1980s epithets combining humour and hostility and evoking an image of a predatory sodomite ('chasing' or 'stealing' excreta). **Turd burglar**, and **chocolate bandit** are synonyms.

brownie points n pl

credit for good deeds, an imaginary award for virtuous actions. An American colloquialism which has caught on in Britain since the late 1970s.

brown-nose vb n

to flatter, behave sycophantically (towards). A vulgarism common in all English-speaking countries at least since World War II. 'Brown-noser' is an alternative version of the noun form. From the image of kissing another person's backside. (Private Eye, the satirical magazine, has instituted a regular column in which the 'order of the Brown Nose' is awarded for nauseating sycophancy.)

● 'Brown-nosing the boss.'

● 'Now he is on his knees, brown-nosing with the rest of them.'

(Private Eye, 1 April 1988).

brown trousers n, adj British

(a) very frightening (situation). A light-hearted reference to the terrified person losing control of their bowel movements. Now mainly middle class in usage, the term probably dates from World War II, but has not previously been recorded in writing.

● 'Getting up in front of all those people was brown trousers.'

● 'A brown trouser job.'

Brum n British

a modern short form of **Brummagem**, Birmingham.

Brummagem n British

Birmingham. A nickname used by

65

inhabitants and outsiders which is, in fact, a dialect version of older forms of the city's name. Nowadays it is usually shortened to **Brum**.

Brummagem screwdriver n
British

a hammer. A humorous term at the expense of workers from Birmingham. Today a more common version is 'Irish screwdriver'.

Brummie, Brummy n, adj
British

a (someone) from Birmingham. From the city's nickname **Brummagem**.

b the speech of Birmingham.

Bruno n American

Brown University, USA. The **preppies'** nickname.

brush n British

a pubic hair.

b sexual activity or potential sex partners. The word is almost invariably used by men of women.

bubbies n pl

breasts. This variant of the more widespread **boobs** is now rare and confined almost wholly to nursery-talk. It dates from the 16th century and probably comes from earlier Common Germanic terms inspired by the noises made by suckling babies.

bubble n British

a Greek. Rhyming slang, from 'bubble and squeak', an inexpensive dish of fried leftover mashed potatoes and greens. The term probably dates from the 19th century, but is still in use in London. In spite of its friendly sound, bubble is not a jocular term and can be used abusively.

● '*They also call him* [George

Michael] *the bubble with the stubble.*'
(*News of the World*, 29 May 1988).

bubblegum n, adj

(something) juvenile and frivolous. A term notably applied to inane pop music in the late 1960s. In that case the pejorative term was adopted by the music industry itself.

bubble-head n

a version of **airhead**.

bubbly n

Champagne, or any other sparkling wine.

● '*A bottle of bubbly.*'

bubs n pl

breasts; a now probably obsolete version of **boobs**. See also **bubbies**.

buck n

1 *American* a dollar. A buckhorn knife handle was used apparently as a counter in 19th-century card games and buckskins were earlier traded and used as a unit of exchange in North America.

2 a young male gang member. A term adopted by British black youth and football hooligans from the streetgangs of the USA, who themselves appropriated a word applied to young Red Indian braves.

bucket n

a pejorative or humorous term for a car or boat.

bucket vb

a to move quickly. Usually but not always in the phrase **bucketing along**. This usage dates from the 19th century.

b to pour (with rain). Usually heard

in the expression *'it's bucketing down'*.

bucket shop n

an establishment selling cheap and/or low quality items in large quantities. The phrase has become a standard British colloquialism for a cut-price travel agency. The expression originated in the USA in the 1880s when it was referred to as share-selling operations, by analogy with cheap saloons.

Buck House n British

the nickname for Buckingham Palace.

- *'"Buck's Fizz, actually", she said, over the teacher. "As distinct from Buck House where the Queen lives."'*
(*Nice Work*, David Lodge, 1988).

Buckley's hope/chance n

Australian

no chance at all or very little chance. The eponymous Buckley was an escaped convict who surrendered to the authorities after 32 years on the run, dying one year later in 1956.

buckshee adj

free, without charge. Like baksheesh, meaning a bribe or tip, this word derives from Persian *bakshish*; something given, a gift, and dates from the colonial era.

buddha sticks n pl

another name for **Thai sticks**.

buddy n

a *American* a male friend, from 'butty', a British dialect or gypsy diminutive of brother. 'Butty', or 'but', is heard in parts of Wales to mean a close friend (of either sex).

b a volunteer companion to an AIDS patient.

buff n

1 an enthusiast, expert or afficionado. An American term which, in forms such as film-buff, opera-buff etc., has become established in other English-speaking countries. The word is said (by American lexicographer, Robert L. Chapman among others) to be inspired by the buff-coloured raincoats worn by 19th-century New York firemen, later applied to watchers of fires, hence devotees of any activity.

- *'Having your life dragged through the popular press for scrutiny by a nation of voyeurs and trivia-buffs ....'*
(*London Australasian Weekly*, 4 September 1989).

2 **the buff** the nude. From the colour of (white) skin.

buffaloed adj American

a bullied, cowed, overwhelmed or bamboozled.

b knocked flat or knocked out. Both senses of the word evoke the crushing force of a stampede.

bug n

a an insect.

b a covert listening device.

c a virus or infection.

d a fault or flaw in a machine or system.

e an enthusiast, devotee. A racier synonym of **buff**.

The word bug originates in Middle English 'bugge' meaning hobgoblin or scarecrow.

bug vb American

to irritate or annoy. The image is of a crawling, buzzing or biting insect. The use of this term spread to Britain in the **beatnik** era but has never fully established itself.

- *'Stephenson said Mark Allen had "kept bugging them to burn down his neighbour's flat".'*

(*Independent*, 1 November 1989).

bug-fucker n American
(a man with) a very small penis. A soldiers' and teenagers' term of derision, often used in conjunction with its synonym **needle-dick**.

bugged adj
1 angry, irritated. From the verb to **bug**.
2 suffering from abscesses. A prisoners' and drug addicts' term.

bugger n
1 a sodomite. The Bogomil ('lovers of God') heretics sent emissaries from their base in Bulgaria in the eleventh and twelfth centuries to contact heretics in Western Europe. These travellers were known as *Bulgarus* (late Latin), and *bougre* (Middle French), a name which was imported into Middle English along with a loathing of the heretics and their practices. One offence which heretics of all persuasions were accused of was unnatural vice, hence the transformation of Bulgarians into buggers. The word is now a very mild pejorative often meaning little more than 'fellow'.
- *'So, if trying to persuade the local authority to stop discriminating and accept its responsibilities in a multi-racial society makes us "buggers" or "pompous prats", as Mr Flounders contemptuously calls us, then we are proud to be so.'*
(Reader's letter, *Independent*, 26 August 1989).
2 an awkward or difficult task or person.
- *'This is a bugger to get open.'*
- *'He's a bugger when he's roused.'*
3 *American* a dark-coloured, potent form of Mexican heroin.
4 a planter of **bugs** (listening devices).

bugger vb
1 to sodomize.
2 to ruin, wreck, incapacitate, thwart. This figurative application of the term is several hundred years old.

bugger-all n British
nothing, none. A synonym of **sod-all** and **fuck-all**. It occasionally denotes almost or virtually nothing.

buggeration n British
ruin, confusion. The word is often used as an exclamation of impatience by middle-class and upper-class speakers.

buggered adj
incapacitated, ruined, useless. This usage is encountered in British and Australian speech.

buggerlugs n British
a jocular term of address or nickname among males. The 'lug' component is either present for its sound or may be a joking reference to homosexual activity as in **buggery grips**.

bugger off vb
to leave, go away. A common verb and expletive in British and Australian speech.

bugger's grips
See **buggery grips**.

a bugger's muddle n British
an absolute mess. A phrase which was in armed-service and middle-class use in the 1950s and although sounding dated, survives.

buggery n
1 anal intercourse. The word is still, in Britain, the official designation of the act in legal terminology.
2 *British* oblivion, destruction, ruin.

The word usually appears in phrases such as 'all to buggery'.

buggery grips n pl British

sideburns or side-whiskers generally. A now-dated jocular or derisory term, popular among servicemen and blunt-speaking middle-class males in the 1950s and 1960s. The phrase invokes the idea of any unorthodox protuberance inviting homosexual attention (compare **fruit loop**).

buggins' turn n British

an automatic privilege that comes in turn to members of a group, regardless of merit, seniority, etc. A piece of bureaucrats' slang. Buggins is an imaginary name, perhaps inspired by **muggins**. The term probably dates from the 1940s and is still heard in local government and civil-service circles.

- 'The committee's leader is still selected on the principle of Buggins' turn.'
  (Recorded, member of Brent Council, London, 1987).

bug house, bug hutch n American

a mental hospital.

bugle n

nose. An old London working-class usage, parallelled in Canada, Australia and elsewhere.

- 'If you go on doing all that cocaine, you'll perforate your bugle!'
  (Recorded, artist, Vauxhall, London, 1976).

bugle-duster n

a handkerchief.

bug out vb American

to leave hurriedly. The **bug** component in this adolescent expression is essentially meaningless.

bugs bunny n British

money. A rhyming-slang term heard in raffish and underworld use since the 1960s.

bug-smasher n American

a light aircraft such as a propeller-driven training plane. The phrase has been used by the USAF since the 1950s (often derisively by jet pilots).

buick vb, n

(to) vomit. An imitative term employing the name of an American make of automobile and recalling such words as **puke** and **hoick**.

built adj

1 physically well-developed; statuesque or strong. An American term of the 1970s, now heard in Australia and Britain. It is used to express appreciation of sexual attractiveness by men of women and vice versa.

- 'Man, is she built.'

2 **built like a brick shithouse** heavily, strongly or solidly built. The term is used usually of people; when referring to men it is generally appreciative, when used of women it is more often disparaging. This is a very popular expression in Australia, but used throughout the English-speaking world. In polite company 'outhouse' can be substituted for 'shithouse'.

bull n

1 a uniformed policeman. A 200-year-old term still heard in North America and Australia, but never in Britain.

- 'But Butch, you can't stay here. This is the first place the bulls will look for you.'
  (Going Bye Bye, film starring Laurel and Hardy, 1934).

2 a shorter and more acceptable version of **bullshit**. In armed-service usage it particularly refers to excessive

regimentation of unnecessary formalities; in civilian speech it often denotes empty talk.

3 *American* a sexually active or aggressive male. A rarely heard 1970s and 1980s alternative to **stud**.

See also **shoot the breeze/bull**.

bull and cow n *British*

a noisy argument, a fight or brawl. Still thriving London rhyming slang for row.

- *'There was a right bull and cow in the pub last night.'*

bull artist n

a more polite form of 'bullshit-artist'.

bulldust n *Australian*

See **bull's dust**.

bulldyke n

a masculine, dominant or aggressive lesbian. An offensive term which was commonly heard until the late 1960s (by which time **gay** women's styles had largely moved away from imitation of male roles). Bulldyke was almost invariably used by men and was invariably pejorative; it was sometimes extended to apply to any lesbian.

See also **dyke**.

bull fiddle n

a double bass. A musicians' term heard since at least the 1940s.

bull's dust n

a less common version of **bull's wool**.

bull session n

a period of earnest or bombastic but shallow conversation. The expression usually refers to energetic group discussions between friends (usually males), talking **bull**.

bullsh n

a lightly disguised version of **bullshit**.

bullshit n

nonsense, or falsehood, especially when blatant or offensive; empty, insincere or bombastic speech or behaviour; tedious attention to detail. The term has become particularly widespread since the late 1960s before which it was more often heard in American speech than British (where it was, however, a well-known part of armed-service language).

- *'I'm not allowed to talk about it . . . [Roald] Dahl grumbled from his Buckinghamshire home. It has something to do with security or some such bullshit.'*
(*Evening Standard*, 8 September 1989).

- *'Listened admiringly as his interviewee expounded the Higher Bullshit of his trade. For example: "Advertising is using products to exemplify how they relate to the way you live, to the way you are".'*
(John Naughton, *Observer*, 15 January 1989).

bullshit vb

to try to impress, persuade, bamboozle or deceive with empty, boastful or portentous talk. Whereas the noun form is sometimes shortened to the less offensive **bull**, the verb form, especially in American speech, is shortened to **shit(ting)**, (as in 'come on, you're shittin' me').

- *'Don't try to bullshit me, I know the score . . . .'*

bullshitter n

a bombastic, verbose or insincere person; a habitual source of **bullshit**.

- *'"Mi-Lords! Laydees! and Gentlemen!!!" A VOICE FROM THE*

DARK SHOUTS, "Go home you Welsh bull-shitter!'" (Spike Milligan, Adolf Hitler, My Part in his Downfall, 1971).

bull's wool n

nonsense, something illusory, ephemeral or non-existent. A phrase that is often employed as an exclamation of dismissal or disbelief. Bull's wool seems to have been a rustic expression for anything fanciful or unnamed, throughout the English-speaking world in the 19th century.

bum n

1 British bottom, backside, buttocks. From the Middle English period to the end of the 18th century it was possible to use this word in English without offending respectable persons. By the 19th century it was considered rude, perhaps unsurprisingly in that its suggested origin was in 'bom' or 'boom', an imitation of the sound of flatulence.

2 a tramp, down-and-out, wastrel. This sense of the word is probably unrelated to the previous one. It is a 19th-century shortening of bummer, meaning an idler or loafer from the German Bummler, layabout (derived from bummeln, to dangle, hang about).

See **on the bum**.

● 'A.A. meetings here I come, even my mother thinks I'm a bum.'
(Lyrics to 'I'm a Wreck', by Mojo Nixon, 1989).

3 a sodomy or the opportunity thereof. A vulgarism used mainly by heterosexuals, referring to homosexual activity.
b sex. A heterosexual synonym for tail.

bum adj

a worthless, inferior, bad.
● 'A bum cheque/trip.'
b incapacitated, out of order.
● 'A bum ankle.'

These usages are inspired by the American noun sense of tramp, idler.

bum vb

to cadge or scrounge. From the noun form bum meaning down-and-out or beggar. This use of the word is predominantly British.
● 'Can I bum a cigarette from you, man.'

Bum and tit

See **B and T**.

bum bag n British

a rubber colostomy bag or improvized sporran, as worn as part of the punk uniform from 1976.

bumboy n British

1 a homosexual or a youth (not necessarily homosexual) who consents to buggery. A term of contempt, originating several hundred years ago and widespread since the 1950s, especially among schoolchildren.
2 a sycophant, an **arse-licker**. The term is rather archaic, having been supplanted by stronger alternatives.

bum chum n

a male homosexual partner. A schoolchildren's term, usually used jokingly to jeer at close friends.
● 'Eventually Lewis procured the help of the head steward who wore white gloves and a white suit, and his two bum chums dressed in blue.'
(Tatler, June 1989).

bumf, bumpf, bumph n British

information on paper; forms, instructions, brochures, etc., especially those considered unnecessary, annoying or in excessive quantity. This term is now an acceptable middle-class colloquialism although its origin is more

71

vulgar. It derives from 'bum fodder', a pre-World War II public-school and armed-forces term for toilet paper. This was applied scornfully in wartime to excessive bureaucratic paperwork. In Australia the usage is sometimes extended to mean unnecessary or verbose speech. The phrase 'bum fodder' in full is now obsolete, but was used from the 17th century to refer to waste paper.

● '*A glimpse of the unpestered life you lead at Cap Ferrat, deluged with fan mail, besieged by the press, inundated with bumpf of one sort or another.*'
(Ian Fleming in a letter to Somerset Maugham, quoted in John Pearson's biography, 1966).

bumface n British
a term of (usually humorous) abuse which was popular among metropolitan youth in the 1980s.

bumfluff n British
light facial hair on a pubescent boy. Usually a term of mild derision, especially referring to a youth's first attempts to grow a moustache or beard.

bumfreezer n British
a short jacket. The term originated among schoolboys in the 19th century to describe their uniforms, particularly the Eton jacket. It was later used by other wearers of uniform and also to describe so-called Italian box-jackets worn by **mods** between 1962 and 1965.

bummed out adj American
disappointed, dejected, having suffered a **bummer**.

bummer n
a bad experience, a disappointment. An American expression (said to have originated in the jargon of the racetrack where it meant a loss which reduced

one to the status of a **bum**) which spread to Britain and Australia in the **hippy** era of the late 1960s. It is still heard, although in the late 1980s it was dated. The meaning of the term was reinforced by the expression **a bum trip**, an unpleasant experience with LSD.

● '*So okay, it looks like a bummer. But maybe . . . maybe you can still get something out of it.*'
(Elmore Leonard, The Switch, 1978).

bump vb
to remove someone surreptitiously from a waiting list, in order to substitute a more favoured client. A piece of jargon from the world of air travel which entered the public consciousness in the late 1980s due to the prevalence of the practice.

● '*We were bumped at the last moment.*'
● '*They offered to bump someone to get us on.*'

bumpers n pl
1 breasts.
2 tennis shoes or baseball boots, especially those (in the style of the 1960s) with extra-thick rubber round the toe-caps resembling the bumpers of American automobiles.

bumph n
an alternative spelling of **bumf**.

bump off vb
to kill. A 'tough-talking' euphemism now largely replaced by more sinister locutions such as **blow away**, **waste**, etc.

bumps n pl
breasts. A mock-childish term.

bump start vb, n British
(to assist in) a sudden rousing to action, whether physical or metaphori-

cal. The expression, employing the image of push-starting a reluctant car, is a fashionable colloquialism in the 1980s, often in a business or sexual context. **Kickstart** is a more popular alternative in American speech.

- 'The poor old boy needed a bump start!'
- 'We had to bump start the bloody project by ourselves.'

bump tummies vb

to have sex. A humorous euphemism invented by adults in imitation of nursery language. Usually said by middle-class speakers.

the bum's rush n

an unceremonious ejection. This is North American saloon terminology of the early 20th century, referring to barmen or doormen grabbing undesirable customers (such as **bums**) by the collar and the seat of the pants and bodily hustling them out into the street. The phrase is almost always used in the expressions 'give someone the bum's rush' or 'got the bum's rush'.

- 'Personally I think Ange should have given Den the bum's rush.'
(Biff cartoon, 1986).

bum tags n pl British

another term for **dingleberries**.

bumwad n

toilet paper. A vulgarism heard in Britain and Australia.

bunce n British

money or profit. A word dating from the 19th century and almost obsolete by the 1960s, except among street traders and the London underworld. In the late 1980s the word was revived by middle-class users such as alternative comedians in search of colourful syno-

nyms in a climate of financial excesses. Bunce may originally have been a corruption of 'bonus'.

bunch of fives n British

a fist. A 19th-century pun on a hand of cards (or, later, a handful of banknotes), typically used in describing threatening or violent behaviour.

bunco n American

a swindle, fraud. A version of **bunk** or bunkum which has not been exported.

bundle n

1 a large quantity of money or of something else desirable, such as narcotics.

- 'I lost a bundle.'

2 British a fight, brawl or rough-and-tumble. Used especially by schoolchildren from the 1950s onward, typically as a cry or chant to attract onlookers to a playground or street fight, it is the British equivalent of the American **rumble**. Bundle is also used as a verb.

3 the male genitals, normally as seen through tight clothing. A term used by homosexuals and heterosexuals since the mid-1960s.

4 American an attractive woman. A condescending term which is probably a shortening of 'bundle of joy'.

See also **drop a bundle**.

bung n British

a bribe. A term used by police and criminals, almost always to refer to a bribe being given to a policeman. This normally implies something more substantial than a **drink**. The earlier verb form **to bung**, meaning to pay a bribe or protection money is now rare but not obsolete.

- 'He wants a bung of a monkey to square it.'

73

bung (someone) vb British

to bribe, pay protection money. An item of underworld and police jargon.
● *'We're going to have to bung him if we want to stay out of trouble.'*

Bungalow Bill n phrase British

a name applied by wits to a male who is either considered to be rather unintelligent (i.e. there is 'nothing up-stairs') or genitally well-endowed (i.e. 'everything is downstairs'), or both. The nickname was applied by the UK press in 1987 to the actress Joan Collins' companion, the property developer, Bill Wiggins.

bunghole n

the anus. A vulgarism found in the works of the celebrator of low life, Charles Bukowski, among others.

bunghole vb

to sodomize, **bugger**.

bungi-jumping n British

a dangerous sport of the 1980s involving jumping from high places attached to an elastic line. The spelling of the familiar schoolboy **bungy** has been changed for the sake of exoticism or on the mistaken assumption that it is from a non-European language.

bungy, bungie, bunjie n British

a rubber eraser. A schoolchildren's term since at least World War II, it was in use among office workers as early as the 1930s. The sound of the word is intended to convey the shape and consistency (influenced by words such as bung and spongey). The 'g' is usually soft.
● *'If i thro a bit of bungy at peason he will bide his time and thro an ink bomb back [sic].'*
(*Back in the Jug Agane*, Geoffrey Willans and Ronald Searle, 1959).

bun in the oven, to have a bun in the oven n British

'to have a bun in the oven' has meant to be pregnant in working-class British usage since the 19th century. The comparison of the stomach or abdomen with an oven is older still.

bunjie n British

an alternative form of **bungy** (rubber eraser).

bunk adj American

unfashionable, **uncool**. A teenage vogue word from 1987 which is a deliberate shifting of the standard sense of bunk and bunkum (as signifying nonsense).
● *'That's bunk, man.'*
● *'A real bunk thing to do.'*

bunk vb American

to cheat. A verb formed from the colloquial nouns bunk and bunkum and the slang **bunco**.

bunk in vb British

to gatecrash, enter illicitly or surreptitiously. Bunk occurs in many contexts as a version of bung, meaning throw forcibly; here the image evolved is of being lifted or hoisted through a window, for example.
● *'I told him I'd never been to drama school, so he said: "RADA [the Royal Academy of Dramatic Arts] is just down the road. Let's go and bunk in".'*
(Philip Roth, *Observer*, section 5, 9 April 1989).

bunk off vb British

to play truant or absent oneself. A term now heard mainly among school-children, bunk off is a variant of 'do a bunk' which has been a common expression since the 19th century. There is no connection with bunk bed, but rather with the sense of bunk (like 'bung') as to hoist or toss.

bunk (someone) up vb British
to lift someone or otherwise help them to climb over an obstruction, such as a wall. A schoolchildren's word of the 1950s, still occasionally heard, it was less common than the form to give someone **a bunk-up**. This is another example of bunk in the sense of hoist or throw
See **bunk in, bunk off, bunk-up**.

bunk-up n British
1 an act of sexual intercourse, especially when furtive and/or brusque. A term influenced more by the notion of being **up someone** than the erotic possibilities of bunk beds.
● *'A bunk-up behind the bike sheds.'*
2 a lift, help in climbing something.
● *'Give me a bunk-up over this wall and I'll scrump us some apples.'*
Both uses were common schoolchildren's currency in the 1950s and 1960s. The sense of bunk is hoist or throw; it is a variant form of bung.

bunny n British
1 incessant talking, chatter. This is a later version of **rabbit** (a shortening of the rhyming slang 'rabbit and pork'; talk). As rabbit entered non-cockney colloquial speech, so working-class Londoners adopted this more raffish alternative. It is sometimes used in verb form.
2 a a foolish, innocent person, victim. A usage recorded in Britain, the USA and Australia.
b a girl or young woman. A patronizing male term with similar implications to the previous sense.

buns n pl
1 *American* buttocks. A popular term since the early 1970s which is not

particularly vulgar and which is not in popular usage outside North America. The origin may be an obsolete Northern British dialect term for 'tail', a variation on **bum**, or simply refer to the parallels in form and texture with edible buns.
2 *Australian* sanitary towels or tampons. A shortening of 'jam buns' used almost exclusively by men. ('To have the buns on' is to be menstruating.)

buppy n
a member of the black middle class, a black **yuppie**. An American categorization of the late 1980s also heard in Britain.
● *'Establishing a black middle class won't help anybody except a few buppies – all yuppies, black and white, are scum.'*
(Reader's letter, NME, 8 July 1989).

the burbs pl American
suburbs. A vogue word of the later 1980s.

burg n American
a town, place. From the Germanic component added to many American place-names.
● *'Let's split this burg for good.'*

burl n Australian
a try. Usually in the phrase **give it a burl**; to make an attempt at, to try (a task or activity). Probably a blend of the colloquial expressions 'have a bash' and 'give it a whirl'. Give it a burl is one of many Australian expressions given currency in Britain by the cartoon strip *The Adventures of Barry McKenzie*, written by Barry Humphries, which ran in the satirical magazine *Private Eye* between 1965 and 1974. Some of the more colourful of these expressions were in fact coined, or embellished, by Humphries him-

self, but this phrase was well-established in Australia by the early 1960s.

burly n, adj American

(something) difficult, hard to achieve, problematical. A teenage vogue term from 1987, in use among the successors of **Valley Girls** and **preppies**, among others. It may originate in black street-slang where standard terms are often appropriated for use as gang code words or from surfers' slang.

burn n

a tobacco.
● *'Got any burn.'*
b a cigarette.
c a smoke.
● *'A quick burn.'*
The first sense is in use in prisons in the UK; the others are also heard in other English-speaking areas.

burn (someone) vb

1 to cheat financially. An Americanism that was part of the **hippy** vocabulary (typically referring to selling phoney drugs) and hence spread to the UK. It is now archaic in Britain. 2 American to kill. A 'tough guy' euphemism.

burn-artist n

a cheat, swindler. The term is applied particularly to someone who (habitually) relieves victims of money by selling worthless or under-strength narcotics.

burn off vb British

to overtake, outstrip and thus humiliate another driver. A term from the language of **ton-up boys** and **boy racers**.

burnt adj American

terrible, hopeless. A teenage vogue term of the late 1980s which is an ex-

tension of the earlier slang senses of cheated or 'burnt out'.

bush adj

provincial or primitive. A term that can mean rural, or second-rate, or both. Much used in Australia in expressions such as 'bush scrubber' and 'bush lawyer' and, to a lesser extent, in the USA where it is often in the form 'bush league', small-town or small-time.

bush n

1 area of pubic hair. The term is used more often by men of a woman's pubic hair than vice-versa.
● *'Naff things the French do on a beach: . . . display enormous pubic bushes.'*
(*Complete Naff Guide*, 1983).
2 marihuana, **grass**. A common term among smokers in the Caribbean and Britain. Bush refers especially to cannabis leaves and seeds sold unsorted and uncleaned.
● *'Want some bush, man?'*
(Recorded, street-dealer, Notting Hill, London, 1985).
● *'Prisoners cut off the cannabis leaves and dry them before smoking the drug in a form known as "bush".'*
(*Observer*, 12 June 1988).

bushed adj

exhausted. A 20th-century version of the 19th-century senses of disorientated, lost in the wilderness.

bushie n Australian

a provincial, rural or barbaric person; yokel.
● *'He thought the stereotype of the sporty, outdoorsy Australian began with the romantic 19th century image created by artists like Banjo Paterson, who had tried to convince us that we were "bushies".'*

- (*Southern Cross* magazine, July 1987).

business n

1 *British* **the business**. The very best, the acme of excellence.
- '*You should try some of this gear – it's the business.*'

2 *British* **the business** a thrashing, a thorough dressing down or beating up.
- '*We gave him the business. He won't try that again.*'

3 a hypodermic syringe. A drug user's euphemism.

4 defecation. To '*do one's business*' was a nursery expression epitomizing Victorian notions of duty and hygiene.

busk it *vb British*

to improvise. From the standard English **busker**, a wandering street musician. **Busk it** at first was a musician's, later a theatrical performer's term, referring to improvisation ('*I don't know it, but if you hum a few bars I'll busk it*') but is now widely used in other forms of endeavour, such as business. The word '**busk**' seems to have originated in an 18th-century borrowing from a Latin language: the Spanish *buscat*; to search; the archaic French *busquer*, to cruise; etc.
- '*If they don't accept our agenda we'll just have to busk it.*'

bust n

1 an arrest, especially for possession of illicit drugs. An item of **hippy** jargon which originated in the early 1960s and which by the late 1980s had become a common enough colloquialism to be used in the written and broadcast media. In American streetgang and underworld usage the word already had the sense of '*catch in the act*' by the late 1950s.
- '*The busts started to happen. People started to go to prison.*'

People started to die. But by then you were too far in.'
(Female ex-drug addict, *Independent*, 17 July 1989).

2 *American* a spectacular achievement or successful coup. A teenage term of approbation of the late 1980s, coming from the jargon of basketball, where it means a good shot.

3 a wild party or celebration.

4 a *Australian* a break-in, burglary.
b a break-out, escape from prison.

bust vb

1 to arrest, particularly for possession of drugs. In the USA the word was being used in this sense by the 1950s.
- '*And then I went and got busted, my old mother was disgusted. I'm never ever going to be trusted, by anybody anymore.*'
(Lyrics to 'Busted' by the Bonzo Dog Band, 1970).
- '*What I say [is] if guys get busted in North Africa and end up in their shitty prisons they got to be dumb in the first place.*'
(Letter to *Oz* magazine, June 1969).

2 *American* to demote. The word is used in this sense in armed-forces jargon as in '*busted down to sergeant*'.

bust one's buns *vb American*

to exhaust oneself by working, to make great efforts. **Buns** in this expression means buttocks, and the phrase is roughly equivalent to the British 'work one's arse off'.

butch adj

a tough, strong and assertive. The term is now often used humorously or to express mild derision; it probably comes from 'Butch' as a male nickname first heard at the end of the 19th century in the USA, which in turn probably derives from butcher.

b assertively masculine in behaviour and/or appearance. The term, typically

77

applied disapprovingly or derisively, is used about heterosexual women, lesbians and **gay** men. During the 1950s the word had a narrower sense of a 'masculine' (active) rather than a 'feminine' (passive) partner in a homosexual relationship, or of a lesbian who behaved and dressed like a man; in this sense butch was also used as a noun.

butcher's n British
a look. Nearly always in the phrases 'have a butcher's' or 'take a butcher's (at this)'. From the rhyming slang 'butcher's hook', which is at least eighty years old, and is still heard in the unabbreviated form.

butch up vb
to become more assertive, tougher or more masculine. This relatively recent expression (heard since the early 1980s in Britain) is often used as an exhortation, normally to a man who is behaving in a weak or cowardly way. (The antonym is **wimp out**.)

butt n
backside, buttocks. In the United States, butt is the most common colloquial term for this part of the body. Although slightly vulgar and generally the monopoly of male speakers, butt unlike **ass** is permissible in 'polite society' or broadcasts. It is rarely heard in Britain or Australia. Butt is historically related to 'buttocks' and in British, Australian and American English is still used to denote the thick end of something, as in the butt of a cue or a rifle, or simply the end, as in cigarette butt.

butterball, butterbutt n
American
a fat person, a **lard-ass**.

buttered bun n
a woman who has had, or often has,

sexual intercourse with a succession of men at a time. A very old expression (recorded in Grose's A Classical Dictionary of the Vulgar Tongue in 1785) which is now rare in Britain, but still heard occasionally in Australia.

buttfuck, butt-fuck n American
a a male homosexual. A heterosexual term of abuse.
b a despicable or contemptible person.
Both senses of the term play on the idea of someone who will submit to anal intercourse.

buttfuck, butt-fuck vb
American
to sodomize, **bugger**. An expression typically used by heterosexual males who are repelled or fascinated by the practice.
● '"Go butt-fuck yourself, Fruitfly." Milo smiled tightly.
"If I were you, I'd worry about my own anal sphincter, Ernie".'
(Jonathan Kellerman, Over the Edge, 1987).

buttie, butty n British
a sandwich. From Liverpool working-class slang (a shortening of 'buttered bread'). The term was spread throughout Britain in the 1960s, largely through the influence of the 'Mersey boom'.
● 'A chip buttie/A jam buttie.'
See also **buddy**.

buttinsky, buttinski n American
someone who interferes, someone who butts in. A humorous imitation of a Yiddish or a Slavic surname. The jocular **-ski** suffix is popular among high-school and college students, for instance.
● 'This is probably not any of my business, in fact I'm sure that it's not my business, and you're

78

probably going to get very mad at me for being a buttinski, but I really couldn't live with myself if I didn't say something.'
(*Moonlighting*, US TV series, 1989).

button n

1 a clitoris. An obvious reference which has been recorded in English since 1879. It gave rise to the now archaic buttonhole for the vagina.

b chin. Most often heard in the phrase 'right on the button', used of a punch that finds its target.

2 a section of the peyote cactus resembling a button, ingested for its hallucinogenic effect.

button it vb

to shut up, keep quiet, zip one's lip. A shortening of button one's lip which is heard as a peremptory imperative.

button one's lip vb

to shut up, keep quiet.

butt out vb American

to stop interfering, keep out, leave. Usually in the form of an instruction to remove oneself, butt out is a fairly mild if brusque expression. The butt component is interesting in that it is probably inspired by 'butt in' in which case it derives from butt meaning strike or push with the head. (It is commonly assumed to derive from butt, backside.)

buttplug n American

a term of abuse among schoolchildren. A slightly milder version of buttfuck.
- *'Sit on this, buttplug!'*
(*My Science Project*, US film, 1985).

butt-ugly adj American

a stronger version of the colloquial 'plug-ugly'.

buy it vb

to die or meet disaster. A euphemism often ascribed to airforce pilots in war comics and films. It may derive from the expression to buy or pay dearly (i.e. with one's life) or may be a shortening of the American buy the farm.
- *'I'm sorry, Madge, but Archie's bought it.'*

buy the farm vb American

to die. An expression which is said to have originated with barnstorming or fighter pilots. The farm in question is either a 'worm farm' (i.e. a grave) or an ironic reference to a symbol of retirement, (if a pilot survived he would often literally buy a farm).

buzz n

1 a rumour. A usage now so widespread as to be a colloquialism rather than slang.

2 a pleasurable sensation, stimulation. In the jargon of drug users, especially the beats and later the hippies, the word referred to a surge of light-headedness, a rush or high. It sometimes also refers to the use of alcohol.

buzz-crusher n American

a killjoy or 'wet blanket'. A teenage vogue term of 1988.

B.V.D.s n American

men's underwear. From a trademark name.
- *'I was standing there in my B.V.D.s.'*

by the cringe exclamation
British

a more moderate or joking euphemism for 'by Christ'. It appeared in the north of England in the 1960s and was popularized by, among others, the TV comedy series *The Likely Lads* and the soap opera *Coronation Street*.

C

C n

cocaine. A rare usage, cocaine having a wealth of more colourful nicknames, from **snow** to **Peruvian marching powder**.

cabbage n British

1 money; a lighthearted 1950s expression rarely heard today. The term was used for instance by 'Flash Harry' (played by George Cole) in the film *The Pure Hell of St Trinians*, in 1960. **Lettuce** was a more popular alternative, with the same derivation from the 'green and leafy' nature of banknotes.

2 a brain-damaged or inert, incapable person.

3 clothes made up from excess material; a perk of the textile industries. This ancient use of the word by tailors and the rag trade is of obscure origin, in spite of ingenious attempts to derive it from a variety of unlikely sources. It may simply compare rejected scraps of material with scavenged cabbage leaves. Cabbage in this sense is still used to mean scraps or rags.

ca-ca n British

excrement, **shit**. A word generally used by parents and children in the home. For the derivation see **cack**.

cack n, vb

shit, defecate. A word which in Britain is fairly rare (it is heard more often in the north of England than in London and the south-east), but remains common in Australia. Cack is a variation of

ca-ca: both are usually 'nursery words' and come from a common and very ancient Indo-European base. There are equivalents in Latin (*cacare*) and many modern European languages – *caca* in French, *kaka* in German, *kakani* in Czech. 'Cakken' was the middle English verb.

- 'He cacks on your "originals", you pee-pee on his boots.'
  (*Psycle Sluts*, John Cooper Clarke, 1979).

cack-catchers n pl Australian

trousers tied at the ankles, as worn by country farm-workers. They are also known as poop-catchers.

cack-handed adj British

clumsy, inept. The term originally meant left-handed, probably deriving from the idea of handling **cack** (excrement). Although the connection seems obvious, this expression is probably too old to be influenced by reports of the Muslim practice of eating with the right hand, wiping away excrement with the left. This pejorative adjective seems to be country dialect in origin; it is now fairly widespread and not particularly offensive.

- 'A cack-handed attempt at patching up the dispute.'

cad n British

An unprincipled, contemptible fellow. A word applied in the 19th century by privileged school pupils and students to their 'common' counterparts. It came to mean an often plausible but dishonourable male. Unknown to most of its users, the word is a short form of 'caddie', a Scottish and Northern English dialect word meaning junior or unskilled helper, itself from the French *cadet*. It remains an emblematic term of the period from the 1920s to the 1950s, suggesting to many the blazered and cravat-wearing character personified by the comic actor Cardew ('the Cad') Robinson.

Caddy n

a Cadillac car.

caff n British

a café, particularly a cheap, unpretentious one. An important word in the vocabulary of **teddy boys**, **ton-up kids**, etc., the word was later given the racier alternative pronunciation **kayf**.

cakehole n British

mouth. A slang term which was extremely widespread (and considered by many to be vulgar) in the 1950s and 1960s. It survives in the argot of schoolchildren.

call vb Australian

to vomit. A shortening of **call for Hughie/Charlie/Ruth**, etc.

● *'I've got to call.'*

● *'He's called all over the stairs.'*

call-boy n

a male prostitute or **rent boy** who may or may not be summoned by telephone. A rare back formation from call-girl.

call for Hughie/Charlie/ Ruth, etc. vb

to vomit. These are variations of **cry Hughie**, etc.

call-girl n

a prostitute who makes assignations by telephone. The term became popular after streetwalking was outlawed in Britain.

camp adj

homosexual, effeminate or affectedly theatrical in manner, gesture, speech, etc. A word which emerged from theatrical slang into general use in the 1960s. The sense of the term has moved from the specific ((male) homosexual) to the general (affected, exaggerated, parodic).

The word was adopted by the theatrical world some time after World War I from London slang, but the ultimate derivation of the adjective is obscure. It may come from the French *camper*, meaning to portray or pose, or from the dialect term 'kemp', meaning uncouth. In the late 1970s the gay phrase '*as camp as a row of tents*', referring to a person who is outrageously or blatantly camp, crossed over into general usage. The word camp was adopted in Australia and the USA before World War II.

● *'To be camp is to be mannered, affected, theatrical. To be camp is to be effeminate.'*
(About Town, magazine, June 1962).

● *'You, Joan [Collins] have earned your place with Judy, Marlene and Marilyn in the great camp pantheon of the sky.'*
(Howard Jacobson, Sunday Correspondent, 17 September 1989).

camp, camp about, camp it up vb

to behave in a **camp** way, using exaggerated, 'effeminate' gestures, speech mannerisms, etc. The phrase '*camp it up*' is particularly used to indicate a scene-stealing or outrageous piece of theatrics (literal or figurative) without necessarily any sexual overtones.

can, the can n

1 the can a toilet. Now a less-than-respectable term, but originally an accurate description of the buckets, tin containers, etc. used in outdoor lavatories, for example. The word was more common in the USA than Britain (except in armed-forces usage) until the 1970s.

2 the can a jail, prison. In this sense dating from the late 19th century, the word is more common in Australia and America than it is in Britain.

3 American backside; buttocks. An inoffensive euphemism.

- '*She fell on her can.*'

4 American a safe or strongbox, in underworld jargon.

can vb American

1 to dismiss from a job, fire. The term probably derives from the American sense of **can** meaning buttocks, **ass**, and the notions of kicking one's **ass** out, or thrown out on one's **ass**.

- '*I got some more news, I got canned last week.*'

(Recorded, executive, Chicago, 1983).

2 to stop, suppress or conceal something. This sense is normally expressed in the phrase '*can it!*'.

3 to jail (someone). A rare term formed from the noun.

canary n

an informer. An underworld term originating in the USA, based on the notion of **singing** (like a bird).

- '*Mob canary slain in Rolls – Had testified in bootleg gas probes.*'

(*New York Daily News*, 3 May 1989).

cancer stick n

a cigarette. A middle-class irony,

used by smokers and non-smokers alike since the late 1960s.

candy n American

a an illegal drug, particularly cocaine, heroin. This use of the word originated before World War I as a specialization of the figurative use of candy as anything enjoyable. (The word was used in black street slang with sexual connotations.)

b a dose of liquid LSD on a sugar cube. This vogue term was heard in Britain about 1967 when LSD was still taken in this form.

c American a dark-coloured form of heroin originating in Mexico.

See also **nose candy**.

candyass n American

a weak or effete person, usually male.

candyman n American

a **pusher** or **dealer** of illicit drugs, especially heroin or cocaine. Originating in black street usage, in which candy could also signify sexual gratification, this expression became part of the addicts' lexicon in the USA by the 1950s. (The original 'candyman' was an innocent peddler of sweets in the early 1900s.) The word features in numerous blues and folk songs.

cane vb British

to beat up, assault. A working-class brawler's and prisoners' term. It is probably a back formation from the more widespread colloquialism a 'caning', meaning a trouncing or defeat.

canned adj

drunk. The word seems to have originated in the USA, but had spread to other English-speaking countries before the 1950s.

cannon n

See **loose cannon**.

canny adj British

sharp-witted, 'street smart', attractive. This term from standard English is applied, particularly in Newcastle and the North of England, as a general term of approval, especially in the phrase '*a canny lad/lass*'. Canny is an irregular adjectival form of the verb 'can', thus meaning able, probably influenced by the dialect 'ken', to know (how).

can of worms n

an extremely complicated and/or distasteful state of affairs. This phrase, from the longer expression '*open up a can of worms*' is now used indepondently and has been popular since the late 1970s.

- '*Honestly, I wouldn't get involved; it's a can of worms.*'

cantaloupes n pl American

breasts. (The cantaloupe is a type of melon.)

Canuck n

a Canadian. The only widespread slang term for Canadians, whether French or English-speaking, it is rarely used by the British. The word has usually been used in a derogatory sense. (The -uck ending is probably an imitation of an Amerindian form, as in Chinook, the name of a North American Indian tribal group and jargon.)

canvas n

See **on canvas**.

cap n

a capsule of an illicit drug. The word appeared in the 1960s and was sometimes applied to a dose of LSD even when this did not come, strictly speaking, in capsule form.

- '*She scored a few caps of acid.*'

cap vb American

to insult, humiliate, **put (someone) down**. A teenage vogue term of the late 1980s. It presumably originates in the idea of capping someone's best stories or achievements, i.e. going one better.

capeesh?, capeeshee?, coppish? question form American

do you understand? The words are anglicizations of the Italian *capisci*?

- '*You dig? capeesh? understand? dig? Didn't they teach you that in Kiev?*'
  (*Red Heat*, US film, 1988).

Captain Cook n British

a look. An old piece of rhyming slang which shows signs of a revival in the late 1980s, as middle-class speakers fashionably imitate working-class usage. It is typically used in expressions such as '*take/have a Captain Cook (at this)*'.

cardie n British

a cardigan.

cark, cark it vb Australian

to die. The origin of the word is obscure; it may be a deformation of **croak** or of **cack**. Like other items of current Australian slang, the word has been introduced to Britain via TV soap operas.

- '*They break down in the middle of nowhere and before you know it they've carked it.*'
  (Recorded, Australian visitor, London, 1988).

carked adj

1 (of a situation) ruined or destroyed.

2 (of a person) exhausted, **pooped**.

This word may simply be an invention, or may be derived from **croak**, **cocked (up)**, or, more plausibly, **cack** (excrement, **shit**, by analogy with **poop**). It is heard in Britain and Australia, but not in the USA.

carn n British

cash, money. A distorted pronunciation of coin, probably taken from, or in imitation of black speech. The word was heard in teenage circles from at least 1990.

● *'You got nuff [enough] carn, guy?'*

carnie, carny, carney, carni n

a a carnival or travelling circus.
b a carnival or fairground worker.

The word is used in Britain and Ireland, but is more popular in the USA, where a subculture of travelling showmen and women with their own habits and jargon has grown up.

carpet rat n

a less common version of **rug rat**.

carrot-top n

a red-haired person. The expression is used all over the English-speaking world; in Britain the earlier carrot-nob, like **copper-nob**, is now almost obsolete.

carrying adj

1 in possession of illicit drugs or firearms. An international English usage.
2 British solvent, 'flush', having plenty of cash on one's person. A London working-class term.

car surfing n riding on the roof of a moving car. A dangerous teenage fad of the late 1980s, influenced by the US film *Teenwolf*.
See also **train surfing**.

carsy, carzie n British
alternative spellings of khazi.

carve vb British
to attack with a knife, to slash or cut (someone). From the vernacular of thugs, street gangs and professional criminals.

● *'They threatened to carve him.'*
● *'She got carved.'*

carve up vb British
1 to deliberately ruin (someone's) chances. It is usually in the passive form as in *'we really got carved up'*.
2 to cut in front of (another driver). A slang term of the 1960s which has become a respectable colloquialism in the 1970s and 1980s.

carve-up n British
1 a swindle or conspiracy that ruins one's chances. A rueful London working-class term probably inspired by a greedy carving up of a chicken or joint of meat and the use of **carve** to mean slash (a person) with a knife. The word was especially popular in the 1950s.

● *'Wot A Carve-Up!'*
(Title of British comedy film, 1962).
2 a sharing-out of loot or booty. A term used by criminals and police, especially in London.

cas adj American
1 relaxed, nonchalant.
2 good, acceptable.

Both senses of the word, which is a shortening of casual and pronounced 'cazz' or, more frequently, 'cazh', are teenage terms of approbation from the late 1980s.

case n
See **get on someone's case**.

case vb
to reconnoitre (premises) in prepara-

tion for subsequent robbery. The well known phrase '*case the joint*' has existed in underworld slang since before World War II. It originated in American usage, first being used with a generalized meaning of to assess

cassava n American

a the female genitals. A euphemism used by men and heard in the 1980s. It may come from the Caribbean, where the cassava root is eaten as a staple.

b a woman, especially an available one. By extension from the more specific first meaning.

casual n British

a member of a working-class subgroup of the early 1980s who were to some extent successors to **skinheads** and **suedeheads**. The characteristic of a casual was that he or she wore fairly expensive designer sports clothes in imitation of Italian or US **preppie** looks. The musical accompaniment to this style was generally home-produced soul or disco music. Casuals were a more materialistic and conformist manifestation from the skinhead and **mod** milieus. Optional elements of the lifestyle included football hooliganism and shoplifting for clothes or profit. Casuals were personified by the 1988 comic character Eddie Loadsamoney, created by Harry Enfield.

cat n

1 a person. In the parlance of **beatniks**, **hipsters**, etc. Deriving from black musicians' argot, cat was an approving form for a fellow (almost always male — females were **chicks**). The word is still in use, unselfconsciously among American blacks and jazz afficionados, and self-consciously in **hip** circles in Britain and Australia.

● '*All the cats and chicks/gonna get their kicks/at the hop.*'

(Lyric to *At the Hop*, recorded by Danny and the Juniors, 1959).

2 a spiteful woman. This sense is now so widespread as to be a colloquialism, rather than true slang. It is probably derived from '*catty*' rather than vice versa, although cat meant prostitute until the end of the 19th century.

3 American the female genitals. A rarer alternative to **pussy**.

4 Australian a passive male homosexual. This sense of the word probably, although not certainly, originated as an abbreviation of catamite.

the catbird seat n American

a very advantageous or privileged position. The catbird is a black and grey songbird which characteristically sings from a high perch.

catch a cold vb

to suffer a financial loss or setback. This expression from business jargon, implies a temporary rather than terminal affliction.

catch some z's vb American

a version of **cop (some) z's**.

cathouse n

a brothel. A widely-known expression, although it is mainly used in the USA; cathouse is based upon cat in its now archaic sense of prostitute (current in British English from the 16th to the early 20th century).

cat lick n, adj British

(a) Catholic. A children's corruption of the word, sometimes used, unaffectionately, by adults.

cavalier n British

(a male with) an uncircumcized penis. This term is from the argot of schoolchildren.

Compare **roundhead**.

ceiling inspector n
a willing woman, female sexual partner. A supposed witticism used, among others, by the Australian comic writer and actor Barry Humphries who may have coined the phrase.

cementhead n American
a stupid person. A coinage on the lines of **rubblehead**, **rock-head**, etc. (The notion of 'rocks in one's head' in place of brains is a well known American concept.)

century n
one hundred pounds or one hundred dollars, the word has been common in the argot of criminals, among others, for the last hundred years.
- *'I put a century on it and it lost.'*

cereb n American
a **swot**, in the language of the more sophisticated **preppies**. The word is from cerebral and may be pronounced 'see-reb' or 'sarebbe'.

cessy adj British
foul, repugnant, disgusting. A fairly rare, and usually middle-class usage, derived from cesspol or cesspit.
- *'Honestly, the whole thing was cessy!'*

the chair n American
the electric chair, used for the execution of criminals in many parts of the world.

Chalfonts n pl British
haemorrhoids. Rhyming slang for piles, from the small town of Chalfont St Giles in Buckinghamshire. **Farmers** and nauticals are synonyms.
- *'Stan was around yesterday, complaining about his Chalfonts.'* (Recorded, pensioner, Bristol, 1989).

chalice n
a large, cup-shaped container, similar to a **chillum**, used for smoking marihuana, especially in the Caribbean. The word expresses both the cup shape and the sanctified nature of **herb** smoking among Rastafarians.

char, cha n British
tea. The words for tea in almost all eastern languages from slavonic through Indian to Chinese, are variants of 'ch'a' or 'chai'.
- *'A nice cup of char.'*

chara' n British
a motor coach. From the word charabanc (French *char à bancs*, carriage with benches), widespread from at least the 1920s into the 1950s as a rather pretentious alternative to coach, and used by tour operators and their customers. The word in full was pronounced 'sharrabong' or 'sharrabang', and the shortening likewise. Elderly speakers still occasionally use the term.

charas n
hashish, cannabis resin. This is the Hindi word for cannabis resin (as distinguished from b(h)ang, the herbal form of cannabis). Occasionally used by smokers in other English-speaking areas in the 1960s and earlier to apply to hashish from any part of the world, charas today is used rarely outside India, and only by those who are, or who affect to be, connoisseurs of the drug.

charge n British
hashish or marihuana. The word was popular in the 1950s and 1960s, especially among **beatniks**, students, etc., who generally did not use hard drugs. This term, no longer heard, refers, (rather inappropriately perhaps in the case of cannabis), to the 'charge', or sudden electrifying sensation felt by

the drug user, possibly reinforced by **charas**. In American usage it was originally applied to the effect of a heroin injection.

● *'Got any charge, man?'*

charity-bang/girl/moll *n*

a woman who gives sexual favours gratis (especially when she might be expected to demand payment, or when the favour is inspired by pity). The 'moll' version was heard in Australia in the 1950s and early 1960s.

Charles *n British*

cocaine.

See **charlie**.

charlie *n*

1 *British* a foolish person. This innocuous word, often encountered in the expression *'a right/proper charlie'*, is in fact derived from the more vulgar cockney rhyming slang Charlie Hunt: **cunt**. In pre-World-War II cockney usage **cunt** merely meant fool, rather than the modern sense of a thoroughly unpleasant person.

2 cocaine. A euphemism from the international alphabet designation for the letter 'C', or simply a nickname. (The full form of the proper name, Charles, is occasionally used, usually facetiously, in Britain in this sense of the word.)

● *'She came steaming into the room when I had a massive great pile of charlie drying out on the floor.'*
(*News of the World*, 29 October 1989).

3 *American* the Viet Cong personified. During the Vietnam war the military alphabet designation 'Victor Charlie' was shortened thus.

4 *Australian* **a** a girl. From the rhyming slang Charlie Wheeler: **sheila**. The term is now dated.

b a (female) prostitute. By extension from the previous sense.

charlie *adj British*

cheap and nasty, flashy or in bad taste. A public-school and **Sloane Ranger** term of disapproval, heard in the early 1980s.

● *'He's really awfully charlie.'*
● *'The flat's a bit charlie, if you ask me.'*

charlies *n pl*

breasts. A word used (almost exclusively by men) since the 19th century. There have been many attempts to explain this term by deriving it from rhyming slang (Charlie Wheeler: **sheila**), from Romany or from the habits of Charles II. It is more probably simply a personification which implies affectionate familiarity.

Charlie's dead! *exclamation British*

your slip/petticoat/underwear is showing. A schoolchildren's cry since the 1950s. Inspired by the notion of flags at half mast (in mourning for a deceased husband).

charver, charva *vb, n British*

(to have) sexual intercourse. A word that is almost unknown in the 1980s, but which was used in criminal, theatrical and other circles in the 1950s and early 1960s. It is Romany in origin (*charvo* meaning to interfere with), and refers to the 'taking' of a woman by a man, so by extension it has been used to signify a woman as a sex object.

chase the dragon *vb*

a to take heroin by smoking it. The specific meaning of this expression (the arrival of which coincided with an influx of cheap heroin into the UK in the late 1970s) is to inhale fumes from a piece of the vaporizing drug through a tube, often literally chasing the smoke across the sheet of foil on which the drug is 'cooked'.

• *'Carmella never injected heroin, her serious involvement came with "chasing the dragon", inhaling a burning trail from a piece of tin foil.'*
(*Independent*, 17 July 1989).
b to flirt with death by using heroin. This more generalized meaning of the sinisterly colourful phrase was adopted by middle- and upper-class drug users when heroin spread to these circles in the early 1980s.

chateau'd *adj British*
drunk. A colourful upper-class and **yuppie** expression of the late 1980s playing on 'shattered' and implying that it is an expensive claret (Bordeaux) or other château-bottled wine which has caused the inebriety.

cheaters *n pl American*
sunglasses or glasses. A word now popular with schoolchildren but which probably originated with cardsharps who supposedly used 'magic spectacles', or with fraudsters who wore dark glasses as disguise.

check *interjection American*
yes. A jargon expression of affirmation (based on the mark of verification on a checklist, for instance) carried over into popular speech.
• *'Hey you, stay cool – Check!'*
(*Panic on the 5.22*, US film, 1974).

check out *vb*
to die. The notion of leaving a hotel or motel carried over into an eternal context. An old euphemism in American English which is now international.

cheese, the cheese *n*
1 an important person. In the form a cheese or the cheese this is a short term of the colloquial 'big cheese'.
2 something or someone unpleasant

or unsavoury, particularly distasteful bodily secretions. From the smell and texture of ripe cheese.
3 *exclamation British* another spelling and/or pronunciation of **chiz!**
4 a Dutch person. A humorous or derogatory term heard in one form or another (*'cheese-head'* or *'John Cheese'* are alternatives) since the 19th century.

cheeseball *n*
an unsavoury or contemptible person. An all-purpose term of abuse borrowing the name of the cocktail biscuit and the notion of **cheesy**.

cheese it *vb American*
to beware, hide or to run away. This old phrase, normally used in the form of an exclamation such as *'cheese it – the cops!'* has become a comic cliché in the USA. It may once have been used by members of the underworld (in Britain) or it may be a pre-1900 invention by writers or journalists. In any case it is actually heard in use today, usually somewhat facetiously by adults, and straightforwardly by children.

cheesy *adj*
unpleasant, unsavoury, squalid, disreputable, underhand. The original notion of smelly cheese has encompassed a number of nuances of distaste.
• *'A cheesy place.'*
• *'a cheesy thing to do.'*
• *'It was a degrading, lying, cheating piece of cheesiness.'*
(John Lydon [characterizing Alec Cox's film *Sid and Nancy*], BBC television, 1989).

cherries *n pl American*
flashing lights on a police car. *'Hit the cherries!'* is the command to turn them on.

cherry n

a a maidenhead, virginity. The word is usually part of the phrase 'to lose one's cherry', said normally of girls but occasionally of boys. The expression is old (dating at least from the late 19th century) but has not been superseded. It derives from the supposed similarity of the fruit to the hymen.

b a young girl, virgin. This is an extension of the preceding sense, although modern users of the word may derive it simply from the notion of sweet or delicious.

See also cherry 'og

cherry adj

new, fresh and attractive. A term used by teenagers and young adults since the 1970s in the USA and subsequently elsewhere. It evokes both the shininess of the fruit and the figurative sense of virginity.

cherry 'og n British

a dog. This working-class rhyming-slang term is still sometimes heard, in full or shortened to 'cherry'. 'Cherry oggs' was a children's pavement game played with cherry stones at the turn of the century.

chesty adj

having large breasts. A male euphemism or pun on the colloquial sense of 'chest cold'.

chevy n

a Chevrolet car.

chew (someone) out, chew (someone's) ass vb American

to chastize, tell off, give someone a severe 'dressing-down'. A colloquial expression heard typically in educational institutions and the armed services.

chi-ack, chi-ike, chiake vb

to tease or taunt. A rather dated term derived from 'to cheek'. It has been more common in Australia where the noun form, meaning impudence or insolence, is also heard.

Chicano n

a Mexican American. Méjicano or Méxicano in Spanish has been anglicized to this word which by the 1980s has few pejorative overtones. It has to a large extent been superseded by **Latino** or 'Hispanic'.

chi-chi adj

excessively cute, pretentious or twee. The word is a direct borrowing from French.

chick n

a a girl, girlfriend. The word has been used as a term of affection for hundreds of years, but was readopted by British slang from America in the **teddy boy** era. It was used unselfconsciously by **hippies** until the mid-1970s, since when it has been disapproved of by the majority of women. The term is now dated.

● 'This year two chicks and I got
enough bread together and flew to
Eilat (Israel) to see what was
happening out there.'
(Reader's letter, Oz magazine,
February 1970).

b also **chickie, chicken** American a passive homosexual partner or sodomized victim of a **rooster**. An American prison term of the 1970s and 1980s.

chicken n

1 a coward. In this sense the word has been in use for several centuries, although the children's taunt or exclamation was an Americanism of the early 1950s.

2 a a young male who is, or is likely

89

to be, preyed on by an older homosexual (**chickenhawk**), in **gay**, police and prison usage.

b an under-age girl as a sex object or partner, in the jargon of pornography. ('Chicken' was a common term of endearment especially to a younger or vulnerable lover in the 19th and early 20th century.)

3 a game in which young people dare one another to attempt something dangerous (e.g. to stand in the path of an oncoming train or car); the chicken, or first to withdraw, is the loser. When motor vehicle races are involved **chicken run** is the usual phrase.

chicken adj
afraid, cowardly.

chickenhawk n
a a male homosexual who 'preys on' younger men. This American term from the **gay** lexicon was given wider currency by press articles in the late 1980s, when Scott Thurston, the entertainer Liberace's lover, referred to him as a chickenhawk in revelations after his death.

b a heterosexual seducer or exploiter of under-age girls.

* '*Lolita at twelve, thirteen, fourteen, fifteen – and chickenhawk Charlie* [Chaplin] *never far away, mistily watching the bud unfold.*'
(Kenneth Anger, *Hollywood Babylon*, 1975).

chicken neck, chicken's neck n British
a cheque. An unusual piece of rhyming slang recorded in the late 1980s. An alternative is **Gregory (Peck)**.

* '*He suggested that £25,000 would be enough for him to spill the whole story . . . He then dropped his price to £5,000 and added "I'll take a chicken's neck".*'
(*Daily Mirror*, 31 March 1989).

chicken ranch n American
a rural brothel. It is not certain whether the chickens referred to are the girls ('cooped up' in the establishment) or the chickens supposed (probably apocryphally) to be given by rustic customers in lieu of cash. More than one brothel has been opened under this name recently, apparently inspired by an original bordello in Gilbert, Texas.

chicken run n American
a teenage game in which drivers aim their cars at each other to see which one will swerve first; **chicken** here is in the colloquial sense of coward(ly).

chickenshit n
anything worthless, petty or contemptible. In American usage the word originally had the specific meaning of oppressive minor regulations and other effects of bureaucracy, particularly in the armed forces in World War II. The noun sense is now rarer than the adjectival use of the word, except when describing paltry amounts of money.

chickenshit adj
a cowardly, afraid. An Americanism which was adopted in Britain, mainly by schoolchildren and teenagers, in the late 1980s.

b petty, contemptible. This sense derives from the American and Canadian armed forces expression to describe small-minded regulations, orders, etc.

chickie, chicky n American
a a young girl.

b a young partner or victim of a dominant male homosexual, particularly in prison. Both senses of the word are (often sinister) adaptations of an original term of endearment.

chief, the chief n American

LSD. A nickname from 1966.

chilled adj

excellent, admirable. A teenage vogue word of the later 1980s. The term is a synonym for **cool**, influenced by the verb form to **chill out** (relax, unwind). British fans of **rap**, **acid house** music and skateboarding introduced the word to schoolchildren's slang.

the chilled article n Australian

a cold beer. A mock-pompous euphemism used by drinkers.

chillin' vb American

relaxing. A teenagers' shortening of chill(ing) out recorded in the late 1980s.

chill(ing) out vb American

to relax, take it easy. A popular phrase in the 1980s, first among teenagers but later among adults, too, it comes from black street talk and is a later variation of **cool out**.

chillum n

a type of container (usually ceramic but sometimes made of wood or stone) which is packed with marihuana or hashish (often mixed with tobacco) for smoking. This item from the lexicon of **hippies** and other cannabis users is not a pipe, but a hollow cone held cupped in both hands, with a 'chillum stone' lodged in it to prevent the contents being sucked into the lungs of an enthusiastic user. Chillum is not, strictly speaking, a slang word, but Hindi in origin. It is, however, the only name for the object in question.

chin vb British

to hit someone (by implication on the face or head, although not necessarily on the chin). An old working-class term still heard in or around bar brawls, playground fights, etc.

- '*He called me a poof, so I chinned the bastard.*'
  (Recorded, pub habitué, London, 1988).

china n British

a friend, 'mate'. Rhyming slang from 'china plate'. An example of London rhyming slang which has survived from the 19th century and is still in working-class use today, albeit often ironically or self-consciously. It is usually part of the phrase '*me old china*',

China brown n

a variety of heroin imported from the far east in the mid-1970s.

China white n

a variety of heroin. China white appeared in about 1974 and was notable (and sometimes lethal) due to its unusual purity, hence strength.

- '*I had turned to Dr. D and cocaine in the first place only because I had come home from London strung out from the China white.*'
  (John Philips with Jim Jerome, *Papa John*, 1986).

Chinese adj

See get chinese.

Chinese rocks n pl

one of several varieties of heroin (including so-called **China white** and **China brown**) imported into the USA and Britain in the mid-1970s from the far east (Hong Kong). The phrase was used as the title of a song by the Heartbreakers (a late 1970s rock group whose dangerous habits were such an open secret that their concerts were advertised with the slogan 'Catch them while they're still alive'). **Rock** implies crystal rather than powder form.

chink n

1 a Chinese person. The word (possibly inspired by Chinese words for their own country and people, actually pronounced 'Joong-') has been used in American and Australian speech since the turn of the century; in Britain it is slightly more recent.

2 money, change. From the sound of coins.

chinkie, chinky n British

a a Chinese restaurant or take-away food service.

b a Chinese meal.

● 'I don't feel like cooking. Let's grab a chinky on the way home.'

c a Chinese person. A more patronizing or dismissive version of **chink**.

chinless wonder n British

an effete or gormless youth, particularly a vacuous upper-class male. The pejorative expression is applied to those literally weak-chinned, but more often to young men, usually in a privileged position, who are irresolute, offensively presumptuous or absurd. **Deb's delight**, **pedigree chum**, and **wimp** have similar overtones.

chipper n American

a an occasional user of illicit drugs (as opposed to a regular user or addict). A term popular in the early 1970s, used with mild contempt by, for example, addicts referring to non-addicts.

b a covert user of an illicit drug while under surveillance, for instance while in prison or on a drug rehabilitation programme.

chippie, chippy n

1 British a fish and chip shop. A nickname which appeared to spread from Liverpool in the early 1960s.

2 British a carpenter.

3 American and Australian a prostitute or promiscuous woman. The etymology of this sense of the word is unclear.

chipping n American

a the occasional use of illicit drugs (as opposed to regular use by addicts).

b secret and sporadic use of illicit drugs while under surveillance, for instance in prison or while undergoing a drug rehabilitation programme.

chippy adj

aggressive and hypersensitive, irritatingly resentful. The word is based on either the 19th-century 'chip in', to interfere; or the later notion of having 'a chip on one's shoulder'.

● 'He's chippy. I find that small people are often chippy.'
(Recorded, **Sloane Ranger**, London, 1984).

● 'Mr Kinnock appears to be sinking under a barrage of criticism to the effect that he is an ill-educated Welsh windbag carried high by chippy class hatred.'
(Evening Standard, 25 July 1988).

chips n

a carpenter. An alternative to the more common **chippie**, inspired by the debris supposedly left behind by these craftsmen.

chiv n, vb

(to) knife (someone). A word originating in Romany (gypsy) speech, used particularly in criminal argot of the 1950s. The word, also written and pronounced **shiv**, often referred to a home-made knife or razor blade used for instance by prisoners or street gangs.

chiz n, exclamation British

a blend of cheat and 'swizz'. A schoolchildren's word of the 1950s kept alive by its liberal use in the

Molesworth series of books by Geoffrey Willans and Ronald Searle.

● '"Let me take you by the handy pandy" and she do chiz chiz chiz chiz while all St Custards cheer.'
(Back in the Jug Agane, Geoffrey Willans and Ronald Searle, 1959).

chocaholic n
a person with an inordinate fondness for chocolate in all its forms. A jocular term punning on alcoholic. Colloquial and slang terms relating to food and indulgence (**foodie**, **couch potato**, etc.) were a feature of the 1980s.

chocolate bandit n British
a male homosexual. Like **brownie hound**, **turd burglar**, etc., this unaffectionately jocular term portrays the sodomist as a covert thief of excrement.

chocolate drop n
a black or coloured person. A usually unaffectionate term used mainly by schoolchildren.

chocolate frog n Australian
1 a foreigner, immigrant, not necessarily non-white. A piece of purely Australian rhyming slang for **wog**.
2 an informer, **stool pigeon**. In this sense the word is probably rhyming slang for dog, as in 'dirty dog', 'low dog', etc.

choirboy n American
a an innocent, naïve or young male.
b a new recruit to the police force, a **rookie**.
c someone feigning innocence or naïvety. In this ironic sense the word was used by the ex-police officer Joseph Wambaugh as the title of his 1973 novel, The Choirboys (filmed in 1977).

choke a darkie vb Australian
to defecate. A vulgarism heard since the 1960s.
See also **strangle a darkie**.

choked, choked-off adj British
overcome with indignation, fury, rancour or another strong emotion. Choked is a very widespread working-class usage, especially in London speech. Choked-off is a less common, and more recent variant.
● 'I tell you I was choked, really bloody choked when she told me they'd given the contract to someone else.'

choke (someone) off vb British
to discourage, repudiate or reject someone. This term is used in a fairly specific sense in the context of prisons where it usually means to frustrate someone who is attempting an official complaint or application.

choke the/one's chicken vb
(of a man) to masturbate. A teenagers' and students' variant of **jerkin' the gherkin**, **flogging the lizard**, etc.

choky, chokey n British
prison or a cell. A word which is still in use in the late 1980s, although it now sounds rather dated. The term comes from the Hindi chauki, meaning a shed or police compound, and was imported from India in the mid-19th century by members of the armed forces.

chomp vb
to eat or bite. An imitative term.

chompers n pl
teeth. A jocular term inspired by the verb to **chomp** and the earlier **choppers**.

93

choo-choo n
a train. Like **chuffer** or **chuff-chuff** this is a nursery phrase often used facetiously by adults.

chook n Australian
a chicken. This is an alternative pronunciation of an old dialect term, imitating the clucking of hens, which gives **chuck** in British English.
- *'I hope your chooks turn to emus and kick down your dunnee.'*
  (Rural Australian curse).

chop n
a cut-down, customized motorcycle. A shortening of **chopper 2a**.
- *'Sarah belongs to the distinctly laid back, Harley-Davidson inclined "lifestyle" bikers. Soon she will be appearing on a customised 550 cut-down "chop".'*
  (*Independent*, 6 April 1988).

chopped hog n
a customized motorcycle. The term originally referred specifically to the Harley Davidsons with lengthened front forks ridden by Hell's Angels.

chopper n
1 a helicopter. This was probably originally a children's version of the longer word, reinforced by the sound and scything action of the rotor blades. It was adopted by adults in World War II.

2 a a customized motorbike, usually having high **apehanger** handlebars and lengthened front forks, as ridden by Hell's Angels. It is derived from **chopped hog** or chopped (meaning cut down, altered). Nowadays it is often shortened to **chop**.

b a young person's tricycle or bicycle designed and manufactured to look like a customized motorbike, that is with a large back wheel and long front forks. From the 1970s when such bikes became popular.

3 *British* penis. A working-class vulgarism dating from at least the 1940s and still heard.

4 *American* a machine gun. Although this use of the word is familiar to many people through films and crime fiction, it has been obsolete in spontaneous speech since before World War II.

choppers n pl
teeth. A lighthearted term used all over the English-speaking world, often referring to false teeth.
- *'A new set of choppers.'*

chops n
mouth or jaws. The word has been heard since the 18th century before which it was usually in the form 'chaps', referring to the jaws of animals.
- *'The punishing dancebeat of late-'80s London smacks you hard in the chops.'*
  (*Time Out*, 26 July 1989).

chop shop n American
a customizing workshop for cars or motorbikes. To **chop** is in this case to cut down or alter.

chopsy adj British
garrulous, inclined to talk out of turn, argumentative, **mouthy**. From the use of **chops** to designate mouth or jaws.
- *'Spurs have turned into a really chopsy team since Venables took over.'*
  (Recorded, Welsh football supporter, London, 1989).

chow n
1 food. The word is about a century old and derives either from far eastern pidgin English 'chowchow', meaning a

94

mixture, or from *jiao(ze)*, (pronounced 'jowzer'), Mandarin Chinese for a dumpling.
2 a Chinese person. The term is usually used derogatively.

chow down *vb American*
to eat, sit down to a meal, 'tuck in'. From **chow** meaning food.
● *'While we're here let's chow down, hey?'*
(*Real Men*, US film, 1987).

Christmas! *exclamation*
an inoffensive euphemism for Christ, mainly used by British and Australian speakers.

Christmas-crackered *adj*
British
exhausted, worn out. Rhyming slang for **knackered**; a less common version than **cream-crackered**.

Christmas tree *n*
1 a spansule (a clear capsule containing different coloured chemical pellets that are released into the bloodstream over a long period of time when the capsule is taken) of drinamyl, an amphetamine or **pep pill**. In this sense the term is from the jargon of drug users of the 1960s, but Christmas tree has been used to describe other multicoloured drug capsules.
2 a garishly-dressed woman, especially one who is heavily built and/or wearing voluminous skirts.

chrome-dome *n*
a bald person. A humorous derogatory term referring to the polished sheen of a hairless head. In their book *The Boy looks at Johnny* Julie Burchill and Tony Parsons consistently referred to the balding musician Brian Eno as a chrome-dome.
● *'Who's the chrome-dome?'*
● *'I never saw him before.'*

(*Cheers*, US TV series, 1987).

chromo *n Australian*
a prostitute. A now dated term, still used in the 1950s and inspired by the image of the stereotypical prostitute's garish make-up and clothing, reminiscent of a chromolithograph, an early, often over-vivid, type of colour print.

chubbette *n*
a 'well-built' or shapely young woman. A vogue term of the early 1980s among some American and British speakers.

chubby-chaser *n*
someone who is sexually interested in or attracted to large or obese people. 'Chubby checker' has also been recorded in London speech for a male who enjoys looking at 'well-built' women, after the name of the American soul singer who popularized the 'twist'.

chuck *n*
a term of endearment literally meaning chicken, in northern English speech. It was originally a rural dialect term imitating the sound of clucking (**chook** in modern Australian).

chuck, chuck up *vb*
1 to vomit. A moderately respectable euphemism.
2 to throw out; specifically in police and underworld jargon to reject (an appeal) or dismiss (a case) or acquit (a defendant).
3 to eat excessively, '*chuck out*', or **pig out**.

chuck a cheesy *vb Australian*
to grin. The colloquial cliché 'a cheesy grin' has given rise to this more recent expression, in use in the mid-1980s among adolescents.

chucklehead n American

a foolish, silly or eccentric person.

chuck you Farley! exclamation American

a variation of 'fuck you Charlie!' used by high-school and college students, **Valley Girls** and others as a cry of contempt or defiance.

● 'Howdy Mr Flakey Foont gimme some skin baby.'

● 'Chuck you Farley!'
(Cartoon by Robert Crumb in Head Comix, 1968).

chuff n British

1 anus, backside. A word which has been heard since the 1940s, and which is innocuous enough to use where other synonyms are taboo. The etymology of the word is obscure, but it may be from dialect meaning plump (which is related to **chuffed**; pleased).

● 'As tight as a badger's chuff.'
(Room at the Bottom, British TV series, 1988).

2 a **fart**. A schoolchildren's and students' vulgarism recently popularized by Viz magazine.

See also **chuffing**.

chuff-chuff n British

a synonym of **chuffer**.

chuffed adj British

delighted, pleased. The word's meaning stretches from flattered to excited. It probably originates in northern English dialect (meaning puffed-up and proud) and is still most frequently heard in the north and midlands. Embellished forms are 'dead chuffed', 'chuffed pink' and 'chuffed to arseholes'. The TV soap opera, Coronation Street, which is set in the north of England, has 'chuffed to little mint-balls'.

chuffer n British

a train. A quasi-nursery word used facetiously by adults.

● 'I'm catching the chuffer down to Bath.'
(Recorded, journalist, 1987).

chuffing adj British

a polite or disguised form of **fucking** as an intensifying adjective. It is heard most often in the north of England.

chuff-nuts n pl British

another term for **dingleberries**.

chug vb British

to drink (alcohol). A coinage, derived from the drinkers' toast or chant 'chug-a-lug', fashionable among young people in London in the late 1980s.

● 'Sloane Rebs all support Chelsea F.C., and can be seen every other Saturday lunchtime "chugging brew" and getting hammered at any number of pubs in the Fulham Road, before charging down to Stamford Bridge for a "frightfully good game of footy".'
(I-D magazine, November 1987).

chummy n British

a term of address used typically by police officers to or about suspects. This condescending word is representative of the menacing use of terms of endearment, understatement, etc. favoured by London police and underworld.

● 'I think chummy here has got something he wants to tell us.'

chunder vb Australian

to vomit. This term, in use among Australian **surfies** and others in the 1960s, was imported into Britain later in the decade by the strip cartoon The Adventures of Barry McKenzie. The writer, Barry Humphries, derives it from the warning cry 'Watch under!', perhaps used by sailors. An alternative derivation is from 'Chunder Loo' as rhyming slang for spew, from the name of a character used in advertisements for boot polish fifty years earlier. Already established in Britain, especially among young sportsmen and drinkers, there are signs that this and other Australianisms are making headway in the USA following the success of the Australian comedy film *Crocodile Dundee* in 1987.

chunder circuit n *Australian*
a pub crawl.

chunky *adj British*
an all-purpose term of approbation briefly in vogue among London **mods** in 1966 and 1967.

chunter, chunner *vb British*
to nag or complain, especially incessantly and in an undertone. Chunter is a common form throughout Britain, while chunner is a northern and midland variant. The word is imitative of the sound.
• *'What are you chuntering on about?'*

church key n
a bottle opener. A (mainly middle-aged) drinkers' witticism.

chutzpah n
daring effrontery, impressive cheek. The word, pronounced 'hootspar', is via Yiddish from the Hebrew *huspah* (brazenness, audacity); it has been in use among non-Jewish Americans since at least the mid-1960s, but only appeared in the mid-1970s in Britain.
• *'I have valued my fleeting acquaintance with Larry Adler over the years because it has always given me an easy way of explaining the meaning of the Jewish word*

chutzpah *to those who have not met this valuable term. As far as I can define it briefly, it's an elegant opportunism, so fast as to deceive the eye, and so successful as to be totally disarming. Or what cockneys call bloody cheek.'*
(Miles Kington, Independent, 27 January 1989).

cig, ciggie n
a cigarette.

cirp, curp n *British*
alternative possible spellings of kirp.

clack n, vb *British*
(to) chatter, talk incessantly. A mainly working-class word, popular in the north of England. **Clack on** is an alternative verb form.

clag n *British*
bad weather. A rural dialect term for clay or mud, **clag** was first adopted in airforce slang to refer to thick cloud or fog. More recently, TV weather forecasters have employed the term lightheartedly.

clam n *American*
1 a dollar. Invariably used in the plural, this is a racier alternative to **buck**, etc.
2 *see* **spear the bearded clam.**

clambrain n *American*
a foolish or stupid person. The image evoked is of someone with the brain power of a mollusc.

clam up *vb*
to keep quiet, refuse to speak. Originally an Americanism (clams are a popular oyster-like seafood), the term is now widespread.

clang vb British

to commit a gaffe, make a mistake. A back formation from the colloquial phrase '(drop) a clanger', which shares the meaning of the shortened form.

clap, the clap n

venereal disease, gonorrhoea. The only widespread slang term for the condition, this word was derived from French (clapoir, meaning a swelling or clapier, brothel) in the late 16th century. It became a taboo and therefore slang term only in the 19th century. The specific reference to gonorrhoea had widened to include other venereal diseases by the 1950s.

- 'Ain't got the clap have you?'
  'God no! It's just a sense of cosmic boredom.'
  (Robert Crumb, cartoon in Head Comix, 1968).
- 'For while he nibbles at her
  Am'rous Trap
  She gets the Mony but he gets the Clap.'
  (Poor Pensive Punck, poem by John Dryden, 1691).

clapped, clapped out adj

worn out, exhausted. The second of these essentially British terms has been adopted in the USA since the 1950s. They are normally applied to machines, particularly cars, although they derive originally from the idea of a person debilitated by the **clap**, or venereal disease. As the origin is forgotten, the terms are now colloquial rather than vulgar.

clapped, clapped up adj

infected with venereal disease, suffering from gonorrhoea. These rather old-fashioned forms have largely been replaced by 'got the clap'.

claret n British

blood. Originally an upper-class the-atrical and boxing euphemism, this word is now heard mainly in London police and underworld circles.

- 'If you prick me do I not spill claret?'
  (The character 'Arthur Daley' in Minder, British TV series, 1983).

clart, clarts n British

trouble, a mess. This dialect term from the north of England and Scotland – probably a variety of 'clot' or 'clod' (of mud, slime, excrement) – is heard occasionally in other parts of Britain, usually in expressions such as 'too much faff and clart' or '(dropped) in the clarts'. 'Clarty', the dialect adjective meaning dirty, sticky and messy, is also still heard.

class act n American

an impressive display, performer or performance.

clat-tale n British

a tell-tale. A northern English children's variant of the standard terms 'tattle-tale' or 'tell-tale'.

clay pigeons n pl British

the cycle and motorcycle couriers' nickname for pedestrians in London heard from at least the late 1980s.

clemmed adj British

starving, hungry. An old word which is a survival of northern dialect (from Middle English 'clemmen', to pinch). It is still heard occasionally among older speakers (and, incidentally, in the TV soap opera Coronation Street).

clever-clogs n British

a know-all, **smartarse** or over-achiever. A now common colloquialism probably originating in the North or Midlands where clogs were until recently part of working-class folklore.

See also **pop one's clogs**.
- 'The exhibition has all the hallmarks of a rushed and ill-considered job, knocked together by a clever-clogs rather than an art historian.'
(Evening Standard, 17 March 1988).

click n American

a clique, small group of friends or confederates. A favourite word with high-school and college students.

clink n

1 a jail, prison. The most common (in Britain) and least racy synonym; it was the name of a prison on Clink Street in Southwark, London, from at least 1509 until the 18th century. The term may also be inspired by the sounds of metal keys, doors and manacles.
- 'You'll end up in clink.'
b British detention, in schoolchildren's jargon.
- 'I'm in Saturday morning clink again.'
2 British money. Like **chink** it is imitative of the sound of cash.
- 'I'm a bit short of clink.'

clinker n American

a failure. A word used particularly with reference to a film or play. In this sense it has been adopted by some British writers; in the USA it may occasionally denote other types of failure or incompetence. The slang use is based on the word's standard meaning of coal residue or cinder.
- 'Most of Hollywood, and especially John's brother Jim, refused to have anything to do with this clinker, adapted from the book by crusading Bob "I've been played by Robert Redford" Woodward.'
(Tatler, October 1989).

clinkers n pl British

another term for **dingleberries**.

clip n British

a blow, usually delivered with the open hand, a cuff. Often heard in the phrase 'a clip round the ear', a time-honoured punishment typically threatened and occasionally carried out by authority figures (policemen, teachers or parents) on misbehaving or cheeky small boys.

clip vb

1 to take (someone's) money dishonestly by sharp practice, deceit or fraud. The word is a euphemism from the jargon of tricksters, with the image of 'trimming' someone of their 'excess' wealth.
2 British to hit someone a glancing blow with an open hand, to smack.
- 'I clipped him round the ear.'

clip artist n American

a fraudster, cardsharp or confidence trickster. A dated term derived from the verb to **clip**.

clip joint n

originally a club or bar which employs hostesses who encourage clients to buy them (inevitably hugely overpriced) drinks in the expectation, rarely fulfilled, that their generosity will be reciprocated with sexual favours. The phrase may now be applied to any overpriced low-quality establishment. **Clip**, like 'trim', is an old euphemism for 'relieve someone of their money'.

clippie n British

a bus conductress or conductor. The word obviously derives from the clipping of tickets; it originated in Britain and Australia around the outbreak of World War II and is still heard wherever these professions survive.

clipping n British

a particular kind of cheating in which a prostitute takes a client's money but does not provide sex. A specific sense of the more general slang meaning of **clip**.

clobber n British

clothes, accessories or equipment. The word is now so widespread as to be colloquial rather than slang. It dates from the 19th century but its origin is obscure; it may be an invention, a dialect form of 'clothes', or from the Yiddish klbr.

clobbered-up adj British

a dressed, dressed-up.
b burdened, encumbered.

clock vb British

1 to notice or see, to look at. A working-class usage widespread, especially in south-east England, since World War II. The middle-class fashion in the late 1980s for imitating working-class speech has brought the word into some prominence and greater respectability. It probably derives from the obsolete use of **clock** to mean a person's face.
● 'Villains call it clocking in Leeds, eyeballing in Manchester and screwing in London's East End ... It came as a shock: juries can be intimidated by a stare.'
(Sunday Times, 5 June 1988).
2 to hit. A usage that was and is popular in Australia and which has been adopted in Britain (where it may have originated) and the USA. This term, used almost exclusively by men, probably also derives from the archaic **clock** meaning face; hence the verb, meaning to punch (in the face).
● 'He finally lost his temper and clocked him one.'
3 to tamper with the mileometer of a car in order to show a low mileage. A

piece of dealers' jargon which has passed into common currency due to the wide extent of the practice.

clock, the clock n British

the period of a particular police inquiry started by a caution and followed by 36 hours in which to question the suspect. An item of police jargon.

clocking n American

selling **crack**. A street-slang term of the late 1980s.
● 'Some of them wear tiny gold charms that look like miniature watch faces – a dealer's trademark, which is probably where the term clocking came from.'
(Sunday Times, 10 September 1989).

clodhopper n

a a clumsy or boorish person. The term originally (two hundred-odd years ago) referred to a ploughman or rustic (treading clods of earth in the fields).
b British a policeman. Rhyming slang from **copper**, rather than a simple pejorative.

clog vb British

to kick.

clog, cloggy n British

a Dutch person. This humorous or derogatory word may date from the 1940s when clogs were still widely worn. **Cheese** is a synonym.

clogger n British

someone who kicks people. The term is usually used dismissively of soccer players whose game is based more on violence than competence.
● 'That team are nothing but a bunch of cloggers.'

cloggy n
See clog.

clogs n pl
See pop one's clogs.

clone n
a a gay man of stereotyped appearance. In the gay male community of the 1970s a 'uniform' of working clothes, leather caps, moustaches, etc. developed. Indistinguishable conformists to this standard code were referred to by others and themselves as clones. In this sense the word is not necessarily pejorative.

b any fashion-follower or imitator who is indistinguishable from others, or blindly conformist to a dress code. A derogatory term since the late 1970s, often added to a prefix to form such epithets as 'Madonna-clone', 'Michael Jackson-clone', etc.

clone-zone n
the male homosexual milieu or gay area of a town where clones congregate. A term from the late 1970s.

closet adj
secret, covert. This general usage derives from the specific terms closet case and closet queen. Since the 1970s it has been applied, often facetiously, to anyone afraid to admit his or her leanings or affiliations.
● 'A closet liberal.'

closet case/queen n
a homosexual who conceals his or her homosexuality; the second version of the phrase refers only to men. Originally part of underground gay terminology, this phrase became well-known in the early 1970s when many previously secretive homosexuals decided to come out. The term was first widely used in the USA although its precise time and place of origin is ob-

scure. The connection between closet and secrecy is obvious; compare the phrase with the well-known 'skeleton in the cupboard'.

Club Fed n American
prison, especially a Federal, rather than state institution. A 1980s pun on Club Med(iterranée), which continues the time-honoured metaphor of a prison sentence as a vacation.

clucky adj Australian
broody, pregnant. From the image of a mother hen clucking over her clutch of eggs, the word has now extended to mean pregnant, wanting to be pregnant, or merely eagerly anticipating something.

clunk n American
1 a stupid, dull-witted person.
2 an old, dilapidated car or truck.

clutch n British
a cheek-to-cheek or arm-in-arm dance. A 'society' word used by Sloane Rangers among others, which is a specialized use of the colloquial meaning of 'embrace'.

Clude n
See Clydesdale.

Clydesdale n American
an attractive male. A humorous term of the late 1980s based on the supposed suggestion of heroic WASP maledom inherent in the Christian names Clyde and Dale. The word, which probably originated on the streets ('Clyde' was used by hipsters in the 1950s to categorize an archetypal square), was used by Valley Girls and preppies among others in the early 1980s. (The literal meaning of Clydesdale is a form of large, handsome, pedigree horse; strong, hardworking and enormously expensive.)

c-note n

a hundred dollars or a hundred pounds (not necessarily always in the form of a hundred-denomination bill). From the Latin numeral C: one hundred, this amount is also known as a **century**.

coasting adj American

under the influence of illicit drugs, moving around in a drug-induced daze or stupor. By extension, being in an euphoric state after listening to jazz, rock music, etc.

cobber n Australian

friend, mate. An unsophisticated term of address among men, which is now virtually obsolete. There are two possible derivations proposed for this well-known Australianism: the archaic English dialect verb 'cob', to take a liking to (someone) or the Yiddish word *chaber* (from Hebrew, meaning comrade).

cobblers n British

nonsense, rubbish, **balls**. A popular example of rhyming slang (from 'cobbler's awls') which is often used in ignorance of its vulgar derivation. Formerly used literally by cockneys to mean testicles, the word is old, but was given widespread currency in the 1960s by such TV comedies as *Steptoe and Son*.

● *'He is dismissive about awards: "A load of cobblers".'*
(*Observer*, Section 5, 9 April 1989).

cock n British

1 a term of address (for men). It probably derives from 'cock-sparrow', or from the image of a brave-fighting cock. Typically, the word is used in an affectionate, bantering way in expressions such as the dated Cockney *'wotcher cock!'*, or *'(my) old cock'*.

Cock has been used in this general sense for at least three hundred years.

2 nonsense, rubbish. This sense of the word has been in use since the 1940s and may be a shortening of poppycock (from the Dutch *pappekak* – 'soft shit' or absolute rubbish), or 'cock and bull', or a euphemistic variant of **cack**.

3 penis. In this sense the word is used all over the English-speaking world. In Britain the usage dates from the 17th century. Its origin is in the image of the male member either as a strutting fighter or as resembling a chicken's neck or water-valve. (In the USA the word rooster is usually prudishly substituted when referring to the male bird.)

cocker n

an affectionate term of address to a male usually in the form *'my old cocker'*. This London working-class expression dates from the 19th century and possibly referred to a fellow devotee of cockfighting.

cock-rock n

a pejorative description of bombastic 'heavy-metal' or hard rock music of the early 1970s, characterized by much **macho** posturing. The group Led Zeppelin epitomized the genre.

cock-shy adj British

(of a man) afraid to be naked in front of others, afraid to reveal his penis. The expression puns on the name of an obsolete fairground game in which missiles are thrown at a target.

cocksucker n

a despicable, contemptible person. This expression is almost always used in this sense rather than its literal meaning of someone who performs fellatio; it is generally an Americanism, applied to males as a term of abuse.

The implication is of a person who is willing to stoop (metaphorically) to disgusting, debasing acts.

cocktail n

1 illicit drugs mixed together or ingested simultaneously.

2 see **corporation cocktail**.

cock-tease, cock-teaser n

a slightly more polite version of **prick-tease(r)**.

cock (something) up vb

British

to make a mess of, to mismanage disastrously. As in the noun **cock-up** the precise origin of the expression is uncertain. It is common in Britain and Australia, but not in the USA.

cock-up n British

a mistake, blunder or shambles. Many different sources have been posited for this expression; cock may refer to some obscure piece of professional jargon (it occurs in the vocabularies of printers, hunters, browers and others), or to the penis; it may be an alteration of **cack**. Alternatively cock may simply have been chosen as a more acceptable complement in a phrase synonymous with **balls-up** and **fuck-up**.

- 'Mercifully these cock-ups don't happen too often.'
(Jeremy Paxman, Breakfast TV, November 1988).

cocky n Australian

1 a cockatoo. 'Cocky cack' is sometimes used to mean something insignificant and/or messy.

2 a small farmer. This expression derives from 'cockatoo' on the basis that, like the bird, the farmer inhabits a small restricted area.

coco n British

a black or coloured person. A pejora-tive or patronizing term used especially by middle- and upper-class speakers since the 1960s.

- 'And there were two cocos changing a wheel in the outside lane.'
(Recorded, public schoolboy, London, 1971).

coco, cocoa vb British

almost always used in the phrase 'I should coco(a)!', expressing disbelief or indignation. This is London rhyming slang for 'say so' (as in 'I should say so!').

coconut n

1 British a non-white person who collaborates with the white establishment, an **Uncle Tom**. This expression, used by young Asians and blacks in the 1980s, refers to the idea that such people are, like the coconut, black on the outside but white on the inside. **Bounty bar** is an alternative.

2 one's head. An obvious but probably obsolescent usage.

3 American a dollar.

cocooning n American

staying at home with one's wife and children (as opposed to going out or socializing in the evening). A **yuppie** term from the late 1980s.

- 'The latest trendy American word for spending an evening at home in front of the TV with your partner is "cocooning". The Yanks say it's a natural new-age protective reaction to the stresses of late 20th century life.'
(Daily Mirror, 16 February 1989).

cods n pl British

testicles. The singular form cod is an archaic word for the scrotum; it is an anglo-saxon word meaning bag (seen in the obsolete terms pease-cod and codpiece). Since the era of Middle English the plural has had this meaning in

British and later Australian usage, although not in the USA.
- *'He got kicked in the cods for his efforts.'*

codswallop, cods *n British*

nonsense, worthless rubbish. A dismissive term, typically applied to something purporting to be true. There is more than one theory as to the origin of the word; the most fanciful is that it referred to the wallop (gassy drink) produced by Mr. Codd (inventor of a patent ginger-beer bottle). Alternatively it may refer to testicles (**cods**) as in **balls**.
- *'Equal opportunities? That's a load of old codswallop!'*
(Recorded, office worker, London 1986).

coffee-bar cowboys *n pl*
British

young men who frequent coffee bars and cafés. The equivalent of America's **drugstore cowboys** and Australia's **milkbar cowboys**, this term was used derisively or disapprovingly of the young (**corner-boys, teddy boys, ton-up kids, rockers**, etc.) who congregated in such places throughout the 1950s and 1960s.

coffin nail *n*

a cigarette. The jocular term predates the public concern over the effects of smoking on health in the last three decades.

cog *n British*

a a gear, in the jargon of motorcyclists and other drivers.
- *'Drop down a cog and rev up.'*
b power, acceleration.
- *'Give it some cog.'*

cojones *n pl*

a courage, 'guts'. A word (pronounced 'co-honays') introduced to

many English speakers by Ernest Hemingway, it is the Spanish slang word for **balls** in both literal and metaphorical senses.
b testicles. The word sometimes has its literal sense in American English, especially when spoken by Hispanics.
- *'She kicked him in the cojones.'*

coke *n*

cocaine.
- *'It's very easy to find women if you've got coke.'*
(*News of the World*, 29 October 1989).
- *'If somebody came and sell coke on our street we kill 'em or beat 'em up bad.'*
(13-year-old US dealer, *Independent*, 24 July 1989).

cokehead *n American*
a (habitual) user of cocaine.
See **head**.

cokie *n American*
a cocaine user or addict. A now rather dated term, heard mainly among non-users.

cold *adj*
untraceable. The opposite of **hot** in its criminal sense, often applied to weapons or cars.
- *'It's OK, these guns are cold.'*

cold turkey *n*
a sudden withdrawal from hard drugs, typically heroin, with attendant hot and cold flushes, goose-pimples, discomfort, etc. The expression is originally American, from the 1940s or earlier, and in the late 1980s was increasingly used, often ironically, to describe a sudden withdrawal from any habitual activity. The phrase refers either to 'goose flesh' or to the general pallor and consistency of cold turkey meat.

104

- 'To go cold turkey/go through cold turkey.'
- 'They gave him cold turkey treatment.'
- 'When you've got cold turkey you think: "If I just had a little bit, I would be perfectly all right".' (Ex-drug addict, Independent, 17 July 1989).

collar n, vb

(to) arrest (someone). The noun form is a later coinage from the verb, meaning to catch, and the idiomatic expression 'to feel someone's collar', meaning to arrest them. Collar is another police jargon term which has passed into general use.

- 'Forget it Friday, this is our collar.' (Dragnet, US film, 1987).

come vb

to experience an orgasm. A Victorian euphemism for a physiological fact that has no other name (apart from the also-euphemistic 'climax') in standard English; this use of the word in fact dates back at least as far as Shakespeare and occurs subsequently in the (now archaic) form 'come off'.

come, cum n

semen. A later derivation from the verb to come.

come across vb

to consent to sex, especially after initial reluctance. A phrase widespread in the English-speaking world since the 1960s, originating from the more general sense of come across, meaning to accede, give, agree.

comedown n

a period of physical and mental depression and exhaustion following a bout of elation from drugs, specifically the after-effects of amphetamine use.

- 'That stuff's terrible – the

comedown lasts longer than the high.'

come hard, come it hard vb
British

to act aggressively or threateningly. A working-class term which is a variation of come it.

- 'Was you comin' 'ard the other day down our playing field?' (Recorded, 12-year old, London, 1959).

come it vb British

to behave in a presumptuous, provocative or aggressive way, to show off. A working-class phrase popular with skinheads, who used it to mean 'invite aggression'.

- 'Don't come it with me you cheeky little bleeder or I'll give you a clip round the ear.' (Recorded, park keeper, London, 1958).

come on vb

to start to menstruate. A euphemism used by women and men.

come-on n

an approach or enticement. The word was formerly slang, usually in a sexual context, but now has become a colloquial term for almost any inducement (especially one of doubtful benefit).

come out vb

to reveal oneself as a homosexual, declare one's homosexuality. The expression is a shortening of 'come out of the closet', dating from the period in the early 1970s when liberalization encouraged more openness among gay men and women in their relations with each other and the straight world. The term has sometimes been extended in the later 1970s and the 1980s to mean 'to declare one's real position' in non-sexual contexts.

come the raw prawn vb
Australian
to try to take advantage of, or deceive someone. This colourful expression probably originated in the 1940s and is still heard. The precise connection between the uncooked crustacean and deceitfulness is not clear, but the suggestion is of cadging by feigning innocence or naîvety.

the Company n *American*
the CIA, the American intelligence agency. A nickname used by its employees and associates.
- *'Gerry Hart used to refer to the CIA as "the Company" to emphasize that he had been on the inside.'*
(Len Deighton, Twinkle, Twinkle, Little Spy, 1976).

completely cute adj *American*
suitably attractive, handsome and/or sexy. An expression used by upper- and middle-class young women to indicate approval of a potential male partner. A code term in the **preppie** lexicon.

compo n *Australian*
(unemployment) compensation. A typical Australian shortening. (Compare **arvo**, **convo**, etc.)

con vb, n
(to perpetrate) a swindle or fraud, obtain money by false pretences. This venerable colloquialism (regarded as slang in the 1950s) is simply a shortening of 'confidence-trick'.
- *'A crazy au pair girl planned to con super-star Eric Clapton out of a fortune by claiming another couple's baby was THEIR love child.'*
(News of the World, 1988).

con n *American*
a convict or ex-convict, felon or prisoner.

conch n *American*
a **swot**. A **preppie** shortening of conscientious.

conchie n
an alternative spelling of **conshie**.

condo n *American*
a condominium (an apartment complex which is jointly owned by its tenants).

conk n
1 a nose. The generally-quoted origin for this comical word is the conch shell (often collected as a curio since the 17th century), or a learned play on the Latin *concha*, meaning shell in general, or trumpet.
- *'Ooh, sir, that's a big conk you've got.'*
(Recorded, schoolgirl, Battersea, London, 1973).
- *'This face, embossed as it is with a vast fleshy conk.'*
(Observer magazine, 15 May 1988).
b head. A less common use of the word.
2 *American* a 'process' hairstyle (one where the hair is straightened by the application of chemicals and/or heat) as worn by **hip** young blacks from the 1930s until the 1960s when it was superseded by the racially affirmative **afro** styles.

connection, connexion n
a drug supplier, a **dealer** or **pusher**. Originally from the language of American drug users of the late 1950s and 1960s, the term has become part of the international jargon of illicit drug users. It particularly refers to a source of heroin. (Connection was used am-

biguously as the title and in the lyrics of a 1967 song by the Rolling Stones.)

conshie, conchie n
a conscientious objector; a (generally pejorative) term from the days of conscription and national service.

convo n Australian
a conversation. A characteristic Australian shortening of the standard word.

cookie-pusher n American
an unmanly man, an effete or sycophantic male. The image is of someone who spends his time (the word never seems to be used of women) passing cookies at tea parties, either because he enjoys such 'effeminate' activities, or in order to curry favour or further his career.
● 'Some little State Department cookie-pusher trying to persuade them all to play ball.'

cooking adj American
going well, moving fast, succeeding. Originally from pre-World-War II street language, this usage spread, especially via jazz musicians, to young whites. It is still often used to refer to musicians performing well and generating excitement. A stronger form is 'cooking with gas'.

cool adj
a unflappable, imperturbable.
b excellent, admirable, acceptable. One of the key items in the vocabulary of jazz musicians, **hipsters**, **beatniks** and **hippies**, cool, with its original suggestion of calm disinterested serenity, is a word which has not dated. It is as much in vogue with teenagers in the late 1980s as it was among the 1930s jazz musicians who probably coined it (to denote gentler, progressive jazz, as opposed to 'hot' jazz).

cool n
sang froid, imperturbability. A back-formation from the adjective.

cool it, cool out vb
to relax, unwind, defuse a situation. A **hipsters'** term which has become a common colloquialism.

coon n
a black person. Originally (and still) a term of racist abuse common in the Southern states of the USA, from raccoon (a black-faced rural pest). The word has been adopted in Britain and Australia to refer to a person of any supposedly inferior race. In Britain it is a widespread racist epithet in use by the police and other working-class whites; **egg and spoon** is the rhyming-slang version.
● 'There were a couple of coons shouting at each other and it's difficult in these circumstances, I suppose.'
(Police officer, quoted in Inside the British Police by Simon Holdaway, 1983).

coose n American
an alternative spelling of **cooze**.

cootie n American
a head or body louse. The word was originally armed-forces slang, from the Polynesian kutu, meaning 'parasite'.
● 'Here you are.'
'No, not if it has cooties on it.'
'I don't have cooties!'
(Roseanne, US TV comedy series, 1989).

cooze n American
a a woman. A fairly vulgar term, used almost exclusively by men, and having overtones of 'sex object', 'victim' or 'slut'.
b the female sex organs. The origin of the word is obscure.

cop n

a police officer. A shortening of **copper**. In Britain until the 1960s **cop** was felt to be an Americanism and only in the late 1980s has it finally found its way into print, albeit in the gutter press.

- *'Don't cry/Gotta go bye bye/ SUDDENLY: DIE DIE/COP KILL A CREEP! pow pow pow.'*
  ('Concentration Moon' written by Frank Zappa, recorded by the Mothers of Invention, 1967).

cop vb

to buy illicit drugs, to **score**. A specialization of the general use of cop to mean obtain.

- *'You wanna take a walk,*
  You wanna go cop,
  You wanna go get
  Some chinese rock?'
  ('Chinese Rock' by Dee Dee Ramone and Richard Hell, recorded by the Heartbreakers, 1977).

copacetic, kopasetic adj
American

excellent, satisfactory, hunky dory. Used usually of a situation or state of affairs, copacetic is as likely to be said by a college professor as a New York **cop**. The college professor might think he is using a newish slang term; the cop may suspect that a word ending in -ic derives from Greek or Latin. Both would be wrong. This bizarre word has rarely been written down, but was recorded as early as 1919. Attempts have been made to derive it from Latin, Yiddish or even Amerindian roots, but its true origin is unknown. It has not crossed the Atlantic in its comparatively long history.

- *'What's your sign love?'*
  'Stop'
  'Well that's copacetic.'
  (*Beach Party*, US film, 1981).

- *'You stick with me and everything will be copacetic.'*
  (*The Secret of My Success*, US film, 1987).

cop a feel vb American

to grope (someone) sexually; succeed in heavy petting. A (mainly male) teenagers' term from the 1950s, when this might be the goal, rather than a way-stage in the process of seduction.

- *'I didn't even get to cop a feel.'*
- *'Then when they start gettin' passionate, start coppin a few feels.'*
  (High-school student, IT magazine, June 1972).

cop a plea vb American

to plead guilty to a lesser offence than the one which is charged to speed up the judicial process (for the prosecutors) and avoid a heavier sentence (for the defendant). A strategy which forms the basis of plea bargaining, a peculiarity of the US legal system.

- *'The guy copped a goddam plea and only went down for three.'*

cop off vb British

to find a sexual partner, to **pull** someone. A term from the North of England.

- *'Down on the disco floor/They make their profits/From the things they sell/To help you cop off.'*
  (Lyric of 'At Home He Is a Tourist', written and recorded by The Gang of Four, 1979).

cop-out vb, n

(to be guilty of) an evasion, avoidance of responsibility. This expression (almost always heard in the noun form) was American slang until the late 1970s at which time it suddenly gained widespread currency, even among 'respectable' speakers in Britain. The phrase arose in the 1960s meaning specifically to 'duck out' of one's obligations to one's peers.

copper n

a police officer. The word originated in Britain in the 1840s, from 'to cop' as a humorous or racier alternative to 'to catch'.

copper-nob n

a red-headed person. An affectionate nickname, now dated but still common in the early 1960s.

coppish question form American

an alternative spelling of capeesh.

copshop n British

a police station. Currently mainly a children's expression.

cop (some) z's vb American

to sleep. A phrase which uses the comic book convention of z's representing snoring.

corgis n pl British

(a) 'couple of really ghastly individuals'. Another in the series of jokey acronyms (on the lines of yuppie, dinkie, etc.) coined by professionals and the media to epitomize special subgroups of the population in the late 1980s.

cork up vb British

to keep quiet. A phrase briefly in vogue among adolescents in the mid-1960s, usually in the form of a brusque imperative.

corner-boy n British

an idle or shiftless youth, a layabout. From their habit of hanging around on street corners. This adult and journalese term of disapproval from the 1950s was applied to supposed hooligans and teddy boys. As long ago as the 1880s 'corner-cove' and 'corner man' were in use with a similar meaning.

cornflake n American

an eccentric, crazy or silly person. An elaboration of the widespread term flake (which has the same meaning). The pun is on the name of the breakfast cereal; 'corn' is otherwise meaningless.

Cornish pasties n pl British

a style of man's shoe considered deeply unfashionable or indicative of a certain social subgroup in the 1970s and 1980s (specified by Judy Rumbold, fashion editor of the Guardian as 'maths teachers countrywide'). The pastie was so-called because of the supposed resemblance of the moulded-soled, heavily stitched shoe to the meat and vegetable savoury.

corporation cocktail n British

milk with coal gas bubbled through it, drunk by alcoholics and drug abusers as a cheap last resort in getting high. The introduction of non-toxic natural gas from beneath the North Sea rendered this habit of the 1950s and 1960s obsolete. The corporation in question was the state-run British Gas Corporation.

corporation pop n British

water. A humorous 1950s term from the north of England, heard in the television soap opera Coronation Street. The corporation in question is the local council, responsible for the water supply.

corpse vb British

(in acting) 1 to be rendered unable to speak or act by the onset of uncontrollable hysterical laughter, in rehearsal or before an audience. The word has been used in the theatre since the 19th century.

2 to cause another actor to break down with laughter or giggling during rehearsal or performance.

These meanings are also true of performers in operas and musicals.

cory, corey n British

penis. A vulgarism used particularly by marginals and the poorer elements of the working class. The word, which is from the Romany word for thorn, *kori*, was more widely used in the 1950s and 1960s than today.

cosh boy n British

a young male thug. A journalese phrase from the early 1950s when criminals frequently carried coshes (US: blackjacks) with which to attack people. The phrase was used as an alarmist codeword for a **mugger**. Ian Fleming (in a letter to Somerset Maugham in 1953) referred jokingly to his first James Bond novel as a 'Cosh-boy's Own Paper'.

costume n

See **in costume**.

cosy n British

an act of sex. A **Sloane Ranger** euphemism, used by girls and perhaps revealing of sexual attitudes in this milieu.

cot-case n

an invalid or someone who has been mentally and/or physically incapacitated. A usually heartless and often derogatory expression, used in Britain and Australia typically by health-care personnel or relatives. The similar term 'stretcher-case' has become an acceptable colloquialism, whereas **basket case** remains slang.

cottage n British

a public lavatory, in the language of the homosexuals who made contact

there. The word and the practice were more common in the 1950s and 1960s before the liberalization of anti-homosexual laws, but are still in evidence. The term is also used in Australia.

cottaging n British

visiting, or hanging around in, public lavatories to make sexual contacts. A male homosexual's term from the 1950s, still in use in the late 1980s.

couch potato n American

a lazy, greedy person. This expression from the late 1980s describes a person whose only activity is to lie in front of a television and eat and drink. (Couch is an American synonym for sofa.)

- *'That new breed of American, the stay-at-home, VCR-watching couch potato, has been good news indeed for the US home video industry.'* (Guardian, 29 February 1988).
- *'"Couch-potato," according to Lindsey Bareham "is American for a television addict": the potato, once again, is defamed as a symbol of dull lethargy.'* (Patrick Skene Catling, *Daily Telegraph*, Christmas Book Review, 1989).

cough vb British

to confess to a crime, to reluctantly give up information. A police and underworld term influenced by the notion of coughing up something stuck in the throat.

- *'If you don't start coughing Keith's going to drive us around all night.'* (*Rockliffe's Babies*, British TV crime series, 1989).
- *'Look, many times I have known prisoners who have coughed to seven or eight jobs when they have been given a quick thump.'* (Police officer quoted in *Inside the*

110

British Police by Simon Holdaway, 1983).

cousins, the cousins n pl
British

the Americans, the American secret services, diplomatic corps, etc. A euphemism employed by diplomats, spies and civil servants, not necessarily affectionately.

cow n *British*

a an unpleasant or obnoxious woman.

b a placid, drab or humiliated woman. The word is often used with real malice, or alternatively can be said with fellow feeling by a sympathetic woman, especially in the phrase 'poor cow'. Cow is not a universal term of abuse (in French for instance it can be a term of affection). It is said that the synonym **moo** was used in the 1960s because cow was still considered beyond the pale for family TV.

● *'When she went bust the Revenue let her keep her bed because it was a tool of her trade. She was a rude old cow but I liked her and we'll all be dead soon.'*
(William Donaldson, *Independent*, 20 August 1999).

cowboy n

a a reckless or irresponsible person, especially someone young, inexperienced and/or wild. The term is typically used by older workers referring to younger ones, or by police about a delinquent loner. The term originated in the 1950s, drawing comparisons with western film heroes or with pre-war gangsters' use of 'cowboy job' or the verb 'to **cowboy**' to refer to a particularly messy or violent crime.

b *British* a bad workman. The meaning of **cowboy a** has been extended and popularized in colloquial language to mean anyone who does a shoddy job in order to make a quick profit.
● *'Cowboy plumber/plasterer.'*

cowboy vb *British*

to behave or perform recklessly. The word is now used in two main senses; to drive dangerously or to perform a professional task in a slapdash and/or hazardous way.

cowboy job/operation n

1 an unauthorized scheme, as in for instance, the field of espionage.

2 *British* a badly finished or skimped example of workmanship.
See **cowboy**.

cowboy outfit n *British*

a firm or organization which specializes in shoddy workmanship or dubious business practices. The punchline of a familiar joke among disgruntled businessmen is that a doting millionaire when asked by his infant son for a cowboy outfit, buys him the company in question.

cow cocky/cockie n
Australian

a small-scale cattle-farmer.
See **cocky**

cow college n *American*

a college in an obscure town or remote place.

cow-horns n pl *British*

high curved handlebars on a motorcycle or bicycle. A synonym for **apehangers**.

coyote n *American*

a person who preys on those illegally immigrating to the USA from Mexico. The word (literally, prairie wolf) is used in Spanish to describe unscrupulous agents, mainly Mexican, who offer to help **wet backs** cross the border, but rob, defraud, denounce or even kill them instead. A term from the late 1970s and 1980s.

crabs n pl
pubic lice, a case of *pediculosis pubis*. The louse is popularly known as the crab louse from its resemblance when viewed under magnification.
● '*A dose/case of crabs.*'

crack, the crack n
1 a purified, addictive form of cocaine. Pellets of crack are smoked; they fizz and crackle, which is probably the origin of the name, reinforced by the precedent of **smack**. The drug became popular in the USA in 1985, but was first described in *The Gourmet Cookbook, a complete guide to Cocaine*, published in California in 1972.
● '*Crack – cocaine mixed with baking soda and cooked in microwave ovens – has been described as the "fast food of drugs".*'
(*Independent*, 24 July 1989).
2 the vagina. An obvious vulgarism, occasionally heard in all English-speaking areas.
3 *Irish* and *British* a good time, from the adjective **cracking** and the Irish notion (sense **4**).
● '*It's a right crack.*'
(Snooker hall manager, ITV telethon, May 1988).
4 the crack *Irish* and *British* what's going on, the latest news, or the current ambience. This word is used all over Ireland and in the late 1980s seemed to be spreading in Britain. The all-purpose term, usually in phrases such as '*what's the crack?*' or '*that's the crack!*', seems to combine two very old popular unorthodox senses of the word: talk, gossip or boast, as in **crack on**; and first-rate, excellent – **crack** as an adjective.

● '*This is the only place to live. I tried Australia but I came back because I missed the crack.*'
(Belfast resident, *The Crack: a Belfast Year*, Sally Belfrage, 1987).
● '*Big Alex is a minder and a fixer. In his words, he knows all the crack.*'
(*Guardian*, 12 December 1987).

crack adj British
top-notch, first-rate. A shortening of **cracking**.
● '*A crack outfit/a crack team.*'

crack vb
1 to share.
● '*Let's crack a bottle.*'
2 to split.
● '*I'll have to crack a fifty.*'
See also **crack wise**.

crack a brown vb Australian
to **fart**. A fairly rare post-World-War II male vulgarism.

crack a fat vb Australian
to have an erection. A vulgarism known in Britain through Barry Humphries' *Adventures of Barry McKenzie*. There are a number of mostly obsolete expressions in Australian English using the word 'crack' meaning achieve or produce.

crack a stiffie vb British
to have an erection. An expression used in **Sloane Ranger** and **yuppie** circles, among others.

crack house n
a place where the drug **crack** is prepared, sold or consumed.
● '*In the depressed inner-city areas of Los Angeles or New York, crack is frequently consumed in "crack houses" or "rock houses" – derelict buildings, often occupied by squatters, where addicts can buy and consume the drug.*'

(*Sunday Times*, 10 September 1989).

cracking *adv, adj British*
extremely (good). A hearty word still used unselfconsciously to show approval or enthusiasm by middle-class speakers and sometimes shortened to the adjective **crack**.
• '*A cracking good story.*'

crack it *vb British*
to succeed in a seduction. Used by and about men, this is a specific use of the general colloquial sense of to succeed, especially to suddenly succeed after long effort, as in 'cracking' a safe or a code.

crackle *n British*
money, banknotes. A word used by street traders, bookies, **spivs**, etc., particularly in the 1950s and 1960s. An alternative to **crinkle**, similarly inspired by the sound of crisp new notes.

crackling *n British*
an attractive female, or women in general seen as sex objects. This male expression was particularly popular in the 1950s and early 1960s, usually in the phrase '*a bit of crackling*'. It derives from the idea of pork crackling being a 'tasty morsel', perhaps reinforced by the vulgar sense of **crack** (see **crack**, sense **2**).

crack on *vb British*
to talk incessantly, browbeat or boast. The phrase, which is now generally used by middle-class speakers, is a successor to a colloquial use of **crack** to mean gossip, brag or tell tales which is at least 300 years old and survives in Scottish and American speech.
• '*He was cracking on about his job and his responsibilities.*'
(Recorded, city financier, London, 1987).

crack wise *vb*
to make witty or cheeky remarks. A back-formation from the noun and verb 'wisecrack'.

crank *n*
1 penis. A rare usage, mainly heard in the USA among sailors, **truckers**, **hard-hats** and others in the 1960s.
2 speed (methedrine or amphetamine), heroin. A drug users' term from the late 1960s which could also be used to refer to any drug which '*cranks up*' or re-stimulates a person's system.

crank up *vb*
to inject (a dangerous drug). A **junkies'** term from the early 1970s derived from the image of inserting a handle into an engine to jerk it back into life.
• '*They're going to crank up/to crank up some smack.*'

crap *n*
1 a excrement, **shit**.
b dirt, rubbish.
c worthless nonsense, **bullshit**
In modern usage crap is generally seen as a more moderate synonym for **shit**; in fact the word comes from Middle English 'crappe', which meant scrapings, scale, residue or chaff, this in turn came from words existing in Old French, German and Dutch, distantly related to 'crop' and 'crabbed'. (The fact that the flush toilet was invented by a Thomas Crapper appears to be pure coincidence.)
2 oppressive, petty or unpleasant behaviour; by extension from **crap 1 a** and **b**. This idea is usually expressed in such phrases as '*he doesn't take any crap from anyone*' or '*she's not going to put up with this crap any more*'.

crap *vb*
to defecate, **shit**. The verb form, which began to be used in the late 18th

century, is derived from the earlier noun **crap**, which originally meant rubbish, rather than excrement.

crapola n American

misleading or worthless information, pretentious, contemptible behaviour. An embellishment of **crap**. (The suffix **-ola**, as in **payola**, etc., is an imitation Spanish/Italian word-ending which adds the sense of big, bad, flagrant, etc.)

crapper, the crapper n

toilet. This vulgarism appears to derive from **crap** and not from the name of Thomas Crapper, a Victorian manufacturer of lavatories who is claimed to be the inventor of the flush toilet.

crappy, crappo adj

worthless, contemptible, of very low quality. From **crap**. Crappo is a more recent variant.

crash vb

1 also **crash out** to go to sleep, lie down and lose consciousness. This word was very popular in the **hippy** era, perhaps because the suggestion of sudden collapse coincided with drug-induced sleep or simply curling up on a floor, exhausted. Crash sounds rather dated in the late 1980s; it originated in armed-services slang in World War II, probably among airmen, and was adopted by bohemian travellers and **beatniks** during the 1950s.

2 to gatecrash. A word made especially popular by the teenage custom (from the 1960s onward) of arriving uninvited at parties.

crasher n British

a (crashing) bore. An upper-, and more recently middle-class term. It has existed in limited circulation since the 1950s, but is currently fashionable among **Sloane Rangers**, **yuppies**, etc.

crash-hot adj Australian

excellent, first-rate. This fairly popular expression is probably a euphemism for **shit-hot**.

crashpad

a place to sleep (temporarily). This term, combining **crash** meaning to sleep, and **pad**, meaning home or shelter, was popularized by the **hippies**; it usually referred to a communal building where sleeping space was available to travellers.

cream, cream one's jeans vb

to have an orgasm, or to become sexually excited (while dressed). The vulgarism can be used of either sex (and now, by extension, can even sometimes mean to become over-excited or over-enthusiastic without the sexual connotation). Cream has been a euphemism for semen or sexual lubricant for at least a century. **Cream one's jeans** dates from the late 1960s.

cream-crackered adj British

knackered; exhausted, worn out. A humorous rhyming-slang version of the more common word. It was probably coined in the 1970s, inspired by the savoury dry biscuits called 'cream crackers'.

creature-features n

a mild term of abuse among schoolchildren. It may originate in 'creature-feature', a showbusiness jargon term for a horror film of the 1950s.

creatures, the creatures n pl British

prison warders. A prisoners' term conveying more bitterness than the more usual **screws**.

cred adj, n British
(having) 'street credibility'. A 1980s adolescent vogue term inspired by the earlier cliché.

creeping Jesus n
an unpleasantly insincere, untrustworthy or complaining person, a creep, sneak or **whinger**. This strange expression of distaste is mainly heard among middle-class speakers in Britain and Australia; it dates according to the Oxford English Dictionary at least to 1818.

creepshow adj
frightening, grotesque, or merely unpleasant. An American teenagers' word, from the title of a horror film released in 1982. The adjective is an elaboration of 'creepy' and the earlier 'creepsville', and has been heard among British teenagers from the late 1980s.
● 'A creepshow party.'
● 'Her creepshow boyfriend.'

cremated adj British
ruined, destroyed, defeated, trounced. A coinage of the 1980s combining the notions of 'killed' and **burned**. The term was briefly in vogue among **yuppies**.
● 'If the market moves in a big way we'll get cremated.'
(Serious Money, Caryl Churchill, 1987).

crew n
a British a gang. A word used since the 1960s by street gangs, especially **skinheads** and football hooligans, to refer to themselves. It was a synonym for band (of ruffians) 300 years earlier.
b American a group of young people. Unlike the British sense which implies violence, this 1980s usage usually refers to hip-hop artists, break dancers or **scratch** musicians.

crim n
a criminal. A term heard increasingly in the late 1980s; it is probably originally an Australian usage.

crim, crimble, crimbo n
British
Christmas. These are adults' nursery words (probably originally from Liverpool) which were popularized, particularly by radio disc jockeys, in the 1970s.
● 'Stevie's determined to have a well wacky Crimble do – even by his standards.'
(Just Seventeen, magazine, December 1987).

cringe n British
a euphemism for Christ.
See **by the cringe**.

cringe (someone) vb British
to embarrass, discomfit or excruciate. A mainly middle-class usage of the late 1980s.
● 'Would it cringe you too much if I used my [cell-]phone here?'
(Recorded, yuppie to companion in opera-house bar, London, June 1988).

cringe-making adj British
sickening, embarrassing. The use of '-making' as a suffix in this way is typical of British middle- and upper-class usage in phrases such as this and sick-making.
● 'I couldn't bear to watch; it was just too cringe-making.'

crinkle n British
banknotes, money. This term was used by bookies, **spivs**, and the like in the 1950s and is now probably obsolete. **Crackle** was a synonym.
● 'I need some crinkle in a hurry.'

crinkly n British

an elderly person or adult. A young person's dismissive (or sometimes grudgingly affectionate) term. It forms part of the group of post-1970 vogue terms which includes **dusty**, **crumbly** and **wrinklie**.

crispy adj American

suffering from a hangover. A teenage and adolescent vogue word of 1988. Its provenance is uncertain; it may evoke the notion of 'brittle' or 'fragile'.

croak vb

1 to die. An unsentimental term derived presumably from the choking death rattle, or rasping dying words. The usage dates from the 19th century.
• *'He croaked before he could tell us anything useful.'*
2 to kill. An American gangster and prison term.
• *'The guy threatened to croak his business partner.'*

croaker n British

a doctor who prescribes for addicts. A drug addicts' and prisoners' term in use since the 1960s, although the notion of the death-dealing doctor thus expressed goes back to the 19th century.

crock, crock of shit n American

nonsense, something worthless and unpleasant. *'It's a crock!'* is an expression (inoffensive enough to be used on TV) employed in the 1970s and 1980s to dismiss, deride or reject something such as false information. In North America the word crock for container is not archaic as it is in Britain and Australia.

crocked adj

1 American drunk. A word used for example by college students in the 1980s. It probably comes from the old

use of crocks as containers for pickling or preserving in alcohol or, particularly in Canada, as containers for whiskey. Alternatively, the derivation may be the same as that of the following sense.
2 American angry. This use of the word is connected with an archaic or dialect use of 'crock' and 'crook' to mean an old, infirm, cantankerous and complaining person.
3 British broken or injured; used particularly of sportsmen incapacitated through injury. From the standard English sense of crock as potsherd or from a dialect term for a decrepit animal.

crook adj Australian

unwell, unhealthy, wrong, dubious. A common term in Australia, crook is either an alteration of archaic slang 'cronk' (from German and Yiddish *krank*) meaning ill, or of crooked, meaning bent out of shape. By 1988 the word could be used in a British newspaper or magazine, due to the influence of Australian soap operas (it has not as yet penetrated British speech).

crucial adj British

a Jamaican code word from the radical self-dramatizing slang of **rude boys** and reggae devotees, crucial became a vogue term of appreciation in London around 1979, first among black youth and later white imitators. Lenny Henry, the black comedian brought the word to a wider audience by including it in the scripts of his television series, in the mouth of the character 'Delbert Wilkins'.

crud n

a anything filthy, disgusting or worthless, including excrement, any encrusted or coagulated substance and (in American English) the effects of skin infection. Crud is from Middle

English 'crudde', a dialect word related to the standard English curd.
b a worthless, despicable person (usually male). A word used widely in the 1960s, in place of taboo synonyms such as **turd**.

cruddy adj
unpleasant, inferior, worthless. A word in vogue in the mid-1960s. It is now heard mainly among schoolchildren.

cruise vb
a (used intransitively) to move around in search of a sexual partner. The word was first used by prostitutes seeking clients, then in the 1960s by **gays** and subsequently in the 1970s by heterosexuals, especially those frequenting singles bars.
b (used transitively) to actively try to attract a particular potential sexual partner. The overtones of cruising a person are a discreet display of oneself with some unmistakeable hints or **come-ons**.

crumb n
a contemptible and/or inconsequential person. The word is now rare but in 1958 the British audience at the Granada, Tooting were reported to have shouted 'go home you crumb!' at the rock 'n' roll singer Jerry Lee Lewis who had married his 13-year-old third cousin, just prior to his tour of Britain.

crumb (it) vb American
to ruin, mess up. From crumble in its standard sense, reinforced by the notion of acting like a **crumb**, and by **crummy**.
● 'You crumbed the play.'
(House of Games, US film, David Mamet, 1987).

crumble n British
a generic term for old or senile peo-

ple. Used in the 1980s in the expression 'a bit of crumble' for instance, or by nursing staff to refer contemptuously to their elderly patients.

crumbly, crumblie n British
a an old person. In spite of the suggestion of crumbling or falling apart, the term is only mildly contemptuous and may even be used affectionately. Coincidentally, the 1960s French slang term for old or 'past it' was croulant, meaning crumbling.
● 'Senior citizens, inevitably, watch 37 hours a week. "Audiences are getting crumbly," says Street-Porter in media-speak.'
(Independent, 23 March 1988).
b a parent or adult. Used by children and teenagers since the mid-1970s. A fairly inoffensive middle- and upper-class word favoured by **Sloane Rangers** among others.
See also **wrinklie**, **crinkly**, **dusty**.

crummy, crumby adj
dilapidated, dirty, worthless. By the mid-19th century this word was in use in Britain as a literal and figurative synonym for lousy, apparently due to the resemblance of body lice to crumbs. The word (usually spelled with double 'm'), has remained in widespread use in Britain and the USA.

crumpet n British
a woman, or women viewed collectively as sex objects. **Crumpet** or 'a bit of crumpet' date from the last decade of the 19th century and conform to a much older pattern of likening women to cakes (**tart**), delicacies (**crackling**), etc. The terms 'crumpet' or 'a bit of crumpet' are now likely to offend most women although both are still widespread, mainly in working-class usage. Women are now beginning to use the terms to refer to males.

117

• *'I don't think we should condemn a doctor simply because he made a wrong diagnosis of what is, or is not, crumpet.'*
(*Carry on Again, Doctor*, British comedy film, 1969).

crumpet man n British
a womaniser, seducer. A working-class expression of the 1960s.

crunchie n American
a lesbian, particularly a lesbian with austere habits and 'utopian' views. 'Crunchies' were one faction of lesbians at Yale University in the late 1980s, the other being so-called **lipsticks**.

crusher n British
a boring, tedious person, a ('crushing') bore. An alternative to **crasher**, typically used by middle- and upper-class speakers in the 1980s.

crust n British
(one's) head. This London working-class usage is almost always heard in the forms **off one's crust** or '*do one's crust*'.

crut n
dirt, distasteful material or unpleasantness in general. A version of **crud** (normally felt to be less offensive than that word).

crutch n British
a pair of matchsticks or a split matchstick used to hold the end of a **joint**; an improvised **roach** clip.

cry Ruth/Hughie/Ralph vb
to vomit. All these humorous equivalents attempt to imitate the sound of hearty or sudden retching. They have been popular, particularly with students, all over the English-speaking world since the 1960s.

crystal n
amphetamine or cocaine. An item of drug users' jargon.

cube n
an extremely **square** person. A derogatory **hipsters'** and **beatnik** term last heard in the early 1960s.

cubehead n American
a user of LSD (lysergic acid diethylamide), the hallucinogenic drug. A term used in the mid-1960s, when LSD was frequently taken orally on sugar cubes.

cuff vb American
to put someone in handcuffs. A police term.
• '*Cuff this asshole, read him his rights.*'
(*The Last Innocent Man*, US film, 1987).

cum n
See **come**.

cunt n
1 a the vagina. This taboo word has ancient origins; related words (French *con*, Spanish *coño*, etc.) exist in other European languages and it seems that in the unwritten prehistoric Indo-European parent languages 'cu' or 'koo' was a word base expressing 'feminine', 'fecund' and associated notions.
b a woman, or women in general. An extension of the above which is probably most commonly heard in the USA.
2 a very unpleasant person. As well as being the most 'obscene' of the common set of sexually-related taboo words, cunt is also used to indicate extreme distaste or dislike. This usage, which is more noticeable in British and Australian English than American, is presumably inspired by deep-seated fear and loathing of women's

sexuality, although in practice the word is usually applied to men.

From Anglo-Saxon times until the 14th century the word was in standard use, but was then replaced by euphemisms in all but rural dialect speech. Most dictionaries refused to acknowledge the word until the 1960s and it is probably the only word that is still banned from British newspapers and television.

cunt-hooks n pl

fingers. An exclusively male vulgarism, also used in Australia as a term of abuse.

cunt-struck adj

a vulgar synonym for 'henpecked', employed by males.

cupcake n American

1 a cute or attractive woman. A deliberately humorous or (consciously or unconsciously) patronizing male term of endearment. Cupcakes are small, usually iced, buns.

2 an eccentric person.

currant bun n British

1 a the sun.
b son.

Both rhyming-slang uses have been in evidence in London working-class use since at least the 1940s.

2 a nun. A rare item of rhyming slang heard occasionally from at least the 1950s.

curse, the curse n

menstruation, a monthly period. This is the standard term used by schoolgirls and women; its probable origin is in Genesis, in which Eve is 'cursed' by God who promises to 'multiply thy sorrow and thy conception: in sorrow thou shall bring forth children'. The 'curse of Eve' thus became a eu-

phemism for the most troublesome aspect of femininity.

● 'I've got the curse, I'm afraid.'

cushdy, cushti, kushti adj
British

fine, wonderful. An all-purpose term of approbation or agreement. This working-class term (recently brought to a wider audience by the television comedy Only Fools and Horses) is related to cushy, the colloquial term for easy or comfortable. Both words derive ultimately from an archaic Persian word khosh meaning pleasant, either via Hindustani, khush or Romany, kushto or both.

cut n

a record, album track or musical extract. An item of musicians' slang which has become a widespread colloquialism through its use by disc jockeys and others. It may also be used as a verb to describe the recording process.

cut vb

to dilute or adulterate (illicit drugs), usually with the intention of increasing weight and hence profit.

● 'The coke was cut with lactose.'

cut (someone) a little slack
vb American

to relax regulations, to make allowances for or give room to move. The image is of tailoring something for relatively unrestricted ease of movement.

● 'Come on, cut me a little slack, will you?'

cut a rug vb

to dance. A lighthearted expression which was fashionable in the jitterbug era and in the post-war language of rock and **jive**. It still survives in jocular use.

119

cutaways, cut-offs n pl
shorts made by cutting the legs off blue jeans at the knee.

cute adj
See **completely cute.**

cut it vb
to succeed, manage. A shortened form of 'cut the mustard' or 'cut some ice'.

• 'Her experience among women rappers trying to cut it in the macho world of Hip Hop, led Charlotte to look again at the girl groups from the Seventies she'd always loved.' (Ms London Magazine, 4 September 1989).

cut lunch n Australian
sandwiches.

D

D *n*

1 dope, illicit drugs. The predictable abbreviation was typically used by British cannabis smokers in the early and mid-1970s.

● *'Hey, man, got any d?'*

2 *Australian* detective. This abbreviation dates from the 19th century and is now almost archaic. It has metamorphosed into **demon**.

D.A. *n British*

1 a hairstyle in which the hair is scraped back and greased into a curl on the nape of the neck. It is an abbreviation of **duck's arse**. The style was popular among **teddy boys** in the 1950s and, to a lesser extent, with the **rockers** of the early 1960s.

2 drug addict. An abbreviation used, generally facetiously, by drug users themselves in the mid- and late 1960s.

dabs *n pl British*

fingerprints. The term has been used by police, criminals and crime writers since the 1930s at least. It derives from the fingerprinting process in which the suspect presses his or her fingers on an ink pad.

● *'We managed to lift some dabs from the wine glasses.'*

daddio, daddy-o *n*

(old) man. A variant of Dad and Daddy, used as a term of address. It originated in the **jive talk** of black jazz musicians in the 1940s, and was adopted by the **beatniks** of the 1950s.

The word implied a degree of respect or affection, usually for someone older or in authority. In later use, by British **teddy boys** and **beatniks** for example, it was often a teasing or mocking form of address.

daddy *n British*

1 a dominant inmate among prisoners.

2 an older and/or dominant male homosexual, in a relationship, group or institution.

dag *n Australian*

1 (a piece of dried) sheep dung. This sense of the word dates from the 16th century, but has become archaic in Britain. It usually refers to the dried flakes adhering to tail wool.

2 a stupid or unpleasant person, by extension from the first sense. In the late 1980s dag has become a fairly mild all-purpose insult or description, freely used for instance in television soap operas such as *Neighbours*.

dage, dayg *n Australian*

a variation of **dago** (the 'g' is hard); now dated, it was heard in the 1950s and 1960s.

dagga *n South African*

cannabis, marihuana. This is the most common term for these drugs in South Africa, and derives from local African languages. It is occasionally heard elsewhere among drug users.

daggy adj Australian

stupid, unpleasant. From **dag**. A brusque but fairly mild expression of distaste (deemed suitable for inclusion in the script of TV soap operas, for instance).

dago n

a a person of Hispanic origin (Spanish or Latin American). This derogatory meaning is probably the original sense of the word in that it derives from the Hispanic proper name Diego (James). The word usually has this sense when used by British speakers.

b an Italian. This has become the most common American sense of the word. Dago is sometimes used as an indiscriminate insult to persons, usually male, of Mediterranean origin.

daily mail, daily n British

1 a the backside, buttocks. Rhyming slang for **tail**.

b sexual activity. By extension from the preceding sense.

● 'Have you been getting any daily lately?'

2 bail. A rare usage in the jargon of criminals.

dainties n pl

(women's) panties, knickers. A jokily coy euphemism heard in both America and Australia in the mid-1970s.

daisy n

a male homosexual or an effeminate man. The word in this sense is not common but occurs occasionally in British, American and Australian usage.

daisy chain n

a group of people taking part in 'serial' sexual activity; cunnilingus, fellatio, penetration etc. in series.

daisy roots, daisies n pl British

boots. A well-known, but now rarely heard, piece of Cockney rhyming slang which dates from the late 19th century. The meaning of the term was sometimes extended to shoes.

daks n pl

trousers. From the trademark name of a brand of casual trousers sold since the 1930s in Britain and Australia. The word's popularity was boosted by its use in the Barry McKenzie cartoon series in Private Eye magazine, usually in the phrase 'drop one's daks'.

damage n

expense, cost, charge. This sense of the word is at least two hundred years old and today hardly qualifies as slang.

● 'What's the damage?'

dame n

a woman. An Americanism usually identified with the criminal, musical, etc. milieus of the 1920s, '30s and '40s. The usage obviously derives from the original British 13th-century title of Dame (itself from Latin domina, via Old French), which quickly became a synonym for woman in dialect and rural speech. Like **doll**, **broad** and to some extent **chick**, the term now sounds dated.

damp adj

1 British a middle-class synonym for **wet** in the sense of ineffectual, feeble.

● 'I always found Jenny's husband a bit damp.'

2 sexually aroused (of a woman).

● 'On the Jonathan Ross show one night I saw a female comic asked how she viewed the prospect of the next guest, a renowned male hunk. "I'm damp," she replied, and went on to repeat the assertion a few times. "Damp. Yes, I'm really damp." There was no joke as such,

no turn or twist or wit, just a blank description.'
(Sebastian Faulks, *Independent* magazine, 28 October 1989).

d and d *adj*

drunk and disorderly. The phrase in full is police or judicial jargon; the abbreviation is a euphemism used by police in the USA and in Britain facetiously by drinkers.

• *'Terry was completely d and d again last night.'*

dang *n American*

1 penis. A rare variant of **dong**.
2 a euphemism for damn.

dangleberries *n pl*

a variation of **dingleberries**.

dangler *n*

1 a penis. A nursery euphemism also used facetiously among adults.
2 *Australian* a **flasher**, a male sexual exhibitionist.
3 *British* a trailer, when attached to a truck or tractor.
4 *American* a trapeze artist.

danglers *n pl*

testicles. An old and predictable euphemism heard, for example, in British public schools and the armed forces.

daps *n pl British*

tennis shoes, plimsolls. The word may echo the sound of light footfalls or derive from an archaic dialect verb meaning to dart or pad. Daps was a particularly popular term among teenagers and schoolchildren in Wales and the southwest in the 1960s.

darbies *n pl British*

a handcuffs.
b hands.

c fingerprints.

All these uses are in fact archaisms but are occasionally resurrected for facetious use by police or criminals, especially in London, and by writers. They are all connected with the original rhyming slang, 'Darby Bands', which in turn derived from a 17th-century moneylender's bond known colloquially as 'Father Derby's [or Darby's] Band'.

Darby Kelly, Derby Kelly *n British*

belly. A piece of Cockney rhyming slang which is probably as old as the century, but which is now rare. The identity of the eponymous Mr Kelly is unclear.

darkie *n*

a black or coloured person. A racist term which first became prevalent in America in the 18th century.

dark meat *n*

a coloured person or coloured people considered as sex objects. The reference, which is simultaneously offensive and appreciative, presumably refers to the distinction between dark and white meat on cooked poultry.

dash *n*

money, a bribe or tip. The term is from West Africa, where it derives from *dashee*, a local African dialect term. It may be the origin of the more common **dosh**.

date *n*

1 *Australian* also **date-locker** the anus. Presumably by association with the colour of the fruit, or just possibly from the archaic British rhyming slang 'date and plum' meaning **bum**.
2 *British* a stupid, silly or weak person. This rare usage (probably by association with the texture of an over-ripe

date) is now nearly obsolete, but was heard until the 1960s, especially in the phrases 'you soft date' and 'you soppy date'. Such phrases now survive only in nursery language.

date mate n

1 *American* a partner of the same sex to accompany one on a double date. A teenage expression of the 1950s.

2 *Australian* a male homosexual partner. Derived from **date 1**.

date roll n *Australian*

a toilet roll. Derived from **date 1**.

Davy Crockett n *British*

pocket. A piece of rhyming slang inspired by the cult film about the American pioneer for which there was a craze in 1956. **Sky rocket** and **Lucy locket** are synonyms.

day-glo *adj*

vulgarly colourful and bright, gaudy or tawdry. Inspired by the luminescent colours with the Day-glo trademark, invented in the 1960s.

● *'She was wearing this sort of garish day-glo outfit.'*

daylighting n

working (usually illicitly) at a second job during daylight hours. An obvious derivation from the colloquial 'moonlighting'.

deadass n, *adj American*

very boring, feeble or very stupid (person).

● *'He's a real deadass.'*
● *'What a deadass town.'*

dead bang *adv, adj American*

caught in flagrante, or red-handed. An American police version of **dead to rights**, or the British **bang to rights**.

● *'I got you dead bang for breaking into Eddie's apartment.'*
(*The Rockford Files*, US TV crime series, 1979).

deadbeat n

a a poor or homeless person.

b a penniless scrounger, freeloader.

c a worthless or stupid person.

All these senses derive from a 19th-century Americanism in which 'dead' means 'completely', and 'beat' is not 'exhausted' but 'loafer' or **hobo**.

deadhead n

1 a very stupid, lifeless or boring person. An obvious derivation of its component parts, this phrase is reinforced by its 19th-century American meaning of non-paying passengers or non-participants (from dead head of cattle).

2 a fan or devotee of the San Francisco rock group The Grateful Dead, which was popular in the late 1960s and early 1970s, and enjoyed a revival in the 1980s. Supposedly archetypically **hippy** in their attitudes, The Grateful Dead, known to their fans simply as The Dead, inspired unusual levels of commitment in their followers.

deadhead vb *American*

to run or drive (a vehicle) empty or without passengers. This meaning, a relic of 19th-century cattle drives, is now rarely heard. (*See also* **deadhead 1**.)

deadleg n, vb *British*

1 a feeble, lazy or disappointing person. This word has been used from the 1950s and may derive from an earlier armed-forces term **deadlegs**, meaning a cripple or someone who refuses to rise from bed.

● *'The usual crowd of airheads, phonies, deadlegs, posers, bimbos,*

wallies, wannabees, hangers-on and gatecrashers.'
(Christina Appleyard, *Daily Mirror*, 11 May 1989).

2 a numb feeling in the leg following a kneeing in the thigh by an attacker or, when used as a verb, the action of kneeing someone in this way. A popular school playground tactic.

dead meat *n*

a person who is dead, about to die or inevitably doomed. Dead meat is an old and heartless euphemism for a corpse. Now the phrase usually forms part of a threat.

● *'Do that, baby, and you're dead meat!'*

deadneck *n American*

a variant of **deadhead, deadbeat**, etc.

deadshit *n Australian*

a contemptible or very unpleasant person. The word is also sometimes used as an adjective as in, *'That was a deadshit party'.*

dead soldier *n*

an empty bottle (of alcohol). The phrase was first used by members of the British armed forces about 200 years ago, likening the aftermath of a drinking bout to a battlefield littered with corpses. In American usage the term is sometimes extended to leftovers other than bottles.

● *'I'll clear up the dead soldiers while you fumigate the place.'*

dead to rights *adv, adj American*

an American version of the British **bang to rights**. Dead to rights is probably the original form of the phrase, dating from the 19th century and now rarely, if ever, heard in Britain. ('Dead' is used in its common colloquial meaning of 'completely'.)

deal *n British*

a portion or amount of a drug, especially hashish. Before decimalization in 1971, very small amounts of cannabis were bought or referred to as a **five-bob deal** or **ten-bob deal**.

deal *vb*

to sell (drugs). The verb is used intransitively, *'does he still deal?'* and transitively, *'she deals dope at the weekend'.*

dealer *n*

a supplier of illicit drugs. The term, imported into other English-speaking areas from the United States in the early 1960s, is a neutral one, implying someone who sells on demand without coercion. It replaced the earlier, pejorative word **pusher** among users themselves.

deb *n*

1 a debutante, that is, a young girl being introduced into the social season. Although principally identified with an upper-class London milieu, the adoption of *débutante*, French for 'beginner', may have occurred in the USA in the first decade of the 20th century.

2 American a female member of a street gang. A term used in the 1960s, usually in the plural, probably originating in debutante, perhaps reinforced by the prevalence of the Christian name Deborah or Debbie. Deb resurfaced in the gang argot of Los Angeles in the 1980s.

de-bag *vb British*

to remove (someone's) trousers. The phrase originated among 19th-century university students but quickly spread to schoolboys for whom the ritual humiliation of fellow pupils by de-bagging was a popular diversion up to the late 1960s at least. **Bags** was a 19th-century slang term for trousers which survived until fairly recently.

debs' delight n British

an upper-class young man, especially one who might be considered an eligible partner or escort by parents (of debutantes), in spite of low intelligence. The phrase was used pejoratively and/or enviously and was popular in the 1960s. A more recent version is **pedigree chum**.

deck vb

to knock (someone) to the ground. A variant of to floor.

deck n

1 a portion or package of illicit drugs, especially heroin. The term, from American addicts' jargon of the 1960s, spread to Britain and Australia where the meaning was sometimes amended to refer to an injection, or the amount (of heroin) necessary for an injection.

2 a skateboard or surfboard, in the jargon of afficionados.

deck up vb

to prepare for injection, or to inject a drug, usually heroin. A phrase from the jargon of drug users and prisoners in the UK. The verb derives from the noun **deck**, meaning a quantity of a narcotic.

decorators n pl British

See **have the decorators in**.

de-dyke vb

to remove or conceal evidence of lesbianism. In British lesbian households of the 1980s, de-dyking generally preceded a visit by heterosexual parents.

deelybobber, deely bopper n

a set of imitation antennae worn on the head by children. This novelty item enjoyed a brief vogue in the USA in 1975, and later elsewhere.

deep sea diver n

a £5 note, 'fiver'. A piece of London rhyming slang heard occasionally since about the mid-1970s.

deep six vb American

to bury, dispose of. The verb form, which has been common in American speech since the 1950s, derives from the earlier noun form **the deep six**, an underworld euphemism for the grave. The ultimate origin is nautical; burials at sea have to be made in water that is more than six fathoms deep.

- *'I've got to exchange all this [money]!'*
- *'You can deep-six it, sir.'*
  (M.A.S.H., US TV series, 1977).

def adj

excellent, wonderful, the real thing. A late 1980s vogue term of approbation deriving from the language of **hip hop**. The word is a shortening of definitive or definite. The use of the word as the title of a BBC2 'youth slot' programme (DEF II) in 1988 may mark its apogee.

- *'This month's music selections are frightfully def, totally treach and all those other hip hop clichés.'*
  (I-D magazine, November 1987).

de facto n Australian

a live-in lover, one's unmarried partner. This phrase is one Australian solution (since the 1970s) to the problem of finding an acceptable term to describe what the British judicial system calls a 'common-law spouse'.

- *'My de facto's out buying groceries.'*
  (Recorded, young woman, Melbourne, 1978).

de-frosted adj American

heated, agitated. An adolescents'

term, inspired by the opposite notion of **cool** or **chilled out**.
- *'Come on, don't get all de-frosted.'*

dekko n British

a look, glance. A word that probably originated in the jargon of tramps, taken from the Romany word for look, *dik*, in the late 19th century. British soldiers overseas also encountered the Hindustani version *dekko*. The word is now less popular than in the 1950s but is still heard in the phrases **take** or **have a dekko (at)**. The word is not unknown but is rare in American slang, where it has been recorded as 'decko'.

See also **dick**.

Delhi belly n

diarrhoea. Since the era of British colonialism this has been the South Asian equivalent of **gippy tummy**, **Montezuma's Revenge**, etc.

deli n

a delicatessen. An Americanism increasingly heard in Britain.

dementoid, demental n, adj American

(a) crazy, demented (person). A high-school term of the 1980s that expresses contempt, grudging admiration or both. The word is also used adjectivally as in *'that was a totally dementoid movie'*.

demo n

1 a political demonstration.
2 a demonstration tape or record made by musicians in the hope of gaining work.
3 a demolition job or a demolition worker.

demon n Australian

a detective. This probably originated in the simple abbreviation D, which

then passed via 'd-man' to demon. The word is fairly rare; when it does occur it is often in the plural form.

Derby Kelly n British

See **Darby Kelly**.

dero, derro n Australian

a homeless person or tramp, a derelict. The term has been in use for about twenty years. It is also heard as a (fairly mild) insult among children and adolescents.

derro n British

1 an unfortunate, inferior or unpleasant person. A derivation from 'derelict', used either of vagrants or of someone pitied or disliked.
- *'And touching someone when you're dancing, Caris intimates, is the act of a derro, a flo-to-tin' yup, a deadbeat, a homebug and a commuter.'*
(*Observer*, Section 5, 7 May 1989).
2 a **derry** (derelict building).

derry, deri n British

a derelict building or similar location, used as a temporary shelter by tramps, etc.
- *'It's not a derry, guy, there are people living there.'*
(Recorded, vagrant, Waterloo, London, 1988).

designer drug n

an illicit drug produced artificially by chemists rather than one occurring in or synthesized from nature. The term also designates a drug produced with a slightly different chemical formula to that of a proscribed drug, such that the effects are similar to the illicit drug but its users can avoid prosecution.

Desmond n British

a lower second university degree, a

2/2 (two-two). This is a student's witticism playing on the name of the black South African community leader Bishop Desmond Tutu. The word was in vogue in 1986 and gave rise to a number of other joky euphemisms, such as **Douglas, Pattie, Taiwan, Richard.**

- '*We all expected Penny to get a James but she ended up with a Desmond.*'
  (*Evening Standard*, June 1988).

des. res. n British
a 'desirable residence'. The spoken form of the abbreviation used in estate agents' advertisements (pronounced 'dezz-rezz') is usually used enviously, of a genuinely attractive home, or ironically of a squalid one.

destroyed adj
completely intoxicated by alcohol or illicit drugs. A widespread colloquialism which has been particularly popular among middle-class speakers since the late 1960s. The word continues the tendency evidenced by usages such as **smashed, bombed, wrecked,** etc.

detox n, vb
(to undertake) a course of withdrawal from 'hard' drugs or alcohol, detoxification, detoxify. A term from health workers' jargon which is now standard among drug users and patients.

deuce n
a two dollars or two pounds.
- '*Just let me have a deuce till tomorrow.*'
b a two-year prison sentence.
- '*He pulled a deuce in Club Fed.*'

dex, dexie, dexo n
a pill or capsule of Dexedrine, an amphetamine (**pep pill**) frequently prescribed and abused in the 1950s and 1960s. Yellow pills of Dexedrine (a

trademark) were popular among English **mods** of the mid-1960s. Dexy's Midnight Runners, a phrase adopted as the name of a late 1970s white soul group was an elaborate nickname for the drug.

diamond adj British
first-rate, superb, admirable. A London working-class and underworld term, often heard in the appreciative phrase 'a diamond geezer'.

dib n
a contribution, portion, amount of money. This word was in use in Britain in the late 19th century, but is now heard mainly in the USA, typically in children's street or playground games. The plural form was common in England until the late 1950s and survives especially in the expression 'to have dibs on something', to reserve or have first rights to.

dib vb, n British
a partly-smoked cigarette saved for relighting later, or the act of extinguishing it. This term, which may originate in a dialect verb meaning to pinch or to stub, is used for instance by workmen, labourers and the armed forces.

dick n
1 penis. This use of the word has been widespread in the English-speaking world since the end of the 19th century. It is probably in origin an affectionate personification in the same way as **willie**, etc. This sense of the word is sometimes extended to mean sex in general, as in '*Suzy loves dick*'.
- '*Not all women in pop are or ever have been, brainless bimbos lured into lurex by cynical rock business shitheads with one eye on their cheque books and the other on their dicks.*'

(*Ms London* magazine, 4 September 1989).

2 a fool (invariably male). Dick has this secondary sense in common with most slang terms for the male member, such as **prick, tool** etc.

3 nothing at all. A vulgar emphatic more commonly heard in America, and in vogue since the mid-1970s. Its sense is roughly equivalent to the British **bugger-all**.

- '*What do those gimps do all day?*'
- '*They do dick.*'

4 a detective. Almost invariably in the phrase **private dick**. This Americanism, popularized in crime fiction, originated in underworld jargon as a corruption of the word detective itself.

See also **dickless Tracy**.

dick vb

1 to have sex (with), penetrate. A predictable but rare term, generated from the noun sense of **dick**.

2 *British* to look at. A variation of the Romany *dik*, to look, from which **dekko** may be derived. This rare term is occasionally heard among tramps, street traders, etc.

See also **dekko**.

3 to mess up, mess around (with). A variant of **dick around** or **dick up**.

- '*She completely dicked the project.*'

dick around vb

to mess around (with), behave in a disorganized or aimless way. The expression employs **dick** (penis) in the same way as **cock, prat** around, etc.

dickbrained adj

stupid, extremely foolish. A term popular among young people in the 1980s. The adjective is American in origin and the sense of **dick** deriving from 'penis' may be reinforced by the German sense of 'thick'.

dickhead n

a fool, idiot. An old, folksy Americanism which became a vogue term among British youth from around 1980. It may be applied to males or females. Abusive compound words ending in '-head' have proliferated since the end of the 1970s.

- '*The outcome of being a dickhead is that I don't possess any Aretha Franklin singles and make do with compilations.*'
  (John Peel quoted in *New Musical Express*, 7 February 1987).

dickless Tracy n Australian

a policewoman. A humorous coinage playing on **dick** (penis) and Dick Tracy, the American comic-strip detective hero created by Chester Gould.

dick up vb

to make a mess of. A variant of **cock up** occasionally heard in Britain and Australia.

dicky adj British

shaky, insecure, faulty. A colloquialism whose origin is obscure but which dates back at least 150 years. Its original meaning of 'ill' survives in the modern phrase '*a dicky heart*'.

- '*Dicky Hart and the Palpitations.*'
  (Name of 1970s London rock group).
- '*Oh, my dicky ticker!*'
  (Catchphrase from '*Allo 'Allo!*, British TV comedy series of the 1980s).

dicky, dickey n British

a a detachable shirt front.

b a shirt, especially an old or favourite one.

c a ready-made clip-on bow-tie, a **dicky-bow**.

d a detachable part of a vehicle such

as a motorbike, for instance a wind-screen or a small extra seat.

The origin of senses **a**, **c**, **d**, which were all current in the 1950s, is obscure.

Sense **b** is a shortening of the rhyming-slang term **dicky dirt**.

dicky bird n British

a word. A piece of London rhyming slang which has become a widespread colloquialism, especially in the phrase 'not a dicky bird'. Unlike most modern examples of rhyming slang, it is invariably used in full, presumably to avoid confusion with 'dickie' and **dick**.

dicky-bow n British

a bow-tie.

dicky dirt n British

a shirt. A piece of cockney rhyming slang which was obsolescent by the early 1970s but was resuscitated and given wider currency in London by the opening of a chain of cut-price clothing stores under the same name.

did n British

a form of **didicoi**.

diddie n British

an alternative spelling of **diddy**.

diddle vb

1 British to cheat. A common colloquialism recorded since the early 1800s. In Old English 'dydrian' meant to deceive or delude; Jeremy Diddler was a fictional swindler (in the 1803 farce Raising the Wind by James Kenney).

● 'Comedian Ken Dodd insisted on cash for shows to diddle the taxman, his former agent told a jury yesterday.'
(Daily Mirror, 5 July 1989).

2 a to have sex with. This sense probably derives from a nursery sense of

diddle meaning fiddle with or agitate (see **diddle 2b**).

b to sexually stimulate (a woman) with the fingers. (In Middle English 'dideren' meant to quiver.)

diddlo, didlo adj British

crazy, silly or unhinged, 'daft'. An inoffensive Londoners' word popularized by the ITV series Minder from the late 1970s.

● 'Right bunch of diddlos, this lot!'
(Minder, British TV series, 1986).

diddly(squat) n American

nothing at all, or something very insignificant, petty or small. Diddly is a nursery term akin to tiddly. The word has been used by adults, alone or in conjunction with other nursery terms (**squat**, **shit**, 'whoop', 'doo', etc.) to express dismissive contempt. A variant form is **doody** or **doodly (squat)**.

diddly-dum adj British

perfect, fine. A term used typically by students in the 1970s and 1980s, usually in phrases such as 'everything's (just) diddly-dum'. The phrase resembles other mock-nursery inventions such as **dinky-di** and **fair dinkum**.

diddy n British

1 a fool. A lighthearted term of abuse, heard particularly in Scotland and the North of England.

● 'You're a genius! How much did he promise?'
● 'Nothing.'
● 'You're a diddy!'
(City Lights, British TV series, 1989).
2 a **didicoi**.
See **didicoi**.

diddy adj British

small, cute and appealing. A variant

of **diddly**, popularized by the Liverpool comedian, Ken Dodd.

didicoi, diddicoy, diddyguy, did n British

a gypsy or a half-gypsy. The word derives from the Romany *didakeis*, meaning the offspring of a marriage between a full-blooded gypsy and an outsider. The word, which can be spelt in many ways, is often used in country districts to denote any type of gypsy or traveller.

- 'The Dancing Didicoi, the Dancing didicoi. Since he was a boy, he's been a dancing did.'
(Song lyric by the British rock group, The Dancing Did, 1982).
- 'There was this didicoi used to go down our snooker club – couldn't sign his own name but he always had a roll of money on him.'
(Recorded, carpet fitter, London, 1989).

diesel (dyke) n

a lesbian who behaves aggressively and/or who is of rough masculine appearance or heavy build. The word, which is pejorative and generally used by men, carries overtones of engineers, engines, trucks and other **butch** associations and perhaps also refers to the overalls, dungarees, etc. worn by some lesbians. The term originated in the USA but was heard in Britain in the 1980s as a pejorative term and also as a simple descriptive phrase used by lesbians themselves.

dig vb

to understand, appreciate or enjoy. A word from the slang of American swing and jazz musicians which was adopted by the beat generation and thence by teenagers all over the English-speaking world. It is now almost always used ironically or facetiously (except in the question form, 'you

dig?'). The ultimate origin is perhaps a metaphorical or religious sense of dig (into), meaning to apply oneself to (a task).

- 'The Seventies were not a decade in which a young artist could kid himself his creative idealism could best be fulfilled grovelling in a muddy field digging Hendrix through a bad acid haze.'
(*Platinum Logic*, Tony Parsons, 1981).

digger n Australian

an Australian. The word was used by gold prospectors in the latter half of the 19th century to address or describe one another. It was adopted by British, Canadian and American servicemen in the First World War. **Aussie** has largely replaced digger since the 1960s.

dike n

a variant spelling of **dyke**.

dilbert n British

a foolish person. A teenage term of mild abuse from the late 1080s, it is probably a blend of **dill** and the (supposedly comical) Christian name Gilbert.

- 'No I'm not – and definitely not with a dilbert like you.'
(Recorded, schoolgirl, London, 1989).

dildo n

1 an artificial penis. The word is approximately 200 years old and probably originates in *diletto*, Italian for (a) delight or darling. Alternatively the term may simply be an invention.

2 a fool, an offensively stupid person. This sense of the word, popular among teenagers since the mid-1970s, may be an embellishment of **dill** as much as a derivative of **dildo 1**.

- 'Oh, come on, he's such a dildo!'

(Recorded, schoolboy, London, 1988).

dill n

fool, idiot, silly person. A word which has been recorded in Australia and the USA since at least the early 1950s, and in Britain since the mid-1970s when it was popular among schoolchildren. The word may be a shortening of dill pickle (gherkins may also be the source of **wally**, used to describe a fool), or of **dilly**.

dillberries, dilberries n pl

a variant of **dingleberries**.

dilly n

1 something remarkable, impressive or outstanding. Typically used in an admiring phrase such as 'that's a dilly! The word may be an invention, a corruption of 'delight(ful)' or a survival of a lost dialect word.

2 a fool. Possibly influenced by dull/silly, this term is most commonly heard in Australia.

3 The Dilly is the Piccadilly section of central London frequented by, among others, prostitutes and drug users.

dimbo, dimmo n

an unintelligent or dull-witted person. These embellishments of dim (also influenced by dumb, **dumbo** and **bimbo**) have been favourite words with British schoolchildren since the late 1970s.

• 'You little dimbo, you've got no idea have you?'
(On Approval, British TV play, February 1989).

• 'He [Bruce Springsteen] is just dead popular with a lot of dimmos because of the unchallenging nature of what he does.'
(Alexei Sayle, Great Bus Journeys of the World, 1988).

dim bulb n American

a dimwit or dullard. The phrase evokes a low-wattage light bulb.

dime (someone) vb American

to inform on someone, betray to the police. A back-formation from **dime dropper**, used especially by prison inmates.

dime bag n American

a package or portion of an illicit drug worth ten dollars. (A dime is ten cents.)

dime dropper n American

an informer. An underworld phrase derived from the dime (ten cents) dropped into a payphone when calling the police.

dimp n, vb British

a cigarette end which can be retrieved, typically from the street, and relit. The word, now part of the language of tramps, is also heard as a verb meaning to extinguish (for later smoking). The term seems to be an invention, possibly influenced by crimp and damp.

din-dins n

dinner or another meal, food. A nursery word which like many others 'choo-choo', **gee-gee**, **wee-wee**, etc.) is used facetiously by teenagers and adults. The conversion of dinner into din-din is by a familiar process known as reduplication.

ding vb

1 to hit.

2 to single out for a reprimand, rejection or for an onerous duty. This use of the word occurs in institutional life in both Britain and America, but its origin is obscure.

• 'They dinged me.'

• 'He was dinged.'

dingaling, ding-a-ling n

1 an eccentric, crazy or foolish person. A word which originated in the USA and was enthusiastically adopted by schoolchildren in Britain in the late 1960s.
2 penis. This obscure nursery word was popularized by Chuck Berry's hit song of 1972, 'My Ding-a-Ling'.

dingbat n

1 an eccentric, crazy or foolish person. Originally this was an Australian word, probably derived from 'dingbats' as an adjective (an embellishment of the colloquial 'bats'). The word is now popular in Britain and the USA.
- 'In fact, editing and voice-over combine to ensure that the man never looks a real dingbat.'
(Independent, 23 December 1988).
2 Australian a Chinese person.
3 a any unnamed or unnameable thing. This mainly American sense is influenced by the Dutch and German Ding; thing.
b a typographical symbol, printers' device. A specialized use of the previous sense.

dingdong n

1 a a noisy to-and-fro shouting match or fight; from the image of bells clashing or being struck.
b a rowdy party. This sense is probably British in origin; ding-dong has been working-class London rhyming slang since the turn of the century for 'sing-song' and hence musical gathering and party.
- 'Let's have a Ding-Dong.'
(Title of rock and roll record by American group Freddie Bell and the Bell-Boys, 1958).
2 a fool or eccentric person. A variant of **dingaling**.
3 penis. A nursery word also used facetiously by adults.

dinge n

a black person, a coloured person. A pre-war American term recorded by Raymond Chandler. In spite of its negative appearance (it derives from dingy) the word is vulgar but not necessarily pejorative in intent.
- 'It was one of those dinge bars off the mainstrip.'

dingleberry n

1 a piece of dung or excrement clinging to hair or wool around the anus. This originally rural notion (applied to sheep and by extension to humans) has curiously given rise to a very large number of colourful terms throughout the English-speaking world. Others are **dangleberries, dillberries, clinkers, winnets** and **wittens, bum tags, chuffnuts**, etc.
2 a crazy or eccentric person, a fool. Most commonly heard among American high-school and college students; it is inspired by the previous sense (although users may be unaware of the fact).

dingo's breakfast n Australian

a piss and a look around. A humorous coinage on the lines of **Mexican breakfast** or 'pelican's breakfast'.

dingus n

a thing, an obscure or unnamed object. Originally a South African and American version of 'thingy' or 'thingummy', it derives from the Dutch ding, meaning thing.

dink n

1 a silly person, fool or eccentric. The word has been used especially by children and young people in both Britain and America, although possibly coined separately in each.
2 Australian and American an oriental person; a fairly uncommon term, nowadays used especially and deroga-

torily for a Vietnamese. It may originally have been a blend of **dinge** and **chink**.

3 *American* also **dinky** one of a childless **yuppie** couple; an acronym for 'double (or dual) income, no kids', coined in New York in 1986. Dink is an example of the American use of acronyms to describe social sub-groups. This tendency, which produced **WASP**, **JAP** and later **yuppies** in the 1970s, became a vogue among New Yorkers in the mid-1980s. In spite of enthusiastic use by some journalists and imitation by their London counterparts, this term, like **droppie**, **guppy**, etc. has achieved only limited currency.

● *'Take Dink, for instance, which I always thought meant idiot. The other day I heard a girl refer to a yuppie couple as "dinks".'*
(*Evening Standard*, 22 January 1987).

4 *American* **a** a penis. A fairly rare teenage term.

b nothing at all. In this sense the equivalent of **dick**.

dinkum *adj Australian*
See **fair dinkum**.

dinky *n*
1 *British* a car, particularly a large, impressive car. Said self-deprecatingly or admiringly by nouveau-riche working-class speakers and **Sloane Rangers**. Dinky Toys were a brand of miniature model cars popular among children in the 1950s and early 1960s.

2 a dink (*see* **dink 3**).

● *'I have had my year of being a dinky (double income, no kids) and I lost all my friends of any worth to it.'*
(Richard Jobson, *The Sunday Times*, 9 July 1989).

dinky-di *n*
a *Australian* the real thing (pro

nounced 'dinkee-die'). Perhaps an embellishment of **fair dinkum**.

b *British* fine, perfect (pronounced 'dinkee-dee'; the spelling is arbitrary). A pseudo-nursery term like **diddly-dum**, probably invented by students.

● *'Don't worry, everything's dinky-di.'*

dip *n*
1 a fool. This word, first heard in the 1970s is either a back-formation from **dippy** or a short form of **dipstick** or **dipshit**.

● *'All those people out there, they're just complete dips.'*
(Recorded, American teenager, London, 1988).

2 *also* **dipster** a pickpocket. A Victorian term, still in police and underworld use.

dip one's/the wick *vb*
(of a man) to have sex. A vulgar euphemism which is about a century old. Wick is either a shortening of the rhyming slang **Hampton Wick**; **prick**, or a straightforward metaphor from candle-wick. Originally British, the term is now used, albeit less commonly, in the USA and Australia.

dipping *n*
picking pockets. The term has been in use since the middle of the 19th century.

dippy *adj*
eccentric, silly, or slightly deranged; daft. A British term now in use throughout the English-speaking world. It seems to be an invented word rather than a derivation.

dipshit *n*
a fool. This vulgarism is sometimes said to be a euphemism for male homosexual or male member (compare

dung-puncher, etc.) but may simply be an elaboration of **dip**.

dipso n

an alcoholic or drunkard. A shortening of the term dipsomaniac (from the Greek dipsa, thirst).

dipstick n

a fool. The word is probably a euphemism for **dipshit**, but with less unpleasant overtones. It has been popularized by television series and films in both Britain and the USA since the early 1980s and is a favourite with teenagers.

dipsy n, adj American

1 (an) alcoholic or drunk. In this sense the word is based on dipsomaniac (see also **dipso**) and/or 'tipsy'.

2 (a) foolish person.

dipsy-doo, dipsy-doodle n

American

a fraud or deceit. A folksy pre-World-War II phrase which is still in occasional use. It may be inspired by a dance step involving 'ducking and diving'.

dirtbag, dirtball n American

a despicable person. These terms of abuse, being strong but not obscene, are frequently heard in films and TV programmes, such as the police series Hill Street Blues.

● 'All right dirtbags, I've had enough.' (Psychopath in Beer, US film, 1985).

dirtbox n

the anus. A vulgarism that is also occasionally used as a term of abuse.

dirty adj

possessing or containing illicit

drugs, a jargon term used by police, customs officers and drug users.

● 'His suitcase came through dirty.'

the dirty mac brigade n

British

the lascivious and/or sexist section of the male population who delight in pornography, frequent strip clubs, or indulge in sexual exhibitionism, etc. A generic term based on the stereotype (largely justified as far as the 1950s and 1960s were concerned) of such a person wearing a grubby raincoat.

dirty old man n

See **D.O.M.**

discombobulated adj

confused, discomfited or distracted. An invented pseudo-latinate verb, normally heard in the adjective form. It dates from the 19th century when such portmanteau words were popular.

● 'I've been feeling discombobulated since we got back.'

discuss Uganda vb British

to have sex. A euphemism coined in the 1970s by the British satirical magazine Private Eye. It has become one of the magazine's long-running jokes and is said to stem from a party at which a female journalist was alleged to have explained an upstairs sexual encounter by saying 'We were discussing Uganda'. (Idi Amin's régime was in the news at the time.) The term Ugandan Affairs is also derived from this source.

disgusto n, adj

(a) repellent (thing or person). A favourite term of **JAPs** and **Valley Girls** among others, this Americanism has been adopted, or separately coined, by British and Australian schoolchildren.

● 'Oh look at all the disgustos [baby crabs]! We don't have them by Lake Michigan.'

(Recorded, American Jewish girl, Brittany, 1982).

dish n

1 a a very attractive woman. This appreciative term (though offensive to most modern women) is one of many that liken a woman to a tasty snack or meal. Unlike **tart** or **crumpet**, for example, dish was introduced, or perhaps reintroduced (the metaphor was not unknown in earlier times) into Britain from the USA in the 1930s.

b a very attractive man. Since the mid-1960s the word has also been used of men by women and this usage may now be more common than the original.

● *'And those photographs of Mustapha – he was so unattractive, and because you'd had him they said "what a dish".'*
(Kenneth Halliwell, quoted in Joe Orton's diary, 2 May 1967).

2 American gossip. From the phrase **dish the dirt**.

● *'Oh my, this is prime dish. I can't wait to tell the girls.'*
(*Cheers*, US TV comedy series, 1989).

dish vb

to defeat, destroy or ruin. The original sense of this British term of the 18th century was to swindle, deceive or make a fool of. The image behind the expression was probably that of 'serving up' something (or someone) that has been well and truly 'processed', exploited, etc.

dish the dirt vb American

to spread scandalous or malicious gossip. 'Dish' here is, of course, dish up in the sense of serve to an eager audience.

dishy adj

very attractive, handsome or beautiful. The adjective form of **dish** is currently more often used by women than men and is so common in Britain as to be a colloquialism rather than true slang.

Disneyland n

a fantasy world, a state of insanity or delusion. The word is often used appreciatively by drug users and pejoratively by those disapproving of such indulgence.

diss vb

to scorn, snub, belittle. This vogue word of the late 1980s entered adolescent speech via the **hip-hop** and **rap** sub-cultures originating in the USA. A typical 'clipping', like **def**, **treach**, etc., it is based on the verbs dismiss, disapprove or disrespect [sic], (perhaps influenced by **dish**).

ditsy, ditzy adj

silly, eccentric, twee, or frivolous. An invented term, popular especially in the USA, since the mid-1970s. The word which is obviously influenced by dizzy is generally applied to females.

ditz n

a silly, eccentric and/or frivolous person, someone who is **ditzy**. An Americanism picked up by some British speakers in the mid-1980s.

div n British

a person who is odd, stupid, weak or deviant in some way. This shortening of **divvy** has become popular among young people of all classes in the 1980s. Before that it was part of the lexicon of criminals, tramps, street-traders and workmen.

● *'Him, he's a bit of a div, isn't he?'*
(Recorded, student, London University, 1986).

dive n

See **take a dive**.

divebombing n British

1 attacking something with spray paints in order to cover it with graffiti. From the late 1970s the term has been used by young graffiti artists, or vandals.

2 picking up cigarette ends from the street (to relight and smoke). A term used by vagrants in the 1980s.

diving n American

1 picking pockets. An underworld term which is the equivalent of the British **dipping**.

2 See **pearl-diver**.

divvy adj British

odd, stupid, deviant, weak or pathetic. This term, of uncertain origin, has existed in the vocabulary of society's 'marginals' since at least the late 1950s (it is unlikely to derive from deviant, but may be related to daft or daffy, or even by a tortuous etymology from 'divino' in the sense of possessed). It has recently been revived as a vogue term by schoolchildren, although the short noun form **div** is more common. (Divvy itself has occasionally been recorded as a noun.)

● '*Who's your friend with the glasses?*
'*E looks a bit divvy.*'
(Recorded, street-gang member, London, 1967).

d.k. vb American

to snub someone or renege on something, to feign ignorance of someone or something. The letters (pronounced 'dee-kay') are an acronym of **don't know**.

● '*He d.k.'d me.*'
(*Wall Street*, US film, 1988).

d.m.'s n pl British

'Doc Marten's' footwear. An abbrevi-

ation of the trademark name of the boots worn by skinheads in preference to **bovver boots** in the 1970s and by **punks** and other youth groups. From the late 1980s, D.M.'s were worn by young women as part of conventional dress and had lost much of their youth-group connotations. The term is used to refer to a style of footwear rather than solely to the authentic trademarked item.

DMT n

di-methyl triptamine, a synthetic hallucinogenic drug developed in the 1970s which was publicized as a 'mini-trip' (lasting approximately one hour, as opposed to the four to eight hours of LSD).

do, doo n

excrement. A nursery word used all over the English-speaking world, although in Britain the plural form **dos** is probably more common. The word in this sense is probably pre-World War II and derives from the Victorian notion of doing or performing one's bodily functions (dutifully).

do (drugs) vb

to take drugs. The term can apply to single instances or to habitual use. Originally an Americanism, it was adopted by British speakers in the **hippy** era.

● '*Well the one [trip] that stopped me from doing acid forever was when I dropped seven tabs.*'
(Zodiac Mindwarp, *I-D* magazine, November 1987).

D.O.A. adj

unconscious, inert. A facetious use of the American police and hospital jargon 'dead on arrival' to mean 'dead to the world', particularly after taking drugs or alcohol.

do a Bertie vb British

to turn Queen's Evidence, to inform on one's accomplices. A fairly rare piece of criminal jargon of uncertain origin. It is possibly from the Edwardian era, when turning King's Evidence would have been joining 'Bertie's' side, and seems to have existed before the days of Bertie Smalls, a 1970s criminal supergrass (high-level informer).

do a job on (someone) vb

to deceive, thoroughly overwhelm, devastate. Originally an Americanism, this unspecific phrase is now in fairly widespread use in Britain and Australia.

do a number on (someone) vb

to cheat, frustrate, defeat, demoralize. Like the previous phrase, this expression, the precise meaning of which depends on its context, originated in the USA and is now used elsewhere.

- 'A talk that made it clear that Ari intended "to do a number on Bolker, he wanted to hurt the fellow, not do him in, but certainly to harm him in some way".'
(Nigel Dempster, writing in The Sunday Times, 24 September 1989).

do a runner vb British

to escape, run away or disappear. A phrase from semi-criminal and subsequent working-class usage which has become a generally popular term since the early 1980s. It originally referred specifically to the practice of leaving a restaurant, bar, etc. without paying.

- 'I decided to "do a runner" i.e. to leg it out of the restaurant without paying the bill.'
(Great Bus Journeys of the World, Alexei Sayle, 1988).

do a train (on someone) vb British

to have serial sexual intercourse (with one partner). A 1980s alternative to gang bang with the implication that the sexual partner is consenting.

dob, dob in, dob on vb Australian

to inform (on someone), tell tales. A schoolchildren's term since the late 1970s which was previously, and still is, part of underworld terminology. Dob was a British dialect word meaning something between drop and lob (it survives in the noun form in colloquial expressions such as 'a dob of butter'). Dob in has been introduced to British audiences by Australian soap operas of the 1980s.

- 'I tell you what you do, dob her in to the governor.'
(Prisoner, Cell Block H, Australian TV series, 1982).

dock asthma n British

gasps of (usually feigned) surprise and disbelief by prisoners in the dock. A part of police and prison jargon since at least the 1950s.

docker n British

a partly smoked cigarette, put out for later relighting. This word, which is more common in the North of England than elsewhere, originates in dock: to cut short, or the related archaic use of dock, meaning the solid part of an animal tail.

Doctor Feelgood n American

a doctor or other person who freely prescribes pleasurable drugs. The name has been used in several blues and soul songs since World War II, but probably pre-dates them as a black underworld term, where it had a more generalized meaning of someone who could provide euphoria or comfort. It was later applied as a nickname, for example to Dr Max Jacobson, physician to President Kennedy, famous for his disbursement of amphetamines to New York high society.

doctors and nurses n

sexual activity or sex play. To **play (at) doctors and nurses** is a humorous euphemism, sometimes used by adults, deriving from the children's game which often involves sexual experimentation.

doddle n British

a pushover, something really easy to accomplish. Formerly slang, now a common colloquialism, the word may be a variation of dawdle, or a blend of dawdle and toddle. According to the late Eric Partridge it comes from pre-World-War II racing jargon in which it denoted a 'walkover'.

dodgy adj British

a doubtful, suspect. A common term in British English and nowadays hardly slang. It arose in the later 19th century and derives from the sense of dodge as an artful or risky ruse. In the 1960s 'dodgy!' was the counterpart of 'swinging!' in the catchphrases of TV compere Norman Vaughan.

b stolen, illegal. A narrower sense of dodgy a, common since the 1960s in such euphemisms as **dodgy gear/merchandise**.

dodgy job, dodgy one n
British

a criminal case or arrest which is difficult to substantiate, in police jargon. An expression employing the colloquialism **dodgy** in its sense of both uncertain and illicit.

● 'A dodgy job is a case in which the circumstantial evidence is slight or the arrest has been provoked by the behaviour of the suspect ... rather

than by evidence of some other substantive offence.'
(Inside the British Police, Simon Holdaway, 1985).

dog n

1 a an ugly, unpleasant or unattractive woman or girl. This sense of the word was in common use in the USA from the 1950s. It was adopted by British speakers in the mid-1970s.

b American something unpleasant or worthless. Expressions in which dog expresses distaste or contempt are almost all American in origin, presumably reflecting the cliché that the British are a nation of dog lovers. Nevertheless there are occasional instances of this sense in British English.

● 'This car's a dog!'

c a company or share that performs badly on the stock exchange, a worthless piece of stock; (these are also known as **bow-wow** stocks)

2 British a wig, toupee. The word usually implies a ragged, ill-fitting or generally unconvincing hairpiece. It has been in use among teenagers at least since the early 1970s.

3 a rogue, (likeable) reprobate. A 19th-century usage, now a colloquialism usually surviving in the form **(you) old dog!**

4 a dog-end.

5 See dogs.

dog vb American

to abandon, reject, get rid of. The word in this sense was used by teenagers and college students in the late 1980s.

● 'Dog the dorm rules now!'
(A Different World, American TV series, 1987).

dog (and bone) n British

telephone. An example of rhyming slang which is still used today. It is usually used of the appliance rather than the action.

• '*Get on the dog to him and find out when he's coming.*'

dog-and-boned *adj British*
stoned. A cannabis smoker's term from the 1960s and early 1970s, now heard in the form **doggo**.

dog (someone) around *vb*
American
a to pester. An expression inspired by the same images as to 'dog someone's heels'.
b to behave badly, cruelly, irresponsibly or unfaithfully, especially to one's partner. This Americanism seems to have its origin in black street talk of the late 1950s, perhaps inspired by the notion of an errant or 'dirty dog'.

dog-ass *adj American*
worthless, inferior, bad. A vulgarism in use for instance among military personnel and college students since the 1950s.

dog-botherer *n British*
a humorous and meaningless term of abuse, inspired by **god-botherer**, but without connotations of religious zeal, bestiality or indeed specific wrong-doing.

dog-end *n British*
a cigarette end. The word usually describes a stubbed-out butt, rather than a partly-smoked cigarette put aside for later relighting, (see **dimp** and **docker**). It has been in use since at least World War II.

dogface *n American*
a common soldier, infantry private in the US army. A term from World War II. It is presumably derived from a hangdog or cowed expression.

dogfood *n American*
a dark-coloured, highly refined form of heroin. A drug user's term from the 1980s.

dogfucking *n*
having (human) sex which involves penetration from the rear; ventro-dorsal intercourse.

(all) dogged-up *adj*
dressed smartly or extravagantly. The term is probably inspired by 'decked out' or 'dolled up', or by the expression **dog's dinner**.

• '*I don't want to have to get all dogged-up just to go out to dinner.*'

doggett *vb British*
to scrounge. An arcane piece of London rhyming slang. Thomas Doggett, an actor, on the occasion of George I's accession in 1715, endowed a prize for an annual race for Thames watermen between London Bridge and Chelsea. The prize for the race, which is still rowed, is a coat and badge, hence 'Doggett's Coat and Badge'; cadge. The word is also used as a noun to mean a scrounger.

• '*He's meeting me at the Hong Kong. He's only trying to doggett a Chinese [meal].*'
(Recorded, pensioner, Bristol, 1989).

doggie bag *n*
See **doggy-bag**.

doggie-do/dos *n*
a dog excrement.
b something worthless and/or repellent.
Both meanings are used, generally facetiously, among adults, though the term originated as a nursery word.

140

doggie-fashion, doggy-fashion adv

(sexual intercourse) involving penetration from the rear.

• 'They like to do it doggy-fashion.'

doggo adj

1 American worthless, inferior, bad. A variation of dog-ass.

2 British intoxicated by marihuana. This unusual term derives from a now obsolete piece of rhyming slang dog-and-boned; stoned, perhaps reinforced by the immobility and furtiveness implied in the colloquial phrase to 'lie doggo'.

doggy-bag n

a bag provided by a restaurant for customers to take away uneaten food. This term, originally American, was slang until the early 1970s when the practice became permitted and widespread.

dog it vb American

to perform badly, fail to do one's best. A campus and high-school expression from the 1970s.

• 'If you dog it again this time, you're off the team.'

dog out vb American

to get (all) dogged up.

dogs n pl

1 a feet. Of obscure origin, this usage has persisted in British and American usage at least since World War II. It usually implies tired, sore feet.

• 'Ooh, that feels better – my dogs are barking today!'
(Planes, Trains and Automobiles, US film, 1987).

b slippers, shoes or boots.

2 the dogs British greyhounds or greyhound racing.

dog's breakfast n

a mess, confused mixture. From the image of a mishmash of unappetizing scraps. The expression (compare the roughly contemporaneous dog's dinner), is commonly applied to a misconceived or botched plan or display. The phrase dates from the 1930s.

• 'My god, he made a real dog's breakfast of that presentation.'
(Recorded, publisher, London, 1986).

• 'I'm afraid the syllabus is a bit of a dog's breakfast.'
(Recorded, lecturer, London, 1989).

dog's breath, dogsbreath n

a repellent, contemptible or unpleasant person. A term of abuse popular in the 1980s, probably because it is colourful without being obscene; another factor in its spread is its usage in TV shows, particularly by the cult character Mick Belker in the US TV police series Hill Street Blues. It originated in American teen usage in the late 1970s (see dog). This term is sometimes heard as dogbreath.

dog's cock, dog's dick, dog's prick n

an exclamation mark. A piece of printers', typesetters' and journalists' slang.

dog's dinner n

a an extravagant display, especially a vulgar, misguided or unsuccessful attempt at smartness. The expression, which dates from the late 1920s, usually forms part of a phrase such as 'all done up like a dog's dinner'.

b a mess. In this negative sense dog's breakfast is currently more fashionable.

do-hickey n American

a an unspecified thing, thingummy.
b a spot, pimple or skin blemish.

141

Hickey alone is a common teenage term for spot or lovebite; the prefix is an embellishment.

c penis. A children's term that is probably a specific application of do-hickey a.

doings n

an unspecified thing or things, especially a mechanism or tool, the name of which is unknown or forgotten.

do it vb

to have sex. An evasive or coy euphemism used by children, those too embarrassed to be more explicit, or, often, facetiously by adults.

dole-bludger n Australian

a person who claims unemployment pay which they are not entitled to, a 'dole scrounger' (see bludger). This common term is sometimes extended to encompass any idle or shiftless person.

● 'Newspapers are always whingeing about the dole bludgers.'
(Girls Night Out, Kathy Lette, 1989).

doley, dolie n Australian

someone who is on the dole (drawing unemployment pay).

doll n

woman. A fairly dated Americanism adopted into British working-class usage in the 1950s and again in the 1970s, since when it may also be used by women of men. The word has condescending or proprietorial overtones when used by teenagers.

dollar n British

five shillings (in pre-1971 non-decimal British currency). This usage derives from the fact that the former five-shilling coin resembled a silver dollar and that at various times in the 20th century the rate of exchange of the US dollar stood at five shillings (25 pence after decimalization).

doll city n American

a a beautiful person (of either sex but implying idealized cuteness, femininity or passivity).

● 'Wow check the new boy out – doll city!'

b a pleasant situation or attractive idea. The expression is often an exclamation of approval.

● 'Paris in the fall – doll city!'
Both instances of the phrase typically occur in adolescent speech.

dollface n American

an attractive or cute person. A term of affection used especially by women to men.

dollies n American

Dolophine, an earlier trademark name for methadone, a synthetic heroin substitute.

dolls n pl American

pills of amphetamine or barbiturate drugs. A term adopted by middle-class users of (often prescribed) drugs. The word was popularized (and probably invented) by the author Jacqueline Susann in her sensationalist novel The Valley of the Dolls in 1965. The inspiration for the term is presumably the fact that the pills and capsules are colourful and comforting.

dolly adj British

excellent, attractive, cute. A vogue word of the mid-1960s, enshrined in the title of Adam Diment's fashionable novel The Dolly Dolly Spy. The word passed from camp theatrical and homosexual use to general currency for a year or so. It survives in middle-class speech, as an ironic or scathing synonym for twee.

dolly bird n British
an attractive girl. This expression, which would now appear hopelessly dated and offensive to many women, briefly epitomized the ideal gamine of the mid- to late 1960s. The word was used only fleetingly by the fashionable young themselves before becoming a journalistic cliché.

D.O.M. n
a 'dirty old man'. A middle-class and **Sloane Ranger** version of the colloquial expression. D.O.M. is applied, usually by females, to anyone male and lecherous regardless of age.

donah n
a girl. A 19th-century usage derived via tramps, showmen, market traders and petty criminals from Italian and Spanish (*donna*, *doña*, meaning lady). The word had virtually died out in British English by the 1950s, but was still in use among street gang members in the USA, and more generally in Australia.

Donald Duck, Donald n
a fuck. A piece of rhyming slang, based on the cartoon character, that is heard in Australian and British English.

dong vb
to hit, strike a resound blow; from the sound of a bell being struck.

dong, donger n
1 penis. This word is common in current Australian English but is also heard in Britain and North America. Its origin is unclear but it resembles synonyms such as **whang**, **schlong**, etc. Unlike most similar terms its use has not been extended to mean a fool. This hearty, brusque word is usually used by males.
2 a blow, strike, from the verb form.

donk n Australian
1 a car engine. This is probably a shortening of donkey, which the late Eric Partridge recorded as being in use in British navy jargon for a ship's engine. The term 'donkey engine' is often used for small, portable or auxiliary engines such as an outboard motor or miniature shunting locomotive.
2 a foolish person.

donkey n British
a slow, clumsy person. A usage beloved of soccer fans who delight in braying at any player (usually on an opposing team) who exhibits these characteristics.

donnybrook n
a brawl, free-for-all. Donnybrook Fair held near Dublin was often the scene of uproarious behaviour.

doob n
1 British an amphetamine pill. The singular form of the more common **doobs**.
2 penis. This rare usage is either an invention or a shortening of **doobry**.

doobie, dooby n American
a marihuana cigarette, a joint.

doobie, dooby adj Australian
shabby, dull, unglamorous. A rare word, used predominantly by the middle-aged and elderly. Its origin is obscure.

doobry n British
1 an unspecified thing, thingummy, or a person whose name is forgotten or unknown. This invented word has existed at least since the 1950s.
2 an amphetamine tablet, or other pill. This is probably a narrowing of the preceding sense and was popular among the **mods** of the 1960s, although

the plural **doobs** was the more common alternative. Doobry in this drug-related sense has also been derived from **double-blues**, a particular type of **pep pill**.

doobs n pl British
tablets or capsules of amphetamine (later known generically as **speed**). This was the 1960s mods' own favourite term for the pills known to the popular press as **purple hearts** or **pep pills**.

doodad n
an unspecified thing, thingummy. The word is American, dating from before World War II. **Doodads** are bits and pieces, odds and ends.

doodah n
an unspecified thing, gadget, thingummy. The British and Australian form of the American **doodad**.

doodle n
1 penis. A nursery word.
2 nonsense, rubbish or excrement.

doodly squat n American
a excrement.
b nonsense, nothing at all. The expression is a common variant form of **diddly (squat)**.
● 'Shoot – I wouldn't tell you doodly squat after the way you've behaved.'
(Night Game, US film, 1988).

doody, doo-doo, do-do n
American
excrement. A nursery word used facetiously by adults, this is one of many similar words, perhaps inspired by the older usage, **do** or **dos**.
● 'Elephant doody. His shit tastes like tutti frutti.'
(Cartoon caption from the schoolkids' issue of Oz magazine, 1969).

doofer, doofa n
1 an unspecified thing, thingummy.
● 'Hand me that doofer.'
2 a partly-smoked cigarette; a pun on '(it will) do for later'. A war-time term that remained in use in the 1960s and may still survive.

doofus n
an alternative spelling of **dufus**.

doojie n American
heroin. A drug-users' term which is probably from black speech of the 1950s in which it denoted either an unspecified thing (cf. **doodad**) or excrement (cf. **doody**).

dook n
a hand, fist. A variation of the better-known **duke(s)**. In rustic and working-class Australian speech this form survives from archaic British usage.
See **dukes**, **duke it**, **duke on it**.

doolally adj British
deranged, crazy. A very popular term derived from the location of a colonial army sanatorium and rest camp at Deolali, Bombay, where soldiers exhibiting signs of fatigue, heat exhaustion, etc. were sent. An early form which is still heard occasionally was **do(o)lally-tap**, the tap meaning fever in Hindi.

doolan n
1 New Zealand a Roman Catholic.
2 Australian a policeman.
Both senses are rather dated, and derive from the common Irish surname.

do one's nut/block/crust/ pieces/taters vb
to lose control, to become furious. Originally working-class alternatives for to 'lose one's head' or to 'blow one's top', all in use in Britain and Australia;

the more colourful second, third, fourth and fifth variants are currently in vogue among young people.

- *'Funny you should say that, because these days I find I do my nut very easily.'*
  (*Alfie*, British film, 1966).
- *'They were freaking about those lost trannies [transparencies]; David was doing his crust.'*
  (Recorded, art director, London, 1989).
- *'Men are always saying they can count the number of times they've cried on the fingers of one hand. Well, I reckon women can count the number of times they've really done their blocks.'*
  (*Girls Night Out*, Kathy Lette, 1989).

doorstep vb

to hang around a private house or accost someone at their home. Used of and by journalists seeking a story, this piece of jargon has entered the general domain due to publicity given to the unscrupulous activity of tabloid journalists.

- *'He was out doorstepping.'*
- *'They doorstepped her all week.'*

doover n

an alternative form of the first sense of **doofer**.

doo-wop n

a type of harmonious, (usually) tenor-led, a capella group-singing popular in the USA in the 1950s, especially among street-corner groups of (mainly) blacks or Italians in major American cities. The expression itself was only applied in the 1960s, long after the style had been subsumed in rock 'n' roll ballad singing. It derives from one of the nonsense phrases typically used by the harmony choruses.

dooze n American

1 something which is very easy to accomplish, an attractive proposition.
2 an alternative form of **doozer**.

dooze vb American

to bamboozle, flatter.

doozer, doozie, doozy n

something or someone very impressive, remarkable or exceptional; a 'humdinger'. This is probably an invented word (though some authorities derive it from a spectacular pre-World-War II car, the Duesenburg). The term is certainly American in origin.

dope n

1 an illicit drug, narcotics. The word was first applied to stupefying drugs such as opium and heroin at the turn of the century, and remained limited to this context until the 1960s. In the late 1960s **hippy** drug users began to apply the then almost archaic form ironically to their preferred soft drug, cannabis (marihuana and hashish), and this remains the most common use today.

- *'He said: "You know how you leave dope lying around? Well, she ate some and she went berserk. She hasn't liked it much since".'*
  (*News of the World*, 29 October 1989).

2 information, news. In this sense the word has been used at least since World War I, especially in America. The word is derived from the idea of something dense or viscous, embodied in the Dutch word *doop*, meaning dip (in the sense of a sauce in which other food may be dipped).
3 a foolish or stupid person.

dope out vb

to work out, discover information. A phrase derived from **dope 2**, it is more common in American English where it originated before World War II.

doped-up adj
under the influence of a (stupefying or tranquillizing) drug.

doper n
a user of illicit drugs. The word, from **dope**, has been in vogue since the early 1970s. It is used about, rather than by drug users, and is applied indiscriminately to users of hard and soft drugs.
- *'He's a doper from way back.'*

do-re-mi n American
money. A pun on **dough**.

dork n
1 penis. A term popularized first among American adults then among teenagers in the 1970s, it is probably inspired by **dick** and, perhaps, **pork**.

2 a fool, offensive buffoon. This is a predictable second (and now more widespread) sense of the word, on the same pattern as **dick**, **prick**, etc. It is not used affectionately (as **plonker** for instance is), but is only mildly offensive. Since the late 1970s this term has been in vogue in Britain and Australia as well as in its country of origin.
- *'I love your husband, but he's a real dork.'*
  'Yes, but he's my dork.'
  (*Someone to Watch Over Me*, US film, 1987).

dorky adj
dull, offensively gauche, silly. From **dork 2**.
- *'Wayne asked me out, but he's real dorky.'*
  (Recorded, young Canadian woman, London, January 1989).
- *'I just wanted to give you something that nobody else could and I knew I couldn't compete with your friends when it comes to expensive stuff so I tried that dorky song.'*
  (*Cheers*, US TV comedy series, 1988).

dos n pl
a version of **do** (in the sense of excrement).
(It is pronounced 'dooze'.)

dose n
a venereal infection. Until the 1960s the word most often referred to a bout of gonorrhoea.
- *'Don't Give A Dose to the One You Love Most.'*
  (Song written and recorded by Shel Silverstein, 1972).

dosed (up) adj
1 infected with a venereal disease.

2 drugged illicitly (as in the case of a greyhound or racehorse, for example) or unwittingly (in the case of a human). The expression is in this sense a synonym for **spiked**, and in the 1970s often referred to LSD.

dosh n British
money. This is a working-class term from the early 1950s which was falling out of use in the 1960s, but which, like many similar words (**bunce**, **loot**, **lolly**, etc.), was revived in the money-conscious late 1980s. It is a favourite with alternative comedians and 'professional cockneys'. The original would seem logically to be the old African colonial term **dash**, denoting a tip or bribe, but other authorities claim that it is influenced by **doss**, in the sense of the price of a bed (for the night).

doss vb
a to sleep.
- *'I need a place to doss for a couple of nights.'*

b to move from place to place, sleeping in borrowed or low-class accommodation.
- *'Old Shawie's been dossing for the last three weeks.'*
  (Recorded, student, London, 1988).
  A 19th-century term which may

146

derive from the Latin *dorsum*, for back. The verb, as opposed to noun forms of the word, are mainly encountered in British English.

doss n

1 a a place to sleep, especially a temporary, free and/or makeshift bed. This word from 19th-century tramps' jargon was probably originally a corruption of *dorsum*, Latin for 'back'. Tramps are unlikely to have coined the term; it may have come from the jargon surrounding pugilism (meaning 'flat on one's back') which was a sport subscribed to by aristocrats and students, among others.
b a period of sleep, nap.
2 a very easy task, pushover. In this sense the word, although based on the notion of lying down, may be influenced by 'toss', as in easily tossing off a piece of work.
- *'You mustn't see this purely as a doss.'*

doss around vb British

to do nothing in particular, lead an aimless existence. From **doss 2**.

dossbag n British

1 a sleeping bag.
2 a scruffy, lazy or slovenly person.

doss down vb British

to lie down to sleep (usually on the floor), bed down.
- *'Just doss down anywhere you like.'*

dosser n British

a a homeless person, vagrant, or down-and-out who sleeps wherever space is available.
- *'Leftovers of our present society, the dossers and meths-heads, the socially inadequates, the power-seekers and the bread-lovers.'*
(*International Times* (IT), April 1968).

- *'We are not tramps, winos or even dossers, we are gentlemen of the road – and we refuse to be moved.'*
(Homeless man *Observer*, 16 August 1987).
b a slovenly, irresponsible person. A favourite term of affectionate abuse between young (usually male) people in the 1980s. (From the noun **doss** or the verb **doss around**.)

doss house n

a dormitory for vagrants or a cheap, shabby hotel.
- *'I felt like pissing off and spending the night in some Arab dosshouse.'*
(Joe Orton's diary, 14 May 1967).
- *'I don't know how you manage to live in this doss house you call a flat.'*

dot vb

to hit. Usually used in the phrase to **dot (someone) one**, meaning to land a heavy and precise (on the 'dot') blow, or to black someone's eye.

do the work on (someone) vb British

to fix, defeat, kill or incapacitate someone. An underworld euphemism for violent action.
- *'And there's always someone who wants to say "I did the work on him".'*
(Recorded, ex-convict, Bradford, 1989).

do time vb

to serve a prison sentence.

double-bagger n American

a hideous or repellent person. A phrase from the vocabulary of **Valley Girls** and other American teenagers from the mid-1970s, probably originating in earlier surfers' slang. The image evoked is of a person who must wear a bag over their head – and provide one for the onlooker too, or alternatively wear *two* bags. The expression in this humorous usage was first borrowed from the language of baseball, where it describes a hit which allows the hitter to advance two bases, or 'bags'.

double-blue *n British*
a tablet of amphetamine sulphate (later called **speed**), of a specific type containing amphetamine and barbiturate. These **pep pills**, used by **mods** among others, were in the 1960s pale blue in colour.

double result *n British*
in the jargon of football hooligans, this denotes a victory against both an opposing team's supporters and the police.

douchebag *n American*
a contemptible or very unpleasant person. The expression is usually a strong term of abuse, indicating real distaste, although like comparable words it is sometimes used lightheartedly, typically by high-school and college students. Rubber bags were a part of douching paraphernalia when that form of contraception was widespread, especially among prostitutes. The word is applied to males and females.
- 'OK, we're going in there and anyone who doesn't act elegant is a douchebag.'
(*Satisfaction*, US film, 1988).

dough *n*
money. This was the most popular American slang term for money from the 19th century until the mid-1960s when it was supplanted by **bread**.

doughboy *n*
1 *American* an army private. The word was most popular at the time of World War I but is still occasionally used. The original doughboy was a sort of suet dumpling served in the armies and navies of the 19th century in Britain and the USA.
2 *British* a blow, heavy punch. In working-class and cockney jargon this rare sense of the word is occasionally recorded. Its derivation may be from the (heavy) dumpling referred to above.
- 'He landed him a real doughboy round the chops.'

Douglas *n British*
a 3rd (third-class) university honours degree. A student witticism of the late 1980s playing on the name, Douglas Hurd, of a long-serving member of Mrs Thatcher's Conservative cabinet, (a **Richard** is a synonym). Compare **Desmond**, **Pattie**, **Taiwan**.

do up *vb*
1 to inject or inhale (a drug). An embellishment of **do** in the sense of take (drugs) common among illicit drug users since the early 1970s.
2 *see* **done up**.

done up *adj British*
an alternative form of **fitted up** or **stitched up**.

dout, dowt *n British*
a cigarette end or stub. A word like **dub**, used by vagrants and working-class speakers. The *Oxford English Dictionary* first recorded the word in use in Glasgow in 1975. It may be a dialectal form of 'dowse(d)' or a contraction of 'stubbed-out'.

down-and-dirty *adj American*
a deceitful, corrupt, savage. An exclamation used in poker (when cards are dealt or slapped on the table) extended to describe base or brutal behaviour.
b basic, primitive, authentic, 'rough

and ready'. In this sense the phrase is usually appreciative rather than pejorative; in rock-music jargon it denotes healthily authentic or **funky**.

downer n
1 a tranquillizing or sedative drug (especially a barbiturate) in the language of illicit-drug users (as opposed to **uppers** or stimulant drugs).
• *'She's on downers.'*
2 a depressing or boring experience. From the slang of American **hipsters** of the 1950s, widespread in the English-speaking world since the 1960s, but now sounding rather dated in British English; although the phrase **on a downer** (going through a depressed or unlucky phase) is currently widespread.

downhome adj American
rustic, ethnic or (agreeably) simple and neighbourly. The word was first used by urbanized northern blacks to refer to their southern roots.

downstairs adj, adv
(in) the genital area or the buttocks. A coy euphemism which was probably inspired by the earlier **upstairs**, relating to the brain or head.

down the block adj, adv British
in solitary confinement, being punished. A prisoners' term.

down the tubes/flush/chute adv
ruined, abandoned, beyond hope. These are racier versions of 'down the drain', 'down the pan' or 'down the toilet', heard in the USA since the late 1970s and in Britain since the early 1980s.
• *'Bright enough to realise he is going down the tubes, he is still drawn to a prodigal self-destruction.'*
(*The Sunday Times*, 26 July 1987).

dozy adj British
slow-witted, foolish. The word is now a colloquialism; in the 1950s it was part of 'vulgar' speech. Originally it meant sleepy or lazy and was (and still is) a favourite term of abuse employed by sergeant majors and officers in the armed forces, teachers and other authority figures.

drabbie n British
a 'frump', 'bluestocking' or puritanical person, usually female. A middle-class term of mild derision or disapproval, based on drab and applied, often by journalists, in the 1980s to literary, academic or other professional women who deliberately eschew a glamorous appearance.

drack n Australian
rubbish. An Australian variant form of the more common **dreck**.

drag n
1 women's clothing, as worn by men, especially homosexuals, transvestites, female impersonators. Originally theatrical slang of the early 20th century in Britain, signifying a long dress (dragging along the ground), the phrase **in drag** crossed into popular terminology in the early 1960s. In the case of women wearing masculine clothing **man-drag** or **male drag** is usually specified.
• *'Marlene in man-drag.'*
(Caption to photograph of Marlene Dietrich in Kenneth Anger's *Hollywood Babylon*, 1975).
2 a thing, event or person considered to be boring or depressing. An Americanism, probably originating in the late 19th century, and remaining in marginal use until the 1960s, it was adopted into teenage currency in Britain and Australia in the late 1950s and was widespread by the mid-1960s.
• *'What a drag it is getting old.'*

(*Mother's Little Helper*, Rolling Stones, 1965).

3 *British* **a** an inhalation of cigarette smoke, a puff.

● '*Give me a drag on that.*'

b a marihuana cigarette, a **joint**. A prisoners' term.

4 a street, especially a long or important street, usually in the form **main drag**. This Americanism gave rise to **drag racing** to describe unofficial races from a standing start over a short, straight stretch of public road. Drag racing is now also an organized sport run over custom-built private **dragstrips**.

drag ass *vb American*

1 a variant of **haul ass**.

2 to move unwillingly, lazily or slowly.

drag-ass *adj American*

boring, tedious, onerous. The word is applied to people as well as to tasks.

dragged-up *adj*

a dressed in **drag**.

b dressed, clothed (especially in flamboyant or unusually expensive clothing). By extension from the first sense to the heterosexual world (although the term does not seem to be applied to women). Dragged-up is a racier version of 'dolled-up'.

● '*Here he comes, all dragged-up in his best things.*'

draggin' wagon *n American*

1 a tow-truck.

2 a car or van used to impress, seduce or transport members of the opposite sex. A high-school and college-boy term of the late 1970s, inspired by the preceding sense.

draggy *adj*

tedious, slow or depressing, from the second sense of **drag**. The word is now rather dated. In the 1960s and 1970s it was more popular in Britain than in the USA.

● '*It was a totally draggy scene.*'

drag queen *n*

a male homosexual who wears women's clothing. The phrase now has overtones of flamboyant, exhibitionist 'femininity' rather than mere cross-dressing.

● '*Kenneth Williams then gave a long portrait of a dismal drag queen writing a witty letter requesting employment.*'

(Joe Orton's Diary, 13 April 1967).

● '*The most important week in my life and I'm going to be spending it with a drag queen?!*'

(*He's My Girl*, US film, 1987).

dragster *n*

a customized car used in **drag racing**.

dragstrip *n*

a stretch of road used for **drag racing**.

the Drain *n British*

the nickname of the Waterloo and City line, used by London commuters. This underground link employs ancient, low-ceilinged carriages that speed through smoky, unlit tunnels.

drainpipes, drainpipe jeans, drainies, drains *n pl*
British

very tight trousers fashionable in the 1950s among **teddy boys** and, later, **rockers**. Although the terms have been fashionable subsequently (during the glitter craze and **punk** era, for instance), they are now more rare.

drain the lizard/dragon/ snake *vb*

to urinate. Colourful euphemisms popular with (invariably male) college students, hearty drinkers, etc. These expressions entered the slang lexicon of teenagers and college students in the late 1960s and early 1970s, although they are probably older, adult coinages on the pattern of **siphon the python**. It is not clear where in the English-speaking world the pattern originated, but it is thought by many to be typically Australian.

• *'He can't come to the phone right now, he's in the can draining his lizard.'*

(*Friday 13th Part VI*, US film, 1986).

drama queen n

a self-dramatizing or hysterical person. The expression was originally (in the 1960s) applied by male homosexuals to their fellows. In the 1970s the phrase was adopted by heterosexuals and applied to women and, sometimes, to **straight** as well as **gay** men.

drape(s) n

a clothes, a suit or outfit. The word was in use in the USA (where 'drapes' are curtains) in the 1950s among black musicians, **hipsters** and **beatniks**. It was then adopted by **spivs** and prisoners in Britain, where it is still heard.

b *British* a drape jacket, the top half of a **zoot suit** and part of the uniform of the **teddy boy** in the 1950s. (The drape has wide shoulders, and is almost as long as a frock-coat, but loose and unwaisted.)

draw n British

a tobacco. In this sense the word, derived from the action of inhaling, dates from the 1950s. It occurs in prison jargon in particular.

b cannabis (hashish or marihuana). Since the mid-1970s this word has been in vogue for smokable cannabis.

draw n British

a 'two-one' honours degree in the late 1980s parlance of university students. (The joke is that a draw means 'two won'.) Alternative names for the same award are **made-in** or **Taiwan**. *See also* **Desmond, Douglas, Pattie, Richard**.

dread n Jamaican

a Rastafarian, someone who wears **dreadlocks**.

dread adj Jamaican

an all-purpose word implying authentic, impressive, etc., in connection with the black reggae and **ganja** culture and Rastafarian religion of Jamaica. The word first conveyed the power and awe felt and inspired by the (**dreadlock**-wearing) devotees of Rastafarianism.

• *'He's dread/It's real dread.'*

dreadlocks n pl

hair in long, tight ringlets that are never cut, as worn by devotees of Rastafarianism (**Rasta**), the Jamaican religion. The style has been adopted by some non-religious black and white exponents of 1980s youth culture. The word is now usually shortened to **locks**.

dreamboat n

a very attractive person of the opposite sex. The word, redolent of Hollywood in the 1940s, is still used, especially in the USA and usually, but not always, facetiously as a description or term of endearment.

dreck n

rubbish, a worthless thing, **shit**. From the Yiddish *drek* and German *Dreck*, which have the same meaning.

• *'Here's some news to gladden the hearts of all devotees of dreck – the*

world première of Prisoner Cell Block "H".'
(Time Out magazine, July 1989).

dreg n British

a despicable or worthless person. A middle-class term of abuse or disapproval which has been rare since the late 1960s. It is a modern back-formation from the standard plural dregs, which itself derives from an Old Norse term for oil or wine residues.

drift vb

leave, go away, escape. The word is sometimes in the imperative form, meaning 'get lost'; otherwise it is a **cool** or 'tough-guy' synonym for to go.

drill vb

1 British to sleep. A middle-class and public-school term deriving from the phrase 'blanket drill', a facetious army expression for sleeping.
2 to shoot (usually to kill). A now dated Americanism adopted by crime and Western movies and fiction.
3 to have sex with. A rare usage on the same pattern as **screw**.

drilling for vegemite n
Australian

sodomy as practised by male homosexuals. One of several pejorative expressions based on the faecal aspects of anal sex. Vegemite is an Australian trademark food (a yeast extract) similar in consistency to Marmite.

drink n British

a small bribe, tip or other financial inducement. Originally, in London working-class usage, it meant literally the price of an (alcoholic) drink. Now it usually refers to a more substantial sum and is sometimes extended to a share in an attractive venture, or a 'piece of the action'. As an item of Brit-

ish police and underworld slang, it was given wider currency by TV series such as *Minder*. The word is a typically cosy euphemism for a more sinister reality, a tendency in London working-class usage exemplified by such terms as **bother**, **seeing-to**, etc. In the case of drink, the implication is usually of something to keep someone happy or 'sweet', rather than something that will make them very rich.

● *'Brian will need a drink, too.'*

drinking vouchers n pl British

coins or banknotes. An alternative version of **beer vouchers/tokens**.

● *'Our Rebels are more likely to be huddled inside an SW William Hill putting plenty of "drinking vouchers" (cash money) on Chelsea thrashing Man United. They can often be spied at pubs like the White Hart.'*
  (I-D magazine, November 1987).

drip n

an insipid, unassertive or boring person. This common colloquialism is probably British in origin, but is also used, especially by school and college students, in the USA and Australia. It is one of many terms (**wet**, **damp**, **dripping**) equating weakness with water.

the drip n British

hire purchase, paying by instalments. The phrase is usually part of the longer expression **on the drip**.

dripping adj British

weak, irresolute, pathetic. An upper- and middle-class term of mild contempt from the late 1970s. It is inspired by the popular colloquialism **wet**.

● *'Her husband's absolutely dripping.'*

drive the porcelain bus/ great white bus/big bus vb
American

to vomit. A popular expression among college and high-school students. The image is of a helpless drunk or hangover victim kneeling before the toilet pedestal, clutching the rim of the bowl in both hands like an oversize steering wheel, as the room spins. (**Kiss the porcelain god** is an alternative form.)

droid n American

a stupid, slow or completely unimaginative person, in the language of teenagers and students. It is a shortening of 'android', of which both the full and abbreviated forms have been used extensively in science-fiction books and films since the mid-1970s.
- '*Man, he's a total droid.*'
- (*Zombie High*, US film, 1987).

drone n

a dull, lifeless and/or parasitic person. This word is an unusual example of a term which existed as an educated colloquialism, but may have been reinvented as slang by speakers who were unaware of it. In the 1920s and 1930s it was applied to idle, upper-class, young men about town – debs' delights – as in the novels of P G Wodehouse. The image was of the male bee who never works but serves only to continue the line. The modern reinvention, heard among adolescents in the 1980s in the USA and Britain, may be inspired by the standard senses of 'monotonous hum' or 'unmanned flying target'.

drongo n

a foolish, unfortunate or unpleasant person. An Australian word which was adopted by British speakers in the early 1970s, probably introduced to it by an influx of young Australian travellers. It is a term of scathing contempt which may have been inspired by a spectacularly unsuccessful racehorse of the same name in the 1920s, although drongo is also the name of an Australian bird. The word seemed to be declining in popularity in the late 1980s.

droob n Australian

a dullard. This word is probably a blend of **drip** and **boob(y)**.

drooly adj

very attractive, appealing or appetizing. A less usual synonym of **dishy** or yummy, often used by adolescent females.

drop n

a an illicit or covert delivery, usually of money.

b a place where money, drugs, stolen goods, etc. can be delivered.

c a person who picks up or delivers an illicit package. The terms are underworld and law enforcers' jargon.

drop vb

1 to take (an illicit drug) orally. The word was most often encountered in the phrase **drop acid**; to take LSD by mouth. Originally an American term, 'drop' replaced the neutral 'take' in Britain around 1966.
- '*Well, the one that stopped me from doing acid forever was when I dropped seven tabs. I completely lost my mind and went to Muppetland – the whole trip lasted for about six months.*'
- (Zodiac Mindwarp, *I-D* magazine, November 1987).

2 to knock (a person) down.
- '*He threatened to drop him.*'

3 to give birth to. A shortening of **drop a pup**.
- '*Has she dropped it yet?*'
- '*She's going to drop in August.*'

153

drop a bollock vb British

to commit a blunder; a vulgar alternative to the colloquial 'drop a brick' or 'drop a clanger'.

drop a bomb vb British

to **fart**. A schoolchildren's expression.

drop a bundle vb

to lose a large amount of money (by gambling or speculative investment, for instance).

See also **drop one's bundle**.

drop a pup vb Australian

to give birth. A vulgar and/or humorous euphemism used mainly by men.

dropdead adj

stunning, extreme, sensational. A vogue word of the mid- to late 1980s among those concerned with fashion. The usage is American in origin.

- 'A dropdead blonde.'

drop-kick n Australian

a 'low', worthless or miserable person. This relatively mild epithet, used in television soap operas of the 1980s for example, is probably a descendant of the vulgar rhyming slang (based on soccer), 'dropkick and punt'; **cunt**.

- 'This makes me seem like a real drop-kick or something.'

drop off the twig vb

to die. A lighthearted expression in vogue in Britain in the late 1980s. Bird imagery features in several colourful, predominantly working-class phrases in British colloquial use, such as 'sick as a parrot', or **rattle someone's cage**.

drop one/one's lunch/guts vb

to **fart**.

drop one out vb British

to exclude someone (such as a suspect) from one's list, surveillance or enquiry. A piece of police jargon presumably based on the notion of people being in or out of the **frame**.

drop one's bundle vb
Australian

to panic. The bundle in question may originate in a **hobo's** pack, or may be a reference to fright's tendency to empty the bowels.

drop one's daks vb Australian

to take off one's trousers. An Australianism (Daks is a trademark for a brand of casual slacks especially popular in the early 1960s in Britain and Australia). A catchphrase from The Adventures of Barry McKenzie, the cartoon strip published in Private Eye magazine in the late 1960s was 'drop your daks and say the magic word', meaning to prepare for instant sexual gratification. The 'magic word' was never specified, but it may mean 'please' and elsewhere it was identified as **fuck**.

drop out vb

to withdraw from conventional society, opt out. The motto of the **hippy** movement, coined by Dr Timothy Leary in 1967 was '**turn on**, **tune in**, and **drop out**' (take drugs and/or become enlightened; make contact with like-minded people or the life force; and leave society behind). The phrase survives in the specific sense of abandon one's education.

- 'Since I dropped out in September last year I have come to the conclusion that the city drop-out scene is a pathetic one.'
(Letter to Oz magazine, June 1968).

drop-out n

someone who has opted out of society. In this sense the word, and the concept, date from the late 1960s when **hippies** renounced capitalism, the education system, etc. to form an 'alternative society'. The term was quickly picked up by the press and others who disapproved and became a pejorative description. In the USA in the 1950s and early 1960s drop-out was used to refer specifically to those who had left full-time education before graduating from high school.

dropped on adj

punished, reprimanded. The expression in full is **dropped on from a great height**; the 'dropping' in question may refer to the weight of authority, or may be a euphemism for **shitting**. Predominantly a middle-class term, it is generally used in the context of a hierarchy.

droppies n pl British

people who become self-employed. An ephemeral acronym from 1986 derived from 'Disillusioned, Relatively Ordinary Professionals Preferring Independent Employment Situations'. This mock-sociological categorization was coined on the lines of **yuppie**, **dink**, etc.

drop trou vb American

to take down one's trousers, usually as part of an undergraduate ritual or **hazing**, as an expression of high spirits sometimes, but not necessarily, involving **mooning**; or in preparation for sex. A **preppie** term.

druggy, druggie n

a user of illicit drugs. The term has been used by disapproving commentators, such as concerned parents, teachers, etc. since the mid-1960s, when **beatniks** were the culprits.

drughead n American

a user of illicit drugs. A non-users' description. (See **head**.)

drugstore cowboy n American

a local (male) show-off; a young man who hangs around cafés, street corners, etc. and tries to impress or accost females. The phrase is dismissive. In Britain the equivalent was **coffee bar cowboy**; in Australia **milkbar cowboy**.

drum n

1 British a house, home or building. The word, which is used especially in police and underworld circles, may come from the Romany word drom, meaning highway, but is possibly a back-formation from **drummer**, someone who knocks (drums) on people's doors, either to buy or sell goods or to find somewhere unoccupied to rob. In the past the word has also meant prison cell and brothel, especially in Canada and Australia respectively.
• 'Go and turn over his drum while we keep him locked up here.'
(Recorded, Detective Sergeant, Canterbury, 1971).
2 Australian a tip, piece of information or news, probably from the notion of 'jungle drums'.
• 'I got a drum that she was in town.'

drummer n

a a door-to-door salesperson, peddler or buyer of junk.
b a housebreaker or burglar.
This now obsolescent term derives either from knocking (drumming) on doors or from **drum** as a vagrants' and criminals' synonym for house.

drumming n British

a selling door-to-door.
b housebreaking or burglary.
Both senses of the word derive from **drum** as a slang term for house or

home, or from drum in the sense of knock.

dry-hump, dry-fuck, dry root
n, vb

a sexual activity (often performed standing up) in which the partners simulate intercourse while they (or at least their genitals) are fully clothed. The term usually describes the behaviour of consenting heterosexuals rather than 'perversions' such as frottage (where the activity is performed on an unwilling victim, as for instance in a crowded lift or train), tribadism (between lesbian partners) or frictation (between male homosexual partners). Dry root is an expression peculiar to Australian speakers.

- '*You can't dry hump good in the car. Unless you're a midget.*'
  (High-school student, *IT* magazine, June 1972).

the D.Ts. *n*

delirium tremens; trembling as a result of alcohol abuse.

dub *n*

1 a kind of heavy reggae-music in which instrumental tracks already recorded are electronically altered and overlaid ('dubbed' one on another) with vocals and sound effects to create a new piece of music. The form was popular in Jamaica and Britain in the late 1970s and early 1980s.

2 *American* a cigarette.

3 a fool, incompetent. An almost archaic word which survives among older speakers in the USA and Australia.

dubbed (up) *adj British*

locked up, incarcerated. A 1950s underworld usage probably deriving from an archaic use of dub to mean key or lock. **Tucked up** is a more recent alternative.

dubber *n American*

a cigarette. The word's etymology is unclear.

dubbo *n Australian*

a fool. An embellishment of the archaic **dub** meaning an awkward or incompetent person, especially a rustic simpleton.

duchess *n British*

a woman, usually one's wife. The image is of a dignified, respectable female who is no longer young. This cockney usage is still in evidence although roughly a century old. The word is either a straightforward simile or a shortening of a rhyming-slang phrase, 'Duchess of Fife'; wife.

duck, duck egg *n*

a score of nil or zero in sport, especially cricket. The term is at least a century old and derives from the resemblance between the written or printed 0 and the egg.

duckburg *n American*

a rural, provincial town. A mildly contemptuous term.

duck's arse *n British*

See **D.A.**

duck's breakfast *n*

a drink of water. A humorous expression on the pattern of **Mexican breakfast**, 'pelican's breakfast', etc. The geographical origin of the phrase is obscure.

duck shoot *n American*

an exceptionally easy task. From the image of shooting sitting ducks.

duck soup *n American*

something which is easy to accomplish, a 'cinch'. A humorous expression immortalized as the title of a Marx Brothers' film in 1933.

ducky adj
cute, delightful. A word which today is almost invariably used ironically or facetiously. It derives from duck as a term of endearment.

dude n
a man. The 19th-century American sense of dude as 'fop', overdressed city dweller, etc. (familiar from Westerns and 'dude ranches') gave rise to a 20th-century black usage meaning first pimp or 'fancy man', then simply (male) person. The term came into vogue in the 1970s and spread to Britain, where in 1973 it was briefly adopted by the **gay** and teenage milieux (appearing for instance in the title of the David Bowie song 'All the Young Dudes'). In the late 1980s the word has again surfaced in teenage parlance, inspired by its continuing presence in black American street speech. Dude was originally a German rustic term for a fool.
● *'There were more commercials ... but no more crime ... nothing about two dudes in Halloween masks breaking into a Bloomfield Village home.'*
(Elmore Leonard, The Switch, 1978).

duds n pl
clothes. A word (the plural is usually used) which is approximately three hundred years old, deriving from Middle English 'dudde', meaning a coarse cloth cloak. The plural of the word later came to mean rags or clothes and now sometimes has the extended sense of an outfit and/or set of accessories.

duff n
1 backside, buttocks. Duff is a 19th-century word for boiled dumpling or pudding (surviving in the British 'plum duff'), from which this usage was probably derived.
● *'Come on you turkeys, get off your duffs and give me some info.'*
(Buck Rogers in the 25th Century, US film, 1979).
2 see **up the duff**.

duff adj
useless, inferior. The word derives from a piece of 18th-century thieves' jargon meaning worthless or counterfeit, related to **duffer** which originally denoted a seller of supposedly stolen goods.

duffer n
an incompetent, awkward or ineffectual person. The word is only mildly derogatory and is applied for example to an elderly person or to a novice or inept sportsman. Its earlier meaning was a peddler of worthless or fake (**duff**) goods.

duff up/over n British
to beat up. Mild-sounding terms for what may be anything from a children's scuffle to a murderous attack. The modern sense, in vogue since the 1950s, seems to derive from an earlier sense meaning to ruin which is related to the adjective **duff**.
● *'Michael threatened to duff him up if he ever did anything like that again.'*
(Recorded, teenage girl, London, 1986).

duffy n
See **duppy**.

dufus n American
a an eccentric person.
b a foolish or gauche person.
c a gadget, intriguing object, thingummy.

All three senses are typically used on college campuses. The origin of the term is obscure. It is probably an invented word with a mock Latin suffix, although there is a possible connection with *doofart*, a Scandinavian word for fool.

dugs n pl

breasts, especially aged and/or flaccid ones. This use of the standard English term for an animal's teats or udders to apply to humans is archaic in everyday speech but still occasionally used.

dujie, duji n American

alternative spellings of **doojie**.

duke it, duke it up/out vb

to fight, brawl or box. Later formulations from the noun **dukes**; fists.

duke on it vb

to shake hands. A slang version of 'shake on it', from **dukes**, fists.

dukes n pl American

fists. This has been part of the jargon of streetfighters and pugilists since the turn of the century. It originates either in the rhyming slang Duke of York: fork, i.e. hand or finger; or from a Romany word meaning palm or hand. The word is most commonly heard in the challenge **put up your dukes** or the phrase **duke it out** (to engage in a fistfight).

dumbass n, adj American

(a) stupid (person). A relatively modern extension of dumb (*see* **dumbo**).

dumb cluck n

a stupid or gormless person. In origin a rustic Americanism, probably inspired by the supposed stupidity of chickens (*see* **dumbo**).

dumbell n American

a stupid person (See **dumbo**).

dumb-head n

a stupid person. An elaboration of the American sense of dumb which is a direct translation of the German *Dummkopf*; fool.

dumbo n, adj

(a) stupid (person). The American use of dumb for stupid, reinforced by the German *dumm*, is as old as the British sense of mute. Since the 1960s the American sense has been adopted in colloquial British English. This variant word may have been reinforced by the Walt Disney film *Dumbo* (which was itself inspired by 'Jumbo', the name of an elephant at London zoo).

dumdum, dum-dum n

a stupid person. An embellishment (by the linguistic process known as 're-duplication', which is common in nursery words) of dumb (See **dumbo**).

dummy n American

1 a fool, simpleton or dupe. From dumb in the American sense (*see* **dumbo**).
- 'The dummy got too chummy in a Bing Crosby number.'
  (*Salome Maloney*, John Cooper Clarke, 1978).

2 a deaf mute. From the British sense of dumb.

3 a portion of a substance sold as an illicit drug but which is extremely low-grade or without narcotic effect.

dummy up vb

to keep silent; refuse to speak. A more robust alternative to **clam up**, used for instance by underworld characters in fact and fiction.

dump n

1 a dirty, messy or dilapidated place. The word in this sense is now so common as to be a colloquialism rather than slang (which it would have been considered to be, say, in the 1950s).

2 an act of defecation, usually in a phrase such as 'take' or 'have a dump'.

● *'What are you doing back there, taking a dump?'*
(*Friday 13th Part VI*, US film, 1986).

dump on (someone) vb

to criticize or chastize, heap blame or responsibility on, denigrate. This expression is now often used as an innocuous colloquialism, although it derives from the decidedly vulgar sense of **dump 2** above.

● *'Stop dumping on me, dad.'*
(*Vice Versa*, US film, 1988).

dung-puncher n

a male homosexual. A highly pejorative term paralleling **fudgepacker**, **brownie-hound** and **turd burglar** in the reference to the faecal aspects of sodomy.

dunkie n British

a girl. The word is probably an abbreviation of 'dunkin' donut', a trademark name of an American chain of doughnut and coffee shops, although there may be a connection with the sexual sense of **dunking**. The overtones of the expression, used by teenagers in the 1970s, were not respectful.

dunking n British

sex. A euphemism which was in middle-class and 'society' use in the early and mid-1970s. It now seems to have fallen out of use but might be revived (on the pattern of similarly predictable terms which are periodically rediscovered). The origin is of course in the practice of dunking biscuits

(Britain) or doughnuts (America) in tea or coffee.

dunnee, dunny n Australian

a toilet, especially an 'outhouse' or outside lavatory. The word was reintroduced to some British speakers via the Australianisms in the cartoon strip *The Adventures of Barry McKenzie* in *Private Eye* magazine in the late 1960s. In fact this term has existed for approximately 200 years in British English as 'dunnakin' (spelt in various ways, including 'dunnigan' in Ireland) and had become obsolete. The ultimate origin of these words is obscure but seems to be related to archaic dialect words for excrement such as 'danna', or its colour (dun).

duppy, duffy n Jamaican

a ghost. The word is an example of Jamaican patois which was also known to, if not extensively used by, white Londoners in the early 1970s, due to its use in reggae lyrics and playground **Jamaica talk**.

Durban poison n

the nickname of a particularly highly-prized strain of marihuana from the Republic of South Africa.

Durex n British

a condom. The trademark name of the popular brand is often used generically. **Trojan** is the US equivalent.

dust n

angel dust, PCP. Among young people the shortened form was considered 'cooler' than the full phrase in the late 1980s.

● *'Johnny does dust.'*
(Graffito, Hammersmith, London, 1987).

dust vb American

to kill. A 'tough-guy' euphemism

implying the casual elimination of nuisances, typically in a gangland or military context. The origin is probably in a now-obsolete use of dust, meaning to hit, which survives in the expression 'dust-up'.

dustbin lids n pl British

1 children, kids. A piece of fairly modern rhyming slang which has spread beyond its working-class London context. The singular form exists, but is rare.

2 Jews. Rhyming slang for **yids**. A fairly rare and now dated usage.

dust bunny n American

a ball of fluff lurking in undusted parts of a household. (Also known as **dust kitty** and many other terms.)

• *'She won't make the bed, she won't sweep up the dust bunnies or nothin'.'*
(*The Rockford Files*, US TV series, 1980).

dust kitty n American

a a ball of household fluff, found for instance under a bed or in other undusted parts of a home. This domestic phenomenon has given rise to a number of colourful expressions in American English (**dust bunny, beggar's velvet**, 'house moss' and **ghost turds** are others), but none in British English.

b the navel. So-called due to its being a repository for fluff, etc.

dusty, dustie n British

1 an old person. A term of mild contempt or even affection to their elders among **Sloane Rangers** and other young people of the late 1970s, becoming more widespread since. A less common alternative to **wrinkly**. In *The Official Sloane Ranger Handbook* (1982) Ann Barr and Peter York attempt to define the ages of adults as fol-

lows: **wrinkly** (40 to 50 years old); **crumbly** (50 to 70 years old); and **dusty** (70 and above).

2 a dustman. Not as common an abbreviation as **postie** for postman, for instance.

dutch n British

1 wife. This hundred-year-old piece of cockney usage is still heard (invariably in the form **my old dutch**) although now often used facetiously or self-consciously. It may be a shortening of **duchess**, (originally 'duchess of Fife', rhyming slang for wife), or she may be so-called after 'an old Dutch clock' (a homely piece of furniture with a broad open dial). There is no recorded proof for these etymologies and it is possible that this sense in fact has the same origin as the following, reflecting the use of 'mate' to mean wife.

2 friend, mate. A second Cockney sense of the word comes from the rhyme 'Dutch plate'.

dweeb n

a foolish, gormless or unpopular person. An American campus and high-school word of the late 1980s, adopted by British youth in 1988.

• *'I didn't even tell her my name – I am a dweeb!'*
(*18 Again!*, US film, 1988).

dyke, dike n

a lesbian. The only common slang term to describe a female homosexual; it was first used derogatorily by heterosexuals, but it is now used by **gay** women themselves, though often wryly. When said by a heterosexual the word usually still carries overtones of the 'aggressive masculine' stereotype of a lesbian. No one has satisfactorily explained the term's ultimate origin; it might be from an old pejorative euphemism for a woman's genitals. Another, rather far-fetched theory is that it is inspired by the story of the little Dutch boy with his finger in the dyke. Whatever its origin the word seems to have been imported into British English from America between the world wars.

dykie, dyky *n*

a like a **dyke**, lesbian.

b (of a woman) 'masculine' in behaviour and/or appearance.

dynamite *n American*

high quality, hence extremely powerful, heroin, from the language of addicts. A specialization from the colloquial sense of dynamite, meaning (something) sensationally good and mythically potent, and typically used since the late 1960s to refer to illicit drugs of all types.

dynosupreme *adj American*

excellent, perfect, outstanding. Often an exclamation, this is a teenage vogue elaboration of supreme using a mock-prefix based on dynamo or dynamic, or a contraction of dynamite.

E

E n

1 the drug **ecstasy**. An abbreviation in vogue in 1988 and 1989.

2 See **the big E**.

each way adj Australian

bisexual. A humorous euphemism from the language of horse-race betting.

● *'If you ask me he's a bit each way.'*

earache n British

incessant chatter, complaining or nagging. The expression usually occurs in working-class speech.

● *'Will you stop giving me all this earache about being late and let me eat my tea in peace.'*

ear-basher/-banger/-bender n

someone who talks incessantly, a person who harangues, nags or bores. Ear-basher is heard in Britain and Australia; ear-banger and ear-bender are predominantly American.

earlies n British

underpants, knickers. A fairly obscure but surving instance of 19th-century London rhyming slang. The rhyme is 'early doors'; drawers. 'Early doors' is from theatrical jargon.

earner n British

a scheme or situation which brings financial advantage, especially when unexpected or illicit. Originally from the language of police and thieves, the

term, especially in the vogue phrase '*a nice little earner*', has entered general circulation in the profit-oriented society of the late 1980s.

● *'The job's hard work, long hours and pretty boring – but at £70 a week it's a nice little earner if you're 15 and living at home.'*
(Teenage truant, Observer, February 1988).

ear'ole n British

a dull, gormless or exasperating person. A word used typically by working-class schoolchildren in the 1970s to refer to tedious fellow pupils or adults. The eighth edition of Eric Partridge's *Dictionary of Slang and Unconventional English* quotes a 1976 article in *New Society* which derives ear'ole from those (pupils) who listen and obey, as opposed to those who act or refuse to conform. This is likely to be a folk etymology (and probably spurious) as the word was in use as long ago as the 1950s as a non-specific term of abuse.

ear'ole vb British

1 to 'buttonhole' (someone); in other words, to detain (someone) in conversation.

2 to scrounge; from **on the earhole**, which earlier in the century meant to try to swindle.

3 to nag, shout at, talk incessantly.

4 to listen to, eavesdrop.

All these senses of the word are in

mainly working-class use and are most commonly heard in London.

earwig n British

an eavesdropper, or someone employed to listen out for news, danger, etc. A working-class and underworld expression.

earwig vb British

1 to eavesdrop, or listen out for news, danger, etc. A working-class word used by the underworld and, more innocuously, by or about neighbourhood gossips, etc.

● 'You cunning git! You was earwiggin' my conversation.'
(Only Fools and Horses, British TV comedy series, 1989).

2 to understand, realize. A less common sense of the word in this rhyming-slang expression (from 'twig').

ear-wigging n British

a synonym for **ear-bashing**, punning on the earwig insect and the 19th-century colloquial use of 'wig' to mean scold.

● 'That didn't stop [David] Puttnam giving [Christopher] Patten a severe ear-wigging from the green pulpit last week.'
(The Sunday Times, 26 November 1989).

easing n British

relaxing, unofficial periods of rest or leisure. Police jargon of the 1970s and 1980s, defined in Simon Holdaway's Inside the British Police (1983).

easter egg n American

a child born nine months after a summer romance. An expression used, predictably, in seaside resorts.

easy exclamation British

a generalized cry of derision, triumph, joy, etc. The word is usually

lengthened to 'eezee!' It originated on football terraces in the 1960s, and is often heard in repetitive crowd chants at sporting events.

easy meat n

a a person who is easy to seduce or take advantage of.

b something easy to achieve or acquire. The phrase has been in currency since the 1920s.

easy-peasy adj British

very easy indeed, posing no problem. A popular phrase with younger schoolchildren since the early 1980s, although common in Scotland and northern England for decades.

easy rider n

a a biker. The term is probably inspired by, rather than inspiring the title of the film Easy Rider (1969).

b a person who seems to succeed without effort, or live well without working.

c a person (usually female) who is promiscuous or easily seduced. A dismissive term used typically by males since the 1970s.

eat, eat out, eat someone out vb

to perform cunnilingus. These Americanisms of the 1960s are heard in Australia and to a lesser extent in Britain.

eat dirt vb

See **eat shit**.

eat it! vb, exclamation American

a euphemism for **eat shit!**

eat my shorts! exclamation American

an exclamation of defiance or contempt, popular among male high-

163

school and college students in the 1980s. The shorts in question are of course (unsavoury) male underwear.

eat pussy vb

to perform cunnilingus. A phrase which originated, and is most widespread, in the USA.

eat shit/dirt vb

a to submit to humiliation, to abase oneself. Until recently the phrase had more currency in the USA and Australia than in Britain.

b eat shit! An American exclamation of defiance or contempt.

eckies, exes n pl British

expenses. Shortenings of the standard word used by businesspeople. Nuances of rank may be ascribed to the terms; the first is most usually heard among sales personnel, the second among executives.

eco-freak, eco-nut n

a person concerned with ecology and the environment. These dismissive or patronizing terms, used by critics or mockers, surfaced in the 1970s.

ecstasy n

the drug MDMA (3,4 methylene dioxy methamphetamine). A preparation which was synthesized and patented in 1914 and rediscovered for recreational use in 1975 in the USA. The drug, related to **speed**, remained a minority taste until the early 1980s; it was used by Californian therapists among others and was legal until 1985. Since that time MDMA, which causes elation, wakefulness and comfortable sensations but is now known to be dangerous even in small doses, has been the favourite drug of afficionados of night clubs and discos, especially those subscribing to the British **acid**

house cult. It is also known as **E, Epsom salts, X** and **adam**.

● *'Every generation finds the drug it needs . . . the cold, selfish children of 1985 think ecstasy will make them loved and loving.'*
(P.J. O'Rourke, *Republican Party Reptile*, 1987).

edge city n

a sensation or situation in which one experiences tension, dread or anticipation. A dramatizing of 'edgy' heard among drug users and progressive music fans.

Edwardian n British

a **teddy boy**. A variant form of the name used seriously on occasions by journalists and facetiously by teddy boys themselves.

eek, eke n British

a face. A word heard in London theatrical and **camp** slang from the late 1950s. The etymology is obscure. One suggestion, unfortunately rather farfetched, is that it is from the scream of fright occasioned by glimpsing the said visage leering through the limelight.

b face-paint, make-up. Also a theatrical term, presumably derived from the first sense. **Slap** is a more common alternative.

eff vb

a euphemism for **fuck** heard in America and Australia but more popular in Britain. It is most often encountered in the phrase *'eff off'* and *'effing and blinding'* (cursing, using bad language).

● *'Mr . . . put his arms around my waist and tried to kiss my neck. I told him to eff off.'*
(Victim of sexual harassment, *Daily Mirror*, 31 March 1989).

effect n

See **in effect**.

egg n

See **lay an egg**.

egg and spoon n British

a black person. Rhyming slang for **coon**; this picturesque working-class expression, its origin in children's egg and spoon races, usually implies contempt and dislike.

eggbeater n

an old or primitive motor or motorized vehicle. A helicopter, car, outboard motor, etc.

egghead n

an intellectual, learned or studious person. A slang term from the early years of the century which has now become a common colloquialism.

ego-trip n

an exhibition of self-aggrandizement, self-indulgence or other selfishness. The term dates from the late 1960s and derives from the notion that under the influence of LSD (on a **trip**) unlightened persons will lose their ego, while the unenlightened may experience a concentration of selfish impulses. Trip later took on the generalized idea of behaviour or idée fixe, and ego, simply egomaniacal or egotistic.

Egyptian PT n British

sleeping. A joking and contemptuous expression dating from before World War II. It derives from the feats of legendary laziness imputed to Arabs in general by the British forces overseas. The phrase survives, mainly in public-school and army slang.

elbow vb British

to dismiss (someone), to dispose of or reject (something). A more modern version of 'give it/them the elbow'. It is often in the passive form 'get elbowed'.

- 'OK, elbow the buskers, we haven't got time.'
  (TV studio crew, One Day in the Life of Television, 1 November 1989).

elbow bender n British

an habitual imbiber of alcoholic liquor; a drunk. From the phrase to **bend the elbow** (in lifting a drink to the lips).

- 'Sam Brown admits she became a big-time boozer when she was a schoolgirl and is still a solid elbow-bender.'
  (Photo caption, People, 23 April 1989).

elders n pl Australian

breasts. The word originated before World War II but the derivation is obscure. Some authorities cite the apocryphal story of Susannah and the elders, or the leaves of the elder tree, but there is no solid evidence for either of these speculations.

electric soup n

alcoholic drink, a strong alcoholic punch. The phrase is predominantly heard in middle-class circles. It belongs to a set of synonymous phrases including **lunatic soup** and **giggle water**.

elephants, elephant's trunk adj British

drunk. A piece of 100-year-old London rhyming slang which is still heard, although usually used facetiously.

- 'I seen him down our local again – completely elephants.'

el ----o noun form American

a Spanish pattern applied jocularly to English words mainly by American speakers. The meaning is 'the supreme ----', 'the quintessential ----' or just 'the ----'. It appears in 'el creepo', 'el sleazo', 'el cheapo', etc. This tendency (in imitation of Hispanic 'low life' speech) has been in evidence since the early 1970s.

See also the entries which follow.

el primo n American

the very best, top quality. From Spanish in which it means the first (quality). The expression is used by **anglos**, blacks, etc. in imitation of Hispanic speech.

el ropo n American

a cigar or **joint**, especially a large and noxious one, from the idea of low-grade tobacco resembling **rope**.

embalmed adj

drunk. A now fairly rare, predominantly middle-class euphemism, it is an old usage, probably coined in the 19th century and inspired by balm (as a euphemism for comforting liquor), balmy (see **barmy**) and the early 20th-century Americanism 'embalming fluid', meaning whisky.

embrocation n British

alcoholic drink. A humorous borrowing of the word for rub-on liniment, said mainly by the middle aged.

● 'I think a spot of embrocation might be in order.'

emmet n British

a tourist, an unwelcome stranger. A dialect word (meaning ant) used in Cornwall since the 1950s to refer disparagingly to swarms of holidaymakers. **Grockle** is another regional term with a similar meaning.

enchilada n American

See **big enchilada**.

endsville n, adj American

the ultimate; the best or the worst. From the language of **hipsters** and **beatniks** in the late 1950s, already sounding dated by the 1960s.

English spliff/joint n American

a marihuana cigarette containing both tobacco and (usually) hashish. So-called by American afficionados, whose **joints** invariably contain only marihuana.

Epsom salts n British

the drug **ecstasy**. A vogue term on the **acid house** scene in 1989. The expression is borrowed from the name of the old-fashioned purgative medicine (hydrated magnesium sulphate).

equipment n

a the male sex organs. An unromantic euphemism used by males and females alike.

b a woman's breasts. A rarer vulgarism, usually indicating unromantic appraisal.

equaliser n American

a handgun, revolver. A pre-World-War II euphemism, now found mainly in crime fiction.

'erb n

See **herb**.

'erbert n British

a foolish person, a cheeky, unwashed child. For many years, in London working-class slang, Herbert or 'Erbert was used to refer to any otherwise unnamed man or boy. Gradually, probably by being used in phrases such as 'silly 'erbert', it came to have the more pejorative sense. There probably never was an eponymous Herbert; it was merely a common working-class name from the Edwardian era.

eric n British

1 an erection. A schoolboy term.

2 a foolish, gauche or unpopular male. This sense of the word also occurs in school argot and may be a corruption of **erk** or **oik**.

erk n British

a vulgar, inferior or tedious person. A piece of armed service and public-school slang which some authorities derive from aircraft. It may in origin be a version of **oik**.

-ers n word-ending British

a termination added to all or part of a standard word. In public-school, armed forces or middle-class speech it confers familiarity or affection. The core-word is sometimes preceded by **harry-**, as in **harry-starkers** for stark naked. This speech-pattern, found risible by many since the 1960s, arose at Oxford and in public schools in the late 19th century.

See also **preggas, honkers, starkers**, etc.

ethnic, ethno n Australian

an immigrant ('migrant' in Australian English). An unaffectionate euphemism, used since the 1970s.

euphemism, the euphemism n British

the toilet. A self-conscious, facetious middle-class usage.

● 'Excuse me, where's the euphemism?'

Eurotrash n

the European 'jet-set' and their hangers-on. A version of 'international white trash', heard in 'society' and journalistic circles.

● 'I enjoyed it, famous bits of Eurotrash enjoy it, but Miss Mouse might not feel altogether comfortable.'
(Rupert Christiansen, Harpers and Queen, November 1989).

eve n British

the drug MDEA, a stimulant related to **ecstasy** which is known as **adam** (from MDMA).

even-Steven(s) n

fair shares, a fair deal, equable arrangement. A 19th-century elaboration of the standard term evens.

evil adj American

impressive, admirable. This use of the word originated in the jargon of black musicians; a rarer variant of **bad** or **wicked**. It is now used by teenagers of all ethnic origins, in Britain and Australia as well as the USA.

ex n

See X.

exercise the ferret vb Australian

to have sex. An unromantic male expression equating the penis with the aggressive, hyperactive animal and its well-known proclivity for wriggling into crevices and tunnels.

exes n pl British

expenses. A variant form of **eckies**.

extract the Michael vb British

to **take the mickey**; to mock. A humorously pedantic version of the well-known colloquialism.

extract the urine vb British

to **take the piss**; to mock. A mock-pe-

167

dantic version of the common, more vulgar expression.

eyeball *vb*

to look at, stare at or inspect. The expression probably originated in the USA in black usage in the late 1940s. By the 1970s it was heard in Britain and Australia, especially among teenagers and the police. In the form 'eyeballing' the term can have the specific meanings of staring threateningly or provocatively.

- *'The male models in leopard-skin-print Gaultier jackets getting eyeballed by Sharons with Bucks Fizz haircuts and pound signs in their eyes at the Limelight.'* (*Observer*, Section 5, 7 May 1989).
- *'Villains call it clocking in Leeds, eyeballing in Manchester and screwing in London's East End . . . It came as a shock: juries can be intimidated by a stare.'* (*The Sunday Times*, 5 June 1988).

eyeball *n British*

a a surveillance operation, in the jargon of the CID and the Flying Squad in particular.
- *'We've been on eyeball for a week now.'*

b 'visual contact', a sighting. Another police term, employed for example during a stakeout or surveillance.
- *'Do you have an eyeball on suspect one?'* (Detective Sergeant, *Flying Squad*, British TV documentary series, February 1989).

eyefuck *vb*

to stare, or look lasciviously at someone.

eye-opener *n*

the first drink of the day; the first shot of alcohol, a drug etc., which supposedly jolts one awake. Sometimes the term is used as a euphemism for **leg-opener**.

eyetie *n, adj*

(an) Italian. A rather unimaginative and dated soubriquet, but fairly inoffensive, as opposed to **macaroni** or **wop**. The term arose at about the time of World War I. In working-class pronunciation (in both Britain and the USA) the first syllable of Italian continues to be pronounced 'eye' (hence the Morris 'Ital', named by car workers after a poll).

F

F.A./Fanny Adams, sweet F.A./Fanny Adams n British

a nothing at all. Fanny Adams is a widespread euphemism for **fuck-all**.

b a pitifully small amount. In 19th-century naval slang, Fanny Adams was tinned or cooked meat, a sardonic reference to a girl of the same name who was murdered and dismembered in 1867. The name was later matched with the initials of **fuck-all** and used euphemistically in its place.

- 'He says Eve behaved like a complete bitch over the kids' custody . . . and he'll get sweet F.A. out of the sale of the house.' (Party gossip in cartoon by Posy Simmonds Guardian, 1979).

fab adj

brilliant, wonderful. This abbreviation of fabulous was adopted as an all-purpose term of approbation by toonagers in the 1960s from **camp** adult parlance and a local usage in Liverpool. The word was revived in the late 1980s, at first ironically, but increasingly in its original sense.

face n British

1 an outstanding person, someone who is more sophisticated, better dressed, etc. than the rest. A vogue word among **mods** in 1963 and 1964, probably originating from the idea of a well-known or recognizable face in the crowd, or possibly from a 'face card', an expression occasionally heard in the USA, indicating an extraordinary, important or famous person. (The word also occurs in underworld and prison jargon, denoting a prominent personage.) The quintessential mod groups of the time were The Who (whose first and unsuccessful single was 'He's the face'), and The Small Faces.

2 a synonym for 'cheek' or **front** sense 1. This use of the word is popular in raffish speech of the late 1980s.

- '"A really good beggar makes maybe £50," Brian says. "I haven't got the face to do it".' (Homeless youth, Independent, 22 December 1989).

faceache n

a an ugly person. A term of mild derision or abuse, now mainly confined to children's badinage.

b an indicated but unnamed person, **whatsisname**.

- 'Old faceache's back again.'

face-case n American

a teenage synonym for **faceache**, heard in the late 1980s.

faced adj American

1 drunk. A **preppie** term which is a milder shortening of **shitfaced**.

2 humiliated, snubbed. This teenage term of the late 1950s describes the result of having been **put down**: it derives from 'losing face'.

fade vb American

1 to leave (a place), go away. A piece

169

of **hipster** and **beatnik** language from the 1950s which has been revived by teenagers in the 1980s.

● *'Come on guys, let's fade.'*

2 to meet or cover a bet. From the language of the dice game craps.

● *'Ten bucks says he doesn't make it. Who'll fade me?'*

faff, faff about *vb British*

to behave in a confused, disorganized or indecisive way. The expression usually indicates exasperation at another's incompetence.

● *'Stop faffing about and play the bloody thing forwards!'*

(Recorded, football spectator, North London, 1988).

fag *n*

1 *British* a cigarette. In Middle English 'fagge' meant, as a verb, to droop or, as a noun, a flap or remnant. These notions gave rise to 'fag-end' and subsequently, in the 19th century, to fag as a stubbed-out or limp, low-quality cigarette. In the 20th century the word was generalized to refer to any cigarette.

● *'"Come on darling give us a fag," says a brass to an elderly tom. "Have pity on a destitute prostitute!"'*

(*Sunday Times* colour supplement feature on the East End of London, 2 June 1968).

2 *American* a male homosexual. This is generally taken to be a shortened version of **faggot**, but may predate it. (There is no discernible connection with the British public-school term meaning a junior boy performing servant duties.)

● *'I'm led into a room where a short fag doctor and a big bull-dyke nurse are waiting for me.'*

(Bill Levy's journal in *Oz* magazine, February 1970).

faggot *n*

1 *British* an unattractive or disreputable woman. This now outdated term, some three hundred years old, is still heard in the phrase 'old faggot', but has otherwise largely disappeared due to the influence of the following American sense of the word.

2 *American* a homosexual man. It is not certain whether this term is an embellished version of **fag**, derives from the old British sense of the word (above), or is a native American invention. The second alternative appears the most likely.

● *'You know I'm a faggot? Well, congratulations.'*

(*Kiss of the Spider Woman*, film by Hector Babenco, 1985).

faggoty *adj American*

(of men) homosexual, effeminate. A pejorative and less common alternative to **faggy**.

faggy *adj American*

camp, effeminate. Unlike **faggoty**, this term has been imported to other English-speaking areas.

● *'Just a faggy little leather boy with a smaller piece of stick.'*

('Memo from Turner', song recorded by Mick Jagger, 1969).

fag-hag *n*

a woman who prefers the company of homosexual men. The expression became popular in the late 1960s with increased awareness of the **gay** community among **straights**. The phrase quickly spread from the US to Britain and Australia. Although originally and usually used pejoratively, it can now be used neutrally, or by a woman of herself.

● *'She [Edith Olivier] became the supreme fag-hag of the 1920s and 1930s, the older woman who acts as* mother-confessor and salonnière to a group of young homosexual men.' (Bevis Hillier writing in The Sunday Times, 26 November 1989).

fag-hole n British
mouth. An alternative to the more common **cakehole**, heard in the late 1950s and early 1960s.

fag tag n American
the outside loop at the back (at the top of the pleat) of a standard American button-down Oxford shirt. The phrase is based on the jocular assumption that the 'tag' is there as an aid to homosexual assault. This college-student term, quoted in the Official Preppy Handbook by Lisa Bernbach (1980) has the alternative designations **fruit loop** and **ripcord**.

fains, fainites, faynits
exclamation British
a cry demanding a truce or exemption from something (such as being caught or penalized in a playground game). The various forms of the word are a survival of the archaic 'fains' or 'fains I' which means forbid and is related to the standard English fend.
- 'The air echoed with cries of pax, unpax, fains, roter, shutup.' (Geoffrey Willans and Ronald Searle, Back in the Jug Agane, 1959).

fair dinkum adj Australian
just, honest, equable, worthy of approval. This well known Australianism originated in a Victorian British dialect version of 'fair play' or 'fair share'. (The exact origin of the 'dinkum' component is not clear.)

fair go/goes phrase Australian
an interjection demanding fair or reasonable behaviour.
- 'Come on, fair goes, give us a break.'

fair suck of the pineapple/ sauce stick phrase Australian
elaborations of the colloquial 'fair crack of the whip'.

fairy n
a male homosexual. The word in this sense probably originated in the American West around the turn of the century. It was commonly heard in Britain by the 1920s.

fall guy n American
a dupe, victim or scapegoat. A prewar Americanism deriving from the phrase 'to take a fall' (to be caught, arrested or imprisoned).
- 'Two fall guys were to be arrested and charged in their place.' (Former detective Inside the Brotherhood, Martin Short, 1989).

fall out vb
1 American an alternative for **nod out**.
2 to fail, blunder, slip up. A teenage vogue term of 1988 and 1989 in Britain. It is an extension of the use of the phrase by skateboarders, to whom it is the equivalent of the surfers' **wipe out** (in other words, to fall off one's board).

falsies n pl British
a padded brassiere or other padding worn to make a woman's breasts appear larger.

family n American
a mafia organization (not necessarily made up of blood relatives). A criminal euphemism.

family jewels n pl
the male genitals, more specifically the testicles. A jocular expression which may be Victorian in origin. Now sometimes shortened to **jewels**.

fan n
1 an aircraft propellor.
2 *American* backside. A shortening of **fanny** sense 2.
- '*She fell on her fan.*'

fancy man n
a male lover, adulterer. The word is usually applied disapprovingly and/or enviously to the flagrant partner of a married woman.

fanny n
1 *British* the female genitals. This old and relatively inoffensive euphemism is possibly derived from the well-known erotic novel *The Memoirs of Fanny Hill*, by John Cleland, published in 1749, or is perhaps simply an affectionate personification of the sex organs, using the short form of Frances. The word is used by women as well as men.
2 *American* backside, buttocks. The American sense of the word probably derives from the earlier British sense. Fanny is sometimes confusingly used with this meaning by middle-class speakers in Britain, too.

fanny about vb British
to **faff about**, dither. The **fanny** element may be present merely for its sound, or proximity to fuss or **faff**, or as a suggestion of femininity, rather than as a direct reference to buttocks or genitals.

Fanny Adams n British
See **F.A./Fanny Adams**.

fanny merchant n British
someone who behaves in an indecisive, weak or supposedly effeminate way.
- '*Stop pratting about, Hoddle and get stuck in. You're nothing but a fanny merchant.*'

(Recorded, football supporter, North London, 1985).

fanny rat n British
a womanizer or seducer. A term used with either contempt or admiration by other men.
- '*A policeman accused of drowning his wife in a holiday villa's Jacuzzi bath was branded "King Fanny Rat" by his colleagues because of his womanizing.*'
(*Daily Mirror*, 15 April 1989).

fantasy n British
a powerful hallucinogenic drug said to be a mixture of **ecstasy** and LSD or mescaline. A native British invention of 1989.
- '*A member of the government-backed standing conference on drug abuse said, "fantasy can totally destroy the mind. It brings on horrific nightmare trips".*'
(*Sunday Mirror*, 16 July 1989).

farley, farly n American
a man or boy, a **gay** male, a ridiculous or unattractive person. A **Valley Girl** term used in the early 1970s.
- '*I can't get behind London. There are all these crazy farleys everywhere.*'
(Recorded, Californian teenage girl, 1970).
See also **chuck you farley!**

Farmer Giles
See **farmers**.

farmers n pl British
haemorrhoids. Rhyming slang from Farmer Giles; piles. The eponymous farmer is a common personification of bucolic heartiness. The longer version, Farmer Giles, was heard, particularly among schoolchildren, until at least the late 1970s.

• *'Send your farmers packing with "Preparation Ouch".'*
(*There's a Lot of it About*, British TV comedy series starring Spike Milligan, 1989).

far-out, farout *adj*

a extreme, eccentric, unconventional.

b wonderful, remarkable. By extension from the first sense, usually as an exclamation in the approval of anything extraordinary.

Both senses of the phrase, originally an Americanism, were beloved by **hippies** from the late 1960s, but far-out was sounding dated by about 1974 and if used in current conversation, would probably invite ridicule.

• *'Marlene's entire range of expression was pretty much limited to "far out", "super" and "gross".'*
(*The Serial*, Cyra McFadden, 1976).

fart *n*

1 an expulsion of intestinal gas from the anus. Not really a slang term, but often included as such because of its vulgar overtones. (For the etymology see the verb form.)

2 a term of abuse, sometimes dismissive, now sometimes almost affectionate, heard especially in the expressions 'old fart' and 'boring old fart', **(b.o.f.)**. Fart in this sense suggests someone inconsequential, ineffectual or otherwise worthy of mild contempt.

fart *vb*

to 'break wind', expel intestinal gas through the anus. The word is a descendant of an old Germanic verb *ferzan* which in turn comes from an Indo-European root *perd-* or *pard-* (giving modern French *péter* among others). In English fart has never been genuine slang, but is sometimes considered to be so because it is taboo in polite company. This was not the case until the 18th century. As with other 'four-letter words' there is no neat equivalent term in polite standard English.

fart around/about *vb*

to mess around, waste one's time or play the fool.

• *'Come on you guys, stop farting around and get down to business.'*

fart-arse, fartarse about/around *vb* British

to waste time, behave ineffectually or indecisively. A common, mildly vulgar term in British and Australian English. It is an elaboration of **fart around**.

• *'I wish they'd stop fart-arsing around and make their minds up.'*

fartleberries *n pl*

another word for **dingleberries**.

fart-sack *n*

a sleeping bag, a bed. A vulgarism popular in the armed services, scouting movement, etc., all over the English-speaking world.

• *'Time to climb into the fart-sack and grab some shuteye.'*

fast one *n American*

the 1970s nickname of Ritalin, trademark name of a type of amphetamine (**speed**).

fat cat *n*

a privileged, wealthy, cosseted person. The term implies offensively ostentatious living and smugness. The phrase was probably coined to describe profiteers from World War I.

fat city *n American*

1 a state of contentment and/or material repletion, a very satisfactory situation.

● *'Wait till you see the set-up there – he's in fat city.'*
2 obesity or an obese person. A high-school and college term of the 1970s and 1980s.
● *'Get a load of fat city, here!'*

fat farm n
a health farm or slimming centre.

fatso n
a fat person. This unfriendly term from the USA largely superseded the more typically British 'fatty' in the 1960s.

fave, fave rave n
a favourite thing or person. The expression was first used in the 1960s. Nowadays it is almost always used humorously or ironically, typically surviving in the journalese of teenage magazines.

faynits *exclamation British*
an alternative spelling of **fainites**.

feathers n British
the pubic area, pubic hair. A schoolboy's term of the 1960s and 1970s. It may be an echo of the archaic 18th-century sense of a woman's pubic hair, or may be a new coinage.
● *'I gave him a kick in the feathers.'*

-features *suffix*
'-face'. In British and Australian English it is often added to other, usually offensive, words as an insult or mock insult as in **bum-features**, **creature-features**, cunt-features, etc.

feature with (someone) vb
Australian
to have sex with, succeed in seducing. A favourite expression of Barry McKenzie. Popularized by the cartoon strip in *Private Eye* magazine in the 1960s, it was briefly current as a result among students and others. It is probably inspired by the journalese 'featuring' as in 'starring', or as in being the main protagonist of a scandal.
● *'If I don't feature with this tart tonight the Pope's a flamin' Jew.'* (*Barry McKenzie*).

Fed n
See **Club Fed**.

the Feds n pl American
law enforcers, FBI agents. The word, used especially by lawbreakers in the USA, was briefly and inappropriately picked up in Britain as a euphemism for police in the early 1970s.

feeb n American
a feeble-minded person, **twerp**. A teenager's term. This is one of a series of expressions for social misfits or peergroup outcasts coined by American school and college pupils. Earlier words such as **wimp** and **nerd** have entered world English, others like **dweeb**, which immediately predated feeb, have not as yet.

feel n
a sexual contact, a **grope** or caress. In American teen jargon the word is often heard in the phrase **cop a feel**.

feel one's oats vb
to behave in a restive, spirited, assertive or aggressive manner. This phrase is viewed as slang by some speakers and as a colloquialism by others. It is sometimes felt to be less than respectable by analogy with the vulgar **get one's oats**, but in fact merely draws upon the image of a horse which has just been fed. According to the slang collector, Eric Partridge, the expression originated in the USA in the mid-19th century.

174

feel someone's collar vb

to arrest or take into custody. An item of police jargon, now more often expressed by the noun **collar**.

feisty adj

spirited, tough and assertive, quarrelsome. The word looks like Yiddish, but is in fact from a southern American English dialect word for a small, fierce dog (a 'feist' or 'fice'), the name of which is distantly derived from 'fist', a variant of **fart**. The adjective was exclusively American until the 1970s when, mainly through the journalistic language of film criticism, etc. it became known in Britain and Australia.

● *'It was this feisty creature [Pamella Bordes] who ended a relationship with Andrew Neil by redecorating the walls of his Kensington flat with obscene graffiti.'*
(*Private Eye*, February 1989).

femme, fem n, adj

a a lesbian accustomed to playing a passive, female role in relationships; the opposite role to **butch**.

b an effeminate or passive male homosexual. Both terms are from the French for woman or wife (*femme*), and have been in fairly widespread use since the turn of the century. Femme (or fem) was a slang term meaning woman in the 17th, 18th and early 19th centuries.

fence vb, n

(to act as) a receiver of or dealer in stolen goods. The word was generally considered slang until the 1960s; there being no equivalent shorter than the definition above. Fence is now a universally understood term. It as at least 350 years old, apparently originating as a shortening of 'defence', although the precise relationship to that word is unclear.

fender-bender n American

a someone who poses as a road-accident victim or stages an accident in order to claim compensation. A law enforcers' and lawbreakers' term.

b a minor traffic accident or 'shunt' in which a car or its wing or bumper is slightly dented.

ferret n

See **exercise the ferret**.

fess up vb American

to confess, own up.

● *'We want the truth!' 'What time is it?' 'Time for you to fess up!'*
(*Out of the Dark*, US film, 1988).

fidget n British

a secret, 'wrinkle', edge or angle. A mainly working-class term used, among others, by fraudsters and petty criminals.

● *'He's got a few fidgets worked out.'*

fifth wheel n

a superfluous or intrusive extra person, an unnecessary thing. The phrase is American in origin.

fillet, fillet of cod n British

a **sod**. A disguised rhyming-slang form of the term of abuse. The word (and phrase) is referred to by the comedian Ronnie Barker in his *Fletcher's Book of Rhyming Slang* 1979), but is not recorded elsewhere.

filleted adj British

a late 1980s version of **gutted**. A fashionable way of conveying intense (or exaggerated) disappointment, bitterness, etc.

● *'When she said she was going and taking the kids, I tell you, I was filleted.'*

fill someone in vb British

to beat someone up. A phrase dating from before World War II.

filth, the filth n British

the police, especially those in plain clothes. A thoroughly derogatory term coined in the 1950s and enthusiastically adopted by radicals, student demonstrators and criminals alike in the 1960s.

- 'I didn't realize he [an ex-boyfriend] was filth.'
  (Recorded, nurse, London, 1985).
- 'They don't call us the filth for nothing.'
  (Comedian Julian Clary, in police uniform, on Friday Night Live, April 1988).

filthy adj British

extremely wealthy. A shortening of 'filthy rich'.

- 'I tell you, she's absolutely filthy.'

fin n American

a five-dollar bill. From the Yiddish finif, five.
See also finski.

finagling n

devious machination, manoeuvre or manipulation. The word, which is sometimes used as a regular verb ('to finagle'), is well-established in the USA. It is said to derive from the archaic British dialect word fainaigue (meaning to cheat).

financial adj Australian

well-off, in funds, solvent.

- 'He's fairly financial just at the moment.'

finesse (someone) vb

American
to outmanoeuvre someone, cleverly manipulate or cheat. From the tech-

nique in contract bridge. Originally a cardsharps' term, now in general use.

finger vb

to inform on someone. From the action of pointing out a culprit.

- 'They fingered him for the Jamaica Avenue job.'

finger, finger fuck vb

to sexually stimulate (vaginally or anally) with the finger(s).

fingers n British

a pickpocket. A police and criminal nickname slang description from the 1950s.

fink n American

an informer or any untrustworthy, reprehensible person. In the late 19th century the word was used for spies, informers, policemen and strikebreakers. It is the German word for finch and was presumably imported by German or Yiddish-speaking immigrants, although the exact meaning is obscure. (It appears not to be related to 'singing like a canary'.) Less plausibly, the name of the Pinkerton detective agency has also been suggested as a source.
See also ratfink.

finski n American

a fin (five-dollar bill). An embellished form of the word used typically by high-school or college students. The '-ski' ending (in imitation of Slavic languages or Yiddish) is thought to add raciness to short everyday words.

- 'See what a finski can do for a man's attitude?'
  (Ferris Bueller's Day Off, US film, 1986).

fired-up adj

a angry, furious.
b sexually aroused.

c stimulated by illicit drugs.
d enthused, aroused, excited.

All these senses of the word are American slang in origin, based on the firing-up or revving of an engine. The term is now a common colloquialism.

fireman's hose n British

nose. A piece of authentic rhyming slang, still heard occasionally in London.

● *'He had to stick his fireman's hose into it, didn't he.'*
(Recorded, hairdresser, Richmond, 1988)

firkin' adj

fucking. This word is generally thought of and used as a joky euphemism, inspired by the similarity of the taboo word with the archaic name for a cask of ale. In fact 'firk' existed as a verb in its own right in early modern English. It meant to strike, and also to copulate, and may even have been in origin a distortion of 'fuck'. The word is typically used as an intensifier, as in *'firkin' cold'*.

firm, the firm n

a British a criminal gang or organization. Also used by and of teams of football hooligans, such as the Inter-City Firm, a much-publicized gang of older West Ham supporters.

b an insider's, or would-be insider's euphemism for an official but clandestine organization, such as a secret-service department or undercover police group.

first base n American

kissing, necking. The first stage in the process of seduction, as described by teenagers and students (usually from the male point of view). The image is taken from baseball, where to get to first base is the first step towards scoring a run; stretching the analogy, a home run or homer is full sexual intercourse.

fishing expedition n

an attempt to gather information while purporting to be doing something else. An expression used in general conversation and, recently, specifically in business jargon where, for example, a company will advertise for personnel in order to interrogate interviewees about rivals' plans.

fishing fleet n British

a group of females arriving en masse in search of partners or husbands. The expression is applied today mainly to visitors to the outpost of upper-class society in Hong Kong; it formerly referred to the same social phenomenon occurring in India, etc. in the colonial era.

fishtank n

a cell or reception area where prisoners are kept temporarily. The significance of the name is in the fact that inmates are mixed and under observation.

fit up vb British

to frame; to manufacture evidence to procure a (false) conviction for a criminal offence. A piece of police and underworld jargon, which by 1989 had become widely known through its use by journalists, scriptwriters, etc.

● *'I know a CID sergeant who had fitted a bloke up with an indecent exposure. They just stopped him as he walked around a corner and gave it to him.'*
(Police officer, *Inside the British Police*, Simon Holdaway, 1983).

● *'Would I be fitted up for betraying him?'*
(Former detective, quoted in *Inside the Brotherhood*, Martin Short, 1989).

fit-up, fit n

a **frame-up**, a situation in which an innocent person is accused or incriminated on the basis of false evidence, perjury, etc. The noun derives from the verb form.

- 'It was an obvious bloody fit-up, but they let it go through anyway.'
  (Recorded, pub customer, London, 1987).

five-bob deal n British

a small quantity of hashish or marihuana. From the late 1960s until decimalization in 1971, the smallest saleable unit of cannabis.

- 'Hi everybody. I'd roll you all a joint but I've only got a five-bob deal.'
  (Recorded, university student, 1970).

five-finger discount n

American

something stolen, especially a shoplifter's booty. This is the thieves' own term, popular, especially in New York, in the 1970s and 1980s.

five-minute mover n American

a very enthusiastic, energetic sexual partner, a passionate and/or promiscuous person (usually a woman). The implication is that the person in question is quickly seduced or climaxes quickly. By extension the expression could also be applied to any **raver**, without necessarily carrying sexual connotations.

fix n

an injection of a narcotic. Originally an Americanism, by the 1960s it was in use throughout the English-speaking world. The word is now also used metaphorically or ironically to describe any habitual action, such as taking a fix of nicotine, or any pleasure which the speaker would not willingly forgo, as in a weekly fix of a television programme.

flack n

See **flak**.

flagged adj American

nabbed, reprimanded, identified and/or warned. It is the custom in American-football matches for the umpires to throw a flag (a sort of yellow duster) when they spot an infringement, to mark the spot where it took place. This is known as there being 'a flag on the play'. Flagged sometimes has the very specific senses of having been refused further drinks in a bar or arrested.

flak n

criticism, antagonism, aggression, trouble. The terms *Flugabwehrkanone* and *Fliegerabwehrkanone*, given to German World-War II anti-aircraft guns, provided this acronym which was adopted as an English colloquialism. It is now sometimes spelled flack.

- 'We've had to take a lot of flak over this.'
- 'They've been getting a lot of flak from head office recently.'

flake n

1 American an eccentric or crazy person. A later formation from **flaky**. The origin is obscure.

- 'Marx stands out as refreshingly creative and literate among a batch of flakes.'
  (Robert Conquest, Independent, 27 January 1989).

2 Australian shark meat.

- 'Flake and chips.'

3 American cocaine. High-quality Peruvian cocaine, for example, is often sold in the form of small flakes.

4 American an arrest made merely to meet a quota or to satisfy public opin-

ion, etc. Police jargon of obscure origin.

See also **flaking**.

flaked, flaked out adj

exhausted, collapsed.

flake out vb

1 American to leave (a place). An American teenagers' idiom in use since the late 1970s.

2 American to act eccentrically. From **flake** and **flaky**.

3 to collapse from weariness, fall asleep. In this sense the word is now a common colloquialism. Its derivation is uncertain.

● 'After twelve hours in that damn factory all I want to do is come home and flake out on the sofa in front of the TV.'

flaking n American

doctoring, manufacturing or planting evidence to secure an arrest and/or conviction. Police jargon of uncertain derivation.

flaky, flakey adj American

eccentric, crazy, unstable and irresponsible. This Americanism was given wider currency when President Ronald Reagan referred to Colonel Gaddafi as 'flaky' in January 1986; the word had to be translated in the press for British and Australian readers. The original connotations of the word are obscure. It seems to have existed in the above senses since the late 1960s, possibly originating in the argot of baseball players and sports journalists. Suggested derivations are from **flake** as a word for cocaine, or from flaking or crumbling stucco, stone, timber, etc. This second derivation, with overtones of disintegration and splitting or dividing, is more plausible.

flamer n

1 American **a** a flagrant or obvious solecism or blunder.

b a person who commits a gaffe or error.

Both these sub-senses of the word are campus terms, used especially in **preppie** jargon.

2 a flagrant male homosexual, in American and Australian slang of the 1970s and 1980s. Since the beginning of the 19th century the word had been employed in British English to refer to something conspicuous.

flaming n

using computer links and networks to carry on obscene or sexually titillating conversations or to send rude messages. A term of the late 1980s.

flaming adj

an intensifying adjective; an alternative to **bloody** or a euphemism for **fucking**. The word is mainly heard in Britain, where it is rather dated, and in Australia, where it is fairly common. Especially in the North of England it forms part of several colourful but inoffensive oaths such as 'flaming heck', 'flaming 'eck' and 'flaming Nora'. In American usage flaming usually has the specific suggestion of 'flagrant' in a homosexual context.

flan vb British

to assault someone with a custard pie or similar gooey confection. A word popular with actors, comics, student activists and others given to practical jokes.

flannel vb, n

(to subject someone to) talk intended to flatter, deceive, bamboozle, cajole, etc. This term is now a well known colloquialism for waffle or nonsense. It was originally (in the 19th century) a scathing term for the pretentious ornamentation on commercial letterheads, etc.

● *'He gave me a load of old flannel.'*

flapdoodle n

fuss, agitation, consternation. An invented nonsense word dating from the 19th century.

flap one's lips/gums vb

American

to speak. A derisive, contemptuous expression. Bat one's gums is a less common alternative.

flaps n pl

1 ears, especially large or protruding ears.

2 the female labia.

flapshot n

an explicit, often close-up photograph of a vagina with the labia pulled aside, a more clinical version of the **beaver shot**. A pornographers' term that became current in the late 1960s and 1970s.

flash vb

to expose the genitals (in the case of a man), or the breasts or underwear (in the case of a woman). The word has been used in this sense since at least the 18th century (then usually with the exposed part specified, as in 'flash the meat' in the male case).

'They caught him flashing in Richmond Park.'

flash n

1 a glimpse of, or deliberate exposure of, the genitals, breasts, underwear, etc.

2 a the sensation felt immediately after the injection of a narcotic; the sudden, initial effect of a drug.

b also **acid flash**. A sudden recurrence of a previous experience of the drug LSD (lysergic acid diethylamide).

3 *British* a street trader's display of goods.

flash adj

ostentatious, showing off. Since the 1960s, especially in Britain and Australia, this form has tended to replace the earlier 'flashy'.

● *'Why do you bring horses if not to sell? It's flash.'*
(Recorded, gypsy boy, Appleby horse fair, 1988).

flasher n

a sexual exhibitionist, a man who deliberately exposes his genitals in public. The word was slang or police jargon until the 1960s when the prevalence of the activity and a lessening of verbal prudishness brought it into common currency.

Flash Harry n British

a show-off, a flamboyant or boastful person. The identity of the eponymous Harry is unknown.

flash on (something) vb

to be inspired by something, have a sudden bond with something, have a revealing intuition about something. A characteristically vague **hippy** term of the 1960s which is now rarely heard except in the context of the 'psychobabble' of alternative therapists, etc. It derives from the specific drug-related meaning of the noun **flash**.

flash the ash vb British

to offer a cigarette. Usually the expression is in the form of a request or demand.

flat adj British

penniless. A shortened form of the colloquial 'flat broke', heard in raffish speech of the late 1980s.

flatfoot n
a police officer, especially a uniformed policeman on the beat or a low-ranking detective. This mildly pejorative expression is pre-World War II and now rather dated.

flavour of the month n
the current favourite or fashionable person or thing. An expression which usually expresses a scathing or critical attitude to fads or ephemeral popularity. (It derives from the use of the phrase in advertising ice cream in the USA in the 1950s and 1960s.)
- 'Looks like she's flavour of the month in the office at the moment.'
- 'Ecology, well it's flavour of the month.'

fleabag n
a a cheap, dirty hotel.
b a scruffy, dirty person or animal.
c an old sleeping bag or bed.

fleapit n
a cheap, dirty cinema. Originally the term usually referred to the front-stalls section and the 'pit' in front of the screen. Before World War II, in the case of rural cinemas especially, the term was often a literal description.

fleas and itchers/itches n
Australian
a cinema, movie show. Rhyming slang for 'pictures', inspired by the idea of the cinema as a fleapit. The term dates from the 1950s and is now virtually obsolete.

flick n
a film. This word was first common slang, then trade jargon in the film business and now, via such American magazines as Variety, is emerging again as a general term for a movie. (For the derivation see flicks.)
See skinflick.

flicking adj British
an intensifying adjective, a euphemism for fucking. It is used for example by schoolgirls and adult women.
- 'I can lay any amount of hands on them no flicking danger.'
(An Evening with Victoria Wood, British TV programme, 1988).

flicks, the flicks n pl
the cinema, films. An early slang term in all English-speaking countries, derived from 'flicker' or from the homemade moving pictures made by flicking cards. This form of the word is now obsolete in the USA and has rarely been heard in Britain or Australia since the early 1960s. The singular form flick is still current.
- 'We're going down the flicks tomorrow night.'

flim-flam vb, n
(to attempt) trickery or deceit, specifically a confidence trick involving a tall story. The word, which is in use in Britain, but more widespread in the USA, probably comes, via Scottish dialect, from an old Scandinavian word flim meaning mockery. The added second syllable is an example of a common linguistic change in comical words (such as knick-knack, etc.) known as 'reduplication'.
- 'I can smell flim-flam, right down to the paperclips you make me buy.'
(Columbo, US TV series, 1976).

fling vb, n British
1 (to give someone) a bribe, illicit payment. A piece of criminal and police jargon which is a more recent coinage inspired by bung.
- 'We'll have to fling him to square it.'
- 'I'd need a fling in that case.'
2 an affair, usually extramarital.

181

flip *adj British*
a shortening of flippant.

flip, flip out *vb*
to lose control, either through delight, anger, etc., under the influence of an illicit drug, or during the course of a nervous breakdown. Both words spread from American English to world English in the 1960s and derive from the earlier **flip one's wig** or **flip one's lid**, in use in the late 1940s and 1950s among **hipsters**, jazz enthusiasts and **beatniks**. To flip out was used to describe temporary insanity caused by LSD in the early days of the **hippy** era. The term is now old-fashioned (although surviving in French, particularly in the form *flippé*).

- '*He was worried about his mother, though. The old lady was flipping out.*'
  (*Requiem for a Dream*, Hubert Selby Jr., 1979).

flipping *adj British*
a euphemism for **fucking** used as a mild intensifier, especially in such phrases as **flipping hell** or **flipping heck**.

- '"*Stop standing there dreaming, lass*", shouts Dad, "*And get the top orf this flipping bottle of 'arp.*"'
  (*Town* magazine, May 1964).

floater *n*
1 a drowned corpse, in the jargon of police, coastguards, etc.
2 a floating **turd**, in a lavatory bowl or the sea.
3 a *British* a sausage in soup or gravy.
 b *Australian* a meat pie swimming in soup.

floating *adj*
euphoric, especially from the effects of illicit drugs. A now dated term common in the late 1950s and early 1960s.

flob *vb British*
to spit. An echoic term heard among schoolchildren since the 1950s.

flog *vb*
to sell. A common colloquialism in Britain which would still be considered slang by some speakers. The word originally referred to selling off military stores illicitly and is said to derive from a 19th-century army expression to 'flog the clock', meaning to put the clock forward to shorten the working day, later extended to other devious behaviour.

flog the lizard/log/dong/ meat/mutton/the bishop *vb*
to masturbate. Colourful expressions used of, and usually by, men. The verb to flog was employed in the formation of a large number of slang terms in the 18th and 19th centuries.

floozy, floosie *n*
a disreputable immoral, 'loose-living' or frivolous female. A late-19th-century word which is still in use (now usually said lightheartedly). The word originated in the USA, but by the end of World War II was in widespread use elsewhere. It is probably a deformation of 'flossy' an archaic word for a prostitute (itself deriving from flossy, meaning 'showy', or from the female nickname).

flop *n*
1 a place to sleep, a temporary bed or shelter. Especially in the USA the term is, and has been, used by vagrants since the early 20th century.
2 excreta. Probably originating in the USA, where **dogflop** is heard, this euphemism is paralleled by the British plop(s).

flop vb

1 (in this sense also **flop out**) to collapse exhausted, go to bed.

2 to consent to sex. In this sense the word has been used, albeit rarely, in the USA at least since Raymond Chandler's private eye Philip Marlowe said of a woman that she would 'flop at the drop of a hat'.

flophouse n

a cheap hotel or dormitory for vagrants. Originally an Americanism, the word is now part of international English.

fluff n

See **bit of fluff**.

fluff vb British

a euphemism for **fuck**, used in the form **fluffing** as an intensifying adjective or in the expression **fluff off!** (an exclamation delivered at journalists by Prince Philip in October 1987).

fluffing adj British

a mild euphemism for **flaming** or **fucking**, when used as intensifiers.

fly a kite vb

to issue a worthless cheque. Originally an underworld term from the jargon of fraudsters, the expression is now a common colloquialism with the meaning of presenting any dubious scheme or idea for approval. It retains its original meaning in criminal and police parlance.

fodder n British

food. A lighthearted or hearty usage, heard typically among middle-and upper-class speakers.

foggin' adj

a euphemism for **fucking** when used as an intensifier.

folderol n

fuss, complications, 'argy-bargy'. 'Fol-de-rol' and 'falderal' are nonsense words used in popular songs in former times.

folding stuff, the folding stuff n

money, bank notes. A common lighthearted euphemism.

● 'The Cali cartel has a gentler reputation, first offering large amounts of the folding stuff and abhoring murder unless it is absolutely necessary.'
(Independent, 12 September 1989).

foodie n

a 'gourmet' consumer, cooking enthusiast. This is a journalistic expression coined to coincide with the increasing interest in the more recherché aspects of cooking and eating among, for example, **yuppies** in the late 1980s.

fool around vb American

to commit a sexual indiscretion, typically adultery. A common euphemistic use of the expression, heard particularly among middle-class and middle-aged speakers since the 1960s. The term in this specific sense has not caught on outside the USA.

footling adj

trivial, insignificant, minimal. The adjective is derived from the nearly obsolete verb to **footle** meaning to idle, trifle or indulge in trivialities. (Originating in the French foutre, to copulate or to bungle, influenced by 'futile'.)

footsie n

See **play footsie**.

footy n

football. An abbreviated form popular in Australasia and in Britain where it is now more common than the older **footer** (which persists in public-school usage).

● *'Ockers on the way out . . . these days more go to theatre than footy.'* (Caption to photo in *Southern Cross* magazine, July 1989).

foozling *adj*

a clumsy, bungled.

b trivial, **footling**. From the verb **foozle** meaning to play or move clumsily or bungle; itself from German *fuseln*, to work carelessly.

foreign *adj British*

outside one's jurisdiction or area of operations. A piece of police jargon.

● *'Refused charge by the station officer over there . . . and it is a foreign court anyway so there we are.'* (*Inside the British Police*, Simon Holdaway, 1983).

form *n British*

a criminal record. A police and underworld term derived from the language of the racetrack where it refers to a record or reputation based on past performance.

● *'Has he got any form?'*

fornicating *adj British*

a jocular euphemism for **fucking** (as an intensifying adjective).

● *'I'm fed up hearing about his fornicating job!'*

four-by-two, forby *n British*

a Jew. London rhyming slang in current usage. A descriptive, rather than an intrinsically offensive term. A four by two is a standard size of timber plank (4" × 2"), used for rafters, etc. (In the US it is known as a two-by-four.)

four-letter man *n*

a contemptible or unpleasant male. This is a term employed by middle- and upper-class speakers in Britain, and by some Americans, to suggest that the object of the comment merits the use of a 'four-letter word'. The four letters are not specified (**shit** seems to be the most likely, although many others have been suggested ranging from the American **dumb** to the British **homo**).

four-on-the-floor *adj, adv*

flat out, extremely, excessively. This term, used typically by the young in the 1980s comes from the hot rodders' term for a 'stick shift' or four-speed gear system.

● *'When I realized I wanted it, I tell you, I went at it four-on-the-floor.'*

● *'She's a four-on-the-floor great girl!'*

fox *n*

a person who is sexually attractive. The word was used in black American slang of the 1940s by men of women (who were also known as 'minks'). Fox was adopted by white speakers in the 1960s and can now also be said of men by women.

● *'She's a fox and she knows it too.'* (Lyrics to 'Deborah', written by Dave Edmunds and Nick Lowe, 1978).

foxy *adj*

attractive in a 'feral', sexually exciting way. Usually but not invariably used of women by men. The word was originally a black Americanism derived from the noun form **fox**; it is now widely known and used.

● *'Young foxy looking chick; Mr Walker say [sic] she lays by the swimming pool without her top on.'* (Elmore Leonard, *The Switch*, 1978).

- 'Lookit all these foxy chicks! Everywhere I turn.'
  (Robert Crumb, cartoon in Head Comix, 1970).

fragging n American

killing (a fellow soldier, typically a superior) by means of a fragmentation grenade. The term (which could extend to other methods of attack), like the practice, dates from the Vietnam War.

frail n American

a female. A now obsolete masculine term from the pre-war era of crime fiction (Raymond Chandler used the expression). The expression was condescending, but not at the time offensive. It is occasionally resurrected for humorous use particularly in parody or pastiche.

frame vb

to falsely accuse someone, or contrive to have someone convicted of a crime they did not commit. The image is of a picture or portrait being fitted within a frame. It should probably not be confused with in the frame. The earlier version of the expression was to frame (someone) up which survives in the noun form frame-up; both date from the early 20th century and were exported from the USA before World War II.

- 'He convinced me that they had both been framed so the two villains who had committed the crime could get off.'
  (Former detective quoted in Inside the Brotherhood, Martin Short, 1989).

framed adj

falsely accused, incriminated or convicted of a crime. The term was first used in the USA in the early years of the 20th century.

frame-up, frame n

a situation in which someone is framed. Originally an Americanism from the early years of the century.

frat vb, n

1 British a schoolchildren's alteration of fart.

2 (to indulge in) fraternization.

freak vb

to lose control of oneself, become hysterical. A shortening of freak out, this term came, in hippy usage of the late 1960s and early 1970s, to have a negative connotation of alarm or overreaction.

- 'I told her I was leaving home and she completely freaked.'

freak n

1 a hippy, a long-haired (if male), non-conformist member of the 'alternative society' of the late 1960s and early 1970s. Freak was originally a term of abuse directed by straights at homosexuals and later at those guilty of outlandish behaviour and/or bizarre appearance. The term was quickly adopted by the objects of abuse and used as a badge of pride in themselves. (Hippies almost never referred to themselves as hippies after 1966, freak remained the acceptable epithet until the movement faded in the early to mid-1970s.) The word has now reverted to its original derogatory sense and is applied for instance to sexual deviants.

- 'I feel like lettin' my freak flag [i.e. long hair] fly.'
  (Song lyric, Crosby, Stills, Nash and Young, 1970).

2 (as a suffix -freak) an enthusiast, devotee. From the mid-1970s the word was used in this sense, as in health-freak, eco-freak, etc. It was originally a hippy usage, as in acid freak. The term

now sounds dated and has partially been replaced by the less radical **buff**.

freaking adj

an intensifying adjective, a euphemism for **fucking**.

● *'You're a narc, you're a freaking narc!'*
(*Magnum*, US TV series, 1981).

freak out vb

to lose one's self-control, to behave in an outrageous, frantic way. The phrase first described the alarming effect of hallucinogenic drugs such as LSD on some users, but was soon extended to any wild behaviour (whether viewed positively or negatively) such as ecstatic dancing. The expression originated in the USA among the first **hippies** and quickly spread to other English-speaking areas; it was sounding dated by the mid-1970s.

freak-out, freakout n

a bout or scene of wild abandon, self-expression or loss of control. Originally, in **hippy** terminology, it was the result of ingesting hallucinogenic drugs, but later came to refer to any simulation of their effects.

● *'These guys that come up and say: "Wouldn't it be a mind-blower if we got 6,000 million kids in red uniforms and had a big freak-out in the middle of Ealing Common".'*
(Pete Townshend interviewed in *Oz* magazine, June 1969).

freak someone out vb

to alarm, traumatize or 'transport' someone. A transitive form of **freak out**.

freaky adj

a unorthodox, non-conformist, pertaining to **freaks**.

● *'Their awful freaky dancing.'*

b amazing, outstanding, **far-out**. A term of approval used by **freaks**.

● *'This freaky chick.'*

freaky-deaky adj

a later elaboration of **freaky** in both senses. This form of the word was generally used pejoratively, condescendingly or sarcastically.

freckle n Australian

the anus. One of many Australian vulgarities (**ace, date**, etc.) to denote this anatomical feature.

freckle-puncher n Australian

a male homosexual. One of many derogatory compound expressions, it is based on **freckle**, when used as a synonym for anus.

Fred Nerk n

a buffoon, fool or poor victim. The name is a personification of the hapless male and was heard in the 1950s in Britain and Australia (notably in the radio comedy-series *The Goon Show*).

Fred's n British

the **Sloane Ranger** nickname for Fortnum and Mason's, the exclusive store (with tea-room rendezvous) in Piccadilly.

freebasing n

taking cocaine by mixing the crystals with various volatile solvents including ether to form a **base** which is then smoked in a pipe. This activity is also known as 'basing'.

● *'... the technique known as freebasing, a method of separating the base cocaine from the hydrochloride salt ... the result is pure crystals of cocaine ...'*
(*Guardian*, 5 September 1989).

french vb

1 to perform oral sex. A jargon term from the world of prostitution and pornography. The word may refer to cunnilingus or fellatio and derives from the British notion that all forms of 'deviant' sexual behaviour are widespread among, if not invented by, the French. This may originate in the widespread accusation or supposition of the spreading of venereal disease by foreign neighbours.

2 to engage in **French kissing**, in the language of teenagers. In this sense the word is most commonly heard in the USA.

See also **Frenching unit**.

French blue n British

a tablet of amphetamine, specifically the 'pep pill' drinamyl. The 'French' (a common, and here meaningless, term of distinction until the late 1960s), is used simply to distinguish this variety of pill from other, similar **blues**. Drug users soon abandoned this term from the early 1960s, which influenced the press.

frenchie, frenchy n

a condom. From the now obsolescent 'French letter', one of many examples of ascribing anything with sexual connotations to the French. (In French the equivalent is *capote anglaise*; English **bonnet** or **overcoat**.)

Frenching unit n American

the mouth or tongue. A humorous euphemism, popular among college students for instance, and derived from the verb, to **french**, in the sense of tongue kissing or oral sex.

French kiss n

an openmouthed kiss with tongue contact. A phrase which appeared in British and American speech shortly after World War I, before which there was, perhaps significantly, no equivalent term. Later alternatives were **soul kiss** and **tongue sushi**.

French tickler n British

a ribbed condom or other sex aid which fits over or around the penis to increase clitoral stimulation of the female during intercourse. Another example of the British tendency to ascribe all things sexual, especially if slightly deviant, to the French.

fresh adj American

excellent. A vogue term among teenagers in 1987 and 1988. Teenage argot is in constant need of new terms of approbation and this fairly obvious example (derived probably from its overuse in advertising hyperbole rather than its standard American colloquial sense of cheeky) will probably be ephemeral.

● 'Hey, check the fresh car!'

friar tuck n British

an act of sexual intercourse. A rhyming-slang form of **fuck**.

frig vb

1 to masturbate (oneself or another person). The ultimate origin of the word is the Latin *fricare*, to rub (from which friction is derived), via the Middle English friggen.

● 'Friggin' in the rigging 'cause there's fuck-all else to do.'
(Chorus from the rugby-song 'The Good Ship Venus').

2 to have sex (with). Since the 19th century the word has been used as a slightly less offensive alternative to **fuck**, although this was not its original sense.

The verb is nowadays rarely used in either sense except in the noun or adjectival form **frigging**.

frigging adj

an intensifier used with adjectives and nouns for emphasis in the same way as **bloody** or **fucking**. It is considered substantially more offensive than the former and slightly less offensive than the latter.

- *'I was talking to my Canadian niece this very weekend; she (a devout Mormon, 22-ish, not given to profanity) used the word frigging and said, "I'm sorry. I keep forgetting it's a bad word over here" or words to that effect.'*
(Recorded, editor, London, 1989).

the frighteners n pl

See **put the frighteners on (someone)**.

frill n American

a girl or woman. A condescending male term which may be related to **frail** rather than to a more obvious origin.

frit adj British

scared, fearful, afraid. A rural dialect form of frightened, used particularly in the taunts of schoolchildren. Margaret Thatcher used the word of her opponents in the British parliament in 1986.

frog, froggie n, adj

1 (a) French (person). The only slang term for this particular nationality dates from the end of the 18th century when the French were known as 'frog-eaters'.
2 *Australian* a condom (*see also* **frenchie**).

frog (and toad) n British

road. A piece of London rhyming slang which is occasionally still heard.
- *'I'm off down the frog for a pint of pig's.'*
(Recorded, financial journalist, York, 1980).

frogspawn n British

semolina or tapioca pudding. A schoolchildren's word for one of the most hated items in the school lunch-menu of the 1950s and 1960s.

front, the front n British

1 courage, cheek, effrontery, **chutzpah**. This use of the word, as opposed to the colloquial senses of bearing or façade, occurs in phrases such as 'loads of front' or 'he's got a front as big as Harrods' (a reference to the large, impressive frontage of the London store).
See **front out**.
2 **the front** refers to an important street, area or demarcation line in a town or city. In the language of gang members, prostitutes, etc., this warlike term has been applied to Oxford Street and Piccadilly in London, for instance.

front bottom, front bum n

the female genitals. A term used by young children of both sexes and, often jocularly, by some adults in Britain and Australia.

front out/off/it vb British

a to face up to someone or something, either with courage or bluff.
- *'She decided to front him out.'*
b also **front off, front it**. To behave aggressively or over-assertively. An activity of young working-class males, often containing an implicit invitation to violence.
The phrase in both its senses became popular in the 1980s.
- *'He was fronting out down our boozer, so me and a couple of mates gave him a good kicking.'*
(Recorded, youth, London, 1988).

front-wheel skid, front-wheeler, fronter n British

a Jew. A racist London rhyming-slang term of the 1970s and 1980s. The rhyme is on **yid**.

frost vb

a to snub or ignore.

b to anger or irritate.

Both senses have been in use (based on social coolness, 'chilling' or 'freezing') since the 19th century. The word is currently fashionable in teenage use in the USA.

frost n

1 a failure, woeful example of inadequacy. This fairly rare usage of the word occurs in educated speech, particularly in reference to a disappointing performance (in the theatre for example; it may originate in a literary or Shakespearian 'killing frost').

2 a snub or silent rebuff. This sense of the word derives from the verb form, currently in vogue among adolescents, particularly in the USA.

fruit n American

1 a male homosexual. From the idea of exotic, 'ripe', etc. A common term of abuse in the USA since early in the 20th century.

2 an eccentric person. A shortening of **fruitcake**.

fruitcake n

1 an eccentric or crazy person. This is a term from the late 1960s, originating in the 1950s catchphrase, 'as nutty as a fruitcake'.

2 American a male homosexual. An elaboration of **fruit**.

fruit-fly n American

a a male homosexual. An elaboration of **fruit** and synonym of **fruitcake**.

b a woman who frequents or escorts male homosexuals, **fag-hag**.

fruit loop n American

another college term for **fag tag**. A play on *Fruit Loops*, the name of an American brand of breakfast cereal.

fruity adj

1 British sexually suggestive or provocative. In the former sense the word has become a common colloquialism as in fruity jokes/stories etc. In the latter sense it remains a more restricted slang term in use especially among British cockneys and their imitators.

- 'Hello, fruity!'

(Mick Jagger's greeting to a female fan during a concert in San Francisco in 1969).

2 American strange or eccentric. The word is often used adverbially as in **acting fruity**. It presumably derives from the noun **fruitcake**.

fry vb American

a to execute someone by electrocution in the electric chair.

b to punish or chastise someone. A college students' and armed-forces recruits' term, used in such expressions as 'he got fried' or 'they fried her ass'.

frying pan n

a banjo. A musician's term dating back to at least the 1940s.

fuck vb

1 to have sex with. The most commonly used 'four-letter' word, used intransitively ('let's fuck') and transitively ('he fucked her/him'); now also of women ('she fucked him/her'). Surprisingly, the age and origins of this word are obscure. It may not be Anglo-Saxon as is often supposed (it was not recorded in writing until the 16th century) and does not occur in Chaucer and Shakespeare, but may have been borrowed from Norse (fukkar in Norwegian, fockar in Swedish). Wherever and whenever the word entered English, it is certain that is is related to a pattern of words in Indo-European lan-

189

guages which give, among many others, *pungere* (Latin; to prick), *ficken* (German; to fuck or strike), *foutre* (French; to fuck). The common semantic feature of these words is that they contain the meaning strike, push or prick.

Fuck has always been a taboo word in all English-speaking countries and is still omitted from broadcasts and generally asterisked if written in the press. In the late 20th century the verb often has the more specialized sense of 'habitually copulate' or 'be sexually willing' as in '*does she fuck?*'.

2 to make a mess of, destroy. A 1980s' shortening of **fuck up** with slightly more emphatic or drastic connotations.

- '*They fucked the experiment totally.*'

3 to damn or disregard.

- '*Fuck art, let's dance!*'
  (T-shirt slogan of the 1970s).

fuck n

a an act of sexual intercourse. The noun post-dates the verb by at least three hundred years.

b a person when evaluated as a sexual partner.

- '*A good fuck/an easy fuck.*'

c a person, especially when viewed as a fool, victim, villain, etc.

- '*The poor dumb fuck didn't have a chance.*'

fuck (someone) over vb

to humiliate, discomfit, distress, or destroy someone or something.

- '*Once the income tax guys get their hands on you they can really fuck you over.*'
  (Recorded, self-employed male, London, 1988).

fuckable adj

sexually attractive, considered as a potential sexual partner (approvingly

or grudgingly). A vulgarism which is no longer exclusively in male use.

- '*She may not have a lot upstairs, but she's eminently fuckable.*'
  (Recorded, male student, London, 1987).

fuck-a-duck exclamation

a virtually meaningless expression of surprise or disbelief.

fuck-all n British

nothing or almost nothing. An emphatic vulgarism.

- '*He walked away with two hundred thousand and I got fuck-all.*'
  (Recorded, businessman, London, 1987).

fuck around/about vb

to play the fool, behave irresponsibly or irresolutely.

- '*OK let's stop fucking around and get down to work.*'

fucked adj

a (of things) ruined, destroyed, rendered useless.

- '*This typewriter is completely fucked.*'

b (of people) completely exhausted, beaten or at a loss.

- '*I'm feeling fucked.*'

fucked-up adj

a (of things or situations) in a mess, destroyed, spoilt or ruined. Originally the expression meant seduced and abandoned.

b (of people) psychologically disturbed, traumatized.

- '*Sadowitz will soon revert to being the fucked-up nonentity he must have been before people like you started dressing him up in the Emperor's New Clothes.*'
  (Letter to *Time Out*, December 1987).

c (of people) temporarily deranged

by drugs or drink (not necessarily a negative term).

- *'I got really fucked-up on that dope.'*

fucker n

a person. the word does not invariably imply dislike or contempt, although it may.

- *'The poor fucker never stood a chance.'*

See **motherfucker**.

fuckhead n

a stupid or unpleasant person. A term of abuse popular in the 1980s and usually applied to males.

fuckin' A, fucking aye

exclamation

a absolutely, definitely.
b splendid, fine.

Usually (in both senses) a hearty cry, emphasizing camaraderie and bonhomie. It probably derives from the armed forces' love of abbreviations, and the 'A' may stand for absolutely, ace or, more probably, **arseholes**.

fucking adj

an intensifier used with other adjectives for emphasis. Like **bloody** it is also one of the very few examples of an 'infix' (a word component inserted before the stressed syllable in the middle of a polysyllabic word) in English.

- *'Jesus, it's fucking cold in here.'*
- *'Abso-fucking-lutely.'*

fucknuckle n

a term of abuse, used of males. The second component is included merely for the purpose of reduplication of sound and signifies nothing.

fuck off vb

to leave, go away. A vulgarism that is used in regular verb forms and as an interjection.

- *'Why don't you just fuck off!'*

fuckoff n American

a useless, hopeless or idle person.

fuckpig n

a very unpleasant, worthless or contemptible person. This is the British version of the American **pigfucker**. It has been part of the London working-class slang repertoire since the 19th century.

fuck truck n

another term for **passion wagon**.

fuck up, fuck (someone) up

vb

1 to make a mess of things, commit a serious error or blunder.

See **snafu**.

- *'Don't tell me, you've fucked up yet again.'*

2 fuck someone up to create an emotional disturbance (in someone), traumatize.

- *'They fuck you up, your mum and dad.'*

(Philip Larkin, *This be the Verse*).

fuck-up n

a a disaster, blunder, error or failure.
b a bungler or blunderer.
c someone who is emotionally or psychologically disturbed.

fuckwit n

an idiot, a halfwit. An Australianism which has caught on in British use since the late 1970s. It usually expresses exasperated contempt.

- *'The guy's a complete fuckwit.'*
- *'You've all been coining it for years. All you fuckwits in the City.'*

(Caryl Churchill, *Serious Money*, 1987).

fuckwitted *adj Australian*
hopelessly stupid, dim-witted.

fudge *n British*
an exclamation of annoyance typically used by socially respectable speakers. When used today it is probably intended as a much milder version of **fuck**, but it seems to have existed independently since the 18th century as an equivalent of 'stuff and nonsense'.

fudgepacker *n British*
a homosexual. A derisive late 1980s term employing fudge as an image for excrement and equating homosexuality with buggery, on the same pattern as **brownie-hound**, **chocolate bandit** etc.

fuggin' *adj*
a euphemism for **fucking**.

full (as a boot/bull/bull's bum) *adj Australian*
drunk. Full or 'full as a tick' were euphemisms for drunk in Britain in the 19th century, but are now obsolete. Earlier Australianisms on the same pattern were *'full as an egg'* and *'full as a goat'*.

funbag *n*
a a woman, particularly an attractive woman or a potential sexual partner.
b *American* a prostitute, in 1980s police jargon.

funbags *n pl Australian*
breasts. A vulgar term from the 1960s inspired by children's 'lucky dip' sweet packets on the same lines as **mystery bags**.

fun-bundle *n*
a condescending term for a female.

fungus face, fungus features *n*

a a bearded man.
b a very unhealthy-looking or ugly person.
Both senses are popular with schoolchildren.

funk *n*
1 a heavily rhythmic, 'earthy' music, particularly soul or disco music. A term applied to varieties of urban black music since the 1950s.
b authentic feeling, earthiness, a quality of unsophisticated, raw vitality. The noun form is a back-formation from the adjective **funky**.
2 *British* cowardice, fearfulness, a fit of panic. A word which is quite unrelated to the musical sense. Funk here comes from the Flemish *fonck*, worry or agitation. (A blue funk is a state of extreme fear.) It has been in use since the 18th century.

funky *adj*
1 a earthy, raw in the style of **funk** music (characteristically having heavy rhythm and bass and simple repeated melodies). This term, applied to urban soul-music which contained elements of African, jazz, blues and rock music, has been heard since the 1950s. It is sometimes elaborated to funky-butt.
b vital, raw, energetic in an unsophisticated way. A term of approval applied to people, objects, ideas, etc. by extension from the musical sense.
2 smelly, fetid. This is the original sense of the word, dating from the early-17th-century British noun funk, meaning a stink or 'fug' of tobacco smoke. This in turn probably derives from the Latin verb *fumigare* (to smoke or fumigate), via French. Senses **1a** and **b** originate in this meaning.

funny farm *n*
a psychiatric hospital or home for mental patients.
● *'They're coming to take me away,*

ha ha, to the funny farm, where life is beautiful all the time.'
('They're coming to take me away, ha-haaa!', song by Napoleon XIV, 1966).

funny money n

a counterfeit money.
b worthless denominations.
c foreign currency.
d excess or unearned wealth. The words in this sense express disbelief or resigned acceptance in the face of 'unthinkably' large amounts of money.

furburger, fur-doughnut, furry hoop, fur pie n

the vagina. Expressions which have been part of the male repertoire of vulgarisms since the 1960s. In the USA, furburger and fur pie are sometimes used to refer to a female or females in general.

futz n American

1 the vagina.
2 a disreputable and/or unpleasant male.
These noun forms are related to the verb form.

futz vb American

to mess or fool around. The word is a deformation of a Yiddish verb arumfartzen, meaning literally and metaphorically to **fart around**.

(the) fuzz n

the police. A 1960s' buzzword nowadays only likely to be used by a hopelessly out-of-date adult attempting to communicate ingratiatingly with young people (who will either not understand at all, or regard the dated term with contempt). The meaning was originally contemptuous, but through widespread use in the late 1960s became a relatively mild epithet. It derives either from the likening of a worthless person to mould, fluff or dust, or it is a black reference to white men's 'wispy' head and body hair.

- 'You're more likely to be damaged permanently in a tangle with the American fuzz though, if you see what I mean.'
(Terry Reid, interviewed in Oz magazine, February 1969).

the f-word n British

a coy reference to the taboo word **fuck**.

- 'He was very coarse, always scratching himself and saying the f-word.'
(Recorded, middle-aged female bus-passenger, London, 1989).

G

G n

1 a gram (of some illicit substance). The abbreviation is typically used in referring to cocaine, which is sold in grams.

2 a thousand, a **grand**.

● *'It cost me two g's.'*

gabfest n American

a talking session. The expression resembles the sort of journalese portmanteau words coined by *Variety* magazine, but is apparently older. The implication is of talk that is high on quantity and low on quality; gossip, platitudes, small-talk or empty rhetoric, used ironically to refer to negotiations, political meetings, etc. 'Gab' is an old term for idle chatter, a shortening of gabble, while '-fest' is an American pseudo-German ending meaning festival or celebration.

gadgie, gadgy n, adj British

(an) old, infirm or senile (person). A schoolchildren's word mainly heard in the north of England. The source is in dialect of the 19th century or earlier but the precise original meaning is lost.

gaff n British

a home or house. In 19th-century slang a gaff was a fair, fairground or any place of cheap entertainment. These notions were expanded in the argot of actors, tramps, market stallholders, criminals etc. and the word came to be used to describe any place or location, hence the current meaning which was racy underworld jargon from the 1920s to the 1950s when **spivs**, **teddy boys** etc. gave it wider currency. (It is still mainly used by working-class speakers.)

● *'If I was you I'd go round his gaff and pour brake fluid all over his paintwork – see how that goes down.'*

(*The Firm*, British TV play, February 1989).

● *'Nice gaff you've got here.'*

See also **blow the gaff**.

gaffer n

a a boss. A rustic term of address or descriptive word for an old man or master current in Britain since the 16th century, gaffer is a contraction of grandfather. It is still widely used, particularly by working-class speakers.

● *'If I were you I'd go and fetch the gaffer; he's the only one who knows what's going on.'*

b an old man. This is probably the most common sense of the word in the USA, where it is also used to refer to a father (but rarely specifically a grandfather), and to a foreman as in the first sense.

gag vb

to vomit. A teenager's specialized use of the colloquial term for choking or retching. Its use is not entirely restricted to the speech of teenagers.

gaga *adj*

senile, crazy, besotted. The word has come into world English from French, via upper-class or educated British English of the 1920s. In French it was probably originally a nursery word, influenced by *grand-père* (grandfather) and *gâteaux* (feeble-minded, infirm).

● *'She's gone completely gaga over this appalling creep.'*
(Recorded, wine bar habituée, London, 1986).

gage, gauge *n*

marihuana or hashish. Gauge was a now obsolete slang term for an alcoholic drink and later also for a pipe or a pipeful or tobacco, coming presumably from the idea of a measure (of something intoxicating). The survival of these senses in American and Jamaican English led to the use of the same word for cannabis. In Britain gage was also heard among **beatniks**, prisoners, etc. in the 1960s when it was sometimes assumed to derive from 'greengage', an allusion to the colour of grass. The term is now dated.

gag me with a spoon!

exclamation American

a favourite **Valley Girl** expression of exaggerated or thrilled disgust or astonishment.

● *'Wow, gag me with a spoon! How gross can you get.'*

gal *n American*

a light-hearted spelling and pronunciation of girl.

See also **gel**.

galah *n Australian*

a fool, a silly, empty-headed person. The galah is a species of Australian cockatoo which characteristically congregates with others and 'chatters'. A rural catchphrase in currency before World War II, was *'as mad as a*

(gum)tree full of galahs'. The word is pronounced with the stress on the second syllable.

● *'Let's forget the whole thing, I feel like a right galah.'*
(*The Flying Doctors*, Australian TV series, 1987).

gam *n*

1 *British* an act of oral sex; fellatio or cunnilingus. In the 19th century the word referred only to fellatio. For the etymology see the verb **gam**.

2 *Australian* a sanitary towel or tampon. The word is probably an alteration of tampon or **jam rag**.

gam *vb British*

to perform oral sex. A shortening of *gamahucher*, a 19th-century French term for this practice which was adopted into the specialist jargon of prostitutes, pornographers and their customers. The word is now a rather old-fashioned working-class and schoolchildren's vulgarism.

game *adj British*

working as a prostitute, available for sex. The word in this sense is a back-formation from the earlier 'on the game'. It is used by **punters** and those involved professionally in prostitution.

● *'She's game.'*

gamp *n British*

an umbrella. A word from the latter half of the 19th century, inspired by the large umbrella carried by Sarah Gamp, a character in Charles Dickens' *Martin Chuzzlewit*, published in 1870.

gams *n pl*

legs, especially a woman's legs when considered shapely. A jocular word which now sounds old-fashioned, unsurprisingly in that it originates in the medieval heraldic term for leg, gamb, which in turn comes from Old Northern French dialect *gambe* (modern French is *jambe*, Italian is *gamba*). Gams is sometimes thought to come from gammon, a word which features in several cockney slang expressions; it does not, but it is distantly related etymologically. It is still heard occasionally throughout the English-speaking world.

● '*Oo Nudge, check out those gams.*' (*Beach House*, US film, 1981).

gander n

a look. The word, which is usually part of phrases such as '*take/have a gander at this*', comes from the bird's characteristic craning of the neck.

ganef, gonef, gonof n
American

a thief, petty criminal. A word from the Hebrew *gannath*; thief, via Yiddish. In the 19th century variant forms of this word were heard in Britain and South Africa, but are now archaic.

● '*I'm curious, what do you remember about the man who robbed you ... I want to know what the ganef looked like.*' (*Hill Street Blues*, US TV series, 1986).

gang bang vb, n

(to take part in) sex involving several males sequentially with one woman; group sex. The word received publicity in the 1960s, largely as a result of articles describing the rituals of Hells Angels and others. It has virtually replaced alternatives such as gang-fuck or gang shag. Gang bang is sometimes used jocularly to describe a wild, uproarious but otherwise innocuous gathering.

gang bang vb American

to take part in the activities of a street gang. A term from the 1980s which is a

play on the well-known sexual term, and bang in the sense of gunshot. The word has been brought to public attention by TV documentaries describing the activities of such gangs in the era of **crack**. (The phrase is now sometimes shortened to **bang**.)

gangbanger n American

a loyal and committed member of a street gang. This 1980s term is used by and about the members of street gangs in Los Angeles. The bang in question is a gunshot; shooting a victim is often part of the initiation process.

gangbusters n, adj American

(something) superlative, excellent, impressive. A schoolchildren's word which is a shortening of the jocular adult phrase '*like gangbusters*', meaning very strongly, energetically or dynamically. The terms originate in the violently heroic actions of the anti-mob law enforcers (nicknamed gangbusters) of yellow journalism and crime fiction.

● '*Hey you know, that set they played was gangbusters!*'

gangie n Australian

a **gang bang** or **group-grope**.

ganja n

marihuana. This is one of the many names for cannabis which has been heard in various milieus over the last fifty years or so. At present the term is popular in the Caribbean and among blacks and young white smokers in Britain. It comes originally from the Sanskrit *gañja*, via Hindi.

gannet n British

a person who eats greedily, someone who bolts their food. Gannet is a 1970s and 1980s term derived, possibly via comics' adaptation of navy argot, from the voracious habits of the fish-gorging seabird.

- *'If you've got any sense you'll keep the best stuff away from those gannets.'*
(Recorded, teacher, York, 1981).

ganny, gannie *n British*

Afghani cannabis. A drug users' abbreviated form, heard since the early 1980s.

gaolbait *n British*

See **jailbait**.

garbo *n Australian*

a garbage man, dustman. The word's first use seems to have coincided with the height of the fame of the Swedish movie actress, Greta Garbo.

garbonzas *n pl American*

breasts. One of many invented terms used lightheartedly by males (**gazungas** is another version). This may conceivably be influenced by the Spanish *garbanzos*; chick-peas.

- *'After totting up the score-sheet of exposed breasts ["garbonzas"], mutilations, rolling heads, gross-outs, auto-collisions, he awards a number of stars and puts his seal of approval on a film.'*
(*Observer*, 9 April 1989).

gargle *n Irish and British*

(an) alcoholic drink. A joke on the lines of **lotion** and **tincture** which is at least 100 years old and is still commonly heard in Dublin, for instance.

- *'Fancy a gargle, John?'*
(Posy Simmonds cartoon, *Guardian*, 1981).
- *'I'll have some gargle, if you don't mind, sir.'*
(Recorded, Irish pub habitué, London, 1987).

garn, g'arn *exclamation British*

an old-fashioned Cockney term not widely heard since the late 1950s, garn is a form of 'go on!' or 'get on!', and was used as a shout of dismissal, defiance or irritation.

gas *n*

1 something which is exhilarating, stimulating or highly enjoyable. In the phrase *'it's a gas'* and *'what a gas!'*, this word became one of the clichés of the **hippy** vocabulary. It probably originated in American black street slang of the late 1950s, inspired by the exhilarating effects of nitrous oxide (laughing gas), although the same word, with the same meaning and origin, already existed in Irish speech.

- *'But it's all right now, in fact it's a gas ... I'm jumping Jack Flash, it's a gas, gas, gas.'*
('Jumping Jack Flash', Rolling Stones, 1968).

2 an idle conversation, period of empty chatter.

gas *vb*

1 to chat, talk idly and volubly.

- *'Whenever we get together we gas for hours.'*

2 also **gas out**: to exhilarate, stimulate. A **hip** back-formation from the noun **gas**.

gas guzzler *n*

an uneconomical car. A term originally applied to American non-compact cars of the 1970s.

gash *adj British*

1 spare, available. This now almost obsolete use of the word was common in the armed services in the 1950s and probably has the same origins as the following senses.

2 attractive, impressive. The origin of this sub-sense of gash is obscure but may be inspired by the attractiveness of 'spare' or available women. It was heard among working-class Londoners until the late 1960s.

3 useless, worn out, broken. In this sense gash is still heard especially in London, among workmen, technicians, musicians etc.

● 'There's nothing in there but a pile of gash tapes.'
(Recorded, video technician, London, 1988).

The various meanings of the term probably all derive from a 19th-century adoption of the French word gâcher (to waste or spoil) or gâchis (mess) for rubbish on board ship. The meaning was ironically extended to cover extra portions, then anything spare. The original French is preserved in the third sense above.

gash n

a a woman or girl. A male term of sexual origin but not necessarily used with sexual connotations. The term existed in the argot of the streets in the 1950s both in the USA and in working-class Britain, (where it usually occurred in the phrase 'a bit of gash'). It was revived in the 1980s by afficionados of **rap** music and hip hop as a fashionable synonym for girlfriend. The origin of the word lies in **b**, which is unknown to many users.

b a woman's genitals, or women as sex objects. The fearful or dismissive male image of a woman's external sex organs as a wound is an ancient one. Gash in this sense was a widespread vulgar euphemism in the 19th century.

gasper n

a cigarette. An ironic witticism from the days before the anti-smoking lobby, when shortness of breath was still a possible subject for levity. (It is probably unconnected with the more recent British cliché 'gasping for a fag'.) The word was at its most popular in the 1950s in the language of **spivs**, **cads**, etc., but is not yet obsolete.

gassed adj

drunk. A popular word among middle-class, middle-aged drinkers in the USA in the mid 1960s, gassed was also a synonym for tipsy in Britain after World War I (probably from laughing-rather than mustard-gas).

gasser n

1 something which is highly amusing or impressive. This sense of the word is inspired by the properties of laughing-gas and is used to denote a good joke, for example. This is an Americanism which is also heard in Britain and may have been coined there independently. It was first used before World War II, and is now heard particularly among teenagers.

2 American a depressing experience, person or situation. The word is rare in this sense, in which the image evoked is presumably of a poisonous, asphyxiating or anaesthetic gas.

gat n

a pistol, revolver. A piece of obsolete underworld slang from the early 1900s derived from Gatling gun (an early revolving-barrel machine-gun). The word is occasionally resurrected by writers invoking the atmosphere of the gangster era, and was the trademark name of a cheap British air pistol of the 1950s.

the Gate n British

Notting Hill Gate. This district of London, the venue of an annual carnival, contains Portobello Road street market and centres of ethnic, musical and drug subcultures.

gauch out vb British

See **gouch out**.

gay adj

homosexual. In late medieval English 'gay' often had the sense of showy or affected as well as happy and light-hearted. In British slang of the 18th and 19th century it was a euphemism for sexually available or living an immoral life, and was invariably applied to women, usually prostitutes. In the early 20th century it was adopted as a code word by the British and American homosexual community, an innocent-sounding term which they could use of themselves and each other. The word had the secondary purpose of reinforcing homosexuals' positive perception of their sexual identity as opposed to the derisive or disapproving terminology of the heterosexual world. 'Gay' was widely used in the theatrical milieu by the mid 1960s and, when homosexuals began to assert themselves openly in the later 1960s, it supplanted all alternatives to become the standard non-discriminatory designation.

gaylord n British

an effete or homosexual male. A schoolchildren's term of the late 1980s. The word, which is an embellishment of gay, may derive from Jamaican argot.

gazump vb British

to cheat (in a house purchase) by raising the price at the last moment, after agreement has been reached but before contracts have been formalized. An old expression from the language of swindlers, revived to denote a practice which became widespread during and after the dramatic rise in property prices in 1972. The word formerly existed in several forms (gazumph, gazoomph, gazumf, etc.) and is from Yiddish.

gazunda, gazunder, gazunta, gozunder n

a chamber pot. A perennial humorous euphemism heard in Britain and Australia, based on the fact that the unnameable article in question 'goes under' the bed. By extension these words are sometimes used to refer to other un-named gadgets, containers, implements or contraptions.

gazungas n pl

female breasts. A male term.

gear adj British

excellent, absolutely right, first rate. An ephemeral vogue word that spread with the popularity of the Beatles and the 'Mersey sound' from Liverpool in 1963 to be picked up by the media (a fact which incidentally marked its demise as a fashionable term). It is related to 'the gear' meaning the 'real thing' or top quality merchandise.

gear n

1 clothes, accessories. Now a widely-used colloquialism, gear was slang, in the sense of being a vogue word in restricted usage, in the early 1960s, when its use paralleled the new interest in fashion among mods.

2 illicit drug(s). Since the early 1960s gear has been used by drug abusers, prisoners, etc. to denote, in particular, cannabis or heroin. In this sense the word is a typical part of the drug user's quasi-military or workman-like vocabulary (works, equipment and artillery are other examples).

● 'Got any gear, man?'

3 a top quality merchandise, the 'real thing'.

b stolen goods. A specific usage of the standard colloquial sense of the word.

● 'Stash the gear in the garage.'

gee-gee n British

a horse. A nursery term adopted by adults to refer ruefully or facetiously to race-horses. In British films of the 1950s the word was characteristic of **spivs** and **cads**.

- 'I lost thirty quid on the gee-gees.'

geek n American

a freak, insane or disgusting person. This old word originated with fairground or **carny** folk to describe someone willing to abase themselves or perform disgusting acts, such as biting the heads off live chickens, or a grotesque person exhibited for money. The word is now firmly established in teenage and schoolchildren's slang, helped by the preponderance of geeks in the horror films of the late 1970s and 1980s. It may be derived from German, Dutch or Yiddish words for 'to peep', or from Dutch and English dialect words for a fool.

- 'I'm gonna marry the geek tycoon.'
  (Cheers, US TV series, 1988).

geek, geek out vb American

a to behave eccentrically, like a **geek**.

b to search desperately for drug remnants, particularly **crack**. This sense is a specialization of the first, used by drug users in 1989 to describe the actions of a crack addict in extremis.

- 'You just want more and more. That's when you go geeking – looking for specks on the floor, just to get some more.'
  (Drug user, Guardian, 5 September 1989).

geek rock n American

another name for **crack**. **Rock** is a generic term for narcotics in (lumpy) powder or granule form, **geek** is a crazy person.

geeze bag n American

an old **fart**, old **geezer**. A term of mild abuse or derision, mainly in adolescent use.

geezer n

a man. A common word in Britain, where slang users often assume that it derives from a bathroom geyser (water heater), by analogy with **boiler**. In fact it probably originates in 'guiser' or 'gizer', a word for a masquerader or mummer who wears a (dis)guise. In the 19th century geezer could be applied to women. The word is also used in the USA, where it is regarded as rather colourful.

gel n British

a girl, particularly a public schoolgirl. The word mimics the upper-class pronunciation (of hearty schoolmistresses or crusty colonels for instance) prevalent until the 1960s and still heard.

gelt n

money. The word is taken directly from Yiddish or German and has been used in all English-speaking areas since at least the 17th century, at first probably in allusion to Jewish moneylenders.

gendarmes n pl British

the police. A middle-class appropriation of the French word in an attempt at raciness.

- 'Had a spot of bother with the gendarmes as I was driving down.'

gentleman actor n British

a 'clean-limbed', bland and handsome member of the acting profession, of either sex. A piece of (usually sarcastic) theatrical slang.

gentleman of the road n
British
a tramp, vagrant. A euphemism first applied to highwaymen and later by tramps to themselves.

geordie n *British*
a native or inhabitant of Newcastle or Tyneside in the north-east of England. The word is a Scottish dialect version of George and probably first arose as a nickname for one of the Hanoverian kings, used by and later applied to soldiers billeted upon Newcastle. The name refers also to the distinctive speech patterns of the area.

george adj *American*
excellent, first-rate, fine. A word from teenage slang of the late 1950s which is periodically revived by modern schoolchildren and college students. It probably derives from gorgeous or is an expansion of the letter g (for good).

George Raft n *British*
a draught (of air). A fairly widespread piece of jocular rhyming slang inspired by the American actor of the same name (famous for his tough guy and underworld roles on and off screen).
• 'Blimey, there's a bit of a George Raft in here, ain't there?'

the gerbil n *British*
the teachers' nickname for the Thatcher government's Education Reform bill which became law in 1988. Commentators who remarked on the benign choice of the name of a children's pet misunderstood the teachers' reading of the acronym; rodent-like and insatiable were more probably the qualities evoked.

germ n *British*
an irritating, unpleasant or contemptible person. A schoolchildren's term of criticism or abuse, typically applied to fellow pupils or younger children.

Germans n pl
hands. A piece of Cockney rhyming slang (from 'German bands') which is now rarely heard, but when it is, is almost always in the shortened form. (Before World War I bands of German musicians played in the streets and parks of London.)

gerry, geri n *British*
an old person. A short form of geriatric, typically said without affection by teenagers or schoolchildren.

gertcha! exclamation *British*
a Cockney cry, roughly equivalent to 'get away!', 'give over!', or 'get out of it!' and expressing disbelief or gentle mockery. The dated expression was revived for use in the musical accompaniment (by Chas and Dave) to a television advertisement for Courage Best Bitter screened in 1983.
'"Gercher", wheezes Dad convulsively over the debris of the saloon bar.'
(*Town* magazine, May 1964).

get n *British*
a bastard, literally or figuratively; an unpleasant or stupid person. This word is more widespread in the Midlands and north of England, generally in working-class usage. In the south of England **git** is more common. Get was originally a derivation of 'beget' and meant a (begotten) child.

get a rift/rush/hustle on vb
British
to hurry up, make haste. These are more colourful working-class London variants of the colloquial 'get a move on'.

get behind vb

approve of, support, empathize with. A phrasal verb (originating in the USA) of the sort popular with the 'alternative lifestyle' proponents of the early 1970s. Compare **get off**, **get down**, etc.

- *'I can't really get behind the idea of God as some bearded dude sitting on a cloud.'*

get Chinese vb American

to get very **stoned**, become euphoric and/or semi-conscious by smoking marihuana. This **preppie** expression is based on the premise that their stupefaction will rival that of Chinese opium addicts or that their glazed serenity will result in an oriental demeanour.

get down vb American

to let oneself go, begin something in earnest. This phrase was originally a piece of black slang, inspired by 'get down to business' (probably first used as a euphemism for beginning sexual activity, then transferred to musical activity). The expression is still heard in a musical context, referring for instance to musicians improvising successfully or to disco dancers 'letting go' (it is often used as a shouted exclamation, sometimes expanded into such forms as 'get down and get dirty' or 'get down and get with it!'). Around 1970 get down was adopted as a catchphrase by the white counter-culture, often with a generalized sense of 'start to communicate' or share experience.

get into bed (with) vb

to merge or agree to liaise closely with. A piece of jargon from the business world which has become widely known since the late 1970s.

get it on vb

a to succeed in having sex, to achieve (mutual) sexual gratification.

An American euphemism, dating from the 1960s.

- *'I'm gonna ask you something right up front. Are you getting it on with that dude with the dog parlor or not?'*
(The Serial, Cyra McFadden, 1976).

b to succeed in something pleasurable or desirable. A generalization of the first sense which was used, sometimes as an exhortation, in the **hippy** era. Both senses became known, and to some extent used, in Britain after 1970, but had largely fallen out of use by the end of the decade.

get it together vb

to organize oneself, one's life and/or environment. A vogue term and cliché from around 1969. The 'it' refers to one's 'act', one's life, one's head, or to things in general.

get it up vb

to achieve an erection. A common vulgarism.

get laid vb

to have sex. A derivation from **lay**, which spread from the USA to Britain around 1968.

- *'Young guys in their twenties, of course they're going to try and get laid, and even if they don't succeed it's hardly big news.'*
(Lenny Henry, Time Out magazine, 26 July 1989).

- *'Now the Commander clearly wasn't someone you could bung 50 quid or take to a nightclub and get laid.'*
(Former detective, Inside the Brotherhood, Martin Short, 1989).

get off (on) vb

a to achieve satisfaction, exhilaration or inspiration (from). This American expression of the early 1970s is an extension of an earlier purely sexual sense of the phrase in which get off means to achieve orgasm. This concept was modified by the drug users' image of leaving terra firma, of flying or floating in a state of euphoria. Since the late 1970s the term has been heard (in Britain and Australia) generalized to include finding pleasure from more innocuous sources, such as music.

- 'Did you manage to get off on those mushrooms?'
- 'I really get off on that guitar solo.'
- 'Would you please define "got off on it"?'
- 'He got a sexual thrill from beating the girls.'
  (The Last Innocent Man, US film, 1987).

b to get someone off retains the sexual sense of bringing someone to a climax; this use of the phrase is fairly rare.

get one's act/head/shit together vb

to organize oneself, arrange one's affairs, start to perform efficiently or effectively. A euphemism from the era of alternative therapy which likens one's behaviour to a performance (it may in fact have originated in theatrical or musical circles); unlike many such phrases it is still in widespread use.

get one's arse in(to) gear vb

to prepare oneself, get organized and get going. A phrase which appeared in Britain and America (with ass) seemingly simultaneously around 1974. It is usually employed as an exhortation to someone who is disorganized or wasting time.

get one's end away vb British

to have sex, succeed in seduction. A masculine vulgarism in widespread use since the 1960s, this is a variation on 'get one's end in', a euphemism dating from the early years of the 20th century.

get one's head together vb

to collect one's thoughts, achieve a state of equanimity. A cliché of the 'alternative society' of the early 1970s (members of rock groups, suffering from the excesses of social and professional life, typically spoke of going to the countryside to get their heads together). This phrase is still heard, albeit more rarely, usually in the sense of pull oneself together or get one's act together.

- 'You know you really should try and get your head together if you intend to carry on in this business.'

get one's jollies vb

to derive enjoyment, obtain sensual satisfaction. The gratification referred to in this phrase is often less innocuous than the light-hearted nature of the words might imply.

- 'It's not my idea of a good time, but if that's how you get your jollies, I won't stand in your way.'

get one's knickers in a twist vb British

to become agitated, flustered or over-excited. This picturesque vulgarism originated in the late 1950s with a purely sexual sense. Now widely used, it is generally heard in the negative form, exhorting someone to calm down.

get one's leg over/across vb British

(of a male) to have sex, to succeed in seduction.

- 'You [Colin Moynihan, minister for sport] can be honest with us. Did you get your leg over or not?'
  (Private Eye magazine, April 1989).

get one's oats vb British

to achieve sexual satisfaction. The phrase originates in the idea of 'sowing one's wild oats', especially in the sense of sexual adventuring outside marriage. Since the 1960s the phrase has been applied to both men and women, and to sex in general rather than adultery in particular. It is heard in all social classes in Britain and Australia.

- 'If he plays his cards right, he should end up getting his oats tonight.'
(Recorded, teenage drinker, London, 1986).

get one's rocks off vb

to obtain sexual satisfaction, achieve orgasm, ejaculate. An American vulgarism which became part of the **hippy** linguistic repertoire; some British users of the expression are unaware that **rocks** is a direct euphemism for testicles. (In American usage **nuts** or other terms could be substituted for rocks.) In the later 1970s the phrase was extended to mean to indulge oneself or enjoy oneself generally rather than in a specifically sexual sense. It now sounds dated.

- 'But I only get my rocks off while I'm dreaming.'
(Lyric from 'Rocks Off', The Rolling Stones, 1972).

get on one's wick/tits vb British

to irritate, annoy or vex. The 'wick' in question, unknown to many speakers, is a now rather archaic shortening of **hampton wick**, rhyming slang for **prick** (which is nowadays more usually shortened to **hampton**). In spite of the implied gender difference, both versions of the expression are used indiscriminately by both men and women.

- 'It really gets on my tits when someone calls me a career woman.'

(Recorded, female journalist, London, 1986).

get on someone's case vb American

to harass, badger or interfere. A phrase used with indignation or resentment, typically by an 'underdog' to or of an authority figure. The notion on which the expression is based is that of a judge or law-enforcer examining one's case. 'Get off my case' is a widespread negative form.

get someone up vb British

a to bribe or pay off, 'square someone'.

b to entrap, **frame** or manoeuvre someone into a disadvantageous position.

Both senses of the rather vague euphemism have been in use in police and criminal parlance since the 1960s.

get the horn vb

to achieve an erection. A vulgarism employing the horn as a penis metaphor, heard more commonly in the adjective **horny**. Get the horn is now mainly heard in uneducated adult speech and the language of schoolchildren. To be 'on the (h)orn' is an alternative form.

get the hump vb British

to become bad-tempered, morose or offended. This common expression is at least 100 years old. The origin of this sense of hump is not clear, although it may refer straightforwardly to a hunchback's deformity, to a back bent with care, a head dropped in gloom, or a traveller's burden. In modern Cockney usage the phrase is often abbreviated to the adjective **humpty**.

get the needle, get the dead needle vb British

to become irritated, bitter or vindictive. This expression is one of a number referring to needle in the sense of provoke or annoy. This particular form of words has survived as a working-class Londoners' phrase since the late 19th century.

getting any? *question form*

a jocular male greeting. The 'any' refers to sex. This hearty vulgarism is no longer confined to masculine speech; the American actress Jamie Lee Curtis announced that she had considered using 'get n' any' as the designation of her California license plate in the early 1980s but had thought better of it.

get up one's nose *vb British*

to irritate, annoy. A colourful vulgarism used by both sexes since its popularization in TV comedies of the late 1960s, notably *Steptoe and Son* and *Till Death us do Part*.

- 'It really gets up my nose the way he harps on about his work.'

ghettoblaster, ghetto box *n*

a large stereo radio-cassette recorder, of the type carried, playing loudly, originally by black music enthusiasts in the late 1970s (just before the spread of personal cassette players with earphones). They were also known as **boogie boxes**, **rasta boxes** and **Brixton briefcases**.

ghost turds *n pl American*

another expression for **dust bunnies**.

gig *n*

a a musical engagement or performance. One of many terms, originating among pre-World-War II jazz musicians in the USA, which were adopted by the rock-music milieu in the 1960s. The exact origin of the word is obscure, but may be related to 'jig' in the sense of a dance.

- 'These lads are professional

musicians and gigs are their bread and butter.'
(*News of the World*, 29 May 1988).
b an appointment, session, stint or activity. Particularly in the 1970s the musicians' term was extended to refer to any one-off engagement or event (thus sometimes performing as a synonym of **trip** or **scene**).

- 'I've got the feeling this party isn't really my gig.'

gig *vb*

to perform at a **gig** or (more often) a series of gigs. An item of musician's jargon.

- 'We've been gigging round the South-west since March.'
- 'These guys [The Grateful Dead] will be gigging beyond the grave.'
(*Independent*, 26 February 1988).

giggle-farm/factory *n*

a psychiatric hospital.

giggle-stick *n*

a **joint**, cannabis cigarette. A jocular expression, typically used by middle-class students or otherwise respectable adults since the early 1970s. It is not part of the lexicon of hardened drug users.

giggle water *n*

alcoholic drink, particularly champagne or exotic spirits. An ingenue's jocular expression for the potential cause of unaccustomed hilarity.

gig-lamps *n pl British*

spectacles, large eye-glasses. A piece of slang that is probably as old as the objects referred to (carriage lamps) themselves. The term is still in occasional use, mainly among the elderly.

gilbert *n British*

See **green gilbert**.

gimp n

a a crippled or lame person, especially an old one. The term is thought to derive from a blend of grandfather and limp. The adjective 'gimpy' is applied, often derisively, to anything or anyone clumsy or crippled.

b an awkward, ineffectual or clumsy person. By extension from the first sense above. The word is popular among schoolchildren.

gin n Australian

an aboriginal woman. An abbreviation of aborigine which is over 100 years old. The term is derogatory and offensive.

ginch n

excellence, stylishness or elegance, expertise or skill. A now-rare term which achieved some popularity among young people in Australia and Britain in the 1960s. It is of unknown provenance and more usually occurs in the adjective form **ginchy**.

ginchy adj

excellent, skilful, smart, elegant. A word of unknown etymology which entered the teenage lexicon in the early 1960s, first in Australia and Britain and shortly thereafter, in the USA. Ginchy is said to have originated in surfing slang, denoting for instance, an expertly executed manoeuvre. The noun form **ginch** also exists, but has been less common; both words are now rare.

ginger n, adj British

a homosexual. Rhyming slang from 'ginger beer'; **queer**. A piece of pre-World-War II London working-class argot which is very much alive in spite of the decline in ginger-beer drinking.

gin jockey/burglar n

Australian

a white man who consorts with an aboriginal woman or women. These are rustic terms of racist disapproval and abuse which are still in evidence; the former pre-dates the latter. 'Burglar' occurs in other sexual contexts (as in **turd burglar**), implying furtiveness and deviance from social norms.

gink n

an awkward, ugly, foolish, clumsy person. The word is at least 100 years old in Britain and America, but its origin is obscure; it may be an invention, or derive from either Scottish dialect or Turkish or Arabic via Romany. Before the 1950s the word also meant simply a person, without the pejorative overtones.

● *'Who's the shortsighted gink in the corner?'*

ginormous adj

huge, vast. A children's blend of giant or gigantic and enormous.

gippo n

See **gyppo**.

gippy tummy n

See **gyppy tummy**.

girl-cott vb

to boycott. A feminist alternative, coined in the 1980s and used both facetiously and seriously.

girlie n British

a weak or effeminate person, sissy. A schoolboy expression of derision adopted facetiously by some adult males.

girl's blouse n British

See **big girl's blouse**.

gism n

an alternative spelling of **jissom**.

gismo, gizmo n
a gadget, unnamed object. An American armed-forces term adopted in Britain since the 1960s.

git n British
an unpleasant or worthless person. Many saloon-bar lexicologists have claimed that this word is an Arabic term of abuse, meaning 'pregnant camel', which was imported by servicemen who had been stationed in Egypt. The Arabic word does exist, but was probably noticed by British soldiers because the word git, a southern pronunciation of get (bastard or fool), was already part of their stock of vulgarisms.

- 'A frightfully clever chap called Stephen Fry, sending up all those smug gits who present kids' TV. (Hmmm . . . comes across as a bit of a smug git himself.)'
(News of the World, 15 May 1988).

give head vb American
(to be willing) to perform fellatio. A male term from the 1950s and 1960s, used typically by college students or servicemen during the hippy period of sexual experimentation. The phrase, and indeed the practice, seemed to assume a real and symbolic importance in male sexuality in the USA far greater than in Britain and Australia. The term has occasionally been applied to cunnilingus. (In the 1980s the words **skull** or 'some skull' have occasionally been substituted for head.)

- 'But she never lost her head, even when she was giving head.'
('Walk on the Wild Side', written and recorded by Lou Reed, 1972).

give it a burl vb
See **burl**.

give it one, give her one vb
British

to have sex (with a woman). A male vulgarism which has been commonly heard from the 1980s, both in boastful or assertive male conversation and in parodies thereof. A common elaboration is 'Give her one for the boys'.

give it some cog vb
to accelerate, increase power and speed. A motorcyclist's term of the 1980s. Cog is jargon for gear.

give it some wellie vb
See **wellie**.

given, givon n British
an unpleasant, despicable or stupid person. A term of abuse heard in the 1950s and 1960s, mainly in working-class and schoolchildren's usage. The word is of obscure origin (one suggestion is that it is a corruption or misunderstanding of 'gibbon') and does not appear to have been recorded elsewhere.

give someone the arse
Australian
to get rid of, jilt or dismiss someone; a variation of **give someone the boot/elbow/heave-ho**.

give the dog a bone vb British
to have sex (with a female). This uncommon male euphemism was popularized by the hit song 'Cool for Cats', recorded by Squeeze in 1978.

glar, glah n British
paint. A term used by house painters and artists in London, which has not apparently been previously recorded in writing. The origin is obscure, although some connection with glare, gloss or glue seems possible.

- 'Go on, slop on some more of the old glar.'
(Recorded, mural artist, Vauxhall, London, 1974).

Glasgow kiss n British

a head-butt. An alternative term of 'Gorbals kiss', meaning headbutt.

glass n

diamonds or other gems, in underworld argot.

glass (someone) vb British

to hit or slash with a glass or bottle. A term from the repertoire of brawlers.

glasshouse n British

an army prison. The military detention centre at Aldershot barracks had a glass roof in the early years of the 20th century and was notorious for the severity of its regime. Known as the 'Glass House' to inmates, it gave its name to other similar establishments.

glim vb, n British

(to use) a dimmed or shaded flashlight, in housebreaking or burglary. A piece of criminal argot.

glitch n

a snag, unforeseen fault or malfunction. This piece of aerospace technicians' jargon from the late 1960s has entered the common vocabulary in the era of high technology, referring particularly to computer problems. It is either a blend of **gremlin** and hitch, or from a Yiddish version of German *glitschen*, meaning to slip.

glitz n

glamour, (pseudo)sophisticated showiness. The word is a blend of glamour, ritzy and glitter and is probably a back-formation from **glitzy**. The term is usually used with a degree of implied criticism; it evokes superficiality and 'brittleness'. The word seems to have been an invention of journalists and writers in about 1984. In 1985 it was used as the title of a crime thriller by the American author Elmore Leonard.

● *'Here [Liberia] there is little glitz to the evangelical churches.'*
(*Sunday Correspondent*, 17 September 1989).

glitzy adj

glamorous, showy. A vogue word from 1985 to 1987, used particularly by journalists evoking materialistic but superficial glamour. It is generally more negative than positive in its connotations (*see* **glitz**).

glop vb British

to drink alcohol, particularly to swill beer. A student term of the 1980s.
● *'Glop, don't stop.'*
(Slogan in urinal, University of Essex, 1987).

glug vb, n

(to take) a drink or drinks of alcohol. A word which imitates the gurgle of pouring or swallowing.

G-man n American

an FBI agent. The underworld and journalese term is either a contraction of 'government man' or a reference to G-division of the Dublin police force in which some New York City policemen had served. The phrase is now obsolete.

G.M.F.U. n British

a 'grand military fuck-up'; a complete disaster or extreme case of ineptitude. An abbreviation used in public schools and by **Sloane Rangers**, as well as members of the armed services.

gnarly adj American

1 excellent.
2 awful, inadequate. Both senses of the word have been beloved by **Valley Girls** and their teenage imitators in the USA since the mid 1970s. The word is

thought to have originated in surfing jargon in the 1960s, referring to the texture of waves. By 1989 *Tatler* magazine reported the word as being in use among schoolboys at Eton. It is sometimes spelled **narly**.

gnaw the 'nana *vb Australian*

to perform fellatio. A masculine witticism recorded by the comic writer and actor, Barry Humphries in the 1960s.

go *vb*

to be sexually active and/or enthusiastic. The word is used in this sense, particularly in Britain, of women by men; its vulgarity was highlighted in the 'Nudge nudge, wink, wink' sketch by Eric Idle in the British TV series, *Monty Python's Flying Circus* (1970), in which he badgers a fellow drinker with importunate questions such as:
 • *'Your wife . . . does she go? I bet she does.'*
 See also **goer**.

go ape *vb*

See **ape**.

gob *n British*

mouth. The word was originally Irish and Scottish Gaelic for beak or mouth, becoming a British dialect term in about the 16th century. It is still more widespread (and considered less vulgar) in Ireland, in Liverpool, where the influence of Irish speech is strong, and in the north of England where the influence of post-Gaelic dialect lingers. In southern England it is mainly a schoolchildren's word.

gob *vb*

to spit. The ritualistic spitting at groups performing on stage indulged in by **punks** from 1976 on was known as *'gobbing'*.

gobble, gobble off *vb, n*

(to perform) oral sex, particularly fellatio. A vulgarism which is most widespread in Britain.

go belly-up *vb*

a to die.
 • *'Just another fat junkie who went belly-up.'*
 (*Tatler*, October 1989).
 b to fail or collapse. Said typically of a business or other venture.
 These senses are based on the image of a dying fish or a supine dead animal.
 • *'He lost all his equity when the firm went belly-up in the recession of '81.'*
 (*Wall Street*, US film, 1987).
 c to give in, yield, submit. This refers to the animal behaviour whereby the soft underparts are exposed to an adversary as a sign of submission.

gob job *n British*

an act of oral sex, usually referring to fellatio. A vulgarism from the late 1960s.

go Borneo *vb American*

a to get drunk.
 b to behave outrageously, go too far.
 Both senses are **preppie** terms indicating a regression to a supposed primitive jungle mentality, influenced by the numerous 'Wild men of Borneo' featured in travelling freak shows and the wrestling ring over the years. (The original tales of wild men living in the unexplored jungles of Borneo probably arose from the first reports of the orangutan.)

gobshite *n British*

a contemptible person. A Liverpudlian and northern term of abuse which, since the 1960s, has spread to other areas of Britain including London. It usually indicates great distaste or contempt (**gob** is mouth and **shite** excrement; both are regional vulgarisms).

gobslutch n British

a slovenly, messy person; someone with dirty personal habits, especially eating habits. A term from the north of England, heard in the long-running TV soap opera *Coronation Street*. (**Gob** is mouth, 'slutch' a variant form of slush.)

gobsmacked, gob-struck
adj British

astonished, struck dumb, left open-mouthed in amazement. From **gob**. These are originally Liverpudlian terms and are now widespread, used even by **Sloane Rangers** and **yuppies**, thanks initially to usage on TV comedies set in Liverpool. The expressions enjoyed a vogue in popular speech and journalistic use in 1988 and 1989. The phrases originally referred to a victim gaping after literally being punched in the mouth.
- *'He had expected to pay one tenth of the price and was said to be "gobsmacked" at the final cost.'* (Independent, 21 September 1989).

gobsmacking adj British

astonishing. A more recent derivation of **gobsmacked**.
- *'... but when Casaubon observes, "Life isn't simple, the way it is in detective stories," the gobsmacking banality can only be the author's.'* (Hugo Barnacle reviewing Umberto Eco, Independent, 14 October 1989).

go bush vb Australian

to go native, become countrified. *See also* **bush, bushie.**

godawful adj

terrible, appalling, pitiful. An inten-sive form of awful using the first element of goddamn.

god-botherer n British

an excessively pious person or a clergyman. A mainly middle-class expression applied particularly to institutional holy men such as prison and army chaplains, or to members of evangelical movements. The phrase has inspired the more frivolous non-specific insult, **dog-botherer**.

go down vb American

to take place, happen. A phrase from black street slang which became widespread in the later 1960s.

go down (on) vb

to perform oral sex. The term is used by and applied to both sexes; until the late 1960s it was a predominantly American expression. Elaborations used by high-school and college students included '*go down like water/ like a submarine*' (usually indicating shock at a person's readiness to indulge in this behaviour).

the God squad n British

the forces of organized religion, especially in evangelical form. The phrase has been applied scornfully to the Salvation Army, doorstep zealots and university Christian Unions alike, from the late 1950s to the present.

goer n

a sexually active and enthusiastic person; in the past, almost always said of women by men. The word can express admiration and approval or astonishment, rarely moral disdain.

gofer n

a minion or assistant who runs errands or delivers messages, etc. The word, originally an Americanism from the film industry (where it is now a job title) is a pun on 'go for (something)' and gopher, the North American burrowing rodent.

gogglebox n

a television set. This term has been in use since the late 1950s. At first used pejoratively by those disapproving of TV, then ironically by viewing enthusiasts, the word is now semantically neutral.

goggles n

spectacles, or someone wearing them. A schoolchildren's word.

goggy n British

a misfit, pupil rejected by schoolfellows. This invented term was reported by the Tatler of September 1989 to be in current use at Eton College. (Synonyms are gunk, spod, Wendy and zoid.)

goldbrick vb American

1 to shirk, idle or loaf. In this sense the word is often used in an armed service context.

2 to swindle. The reference is to painted 'gold' bricks sold by fraudsters.

gold-card vb

to assert oneself, behave ostentatiously or resolve a situation by the use of wealth. This probably ephemeral yuppie term of 1989 is inspired by the use of 'gold' versions of credit and charge cards such as American Express.

● 'Old Milward just gold-carded him.'

golden showers n

urine or urination. A jokey euphemism derived from the jargon of prostitution, in which urination is part of the sexual repertoire. An alternative term is water sports.

gollum n

a wild, uncatchable throw in a game of Frisbee. The term, from the vocabulary of American frisbee players, invokes the malevolent, puckish character from J.R.R. Tolkien's The Hobbit and The Lord of the Rings.

golly n

1 British a black or coloured person. Now a racist term only slightly less offensive than wog. The figure of the gollywog (a stuffed doll representing a black man or woman) has been vilified for its unfortunate connotations. (It was originally spelled Golliwogg, a character in childrens' stories by the American writer Bertha Upton.) This word was in fact used with two different intentions in the 1950s and 1960s. Among pro-black London bohemians it was an affectionate term; in the speech of others it was abusive.

2 Australian a gob of spittle. This vulgarism is also derived from gollywog, since wog is an Australian slang verb meaning to spit.

gome, gomer n American

a tediously studious fellow pupil or student, a swot. A preppie and teenage term based on the name (Gomer Pyle) of a fictional comic television character who personifies cloddishness. Perhaps coincidentally, gomeril or gomerel are archaic British dialect words for a simpleton.

gone adj

a in a euphoric state; ecstatic from the effects of drugs or music. The term is from the slang of jazz musicians of the 1950s, adopted by beatniks and hipsters. It now seems comically dated.

● 'I tried talking him out of it, but he was totally gone on booze and reefer.'

b inspiring ecstasy or euphoria; said

especially of music and usually preceded by 'real'.

- *'Some real gone jazz.'*
- *'A real gone chick.'*

gonef *n American*

an alternative spelling of **ganef**.

gong *n*

1 *British* a medal. The use of the word derives predictably from its resemblance to the metal gong which was ceremoniously sounded in colonial days, itself named from an echoic Malayan word.

- *'Tony Hart, Tory leader of Kent County Council, may not be in line for the usual gong dished out to holders of his office.'*
(*Private Eye*, April 1989).

2 *Australian* opium or an opium pipe. This usage may simply be an identification of both opium and gongs with the orient, or just possibly from the idea that being struck by sudden opium-induced euphoria is reminiscent of the striking of the gong. More prosaically it could be an alteration of the better known **bong**.

gongol *n British*

an idiot, an unfortunate simpleton or buffoon. The word is a blend of **goon** and mongol and was briefly a vogue term among London schoolchildren from 1979.

gonk *n British*

a dull-witted, buffoonish or grotesque person. Gonk was services slang in the 1950s for sleep (probably from 'conk out') but the word was used as a trademark name for troll-like dolls in the late 1960s. It is from this source that the word as a term of abuse or contempt arose, just as **muppet** did in the late 1970s. Gonk was applied by schoolchildren to unfortunate fellow-pupils and by hospital staff and police to the mentally retarded.

gonof *n American*

an alternative spelling of **ganef**.

gonzo *adj*

unrestrained, hedonistic, extremist as a style, particularly a journalistic style popularized by Hunter S. Thompson in his articles for *Rolling Stone* magazine in the early 1970s. Gonzo is said to be an earlier **hipster** term made up of **gone** and the '-o' ending (with a median s or z to aid pronunciation), but is more likely to be a straightforward borrowing of the Italian *gonzo*, meaning foolish.

- *'He was responsible for pioneering the style of modern journalism known as "Gonzo": the freewheeling and often self-indulgent method which has been copied by countless writers.'*
(*I-D* magazine, November 1987).

gonzo *n*

a a **gonzo** person (see adjective form).

b a fool, buffoon. This is the meaning of the Italian word *gonzo*, often used in that language to denote a simpleton.

goobatron *n*

a foolish person, **nerd**. An adolescent elaboration of **goober**, heard in the late 1980s.

goober *n American*

a a spot or pimple.

b a foolish person, especially one small in stature.

c a gob of spit.

All senses of the word are derived from a Southern American term for a peanut which is an Americanization of the Kongo word *nguba*.

the goods n

1 the real thing, first rate merchandise.
2 incriminating information, evidence.

goody-goody, goody-two-shoes n

an offensively virtuous or diligent person. The second phrase is more often heard in the USA; it derives from the heroine of a children's story, and implies a dislikeable prissiness.

● 'Superman's naive, a goody-two-shoes. Batman busts heads,'
(Joe Lihach of Village Comics, Observer, July 1989).

gooey n American

girlfriend. A fashionable but probably ephemeral term among teenagers in late 1987 and 1988. It is probably influenced by 'gooey-eyes' (romantic looks).

● 'How's your gooey?'

gooey nectar n American

an attractive girl, a particularly good-looking girlfriend. A teenagers' vogue word from late 1987 combining gooey (girlfriend) with 'nectar' (pretty girl).

goof n

a gormless, awkward or foolish person. Originally a rural British dialect word, goof became widely-used between the two world wars all over the English-speaking world, particularly in the USA.

goof vb American

1 to blunder, make a mistake, fail. The verb post-dates the noun form of the word.
2 to stare or look vacuous. A teenage term from goofy.
3 to indulge in wordplay, improvise

poetry. A word and an activity popular with the more literary **beats** in the 1950s.

goofball n American

1 a slow-witted and/or clumsy person. A mildly derogatory term derived from **goof** and **goofy**.
2 an illicit drug, typically a tranquilizer or barbiturate which renders the user slow or inert.

goof off vb American

to avoid responsibility, refuse to take things seriously. An Americanism since the 1940s, the word was briefly adopted by British **beatniks** in the early 1960s but did not establish itself.

goof-off n American

a a lazy or irresponsible person, a shirker. From the verb to **goof off**.
b an instance of or an excuse for shirking.

goof up vb American

to make a mistake, blunder. (An elaboration of **goof**.)

goofy adj

gormless, clumsy or slow-witted. A back formation from the noun goof.

googy-egg, googie, goog n

Australian
an egg. A piece of 'baby talk' transferred from the nursery to facetious adult usage.

gook n

1 American a North Vietnamese or any oriental. A derogatory term widely used by American soldiers in the Vietnam war, but originating much earlier, probably in the Filipino uprising of 1899, in which US troops referred to Filipinos as 'gugus' from a native word meaning tutelary spirit. Coincidentally, kuk is a Korean word-ending meaning person, and gook was also heard in the Korean conflict.

- ' . . . dinks, gooks, slopes – all sorts of slang to dehumanize them.'
  (Veteran of My Lai massacre, Channel 4 TV, 22 June 1988).

2 an alternative spelling of **guck**.

goolies, ghoulies n pl British

testicles. In northern Indian languages *gooli* means pellet or pill. The word was picked up by British colonial troops at the turn of the century as a euphemism for testicle. This sense was reinforced by a more circuitous route; the gypsies' language, Romany, also adopted the Indian word *gooli*, from which the English and Australian schoolchildren's word 'gully', a marble, derived. **Marbles** itself was a common euphemism for testicles.

- 'The temperature further increased each time we dipped a deep fried fish ball into the special Oh' Boy sauce. "It's enough to take your goolies off," gasped my sister-in-law.'
  (Craig Brown, The Sunday Times magazine, 8 October 1989).

goon n

a a foolish, clumsy or clownish person. This sense of the word was popularized in Britain by the zany radio series The Goon Show in the 1950s, and was earlier used in the Popeye cartoons for 'Alice the Goon', a huge dull-witted character. This in turn was probably influenced by a pre-existing word in British dialect meaning vacuous or simple (and distantly related to 'yawn').

b a thug. The word was already being used in this sense in the USA in the late 1930s, typically of hired strike-breakers. It was later applied particularly to strong-arm men of low intelligence

used by gangsters to intimidate or punish.

- 'Tell Simpson to get his goons to lay off – then we'll talk.'
  (Rockford Files, US TV series, 1978).

goony n American

a foolish person. A variant form of **goon**, mainly heard among children and teenagers.

goop, goopy, n

a fool, **goof**. A fairly rare but long-lived word. It seems to date from the turn of the century and is now more common in Australia than Britain or America. It appears to be an invention influenced by **goof** (which existed as a rustic dialect term before becoming a general colloquialism), dupe, etc.

gooper n American

a gob of spit. This is probably a variant form of **goober**.

goopy adj

foolish, clumsy or unfortunate. An uncommon adjective influenced by **goop** and **goofy**.

- 'To keep goopy stills from love scenes out of circulation, his contracts stipulate that the studio can't release his photograph without his approval.'
  (Elle magazine, May 1989).

gooseberry n British

See **play gooseberry**.

goosegog n British

a gooseberry, in the literal sense. A nursery term also used by adults and teenagers.

go south vb

to perform oral sex. A rarely-heard euphemism.

goss n British

gossip (in the sense of rumour, scandal and chatter, not of a person). A vogue term which appeared in 1988 and established itself in the language of teenagers and writers in teenage magazines. Although the shortened form resembles the abbreviated journalese of *Variety* magazine in the USA, it appears to be a native British coinage.

● '*A triff new weekly mag with all the goss on your fave TV stars.*'
(BBC TV advertisement for *Fast Forward* magazine, 1989).

goth n British

a young person characterized by a devotion to a 'doom-laden' or bombastic style of 1980s post-punk rock music and the wearing of black clothing and quasi-medieval insignia jewellery, etc. Goths formed one of the persistent youth sub-cults throughout the 1980s (as opposed to **anoraks, Sloanes**, etc.).

● '*Goth metal, grunge rocking, thrash merchants with a grebo edge.*'
(*Independent*, July 1989).

go the full distance vb

to be arrested, tried, convicted and sent to prison. A euphemism heard among the criminal fraternity and the police in the 1970s and 1980s. The metaphor is taken from boxing jargon.

go troppo vb Australian

See **troppo**.

gouch out vb British

a to botch a drug **fix**, fail to hit a vein. A term used by drug addicts in the mid 1960s.

b to become semi-conscious, **nod out**. The difference between these two meanings seems to be based on a misunderstanding, but since the origin of the term is obscure (a rather far-fetched

notion is that the supposedly somnolent South American gaucho is the inspiration, although gauchos in fact are anything but somnolent) it is not clear which is the 'true' meaning.

gouge vb American

to intimidate, damage, do down. A business term of the 1980s.

gouger n Irish

a **yob**, lout or thug. The word is Dublin slang of the 1980s.

gourd n American

head. The word is almost always heard in the phrase '*out of one's gourd*'.

governor n British

See **guvnor**.

go walkabout vb

to daydream, lose concentration. The term derives from the Australian aborigine practice of leaving the community to go into the bush on a mystical quest (when they are said to 'go walkabout'). It was applied by journalists to the tendency of the tennis player, Evonne Goolagong, to allow her concentration to slip during matches and now is applied to any sort of aberrant mental behaviour.

gozunder n

See **gazunda**.

grab n British

1 overtime. An old London working-class term used, for example, by workers in the public services such as railway personnel.

● '*Do some grab/get some grab/he's on (the) grab.*'

2 a bag. A word used in the north of England and Scotland.

215

graft n

1 a work, particularly hard, unrelenting or persistent work.

b a job, one's occupation.

2 *American* dishonesty, bribery, or peddling influence in public or political life.

Both the British and American senses of the word ultimately derive from a British dialect word descended from the Anglo-Saxon verb *grafan*, related to grave, and meaning to dig.

graft vb British

a to work, in particular to work hard and constantly.

b to engage in clever, devious or dishonest money-making schemes, especially those involving selling in street markets, fairs, etc.

c to pursue criminal activities.

All the senses of graft originate in a dialect word meaning to dig, from the Anglo-Saxon verb grafan.

grafter n British

a a worker, especially a humble, hard-working or long-suffering worker.

b a person who makes a living from clever, devious or dishonest schemes. This word is applied in particular to street traders.

c a criminal, particularly an habitual petty criminal. These senses all derive from the verb to **graft**.

grand n

a thousand pounds or a thousand dollars. The word originated in the jargon of American sportsmen, gamblers and, later, criminals. It was adopted in the same milieus in Britain by 1950.

- *'Zackerman rings and – this'll make you smile – he goes, he goes, I'll give you a hundred grand plus the car and that, and fifty in your hand.'*

(*Serious Money*, play by Caryl Churchill, 1987).

- *'I was buying it by the grand.'*

(*News of the World*, 29 October 1989).

grandstand vb American

to put on a bravura display, show off to an audience. The expression comes from the world of sport and was originally an Americanism. It is often used as an adjective as in 'a grandstand play'.

grass n

1 herbal cannabis, marihuana. British smokers traditionally preferred hashish, but began to import more marihuana in the mid 1960s. Grass was the predominant American term and had largely supplanted **bush**, **pot**, **herb**, etc. in British speech by 1970.

- *'Well, the first thing they wanted was some grass.'*

(Rockstar's minder, *Guardian*, 12 December 1987).

2 *British* an informer. Originally the expression was 'grasshopper' as rhyming slang for copper; the meaning was then transferred to the '*copper's nark*' or informer and by the 1940s grass had become established in the underworld lexicon. By the 1970s the word was also widespread among schoolchildren and others. 'Supergrass' was a journalese elaboration denoting a highly significant informer.

grass (someone up) vb British

to inform (on someone), betray (someone) to the police or authorities. The usage was originally to '*grass on someone*' or to '*grass to the authorities*'. In the 1980s the London underworld expression to **grass someone up** is widely used, not least among schoolchildren, who had adopted it from TV police dramas and documentaries. For the etymology see the noun, **grass**, sense **2**.

graze vb
to eat while standing up and/or occupied in some other activity. A piece of **yuppie** jargon from the late 1980s.

grease n American
money. An underworld term of the early 20th century, adopted by **beatniks** among others and, more recently, by teenagers. From the notion of greasing the wheels of commerce, or money as a social lubricant.

● 'If we had some grease we could hit town this weekend.'

grease vb American
to kill. The word appears to have had the specific meaning of shoot (probably inspired by 'grease-gun') until the 1970s when it acquired its additional and more general sense.

● 'One move and we grease your friend.'

greaseball n American
a a person of Hispanic or Mediterranean origin or appearance. An offensive term which has been in use since before World War II.

b a person, such as a cook or mechanic, who works in literally greasy conditions.

greaser n
1 British a **rocker**, motorcycle enthusiast, scruffy unfashionable person. A scathing term adopted by **mods** and students to refer to **rockers** in 1964. The word has gradually fallen out of use since that time.

2 American an Hispanic or person of Mediterranean origin. The term refers to a supposedly greasy complexion; it implies great contempt and causes offence.

● 'Crazy greasers – they've always

got bees in their panty hose about something.'
(P.J. O'Rourke writing on Panama in Holidays in Hell, 1988).

3 a petty criminal, juvenile delinquent, etc., specifically one who wears hair oil, a leather jacket, etc.

4 a toady, sycophant or hypocrite, from the notion of greasiness equated with unctuous, devious behaviour.

grease-up n British
a meal of fried food, particularly a cooked breakfast; the sort of meal served in a **greasy spoon**.

greasy spoon n
a transport cafe, diner or other cheap restaurant. A mildly derogatory but generally affectionate term for the kind of eating place where most if not all of the hot dishes are fried in animal fat. The expression seems to have originated in Canada or the USA in the 1930s.

● 'There's nothing for breakfast except toast. Let's go down the greasy spoon – I fancy a good grease-up.'
(Recorded, teacher, London, 1987).

grebo, greebo n British
a scruffy young rock-music enthusiast, typically long-haired, unkempt and leather-jacketed. The word was coined in 1985 in the Midlands to describe a youth sub-group of gauche but earnest heavy-rock devotees. Grebo does not so much denote a separate cult (its proponents display characteristics of **rockers**, **hippies**, **goths** and **punks**) but a new term for a pre-existing phenomenon (as in the case of **anorak**).

● 'Brummie "grebo" boors Pop Will Eat Itself sound frightful on paper and even worse (in the best possible sense, you understand) in the flesh.'
(Independent, 11 May 1989).

● 'Greboes drink stout and snakebite,

smoke *Players No.6 (packets of ten),
wear y-fronts and dirty torn jeans,
drive big bikes, and go out with girls
who don't shave their armpits.'*
(*I-D* magazine, November 1987).

● *'Goth metal, grunge rocking, thrash
merchants with a grebo edge.'*
(*Independent*, July 1989).

green, green stuff n

money. Banknotes of all denominations are green in the USA (see also
long green). In Britain, pound notes
were green until replaced by coins in
the 1980s.

green and blacks n pl

Librium capsules. Librium is the
trade name of a tranquilizer
(chlordiazopoxide) much used by narcotics abusers in the 1960s and 1970s,
often to counteract the effects of stimulant drugs. The preparation did indeed
come in green and black capsules.

greenback n American

a banknote. US paper money is
predominantly green in colour.

greenback vb American

to subsidize, underwrite, finance. A
recent derivation of the well-established noun form, greenback is employed as a novel synonym for bankroll.

greenery n

money, banknotes. The term is a
popular one in the USA where all denominations of banknotes are green. In
Britain the word was used while green
one-pound notes were in circulation
and fell into desuetude in the 1980s
when they were replaced by coins.

green gilbert n British

a thick piece of mucus from the nose.
A schoolchildren's term which has
been in use since the 1950s and is now

considered respectable enough to be
said on television. The choice of Gilbert is due to the supposed inherent
comicality of the name and to its echoes of gobbet, glutinous, etc.

greenie n

1 *British* a one-pound note. From the
predominant colour.

2 *American* a (Heineken) beer. A
preppie term, often extended to refer
to other brands, from the colour of the
bottle and label of the popular import.

green welly, green-welly brigade adj, n British

(in the style of or characteristic of)
upper-middle-class young people who
indulge in country pursuits such as
riding and hunting and who typically
wear Barbour jackets and green wellington boots. The term **green-welly
brigade** is used pejoratively to refer to
wealthy townspeople who visit the
country at weekends (usually staying
in second homes), and comments of
their habit of 'dressing-down' in a
pseudo-country style. The urban
equivalent is **Sloane Ranger**, although
that term was out of favour by about
1988. The phrase 'green welly' was
sufficiently well known to be used as a
caption in a press advertisement for
'environment-friendly' Saab cars in
1989.

gregory n British

a cheque. A piece of rhyming slang
from the late 1980s, playing on the
name of the film star Gregory Peck. The
same rhyme has also been recorded
with the alternative meaning of 'neck',
but this, given the rarity of conversations concerning that part of the body,
seems unlikely to supplant the financial sense.

● *'I'm just popping out to sausage
[and mash: cash] a gregory.'*

(Recorded, property speculator, Bath, 1988).

grem, gremmie n Australian

a a novice or incompetent surfer.

b a novice or incompetent skateboarder. A teenage term imported into Britain in the late 1970s. The variant forms are probably based on **gremlin**.

gremlin n

an unexplained flaw, malfunction or error. A word used particularly by British soldiers in World War I, and American airmen, in World War II, evoking a malicious spirit. (The word is a form of the Irish *gruaimin* meaning a bad-tempered little fellow.)

grey, the grey n British

1 a a conventional, conformist person. A vogue term in British counterculture circles from about 1966 to 1968. The word had the same dismissive or pitying overtones as **straight** which had supplanted it by the end of the 1960s.

b the grey denoted the collective mass of conformism, dullards and authority figures, as opposed to the (literally as well as metaphorically) colourful **hippies**.

These terms had greater resonance for British nonconformists than may now be apparent, in that prior to 1968 most British males did in fact dress predominantly in grey or other muted colours.

2 *American* the 'white' man. A derisive term used by blacks.

greybeard n

an 'old-timer'. The word probably originates (as 'graybeard') in the USA where it is a jargon term for a long-serving senior officer in various fields, such as civil aviation, from the literary term for an old man.

See **longbeard**.

griefy adj British

depressing, troublesome. A fairly rare middle-class teenage and student term from the early 1970s.

● '*I mean we've all tried to fly from upstairs windows . . . we know those griefy scenes, man!*' ('American ethno-botanist' in cartoon by Posy Simmonds, *Guardian*, 1980).

grifter n American

an untrustworthy, suspect or dishonest person, typically a gambler or minor fraudster. Grifter is a word from the early 20th century which is a blend of graft and drifter. It was used by Raymond Chandler in his detective fiction and was still occasionally heard in the late 1980s.

grill vb

to interrogate. Police and armed-forces slang of the 1950s which has become a widely-used colloquialism.

grind vb

to have sex. An unromantic description, widespread in the 1960s, via an earlier phrase 'bump and grind', describing sex or a suggestive dance, especially the motions of a striptease or burlesque artist. Grind in the noun form has been used in a sexual sense for approximately 400 years.

grind n

1 an act of sexual intercourse. A widespread vulgarism since the 1960s. 'Bump and grind' was considered an apt metaphor for sex, or a simulation of the sex act. Grind itself has been used with a sexual connotation since the 16th century.

2 *American* a **swot**, a tediously diligent student, in high-school and college terminology.

3 the quotidian reality, oppressive routine, as in the 'daily grind'.

grit n

courage and integrity, determination. A word which appeared in British English in the mid 19th century, probably imported from America. The adjective 'gritty' is a British colloquialism with the rather different meaning of rugged and abrasive.

groceries n pl

See **blow one's cookies/groceries**.

grockle n British

an unwelcome outsider, tourist or visitor. A Devon dialect term applied contemptuously to summer visitors by local residents since the 1960s. The word has been adopted by the many non-native **hippies** and travellers living in the West Country to refer to anyone who is not approved of. (The term has also been heard in other parts of Britain.) Grockle is claimed to derive from the name of the famous clown Grock. In Cornwall the equivalent is **emmet**.

● 'That unmistakeable grockle smell – stale fat and farts.'
(Recorded, resident of Torquay, 1976).
● 'We never go in that pub – full of grockles.'
(Recorded, resident of Parracombe, North Devon, 1986).

grody adj American

an American version of **grotty**, used typically by **Valley Girls**. A word dating from the mid 1970s which now seems established in the teen lexicon. It is often intensified in the phrase 'grody to the max'.

grog vb, n

(to indulge in) alcoholic drink. The noun form, from the rum and hot water served in the British navy since the 18th century, can now refer to any strong drink, or even beer. It is generally heard among middle-aged speakers. The verb 'to grog' or 'grog up' (in Australian English to 'grog on') is rarer and restricted mainly to a younger age group. It implies heavy and constant imbibing. 'Old Grog' (from the grogram, or silk and wool cloak he wore) was the nickname of Admiral Vernon who aroused his sailors by ordering the dilution of their rum ration in 1740.

● 'Not realizing one's dependence on the grog is where the wheels touch the road, eh?'
('Edmund Heep' in a cartoon by Posy Simmonds, Guardian, 1979).

groid n

a black person. This racist term of abuse, a shortening of the adjective negroid, was particularly prevalent in police usage in London in the late 1980s. It also exists in American speech.

● 'Travelling around – being an International Knee-grow (or a "groid" as the Met would have it) – thanks chaps!'
(Lenny Henry, Time Out magazine, 26 July 1989).

grolley, grollie n British

a look or glance. A word of unknown origin heard in London speech in the late 1980s, usually in the phrase 'have/take a grolley at that'.

grommet n British

1 an imaginary fixture, component or part, an unspecified or unnameable object. A grommet is actually an eyelet or metal ring, originating in a nautical context and deriving from the archaic French gourmette or groumette, meaning bridle ring.

2 a a woman or women regarded as sex objects.

b sexual activity.

These now obsolescent uses of the word were in use in the 1950s among male speakers. They arise from the nautical term for ring or eyelet, used as a euphemism for the female genitals.

groove n

an enjoyable experience or situation. An Americanism derived from the verb to **groove** (on) and the adjective **groovy**. The word was **hip** jargon of jazz musicians since the 1930s, later becoming part of the **hippy** lexicon and as such was also heard outside the USA until the mid 1970s. It now sounds very dated.

See **in the groove**.

groove vb

to experience a sensation of well-being, fellow-feeling, to feel in tune with one's surroundings. This well-known and characteristic **hippy** term originates in the slang of jazz musicians and others for whom being in the groove meant being at one with the melody, with one's fellow players, etc (like a needle in the groove of a record). The word subsequently became a pivotal one for hippies, for whom it expressed a notion of enjoyable one-ness with one's environment that hitherto lacked a name. The expression was hackneyed by the time James Taylor was ridiculed by British rock journalists for his declaration at a mid-1970s concert at the Royal Albert Hall that he 'grooved to the vibes'. To 'groove on something' was another typical form.

- '*Groovin' down a crowded avenue/ doin' anythin/ we like to do.*'
  ('Groovin', recorded by the Young Rascals, 1967).

groover n

1 a fashionable, dynamic **hip** person. A 1960s formation from **groovy** and the verb to **groove**.

2 a tedious person, **swot**. A probably ephemeral usage of the late 1980s, based on the newly pejorative teenage sense of **groovy**.

- '*Charmless college swats are no longer known as "nerds" but are on the receiving end of a whole variety of new insults including "dweeb", "geek", "goober", "wonk", "corndog", "goob-a-tron" and "groover".*'
  (Independent magazine, 24 December 1988).

groovy adj

1 satisfactory, satisfying, fine. A term of approval, sometimes in the form of a mild exclamation from the **hippy** era. The adjective is derived from the verb to **groove**; originally an American term, it was adopted by British rock musicians, **beatniks**, and, later, **hippies** from about 1965. It now sounds risibly dated, unless used ironically.

- '*Wouldn't you agree, baby you and me, we've got a groovy kind of love.*'
  ('Groovy Kind of Love', Patti Labelle and the Blue Belles, 1965; also recorded in the late 1980s by Phil Collins and used as the title track for the film Buster, 1989).
- '*You see we have a lot of other groovy things going for us, and not just concerning music.*'
  (Mick Jagger, Record Mirror, 26 August 1967).

2 American tedious, dull. A vogue word of 1988 among adolescents. It is probably inspired by ironic use of the dated term of approbation.

- '*Another 1960s catchword, "groovy", has mysteriously turned into its opposite, now signifying stodgy or old-fashioned.*'
  (Independent magazine, 24 December 1988).

grope n

an act of fondling or sexual caressing, 'heavy petting'.

● 'A quick grope in the back of a car.'

grope vb

to fondle sexually, particularly in a clumsy fashion. A teenage code word of the 1950s which is now widespread in informal English.

See group grope.

gross n British

the offence of 'gross indecency', in police jargon.

● 'They got him for gross.'

gross adj

disgusting, distasteful. An Americanism of the mid 1960s, particularly popular among teenage girls. It is a fashionable usage of the standard term (from Latin grossus, thick, via French and Middle English) in its sense of excessive, vulgar or obscene.

● 'Like Joan's, Marlene's entire range of expression was pretty much limited to "far out", "super" and "gross".'
(The Serial, Cyra McFadden, 1976).

gross-out n American

a disgusting act or situation. A favourite term of teenagers since the mid 1960s, usually said with excited or exaggerated distaste.

● 'After totting up the score-sheet of exposed breasts ("garbonzas"), mutilations, rolling heads, gross-outs, auto-collisions, he awards a number of stars and puts his seal of approval on a film.'
(Observer, 9 April 1989).

gross (someone) out vb
American

to disgust or repel. The expression is normally used by a speaker to refer to

their own distaste. It is a teenagers' term, popular since the late 1960s.

● 'Would you move your socks. Like out into the patio or something? I mean they're really grossing me out.'
(The Serial, Cyra McFadden, 1976).

Grosvenor Squares vb British

rhyming slang for flares, i.e. bell-bottom trousers. This phrase was an ephemeral youth term of the late 1970s used contemptuously of the (by then) unfashionable style and the remnants of the hippy movement who still favoured it. London's Grosvenor Square, the site of the US embassy, was the scene of peace demonstrations by students and hippies during the Vietnam war. A later, more lasting alternative piece of rhyming slang for the same item was 'Lionel Blairs'.

● 'Belinda has discovered an important pair of "jeans" dating from the late 1960s. These are most certainly rare items, known by collectors as "Grosvenor Squares".'
(Caption to cartoon by Posy Simmonds, Guardian, 1981).

grot n British

a dirt, squalor, unpleasantness. Although this word was a back-formation from the adjective 'grotty', it no longer reflects that word's origin in 'grotesque'.

● 'I can't go on living among all this grot.'

b a dirty, slovenly or disreputable person.

● 'He really is an awful grot.'

grotty adj British

unpleasant, revolting or distasteful. The word became extremely popular in the early 1960s and quickly passed into the middle-class lexicon where it is still found. Grotty, a typically Liverpudlian shortening of grotesque, became popular among young people, via the influence of the 'Mersey boom' in the early 1960s. It was adopted by some Americans in imitation of British usage, although an American form, **grody**, arose in the 1970s.

the ground n British

the area under the jurisdiction of a particular police station, the '*manor*' or **turf**. A psychological rather than official delimitation.

- '*Members of the force from adjoining stations have no right of entry into or patrol of the ground save by invitation.*'
(Inside the British Police, Simon Holdaway, 1983).

grounded adj American

confined to one's home, deprived of one's car keys. A popular parental means of chastizing American teenagers. The image is of course that of a plane and/or pilot prevented from flying.

- '*I can't go out tonight, I'm grounded too, you know.*'
(The Stepford Children, US TV film, 1987).

group-grope n

a group 'heavy-petting' session. A teenagers' term from the early 1960s. The phrase was later applied to full scale **gang bangs** or orgies, and scathingly to group therapy sessions.

groupie n

a girl who associates with or follows a musical group or star. The term originally assumed and still implies the sexual availability of the girl. The word and the phenomenon were publicized in the late 1960s, particularly in the semi-autobiographical book *Groupie* by the British writer Jenny Fabian in 1968 and the US film *Groupie Girl*, 1969. Groupie was a con-

descending or pejorative expression used by the musicians themselves, and by jealous or disapproving fans in the mid 1960s in Britain whence it spread. Nowadays the word is usually used in the general sense of devotee, admirer.

the Grove n

Ladbroke Grove and its Notting Hill environs, one of the focuses of the black community during the 1960s and 1970s. Many social subcultures were centred on this area.

grub n

1 food. The word has existed with this meaning since at least the 17th century, inspired by the action of grubbing around.

- '*At the weigh-in, Reynolds, in the red corner, weighed eight stone, two pounds.*'
- '*Give the poor sod some grub!*'
(Spike Milligan, Adolf Hitler, My Part in his Downfall, 1971)

2 a Australian a dirty, slovenly person. This sense of the word was in British use until the early 20th century, but is now obsolete there.

b British a younger child, especially a grubby or defiant one. From the terminology of prep and public schools.

Both these senses of grub derive from the lowly insect larva.

gruey, gruie adj British

'gruesome', distasteful, unpleasant. A middle-class teenagers' and students' term from the early 1970s.

grumble (and grunt) n British

the female genitals or a woman or women in general seen as sexual partners. The word or phrase is rhyming slang for **cunt**.

grunge n American

a anything dirty, distasteful, squalid

or sordid. This adolescent coinage is now heard in Britain.

- '*For Martin Amis is the Wodehouse of grunge . . . '*
(David Sexton, *Sunday Correspondent*, 17 September 1989).
b a boring or irritating person or task.

grunt n American

a (dog) soldier, an army private. A derogatory term sometimes used ironically by the soldiers themselves, deriving from the supposedly low intelligence and predilection for grumbling of the humble enlisted man or conscript.

- '*The grunts were conscious that they were involved in a drug-and-rock 'n' roll extension. Most of the combatants, black and white, came from the working class.*'
(Michael Herr, *Observer*, 15 January 1989).

grunter n

a a very primitive, slovenly or ignorant person.

b *Australian* a sluttish woman with whom only sex and the most rudimentary conversation are supposedly possible.

- '*Man, she's a grunter.*'
(*Razorback*, Australian film, 1984).
c a bad-tempered adult. In schoolchildren's and teenagers' jargon of the 1980s.

gruntled adj

satisfied, gratified. A jocular back-formation from the standard disgruntled (in which 'gruntle' in fact means grumble and is related to grunt). This rare word is typically used by educated speakers, saloon-bar philosophers and amateur or professional comedians.

- '*I was feeling extremely gruntled following my success.*'

G.T.P. adj British

'good to police'. A police jargon designation of people and places where the police can expect a warm welcome.

gubbins n British

a a gadget or unnamed object; equipment, paraphernalia. The term comes from a Middle English word *gobyn* (related to gobbet), meaning a bit or portion. Until the 1920s the word usually meant one's necessary (army) equipment. It has retained this idea of something useful or necessary, but unnamed or unnameable.

b extras, 'trimmings'. This sense of the word, typically applied to meals, is inspired by sense **1**.

- '*I'd like it with all the gubbins.*'

guck n

a sticky substance, muck. A mainly American nursery word blending 'goo' and 'muck'. Also spelled **gook**.

guff vb, n British

(to) **fart**. An old childish vulgarism which has been revived in the late 1980s as part of a vogue for pseudo-nursery slang among students and others.

- '*The force of the gigantic guff you used has wrecked the entire drainage system.*'
(*Johnny Fartpants*, Viz Comic, April/May 1988).

guffie n British

a **fart**. A variation of **guff**.

guinea n American

an Italian. An offensive term, the origin of which is obscure, but which might derive from a proper name such as Gianni or Giovanni, or else by a tortuous process from the name of the African country (whence slaves were exported).

gumball n American

a dark-coloured, highly-refined form of heroin. A drug-users' term from the late 1980s.

gumballs n pl American

the flashing lights on the roof of a police car, from their supposed resemblance to multi-coloured chewing gum or boiled sweets.

- '*He'd be on him before he hit Woodward, nail him with the gumballs flashing blue and siren turned up to high yelp.*' (Elmore Leonard, *The Switch*, 1978).

gumbo n

See **hippy gumbo**.

gumby n

an aggressively gormless, clumsy and/or dull person. From the name of a character personifying these qualities in the TV comedy series *Monty Python's Flying Circus* in the 1970s (in turn partially inspired by Peter Cook's earlier invention 'E. L. Wisty'). The personification and name were taken up by British and American teenagers in particular.

gumshoe n, vb

a detective, private eye or plainclothes police officer. The term was first used in the USA early in the 20th century and referred to the silent rubber-soled shoes that detectives supposedly wore as opposed to uniformed police officers' heavy boots. Gumshoe (now a word largely confined to humorous or literary use) has also been employed as a verb meaning to plod the beat or follow a trail of clues.

gunge n British

a sticky substance, muck. A slang term of the 1960s which has become a middle-class colloquialism.

gung-ho adj

excessively eager, enthusiastic and/or assertive, especially in the context of patriotism, jingoism and military aggression. This phrase was thought to be a Chinese rallying cry. (The words 'gung ho' were part of the Chinese title of an Industrial Cooperative and were assumed wrongly to mean 'work together'.) It was adopted by the Marine Corps and later for general American military use in World War II. It became known outside the USA to a limited extent during the Korean war and more particularly during the Vietnam war, now being so well known as to constitute a colloquialism rather than slang term.

gunk n

1 muck, goo, sticky stuff. An American version of the British **gunge**, now heard in Britain, too. By extension it can also mean debris or rubbish.

2 British a school misfit. A schoolboy term reported to be in current use in Eton College by *Tatler* magazine in September 1989.

gunsel n American

a a callow youth.

b a gunman.

The latter meaning is now more widely encountered, but the former, with overtones of punkishness, comes from the Yiddish slang for young man (*gantsel* or *ganzl*; gosling), and was the sense in which it was used in crime novels and *films noirs* in the 1930s. The second meaning is based on a misreading of the first.

gunship n British

an unmarked police car, in the jargon of the late 1980s. Although partially ironic, the choice of term illustrates the shift in self-perception since the days of the **bobby** on his 'manor'.

- '*They call their specially souped-*

up cars gunships and when the order comes to go in the command is: "Attack! Attack! Attack!".'

guppy n

an environmental **yuppie**. An ephemeral journalese coinage blending green and yuppie, inspired by the popular tropical fish.

gurgle n British

(an) alcoholic drink. A fairly predictable euphemism, used typically by pub habitués and other hearty drinkers. It is probably influenced by **gargle**.

● *'Fancy popping down to the Swan for a bit of a gurgle?'*
(Recorded, middle-aged drinker, Pangbourne, 1986).

gurgler n Australian

a toilet. The word usually occurs in the phrase *'down the gurgler'*.

gurk vb, n

a British (to) belch, burp.

b Australian (to) fart.

Imitative words used, mainly by children, since the 1950s.

gutless adj British

cowardly, feeble. A word which is usually used with great contempt or dislike, whether of a person, or, for example, a poorly performing car. It often occurs in the form of the phrase *'gutless wonder'*, probably inspired by **chinless wonder**, heard in Australia as well as Britain.

gut-rot n

cheap, low-quality alcoholic drink. This phrase is probably more widespread in Britain and Australia than the alternative **rot-gut**. Unlike rot-gut, it is occasionally also used to refer to food.

gutsache n

a miserable, complaining person, **misery-guts**. The expression is particularly popular in Australia, but is also heard in Britain. The image evoked is of someone perpetually suffering from dyspepsia or provoking indigestion in others.

gutted adj British

devastated, deeply disappointed, saddened or shocked. A vogue word among working-class and lower-middle-class speakers in the late 1980s, perhaps encouraged by the over-use of the word by sportsmen and sports commentators. The concept has also been expressed subsequently by the alternatives **kippered** and **filleted**.

● *'Slaughtered, gutted and heartbroken/ With no spirit or no soul/ My emotions have been stolen/ Love has left me with this hole.'*
('Slaughtered, Gutted, and Heartbroken', recorded by Squeeze, 1989).

● *'24 hours before work on the commercial was due to start the answer came from Central. It was no. After all those years – just no. I was gutted.'*
(Paul "Benny" Henry, News of the World, 8 January 1989).

gutty, gutsy adj British

bold, brave or 'bolshie'. A late 1980s coinage, popular in unsophisticated speech, which is a back-formation from the well-established colloquial sense of guts as courage.

guv n British

a respectful term of address to a male, in working-class usage. Said invariably by as well as to men, guv is a shortening of the almost equally widespread **guvnor**, meaning boss.

guvnor, governor n British

a boss, chief or leader. A descriptive term or term of address used by, to and about males in working-class speech. This widespread colloquial form of governor arose in the early 19th century and shows no sign of dying out. Governor, then spelled correctly, was recorded as a slang term for one's employer as early as 1802; Charles Dickens later referred to it as a slang synonym for 'old man' or 'boss' when referring to one's father. In the 1980s it acquired a further nuance in the form 'the guvnor' as an acknowledged expert or leading exponent (for instance among rock musicians and fans).

● 'I'll be alright 'cos I believe in the life hereafter. I mean, Jesus was the governor wasn't he?'
(East Ender, The Sunday Times, 2 June 1968).

guy n

a man, person. This now well-established term, occasionally applied to females, too, was considered an Americanism and slang in British English before the late 1960s. The term originally referred to an awkward or grotesque person, by analogy with the effigies of Guy Fawkes made for burning on November 5. The similarity with the Yiddish goy (a gentile, from the Hebrew goi, tribe) is almost certainly coincidental.

gweeb, gweebo n American

a stupid, dull, person. A late 1980s variation on **dweeb**, coined by teenagers. It is probably unrelated to the British **grebo**.

gwot n American

a contemptible person. This high-school term of great distaste, heard in the late 1980s, is an invention, obviously influenced by other evocations of unpleasantness such as grotesque, **weed, twat**, etc.

● 'Oh god, not him, he's such a gwot.'
(Some Kind of Wonderful, US film, 1987).

gyppo n

1 a gypsy.

2 an Egyptian. A neutral rather than pejorative term in origin, gyppo was, and is, sometimes extended in uneducated speech to encompass other Arabs or Muslims.

gyppy tummy n British

an attack of diarrhoea. A phrase from the colonial era. The equivalent of **Delhi belly**, **Montezuma's revenge**, etc.

gypsy n British

a dancer or chorus girl. A theatrical term for those continually on the move from show to show seeking a living.

● 'It's been a boom time for dancers, known as gypsies in the trade, with a glut of big-budget musicals.'
(Sunday Mirror, 20 January 1989).

H

H n

heroin. This was the most popular term among British drug users in the 1950s and 1960s before being supplanted by **smack, scag**, etc.

- *'He's been on H for years.'*

h. a. n British

home address. An abbreviation from the jargon of the police, particularly the Flying Squad, in the 1980s.

- *'We'll have to stop him before he gets to his h.a.'*

habit n

an addiction, a 'drug habit'. A drug user and law enforcer's term, sometimes extended to refer to more innocuous addictions.

- *'A $100 a day habit.'*

hack n

1 a journalist, professional writer. The word, inspired by the image of a worn-out workhorse, has traditionally denoted a disreputable, unprincipled, mercenary reporter or writer. Since the late 1960s, if not earlier, journalists have appropriated it to refer to themselves proudly rather than self-deprecatingly. Hack is still used in publishing as a simple descriptive term for a journeyman writer prepared to tackle any subject, as distinct from a specialist.

2 a cough, particularly a dry, rasping cough. The word imitates the sound in question.

hack vb

1 to cough and/or spit. This verbal sense is probably a back-formation post-dating the imitative adjective hacking and the noun **hack**.

2 also **hack into** to penetrate a computer system.
See **hacker**.

3 to drive a taxi.
See **hacker**.

4 to work as a writer.
See **hack** (noun).

hacked-off adj

annoyed, irritated, resentful. From the late 1980s, this phrase has enjoyed something of a vogue as a replacement for the better-known 'brassed-off', 'cheesed-off' and as a euphemism for **pissed-off**. It has been recorded in both the USA and Britain since the early 1950s, sometimes shortened to **hacked** alone.

hacker n

1 someone who **hacks into** a computer system. The hacking in question is the evocation of a person chopping their way through dense undergrowth to their destination. Hacker in this sense appeared as part of data-processing jargon in the early 1980s. Spectacular instances of the penetration of computerized systems brought the word to public awareness.

2 a taxi driver. A 'hackney cab' (the archaic version of taxi cab) takes its name from 'hackney' meaning a horse used for transportation. The short version of the phrase survives in this sense.

3 a clumsy worker. Here hack evokes chopping clumsily, rather than handling or cutting finely.

hackette n British

a female journalist. A jocular term coined by journalists (on the basis of **hack**) and popularized in the 1980s by *Private Eye* magazine (who referred to society gossip columnist Lady Olga Maitland as '*the fragrant hackette*') among others.

hack into vb

See **hacker**.

hack it vb

to succeed, to manage (in spite of adversity). A slang usage which remained relatively obscure until the early 1980s since when it has become a common colloquialism. The original sense of hack is uncertain here; it may mean to drive, to strive or to chop (one's way through). The phrase is a near-synonym for 'cut it' (which, however, probably derives from 'cut the mustard').

● '*The poor guy's finished, he just can't hack it anymore.*'

ha-ha n British

marihuana or hashish (cannabis), or another 'euphoric' drug. A light-hearted reference by middle-class soft-drug users to the hilarity induced by smoking, ingesting or sniffing the chosen substance.

hairball n American

an unpleasant and/or despicable person, by analogy with something vomited by a cat. The phrase owes its usage from the 1980s partly to the fact that, while offensive, it is not obscene and can therefore be used in television

dramas and by children in the presence of adults.

hairburger n

an alternative version of **furburger**.

hair pie n

a cunnilingus.

b the female genitals.

The phrase is a male vulgarism heard in Britain but more widespread in Australia and the USA. It may possibly be influenced by an earlier London slang phrase, '*air pie*' meaning (living on) nothing at all.

hairy adj

dangerous, frightening. The word was used in the early 20th century in Britain by university students to mean difficult, and later in the armed forces to mean dangerous. It is not clear whether the image inspiring the term is that of a hairy animal or monster, or of one's own hair standing on end.

● '*That was a pretty hairy drive down to Donovan's place.*'

hairy, hairies n British

a bearded, long-haired person and by extension a **beatnik**, 'bohemian' or intellectual. A disparaging term typically used by middle-class speakers in the mid 1960s.

● '*Honestly, she spends her time with all these weirdos and hairies.*'

hairy-arsed adj British

wild, primitive, uncouth or rugged. A term in armed-forces and middle-class use which is often, but by no means always, appreciative in tone.

● '*I tell you, they're a hairy-arsed bunch over there.*'

● '*The place was full of hairy-arsed builders.*'

hairy-legs, hairy-legger n

an uncouth, primitive person, particularly a supposedly masculine or unkempt feminist in the language of male critics. The terms are British and Australian and refer to the liberated woman's noticeable and supposedly typical refusal to shave her legs.

half a bar n British

before decimalization in 1971 half a bar was ten shillings; since then it has meant fifty pence. The phrase is London working class or Cockney. 'Bar' is an archaic term, still occasionally heard in London, coming from a Romany word (bar or baur(o)) meaning a sovereign and, later, one pound.

half a dollar n British

two shillings and sixpence in pre-decimalization currency, 'half a crown'.

See **dollar**.

half-arsed, half-assed adj

ill-considered, incomplete, ineffectual. An expression which appeared in British and American usage around the turn of the century. The term may originate in the notion of something which has less than a whole solid base or, according to a more fanciful theory, derive from a jocular deformation of 'haphazard'. In modern British speech it is sometimes used as a more vulgar version of half-hearted (its more probable inspiration).

● 'A half-arsed attempt to take over the department.'

ham n

1 an amateur radio enthusiast and broadcaster. The word is a form of amateur.

2 a histrionic, exaggerating or otherwise unconvincing or incompetent actor or actress. There are three possible etymologies for this usage: ham fat (formerly used for removing grease-paint), 'ham-bone' (an archaic Ameri-

can term for a provincial showman or performer), or a distortion of the word amateur. In its theatrical sense, ham is also used as a verb and an adjective.

hammered adj British

drunk. A briefly fashionable word among young people in 1986 and 1987.

● 'Sloane Rebs all support Chelsea FC, and can be seen every other Saturday lunchtime "chugging brew" and getting hammered at any number of pubs in the Fulham Road, before charging down to Stamford Bridge for a "frightfully good game of footy".'

(I-D magazine, November 1987).

Hampsteads n pl British

a short form of the Cockney rhyming slang 'Hampstead Heath'; teeth.

hampton, Hampton Wick n British

penis. Hampton Wick is a south-western suburb of London, providing a rhyme for **prick**. In modern usage the short form of the phrase is usually preferred. Since the mid 1970s the term has been considered well-established and inoffensive enough to be used in television comedies.

● 'Then there were these telephone calls from ... groupies. Somehow they'd learned a hell of a lot of cockney slang. They'd phone up and say "Hi Jeff [Beck], how's your 'Ampton Wick?" Ridiculous!'

(Jimmy Page, Oz magazine, April 1969).

handbag n British

a male escort, a 'walker'. Handbag refers to a 'decorative appendage' to a fashionable lady, often a homosexual male. The term was popular in high society and journalistic circles in the mid 1980s.

handbag vb British

to frustrate, obstruct or attack. A jocular version of **sandbag** seen in the 1980s, often in journalistic references to Margaret Thatcher. The term evokes shrewish intransigence.

hand-job n

an act of manual sexual stimulation, usually masturbation of a male by a female. A common vulgarism in use since the mid 1960s.

handle n

a name, nickname, alias or title. The first sense of the word was that of title (an appendage to one's name) in the early 19th century.

handsome adj British

excellent, impressive. An all-purpose term of approval used by Cockneys and other Londoners, sometimes standing alone as an exclamation. The 'h' is usually dropped.

handy adj British

a catch-all London working-class term, invariably pronounced without the 'h' and signifying adept, devious, virile, brutal, etc., usually in a context of immorality or illegality.

hang a louie vb American

to take a left turn. A teenage expression from the early 1970s.

hang a ralph vb American

to take a right turn. A teenage expression from the early 1970s.

hang a yooie vb British

to make a U-turn when driving a car. A mock-racy expression from the 1980s.

hang five vb

to ride a surfboard (at near-optimum speed or full stretch) with the toes of one foot hooked over the front. From the jargon of American surfers since the early 1960s.

See also **hang ten**.

hang loose vb American

to stay relaxed, keep **cool**, chill out. A vogue term from the late 1950s and early 1960s when it characterized the nonchalant state of detachment aspired to by **beatniks,** jazz musicians, etc. The phrase (still heard occasionally) is often an exhortation to a friend on parting. It probably originates in the use of **loose** to describe a free, unstructured style or mood (although some have interpreted it as referring to the male genitals in an unencumbered position).

hang one on vb

an alternative form of **tie one on**.

hang one on someone vb

to hit, punch. An expression, used particularly by brawlers, which may also be expressed with the verbs 'land', 'stick' or 'put'.

hang out vb

See **let it all hang out**.

hang ten vb American

to ride a surfboard (at near-optimum speed or full stretch) with the toes of both feet hooked over the front. From the jargon of American surfers since the early 1960s. The phrase is sometimes used figuratively to mean something like 'go full-tilt on a risky course'.

hang-up n

a neurosis, obsession. From the image of being hung on a hook. This **beatnik** term was seized upon by the **hippies** to describe the concerns of the **straight** world. Unlike many contem-

porary terms, hang-up has not dated significantly and is still in use today.
- *'He's got a hang-up about young chicks in uniform.'*

ha'porth n British

an inconsequential person. A person of no account or importance was likened to a halfpenny's worth. Usually in the phrase *'silly ha'porth'* (with the 'h' often dropped) this mild expression of contempt or derision was common until the early 1960s.

happening adj American

exciting, stimulating and/or up-to-date. A fashionable term from the vocabulary of teenagers since the mid 1970s. It is influenced by the earlier black catchphrase greeting 'what's happening?' and the **hippy** cliché, 'it's all happening'.
- *'A really happening band.'*

happening n

a spontaneous artistic event or a staged event at which participants ad-lib or interact as inspiration takes them. This expression from the **hippy** counterculture in the USA (circa 1966) was quickly appropriated by the avant-garde art world, bogus entertainers and the press.

happy dust n

a narcotic in powder form. The term has been applied to cocaine, **PCP** and amphetamines among others.

happy stick n

a **joint** (cannabis cigarette). A rare euphemism.

hard-arse, hardass n

a tough, unyielding and/or severe person, martinet. This noun form postdates the adjectival form **hard-arsed**.

hard-arsed, hardassed adj

severe, aggressive, tough, uncompromising. In the 19th century the term referred particularly to a hard bargainer or miser. It has since become generalized to encompass anyone of unyielding attitude.

hardass n American
See **hard-arse**.

hardball n
See **play hardball**.

hardbody n American

a young Californian male, especially one interested in physical culture and body-building. A vogue term of the late 1970s and 1980s heard among those frequenting the beach and boardwalk.

hardcore adj

thoroughly criminal, deviant or sexually debauched, this is a specific sense of the colloquial meaning of hardcore (committed or uncompromising, as applied for example to political beliefs or pornography). In the 1970s in the USA the word took on a narrower connotation in the jargon of the street and underworld, coming to mean irredeemably criminal. It was often used in this sense to indicate admiration or awe.
- *'That guy's real hardcore.'*
- *'The hardcore life.'*

hardcore n

a style of fast, loud, aggressive music, a development of **punk**. The term originated in America in the early 1980s, perhaps influenced by the adjectival use of **hardcore** to mean (uncompromisingly) rebellious, anarchic or criminal, spreading to Britain around 1985. The genre has since spawned sub-cults such as *'deathcore'* and *'speedcore'*.

hard dog n American

a trained attack dog as used by, for instance, drug dealers to defend their territories. An item of 1980s police jargon.

hard-hat n American

a construction worker or other labourer, especially one displaying stereotyped, illiberal right-wing attitudes. The expression dates from the time of the Vietnam war when such workers, often wearing their hard-hats (safety helmets) clashed with anti-war protestors.

hard-on n

a an erection. To 'have a hard-on' has been the most common way of expressing male sexual tumescence since the early 20th century. It derives from a slightly earlier adjectival form (to be 'hard-on') which follows a pattern of Victorian euphemism which includes 'fetch off' (to have sex or orgasm), etc.

- 'Don't go home with your hard on/It will only drive you insane.'
  (Lyrics from 'Don't go home with your hard-on', Leonard Cohen and Phil Spector, 1977).

b a sudden strong desire or affection. This specialized sense is a piece of macho business jargon from the late 1970s. It suggests an aggressive and uncompromising wish to acquire or cement relations with a business partner, for example.

- 'I think Ingrams is nursing a hard-on for United Mills.'

the hard word n

a a rejection or condemnation.

- 'It was the one thing that would bring Christina [Onassis] and her father together again. It was only a matter of time before Christina gave me the hard word.'

(Joseph Bolker quoted in Heiress, by Nigel Dempster, 1989).

b a difficult request or ultimatum, particularly a demand for money or sex.

The phrase is normally part of longer expressions such as 'put the hard word on' or 'give someone the hard word'. The origin of the expression is obscure, but it is most prevalent in Australian use.

haricot (bean) n Australian

a male homosexual. Rhyming slang on queen.

Harold (Lloyd) vb British

to slip a lock using a strip of celluloid or plastic. A now archaic term for this practice, employed by housebreakers, etc. Since the 1960s loid has been the version preferred by police and criminals. (Harold Lloyd was a star comedian of the American silent cinema between the World Wars.)

harolds npl Australian

trousers or underpants. The etymology of this jocular usage is unclear: it is thought to originate in rhyming slang based on a real or imaginary proper name such as 'Harold Tagg(s)' or 'Wragg(s)' bags.

harp, harpoon n

a harmonica. Long known as a 'mouth harp' among black American blues musicians, the harmonica became known worldwide as a harp during the rhythm and blues boom of the early 1960s. Harpoon is a later and fairly rare elaboration.

- 'Seriously he [Stevie Wonder]'s a knockout harp player, but this singing-only effort is a swinger.'
  (Rave magazine, March 1966).
- 'Gimme dat harp, boy, that ain't no young man's toy.'

('Gimme Dat Harp Boy', Captain Beefheart, 1968).

- *'Jagger especially, increasing his role in the band, chipping in on guitar, keyboard and percussion as well as contributing his best blues harp for years.'*
(*Independent*, 15 September 1989).

harpic adj British

crazy, deranged. A pun which was popular for instance among schoolchildren in the 1960s. The person so described was '*clean round the bend*', from the slogan of the Harpic toilet cleaning preparation which claimed in a TV advertisement to '*clean round the hidden bend*'. The word was used on *Whacko!* a parody of public-school life starring the late Jimmy Edwards.

harpoon n

1 a hypodermic syringe. Another example of the self-dramatizing language of drug abusers.

Compare **artillery, shooting gallery,** etc.

2 a version of **harp** in the sense of harmonica.

harry n British

heroin. An addicts' term from the 1960s, personifying the drug in the same way as **charlie** for cocaine.

harry- prefix British

a prefix used in public-school, university and armed-services slang, almost always by males, to add jocular familiarity to a standard term. It is often used in conjunction with the **-er(s)** word ending. The **er(s)** form is probably earlier; 'harry-' seems to have originated in armed-forces speech pre-World War II.

- *'Fiona's harry-preggers again.'*

harry-starkers adj British

naked. An upper-class or armed-services jocularity.

hash n

hashish (cannabis resin). Hashish from North Africa, the Middle East and the Himalayas is the most widely-used form of cannabis in Britain, especially among white smokers, while **grass** (herbal cannabis) is more common in the USA. This shortened form of the word was probably the most widespread term in use among British cannabis smokers in the early 1960s. It was then largely supplanted by more colourful terms such as **charge, shit, dope,** etc.

- *'Hash smoking is now a widespread social habit, almost in the same class as whiskey and soda.'*
(Letter to *Oz* magazine, June 1969).

Hashbury n American

the Haight-Ashbury district of San Francisco which formed the epicentre of the **hippy** community of the mid to late 1960s in the city. The nickname is a play on **hash.**

hassle vb, n

(to subject someone to) bother, harassment, intrusive complications. This term had existed in American English since the 19th century; in the 1960s it formed part of the **hip** and counterculture jargon which became established throughout the anglophone community. In origin it is either a blend of harass or haggle and tussle or wrestle, or an Anglicization of the synonymous French verb *harceler*, or (more convincingly), a version of **hustle.** In Britain hassle replaced hustle as a vogue term among **beatniks** and **mods** in about 1967.

hatch vb British

to drink, drain (one's glass). A matter-of-fact beer-drinkers' term, derived from the exclamation 'down the hatch!'.

● 'I think we'd better hatch these [beers] and get going.'
(Recorded, wedding guest, Bristol, 1988).

haul ass vb

to get moving, go into action. An Americanism, usually in the form of a command or exhortation, which is heard in British and Australian speech of the 1980s.

haul off vb American

to get ready to strike someone or to launch an attack. The term may be used literally (of leaning back before aiming a blow) or figuratively.

have (someone) over vb British

to trick, dupe, deceive. A London working-class expression.

● 'Similar themes run through stories about social workers who are reckoned to be easily "had over" by "villains" and even by juvenile offenders.'
(Inside the British Police, Simon Holdaway, 1983).

have a scene (with someone) vb

to have a sexual relationship, have an affair. This phrase, now sounding rather dated but as yet lacking a more fashionable alternative, was the standard term throughout the late 1960s and early 1970s for an unmarried relationship. The expression, particularly popular with middle-class British hippies, avoided the juvenile, frivolous or banal implications of 'going out with' and the middle-aged overtones of the word 'affair'.

have a word with (someone) vb British

to beat up. A euphemism used by brawlers, street gang members and police officers, particularly in the late 1960s.

have it away, have it off vb

to have sex. These phrases, which have been commonly used in Britain and Australia since the 1940s, seem to derive from an earlier sense of the same terms meaning to succeed in stealing or succeed in accomplishing (something illicit). There is also significant similarity with 19th-century sexual euphemisms such as 'fetch off'. Both expressions are used by all social classes.

● 'He later told me he'd had it off with a photographer the previous night and so wasn't much concerned with having it away himself.'
(Joe Orton's Diary, 14 May 1967).

have it (away) on one's toes vb British

to escape, run away. A phrase from the repertoire of criminals, prisoners and the police since the early 1950s. It is still current among these and working-class Londoners in the late 1980s.

have the decorators in, have the painters in vb

to menstruate. A women's euphemism; both phrases are heard in Britain and Australia, the second version in the USA.

have the hots (for someone) vb

to nurse a sexual desire for someone, to lust after. The phrase is a variation of now obsolescent phrases ('to be hot for', to 'have the hot ass', etc.) in which hot equates with sexually excited. First heard in the United States in the

1960s, the term quickly spread to other English-speaking countries.

Hawaii n British

a £50 note or sum of fifty pounds. A raffish expression inspired by *Hawaii-Five O*, the title of an American TV crime series of the 1970s.

- '*I got him to do it, but it cost me a Hawaii.*'

the hawk n

1 a short-lived nickname for LSD in 1966 and 1967. The significance of the word is lost; it may have had some connection with the increased visual awareness brought on by the hallucinogen.

2 a short form of **chickenhawk**.

hawk one's fork, hawk the fork vb Australian

to sell one's body, engage in prostitution. A colourful vulgarism playing on the medieval sense of fork as the join of the legs. In archaic British slang 'hawk one's mutton' and 'hawk one's meat' were terms with the same meaning.

hay n American

marihuana or hashish (cannabis). A slang term popular among drug users in the 1950s and 1960s, now dated.

hazing n American

teasing or humiliation, especially as part of a student initiation rite. An American version of the British 'ragging', but often with less light-hearted overtones. The word originated in naval use where it meant to oppress or harass. It probably has no etymological connection with other senses of haze, deriving instead from the archaic French *haser*, to irritate.

head n

1 an afficionado of the drug-using counterculture; a drug-user. A word used by **hippies** to refer to themselves. The term originally simply meant a person or individual in the slang of black jazz musicians and, later, white **hipsters.** It became a suffix used to denote different categories of drug users ('pot-head', acid head, etc.) and subsequently was generalized again. It now sounds dated and has fallen out of use save among the remnants of the 'alternative society'.

- '*Those were the days of heads and freaks. And if getting high was where it was at, then Vietnam was the ultimate trip.*'
  (Michael Herr, *Observer*, 15 January 1989).

2 a toilet. This is the singular form of **the heads**, the earlier designation for shipboard latrines.

3 oral sex, particularly fellatio. The word in this sense is usually encountered in the phrase **give head.**

headbanger n

a a devotee of heavy-metal rock music who expresses excitement by frenzied shaking and even literal banging of the head in time to the music. The practice and term originated in the early 1970s.

b a person who behaves in a relentlessly frenzied or dangerous way. This usage, deriving from the first sense of the term, usually expresses a certain shocked admiration. It has been current among British schoolchildren and students since the late 1970s, and is rapidly becoming 'respectable' by its use in the press and elsewhere by adults, typically with reference to political extremists.

- '*I'd like to meet her father; he sounds like a right headbanger.*'
  (Contestant on *Blind Date*, TV show, September 1989).

c a madman, psychotic, **headcase.**

• *'Another bloody headbanger, that's all. Probably didn't get enough sugar on his cornflakes, so he takes it out on innocent folk.'*
(Victim of random shooting, *Daily Mirror*, 2 May 1989).

headbanging *adj*

a shaking or banging one's head in response to rock music.

b behaving in a wild, unrestrained, relentless or excessive manner. The second generalized sense is an extension of the first and was coined to describe the behaviour of (mainly male) rock-music fans in the early 1970s.

headcase *n*

an unhinged or deranged person. The word, originally an Americanism of the early 1970s, is typically used by teenagers to indicate awe or dismissive contempt; it rarely refers to the genuinely insane.

head honcho *n*

the top person in a hierarchy, the most important boss.
See **honcho.**

• *'I can't be bothered dealing with assistants. Who's the head honcho around here?'*

head job *n*

1 an act of oral sex.
2 a crazy or deranged person, **headcase.**

headlamps, headlights *n pl*

breasts. These are jocular male terms from the earlier 20th century, when large, raised car headlamps were the norm. The first version is British, the second American and Australian. **Bumpers** and **hooters** are other slang terms for breasts using automotive analogies.

heads, the heads *n pl*

a toilet, latrine. This plural form is now rather dated, except in armed services' usage. It originated in naval terminology where it referred to the for'ard location of the privies on a ship. (The) Head is more common.

headshrinker, headshrink *n*

a psychiatrist, psychoanalyst. A jocular term of the 1950s originating in the United States and reflecting the mild contempt, tinged with fear, felt towards the practitioners of these professions. Since the late 1960s both terms have normally been shortened to **shrink.**

head trip *n*

a an instance or period of self-obsessed behaviour. An expression from the **hippy** lexicon, originally supposedly describing a specific category of LSD-influenced behaviour, which was later extended to describe any thoughtless egoism

b an instance or period of delusion, incoherence, self-absorption or contemplation, especially one provoked by drugs such as LSD. In this sense the phrase is not necessarily pejorative, and was used in the **hippy** era to describe 'self-exploration'.

heart *n American*

a dexedrine pill, from the shape of the amphetamine pills prescribed and abused in the US in the 1950s and 1960s. Not to be confused with **purple hearts.**

heat, the heat *n American*

the police. A black street form of the early 1960s (using the image of heat as pressure, oppression, something stifling) which was adopted by **hippies.** *'The heat's on the street!'* was a warning among black communities and white activists alike.

• 'Her man got took away by the heat/
we're lost and incomplete.'
('Endgame', song by Doll by Doll,
1979).

heater n American

a handgun. A pre-World War II term
which was appropriated by writers of
crime fiction.

heave vb

to retch or vomit. A literal, rather
than metaphorical usage.

heave-ho, the old heave-ho, heave-o n

a rejection or dismissal. A worldwide English expression, typically referring to being jilted by a lover, or being fired from one's job. It originates in
the shouts of exhortation made by men
engaging in physical exertion. It was a
sailors' call in the 17th century.

• 'It was evens . . . four men had
broken her heart and she had given
another four the old heave-ho.'
(A Touch of Spice, British TV
comedy, 1989).

heaves, the heaves n

an attack of retching or vomiting. A
literal description of these spasms, although the expression is, by its context, considered slang.

heavy n

a thug, **minder,** someone employed
for their intimidating physical presence rather than their intellectual
qualities. Originally an Americanism,
the term has spread to world English
via crime fiction and films. In current
British colloquial speech it is sometimes used in the phrase 'come the
heavy', meaning to act in a threatening
manner.

heavy vb

to intimidate, threaten or pressurize
(someone). The verb forms (expressed
as 'to heavy someone, to heavy someone into (doing) something' or to 'come
the heavy') post-date the adjective and
noun forms.

heavy adj

1 violent, oppressive, intimidating,
powerful.
2 a (of a situation) emotionally
charged.
b (of a person) difficult to cope with,
having a powerful personality.
These senses of the word, which
were slang terms of the 1960s, have become common colloquialisms.

hebe, heeb, heebie n

a Jew. Based on the word Hebrew,
these words originated in the USA.
They have been heard in Britain and
Australia since the early 1970s, sometimes jocularly lengthened to **heebie-
jeebies.** Hebe is less offensive than **yid,**
kike, etc., but discriminatory nonetheless.

hedgehopper n, vb British

a pilot or airforce recruit. The term
dates from World War I and is still used
by younger airmen to refer to themselves. Hedgehoppers Anonymous, a
pop group including members of the
Royal Air Force, had a number one hit
in Britain in 1967 with 'Good News
Week'.

the heebie-jeebies n pl

1 a state of nervous excitement,
brought on by fear, anticipation, drugs,
etc. Originally an Americanism,
coined by the cartoonist W. DeBeck
before World War II, the term soon entered world English and is now a common colloquialism.
2 Jews. A jocular elaboration of **hebe**
or **heebie.**

heel n American
someone who behaves in an unworthy or base way. This use of the word appeared at the turn of the century.

heesh n American
an altered pronunciation and spelling of **hash** (hashish). The term was used on the street in the 1960s and 1970s, since when it has been adopted by schoolchildren and **preppies** in imitation of more louche speakers.

heifer n
a young woman. A usage which is mainly restricted to the slang of the USA and Australia. In Britain the word was common in the 19th century, but has been archaic since before World War I.

height adj American
excellent, first-rate. A term of approbation from the hip-hop youth culture of the 1980s, coined by black teenagers (as a shortening of 'height of fashion'), in the USA and spread with the music and dance trend to Britain. The word is ephemeral and perhaps unlikely to outlast the 1980s.
● 'Don't reach for a tape measure the next time someone refers to your bullet-proof safari jacket as "height". They just mean it's cool.' (Charles Maclean on New York terminology, Evening Standard, 22 January 1987).

heimie n
an alternative spelling of **hymie**.

heinie n American
backside, buttocks. A coy diminutive of hind(quarters) or behind, although spelled as if it were Yiddish. The term is innocuous enough to be used by mothers and children.
● 'He hit me daddy – and then he kicked me in the heinie.'

(Date with an Angel, US film, 1987).

heist vb, n
(to commit) a robbery or hold-up. The word, redolent of American gangsterdom, dates from the first two decades of the 20th century. It is probably a variant form of **hoist**, like 'lift' a 200-year-old euphemism for steal, influenced by German and Yiddish speakers who would know the verb as heisst. Heist in its current usage usually suggests a carefully staged major robbery or criminal operation.

hella prefix American
very. A variant form of 'helluva' and 'hellish', influenced by the fashionable prefix **mega**. The most popular use of the device is in the combination 'hellaoool', heard among American teenagers in 1987 and 1988.

hellacious adj American
a appalling, awful, horrifying. A hyperbolic term mainly used and presumably coined by educated speakers, this is an invented elaboration of 'hellish'.
● 'Hellacious wet scene.'
'Multiple wounds?'
'Uh-huh.'
'Same as the other Slasher murders?'
(Over the Edge, Jonathon Kellerman, 1987).
b impressive, excellent. The term, like **bad, wicked**, etc. has since the early 1980s been used by the young to indicate approval.
● 'Hey, they're a hellacious band.'

hen n
a woman. A now colloquial pejorative or dismissive term which has been in use since at least the 17th century. It implies an empty-headed, fussy person, usually a housewife, although it has also been used as a rustic term of

endearment (it is still used in this way in the north-east of England and Scotland). This use of hen is paralleled in many other European languages, including for example the Czech *slepice*.

hen party, hen night *n*

the female equivalent of a pre-wedding stag night (British and American) or '*buck's night*' (Australian). By extension, any exclusively female social gathering.

henry *n British*

1 heroin. A personification used by addicts in the 1970s, perhaps influenced by the use of the name 'Henry the Horse' in the song 'For the Benefit of Mr. Kite' on the Beatles' 1967 LP, *Sgt. Pepper's Lonely Hearts' Club Band*.
See also **Harry**.
2 an eighth of an ounce (of cannabis). A drug dealer and user's jargon term of the later 1980s inspired by King Henry VIII. (A **louis** is one-sixteenth of an ounce.)

hep *adj*

aware, in touch with the latest (cultural) trends. An Americanism from the jargon of jazz musicians in the early part of the 20th century, hep was adopted by the white intellectuals of the **beat** generation in the mid 1950s and slightly later by teenagers. The word metamorphosed into **hip** (although the two terms coexisted in the early 1960s), which itself prompted the coinage of **hippy**. The precise dates and derivation of hep are somewhat obscure, although it almost certainly originates in a shout of exhortation or encouragement; either the noise used by riders, ploughmen, etc. to horses, or (perhaps more likely, given the importance of marching bands in the early history of jazz) that used by parade leaders, drill sergeants, etc. to keep time. To 'get hep' or 'be hep' then signifies to be working in harmony or in step.

hepcat *n*

an afficionado of **jive**, jazz and other aspects of progressive popular culture of the 1940s and 1950s. Originally a black term combining **hep** (fashionably aware) and **cat** (man), it was adopted by white bohemians, intellectuals and proto-**beatniks** and used until replaced by such terms as **hipster** in the 1960s. British jazz fans also picked up the expression and used it self-consciously or humorously until the mid 1960s.

herb *n*

1 marihuana, herbal cannabis. This is probably the most common name for the drug in Caribbean use (usually pronounced **'erb**). The word has been given especial prominence since the early 1970s by reference to it (in popular songs and elsewhere) by Jamaican Rastafarians, for whom it is sacramental. White British cannabis smokers adopted the term as an alternative to the more commonplace **grass**, **bush**, etc. in the mid 1970s.
2 *British* a street urchin. A rare shortening of **Herbert**, typically pronounced 'erb.

Herbert *n British*

See **'erbert**.

her indoors *n British*

one's wife, female partner or boss. A London working-class circumlocution which was popularized by its use in the TV series *Minder* (broadcast between 1979 and 1988). The expression has established itself as a facetious or ironic reference to an unseen (and by implication oppressive) female presence.
● '*All right I'll stop off for a quick*

drink, but for God's sake don't tell her indoors.'
(Recorded, teacher, London, 1988).

hey diddle diddle n
an act of urination, a **piddle**. A piece of rhyming slang in use in London and Australia. (**Jimmy Riddle** is a more common alternative.) The words are from the first line of a well-known nursery rhyme.

the hey-diddle-diddle, the hi-diddle-diddle n British
the middle. An authentic piece of rhyming slang.
● 'A long ball straight down the hi-diddle-diddle.'
(Jimmy Greaves the footballer and sports commentator, January 1988).

hickey n American
a a love bite.
● 'I like your date, Sam. Be careful she doesn't lose a baby tooth when she's giving you a hickey.'
(Cheers, US TV comedy series, 1986).
b a spot or other skin blemish.

Hicksville n American
a backward provincial place. A racier version of 'hick town', based on 'hick' meaning rustic or unsophisticated. (Hick was originally a diminutive of Richard, influenced by 'hickory'.)

hide-and-seek n British
a boutique. A piece of London rhyming slang of the period 1965–1970 when boutique itself was a vogue term.

hide the sausage/salami/weenie n phrase
to have sexual intercourse. Usually preceded by 'play', these phrases are adult imitations of baby talk, used facetiously since the late 1960s. The first

version is British and Australian, the second and third American.

high adj
intoxicated by alcohol or drugs, euphoric. The expression 'high as a kite' preceded the shorter usage which became widespread in the late 1960s.
● 'I feel like getting high.'
'High on life.'

high-hat vb American
to behave condescendingly or 'high-handedly' (towards someone). A fairly rare but long-established expression. The silent-film star Clara Bow claimed that more sedate members of the Hollywood community high-hatted her.

high muckamuck n American
See **muckamuck**.

high yellow n, adj American
(a black person, usually female, who is) light skinned. The term is descriptive rather than appreciative or pejorative.

hike vb, n
(to make) a departure or journey.
● 'Take a hike.'
● 'It's time to hike.'

hinky adj American
inspiring doubt, or suspicion; of uncertain loyalty, origin, etc. This term of unknown derivation is roughly equivalent to the British **dodgy**.

hip adj
a in touch with current trends, up-to-date, culturally aware. This word coexisted with, and then supplanted **hep** in the 1960s in the argot of musicians, **beatniks** and other bohemians. It implied identification with an ideal of **cool** behaviour characterized by a nonchalant, enlightened detachment

and a rejection of 'bourgeois' values. The word is still used in this sense, but is no longer a vogue term; it is rather a descriptive or ironic designation used typically by journalists and social commentators.

- *'Now, the truly hip stay at home with the baby and open a bottle of wine with a couple of friends; if they do go out, they dress down in T-shirts, jeans and sneakers.'*
  (*The Sunday Times*, 9 July 1989).

b aware, 'in the know'. Hip now divested of its counter-culture overtones, is used in popular speech to denote an unspoken understanding of a certain state of affairs.

- *'There's no need to give me all this bullshit, man. I'm hip to what's going down.'*

hippy, hippie *n*

a proponent and member of the 'alternative society' or counterculture movement which opposed orthodox bourgeois values during the late 1960s. The hippy movement was a much wider-based successor to the **hipster** and **beatnik** tendency, reaching public notice in California in 1966. By the summer of 1967 (known as the 'Summer of Love') manifestations of hippiedom had spread to Britain. True hippies never referred to themselves as such (but rather as **freaks** or **heads**); the term was originally a slightly condescending nickname (based on **hip** or **hipster**) bestowed by older musicians and other bohemians. By 1975 the main impetus of the movement had ebbed, although, in the 1980s, recognizable hippies still existed, albeit as afficionados of a self-conscious style.

- *'In punk's style degradation, there is still no worse insult than "hippie".'*
  (*Observer*, 24 May 1987).

hippy gumbo *n*

the scruffy, squalid or loutish aspects of 'hippiedom'. This term originated in the early 1970s when it referred to a **hippy** adoption of cajun music and accompanying black magic and poor white culture. (Gumbo is a Louisiana stew.) The phrase came to mean a particularly dirty or **funky** aspect of the 1970s counterculture music and lifestyle currently resurrected to some extent in the British **grebo** movement.

hipster *n*

a culturally aware person, a **cool** bohemian. Predecessors to the **hippies** of the late 1960s, hipsters were the afficionados of jazz, oriental philosophy, modernist art-forms, etc., who themselves succeeded the **hepcats** of the 1940s and 1950s. Hipster and **beatnik** are in a historical perspective almost identical, although the word hipster, unlike beatnik, was used by those in question to describe themselves. For the etymology of the word, see **hep**.

hit *n*

1 a a puff on a cigarette or pipe containing marihuana or another illicit drug.

- *'Give me a hit on that joint.'*
- *'It opens my head, opens my membranes. If you get a good hit, maybe you go comatose for ten minutes.'*
  (**Crack** user, *Guardian*, 5 September 1989).

b a single dose of a drug, particularly LSD.

- *'Laura just sold me three hits of acid for six quid.'*
- *'At work it got more and more difficult. To start with she would have a hit in the morning, another in the evening, and then at night.'*
  (*Independent*, 4 April 1988).

Both uses date from the late 1960s and are still current.

2 a killing, assassination. An underworld euphemism from the USA, since the early 1970s used or understood all over the English-speaking world. The term invariably refers to a professional murder.

hit vb

1 to assassinate or murder. The verb probably post-dates the noun form.

2 *American* to serve a drink to. Usually in a form such as '*hit me again with one of those*'.

3 to solicit money from, borrow from. A more robust version of the colloquial 'touch'. A racier and more recent American version is '*hit someone up*' *(for)*.

● '*He hit me for $20.*'

hit-and-miss n British

an act of urination, **piss**. London rhyming slang.

hit-and-missed n British

drunk, **pissed**. An item of London rhyming slang.

● '*If you ask me, he was a bit hit-and-missed.*'

hit-man n

a professional killer, paid assassin, this euphemistic term from the jargon of the American underworld and law enforcers had spread to other English-speaking areas by about 1972.

hit on vb American

a to 'chat up', attempt to seduce, accost sexually or romantically.

b to aggress, bully or criticize.

c to importune or beg for money.

All senses of the term became popular in the 1980s, especially among teenagers. The unorthodox verb form probably originates from an immigrants' error, or a deliberate elaboration by black speakers.

hitter n

1 an impressive performer, successful or dynamic person. The term originates in sports jargon, specifically denoting a baseball star.

2 a more recent, racier variant of **hitman**.

3 *See* **switch-hitter**.

hit the bricks vb American

a more fashionable version of the colloquial 'hit the road' and later '*hit the street*' (to get going or appear in public). Originally the phrase specifically referred to released prisoners.

hit the hay/sack vb

to go to bed, lie down to sleep. Both expressions have been widespread in English since the turn of the century and probably originated in tramps' jargon.

hit up vb

1 to inject oneself with an illicit drug, particularly heroin. An American addicts' expression of the 1960s, since adopted elsewhere. It may be used intransitively as in '*she's hitting up*', or transitively as in '*hit up some smack*'.

2 hit someone up *American* a racier version of **hit** in the sense of borrow (money) from.

hobo n American

a tramp or vagrant. The word is now a common colloquialism and no longer considered to be slang by most speakers. Authorities disagree on the origin of the term; it may be from a greeting ('*Ho! Boy*' or '*Ho Bro*'!') or refer to 'hoeboys' (agricultural migrant workers).

hobo jungle n American

an urban skid-row or shanty town.

hobson-jobson n British

the linguistic process whereby foreign words or phrases are anglicized for use by English speakers. The practice was particularly noticeable during the colonial era and World War I. Hobson-Jobson is itself a rendering of the Moslem religious cry '*Ya Hasan, Ya Hosain!*' (praising or lamenting Hassan and Hussein, grandsons of Mohammed).

Plonk (an alteration of the French *vin blanc*) and hocus-pocus (from the Latin *hoc est corpus*) are examples of this type of pun or folk etymology.

hock vb

to pawn. The word comes from the Dutch *hok*, the literal meaning of which is 'hook'. In 19th-century Dutch slang, *hok* meant both debt and the clutches of creditors or the law, whence the English term.

hockey, hockie n

a an act of (hawking and spitting).

b a gob of spit.

c a piece of any disgusting substance, such as excrement. The term is imitative either of clearing the throat and spitting or of a choking reaction to a disgusting sight.

d *American* nonsense, rubbish. A generalization of the previous senses.

hockle vb, n British

to hawk and spit, or an instance or result of hawking and spitting. The echoic word is mainly heard in the north of England.

hockshop n

a pawnshop, pawnbrokers. An expression (from **hock**) used all over the English-speaking world. In Britain popshop is a synonym.

hod n British

a short-lived generic term for women or female sex partners. The word was a vulgarism used by **spivs, teddy boys** and others in the 1950s. It is of uncertain origin, but may in some way equate the female sex organs with the standard British term for a brick cradle as used by labourers.

● '*A bit of hod.*'

hog n

1 a motorcycle. A word popular with American Hell's Angels of the late 1950s and 1960s, and their British and Australian imitators. The word originally referred specifically and affectionately to Harley Davidsons, the Hell's Angels' preferred machines. (Hog is the standard American term for pig.)

See **chopped hog**.

2 an angry or unpleasant woman. An Americanism which, unlike the similar **pig** or **dog**, has not been adopted in other English-speaking areas.

3 PCP, angel dust. This disorienting narcotic, phencyclidine, is an animal tranquilizer used on pigs, among other species.

hog-tied adj American

incapacitated, rendered helpless. Hogs (the standard American word for pigs) were hobbled by having all four legs bound.

hog-whimpering adj British

a abject, bestial, helpless.

b abjectly or bestially drunk.

A colourful term popular among **Sloane Rangers** in Britain since the mid 1970s. The word is probably an original public-school or army coinage, but may echo the many now obsolete slang terms containing the word 'hog' that invoke wallowing, snorting and other excessive behaviour; expressions such as 'hog-rubber' (peasant), 'hog-trough' (ship), 'hog-fat' (slovenly person), etc.

• *'Old Ollie was absolutely hog-whimpering last night.'*

hog-wild *adj, adv*
uncontrolled, unrestrained in behaviour. A folksy Americanism from the turn of the century which is normally heard in the form of *'go hog-wild'* or *'run hog-wild'*. (Hog is the standard term for pig in the USA.) The term was immortalized as the title of a Laurel and Hardy short film in 1930.

ho-hum *n, adj*
(something) dull, tedious, of mediocre quality or little interest. When used by Americans this expression usually denotes boredom, by British speakers it may rather suggest uncertainty. In American English the adjective occasionally doubles as a noun, or more rarely a verb (meaning to be bored by or to declare boring).
• *'As far as the presentation went, well it was kind of ho-hum.'*
• *'A big ho-hum.'*
• *'They ho-hummed the lecture course.'*

hoick *vb British*
to spit, or to clear the throat and spit. The word is a more echoic version of the standard English 'hawk'.
• *'He hoicked over the fence into the garden.'*

hoist *vb*
1 to steal, particularly by shoplifting or picking a pocket. The term is around 200 years old in underworld jargon, and was still heard in the late 1980s.
• *'He managed to hoist a couple of watches.'*
2 American to raise and down a drink, usually beer. A masculine term with overtones of heroic or hearty drinking sessions. (The word may occasionally refer to eating, as in *'hoist some oysters'*.)

• *'What say we go hoist a few?'*

hoist, hoister *n*
a a thief, specifically a shoplifter or pickpocket, or a thieves' accomplice.
b a robbery or an act of shoplifting or pickpocketing. The racier **heist** is a variant form of this 100-year-old expression.

hoity-toity *adj*
affectedly arrogant, condescendingly superior. A 19th-century term which derives from the earlier 'highty-tighty' (meaning 'high and mighty') and is influenced by haughty.

hokey *adj American*
phoney, counterfeit, of dubious quality, third-rate. A back-formation from **hokum**.

hokum *n*
nonsense, trickery, a deceptive but empty display. An American word, probably inspired by 'hocus pocus' and 'bunkum'; it had become world English by the 1930s.

holding *adj American*
In possession of illicit drugs. A legalistic, officialese term, also adopted by drug abusers.
• *'When they found him he was holding but they had to let him go on a technicality.'*

hole *n*
1 a anus or vagina. The word is barely a euphemism but a simple description of an orifice, in common use since at least Chaucer's *Canterbury Tales* (begun sometime in the later 1380s).
• *'Dark was the night as pitch or as coal and at the window out she [Alison] put her hole.'*
('The Miller's Tale', *Canterbury Tales*, Geoffrey Chaucer).
• *'Does anyone need another*

politician/ caught with his pants down/ money sticking in his hole.' (Lou Reed, 'Strawman', from the LP *New York*, 1989).

b mouth. In this sense the word is often used by schoolchildren, especially in the phrase *'shut your hole!'*.

2 a an unpleasant place. This term is now so common as to be a colloquialism rather than slang, as it probably would have been considered until the early 1960s. **Rat-hole** is a more vivid modern embellishment.

b a one-person cell, a place of solitary confinement.

home, homes

shortenings of **homeboy**.

homeboy n *American*

a street-gang member ready and old enough to defend his area or **turf**. The word, now part of the code of Los Angeles street gangs, was originally an innocuous American term for a good neighbour or good citizen.

● *'And some homeboys looking for trouble down here from the Bronx.'* (Lou Reed, 'Halloween Parade', from the album *New York*, 1989).

home run, homer n *American*

an instance of sexual satisfaction or conquest; full sexual intercourse. This adolescents' expression, inspired by baseball and typically used by males, denotes the successful culmination of a heavy petting session or attempted seduction. Partial success is referred to as reaching **first base**.

● *'Danny managed to score a home run.'*

● *'He made a homer.'*

homeys, homies n pl

'homeloving young professionals'. This ephemeral coinage on the lines of acronyms such as **yuppie**, **dinky**, etc. describes the state following yuppie cohabitation in which partners become settled, homeloving and houseproud. It dates from 1988.

● *'Advertisers flood the show because it targets their pet plug: the "homie" generation. ('Homies' have much more disposable income than the yuppie generation).'*

homo n

a male homosexual. This was probably the most common term in colloquial use among heterosexuals until the popular adoption of the non-discriminatory **gay** and its many pejorative alternatives in the late 1960s.

honcho n

a boss, important person. This word from American English of the late 1950s is not, as is often supposed, Chicano in origin, but from the Japanese *hancho* meaning squad-leader; the term was adopted by Americans during the Korean War. It is now used typically in a business context, often in the phrase **head honcho**.

● *'He [Reagan] was surrounded in his own White House by the portly honchos of the Democratic Party. The message was unwitting but clear: these are the people who count in Washington today.'* (*Observer*, 22 November 1987).

honeypot n

the vagina. A euphemism which was first recorded in the 17th century and is still employed today, particularly in the USA.

honk vb

1 to vomit. The term is echoic and has existed in British slang since the 1950s.

2 to stink. Related to the Liverpudlian **ronk**, this sense of the word is widespread in Australia and not unknown in Britain.

3 to drink (to excess). A middle-class and high-society term of the 1950s in Britain, now rarely heard.

See **honkers** and **honking**.

honk n

1 a a stink, bad smell. A variation of **ronk**, perhaps influenced by **hum** and stink. A usage popular in Australia and to a lesser extent in Britain.

b an evil-smelling person or animal.

2 an act of vomiting, from the verb to **honk**.

3 a wild, noisy, drunken party. A British term of the 1950s, probably from **honk** meaning to drink and **honked**, drunk.

honked *adj British*

drunk. The 'honk' in question may echo the hooting and vomiting of drunkards, or else the gulping or quaffing. **Honking** and **honkers** are synonyms.

honker *n American*

nose. An American version of the British **hooter**.

honkers *adj British*

drunk. A middle-class term perhaps originating in armed-service slang, where it has been heard since the 1950s. The **-ers** ending is typical of public-school and army expressions.

Honkers *n British*

Hong Kong, in the terminology of the armed-services and of the many **Sloane Rangers** who serve apprenticeships there, particularly in the Hong Kong and Shanghai Banking Corporation, known as 'Honkers *and* Shankers'. (The **-ers** ending is a typical pattern in public-school and army slang.)

honkies *n American*

backside or buttocks. An Americanism of the 1970s, derived from the colloquial verb to 'hunker down' (i.e. to squat), which in turn is related to the word haunches (in mock-rustic English 'hunkers').

honking *adj British*

drunk. A middle-class usage, heard less often nowadays than in the 1960s, which may have originated in armed services slang. The 'honk' denotes either drinking in gulps, the braying made by drunken revellers or, more probably, vomiting.

honky, honkey, honkie *n American*

a white person. A pejorative black term which became widely known in the early 1970s. The word's origin is unclear; it is said to be a deformation of 'hunk', meaning an immigrant (ultimately from 'Hungarian'), but may equally well be inspired by the honking of pigs.

honky-tonk *adj*

cheap and disreputable, rickety and shoddy. The adjective comes from the noun honky-tonk, describing the cheap American taverns and dance halls of the late 19th and early 20th century (where the jangling sound of out-of-tune pianos inspired the expression). A style of piano playing, heard in old-fashioned British pubs, is known as honky-tonk.

hooch n

alcohol, particularly illicitly produced alcoholic drink. The word originally referred to strong liquor made by the Hoochino Indians of Alaska.

hood, hoodlum *n American*

a criminal, (small-time) gangster. The longer form of the word was in use in the USA by the end of the 19th century; hood became widespread from the 1940s. Many suggestions have been offered as to the origin of the terms. The least unlikely are: a deformation of an Irish surname such as Hoolahan; an altered backslang version of Muldoon; a corruption of 'huddle-'em', supposedly the cry of a gang of muggers; and *hodalem* or *hudilump*, respectively Bavarian and Swiss dialect terms for wretch or naughty boy.

- '*Go tell your hoodlum friends outside/ you ain't got time to take a ride.*'
  (Lyrics to 'Yakety-Yak,' by The Coasters, 1958).

hoof n

See **iron** (hoof) and **horse's hoof**.

hoofer n

a dancer, particularly a chorus girl, tap dancer, or other hard-working professional dancer.

hoofing n

dancing.
See **hoofer** and **hoof it**.

- '*Also on the strength is Ruth Brown as Motormouth Maybell, Pia Zadora as a beatnik and plenty of vigorous hoofing to the unlamented Madison.*'
  (Review, *Time Out* magazine, March 1989).

hoof it vb

a to go on foot, walk. In this sense the term has been used since the 17th century.

b to leave, walk away. This sense of the verb dates from the 19th century and enjoyed a vogue in Britain in the late 1980s as a fashionable synonym for **leg it** or **hook it**.

c to dance. A usage popularized in the context of pre-World-War II Holly-

wood musicals. The predictable use of hoof (animals' foot) is probably reinforced by the word's echoing of the panting of hard-working chorus dancers.

hook vb British

1 to steal. This euphemism, which is still in use in London working-class speech, is at least 200 years old. The 'h' is almost invariably dropped.

- '*Barry's been out hookin' again.*'
  (Recorded, street trader, Islington, London, 1986).
- '*She managed to hook a few videotapes.*'

2 hook someone (one) to hit, punch.

hooker n

a prostitute (invariably female). This American term has been imported into British and Australian usage since the mid 1970s, possibly finding a niche since it is less offensive (and therefore broadcast-able) than alternatives such as **whore**, pro, **tart**, etc. The origin of the word is stated authoritatively by many works of reference. However, they disagree. The most popular version cites the Civil War commander, General Hooker, who supposedly encouraged his men to frequent brothels. Another source gives Corlear's Hook, the name of a New York red-light district, as the inspiration for the term. In fact hooker seems to have been in use with its current meaning as early as 1845 (which invalidates the Civil War explanation) and may simply be a figurative use of the literal meaning as 'enticer', 'ensnarer', a sense which it has in Dutch slang (*hoeker* would be known to the large Dutch-American population of New York as meaning 'huckster', for instance). Hooker was obsolescent by the 1920s, but was revived in the late 1960s.

- '*A high class hooker.*'

• *'Down on the strip where the hookers hang out.'*

hookie n British

a Jew. A dated piece of racist language, typically used by schoolchildren, referring to the supposed hooked noses of Jews.

• *'They did it with the hookies years ago.'*

• *'Hookies?'*

• *'Quarter to twos, Stan calls them.'*
(A.N. Wilson, *Scandal*, 1983).
See **hooky**.

hook it vb British

to leave, run away. A current London working-class expression popularized by the TV series *Minder* among others. London users almost invariably drop the 'h'. The phrase, a variant of '*hook off*', an earlier and now obsolescent Cockney expression, is over 100 years old and is also heard occasionally in the USA. The origin of the hook reference is obscure but may be related to its use to mean anchor (whence the expression to **sling one's hook**, to weigh anchor, although this etymology is disputed).

hooks n pl

hands. For obvious reasons this metaphorical usage, associated with the images of 'getting one's hooks into' someone or something, and to **hook** meaning to steal, has existed for several hundred years. In vulgar parlance hands are also known as **bread hooks**, shit(e) hooks and cunt hooks.

hooky n

truancy, especially from school. Almost always found in the expression **play hooky**.

hooky adj British

stolen, of dubious provenance, **hot**. A London working-class and under-

world term from **hook**, to steal. Hooky is often pronounced with a dropped aspirate.

• *'Last time I saw John 'e was sellin' 'ooky watches out of a suitcase down Brick Lane.'*
(Recorded, young male, London, 1988).

hoolie n

a wild, noisy party or celebration. The word is Irish in origin and is probably an anglicization of the Irish Gaelic term *ceilidh*, meaning an informal gathering for folk music and dance.

hoon n Australian

a lout, hooligan or disreputable youth. Originally this word (of unknown etymology) signified a man 'living on immoral earnings'; its meaning has now been generalized to denote, for instance, a member of a gang of ne'er-do-wells.

hoop out vb American

to play basketball. A high-school and campus term. To '*hoop down*' is to play particularly earnestly or dynamically.

hooray, Hooray Henry n
British

a young upper-class male, particularly one who indulges in offensive, rowdy, hearty, and/or vacuous behaviour. This pejorative term arose in the late 1960s to describe the more exhibitionist members of a social subgroup which was later anatomized under the name **Sloane Rangers**. Hooray is a later shortening. A version of this epithet first appeared in Damon Runyon's story *Tight Shoes*, in which a young man called Calvin Colby was described as '*without doubt, strictly a Hooray Henry.*' In March 1990 Viscount Linley won libel damages from *Today* newspaper, which had, among more serious allegations, referred to him as a Hooray.

- 'Hooray Henrys sometimes cruise down here just looking for an old codger to beat up. The last time they did it, we smashed up their flashy car.'
(Homeless **dosser**, Observer, 6 August 1987).
- 'The Hooray Henry, who is living in his father's London flat in Westminster, added that the little white dog had also scoffed cannabis.'
(News of the World, 29 October 1989).
- 'One long-standing member [of Annabel's nightclub] says he is thinking of allowing his subscription to lapse. There are now, he says, "too many Arabs and Hooray Henrys".'
(The Sunday Times magazine, 15 October 1989).

hootch n

an alternative spelling of **hooch**.

hootchie cootchie n American

sexual caresses or erotic dancing. A phrase familiar to blues music enthusiasts, from black slang of the early 20th century. A hootchie cootchie man is a lover or **stud**. The phrase hootchie cootchie first appeared in the USA in the 1880s, when it denoted a sort of belly-dance. The words may be a pseudo-exotic invention or a distortion of a now-forgotten foreign term.

hooter n

1 British nose. A common term of the 1950s and 1960s which is still heard. A synonym less widespread on the same lines is **bugle**.

- 'The doc says the 30-year-old vain singer [Michael Jackson]'s hooter is collapsing after being broken so

often in four operations to change his looks.'
(News of the World, 7 May 1989).

2 American a **joint** (marihuana cigarette). A college and high-school term.

hooters n American

breasts. A favourite term of college boys reminiscent of **bumpers**, **headlamps** and other automotive similes. The usage also plays on the supposed similarity in action between pressing a rubber bulb and manipulating and fondling a breast.

hoover (up) vb

to devour, eat or drink rapidly or greedily. A popular use of the vacuum cleaner's household name since the late 1960s. The expression is most common in Britain but is known in the USA. During World War II hoovering was the name given to an airborne mopping-up operation by the RAF.

- 'We laid out a spread and they hoovered it up in minutes.'
(Recorded, hostess, Weybridge, England, May 1986).
- 'He hoovered up five pints and got poleaxed.'
(The Crack: a Belfast Year, Sally Belfrage, 1987).

Hooverville n American

a shanty town, or any place where homeless people gather to sleep. The term originated in the Great Depression of the 1930s, when Herbert Hoover was President of the USA. It is still heard today, especially in reference to the cardboard box 'cities' that grow up under urban freeways, etc. In the late 1980s the British group The Christians recorded a song entitled 'Hooverville'.

hop a babe, hop on a babe vb American

to have sex (with a woman). A gauche **preppie** term from the 1970s.

hophead n American

a narcotics user. Hop was a late 19th-century term for opium, later extended to any 'stupefying' drug including marihuana. Hophead, dating from the 1940s, was one of the first words for a category of drug-users to use the -head suffix. By the 1960s the word was used mainly by law enforcers and other disapproving adults. It is now rare.

hopped-up adj

under the influence of narcotics. 'Hop' was a late 19th-century term for opium in the USA, later generalized to refer to any intoxicating drug. Hopped-up is a phrase from the early 1960s which does not however usually refer to opiates or other stupefying drugs but rather to stimulating **uppers**. It is characteristically used disapprovingly by non-drug users of abusers.

hopper n American

a toilet (bowl). A term favoured by **hard-hats** and **jocks** among others. (A hopper is a large metal foodor container in grain silos.) Coincidentally or not, 'the hopper' is also in American usage the place where schemes are hatched and ideas nurtured.

In business jargon or office slang to 'put something in the hopper' is to 'feed it into the system' or to 'put it on file'.

- 'He's been on the hopper for hours.'
- 'It's all in danger of going down the hopper.'

horizontal dancing n phrase

sexual intercourse, a jocular euphemism typically used by American college students, etc. from the early 1980s. The term probably originated as a joke among middle-class adult sophisticates.

horizontal rumble n American

a **preppie** version of **horizontal dancing**.

See **rumble**.

horlicks n British

a mess, an unpalatable or confused mixture. The trade name of a bedtime drink has here been appropriated as a euphemism for **bollocks**. The word is used by all social classes and began to appear in print in the late 1980s.

- 'How to make a total horlicks of it in five easy stages.'

the horn n

1 a the penis, particularly when erect. This obvious metaphor has been commonly employed in English for at least 200 years. Prior to that horn more often referred to the cuckold's emblem.

b an erection. Usually found in phrases such as to 'have the horn', to 'get the horn' or 'on the horn'.

2 a telephone. In this sense the word usually occurs in the form '(get) on the horn'. This usage is encountered more often in the USA than in Britain.

horn bag n Australian

a woman or girl, particularly a sexually attractive female.

hornswoggle vb

to swindle or bamboozle. A jocular 19th-century Americanism, familiar worldwide through its use in Western movies and still heard occasionally. Its origin is obscure; it may simply be a fanciful invention, or is perhaps a reference to cuckolding (the cuckold traditionally wearing horns as a symbol of his condition).

horny adj

sexually aroused, lustful. Although the **horn** in question is the penis (in an image which dates from the 18th century, if not earlier), the expression is now used by and about both sexes, sometimes in colourful phrases such as '*horny as a hoot-owl*'. It is a 1960s successor of longer phrases such as '*get the horn*', to be '*on the horn*', etc.

- '*The total absurdity of it all; seven or eight able bodied policemen keeping 24 hour watch on this horny endomorphic Jewish intellectual.*'
(Bill Levy, *Oz* magazine, February 1970).

horrorball n
a repellent or unpleasant person. A children's term of abuse or joky disapproval of the 1980s. It is a pun on the adjective horrible, influenced by **sleazeball**, **slimeball**, etc.

the horrors n
1 a bout of terror or fit of existential despair. The term applies especially to the sudden uncontrollable feelings of dread and horror experienced as a result of drug or alcohol abuse (as for example in cases of delirium tremens, heroin withdrawal, amphetamine **comedown**, **acid flashes** or the fits of paranoia associated with over-indulgence in strong cannabis). The expression was used in the 19th century to refer to the effects of alcoholism.

2 menstruation, monthly periods. A rare schoolgirl alternative to (**the**) **curse**.

horrorshow adj, n
a (something) shocking or horrifying.

b (something) sensational, impressive or excellent.

Like **bad**, **creepshow**, **hellacious** and other similar teenage terms of the 1980s horrorshow has undergone the process (technically known as 'amelioration') whereby a pejorative or negative term acquires a positive meaning.

This word, inspired by horror films and comics, has the dual implication of awful and thrilling, the intended meaning apparent only in the tone of voice or context.

horse n
heroin. A word used by drug addicts and **beatniks** in the 1950s, it was already dated by the late 1960s and was generally supplanted, first by **H**, and subsequently by **smack**, **scag**, etc.

horsed (up) adj
under the influence of heroin (known, especially in the early 1960s, as **horse**). An expression used by addicts from the late 1950s until the mid 1960s, now obsolete.

horse feathers n American
nonsense, 'baloney'. Usually an exclamation of disbelief, this folksy early 20th-century expression (possibly a euphemism for **horseshit**) was first recorded in a 'Barney Google' cartoon of 1928 and later was ensured survival by its use as the title of a Marx Brothers film. It is still heard in the USA, but was yet to pass into British or Australian usage.

horse's ass n American
a fool, especially an annoying or contemptible one. A common folksy phrase among adults. Like other expressions based on 'horse', the term has not spread to British usage.

horseshit n
nonsense, foolish or empty talk. A popular term in the USA where it is similar in meaning to **bullshit**, with perhaps the suggestion that horseshit is more transparently ludicrous or frivolous. The British apparently still view the horse with more respect or affection; neither horseshit, **horse's ass**

or **horse feathers** have caught on in British English.

- *'You see, there's got to be some respite from the horseshit. And cars give you that. They're primitive.'* (Paul Newman, *Elle* magazine, May 1989).

horse's hoof n Australian

a (male) homosexual. Rhyming slang for **poof**. The British version is **iron (hoof)**.

hose vb American

to have sex with. A mainly male vulgarism.

- *'There must be someone here that I could hose . . . Better get some more sherry to smooth out my brain.'* (S. Clay Wilson cartoon, *Head Comix*, 1968).

hoser n American

1 a fraud, deceitful person, cheat.

2 a promiscuous person, usually female. Both senses of the term are found in the vocabulary of high-school and college students. The etymology of the word is not certain, but probably derives from **hose** as a noun meaning penis and a verb meaning copulate or **screw** in the figurative sense of defraud.

hospitals n pl

See **play hospitals**.

hot adj

1 stolen, from the image of something 'too hot to handle'. The word was used in this sense in *The Eustace Diamonds* by Trollope in 1875.

- *'D'you reckon that video is hot?'*

2 exciting, fashionable. A slang usage (from the language of jazz musicians in which 'hot', frenzied and fast, is contrasted with 'cool', relaxed and slow) which by the mid 1970s had become a common colloquialism.

3 sexually excited or aroused. The adjective has always been used in this sense both literally and figuratively.

- *'She's hot for him.'*
- *'Talk dirty to me. You know it gets me hot.'*

hot cack adj, n Australian

a an Australian version of **hot shit** or **hot poop**.

b good news.

hot-dog vb American

to perform spectacularly and brilliantly and/or to show off. The term is applied especially in sports' contexts (the sport of stunt skiing, for example, is known as 'hot-dogging'), or to high-achieving students.

hot-dog, hot-dogger n, adj American

(someone or something) outstanding, spectacular and/or successful. The term is used as an exclamation, showing amazement and approval, but when applied to people may often indicate envy or disapproval.

- *'Hot dog! we're havin' a great time here!'*

hot pants n

1 a sexually aroused state; lustfulness, particularly in a woman.

2 brief shorts as worn by women in a 1971 fashion.

hot poop n

the very latest news, most up-to-date information. An American term of the early 1960s which had spread to Britain, especially in the armed services and in journalistic speech, by the early 1970s. **Poop** is a nursery term and adult euphemism for **shit**.

hot roller n American

a stolen car, in the language of car thieves and police alike. A term of uncertain age, heard in the early 1980s.

the hots n pl

See **have the hots**.

hot shit n, adj

(something) impressive, exciting, superlative. The common colloquial terms 'hot stuff' and 'hotshot' are in fact euphemisms for hot shit, a term both of contempt and approbation common since the beginning of the 20th century in the USA (still heard more often there than in Britain or Australia).

• 'Some hot-shit record producer.'

hotshot vb, n American

(to administer) a lethal injection of a narcotic, usually heroin. This term from the vocabulary of addicts and the underworld refers particularly to a deliberate lethal dose, either self-administered or as a gangland method of punishment and murder. Sometimes the hotshot is a high-strength overdose, sometimes a normal dose of the drug mixed with a toxic substance.

• 'The guys put him away with a Drano hotshot.'

hotsie, hotsie-totsie n British

an alternative form of **tottie**.

hotsy-totsy, hotsie-totsie adj

splendid, perfectly satisfactory. An expression from the 1920s when it was coined in the USA by the cartoonist Billy de Beck. The phrase is still used, usually facetiously or ironically.

hot tamale n American

a sexually arousing or provocative woman. A male expression of admiration or approval first coined by adults but now probably more popular among enthusiastic if unsophisticated high-school and college students. A *tamale* is a Mexican speciality, a spicy rolled pancake.

hottie, hottie-tottie n

1 a hot water bottle. A short form used in Britain, particularly by children, and in Australia, where it often characterizes an elderly, suburban cosiness.

2 also **hottie-tottie** an alternative form of **tottie**.

hot to trot adj

eager and enthusiastic for sex, and by extension for any activity. A jocular rhyming phrase probably deriving from black American usage in the late 1950s, it was adopted by **hippies** and subsequently enjoyed a vogue in the language of disco dancers, devotees of nightclubs, etc. in the late 1970s, when it usually had the innocuous sense of ready to dance.

• 'Honey get ready – I'm hot to trot.'

hot-wire vb

to start (a car) by tampering with the ignition electrics rather than using the key. A thieves' and law enforcers' term.

hound n British

1 a reprehensible person. The word is typically used as mild criticism or affectionate disapproval.

2 See **brownie-hound**.

house n

a type of disco music typically played in amateur or impromptu club sessions in the late 1980s. House music is electronically enhanced versions of black and European dance records, growing out of the **rap** and **scratch** embellishments of 1970s disco. This style of music coupled with the taking of **ec-**

stasy and other stimulants and hallucinogens produced the **acid house** cult of 1988 and 1989. The word house itself refers to the Warehouse club in Chicago where this form of music was pioneered.

house moss n American

another term for **dust bunny**.

how d'you do n British

a fuss, commotion or brawl. A jocular Victorian euphemism which is still heard, especially in the speech of older adults.

- *'Fancy all that how d'you do about a little thing like that.'*
 (Recorded, female pensioner, London, 1986).

hubba n American

a pellet of **crack**, or crack in general. An ephemeral drug user's term of 1988, hubba is inspired either by 'hubba-hubba!', a chant of enthusiasm or hubble bubble as a synonym for a pipe or imitation of the sound of smoking.

Huey n

A helicopter. This nickname originated in the 1970s.

huff n

See **take the huff**.

huff vb

1 to sniff, **snort** (an illicit drug). A late 1970s alternative to the more common **snort** in connection with cocaine. The term has a more specific relation to solvent and glue abuse. It is American in origin.
2 British to fart. A schoolchildren's term. **Guff** is a synonym.

huffy adj

irritable, indignant, angry. The word (a colloquialism rather than slang

since the 1960s) is inspired by the 'huffing and blowing' of a furious adult. It has been in use at least since the middle of the 19th century.

hum vb, n

(to) **fart**. Especially popular in Australia, this jocular term probably relates to the surreptitious sound rather than the colloquial meaning of hum as 'stink'.

humdinger n Australian

a spectacular **fart**. This vulgarism is a specific usage of the well-known colloquialism denoting anything resounding or impressive.

hum-hole n

mouth. An American high-school word, usually employed as part of an insult or challenge. It appears to date from the early 1980s.

- *'Tell him to shut his hum-hole.'*

hump vb

1 to have sex (with). 'Once a fashionable word for copulation', according to the *Dictionary of the Vulgar Tongue* by Grose, 1785, hump is now scarcely fashionable but still a widespread vulgarism, often in the form 'humping'.
 See **dry-hump**.
2 to carry. This now common informal sense of the word was considered unorthodox in the 1950s.

hump n

1 **the hump** a feeling of annoyance, resentment or depression. To '*have the hump*' or '*get the hump*' has meant to be bad-tempered or to take offence since the 18th century. It comes from the notion of a hunchback's burden.

- *'"I've got the 'ump today!" he told us cheerfully.'*
 (Security guard, *Evening Standard*, 12 June 1989).

2 American nickname for a Camel cigarette.

humpty adj British

1 having the **hump**, annoyed, resentful.

- 'He's a bit humpty this morning.'

2 wanting to **hump** someone, priapic, **horny** or sexually aroused. Both senses of the word were current in London working-class usage in the late 1980s. The 'h' is usually silent.

humpy adj British

having the **hump**, annoyed, resentful.

humpy n Australian

an aboriginal's shack. This 19th-century term from a native word *oompi* is now sometimes extended to refer to any makeshift cabin or shelter.

humungous, humongous adj

enormous, terrifying, tremendous. A popular word among schoolchildren and teenagers since the late 1970s, this is an invention combining elements of huge, tremendous and enormous, on the lines of **ginormous**, 'sponditious', etc. It seems to have originated in the USA.

- 'Darlene and I just killed a huge spider – we hadda use a whole can, it was humungous.'
  (Roseanne, US TV comedy series, 1989).
- 'Man, I got a humungous thirst on me.'

hung adj

1 a sexually endowed (referring to men). A coarse euphemism which is probably Victorian, perhaps older. The word is often part of colourful comparisons such as 'hung like a horse/bull/ jack donkey' or, alternatively, 'hung like a fieldmouse'.

- 'Her opener had a certain showgirl

candor: "Is it true what all the girls say – that you're hung like a horse?"'
(Kenneth Anger, Hollywood Babylon, 1975).

- 'Looks like you're doing alright Howard, nice chick too – I'm hung like a horse . . . Work out baby.'
  (S. Clay Wilson cartoon, Head Comix, 1968).

b sexually well-endowed, having large genitals. This shortening of **well-hung** has been part of male **gay** jargon since the early 1970s.

- 'Wow, he's really hung.'

2 a variation of **hung-up**.

- 'You got me to/ Fall in love with you/ Though I'm not free to/ Fall in love with you/ Oh, why/ Did I/ Have to get so hung on you?'
  (The Righteous Brothers, 'Hung on You', written by Spector/King/ Goffin, 1965).

- 'Nothing to get hung about.'
  (The Beatles, 'Strawberry Fields Forever', 1967).

hung-up adj

a suffering from a complex; neurotic, inhibited. A popular **putdown** used by **hippies** to categorize socially or sexually repressed, **uptight** behaviour, especially on the part of **straights**.

b hung up on (someone) obsessed with, in love with (someone). A hippy usage which persisted into the 1980s, and is still in common currency.

hunk n

a well-built sexually attractive male.

Hunkie n American

a Hungarian. A term applied (with pejorative connotations) to immigrants.

hunky-dory adj

fine, in good order, perfect. A well-established colloquialism, adopted in

Britain some time after World War I. The phrase arose in the USA in the mid 19th century. The 'hunk' component is from the Dutch honk meaning a post used as a 'home' in a game of tag; 'dory' is probably a meaningless elaboration.

huntley n British

karma (personal destiny). An ephemeral and unusual collision between the worlds and concerns of the hippy and rhyming slang, this humorous coinage is from Huntley and Palmer, a well-known British biscuit manufacturer.
- 'Hello love, how's your huntley?' (Recorded, social worker, London, 1987).

hurl vb

to vomit. A usage common in Australia and to a lesser extent in Britain.

hurry up van/wagon n

a black maria. Now dated terms from the 1950s.

hustle vb

a to work as a prostitute, solicit sexual clients.
b to importune, pressurize, take advantage of.
c to make great efforts (often selfishly). All senses of the word (introduced from the USA into other areas in the mid 1960s) derive from its origin in the Dutch husselen or hutseln meaning to shake up or jostle. This gave rise to an American version of the word meaning hurry or shove, later used in the specific senses above.

hustle n

a a high-pressure scheme, an attempt to obtain money, bully or browbeat someone.
b a rush, energetic action. The noun forms derive from the earlier verb form.

hustler n

a a prostitute (of either sex). This specific and euphemistic sense of the word remains exclusively North American.
b any intrusive, importunate or over-assertive person. A word which entered world English in the late 1960s, from American usage. Both senses of the word post-date the verb form hustle.

hymie, heimie n

a Jew. An unaffectionate, if not strongly offensive term inspired by the short form of the Jewish male forename Hyman. The word has been used in British English since the 1950s.

hype vb, n

(to create) excessive, overblown or misleading publicity. A term applied first to the activities of the pop music industry in the early 1970s, hype is a shortening of hyperbole. The word was apparently in use in the USA for many years among swindlers and tricksters before becoming part of commercial jargon (where it is now widespread).
- 'If hyping is the pursuit of profit over performance, and anticipation over delivery, then there is a mystical link between the garish posters of the Ringling Brothers ("Giant Two-Storey Elephant") and all those trailers for movies you slept through or ran screaming from into the night.' (Time Out, March 1989).

hype, hypo n

a hypodermic syringe. This short form was used by drug abusers in the 1950s and early 1960s, but was always rarer than the more colourful alternatives such as harpoon, works, artillery, etc. It persists in the vocabulary of doctors, paramedics, etc., particularly in the USA.

hyped-up *adj*
1 exaggerated, inflated, overpublicized. From the verb to **hype** (itself from hyperbole).
2 excited, over-stimulated, tense. This sense of the word probably originates in hypersensitive, hyperactive or hyperventilate rather than in hyperbole.

hyper *adj*
an abbreviation of hyperactive and/ or hyperventilating. The word, which was especially popular among American devotees of group therapy, 'consciousness-raising', etc., has now taken on a generalized sense of agitated or keyed up.

I

ice n

1 diamonds or other jewellery. An underworld term in all English-speaking areas, this word has also been heard in everyday speech.

2 an illicit drug which appeared in Hawaii in 1989 and seemed poised to replace **crack** as a major social scourge in the USA. Ice is a highly synthesized version of methamphetamine (the archetypal **speed** as abused in the 1960s and 1970s under the name of methedrine).

ice vb

to kill. An American underworld term which may initially have been a shortened form of 'put someone on ice'. The word has been popularized by its use in crime films and TV series.

● 'Maybe he saw the Hellinger killing go down – they iced him to keep him quiet.'

(*The Rockford Files*, US TV series, 1978).

ice cold n

a beer. An American and Australian term of the 1970s adopted by some British lager drinkers.

● 'Set up some ice colds, will you.'

ice cream n British

1 a man. This piece of now obsolete low-life and demi-monde slang of the 1950s derives from 'ice-cream freezer', rhyming slang for **geezer**.

2 a white person. This is a quite separate coinage from sense 1 and is mainly used by black and Asian schoolchildren to refer dismissively to whites. The term is not widespread or well-established. There is as yet no universal offensive epithet with which to refer to whites; **honkie** and **whitey** are probably the most common, 'pinky' is a less well-known alternative.

ice creamer n

1 British an Italian. From the 19th century to the 1960s, small-scale ice-cream selling was identified with Italian immigrants. The phrase is usually said dismissively.

2 American an occasional drug user. This term, coined by habitual or addicted drug-takers to refer condescendingly or contemptuously to irregular, 'recreational' users, dates from the 1950s.

ice man n American

1 a jewel thief. From ice in the sense of diamonds or other games or jewellery.

2 a **hit-man**, professional killer. From the verb ice meaning to kill.

icky (poo) adj

a distasteful, unpleasant.

b sickly sentimental, cloying.

The word originated as a baby-talk version of 'sticky'. It is now used by adults and particularly by teenagers to refer to something either literally or metaphorically viscous.

iddy, iddy-boy n British

a Jew. A London working-class term of disparagement and abuse which is a distortion of **yid**.

idiot box n

a television set. A less common alternative to **gogglebox**, dating from around 1960, by which time the mind-numbing effects of TV-viewing were attracting critical comment.

● 'An entertaining and salutary study of the tangled, dishonest and sometimes demented relationships our premiers have had with the idiot box.'
(Sunday Correspondent, 13 September 1989).

idiot dancing n British

a style of frenzied, abandoned dancing on the spot (invariably consisting of writhing hand and arm movements and shaking of the head) to rock music, particularly the **psychedelic** style (a precursor of heavy metal) of the late 1960s. Idiot dancing was influenced by a notion of Indian and oriental religious ecstatic dancing and, more prosaically, by the limited space for any more expressive movement allowed by the packed concert halls and festival sites that were the natural habitat of the idiot dancer. By the mid 1970s it had mutated into the less picturesque **headbanging**.

idiot's lantern n

a television set. A less common version of **idiot box**, heard in the early 1960s.

iffy adj

a questionable, doubtful or suspicious. In the 1960s this was a slang term heard predominantly in London working-class usage. It enjoyed a vogue among the fashionable in the late 1970s, by which time it was also widespread in the USA. The term is now a common colloquialism.

● 'Paid-for lessons at some professional club in Romford; and the use of such iffy stimulants as "Matchroom" aftershave.'
(GQ magazine, August 1989).

b British (of a person) dishonest, probably criminal or (of a thing) probably stolen. A milder version of **bent** or **moody**.

ikey (mo) n British

a Jew. A derogatory term dating from the 19th century. Ikey is a diminutive form of Isaac and Mo (Moses). Ikey Mo was a character in the Ally Sloper cartoons at the turn of the century.

illin' adj

1 a unhealthy, sick. This conversion of the adjective ill has been a feature of many English dialects, particularly black and rural ones, since the 18th century.

b stupid, crazy, unbalanced.

2 bad, **uncool**. This sense results from the appropriation of the older expression by black youth and later white emulators in the USA in the early 1980s. The word enjoyed a vogue in Britain in 1987 and 1988, having been imported as one of the buzz-words of the **rap** and **hip-hop** cultures. The word was particularly common in the lyrics used by the band The Beastie Boys.

imbo n Australian

an imbecile. A characteristic Australian shortening.

impot n British

an imposition (a written task imposed as a punishment for misbehaviour), in the jargon of public school and grammar school boys. The abbreviation is usually pronounced 'im-poh', as if it were French; occasionally 'im-pot'.

imshi *exclamation*

go away. An Arabic imperative adopted by members of the armed forces, particularly in Egypt, and imported to Britain where it is still heard occasionally among the older generation.

in *adj*

fashionable, modish, in vogue. This well-known expression was considered jargon or slang in the early 1960s. It subsequently became emblematic of the successive fads of the 1960s and passed into common speech. By the mid 1970s the word was no longer used by those who consider themselves fashionable. It remains a rather dated colloquialism.

in-and-out *n*

a version of **in-out**.

in-and-out man *n British*

an opportunist thief. An underworld and police term describing an offender who takes advantage of an open door, unprotected premises etc. to steal on impulse.

in bother *adj British*

in trouble, endangered. From **bother**.

- '*I thought you was in bother.*'
(*Only Fools and Horses*, British TV comedy series, 1989).

in costume *adj American*

in uniform. Police jargon of the 1980s.

in deep shit *adj*

a later elaboration of '*in the shit*', meaning in trouble. This version of the

expression became fashionable in the late 1980s.

India *n British*

marihuana or hashish, cannabis. A rare drug-users' term inspired not by the fact that India is the actual place of origin of a particular piece of imported cannabis, but by the drug's being known for many years in official circles as **Indian hemp**. (The plant's botanical name is *cannabis sativa indica*.)

Indian hemp *n*

cannabis; marihuana or hashish. Very little illegally imported cannabis originates in India, but the potent, smokable strain of the hemp plant has the botanical name *cannabis sativa indica*. **Indian hemp** was a term employed by official and quasi-scientific authorities in the early 20th century (*The Charms of Indian Hemp* was the title of a 1907 publication). In the 1950s smokers of the drug also used the expression, but by the 1960s it was confined to judicial or journalese usage. The word cannabis largely supplanted the term in the 1970s.

indie *n British*

an independent record label (i.e. one not affiliated to one of the big business conglomerates known as 'the majors'), or a record issued on one of these. The expression and the phenomenon date from the mid-1970s when small-scale record companies, boosted by the advent of punk rock, with its do-it-yourself ethic, began to threaten the virtual monopoly of the majors. Indie had previously referred to independent films produced in the USA.

- '*Apologists for the "indie ghetto", forever championing obscure and unlistenable bands with silly names.*'
(*Independent*, 1 December 1989).

indijaggers n British

indigestion, a stomach upset. A public-school term which perhaps originated as a nursery word in the early years of the century.
- *'I've got frightful indijaggers!'*
  (*Guardian*, Posy Simmonds cartoon, 1981).

in drag adj

See **drag**.

in Dutch adj

in trouble, in a vulnerable condition or delicate situation. This expression is a surviving example of the tendency (dating from the Anglo-Dutch wars of the 17th century) to use Dutch as a pejorative, as in 'Dutch courage', 'Dutch treat' or 'Dutch Uncle'. In Dutch appears to date from the beginning of the 20th century. An alternative etymology would derive the expression from American English in which Dutch refers to the habits of Dutch settlers and indicates peculiarity rather than any more negative qualities.

in effect adj, adv British

in action, at large or happening. A black euphemism used particularly by street gangs in the 1980s. The expression has been picked up by black and white schoolchildren.
- *'Posse in effect.'*
  (Graffito on wall, Clapham, London, 1988).

in hock adj

a pawned.
- *'I'm living on a Chinese rock/All my best things are in hock . . .
  Everything is in the pawn shop.'*
  (Lyrics to 'Chinese Rock', The Ramones, 1980).

b in debt.
- *'They're in hock to the tune of £2,000.'*
- *'He's in hock up to his eyes.'*

The term comes from **hock** meaning to pawn.

inked, inky adj

drunk. These terms, although rare, are not yet obsolete and are common to Britain, Australia and the USA. The origin of the expressions is unclear. They may be humorous parallels to blotto, or perhaps (and more probably) derive from the fact that cheap red wine was in the early years of the 20th century referred to as 'ink'.

in like Flynn adj

successful, in a very comfortable or advantageous position. A phrase which originated in the late 1940s and which shows no signs of disappearing despite the death of Errol Flynn, its inspiration. Flynn, the Australian hero of swashbuckling adventure films, was turned, especially in Australia and Britain, into a folk symbol of male sexual prowess by the press coverage of his trial on trumped-up statutory rape charges. The expression originally referred to success in seduction, but is now generalized to any impressive achievement, piece of opportunism or stroke of luck.

in-out n

sexual intercourse. A euphemism heard among English speakers everywhere since before World War II. In British usage it is often part of expressions such as '(a bit of) the old in-out'. An earlier version was 'in-and-out'.

in shtuk/shtook/stook/ schtuk adj British

in trouble. A very widespread expression which moved from a restricted demi-monde and theatrical usage to common currency in the mid 1960s, partly through its use in the entertainment media. *Shtuk* in its various spellings is Yiddish for difficulties. 'In sh-

262

tuk' often refers to financial difficulties.

inside *adj, adv*

in prison. Formerly a piece of euphemistic underworld slang dating from the 19th century, this word has become so widely known since the late 1950s as to be a colloquialism rather than true slang.

instant karma *n*

an hallucinogenic drug such as LSD. Karma was a term and concept much used, if often misunderstood, by the **hippy** generation. It refers to the Indian religious notion of personal destiny and responsibility. In western usage the term often has connotations of reward and retribution or poetic justice. The phrase was used as the title of a hit single by John Lennon and the Plastic Ono Band in 1970.

instant zen *n American*

LSD or another hallucinogenic drug. A short-lived late 1960s nickname inspired by the premise that the **psychedelic** effects of LSD replicate the sudden enlightenment experienced in Zen Buddhist meditational practices.

in stir *adj*

See **stir**.

intense *adj American*

good, positive. This all-purpose term of approval, with overtones of exciting, energetic, vital, etc., has been in vogue, particularly among teenagers, since the late 1970s.

intercourse *vb*

From 'sexual intercourse', this term has been used as a humorous euphemism for **fuck** since the late 1970s. It is largely confined to middle- and upper-class speakers such as **yuppies, Sloane**

Rangers and university students. The word is employed in various forms according to the usages of **fuck**; '*Oh, intercourse!*' as an exclamation, or '*(I'm totally) intercoursed*', meaning exhausted, for instance.

interfacing *n*

communicating or getting on well. A piece of jargon from the world of computing, transposed by **yuppies** and others into a humorous (or straightforward) synonym for communicating (with) or relating to others.

interior decorating *n British*

sexual intercourse. A jocular euphemism heard in the 1970s and 1980s.

in the bag *adj American*

1 drunk. A popular expression in American usage.

2 a ruined, botched. The original image evoked is either of a corpse zipped up in a body bag or a gamebird in a poacher's sack.

b demoted, in American police jargon. This is probably an extension of sense **2a**.

in the club *adj British*

pregnant. This very common expression is in origin a shortening of 'in the pudding club', which dates from the 17th century, and is one of many folk expressions using baking metaphors in a sexual context. Pudding is an obsolete euphemism for semen and, more rarely, for the female sex organs.

in the frame *adj*

identified as a suspect in a crime. This example of police jargon, in use both in Britain and the USA, is derived either from the simple image of a portrait in a frame or from horse-racing parlance, in which it refers to the practice of displaying the numbers of the winning and placed horses in a metal frame at the end of the race.

in the groove adj, adv
a proceeding smoothly, working well.

b in harmony with others or with one's surroundings, au fait with what is going on. Both terms come from the jargon of pre-World-War II jazz musicians.

in the nuddie adj British
a coy or facetious deformation of 'in the nude'.

in the shit adj
in trouble. This common expression has been in use since the mid-19th century if not earlier. It is a vulgar version of 'in the soup'.

in your eye, in a pig's eye, in a pig's arse exclamation
an all-purpose expression of violent negation; usually denial, refusal or dismissal. The first two versions are euphemistic alternatives to the third.

irish n British
a wig. Rhyming slang from 'Irish jig'. Wigs and toupees, which attract much notice and derision in Cockney circles are also known as **syrup of figs**, **rugs**, 'mops' or **dogs**.

Irish apricot/apple/plum n
a potato. These predictable witticisms have been heard since the 19th century in both Britain and the USA.

Irish confetti n
stones, rocks and other debris thrown during riots and demonstrations.
- 'The "Irish confetti" was dancing off upraised shields and bouncing

and ricocheting all around in the courtyard.'
(P.J. O'Rourke, Holidays in Hell, 1988).

iron n
a pistol or revolver. A slang term of the 19th and early 20th century (short for the American 'shooting iron') which survives in the pages of 'Westerns' and crime fiction.

iron (hoof) n British
a male homosexual. London rhyming slang for **poof**, the expression is an authentic Cockney folk term which is still very much in currency.

Irving n American
a boring person, nonentity. The Christian name was thought in the 1950s to be quintessentially mundane, personifying an urban dullard.

item n
1 a current (sexual) relationship, a couple. An Americanism of the 1970s which became widespread in the 1980s in expressions such as 'they're an item'. This use of the word began as journalese or jargon of the sort practised by Variety magazine, it then passed into showbusiness, 'society' and subsequently teenage usage.

2 an actual or potential sexual partner. A de-personalizing reference, like **unit**, heard typically in the context of US singles' bars since the 1970s.

Ivan n
a Russian. The most widespread Russian male forename provides the nickname for Russians ('russkie' is the only alternative). The same name is used in the same sense in other Slavonic-speaking Eastern European countries.

ixnay *adj, adv, n*

no, not, none. An all-purpose negative formed by the principle of **pig Latin** from the word **nix**, itself derived from the Yiddish and German for not or nothing. Ixnay was heard, particularly in the USA, in the 1950s and 1960s, but is now virtually obsolete apart from the phrase '*ixnay ofay*', meaning no white people allowed.

J

j *n*

a **joint** (a cigarette containing cannabis). An abbreviation from the jargon of drug users, dating from the mid 1960s.
- *'I rolled a couple of js for the concert.'*

jack *n*

1 nothing. This fairly widespread sense of the word may derive from an earlier and now obsolete sense of jack meaning very little or a small or insignificant amount. (A synonymous expression is *'jack shit'*.)
- *'We didn't get jack.'*

2 a a police officer.

b an informer.

These British and Australian senses of the word have existed at least since the 19th century.

3 meths (methylated spirits) as drunk by tramps, **dossers**, etc.

4 money. A common term in the USA which is also found in Britain and Australia.
- *'Listen, I just need some jack – in a hurry.'*

5 a heroin. In the argot of prison inmates and addicts in the 1960s.

b a single dose of a narcotic, specifically a tablet of prescribed heroin or heroin substitute. A term from the jargon of addicts since the mid 1960s, probably originating in **Jack-and-Jill**, rhyming slang for pill, reinforced by the verb **jack (oneself) up**, to inject.
- *'I just scored ten jacks of H.'*

c an injection (of an illicit drug). From the verb **jack (oneself) up**.

- *'Give me a jack of that shit you're banging.'*

6 *British* the anus or buttocks. A rarer euphemism than **jacksie**, typically used in provincial working-class speech.
- *'A kick up the jack.'*

7 venereal disease. In this sense the word is common in Australia, although it is also heard in Britain. The origin of this usage is either in archaic rhyming-slang, jack in the box: **pox**, or from the archaic use of jack to mean penis or semen.

8 *British* 'on one's jack', on one's own, from the rhyming slang 'Jack Jones', alone.

As a racier version of John, the most common Christian name, Jack has long been used as an all-purpose nickname, usually with overtones of raffishness.

jack *adj Australian*

fed up, tired, weary. To be jack of something or someone has been heard in Australian speech since the early years of the 20th century. It is probably not directly related to the more recent near synonym **jacked off**.

Jack-and-Jill *n British*

a pill, tablet of an illicit or prescribed drug. A rhyming-slang phrase used by drug abusers since the 1960s.

jacked off/out *adj*

annoyed, angry. These 1980s expressions (the first international English, the second primarily North American) are typically used by teenagers and young adults as milder synonyms for **hacked-off** and **pissed-off**.

jacked-up adj

excited, agitated, **hyper**. This usage, encountered in all anglophone areas, is perhaps related to the verb **jack up** by (probably false) analogy with **hyped up**.

jacket n American

a personal file, record; particularly a police file or prisoner's dossier. A law enforcer's term, from the jargon of office-workers.

● '*Let's take a peek at his jacket.*'

jacking n British

talking, gossiping. A version of 'yakking' heard particularly in the north of England.

jack off, jackoff vb, n American

to masturbate. This phrase may be a euphemistic version of **jerk off**, or may be based on 'ejaculate' or on the archaic meaning of **jack** as semen.
See also **jill off**.

jack shit n American

nothing. A dismissive or contemptuous term, originally with folksy southern overtones, but now common.

● '*Man, I worked hard all my life and ended up with jack shit.*'

jacksie, jacksy n

arse, anus, buttocks. A fairly inoffensive working-class word, particularly popular in the north of England, jacksie (the form jaxy has also been recorded) dates from the 19th century. It is probably an affectionate diminutive form of the commoner nickname **jack**. Instances of the word in American speech point to a recent borrowing from British usage.

● '*The jewel in the jacksie of South London, this place is.*'
(*My Beautiful Laundrette*, British film, 1985).

● '*I've got ten minutes to spare. If you like I can redecorate the front room. A better idea still, why don't we shove a broom up my jacksie and I could sweep the floor at the same time.*'
(*Moonlighting*, US TV series, 1989).

Jack-the-lad n British

an individual who is cleverer, more successful, more attractive than the rest. Originating in the working-class language of Liverpool and the surrounding area, the phrase had spread to the rest of Britain by the mid 1980s, probably due to the influence of television drama, films, fiction, etc. It can be used to express either approbation or contempt and is a modern example of the coining of male epithets with 'Jack' since medieval times.

● '*He's Jack-the-lad now, but he'll get his come-uppance.*'

● '*"Nobody in England today seems to like a Jack-the-lad," said Mr King – but when did they ever?*'
(Kate Saunders, TV review, *Evening Standard*, 17 May 1989).

Jack the Ripper n British

a kipper. An authentic piece of London rhyming slang which is still heard, albeit rarely, and which probably originated at the turn of the century.

jack up vb British

to arrange, organize (especially at short notice). This sense of the phrase, used typically by working-class speakers such as police and gang members, suggests mounting an improvised operation or rigging up a contraption. It is presumably an extension of the specific use of the term as employed by car mechanics.

jack (oneself) up *vb*
to inject (oneself), usually with heroin, but possibly with amphetamines, etc. Apart from **shoot up**, this was probably the most common expression for the practice in the 1960s.

jag *n*
1 a binge, as in a crying jag, cocaine jag, etc. This sense of the word derives from a 17th-century English dialect-term originally meaning a burden, later extended to mean a bout (of drunkenness). The word virtually disappeared from British usage in the 19th century, but survived in American slang, whence it was re-imported.
2 a an injection.
b an inhalation of glue or another solvent. These invented terms are probably influenced by 'jab', **jack**, **jack (oneself) up** and **jagged**, as well as the first and more widespread sense of jag itself. The first sub-sense dates from the early years of the century, the second from the 1950s.
3 a Jaguar car.
- 'I was riding in my Stingray late one night/When an XKE drove up on the right./He rolled down the window of his shiny new jag/And challenged me then and there to a drag . . . '
(Jan and Dean, 'Dead Man's Curve', 1963).

jag *vb*
to inject. A prisoners' and addicts' term influenced by the verb **jack (oneself) up** and the noun **jack**, as well as 'jab'.

jagged *adj*
drunk. This predominantly American term (used by **preppies** among others) can be pronounced either as 'jaggid' or, more often, as 'jagg'd'. It de-

rived from **jag** in the sense of a drinking bout.

jailbait *n*
a sexual partner or potential sexual partner under the legal age of consent. The expression is typically used to refer to sexually attractive young girls; it is also part of the gay vocabulary. Jailbait (also 'gaol-bait') has been heard in Britain since the 1950s, but has only been in widespread use since the period of sexual liberation in the late 1960s.
- 'Look again, Billy, this is jailbait – could get you into a lot of trouble.' (Hardcore, US film, 1979).

jake *n British*
meths, methylated spirits as drunk by tramps, **dossers**, etc. It is also known as **jack**.

jake *adj*
excellent, satisfactory, correct. A word of unknown origin, used since the turn of the century in Canada and the USA, where it is now rare, and subsequently in Australia, where it is still heard. The word has not appeared in British usage.

jakes *n*
a toilet. A word from the 16th century which is still in use. The expression may originally have been a euphemism using the proper name Jake, Jack or Jacques, or may have referred to an archaic sense of jack or jake meaning excrement.

jalopy, jalloppy *n*
an old car. A word which has passed from slang of the 1950s into widespread colloquial use. The word was first used in the USA before World War II and could also refer to an aeroplane. It is of uncertain origin.

jam n British

cement or concrete. The term refers to the mixture's consistency when used in road or house building, etc. Jam is part of the jargon of **navvies**, builders and other labourers.

- 'And shovelling jam up in a hydro dam or underneath the Thames in a hole.'

(The Dubliners, lyrics to 'McAlpine's Fusiliers').

jam, jamlt vb

1 a to play music informally, to improvise. The phrase originally referred to loose aggregations of jazz musicians, typically playing 'after hours', later to rock and blues.

b to make up an improvised **rap** chant. The word and the practice arose in New York in the late 1970s. Rapping, like the original jazz improvisation, took place in informally composed groups, often competing among themselves.

2 American to take part in a wild celebration, to 'party'. An extension of the original musical sense of the word.

3 American to have sex (with). This vulgarism usually occurs in the form 'jamming', and is heard typically among adolescents. Slang uses of the word jam as verb or noun play on its standard sense of crush(ed) or wedge(d) together. The additional sense of sweet confection also influences the use of the word in sexual euphemisms.

4 also **jam it** American to move quickly, leave hurriedly. This sense is of uncertain origin, but may refer to jamming the foot on the accelerator.

5 American to sniff cocaine. This use of the word presumably refers to jamming the substance up one's nose. It may alternatively refer to jam as something sweet.

jam n

1 a a shortening of jam session, meaning a group improvisation or informal performance. The term was originally applied to jazz, and later to rock.

b a **rap** session.

2 American **a** party (usually a wild, crowded affair).

3 a a sex act.

b a sexual partner (of either gender).

c the vagina.

The many sexual sub-senses of jam are based on the two standard meanings of squeeze or wedge and something sweet.

4 an illicit drug, particularly cocaine. The term, which is either a specific instance of the colloquial use of jam to mean anything tasty or attractive, or a reference to jamming something into oneself, has been applied to a variety of substances.

Jamaica talk n

the local patois or slang of Jamaica, heard in Britain among immigrants and their descendants. Black schoolchildren brought up in London for instance switch from Cockney to Jamaica talk to assert their identity or to converse in secret. Words such as **duppy**, **dread, illin'** etc., have emerged from Jamaica talk into more widespread and non-black usage.

jamas n pl

See **jarmies**.

jamboree bags n pl British

breasts, a vulgarism mainly heard among males in their thirties and forties (in the 1980s), who remember the lucky-dip sweet and toy packets of the same name.

James n British

a 'first' (first-class honours degree).

269

Students' rhyming slang from 'James the First'.

● *'We all expected Penny to get a James but she ended up with a Desmond.'*
(*Evening Standard*, June 1988).

jam jar n British

a motor-car. A piece of rhyming slang which dates from the 1920s and is still in use in working-class London speech. An alternative is 'la-di (dah)'.
● *'He had to blag a jam jar for the getaway.'*
(Recorded, petty criminal, Vauxhall, London, 1976).

jammed adj American

drunk. A rare synonym, coined in the tradition of designating drunkenness by any handy adjective with connotations of difficulty, damage or destruction.

jammies n pl British

pyjamas. A nursery term. Alternatives are **jarmies**and **jim-jams**.

jammy adj British

enviably lucky, very fortunate. This common expression, which is particularly popular among schoolchildren (typically expressed in such phrases as 'jammy dodger', 'jammy bugger', 'jammy sod' or 'jammy bastard') marvelling at a fellow pupil's luck in escaping punishment, derives from the 19th- and early 20th-century colloquial sense of jam as reward, luxury, indulgence, etc.

jam rag n British

a sanitary towel. A schoolchildren's term in use since the 1950s. It may also refer to a tampon. (A variant form is **tam rag**.)

jam raid n British

a menstrual period. A schoolchil-dren's word from the late 1950s and 1960s.

● *'She's excused swimming because she's having a jam raid.'*
(Recorded, schoolboy, 1960).

jam roll n British

parole. A rhyming-slang term from the vocabulary of prison inmates and the underworld.
● *'He's out on jam roll/up for his jam roll.'*

jam sandwich n British

a police car, in the argot of schoolchildren, tramps, **dossers** and the homeless.
● *'I'm not going to be moved. The jam sandwiches [police cars] will have to cart me off.'*
(Homeless man, *Observer*, 16 Aug 1987).

jam tart n

1 *Australian* a girl or woman. This is a 19th-century British rhyming-slang expression formed to rhyme with sweetheart and influenced by the well-known sense of **tart** as woman.

2 *Australian* a **fart**.

3 *British* heart. A fairly rare item of London rhyming slang.

jane n

1 a women's toilet. A feminine version of a **john**. A term probably coined separately by feminists and humorists of both sexes in the 1970s.

2 a a woman.

b a female prostitute. Both senses of the words are counterparts of **john**.

Jane Doe n American

an unnamed or anonymous woman. A later coinage by analogy with **John Doe**.

Jane Q. Citizen, Jane Q. Public n American

the woman-in-the-street, typical woman, 'Mrs or Ms average'. The female counterpart of **John Q. Citizen**.

jang n American

penis. A rare version of **yang** or **whang**.

jangle vb British

to gossip, chat. A word which is popular in northern England, particularly in the Liverpool area where jangling describes the working-class ritual or pastime of gossiping over the back fence or front gate.

jangle n British

a gossip, chat. The noun post-dates the verb form.

jangled adj

disturbed, nervous, tense or irritated. A 1980s usage, from the colloquialism 'jangled nerves'. (Jangle is not related to jingle but is from a Middle English word meaning grumble.)
- 'I'm feeling a big jangled today.'

jankers n British

military punishment, punishment detail. An army, navy and RAF term heard particularly in the 1950s, when national service was still in force in Britain. The origin of the term is obscure, but it may be related to **jangle**, which had an archaic sense of 'to grumble', hence jankers were either the grumbling servicemen or the punishments which caused them to complain.

Jap n

a Japanese person or an object manufactured in Japan, the word is generally more pejorative in American and Australian speech than in British.

JAP n American

a young Jewish girl, especially a wealthy or spoilt one. An acronym of 'Jewish American Princess'. A member of a social sub-group supposedly characterized by behaving in a comically spoilt, acquisitive and/or self-indulgent way. The mildly derogatory term is pronounced identically to the abbreviation of Japanese, which caused some confusion when the word achieved popularity in the mid 1970s. Originally used humorously by Jewish speakers themselves, there were signs of its derogatory racist and sexist undertones becoming more overt in the late 1980s. Princess here recalls the indulgent term of (usually paternal) affection, and the haughtiness of the subject. Following the Preppie Handbook, a Jap Handbook was published in 1983, analysing every aspect of the phenomenon.
- 'What does a JAP make for dinner? Reservations.'
  (Evening Standard, 9 May 1988).

jar n British

a pint of beer. A pub habitués' term which has been widespread since the 1950s. At the turn of the century, ale was served in china mugs, known as jars, as well as glasses.
- 'Hey Tom I fancy a bit of lunch. Let's stop at that pub for a few jars.'
  (Roger Mellie, cartoon in Viz magazine, 1989).

jarmies, jarmas, jamas n pl British

pyjamas. Alternative nursery terms to **jammies** and **jim-jams**.

J Arthur n British

an act of masturbation. Rhyming slang from J Arthur Rank (the British cinema magnate); **wank**. A very popular word in the 1960s, used almost invariably by and about men. (In the

1940s the same phrase was used to refer to a bank.)

● *'He was having a J Arthur behind the bike shed.'*

java n

coffee. An Americanism that spread worldwide through the influence of Hollywood and pulp-fiction writers. Coffee was imported from Java in the 19th century.

● *'Fancy a cup of java?'*

jaw vb

to talk, chat, gossip. A colloquialism used since the 18th century.

jaxy n

See **jacksie.**

jay n

1 a joint. An alternative rendering of J.

2 *American* a dupe, victim, in the language of criminals, gamblers and confidence tricksters. The reference is to the jay-bird, popularly supposed to be garrulous and dim-witted.

jazz vb

1 a to talk deceitfully, bamboozle, **bullshit.**

b to tease or provoke.

Both sub-senses originated in black American slang and have, since the 1970s, become established in general American colloquial speech. In these meanings, **jive** is a synonym.

2 *American* to have sex with.

A black slang term from the early 20th century, jazz is still used, albeit rarely, in this sense. The word jazz is said to be a New Orleans Creole patois term for sex, or erotic dancing or music.

jazz n

1 a empty, pretentious or deceitful talk.

b provocation, obfuscation, nuisance.

2 a stuff, unspecified things. Often heard in the dismissive phrase *'all that jazz'*.

b ornamentation, decoration, showiness. The precise origin of the word jazz is uncertain. It was first used in New Orleans in the early years of the 20th century in the form 'jass', referring to music and dances inspired by African rhythms. The word also had sexual overtones in its Creole origin. It was later applied to improvised music and, later still, to other forms of exciting display.

jazz up vb

a to decorate, ornament.

b to enliven, stimulate.

Considered slang until the early 1960s, this phrase has subsequently become a common colloquialism.

jazzy adj

showy, glittery, **jazzed up.** Particularly used of vivid, striking colours or excessive ornamentation.

jeez exclamation

a less offensive form of Jesus, originally American, but now heard elsewhere.

Jeffrey n British

£2,000. A probably ephemeral invention by an anonymous wit in the tradition of a **monkey,** a pony, etc. It refers to the sum paid by the author and politician Jeffrey Archer to Miss Monica Coughlan, a prostitute, to enable her to go abroad. Her return in 1987 resulted in Mr Archer bringing a case for libel against the *News of the World,* which he won. This figure has also been referred to as an **Archer.**

jekylls n pl British

trousers. The word is rhyming slang
– Jekyll and Hydes; 'strides'.
● 'That's a fancy pair of jekylls
you've got there.'

jellies n pl British

cheap sandals made of brightly coloured transparent plastic as worn by
art students, etc. in the early 1980s.
The footwear resembled confectionery
of the same name.

jelly n British

gelignite. This is an underworld
term for the explosive favoured by
safebreakers and other criminals
throughout the 1950s and 1960s.

jellybeans n pl

amphetamine tablets, 'pep pills' or
barbiturates. A drug users' term of the
late 1950s from the USA. Many drug
terms are inspired by children's sweets
(for example **candy**, **lollies**). In this
case the usual connotations of indulgence and desirability are reinforced
by the similarity of the multi-coloured
jelly beans to rainbow-hued pills.

jelly-belly n

a fat, overweight or paunchy person.

jelly-roll n American

a a woman's sex organs.
b sexual intercourse.
c a woman seen as a sexual partner,
sex object or sweetheart.
d a male lover or seducer.
All these terms, popularized by their
use in jazz, blues and rock music, derive from black American argot of the
late 19th century. A jelly roll is literally
a jam or Swiss roll. The triple metaphor implied in the first three senses
derives from the rolling motion, the
supposed resemblance of the cake to
the vulva, and the notion of 'sweet reward'. In the case of the fourth sense,

which is less common but may historically antedate the others, the word represents the sweet element of 'sweetheart'.

jerk n

a foolish, despicable or obnoxious
person. This American term crossed
over into limited British usage during
and after World War II. It is usually pejorative, although it is sometimes used
with pitying or even affectionate connotations in American speech. The
word seems to derive from **jerk off**,
meaning to masturbate, and was probably originally a rural term for an idle
or immature boy.
● 'Poor Michael Reagan. As if it
weren't bad enough being the son of
Ronald Reagan, the guy happens to
be a complete jerk as well.'
(Nigella Lawson, book review, The
Sunday Times, April 1989).
● 'Another typical computer
"bulletin-board" message begins:
"There's a jerk at my school who
steals stuff from other students . . .
".'
(Observer, 3 April 1988).
● 'We stand by our story. You are a
Mussolini-loving little jerk.'
(Editorial response to reader's
letter, Time Out, December 1987).
See also **jerkoff**.

jerkin' the gherkin n

male masturbation. A rhyming witticism from around 1960, it replaced
other rarer phrases employing the
word jerk which had been in use since
the mid 19th century, such as 'jerk the
turkey', 'jerk the jelly', etc.

jerk off vb

to masturbate. An Americanism
which has gained currency throughout
the English-speaking world since the
late 1960s when it became a **hippy** and
student vogue term. The phrase exist-

ed in British English in the 19th century but was never widespread.

- *'Plus the exhibitionist jerk off fantasia of "let's do it in the road".'* (*Oz* magazine, 1970). See also **jerkoff**.

jerkoff n American

a despicable or obnoxious (male) person. The American equivalent of **wanker** (to **jerk off** is to masturbate). A word which became particularly popular in the USA in the late 1960s and which had spread to other English-speaking areas by the end of the **hippy** era.

- *'The guy turned out to be a complete jerkoff.'*

jerk someone around, jerk someone's chain vb American

to irritate, harass, subject to minor humiliations. The image evoked is of an animal on a rope or lead being tugged at the whim of its owner.

jerkwad n American

a term of abuse meaning literally a (male) masturbator, a **jerkoff**. ('Wad' figures in many expressions involving male sexuality and may denote penis or semen, or more recently, tissue or toilet paper.)

jerkwater adj American

remote, insignificant. This expression does not, as is often thought, have any implication of urination or masturbation. It derives from the rural American practice of stopping trains in remote country areas to take on water, by pulling across a connection and sluice, or ladling from a trough.

- *'When you work for a jerkwater [TV] station like this you learn to do everything.'* (*Prime Suspect*, US film, 1982).

Jerry n

1 a German, or Germans in general. This was the most widespread term in British use in the two World Wars, replacing the earlier 'Fritz' and now largely supplanted by **kraut**. Jerry was reinforced by the following sense (the standard German military helmet was thought to resemble a chamber pot). The word is a shortening and alteration of German.

2 a chamber pot. In spite of the supposed resemblance to a German helmet, this word is in origin a humorous corruption of jeroboam.

jessie n British

a weak or effeminate man. A Scottish and northern English term of ridicule which has become widespread since the mid 1970s, partly due to the influence of comics such as the Scot, Billy Connolly. It is synonymous with **nellie** and **big girl's blouse**. There are two proposed derivations for the word; the first is simply a borrowing of the female name as a term of endearment, the second is a Biblical reference to '*a rod out of the stem of Jesse*' giving rise to jokes on the subject of masturbation, etc.

- *'Oaw, come on you big soft jessie.'*
- *'Peelie [John Peel] blubbed throughout, the big jessie, and before long we all joined in.'* (*Evening Standard*, 31 August 1989).

Jesus n

See **creeping Jesus**.

Jesus boots n pl British

sandals, particularly thong-type sandals which were characteristic of the **beatniks** of the late 1950s and early 1960s. The jocular term was used by students, **mods** and other teenagers, particularly at the time (between 1962 and 1966) when 'chelsea boots' or 'beatle boots' were also fashionable.

jesus freak n

a born-again Christian, particularly a member of a Christian evangelical or mystical cult of the **hippy** era. A disparaging term, also applied by students in the late 1960s and early 1970s to members of university Christian Unions, etc.

jew (someone) vb

to outmanoeuvre in a financial deal, cheat, behave avariciously (towards someone). This offensive expression, also encountered in the form **jew (someone) down**, is common to all English-speaking communities and derives from popular resentment at the supposed commercial skills of the Jews.

jewels n pl British

See **family jewels**.

jewie louie adj British

in bad taste, showy, flashy, ostentatiously expensive. A term used by **Sloane Rangers** among others to express distaste at nouveau-riche accoutrements and décor.

jewish adj British

mean, avaricious, penny-pinching. An offensive term which is, however, typically used by schoolchildren who are only dimly aware of the racist implications.

- 'Come on, don't be Jewish, lend us some.'

(Recorded, schoolgirl, Battersea, London, 1973).

Jewish American Princess n

American

See **JAP**.

Jewish lightning n American

arson, the deliberate burning of insured property. A type of fraud supposed to be typically perpetuated by Jewish businessmen or landlords.

Jewish typewriter/piano/pianola/joanna n

a cash register. Supposedly jocular racist terms, referring to Jews' presumed love of money. Jewish piano has also been used in Britain for a taximeter.

Jew's canoe n British

a Jaguar or other large car. A racist epithet heard in the late 1960s, particularly in provincial cities. A variant form is **Jew's Rolls Royce**.

Jew's Rolls Royce n British

a Jaguar car. This racist jibe dates from the period (pre World War II to the late 1950s) when it was possible to regard a Jaguar as a more vulgar, showy car than a Rolls Royce.

jewy louie adj

See **jewie louie**.

jig-a-jig, jiggy-jig n

sexual intercourse. Since at least the 18th century there have been various slang terms for copulation using versions of the word jig. 'Jiggle' and 'jigger', for instance, are now archaic, but jig-a-jig has survived, probably because of its use by non-English speakers and those imitating lewd invitations in broken English.

jigger n

a penis. An 18th-century word which is still heard, albeit rarely, and mainly in the north of England.

jiggered adj

a British exhausted.

b nonplussed, astonished. The usual form of words employed is *'I'll be jiggered'* as an exclamation of surprise on the pattern of *'I'll be blowed'* or *'I'll be damned'*.

Jiggered in both the above senses probably originates as a 19th-century euphemism for **buggered**.

jill n British

a policewoman. A term used predominantly in the north of England, particularly in the Liverpool area. It is coined by analogy with **jack**; a policeman (itself usually in the plural form).

jillion n American

an almost inexpressibly large number or amount. A teenagers' coinage to refer to uncountable figures in excess of millions and billions. Other similar terms are 'trillion' (in fact a real number) and **zillion**.

jillock n British

a foolish person, buffoon. A variant form of **pillock**, heard since the late 1970s.

jill off vb

(of a woman) to masturbate. A term coined by women in the 1970s by analogy with the male **jack off**. The term is not widespread but is used both jocularly and seriously, by gay women in particular.

jimbo n American

crack, the refined smokable form of cocaine. An ephemeral ghetto term of the late 1980s.

jim-dandy adj American

excellent, fine. An elaboration of the popular American colloquialism, dandy (jim, like john and jack, was a widespread prefix conferring familiarity).

This expression is often used ironically in modern speech.

jim-jams n pl

1 pyjamas. A nursery word, especially popular in Britain and Australia.

● *'They knew that he [Ronald Reagan] was really an old man in his jim-jams, playing with his dog. Why tell him anything? What would be the point?'*
(Observer, 22 November 1987).

● *'A coat that can double as a dressing-gown, nice stripy jim-jams – such are the staples of male Anglo-Saxon sartoria.'*
(Tatler, November 1985).

2 an attack of nerves, the **heebie-jeebies**. This expression has been applied to delirium tremens (the **DTs**) and to drug-induced terror as well as more mundane jitters. It was first recorded in the mid 19th century.

● *'When the smack begins to flow/ I really don't care any more/ About all the jim-jams in this town/ And all the politicians making crazy sounds.'*
('Heroin', written by Lou Reed and recorded by the Velvet Underground, 1967).

the jimmies n pl Australian

1 an attack of nerves; a variant form of the second sense of **jim-jams**.

2 an attack of diarrhoea; a variant form of the **Jimmy Brits**.

jimmy n British

1 an injection of a narcotic, especially heroin. A word from the lexicon of prison inmates and drug addicts.

2 a shortening of **Jimmy Riddle**, an act of urination.

● *'Hang on to me pint for a minute, I've got to go for a jimmy.'*
(Recorded, young drinker, London, 1987).

Jimmy n British

a familiar (friendly or menacing) form of address, popular in Glasgow and other parts of Scotland and invariably ascribed to all working-class Scots in English jokes and stories. Compare **John**.

Jimmy Brits, the Jimmy Brits

n pl Australian

an attack of diarrhoea. Australian rhyming slang for **the shits**, inspired by the name of a British boxer who toured Australia in 1918. (The surname is sometimes spelt Britt.)

Jimmy Riddle n British

an act of urination. A childish and jocular term derived from rhyming slang for **piddle**.

Jingle n

1 British cash, money, coins. A term used in raffish circles since the 1930s, if not earlier. It has also been recorded in Australian speech.

● '*I'm a bit short of jingle.*'

2 American a telephone call. An American version of the British **bell** or **tinkle**, as in '*give me a jingle*'.

Jingle-jangle n American

money, cash. A term echoing the sound of coins, paralleled in British English by **jingle**.

jin-jang, jingjang n

a penis.

b a woman's sex organs.

Both versions of the term are rare and are originally Americanisms, probably coined under the influence of similar words such as yin, yang (the Ancient Chinese male and female categorization of the life force), **yang** and **whang** (both meaning penis).

jissom, jiss, jizz, jism, jissum, gism n

semen. A word of unknown origin, dating from the 19th century in the USA and by the early 1970s in use all over the English-speaking world.

jive n

1 deceitful or pretentious talk or behaviour, nonsense.

2 a style of fast dancing to accompany swing music or rock 'n' roll.

Both senses of the term originate in black American slang of unknown etymology (it may be from jibe in the sense of change tack, manoeuvre – in conversation or dance – but is more probably derived from a West African dialect term).

3 American marihuana. A now obsolete term.

See also **jive talk**.

jive vb

1 to deceive, tease, browbeat. A black American term from the early 20th century which has enjoyed a vogue among black and white speakers in the late 1980s. For the possible origins of the word, see the noun form.

● '*It was always about the man, how they were going to jive the man into giving them a million dollars.*'
(Elmore Leonard, The Switch, 1978).

2 to dance in a fast energetic style which corresponded in the 1940s to swing music and from the 1950s to rock 'n' roll.

jive-ass adj American

deceitful, pretentious, worthless. A black expression combining **jive** (worthless or deceitful talk or behaviour) and the suffix **-ass**.

● '*I don't want no jive-ass honky lawyer jerkin' me around.*'

jive talk *n*

a style of speech using black musicians' slang and picturesque rhythmic phraseology, originally developed to accompany swing music of the 1930s and 1940s. The vocabulary and cadences of jive talk were adopted by American teenagers in the early 1950s. Jive talk was combined with **bop** talk to influence much of the vocabulary of the later **hipsters** and **beatniks**.

joanie, joany *adj American*

old-fashioned, boringly outdated. A term from the **Valley Girl** lexicon of the 1970s. Its origins are obscure; it may reflect an original antipathy to an individual such as Joan Crawford or Joni Mitchell or may simply be a choice of Joan as a quintessentially older-generation first-name.

joanna *n British*

a piano. A rhyme on the Cockney pronunciation of the instrument.

See also **Jewish typewriter/joanna**.

- *'Give us a tune on the old joanna.'*

Joan of Arc *n Australian*

a shark. A piece of native Australian rhyming slang. An alternative is Noah's Ark.

job *n*

1 a crime. This widespread term occurs in expressions such as '*pull a job*' and in specific forms such as '*bank-job*', '*safe-job*', etc. The word was first used in this sense in the 17th century, usually in the context of theft.

2 a person, thing or action. An all-purpose term for a contraption, specimen or piece of handwork.

- *'Who's the little blonde job by the door?'*
- *'A six-cylinder job.'*

job (someone) *vb*

1 to hit or beat up. Job is an old dialect variant of jab which has been preserved in this working-class Australianism. The word was used in the same sense in Britain in the 1950s, by street-gangs for instance.

2 *American* to deceive, cheat or ruin. A rare late 1980s usage which is a shortening of '*do a job on (someone)*'.

jobbed *adj*

framed, **fitted-up**, informed upon, deceived, victimized or otherwise taken advantage of. An item from the vocabulary of the underworld.

jobbie *vb British*

to defecate. A back-formation from the noun.

jobbie, jobbies *n British*

an act of defecation, excrement. A mock nursery word which is used euphemistically by adults, deriving from expressions such as **big jobs**.

jobsworth *n British*

an obstinate petty official, especially a doorman, bouncer or car park attendant, from their turning down of reasonable requests on the grounds that '*It's more than my job's worth*'. The term was popularized in the rock-music press in the early 1970s when it referred to the officials (often ex-servicemen) who prevented music fans from expressing their enthusiasm or meeting their idols.

- *'There's always some jobsworth between you and the action.'* (Recorded, amateur musician, London, 1987).

jock *n*

1 *British* **a** Scot. Since the 19th century this has been the universal nickname for Scottish males, derived from the northern diminutive for John.

b an un-named male. The word is

used, sometimes dismissively, either as a term of address or as a description.

● *'Ask jock over there what he's drinking.'*

2 a disc jockey. A piece of American radio jargon adopted in other English-speaking areas in the 1970s.

3 *American* an athlete or sportsman. This campus term can now also apply in some cases to sportswomen, in spite of its origin as a shortening of jock strap. Although it can be said affectionately and is a term used by sportsmen about themselves, the word often has overtones of excessive heartiness, brawn, aggression or lack of intelligence.

● *'And the jock shall dwell with the nerd and the cheerleader lie down with the wimp and there will be peace upon the campus.'*
(*Observer*, 29 May 1988).

● *'Loughborough is a university of engineers and sporty types (known as "jocks") – not the sort to have a dangerous reputation.'*
(*The Sunday Times*, 26 November 1989).

jockey *n British*

1 a prostitute's client, a **punter**. A term used by female prostitutes of their customers, playing on **ride** as a metaphor for sexual intercourse.

2 a a male. An all-purpose term of address or designation used in the 1950s.

b a police officer or other official. A specific instance of the former sense. These usages may be versions of **jock** or may be inspired by sense **3**.

3 a driver or pilot.

joe *n*

1 an ordinary man, chap, **bloke**. Originally an Americanism, this use of the name spread to other English-speaking areas in World War II.

2 a victim, dupe or weakling. In this sense the word is used by tricksters, prostitutes and prison inmates, among others, and probably derives from the Cockney **joey**, itself short for **Joe Hunt**, rhyming slang for **cunt**. (Cunt previously meant a foolish, unfortunate or pitiable person, rather than a despicable one.)

3 coffee.

● *'I'm not just some kind of machine you can turn on. I need a cup of joe, a trip to the little boys' room, a glance at the sports pages. Then we'll talk.'*
(*Moonlighting*, American TV series, 1988).

Joe Blake *n Australian*

a snake. An item of native Australian rhyming slang. The eponymous Joe Blake is probably fictitious.

the Joe Blakes *n Australian*

the **DTs** (delirium tremens) as a result of alcoholism, a fit of uncontrolled trembling. Australian rhyming slang for the **shakes**.

See also **Joe Blake**.

Joe Blow *n*

an average man, ordinary person. A rhymed elaboration of **joe**.

Joe Hunt, Joey Hunt *n British*

archaic rhyming slang for **cunt**, in the earlier sense of fool, dupe.

Joes, the Joes *n pl Australian*

a fit of depression, the blues.

Joe Shmo *n American*

1 an average man.

2 a victim, dupe, a simpleton. This Americanism is a personification of *'schmo'* which has also been recorded in British usage.

Joe Soap n British

a an average, ordinary man. The equivalent of a **joe** or **Joe Blow**.

b a dim-witted male drudge or victim. This is the original sense of the name, which is rhyming slang for dope.

joey n

1 British a fool, dupe, victim or weakling. The word is from London working-class usage, deriving from **Joe** or **Joey Hunt**, rhyming slang for **cunt**, which in Cockney speech until the 1950s, referred to a foolish or unfortunate, rather than despicable person. Joey is currently used by teenagers to refer to a timid or unpopular fellow-pupil or gang member.

2 Australian an effeminate man, fop, hermaphrodite or sodomite. It is uncertain whether this usage is derived from the previous sense or the following one.

3 a Australian a young kangaroo. The origin of this term is not the English Christian name but an identical Aboriginal name.

b Australian a baby.

4 British a package smuggled in or out of a prison, in the jargon of prison inmates.

john, the john n

1 a prostitute's customer. John was a 19th-century term for a male sweetheart which was adopted by prostitutes as an all-purpose form of address and later as a synonym for client.

- 'He liked it during the day, the cute ladies sitting around playing music, laughing at things he said. But he didn't care for the white Johns any, their attitude.' (Elmore Leonard, The Switch, 1978).

2 the john a toilet. Originally a more genteel American version of the archaic 'jack' or 'jock' and the almost obsolete **jakes**, all euphemisms for privy.

3 British an arrest. A rare example of police and criminal jargon of the 1960s from the rhyming slang 'John Bull'; **pull**.

4 penis. A fairly rare but recurring usage. Other personifications, such as **John Thomas**, **Willie**, **Peter**, **Percy**, etc., are much more common.

5 British a condom. A shortening of 'johnni (bag)' or **rubber johnny**.

6 John is also used in many local contexts to refer to a male worker, servant, official, etc., and among male homosexuals with a number of meanings, the most prevalent of which is an older protector of a younger man.

John n British

an all-purpose term of address, used typically by a male to another male to express overfamiliarity and/or menace. This working-class usage, common in Greater London, was publicized in connection with the quoted threats by **skinheads** in the early 1970s.

- 'Who you screwing [looking at] John?' (Skinhead challenge used in picking fights).
- ''Ello John, got a new motor?' (Song title, Alexei Sayle, 1984).

John Bull adj Australian

drunk. This witticism is a rhyme on **full** in its euphemistic sense of intoxicated.

- 'He was totally John Bull by three-thirty in the arvo.'

John Doe n American

a an un-named male. This term is used particularly in official parlance to refer to a prisoner of unknown identity, an anonymous male corpse, etc.

- 'We have a John Doe downstairs in the freezer.'

b one's signature.
● *'Stick your John Doe there.'*
See also **John Hancock**.

John Dory n

a story. A rhyming-slang expression heard in Australia, particularly in the inquiry *'What's the John Dory?'*. (A John Dory is an edible fish, *zeus capensis*.)

John Hancock n American

one's signature. John Hancock was the first signatory of the American declaration of independence.

johnnie, johnny n British

a condom, contraceptive sheath. This is the most widespread slang term in British use since the 1940s, although in the 1960s and 1970s it was more usually in the phrases 'johnnie bag' or **rubber johnny**. John or Johnny is, among many other appellations, a 19th century personification of the penis.

John Q. Citizen, John Q. Public n American

the man-in-the-street, typical male, 'Mr Average'. The Q is a jocular reference to the American custom of including middle initials in names recorded in official contexts.

johnson n American

a penis.
b backside, buttocks.

Both senses are personifications used humorously or straightforwardly, especially in black speech. They date from the late 19th century and are elaborations of the use of **john** to designate anything male.
● *'He can kiss my johnson.'*
(*The Bosses' Wife*, US film, 1986).

John Thomas n British

penis. A hearty and/or affectionate personification in use since the mid 19th century. It was used by D. H. Lawrence in *Lady Chatterley's Lover*, written in 1928 and first published in an unabridged edition in Britain in 1959. The phrase now seems to be used particularly by women.

joint, the joint n

1 a marihuana cigarette or a cigarette containing a mix of hashish and tobacco. Joint supplanted **reefer** as the universal term for a cannabis cigarette in the early 1960s. The precise dating and etymology of the word are obscure.
● *'Several large joints passed along the room before someone suggested it was time to go outside and play with the Kalashnikovs.'*
(*Tatler*, April 1990).
2 **the joint** American prison. A specialization of the colloquial sense of 'joint' as a place, building or premises.
3 American penis. A metaphor based on images of meat and (an imaginary) bone.

jollies n

gratification. The expression can cover indulgences ranging from innocent enjoyment, through thrills, to more sinister and/or sexual stimulation. The word usually occurs in the phrase **get one's jollies**.

jollop n

1 medicine, especially a liquid laxative. The word is either a blend of juice and dollop or, more probably, derives from 'jalap', a Mexican root formerly used in laxative powders.
2 a large portion, lump or serving. A variant form of dollop.

jolly n British

a **joint**, marihuana cigarette. A term

281

used, mainly by middle-class smokers, in the 1970s and 1980s.
- *'We were stuck in the queue, so we just decided to sit back and roll a jolly.'*
(Recorded, ex-hippy, London, December, 1988).

jolly-bean n British

a benzedrine tablet or other amphetamine pill, in the jargon of drug users and prison inmates of the early 1960s. The word is inspired by the American **jellybean**, used to describe any illicit drug in pill or capsule form.

jolly d. adj British

'jolly decent'. A public-school or upper-class term of approbation, often used ironically or sarcastically. It is usually an interjection, rather than a description.

jolt n

a the sudden initial effect of an illicit drug, a **rush**.
b an injection of a narcotic.
c a drink of strong alcohol, usually a spirit.

jonah n Australian

a shark. This is not a reference to the whale but a contracted form of the rhyming slang **Joan of Arc**.

jones n American

1 penis. Now predominantly a term used by black speakers and their imitators. It may derive from a 19th-century personification of the male member as 'Mr. Jones'.
2 a drug habit.
- *'They said they had to knock over a couple of stores for money to support their scag jones.'*

josser n British

a foolish or obnoxious person. Used as a less offensive version of **tosser**, the

term was heard particularly in the north of England in the 1980s. The word in fact has had a separate existence since the 19th century during which time it has designated a simpleton, a codger, a fop and a parasite among other senses. Its ultimate origins are obscure, although joss is said to have been a dialect term for bump or jostle.

journo n Australian

a journalist. A characteristic Australian shortening which showed signs of catching on in Britain in the late 1980s.

joy bang vb, n American

(to take) a dose or injection of a narcotic for occasional pleasure, rather than to satisfy a regular habit or addiction. A drug users' term from the late 1950s. **Joy pop** was a more widespread synonym.

joy juice n

1 alcoholic drink. A regularly revived term popular with American teenagers and students in the late 1980s. **Juice** is a common synonym for alcohol.
2 semen. A predominantly American usage.

joy pop vb

a to take illicit drugs on an infrequent and casual, rather than habitual, basis.
b to inject a drug intramuscularly, to **skin-pop**.
See also **joy bang**.

joy popper n

a an occasional drug user, specifically a user of hard drugs who injects infrequently for pleasure rather than regularly to satisfy an addiction.
b a user of heroin, morphine, etc., who injects the drug into the flesh or intramuscularly rather than directly

into a vein. An addicts' term of the late 1950s. The activity is also known as **skin popping**.

joy smoke n

marihuana, hashish. A term popular with some American teenagers and students in the 1980s.

joystick n

1 penis. A pun on the name of the steering control column of aeroplanes, although some authorities claim that the slang euphemism for the male member actually preceded the aeronautic usage (which may in fact derive ultimately from joist).

2 a cannabis cigarette, a **joint**. A fairly rare euphemism.

J.T. n British

1 an abbreviated form of **John Thomas** (penis).

● '*J T Izzard.*'

(Pen-name of British pornographic-magazine writer of the 1980s)

2 Jamaica talk.

jubbies n pl British

a woman's breasts. This childish sounding term was used by (predominantly middle-class) teenagers and adults from the 1980s and is probably a blend of **jugs** and **bubbies**.

jubbly n British

money, wealth. The word is used in London working-class speech, especially in the phrase '*(lots of) lovely jubbly*'. Jubbly was the trade name of an orange drink sold in a triangular carton. Especially when frozen, it was popular with schoolchildren in the 1950s and 1960s. *Lovely Jubbly!* was its advertising slogan. In the late 1980s the term was particularly popular with the nouveau riche, **yuppies** and criminals.

jubnuts n pl British

a southern English rural term for **dags** (fragments of dung clinging to the rear of sheep and other shaggy animals).

judy n British

a girl or woman. A very common word in working-class use in the north of England in the 1950s and 1960s. Judy was a popular 19th-century Christian name, seen as typical of common women (as in Punch and Judy, for example). The word is also used in Australia as an alternative to **Sheila**.

jug n

prison. This term from the beginning of the 19th century is usually part of the phrases '*in jug*' or '*in the jug*'. It probably derives from 18th-century dialect '*jougs*' meaning stocks or pillory (from the French joug, yoke) rather than from jug as a container of liquid. In modern usage the term is jocular.

jug, jug up vb British

1 to imprison. From the noun **jug**.

2 to drink alcohol, especially heartily and to excess.

jugged adj

1 imprisoned. From the noun **jug**.

2 drunk. A rare but recurrent term.

juggins n British

a silly person. A mild middle- and upper-class term of abuse, originating late in the 19th century and used in recent years typically by parents and schoolteachers.

● '"*O, you juggins,*" *said Miss Trent, the games mistress crossly. Mavis bit her lip.*'

(*Back in the Jug Agane*, Geoffrey Willans and Ronald Searle, 1959).

jug handles n pl British

ears, particularly large prominent ears. The term is used by all ages and social classes in poking fun.

jugs n pl

1 a woman's breasts. Originally an Australian vulgarism, inspired by milk-jugs, and probably influenced by the much older term **dugs**. This expression has also been used in Britain and the USA.

2 ears, particularly large prominent ears. The word used in this sense, primarily in Britain, is a shortening of 'jug-ears' or **jug handles**.

juice n American

1 alcohol, **booze**. A pre-World-War II American term still in widespread use.

2 electricity, power.

- *'Give it some more juice.'*

3 American gossip, interesting news. A teenage term of the late 1970s and 1980s which is probably a back-formation from 'juicy'.

juiced, juiced-up adj

drunk. Unlike other slang terms deriving from **juice**, this is not exclusively American.

- *'Howard you never used to talk to me that way.'*
  'I'm just juiced, that's all.'
  (S. Clay Wilson cartoon in *Head Comix*, 1968).

juice joint n American

a bar, liquor store or refreshment stand.

juicer, juice head/freak n

American

an alcoholic, drunkard or habitual heavy drinker. These terms probably originated in black slang of the 1940s.

ju-jubes n pl

a woman's breasts. The term is inspired by the brand-name of a fruit-flavoured gum lozenge.

jumbly, jumblie n British

a jumble sale. A word used particularly by students and teenagers.

jumbo

1 British a fool, a slow, large and/or dimwitted person. A mainly working-class term, used for instance by the CID to refer to uniformed police officers. (Jumbo as applied to elephants derives from the African word *jamba*, anglicized as a name for P. T. Barnum's famous animal exhibit.) In this case the image of a slow, ponderous person is probably also influenced by **dumbo**.

2 British backside, buttocks.

3 crack this is one of many ephemeral nicknames used on the American streets for this powerful drug. Jumbo in this sense was recorded in 1986.

jump vb

to have sex with. This term implying male assertion, domination or assault has been in use in English since the 17th century. It is paralleled in many other languages (the French equivalent is *sauter*). The word is now often used by street-gang members, etc. to refer to indecent assault, influenced by the term's colloquial meaning of attack unexpectedly.

jump n

an act of sexual intercourse. This term has been in use since the 17th century. It is almost invariably said by men, implying as it does an active, possessive male and a submissive or victimized female.

jump someone's bones vb

American

to have sex with someone. The expression, first heard in the 1960s, has rough-and-ready, crass overtones. It invariably refers to the sex act from the male point of view.

- *'I guess she realised I just wanted to jump her bones.'*

Junction, the Junction n
British
the Clapham Junction area of London. The familiar form was popularized by Nell Dunn's novel (later filmed) *Up the Junction*, which also inspired a hit record by the pop group Squeeze.

jungle bunny n
a negro or other dark-skinned person. A racist epithet which is usually applied to Afro-Caribbeans, and is also used by Australians to refer to Aborigines and South Sea Islanders. It has been heard from at least the 1950s.

jungle juice n
strong, low-quality alcoholic drink. This was the term applied in the armed services during World War II to various home-made alcoholic concoctions. (It was previously a nickname for African rum.) The phrase is now used to refer to any cheap, potent drink.

jungly adj British
disorganized, messy, primitive or unsophisticated. An upper-class term of disapproval, employed by **Sloane Rangers** among others. It is in fact an Anglo-Indian word from the colonial era. It was then spelled *jungli* (from Urdu).

junk n
narcotics, hard drugs. The word

(originally a Middle English term for nautical paraphernalia and detritus) was applied to opium in American underworld argot in the late 19th century. It was used to designate heroin by the first decade of the 20th century and has remained one of the most widespread synonyms for this and other addictive drugs. The word spread as the drug-taking habit spread in other English-speaking areas, becoming well-known in Britain during the 1950s.

- *'Fuzz against junk.'*
(Title of book by the pseudonymous Akbar del Piombo, 1965).

junker n American
1 a dilapidated car, **banger**.
2 an alternative (and rarer) version of junkie.

junkie, junky n
a drug addict, a habitual user of 'hard' drugs such as heroin or morphine. The term, derived from the word **junk** became popular in the USA in the 1920s and spread to Britain and Australia in the 1950s.

- *'When we think of a junkie we picture the reckless youth, squatting in the rubble of his life, a hypodermic in his hand.'*
(Independent, 17 July 1989).

juve, juvie n
a a juvenile offender or delinquent. The shortened form is now more common in the USA than Britain, but in the late 1950s and early 1960s 'juvenile delinquent' and its short forms became catchphrases in the British press.
b juvenile court or juvenile custody.
c a 'juvenile lead', in show-business parlance.

K

K *n*

1 one thousand. This abbreviation existed in limited slang usage in the 1970s (based on the k of kilo), but it was its use in computer jargon (to mean a storage capacity of 1,024 bytes) which was first transposed to express sums of money when discussing fees or salaries. It then entered general colloquial use in the 1980s.

- *'He's on 35K a year.'*

2 *British* a knighthood, from the initial letter, or that of KBE, KCMG, etc.

- *'Brenda has now let it be known to Downing Street that Milne should be given a "K" in the birthday honours list. Surprisingly enough Thatcher seems to approve.'*
  (*Private Eye* magazine, April 1989).

kack *n*

an alternative spelling of **cack**.

kafe *n British*

an alternative spelling of **kayf**.

kaffir *n*

a black person. A racist term used initially (and still) in South Africa to refer to indigenous blacks. (Kaffir was one 19th-century name for Bantu-speaking South African tribespeople, originating in the arabic *kafir*; infidel.) The word is sometimes used, mainly by middle-aged or elderly speakers, in other English-speaking areas.

kahsi *n British*

an alternative spelling of **khazi**.

kaifa *n British*

an alternative spelling of **kife**.

kale *n*

money. A word from the vocabulary of **cads**, **spivs**, the pre-World-War II British underworld and their American counterparts. It is occasionally resurrected today, normally in a humorous context. The inspiration for the word (a kind of cabbage) parallels contemporary alternatives such as **lettuce**, **cabbage** and **long green**.

kalied *adj British*

drunk. A fairly popular word in the north of England (usually pronounced 'kay-lide') which has been used in the long-running TV soap opera *Coronation Street*. Some authorities claim that kay-is a dialect prefix meaning askew or awry; Paul Beale in Partridge's *Dictionary of Slang and Unconventional English* derives kalied from 'kali', a children's sherbet dip.

- *'And all he could do was go out and get kalied.'*

kanga *n Australian*

1 a pneumatic drill. The term compares the pounding, up-and-down motion of the drill (and its operator) to the bounding of a kangaroo.

2 a prison warder. This expression is derived from rhyming slang, 'kangaroo'; **screw**. The same usage has been recorded in Britain in the 1980s, both by prisoners and by schoolchildren referring to teachers.

3 money. An alternative piece of rhyming slang gives **screw** in the sense of money earned.

kangaroo (it) *vb Australian*

to squat, particularly in order to defecate; from the kangaroo's habit of sitting back on its rear legs, supported by its tail.

- *'Not wanting to contract any trendy venereal fauna, I kangaroo-ed it.'* (Kathy Lette, *Girls' Night Out*, 1989).

kangaroos in the top paddock *adj Australian*

crazy, eccentric or deranged. A picturesque coinage, probably based on the colloquial 'bats in the belfry'.

kangaroo valley *n British*

a nickname for Earls Court, the area of London in which the first influx of young Australian tourists and travellers settled or stayed in the 1960s and which still houses a large Australian community today. The name is used by Australians and by local people; it was publicized in the cartoon *The Adventures of Barry McKenzie* by Barry Humphries and Nicholas Garland.

- *'Oh well, better get back to Kangaroo Valley via the North Circular.'* (London taxi driver in *The Wonderful World of Barry McKenzie*, 1988).

kaplonker *n British*

a crowbar, in the late 1980s jargon of the London Flying Squad. The word is probably in origin a nursery term for any unnamed heavy object.

- *'Another funny moment came during a Sweeney raid. The cops use an iron bar nicknamed a "kaplonker" to lever open doors.'* (*News of the World*, 5 February 1987).

kark (it) *vb Australian*

an alternative spelling of **cark it**.

karma *n*

a one's personal destiny, fate.

b an aura, impression or influence, **vibes**.

Both senses of the word are inaccurate borrowings, dating from the **hippy** era, from Hindu and Buddhist writings in which the Sanskrit word denotes actions determining one's future state of incarnation.

See also **instant karma, huntley**.

karzi *n British*

an alternative spelling of **khazi**.

Kate and Sidney *n British*

steak and kidney. A witticism heard in canteens and homes when steak and kidney pie or pudding was a staple dish. The phrase was recorded in 1914 and is still heard.

Kate Carney *n British*

the army. A piece of approximate rhyming slang inspired by the name of a music hall singing star of the late 19th century. The phrase was still in use in the 1950s, but is now archaic.

kayf, kafe *n British*

an alternative rendering of **caff** (café), imitating the jocular or unwitting mispronunciation of the original French.

kaylied *adj British*

an alternative spelling of **kalied**.

kazi *n British*

an alternative spelling of **khazi**.

kazoo *n American*

the backside, buttocks. A word of unknown origin (it is probably unconnected with the musical instrument, the name of which imitates its sound); other jocular terms using the same median sounds include **mazoomas**, **gazungas**, etc. (all synonyms for breasts).

kecks n pl British

trousers. This word is the northern English version of the archaic 'kicks', heard in other parts of the country from the 17th century until the 1940s but now obsolete. Liverpool **mods** of the mid 1960s used to refer contemptuously to 'half-mast kecks', that is unfashionably short trousers which flap around the lower calves or above the ankles. 'Strides' was the slang synonym usually preferred further south. **Underkecks** are, of course, underpants, worn by either sex.

keen adj

excellent, great. A teenage vogue word in North America in the late 1950s and 1960s. The enthusiastic term now sounds dated but is still heard, usually said by ingenuous and ironic adults, although there are some signs of a revival among younger speakers both as a description and exclamation (**neato-keeno** was an elaborated version).

keeno n British

a keen, enthusiastic person. A schoolchildren's word, usually said scathingly of a **swot** or excessively hearty fellow pupil.
• 'We just sat at the back and let the keenos volunteer.'
(Recorded, London schoolgirl, 1987).

keep cave vb British

to keep quiet, be wary and/or keep a look out. A schoolboy term of the 1950s from the Latin imperative cave; beware. In English the word is pronounced 'kay-vee'.

• 'They asked me to keep cave in case old Goatman came along.'
(Recorded, former grammar-school boy, 1986).

keep one's cool vb

to maintain one's sang froid, keep one's composure. A phrase which was slang in the 1950s but which is now a common colloquialism. The expression was a musician's **hip** version of 'keep cool', which has been used to mean keep calm, etc. since the last century.

keep on trucking vb

carry on, keep going. A black dancers' slogan used as a catchphrase exhortation by American and later British **hippies** from about 1970. **Trucking** has various associated meanings including an exaggerated sauntering stride or simply 'soldiering on', all deriving from jitterbug dance contests of the 1930s and 1940s in which trucking was a dance step.

keester n American

an alternative spelling of **keister**.

keflumix vb

an alternative spelling of **kerflummox**.

kegged adj

drunk. A fairly rare word used typically by college and high-school students in the USA and occasionally by their counterparts in Britain. The British usage may be a separate coinage, also from keg beer.

kegger n American

a beer party. An adolescents' term.

keister, keester n American

backside, buttocks, anus. This fairly common term is from Yiddish kiste, in turn deriving from Middle and Old Germanic *Kista* and from the Latin *cista*, a chest. The Yiddish word denoted a portable chest and was adapted by English speakers to mean anything used as a travelling container, including a hawker's display cabinet, a satchel and a trouser pocket. The transition from these senses to a part of the human body is not completely clear; it has been suggested that it became an underworld synonym for the anus as used to smuggle contraband across borders or into prison. The term is now rather old-fashioned but was used by Ronald Reagan in the late 1980s.

kelper n British

an inhabitant of the Falkland Islands. This nickname became known during and after the Falklands War of 1982 and by 1989 was established enough to be used without explanation (but with comic intent) in the press. It derives from kelp, the seaweed gathered for fuel and fertilizer by the inhabitants of many rocky island outposts.

kelt n British

money. A variant form of **gelt**, heard in the East End of London in the 1950s.

Ken American

a male dullard, (clean-cut) bland conformist youth or man. Ken is the name given to the male counterpart of the **Barbie Doll**.

Kensington Gore n British

artificial blood. This expression, which is an elaboration of the literary 'gore', has been theatrical slang since before World War II and is still heard. It is a pun on the name of the road connecting Kensington and Knightsbridge in London.

kerflummox, kerflumix vb

to baffle, confuse, bamboozle. A hu-morous embellishment of the colloquial 'flummox'. Ker- is a prefix indicating force, effort or impulse, reminiscent of Anglo-Saxon and modern German ge-: 'made'.

- '*After all their explanations I've got to say I'm totally kerflummoxed.*'
(Recorded, US diplomat's wife, London, 1988).

kermit n British

a French person. A jocular nickname used by students in the 1980s. It is inspired by the character 'Kermit the Frog' in the 1970s US television series, *The Muppet Show*.

- '*Don't forget to send invitations to the kermits.*'
(Recorded, student, London, 1988).

Kevin n British

a common, vulgar or boorish young man. This disparaging term of the 1970s and 1980s is typically used by snobs or wags to designate a working-class or lower-middle-class youth without taste or sophistication. The Christian name supposedly epitomizes this social sub-group (the female equivalent of a Kevin is a **Sharon**). **Wayne** is sometimes suggested as an alternative for Kevin.

- '*That pub's full of Kevins, we never go in there.*'
Compare **Brian**.

kevinish adj British

common, uncouth, and/or vacuous. From the noun form **Kevin**. A disparaging term used by middle-class speakers since the late 1970s.

- '*Other schools just can't understand why they look so "Kevin-ish" – a term describing the white socks and footballers' haircuts (long at the back) which are so popular there.*'
(Tatler March 1987).

kewpie doll n

an excessively cute and/or over-dressed or over made-up girl or woman. The original American Kewpie Doll (a trademark name based on Cupid) is a fairy-like baby. In Australia the name is used as rhyming slang for **moll** in the sense of prostitute.

key n American

a kilo of an illicit drug, typically marihuana, which could be brought by street dealers in this quantity (in Britain the standard quantity is the non-metric **weight**).

- 'He scored a couple of keys and brought it across the border.'

See also **church key**.

key adj

essential, emblematic or supreme. A **preppie** term of approval or endorsement.

- 'Those shoes are key.'
- 'A pair of real key shoes.'

keyhole vb British

1 to pick a lock or enter and rob a building by tampering with a door lock. A police and underworld term.

2 to **busk** at the front door of a pub or other building.

khazi, kharzie n British

a toilet. A term dating from the 19th century which has been in widespread use in working-class speech and in the armed services. There are many alternative spellings of this word, which is often assumed to be of African or Far Eastern colonial origin, perhaps by analogy with khaki. In fact it derives from the Latin word for house and its derivatives, such as *casa* in Spanish and Italian or *case* (meaning 'hut') in French. The word entered working-class speech in **parlyaree**, the latinate jargon of tramps, peddlers and show-

people. Khazi was first thought suitable for broadcasting in the late 1960s and was popularized by such TV comedies as *Till Death us do Part* (written by Johnny Speight).

khyber n British

the anus. From the rhyming slang 'Khyber Pass'; **arse**. This London working-class expression was used in TV comedies of the late 1960s, trading on the fact that most viewers were only vaguely aware of its vulgar provenance. The word appeared in working-class speech after the Khyber Pass was introduced into the public perception by the Afghan wars of the later 19th century.

- 'A kick up the Khyber.'

khyfer n British

an alternative spelling of **kife**.

kibble n American

food, meal. Kibble is a word of unknown origin which literally means coarse-ground dogfood.

- 'OK I've got it, we'll chloroform her kibble!'

(M*A*S*H, US TV comedy, 1981).

kibitz, kibbitz vb American

to pass comment on or offer (normally unwelcome) advice. The verb, which typically applies to an annoying onlooker at a card game or sports performance, comes from the Yiddish *kibitsen*, which in turn derives from *Kiebitz*, the German name for a lapwing, a supposedly raucous, insistent bird. The term is sometimes used to mean simply spectate without the pejorative overtones.

kibitzer, kibbitzer n American

a person who **kibitzes**, a spectator or onlooker. For the word's derivation see **kibitz**.

kibosh n British
See **put the kibosh on.**

kick vb

1 give up (a habit). A piece of drug addicts' jargon which entered general currency in the 1950s.

2 American to be exciting, successful, impressive. This is a shortened form of **kick ass** in its secondary meaning of 'make a strong impression'.

- 'That suit really kicks.'

kick n

1 a sudden sensation of excitement, thrill. This Americanism spread to the rest of the English-speaking world in the 1940s, helped by Cole Porter's song, 'I get a kick out of you'. The plural form **kicks** was a vogue term of the early 1960s.

2 American a particular activity or period of involvement. In the language of **hipsters, beatniks,** etc.

- 'She's on a health kick.'

kick ass vb American

to punish or forcibly restore order, make trouble or behave aggressively. An expression used typically of an authority figure such as an army officer or sports coach. 'Kick ass and take names' is an elaborated form of the expression (meaning identify and chastize). By extension, kick ass can simply mean to express oneself or enjoy oneself boisterously.

- 'That band really kick ass!'

kickass adj American

aggressive, rousing and forceful, tough. A word usually indicating admiration or approval (although sometimes grudgingly).

- 'I think they kind of appreciate his kickass attitude.'

kickback n

money returned or paid as part of an illegal or covert agreement. This term, which is no longer slang, originated in the pre-World-War II American underworld, in which to kick back meant to pay a fixed part of one's income, or a fixed commission, in return for favour or protection. (The original image evoked was probably that of kicking back a portion of booty across a floor.)

kicker, the kicker n American

a the 'final straw', clincher.

b a hidden catch.

c something exciting or stimulating.

kickers n pl

shoes, boots. This slang term from the 1950s and 1960s (heard mainly in the USA) was appropriated by the French manufacturers of casual sports boots in the 1970s.

kick in vb

to contribute, subscribe or pay up. The phrase is more popular in the USA than in Britain. It is presumably based on the image of a circle of gang members each kicking a portion of their booty into a central pile. It usually has overtones of illegal or at least unofficial activity, such as bribery or a 'whip-round' to buy liquor.

- 'If everyone kicks in we should be able to afford to give her a decent sendoff.'

kicking, kick-in n British

a physical assault, beating. This term may literally indicate an assault with the feet or may refer to any savage and concerted attack. It is a working-class expression used by street fighters and the police among others.

- 'We caught him down the alley and give him a good kicking.'

kick it vb

to die. A shortened version of **kick the bucket.**

kick off vb American

1 to die. A later variation of **kick the bucket**, the equivalent of the British and Australian **kick it**.

2 to leave, go away.

kick out the jams vb American

to 'let rip', get rid of all inhibitions and restrictions. A catch phrase in the rock-music world of the late 1960s, to which it was introduced by the rock group the MC5, who were allied to the anarchistic White Panther movement in Detroit. The phrase probably comes originally from an instruction to remove the chocks or wedges restraining a dragster car or aircraft.

kicks n pl

1 British trousers. An alternative and now archaic form of **kecks**, dating from the 18th century.

2 American sports shoes. A rarer version of **kickers**, used particularly by school and college students.

3 thrills. The plural form of **kick**. A usage which became popular in the late 1950s and notorious for its adoption by juvenile delinquents and other nihilists to explain their motives.

- *'They killed for kicks.'*
  (Headline in *True Detective* magazine, 1963).
- *'Kicks just keep getting harder to find/ and all your kicks ain't bringin' you peace of mind/ before you find out it's too late/ girl, you better get straight.'*
  (Barry Mann & Cynthia Weil, 'Kicks', recorded by Paul Revere and the Raiders, 1966).

kicksies n

trousers. A diminutive form of **kicks**, heard since the 19th century, although now rare.

kickstart vb, n

(to urge into) sudden action. A meta-phor taken from motorcycling and applied to a variety of contexts in both literal and figurative senses. **Bump-start** is a synonym.

- *'The chick really had to kickstart the old goat.'*
- *'We need to give the project a quick kickstart.'*

kick the bucket vb

to die. The phrase dates from the 17th or 18th century and the bucket in question may be either a suicide's prop or more probably a British dialect word (also in the form 'bucker') for the beam from which slaughtered animals were hung.

- *'Ches hasn't been the same since his old lady kicked the bucket.'*
  (Recorded, barman, London, 1988).

kick the habit vb

to give up an addiction. This now common phrase was a heroin addicts' euphemism of the 1950s.

kicky, kicksy adj American

exciting, stimulating, spirited. From the noun **kick** or **kicks** in the sense of excitement. In the 1970s and 1980s the word has taken on an extra nuance of up-to-date or modish. (The comparative and superlative forms are kickier and kickiest.)

- *'That kicky little red sportscar of yours.'*

kiddo n

a (usually patronizing or provocative) form of address to a younger person. An elaboration of the colloquial kid.

kidlet n British

a small child. A middle-class term employing the otherwise archaic diminutive suffix '-let' (also seen in **quidlet**).

kid stuff n

a pornography featuring young children.

b sexual abuse of children or paedophiliac practices.

These are bland euphemisms from the jargon of police and pornographers.

kif, kief n

marihuana or hashish. The word, pronounced 'keef', is North African Arabic slang for the cannabis (usually in herbal form) smoked there. More specifically, kif may designate refined powdered hemp plants mixed with powdered tobacco or, as in the Berber stories of Mohammed Mrabet, to uncleaned **grass**. The word's literal meaning is 'pleasure'. Many British drug users of the late 1950s and 1960s had their formative experiences of cannabis in Morocco.

kife, kifer, kyf, kyfer, kaifa, khyfer n British

a a woman or women as a sexual partner or sex object.

b sexual activity (invariably heterosexual). This word in its various spellings is now rarely used. It was nearly always restricted to working-class, underworld or armed-services slang, with an area of meaning now more often catered for by words such as **crumpet**, **tottie** or **rumpo**. The exact etymology of the term is obscure; it may be a 19th-century alteration of an Arabic word keyif, meaning sensual consolation. As the definition implies, the word is used exclusively by men.

● 'Bangkok was OK – plenty of kifer.'
(Recorded, petroleum engineer, London, 1987).

kifer, kyfer vb British

to have sex (with). A rare and now virtually obsolete derivation of the nouns **kife**, **kifer**, etc. (meaning women or sex). The word was exclusively used by males.

kike n, adj

a jew. An old-fashioned racist term which some authorites derive from diminutives of the name Isaac (see **ikey (mo)**). Others, including the Yiddish expert and humorist, Leo Rosten, ascribe to the practice of illiterate Jewish immigrants signing their names with a circle (kikel in Yiddish) on arrival in the USA. The word was adopted by British and Australian speakers and is still occasionally heard.

● 'Take her, kike, she's all yours ... a wop whore and a kike fag in a one-room office on the strip should go a long way together.'
(Platinum Logic, Tony Parsons, 1981).

kiki n, adj American

a (a) bisexual.

b (a) male homosexual.

A fairly rare descriptive term of uncertain origin. It may be a corruption of an Hispanic word, or of he/she.

kilburn n British

a (police) diary. A piece of London rhyming slang; the rhyme is with Kilburn Priory, a street and area in the north-west of the city.

kill vb

to finish off.

● 'Let's kill these beers and go back to my place.'

killer, killer-diller n, adj

(something) superlative. Killer-diller was an Americanism of the 1940s which was briefly in vogue in Britain in the late 1950s among **teddy boys** and bohemians. Killer was a popular teenage term in the USA, particularly among black youth in the 1960s and 1970s, spreading to Britain and Aus-

tralia in the 1980s with disco and hip hop music, break dancing, etc.
- *'That band's a killer.'*
- *'Man, that's a killer-diller car.'*

killing floor n American

a place where sexual intercourse takes place. A phrase which figures in the lyrics of many blues and rock songs until the 1970s. The expression may originally refer to an abattoir in which case the transposition to a sexual context is evoking brutal carnality. Alternatively the sexual usage may arise via a sense of a place where punishing work or effort takes place. The phrase was used as the title of a Howling Wolf record of the early 1960s.

kilt n British

a a girl or woman.

b women as sex objects or sexual activity in general.

In both senses the word is usually found as part of a phrase such as *'a bit of kilt'*. It is part of non-regional working-class slang and is occasionally used self-consciously or facetiously by speakers from other backgrounds. In origin it is a humorous substitute for the more widespread but now dated **skirt**.

kindy n Australian

a kindergarten. Another example of the modern Australian tendency to abbreviate many everyday terms (**arvo**, **blowie**, **hottie** are others).

king hit n Australian

a a hit from behind, stab in the back.

b a knockout blow.

kink n

a a sexual deviant.

b a sexual perversion or perverse idiosyncrasy, an unhealthy trait.

Kinky has been used since the 1920s for deviant, becoming a vogue word of

the early 1960s. The noun form (borrowed as the name of the pop group, the Kinks) is a later adaptation, usually used to express mild disapproval. In colloquial speech the word has now acquired an innocent sense of 'minor problem', flaw or irregularity.

kinky adj

perverted or perverse, unorthodox. In Britain in the early 1960s kinky became so widespread a vogue word that its meaning became diluted to denote merely fashionable/interesting. The term began in the 1920s or earlier as an underground euphemism for sexually deviant, and later as an ironic **gay** term of approbation. In spite of its suggestion of perversities such as fetishism the word was inoffensive enough to be used in 'polite' company, hence its popularity in the first flush of sexual liberalism in the 1960s.

- *'He looks at me like that, at least he's not kinky. That's a relief. He's too fat to be kinky, too fat and forty guineas at least.'*
(*About Town* magazine, June 1962).

kinky boots n pl British

women's knee or thigh-length leather boots as worn from 1962 to 1965. This kind of footwear, inspired by fetishist styles, was considered daring at the time and emblematic of the 'swinging sixties'. The leather style, of which kinky boots were a part, was one of the first 'underground' modes to be adopted by ordinary members of the public. It was disseminated via the media, particularly by way of *The Avengers* TV series. Diana Rigg and Patrick MacNee, the stars of the cult programme, actually recorded a song called *Kinky Boots* in 1965.

- *'Kinky? Kinky is British for weird, you know what I mean?'*
(*Harper*, US film, 1966).

kip n

a a period of sleep.

- '*If I don't get my full eight hours' kip I'm ratty all day.*'
  (Recorded, teacher, Bristol, 1989).
- '*I pulled into the layby for a quick kip in the back of the van.*'

b a bed or place to sleep.

- '*A kip for the night.*'

The word kippe meant a brothel in 18th-century English, probably deriving from a similar Danish word signifying a low-class inn. In the 19th century the word was extended to denote a **doss house**, and by the early 20th century was acquiring its modern meanings. The word is not unknown in the USA but is much more commonly used in Britain.

kip, kip down vb

to (lie down to) sleep. The verb comes from the noun **kip**, ultimately deriving from a Danish word for a tavern or hovel.

Kipling adj British

a term of approval among schoolchildren in 1989. The term is explained by the following elaborate pun:

- '*If training-shoes provoke an excited exclamation of "Hey, man, they're Kipling!" the wearer can rest assured that their street-credibility is intact. Slur "ruddy hard" into Rudyard, and there you have it.*'
  (*Guardian*, 26 September 1989).

kippered adj British

devastated, trounced, **stitched up** or **gutted**. A working-class term which is currently in vogue among the fashionable young in London. The metaphor is 'dead, gutted, skinned and cooked', in the sense of thoroughly humiliated or taken advantage of, and is probably inspired by the earlier 'done up like a kipper'.

- '*I wouldn't advise you to try doing business with them. I tell you, I was kippered . . .*'
  (Recorded, advertising executive, London, 1988).

kirp n British

penis. A rare **backslang** deformation of **prick** (the spelling is arbitrary since the word is never written). Backslang is rare in modern English slang, but persists in some restricted social milieus and trades (notably butchers and meatpackers, market traders, etc.).

kiss n

See **French kiss, soul kiss**.

K.I.S.S. exclamation

'keep it simple, stupid!', avoid unnecessary complications. A business catchphrase pronounced like the word 'kiss', when giving an instruction or citing a principle. The expression originated in American computer jargon.

kiss ass vb American

to abase oneself, flatter or curry favour. A contemptuous description of obsequious or toadying behaviour.

- '*You wouldn't like it [working in a large corporation]; the first thing you'd have to do is to learn to kiss ass.*'
  (Recorded, American female executive, London, 1984).

kiss-ass n American

a sycophantic person 'crawler'. This term of contempt can also be employed as an adjective as in a '*kiss-ass speech*', for instance.

kisser n

mouth. A now rather dated word which probably originated among boxers and their entourages in the mid 19th century. Its meaning is occasionally extended to 'face', particularly as part of an expression such as 'a punch/smack in the kisser'.

- 'Wipe that silly expression off your kisser.'

kissing tackle n British

mouth, lips. A joky euphemism coined in the late 1980s on the lines of **wedding tackle** and **laughing gear**. The phrase is used by teenagers and young adults.

- 'There's a Fosters; get your kissing tackle round that.'

kiss-off n

a dismissal. Originally an Americanism, the term has entered international English with the connotations of offhandedness, abrupt thoughtlessness or condescending rejection.

kiss the porcelain god vb

to vomit. A picturesque euphemism which is particularly popular among American college students; an alternative form is 'kneel to the porcelain god' or **drive the porcelain bus**. The image is one of bending over to kiss the feet of an idol. An attack of diarrhoea involves **riding the porcelain Honda**.

kiss up vb American

to behave as a sycophant (towards), 'crawl' to or flatter. A rarer version of **kiss ass** or the British suck up.

kissy, kissy-kissy adj

affectionate, sentimental. The words may be applied good-humouredly or pejoratively, suggesting cloying or exaggerated affection.

kit n British

clothes. A working-class expression typically used by ex-servicemen which enjoyed a vogue in the late

1980s among working-class speakers and their imitators. It is synonymous with **gear** or **clobber**.

- '"People have really put some kit on", remarked a taxi driver as a stream of Philip Somerville hats filed out of St Martin-in-the-Fields.' (Tatler magazine, June 1985).
- 'His idea of romantic chat was to say "get your kit off and come over here".' (Recorded, female social worker, London, 1987).
- 'Here we see Debbie with her group Blondie. She still hasn't whipped her kit off!' (Smash Hits magazine, November 1989).

kite n

1 an aeroplane. A piece of airman's slang from World War I, well-known to afficionados of adventure stories or war films.

2 a worthless cheque. In the 19th century the word was used to describe any false or worthless bill or document.

kite vb

to pass a worthless cheque.

- 'You wouldn't try to kite a cheque on me, would you?' (Budgie, TV series, 1971).

kite man/dropper/flyer n

an issuer of worthless cheques. **Kite** has meant a dud cheque or other financial document for the past century. These terms, heard in all anglophone areas, usually refer to professional criminals who specialize in **kiting**.

kiting n

passing dud cheques. In the 1980s the term invariably described a deliberate criminal activity, although it could formerly refer also to issuing a cheque in the hope, possibly ill-founded, of finding the funds to support it. The word is international English.

kitty n
See **dust kitty**.

kiwi n
a New Zealander. The flightless kiwi bird is New Zealand's national emblem.

klepto n
a kleptomaniac, compulsive or habitual thief. A short form first heard in American speech in the 1960s.

kludge n
a cumbersome, overcomplicated system or situation. A piece of computer jargon, originating in the USA, blending 'clumsy' and 'sludge'.

klutz n American
a foolish, clumsy person. The word is from the Yiddish *klots* which literally means lump or block. (It comes from the German *Klotz* with the same meaning, which is related to the English 'clot' and 'clod'.) In the 1980s the word has passed from being an Americanism into world English, particularly among adolescents.
- 'As the incidents repeated themselves, Ms Reagan told her fellow workers and friends that she was a "klutz" who kept banging into doors and falling down stairs.' (Guardian, 4 April 1989).

klutzy adj American
foolish and/or clumsy. A back-formation from the more common noun **klutz**.

knacker vb British
to tire or exhaust. A back-formation from **knackered**.
- 'I knacker myself at my job to keep

her nice and warm in my house, with my kids and my dog.' (Divorced husband in cartoon by Posy Simmonds, Guardian, 1981).

knackered adj British
exhausted. This is not strictly speaking a slang word, as it derives from 'knacker', a worn-out horse or a slaughterer of horses, but has come to be seen as slang because of confusion with **knackers**, in the sense of testicles. The ultimate origin of the word is probably a dialect word meaning saddle-maker and based on a version of the word knock.
- 'That washing machine's about knackered, gel, and we ain't even finished payin' for it yet!' (Biff cartoon, Guardian, 1986).

knackers n pl British
testicles. Originally a dialect or rustic pronunciation of knockers (with the sense of 'clappers'), this is the form of the word which has predominated. In the 1950s and 1960s the word was often used in the form of an exclamation on the lines of the now more widespread **balls**, **bollocks** and **cobblers**, expressing defiance or contempt.
- 'Your boyfriend burned his jacket his ticket expired his tyres are knackered his knackers are tired.' (Psycle sluts, poem by John Cooper Clarke, 1978).

knapper n British
a rare alternative spelling of **napper**.

knave n British
an unwitting courier of explosives, a sacrificial bomb-carrier. This was the term used by security forces to designate an air passenger in whose luggage explosives had been planted without their knowledge, a terrorist tactic of the late 1980s.

knee-jerk n, adj

(a person displaying) a reflex action, an unthinking, automatic reaction. This piece of American slang of the early 1970s has passed into general colloquial use since its adopting as part of disparaging descriptions such as 'knee-jerk liberal' or 'knee-jerk reactionary'. The expression of course derives from the doctors' testing of the patellar reflex, featured in cartoons and situation comedies since the mid 1950s.

knees-up n British

a boisterous party, celebration and/or sing-song. The popular Cockney song 'Knees up, Mother Brown' probably produced the expression.

kneetrembler, knee-tremble n British

an act of sexual intercourse while standing up. A popular term in the 1960s, when furtive assignations outdoors were perforce more prevalent. The word was used in TV comedies such as The Likely Lads; it originated in the 19th century and is still heard.

- 'Lugged their possessions from one digs to another in a cardboard suitcase, and, by way of recreation, enjoyed a quick "knee-trembler" up against a tree in a twilit local park.'
  (The Sunday Times, book review, 18 March 1990).

knicker-bandit n British

a fetishistic thief who steals women's underclothes from washing lines, launderettes, etc. Also known as a snowdropper.

knickers! exclamation British

a cry of dismissal, defiance or contempt. This primary and junior school-children's rude word has been adopted for humorous use by adults since the early 1970s. Some authorities claim that it was originally a euphemism for the more offensive knackers but this seems unlikely in that underwear in itself is a favourite subject of prurient interest in pre-pubescent children. (Knickers is in origin a shortening of knickerbockers, meaning baggy knee-length trousers as worn in 19th-century Holland.)

knicker-wrecker n British

a sexually aggressive and/or successful male, seducer. A middle-class schoolgirl's term of the 1960s.

knicks n British

underpants or swimming trunks. An abbreviation of knickers.

knob vb British

to have sex (with). This is a variant of nob, and is said by users of the word to be the incorrect spelling, in spite of the derivation.

- 'If you were in with the Royal Family and you were a girl, you'd definitely want to knob Prince Andrew or someone.'
  (Boy George, NME, 4 June 1988).

knob n

1 British penis. The word has been in use with this sense since the 19th century and was the most common vulgar synonym in Britain and Australia in the 1950s and 1960s, since when such words as dick and prick have increased in popularity.

2 American head. A fairly rare and old-fashioned usage. Knob had this sense in British slang from the 18th century until the early 1950s; it survives only in the dated word 'copperknob' or copper-nob for a red-headed person.

knob-cheese n British

smegma. A term from the 1980s, which is a recent variation on the theme of cheese being used to describe distasteful by-products of bodily functions.

knob-end n British

a stupid, unfortunate or unpleasant person. A fashionable term of adolescent abuse in the late 1980s. (There are no sexual connotations, in spite of the word's provenance.)

knob job n

an act of (male) masturbation or fellatio. A vulgarism in use since the 1960s, knob being one of the commonest terms for penis in Britain and Australia. Although knob alone is rare in this sense in the USA, 'knob job' is commonly heard there.

knobs n pl American

breasts. A fairly rare word, used for instance by (invariably male) college students. It is virtually unknown in Britain and Australia where the sense of knob as penis is prevalent.

knock vb British

1 to kill. A recent, racier variant of knock off or hit.

● *'I've never spoken to anyone I'm going to knock.'*
(Hit-man quoted Observer, 31 May 1987).

2 to have sex (with). A 300-year-old usage which has been rare since the early 1960s. It now survives mainly in variations such as knock off, knocked up or knocking shop.

3 to criticize, disparage. The use of knock to mean deprecate is no longer strictly speaking slang; it has been employed in this sense since the 19th century.

knock n British

an act of sexual intercourse. A word which is now heard less often than in the 1950s and 1960s.

● *'All I wanted was a bit of a knock with Clive, I'm not interested in futile relationships.'*
(Joe Orton's diary, 2 May 1967).

the knock n British

1 stolen goods, criminal booty. A police and underworld term derived from knock off in the sense of to steal.

2 a credit, hire purchase. This meaning is usually expressed by the phrase to buy something 'on the knock'.

b a loss or bad debt (a knocker is a debtor or welsher). The phrase usually forms part of a longer expression such as 'take the knock' or 'get the knock'. Knock here may originally refer to 'financial damage' or to the rapping of the table by a player who cannot take his or her turn in cards or dominoes.

3 the arrival of the police at one's home, or of a summons to appear in court. From the ominous knock at the door.

● *'Charlie got the knock last night.'*
See also knocker, on the knock.

knockback n British

a a rejection of an application for parole.

● *'Jacky's hopeful but if you ask me he's going to get a knockback.'*

b a rejection of sexual advances.

● *'Don't worry about it Jane. I was expecting a knockback anyway.'*

These terms are specific instances of the more general colloquial sense of knockback as any type of disappointment or rebuff.

knocked out adj

bowled over, very impressed. Now a fairly widespread colloquial expression, this was considered both an Americanism and slang until the late 1970s.

See also knockout.

knocked up *adj, vb*

1 *American* made pregnant. Amateur lexicologists never tire of pointing out the possibility of confusion between the American sense and the innocently colloquial British sense of waken (someone) up.
- *'Garp? My daughter got knocked up by a goddam fish?'*
  (*The World According to Garp*, US film, 1982).

2 *Australian* exhausted.

knocker *n British*

1 a borrower of money, debtor, defaulter. The word is used to refer to personal debtors, those reneging on hire purchase agreements or, by prisoners in particular, to those who **welsh** on a bet − a sense in which the word was used in sporting circles before World War II. The origin of this use of knock is not completely clear; it may simply have the sense of to damage (financially), come from an obsolete word meaning to borrow, or may refer to some more specific practice such as rapping on a table to indicate one's inability to continue in a card game.

2 a a door-to-door salesperson.

b a door-to-door tout for an antiques dealer, hoping either to trick the gullible into parting with valuables or occasionally to identify items for later theft.
See also **on the knocker**.

3 a breast. A rarely heard singular form of **knockers**.

knockers *n pl*

1 breasts. A widespread usage which seems to have arisen as recently as the 1940s. It has been suggested, but not convincingly demonstrated, that the word comes from **norks** and was first coined in Australia, whence it spread to the USA and Britain.
- *'Aliens have enormous knockers, according to the Sunday Sport.'*

(Recorded, sub-editor, London, July 1989).

2 testicles. This usage is rare. **Knackers** is the usual term.

knockie(-knockie) *n British*

sex. A humorous euphemism heard since the early 1980s. It derives from the sexual connotations of the verb to **knock** and is probably also influenced by **nookie**. The expression is sometimes in the form 'play knockie(-knockie)'.

knocking shop *n British*

a brothel. A popular light-hearted term now used to refer to a seducer's lair or any scene of promiscuity, as well as to a genuine bordello. The euphemism was recorded with the latter meaning in the mid 19th century.
- *'Life here was hell with that girl. We thought she was running a knocking shop and it drove us all mad.'*
  (Resident of block of flats, *News of the World*, 19 February 1989).

knock off *vb British*

1 to kill.

2 to steal or rob.
- *'They knocked off a lorryload of antiques.'*
- *'The boys tried to knock off a bank.'*
  See also **knock over**.

3 to have sex with, succeed in seducing. In American English to 'knock off a piece' is a depersonalizing description of a sexual conquest.
- *'The 18-year-old he had been knocking off since she was 14.'*
  (*Daily Mirror*, 11 May 1989).

All these uses of the phrase are variations of the underlying meaning of 'to account for' or 'accomplish hurriedly'.

knock-off *n British*

a cheap, cut-price and/or mass-produced article. This use of the term derives from the colloquial sense of the verb to knock off, meaning to accomplish easily, turn out quickly.

knock out vb British

to sell or distribute. In this sense the phrase probably originates in illegal auctions where the apportioning of the (usually stolen) goods was accompanied by the rap of a gavel. The term is now typically used by or of street traders.

- 'We've been knocking out over a hundred of those every week.'

knockout adj

wonderful, impressive, first-rate. Originally an Americanism, deriving from the noun form meaning something stunning, the word was introduced to Britain and Australia in the hippy era and by the mid 1970s sounded somewhat dated. It was often used in the form of an exclamation of (over)enthusiasm.

- 'I met this knockout chick.'

knock over vb

to rob. A racier euphemism than knock off, this American underworld expression was picked up by British speakers in the early 1980s.

- 'Willis is suspected of knocking over a bank in Oregon.'

knock someone's block off

vb British

to beat someone up, to hit someone very hard. A popular, usually jocular expression heard until the 1970s, since when it has sounded rather dated.

- 'The park-keeper threatened to knock William's block off.'

knot-head n

a fool or dim-witted person. A term heard all over the English-speaking world. The knot in question is probably that normally found in pieces of

timber (recalling 'wooden-headed') rather than in string.

the knowledge n British

an examination proving close familiarity with London's streets, a qualification necessary to the granting of a taxi licence in the capital. The term comes from the jargon of taxi drivers themselves, who typically familiarize themselves with London's streets by driving around them on a moped while memorizing a route plan from a clipboard on the handlebars. Aspiring taxi drivers 'on the knowledge' are also known as 'knowledge boys', whatever their age or sex. All three terms were popularized in 1983 by a TV play, The Knowledge, written by Jack Rosenthal.

knuckle vb

to hit, beat up. A word used in Britain by street-gangs and other 'toughs'.

- 'He knuckled the geezer.'

knuckle, knuckle-up n British

a brawl, fistfight.

knucklehead n

an idiot. A variation of the older bonehead, the term originated as a folksy Americanism, entering world English in the 1950s.

- 'The most startling language occurs on a thing called "Bob George", which features a monologue from some knuckle-head having it out with his lady.'
  (Independent, 26 February 1988).

knuckle sandwich n

a blow from a fist, a punch in the mouth or face. A humorous phrase which is often used in unfunny situations in all English-speaking countries. The expression dates from before World War II when it probably originated in a euphemism such as 'feed someone a knuckle sandwich.'

301

knucks n pl

a knuckleduster, brass knuckles. Like the device, the word is part of the repertoire of street-gangs, thugs, etc., especially in the USA.

kode n

the complex system of language and signals used by **gays** in order to secretly communicate with one another, particularly about their sexual proclivities or preferences. This includes the wearing of key rings, chains and specific colours of handkerchiefs in specific pockets, etc. The language is literally code in that it takes terms from standard English such as **straight**, **clone**, **boystown**, etc. and uses them ironically. The alternative spelling of code is an example of the use of K to render English words more Germanic or Slavonic and thus lend them totalitarian overtones, as in 'Amerika' or 'klan'.

konk n

an alternative spelling of **conk** in its sense of hairstyle.

kook n American

an eccentric, quirky or crazy person. This word is an alteration of cuckoo which has been popular in the USA since the 1950s. It has spread to Australia, but although understood in Britain is rarely used there.

kooky adj American

eccentric, quirky, crazy. This adjective probably post-dates the noun **kook**.

koorie n Australian

an alternative spelling of **kuri**.

kopacetic adj American

another spelling of **copacetic**.

kosher adj

correct, proper, above-board. This Yiddish term (usually referring to food prepared according to Talmudic law) is originally from the Hebrew *kasher*, meaning fitting or proper. The word was adopted in the late 19th century by non-Jewish speakers, particularly in the underworld, market trading or other raffish contexts. By the 1970s kosher was generally understood and used by speakers from a wide variety of backgrounds.

- *'Don't worry, it's quite kosher.'*
- *'Let's check out his so-called company and see if its a kosher set-up.'*

kraut n

a German. The word, which originated in the USA, has supplanted hun and later **Jerry** in British slang usage. It is a shortening of *sauerkraut*, thin-cut cabbage pickled in brine, which is a popular German food.

kraut rock n

German rock music of the 1970s, encompassing 'progressive' electronically synthesized music such as that of Kraftwerk and, slightly later, bombastic heavy-metal music such as that of the Scorpions. The term was coined by British rock journalists.

Kremlin, the Kremlin n British

the Metropolitan Police's nickname for their headquarters at New Scotland Yard.

kuri, koorie n New Zealand

a a Maori.

b an unpleasant or unpopular person.

c *Australian* an aborigine. This racist epithet is the Maori word for mongrel.

kushti *adj British*
an alternative spelling of **cushdy**.

Kuwaiti tanker *n British*
rhyming slang for **wanker**. The probably ephemeral phrase arose during the Gulf crisis of 1986 and 1987 when Kuwaiti tankers among other craft were escorted through the straights of Hormuz to prevent attack by Iran. A contemporary synonym was **merchant banker**.

kvetch *vb*
to complain, whine, **whinge**. An Americanism that has been adopted by fashionable and literary sectors of British and Australian society. It is the Yiddish verb meaning to squeeze or press.

kvetch *n*
a person who complains constantly, a whiner or **whinger**. The word comes via the USA from the Yiddish verb meaning to squeeze or press.

kybosh *n*
See **put the kibosh on**.

kyf, kyfer *n British*
an alternative spelling of **kife**.

kyfer *vb British*
an alternative spelling of **kifer**.

L

la n Australian

a toilet. An abbreviated form of lavatory.

labonza n American

a belly or paunch.

- 'A punch in the labonza.'

b backside, buttocks.

A word used particularly by pugilists, criminals and working-class speakers. It is mock-Italian or Spanish, probably based on *la pancia* or *la panza*, both related to the English paunch. The second sense referring to the posterior is rarer.

lace curtain n

a foreskin. A term from the homosexual lexicon, punning on a symbol of coy respectability which pre-dates **gay** emancipation.

laced up adj British

a (of a person) fully occupied, obligated, embroiled.

b (of a thing) completed, accomplished, 'in the bag'. Both senses are variant forms of standard metaphorical meanings of tied up.

c repressed, inhibited. In this sense the phrase is influenced by straitlaced.

- 'She's a bit laced up isn't she?'

lacks, lax n British

the game of lacrosse. An abbreviated form used by schoolgirls.

laddish adj British

boisterous, uncouth and **macho**. The word, which appeared in the late 1970s, refers to the typical behaviour of adolescent males in groups. It is inspired by 'male-bonding' expressions such as 'one of the lads' and the **geordie** battle cry, 'howay the lads!' but is more often used disparagingly or dismissively by women or more mature males.

Lady Godiva n British

a £5 note, a sum of £5. London rhyming slang for 'fiver'. The phrase is still heard although alternatives such as **deep sea diver** are now probably more popular.

Lady Jane n

1 the female sex organs. A popular Victorian euphemism later used by D. H. Lawrence in *Lady Chatterley's Lover* (1928) and which is almost certainly quite obsolete today.

2 marihuana. A variation of **Mary Jane**.

Both uses have been cited as keys to understanding the Rolling Stones' song 'Lady Jane' from their *Aftermath* LP of 1966, although its lyrics may simply refer to the historical figure Lady Jane Grey.

Lady Muck n British

a woman thought to be 'putting on airs' or behaving high-handedly. The female equivalent of **Lord Muck**.

- 'Who does she think she is, carrying on like Lady Muck?'

laff n

a source or occasion of amusement. A jocular, ironic or journalese form of laugh. When said by southern British speakers it is distinguished by a pronunciation rhyming with 'chaff'.

lag n

a a convict or former convict or recidivist. In non-criminal circles the word is usually heard only in the phrase **old lag**.

b a term of imprisonment. At different times in different areas the term has denoted specific periods. **Lagging** is now the more usual form of the word.

lag, lag up vb British

a also **lag up**, to send to prison.
b to arrest.

Both words, which are now rare, date from the beginning of the 19th century, when lag meant specifically to transport to a penal colony. (An archaic meaning of the word was 'to carry away'.)

lag, lag on vb Australian

to inform (on someone), to tell tales. A prisoners' and schoolchildren's word, this was British slang of the 19th century with the meaning of 'betray to the authorities'. It has survived in Australia but has not been heard in the UK since the turn of the century. Its frequent use in Australian TV soap operas of the late 1980s may result in the reintroduction of the term.

- 'Don't worry – 'e won't go laggin' on us.'
(Prisoner: Cell Block H, Australian TV series, 1985).

lagging n British

a period of imprisonment. The word has sometimes had the specific sense of a term of three years or more.

lah-di n British

a motor car. Rhyming slang from 'la-di-dah'. An alternative 'cockney' term to **jam-jar**.

laid

See **lay**.

laid back adj

relaxed, easy-going. This expression was first widely propagated in the USA in the **hippy** period and was particularly appropriate to self-consciously relaxed attitudes prevalent in the Californian counter-culture and later alternative therapy circles. It may simply derive from the notion of lying back and relaxing or perhaps be influenced by a more specific jargon such as that of American **bikers** for whom laid back was the driving position when cruising.

- 'The President and Nancy like to change into pyjamas at 6 pm. This method – not laid back so much as lying down – didn't matter when things were going well . . . .'
(Observer, 22 November 1987).

laid out adj American

a drunk. Another synonym for inebriated. Although the original metaphor is of someone knocked unconscious (or placed in a mortuary), the use of the phrase does not necessarily indicate intoxication to the point of stupefaction.

b under the influence of drugs. This sense of the term, deriving from the previous one, is most commonly used by teenagers.

lair, lare n Australian

a layabout, flashy young tough. This modern usage post-dates an earlier sense of the word denoting an overdressed, showy or beautiful man. Since the 1940s the term has been identified specifically with delinquent or disreputable young males. It forms the basis of many combinations such as 'come the lair', 'lair it up' or 'ten-cent lair'. Lair is based on a variant form of older British words such as **leery, leary**, etc.

lairising vb Australian

behaving like a **lair**. Acting bumptiously and/or dressing in a flashy, disreputable style. (For the ultimate origin of the word see **leery**.)

lairy adj

a flashy, showy, especially in an ostentatious, provocative or vulgar way. This term is especially popular in Australia but was also in use among British youth in the late 1980s.

- 'Wow, Ches's got a really lairy T-shirt.'
  (Recorded, youth, Portobello Road, London, 1986).

b vain, presumptuous or boastful. This sense of the term was in use among working-class speakers, particularly **teddy boys**, in Britain in the 1950s and early 1960s.

Both sub-senses of the word come from the earlier **leary** or **leery**.

lala n Australian

a toilet. The word is a reduplication of **la**, which is itself a shortening of lavatory.

la-la-land n

a state of drugged or drunken euphoria. An expression usually used disparagingly by abstainers.

- 'Cameraman Gerry McGough, who snapped these shots, said "She was completely in la-la land".'
  (Caption to pictures of drunken celebrity, Daily Mirror, 9 February 1989).

lallies n pl British

legs. A word used in theatrical circles and by dancers, art students, etc. in the 1960s. Lallies was given exposure in the radio comedy shows Beyond our Ken and Round the Horne in the exchanges between Kenneth Horne and the **camp** characters 'Julian' and 'Sandy', played by Kenneth Williams and Hugh Paddick. The word, of unknown origin, is still in limited use.

lam vb

to run away or escape from prison. The verb form is probably a back formation from the phrase 'on the lam', although 'lam' originates in a verb, lambaste, meaning to hit or beat.

lame adj

poor quality, disappointing, bad. The common colloquialism was adopted as an all-purpose teenage vogue word in the late 1980s.

lame-ass n, adj American

(a) feeble, disappointing, unconvincing (person). An embellishment of the colloquial 'lame'.

- 'Another lame-ass excuse.'

lamebrain n, adj

(a) dim-witted (person). Lame has been used to mean feeble or weak in colloquial speech throughout the Anglophone community. This compound form was coined in the 1960s in the USA, whence it spread in the 1970s.

- '"English people don't expect high standards because they don't know how to go out and eat in restaurants," scolds Payton. "We're also lamebrains when it comes to going to the cinema".'
  (Evening Standard Magazine, May 1989).

lamp vb

1 to look (at), to eye. The term, (currently in vogue among fashionable adolescents in Britain), comes from a now archaic three hundred-year-old use of lamp as a slang synonym for eye.

2 *British* to hit, beat up or attack. A now dated usage perhaps combining elements of 'lam', in the sense of beat, and lump. The word was frequently used with this meaning in the 1950s.

the landscape *n British*

the scene, environment (surrounding the location of a crime or stake-out) or the general state of affairs in connection with an investigation. A word from the jargon of the police, particularly detectives, in the 1980s. Many other items of police jargon contribute to the image of a tableau, painting or schema (**in the frame, drop one out,** etc.).

lard-ass, lard-bucket *n*
American

a fat person. The American equivalents of the British 'tub of lard'.

lard-head *n*

a stupid or slow-witted person. An expression used in Australia and the USA.

lardo *n*

a fat person. An innocuous variant of **lard-ass.**

- 'Apart from being a congenital lardo, [Clive] James has a further hurdle before he can reasonably take part in the pro-celeb car chase: he can't drive.'
(*Independent*, 23 December 1988).

lare *n Australian*

an alternative spelling of **lair.**

large *n, n pl British*

one thousand, a **grand.** A shortening of 'large one(s)', used typically by

criminals, market traders, gamblers, etc.

- 'I give him five large and asked him to get hold of some gear for me.'

larrikin *n Australian*

a ruffian, ne'er-do-well. The word has been in use in Australia since the mid-19th century and may be a native coinage or an imported British dialect term based on 'lark'. It is not usually strongly pejorative, having the sense of (fairly harmlessly) rowdy and cheeky.

larrup *vb*

to beat, spank, thrash. A word used by toughs in Australia but mainly by parents to children in Britain, where it now sounds rather dated. The term may be a blend of 'leather' and wallop or may be an attempt to imitate the sound of blows landing.

lary *adj*

an alternative form of **lairy** or **leery.**

lash *n Australian*

1 a rampage, bout of wild behaviour.
- 'To go on a lash/have a bit of a lash.'

2 an attempt, try. A variant of bash as in 'have a bash (at)'.

laughing boy *n British*

a a morose, grumbling, sullen or excessively serious-looking person. The phrase is used with heavy irony to deride or provoke someone thought to be unnecessarily grumpy, stern or self-pitying.
- 'Why don't you go and ask laughing boy over there.'

b someone who is smirking or offensively cheerful. A less common sub-sense of the term.

laughing gear *n British*

mouth. A joky euphemism playing on the notion of body parts as equipment on the lines of **kissing tackle** or

wedding tackle. It probably dates from the 1970s.

● *'Get your laughing gear around this!'*
(Dialogue in TV advertisement for Heineken beer, 1988).

laughing soup/water/juice *n*

alcohol. These are middle-class witticisms applied particularly to champagne or gin. Laughing water also recalls the Indian princess in Longfellow's long narrative poem *Hiawatha*. Similar terms still in use are **giggle water** and **electric** or **lunatic soup**.

launder *vb*

to legitimize cash gained illegally or immorally. A euphemism used by American criminals and law enforcement agencies in the 1960s which has become part of world English since the mid-1970s. The word has been used in this predictable sense by financiers since the early part of the century.

lavender *adj*

homosexual (male), **gay**. A facetious term appropriated from the vocabulary of heterosexual mockers for use by the gay community itself; the colour and scent of lavender being thought as quintessentially feminine and 'old-maidish', respectively.

lax *n British*

an alternative spelling of **lacks**.

lay *n*

a a person viewed or evaluated as a sexual partner.
b an act of sexual intercourse.
● *'He's not interested in her, he's just looking for a lay.'*
These uses of the word spread to British English from the USA with the verb form during the 1950s and 1960s, becoming established by the early

1970s. In the first sense the word is nearly always used in combinations such as 'a good lay' or 'an easy lay'.

lay *vb*

to have sex with. The verb was absorbed into British English gradually during the 1950s and 1960s from the USA, where it had been current since the turn of the century. The term implies sex from the male viewpoint but during the **hippy** era began to be used by women. The word is a development of the literal sense of to lay someone down, and of the euphemistic 'lie with', meaning to copulate with, well known from its use in the King James translation of the Bible.

● *'One time I thought she was trying to make me come lay her – flirting to herself at the sink – lay back on huge bed that filled most of the room, dress up round her hips.'*
(*Kaddish*, poem by Allen Ginsberg, 1958).

lay an egg *vb*

1 *American* to fail, to be responsible for a dismal or disappointing performance. This expression comes from the Victorian British 'lay a duck's egg' meaning to score zero (now extinct in British speech).

2 *Australian* to behave in an agitated, over-excited way. One of many farmyard metaphors in Australian use.

lay by *vb Australian*

to put a deposit on an article in a shop, reserve, put aside. Not really a slang term but a local usage, the phrase also occurs in the expression **on the lay-by**.
● *'Lay that by, will you?'*
● *'She wanted to lay by the garden furniture.'*

lay down *vb*

See **lie down**.

lay (something) on (someone) vb

to inflict or impose on. This is one of many expressions originating in black speech which were disseminated during the **hippy** era, often in the form '*lay a (heavy) trip on*', for example.

lay one on someone vb

to hit, punch. A euphemistic expression on the same lines as '*stick one on*', **put one on someone**, **hang one on**.

● '*If that joker doesn't stop mouthing off I'm going to be forced to lay one on him.*'

lay rubber vb American

to drive very fast, especially from a standing start, in a car or on a motorcycle. The phrase is inspired by the shedding of tyre rubber when spinning the wheels at speed, a technique used in **drag** racing to ensure good road adhesion at the beginning of a race.

lay some pipe vb American

to have sex (from the male point of view). A vulgar play on words, used typically in black and working-class speech.

Lazy Y n

See **lunching at the Lazy Y**.

leaf n

marihuana. A predictable nickname for herbal cannabis.

● '*We blew some leaf and mellowed out.*'

leak n

an act of urination. Usually in the expressions '*have a leak*' or '*take a leak*'. The origin of this predictable usage may be nautical.

leak air vb American

to talk nonsense, jabber crazily. The image evoked is that of a collapsing inflatable or punctured balloon or tyre.

● '*Take no notice – the guy's just leaking air.*'

leaper n

a stimulant drug such as an amphetamine, a **pep pill** or **upper**. This term was briefly adopted by (mainly middle-class) British drug users in the late 1960s, giving way to more widespread terms such as uppers or **speed**. It was probably coined by analogy with sleeper in the sense of sedative or tranquillizer.

leary adj

an alternative spelling of **leery** or **lairy**.

● '*If you are dealing with a leary and insolent young brat, do you put that down as information?*'
(Police officer quoted in *Inside the British Police*, Simon Holdaway, 1983).

the least n, adj American

(something) very bad, disappointing, of the worst quality. This term, which is popular especially with teenagers, was probably coined in the 1970s as a humorous complement to the older **hip** expression **the most** (meaning superlative). 'The very least' is a stronger term.

● '*Boy, that movie was the least.*'

leather n British

1 a middle-aged male jet-setter, an ageing sun-tanned playboy. This term was coined by the upper-class young and their imitators in the late 1970s to refer disparagingly to the more prominent members of the international **white trash** frequenting ski resorts, yacht basins, etc. The word could occasionally be extended to apply to women, too. Leather refers to the skin texture of the sub-group in question (perhaps compounded by their characteristic wearing of expensive leather clothes in the period in question).

2 a wallet or purse. A long established item from the underworld lexicon.

leatherboy n

a a motorcycle enthusiast, **rocker** or **biker**. A word popular with parents and journalists in the early 1960s.

● *'The mean and moody leatherboy on a thundering bike is the strongest image of pop culture.'* (Johnny Stuart, Rockers, 1987).

b a young male homosexual, male prostitute or androgynous youth wearing leather.

● *'A faggy little leatherboy with a smaller piece of stick.'* (Lyrics to 'Memo from Turner', by Mick Jagger, 1969).

lech, letch n British

a a carnal desire, brief sexual infatuation. This word, often used by women, was particularly popular in the 1960s and early 1970s in upper- or middle-class speech. It was often (and sometimes is still) used in the form *'letch, letch!'* as a jocular or coyly prurient exclamation (although this more probably refers to the verb form to **lech after** or **lech for**).

● *'Leched over by managers, stitched up by agents, girls in the music biz have traditionally paid a high price for succumbing to the lure of lurex.'* (Ms London magazine, 4 September 1989).

b a lecherous person, usually male. A word expressing attitudes ranging from light mockery to angry rejection.

● *'He's nothing but a boring old lech.'*

lech/letch after/for/over/on
vb British

to nurse or exhibit a carnal desire for, to behave lecherously towards (some-

one). A back formation from the adjective lecherous.

● *'He's always letching after young girls.'*

lechy, letchy adj British

lecherous. A popular form of word heard particularly from the 1960s to the mid-1970s.

lecky, the lecky n British

the Electricity Board. The electricity supply, electricity. A Liverpudlian contraction which seems to be gaining popularity elsewhere.

● *'We had the lecky round to check the meter yesterday.'*

lecky adj British

electric(al). A Liverpudlian contracted form, probably originating in baby talk.

leech off (someone) vb

to behave as a parasite. An extension of the colloquial use of the noun form.

leery, leary adj

a wary, suspicious, shy, cautious. This sense of the word is standard in all English-speaking areas.

b British alert, clever, cheeky. This sense of leery is related to **lairy**, meaning both flashy and conceited.

c British bad-tempered, 'sour'.

d British untrustworthy, devious, cunning.

These nuances of meaning within the same term are difficult to disentangle, given that modern usage is probably derived from two originally separate words: the archaic 'leer', from an Anglo-Saxon word meaning face or cheek, and the obsolete dialect term 'lere', related to learn and lore and similar in meaning to know-how.

left field n, adj

(something) unorthodox, bizarre,

unexpected. An American usage which was picked up by British journalists, musicians etc. in the mid-1970s. The term arises from an earlier colloquial expression '*out of left field*', used to describe something startling or totally unexpected coming from an improbable source. The field in question is the baseball field and left field, (the area to the batter's left and beyond third base), is an area of the park which sees little action and from which the ball rarely arrives. The same thing can be said of right field, however, and the choice of left perhaps has something to do with the overtones of unorthodoxy and radicalism inherent in 'left' in its political context, or simply by analogy with left-handed.

leg-biter n

a small child, a toddler or baby. A less common alternative to **ankle-biter**, heard in the 1980s.

leg it vb British

to run away, escape or leave. A working-class expression, formerly popular with police and criminals, which has become fashionable in middle-class circles in the later 1980s in keeping with a tendency among **yuppies**, students and those in the media, among others, to affect 'cockney' styles of speech.

- '*His pals sprung him by blowing a hole in the wall. He then legged it to Amsterdam, where he changed his name.*'
  (Charles Catchpole, News of the World, 5 February 1989).
- '*He extinguishes a cigarette and gets to his feet, searching for someone to pay. "Shall we leg it?" he picks up a bag containing two large art books and heads for the exit.*'
  (Tim Roth, quoted in Observer, Section 5 magazine, 9 April 1989).

legless adj

drunk. The word originally denoted someone who was helplessly or falling-down drunk; nowadays 'getting legless' can simply mean getting drunk. It has moved from being a raffish slang term to a common colloquialism over the last 25 years.

- '*The doctor's had his bike nicked and his place turned over, and the only time we've seen the Old Bill is when they're in here getting legless.*'
  (Biff cartoon, 1986).
- '*LEGLESS BUT LOVELY: Blonde beauty Sam Brown admits she became a bit time boozer when she was a schoolgirl.*'
  (People, picture caption, 23 April 1989).

leg-man n

a male whose preferred part of the female body is the legs, as opposed to an **arse-man** or **tit-man**.

leg-opener n

a strong alcoholic drink, or an innocent-seeming drink laced with alcohol, thought by some unsophisticated would-be seducers to produce an automatic willingness in their intended victim.

Compare **eye-opener**.

legover n British

an act of sexual intercourse (usually from a male perspective). The term originates in the expression **get one's leg over**, one of many 18th- and 19th-century phrases in which leg is meant both literally and as a euphemism for the parts of the lower body ('leg-business' is one archaic example). In the 1980s the satirical magazine Private Eye has regularly referred to a 'legover situation', a supposed middle-class code for copulation.

lemon n

1 something substandard, useless or worthless. The word is used, particularly in the USA, to apply particularly to cars which are unsaleable. It may also denote any 'dud', from an unattractive woman to a badly-performing share in the stock exchange. This negative sense of the name of a fairly popular fruit derives from the unavoidably sour taste.

2 a fool, embarrassed or discomfited person. To 'feel a lemon' is to be put in an uncomfortable or humiliating situation.

3 the penis. In black American slang the word has been used in this sense which, although no longer common, is immortalized in the lyrics of many blues songs.

● 'Squeeze my lemon, baby/ 'till the juice runs down my leg.'

4 American a quaalude, **'lude** (a hypnotic tranquillizing drug, the equivalent of the British Mandrax or **mandy**).
See **lemons**.

lemons n pl

the breasts. Another image of fruitfulness and rotundity on the lines of **melons**, **cantaloupes**, **apples**, etc. The term is probably most widespread in Australian speech.

lemon-squeezer n British

a man. This phrase, rhyming slang for **geezer**, occurs in anthologies of such expressions but is rarely actually heard in everyday speech. **Ice cream** is a synonym.

length n British

1 a six-month prison sentence.

2 the penis. The word is almost invariably used in the phrase **slip someone a length**.

lerg(h)i, lurg(h)i British

an unspecified disease, a mysterious infection or illness. An invented word (the 'g' is hard) in imitation of exotic or tropical complaints, much used by schoolchildren in the 1950s and still heard today, often in the phrase 'the dreaded lergi'.

● 'Hilary was supposed to come but she's gone down with the lergi.'
(Recorded, housewife, London suburbs, 1986).

les, lez n

a lesbian. Shortened forms of the word in use throughout the English-speaking community.

lesbo n

a lesbian. A contracted form used particularly by young people in Britain in the 1960s and early 1970s, before terms such as **gay** woman or the pejorative **dyke** were in common currency.

lessie, lezzie n

a lesbian. This shortened form was especially popular in the vocabulary of British schoolchildren of the 1970s.

letch n, vb British

an alternative spelling of **lech**.

letchy adj British

an alternative spelling of **lechy**.

let it all hang out vb

exclamation

to express oneself or otherwise behave without inhibitions, act without restraint. This euphemism became a catchphrase of the late 1960s 'counterculture', spreading with it from the USA to other English-speaking areas. The phrase survived mainly among **straight** commentators who employed it disapprovingly or ironically. (The nature of the unspecific 'it' is not recorded: sexual characteristics or hair are likely candidates.)

let off, let one off, let one go
vb British

to **fart**. The first variant is a common schoolchildren's term, the other forms tend to be used by adults. **Blow off** is one synonym among many.

lettuce *n*

money. Another term like **long green, cabbage**, etc. that makes the connection between green banknotes and succulent vegetation. The word was probably first heard in raffish use in the USA, where banknotes of all denominations are and were predominantly green.

lez *n*

an alternative spelling of **les**.

lezz, lezzie, lezzo *n*

a lesbian.

libber *n*

a feminist or other person with progressive and/or libertarian views. A blanket term, usually used with condescension or disapproval, which originates as a shortening of 'women's libber'.

libs *n pl*

librium capsules. Since the early 1960s librium has been one of the most widely prescribed tranquillizers. It has been used extensively by illicit drug abusers to mitigate the after-effects of their activities. Another nickname for the same drug was **green and blacks**.

lick *vb American*

to smoke **crack**, by sucking the smoke from a burning pellet of the drug through a glass pipe or tube. The term is from the users' own jargon.

licks *n pl*

plangent sequences of notes played on the electric guitar, short improvized musical solos. The term was adopted by rock guitarists from earlier jazz musicians who had adapted the colloquial 'lick', meaning both a stroke or hit and an attempt. The word is part of the terminology which includes **chops** and **riff**.

- *'Jimi [Hendrix] has got some licks that none of us can match.'*
(Eric Clapton, speaking in 1970).

lid *n*

1 *American* a measure of marihuana (about one ounce), so called because it is approximately the amount which can be held on the lid of a beer can or tobacco tin.

2 a military or motorcyclist's helmet.

liddy *adj American*

crazy, eccentric. A term deriving from the expression to flip one's lid. **Wiggy** is a word of similar provenance.

lie down, lay down *vb*

to surrender, abase oneself. A fashionable euphemism in the late 1980s, particularly in the contexts of business and politics. It normally has the sense of giving up without a struggle in an adversarial situation. **Sit down** and **bend over** are used similarly.

- *'I'm damned if I'm going to lie down for them.'*

lifer *n*

a a prisoner condemned to life imprisonment.

b a member of the armed services who has volunteered for long service; a career soldier, sailor or airman/woman.

Liffey water *n Irish & British*

Guinness. The Liffey is the river flowing through Dublin, where Guinness is brewed, and Liffey water is an archaic rhyming-term for porter, of which Guinness is an example.

lift vb

1 to arrest or capture, in police jargon and a 'sanitized' euphemism of Vietnam-era military parlance.

2 to steal. Lift has been used euphemistically in this sense since the 16th century.

3 to drink (alcohol). A beer-drinkers' euphemism inspired by the raising of glasses; **hoist** is an American synonym.

• 'What say we go and lift a few?'

lifties, lifts n pl American

'elevator shoes', height-enhancing soles worn inside shoes.

lig vb British

to freeload, enjoy oneself at someone else's expense. The word, coined in Britain in the early 1970s, refers to the activities of hangers-on, **groupies**, music journalists, etc., who attend receptions, parties, concerts, and other functions, usually financed by record companies. The origin of the word is obscure, it has been suggested that it is made up of the initials of 'least important guest' or is a blend of linger and **gig**. Alternatively it may be an obscure vagrants' term from a dialect survival of Anglo-Saxon liegan, to lie.

lig n British

an opportunity for freeloading, a party, reception or other occasion when it is possible to enjoy oneself at someone else's expense. The word refers to the rock and pop-music world, and probably postdates the verb form **lig** and the noun **ligger**.

ligeratti n British

a journalese blend of **ligger** and 'glitteratti'.

• '"The club animals" own Johnny Morris, Caris Davis, who wrote about clubland's scenestealers, wimp-bods and ligeratti in his novel, "Stealth".'
(Observer, Section 5 magazine, 7 May 1989).

ligger n British

a freeloader, hanger-on or gatecrasher at concerts, receptions, parties, etc., in the rock and pop-music milieus. The word is part of rock music's jargon and was adopted enthusiastically by journalists in such publications as New Musical Express in the 1970s to describe those enjoying themselves at the expense of record companies.

• 'Julia Riddiough, 27 "going on 180", is a world-class ligger who could club for Britain.'
(Observer, Section 5 magazine, 7 May 1989).

lighten up vb

to relax or take things less seriously, calm down and/or cheer up. This expression moved from US parlance into the rest of the English-speaking world in the early 1980s.

• 'Lighten up will ya – do you have to take the fun out of everything?'
(Cheers, US TV comedy series, 1985).

lightning n American

1 another name for the drug **crack**.
2 see **white lightning**.

likely lad n British

an alert, smart and/or cheeky youth. A colloquial working-class phrase used particularly in the North of England to describe a young man who shows promise or self-confidence. The expression was adopted as the title of a popular Newcastle-based TV comedy series in the 1960s.

lilac *adj*

(male) homosexual or effeminate. A rarer synonym for **lavender**.

lils *n pl British*

breasts. A vulgar schoolchildren's word of the 1950s and 1960s, which may be a shortening of an earlier 'lily-whites' or an invention, possibly influenced by 'loll' and 'spill'.

lily *n*

an effeminate male, sissy.

limer *n Caribbean*

a hanger-on. A back-formed verb, to lime, is also heard. Both are inspired by the adhesive qualities of birdlime or quicklime. The word was adopted by some white speakers in London in the later 1980s.

limey *n, adj*

(an) English (person). The word, used mostly in North America, is a shortening of 'lime-juicer', a usually pejorative term applied originally to British sailors who were issued with rations of lime juice as a protection against scurvy. The word limey is now rather dated; Brit is increasingly taking its place.

limo *n*

a limousine, luxury car. An American abbreviation, employed by chauffeurs, then showbiz journalists among others, in the early 1970s and now widely used.

limp-dick *n, adj*

(someone who is) weak, ineffectual, irresolute. The metaphor is one of impotence, but the term is invariably used to express generalized rather than sexual contempt. The phrase probably originated in the USA as a harsher version of **limp-wristed**.

limp-wristed *adj*

effete, effeminate, **camp**, ineffectual. A pejorative term applied especially by men to those considered less masculine or less resolute than themselves. The phrase is sufficiently established to count as a colloquialism, rather than slang.

line *n*

a portion of cocaine, amphetamine or other drug ready for **snorting**. The powdered crystals of the drug are scraped into a strip (quite literally 'a line of coke/speed'), typically on a mirror, tile or similar surface, so that they can be sniffed through a straw, rolled banknote, or any other improvised tube.

- 'We had dinner at 192 and then I went back to Sophie's place to do a few lines.'

  (Recorded, record company executive, London, 1983).

line (up/out) *vb*

to sniff **lines** of cocaine or amphetamine. A drug users' euphemism of the 1980s.

lingam *n*

the penis. This Sanskrit word was introduced to English speakers via the Kama Sutra, the Hindu treatise on sexual love which was widely bought for its erotic content in the early 1960s. Lingam means male principle and phallic symbol as well as phallus; it is contrasted with the female equivalent, **yoni**. Lingam was adopted, particularly in magazine articles, as an inoffensive and poetic term for something otherwise difficult to name in print without using either taboo or clinical terminology.

lingo *n*

a language, jargon or way of speaking. The word, which often indicates puzzlement, amusement or xenophobia on the part of the speaker, obviously derives ultimately from the Latin word *lingua*, meaning tongue and language. The question as to which romance language inspired the modern slang word is difficult to resolve; it may be a corruption of the Latin word itself, or of Italian, Spanish (*lengua*), or Portuguese (*lingoa*). Provençal is the only modern language in which the correct form of the word is *lingo*.

- '[Oxford University] *aristocrats disguise themselves with lingo like: "It's wicked, guy."'*
  (*Evening Standard*, 16 June 1988).

lint-brain, lint-head n

American

a dim-witted or foolish person. This adolescent term of abuse draws on the American use of lint to denote fluff, particularly that lodged in the 'belly-button'.

lip n

cheek, back-chat. The expression dates to at least 1818, and is typically used by authority figures to characterize the utterances of unruly subordinates. It is a common usage in Britain and Australia, but less so in the USA.

- '*Less of your lip, you cheeky little bleeder, or I'll clip you round the ear'ole.*'
  (Recorded, park-keeper, London, 1958).
- '*Lesson number one: learn to give less lip and do more work.*'
  (*Neighbours*, Australian TV soap opera, 1987).

lip vb

1 to cheek, speak insolently (to).
2 to play a wind instrument, blow. A jazz musicians' term.

- '*Lip that thing.*'
- '*Cool lipping.*'

lippy adj

cheeky, insolent. This usage comes from the noun form **lip**, which was first recorded in 1818.

- '*He's a bit too lippy for his own good.*'

lip service n

fellatio. A humorous euphemism from the professional jargon of prostitution and pornography (punning on the standard idiom 'to pay lip service to').

lipstick n American

a lesbian interested in high-fashion, a 'feminine' lesbian. A Yale University term of the 1970s. Lipsticks are contrasted in this setting with the more aggressive or 'masculine' **crunchies**. The word lipstick has subsequently entered the **gay** female lexicon.

liquid laugh n

a bout of vomiting. The term probably originated in Australia. It is now heard in Britain (where it was part of the vocabulary of the influential late 1960s cartoon character Barry McKenzie, the Australian boor and ingénu) and, especially on campus, in the USA.

liquid lunch n

a lunchtime session of alcoholic drinking (usually as an alternative rather than an accompaniment to eating).

liquored up/out adj American

drunk. The same phrase was in use in Britain in the 19th century.

Little Big Horn, the Little Big Horn n British

the cycle and motorcycle couriers' nickname for Hyde Park Corner. The name, heard since about 1986, reflects the danger associated with negotiating the area.

little boy's room, the little boy's room n

a gentlemen's toilet. Originally a coy euphemism, used by some Americans in all seriousness, this expression has come to be used facetiously all over the English-speaking world.

● '*I'm not just some kind of machine you can turn on. I need a cup of joe, a trip to the little boys' room, a glance at the sports' pages. Then we'll talk.*'
(Moonlighting, American TV series, 1989).

little girl's room, the little girl's room n

a ladies' toilet. A coy euphemism now almost always used humorously, but originally (in the USA in the late 1940s) used to spare the blushes of the speaker and audience.

little jobs n British

an act of urination, as opposed to **big jobs** (defecation), in the now rather dated euphemistic language of the middle-class nursery.

little man/boy in the boat n

the clitoris. So-called because of a supposed resemblance, though it is unclear why the pilot of this particular craft is invariably male. In the 19th century the same phrase referred to the navel.

little number n

See **number**.

lit up, lit adj

drunk. Originally an American expression, this phrase derives from the visible effects of alcohol (a 'glow', red nose, etc.) as well as the sensation of heat and the notion of alcohol as firewater or fuel. Embellishments of this usage are '*lit up like a Christmas tree*' and '*lit up like a dime-store window*'. The shorter form, lit, often signifies tipsy or merry rather than thoroughly inebriated.

● '*As a whiskey salesman . . . I'm often lit up by elevenses, loop-legged by luncheon and totally schnockered by 6.*'
(Cartoon by Posy Simmonds, Guardian, 1979).

live-in lover n

an unmarried cohabitee. A phrase invented in the search for an acceptable term to designate a common-law spouse or temporary partner. An Australian equivalent is **de-facto**.

● '*Then Bob's your aunty's live-in lover!*'
(Grange Hill, British TV series, 1988).

livener n British

a strong alcoholic drink.

Liverbird n British

a girl or young woman from Liverpool, specifically a working-class or lower-middle-class girl like those portrayed in Carla Lane's TV comedy series of the same name. The term, (the first part of which is pronounced as in 'alive'), puns on the use of **bird** to mean young woman. It also refers to the statues of fanciful birds on the roof of the Liver building on the Liverpool waterfront, which have become emblematic of the city.

lizards n pl

snakeskin, crocodile-skin or iguana-hide footwear. Part of the sartorial repertoire of many social sub-groups including cowboys, pimps, street gangs, etc., lizards are also known as **reptiles**.

load vb Australian

to plant (someone) with illicit drugs or stolen goods, or to **frame** by manufacturing evidence. A term from the Australian criminal milieu which was first recorded in the 1930s and is still in use. The noun form is occasionally used to mean either an act of framing or the supposed evidence used.

load n

1 ejaculated semen. The word usually occurs in the phrases '*come one's load*' or '*shoot one's load*'.

2 *Australian* a venereal infection, a **dose**.

3 a a quantity of an illicit drug prepared for smoking, inhalation or injection.

b a cache or personal supply of an illicit drug, **stash**. These specific instances are from the post-1970 terminology of drug abusers.

loaded adj

1 a drunk. An Americanism in use since the turn of the century, now heard elsewhere in the English-speaking world. The original metaphor may refer to a burden or a large quantity being imbibed or, more dramatically, to the person being charged like a firearm.

• '*Dropped into a tavern/ Saw some friends of mine./ Party was gettin' under way/ And the juice was really flyin' and I got loaded.*'
('I Got Loaded', song recorded by Peppermint Harris, 1957).

b intoxicated by illicit drugs. An American term popular in the late 1960s and early 1970s. It was this sense that inspired the title of the fourth LP by the seminal New York rock group The Velvet Underground in 1970.

2 rich. This term, formerly slang, is now a common colloquialism.

loadie n American

a drunkard or habitual drug user; someone who is often or permanently **loaded**. A teenage and campus expression of the late 1970s, usually indicating disapproval.

loadsamoney n British

(someone flaunting) excessive wealth; vulgar, conspicuous consumption. The eponymous comedy character Loadsamoney, created by Harry Enfield in 1987, was based on observation of a specific social group. This group comprises bumptious and philistine skilled and semi-skilled working-class young people from South-Eastern England, who use their comparative wealth – often gained as part of the black economy – to taunt and provoke those worse off than themselves. This attitude was epitomized at football matches where supporters of London teams playing at home would wave banknotes at supporters of Northern clubs and chant slogans about unemployment (from a safe distance).

The catchphrase 'loadsamoney!' was seized upon by journalists and by the leader of the Labour opposition, Neil Kinnock, who in May 1988 accused the Thatcher administration of fostering an uncaring 'loadsamoney mentality'. In journalese 'loadsa-' was a vogue prefix in 1988 and 1989.

• '*Singer Mike Rivers has vowed never again to work for the Hooray Henry set – "I hate those loadsamoney thugs," he declared.*'
(*News of the World*, 29 May 1988).

load up vb American

to take illicit drugs. A campus and high-school term of the late 1970s.

• '*Listen, if you're loading up, that's it between us.*'

loaf n British

a head. The shortening of the cockney rhyming-slang phrase 'loaf of bread' is now more a colloquialism than slang. Since the late 1950s, it has largely been confined to the phrase 'use your loaf!'.

b life. The more common sense of 'head' and the word 'life' itself are blended in the cockney oath 'on my mother's loaf'.

lob vb British

to throw away, dispose of. A fashionable narrowing of the standard English meaning of the word, heard, particularly in the London area, since the beginning of the 1980s. A near-synonym to **bin**.

● 'It's no use any more – just lob it.'

lobe n British

a dull, conformist person. This word, used typically by schoolchildren of a tedious or unpopular fellow pupil is a shortening of 'earlobe' itself inspired by the long established working-class **ear'ole**.

lock n American

a certainty, usually heard in the teenagers' phrase 'it's a **lock**'. This sense of the word is an adaptation of the colloquial phrase to 'have (the situation) all locked up'.

lockjawed adj British

drunk. A lighthearted usage evoking speechless inebriation.

loco adj

mad, crazy. This word, popularized worldwide by its use in Western movies and cowboy fiction, is the standard informal Spanish word for crazy, deriving from the Latin ulucus; owl (which is incidentally related to the English ululate).

loco n American

a locomotive.

loco weed n American

marihuana. An elaboration of **weed**, punning on the popular name of plants inducing fits of craziness in cattle, (oxytropis or astragalus).

log n

1 Australian a lazy, inert person.

2 a piece of excrement, a **turd**.

log-rolling n

unofficial or dubious collaboration for mutual advantage, especially in the word of politics. This expression has been in use since the 19th century when it referred to lumberjacking, where pioneer neighbours would help each other move the timber required for building by physically rolling the logs to their destination before cutting them up; it has recently become popular in British journalistic circles under American influence.

loid, lloid vb

to open a door by moving a strip of celluloid or piece of plastic, (e.g. a credit card), up and down in the gap between the door and its frame, slipping the lock. A police and underworld term, like the practice in use since before World War II.

lollapalooza, lolapaloosa n American

something wonderful, outstanding, enormous and/or spectacular. This invented term is a synonym for words like whopper, **lulu** or **humdinger**, depending on the context. (Like whopper it can sometimes refer to an outrageous lie.) The word is used in particular by schoolchildren and parents.

lollies n Australian

sweets, candy. Australasia has retained the more general meaning of the word, narrowed in Britain to refer only to lollipops. (Lolly originated as a rural British dialect term for tongue, related historically to the verb to loll.)

lollipop vb British

to inform on someone, betray (to the police). This is London rhyming slang for the term to **shop**. It is sometimes shortened to **lolly**.

● 'It wouldn't be like Smoky to lollipop his mates.'

● 'If you ask me they were lollied.'

lolly n British

money. A well-established, light-hearted word, popular in the 1950s and 1960s and enjoying a revival, significantly, in the 'Thatcher years' (the mid- and late 1980s), when many obsolescent euphemisms for money have received a new lease of life. It is said to originate in the Romany word loli, meaning red, used by gypsies to mean copper coins, and hence money in general. It is perhaps easier to derive the word from lolly, meaning sweet or candy which itself originated in dialect with the meaning of tongue. (The sense of lollipop is later.)

● 'Lots of lovely lolly – that's what we want.'

lolly vb British

a short form of the rhyming slang **lollipop**.

lolly water n Australian

soft drink(s). The expression, from the Australian sense of **lollies** as sweets, is often used scathingly by committed drinkers of alcohol referring to non-alcoholic beverages, or even by **macho** drinkers to refer to alcoholic drinks considered unmanly.

lombard n British

a wealthy but stupid and/or unpleasant person. A late 1980s acronym from 'loads of money but a real dickhead', coined by **yuppies** to refer particularly to young moneymakers in the City of London, on the lines of expressions such as **dinky, nimby, homey**, etc. The word's resonance is enhanced by the role of London's Lombard Street as the home of banking and insurance companies. (The historical Lombards were incidentally a 6th-century Germanic people who invaded Northern Italy and became known as money-lenders.)

● 'If they were not Sloanes or yuppies they had to be dinkies (dual income no kids), lombards (lots of money but a real dickhead) or even swells (single women earning lots of lolly).'

(Evening Standard Magazine, May 1988).

longbeard n

an old person. A quasi-folksy term from science or fantasy fiction adopted facetiously by rock-music journalists to describe members of the older generation (or themselves when reminiscing). **Greybeard** is a slightly more widespread alternative.

long drink of water n

a an insipid, bland, ineffectual person.

b a tall, thin person.

c someone combining both the above sets of characteristics.

The second sense of the expression is the original one, but its implications of weakness, etc., have given it an alternative usage. More often than not, as in sense **c**, both sets of associations are intended or implied. (More offensive near-synonyms are the British **long streak of misery/piss**.)

long green n American

money (dollar bills of all denominations in America are coloured green). The euphemism is old, dating from the turn of the century, and is still in use.

- 'We'll soon have enough of that long green to choke a horse.'
(Knight Rider, US TV series, 1981).

long streak of misery n British

a tall, thin person who may or may not be morose, gloomy or habitually pessimistic. This expression, like the less common **long drink of water** and the more vulgar **long streak of piss** is normally part of the working-class catchphrase announcement 'here he comes again – the long streak of misery!' which may indicate affectionate recognition or genuine dislike. The phrase can refer to women as well as men.

long streak of piss n British

a tall, thin person. An expression of contempt or dismissiveness, usually implying weakness or insignificance as well as an ectomorphic body shape. The expression is almost always applied to males.

loo n British

a toilet. The most widespread and socially acceptable euphemism for lavatory, privy, etc. This word, which became firmly established in the mid-1960s, is a favourite of amateur etymologists who derive it variously from lieu ('place', as in the French euphemism lieu d'aisance, 'place of ease'); from l'eau (water) or gardez l'eau (mock-French for 'watch out for water', said to be the cry of someone emptying a chamber-pot from an upstairs window into the street below in 17th-century British cities); from 'bordalou', a type of travellers' chamber-pot; from an abbreviation of the name of Lady Louis Hamilton (apparently affixed to a lavatory door) in Dublin in 1870; or, least convincingly of all, from leeward (the side of a boat from which one would logically urinate). It may be significant, however, that this rather refined euphemism for water-closet was not recorded until well after the battle of Waterloo and the naming of the London railway station.

- 'And a bit about doing up the loo in chintz is sure to do the trick.'
(About Town magazine, June 1962).

looker n

an attractive person. The word can now be applied to either sex; formerly it was invariably used appreciatively (if sometimes patronizingly) by men of women. It originated as a truncated form of good-looker.

loon n

a a crazy, eccentric or silly person. This word is in its modern usage a convergence of three sources. It is both a shortening of lunatic and the name of an American diving bird with a cry like a demented laugh. In addition, it probably also recalls an archaic Middle English and later Scottish dialect word, 'loun', meaning a rogue. Keith Moon, drummer with the English rock group The Who, who was notorious for his wild and outrageous behaviour, was dubbed 'Moon the loon' in the late 1960s by acquaintances and the press.

b British a bout of uninhibited and eccentric behaviour. In this sense the noun is derived from the following verb.

loon, loon about, loon out vb British

to behave in an uninhibited, light-hearted and/or outrageous manner. The expression was coined at the end of the 1960s to describe a bout of high-spirited, anarchic play typical of those liberated from convention by drug use and/or progressive ideas.

● 'Gone is the rampaging looner of old, the very sight of whom would strike fear into the hearts of publicans and club owners throughout the land.'
(Record Mirror, 26 August 1967).

loon pants n pl British

flared trousers in cotton, canvas or velvet, sold in London around 1970s and emblematic of the **hippy** style of the time. Loon pants, which began as cut-down naval bell-bottoms, were so-called by sellers and wearers under the influence of the verb **to loon**. This apparel, especially the once-ubiquitous purple cotton variety was singled out for particular derision by later, post-**punk** disparagers of the hippies.

loony, looney adj

crazy. An adaptation of lunatic (see the noun **loon** for other influences) which is now a common colloquialism.

loony bin n

a hospital for the insane or mentally subnormal, an 'insane asylum'. The most common slang expression for such an institution in the English-speaking world since the end of the 19th century. In modern British parlance it is usually shortened to **the bin**.

loony tune/tunes/toons n, adj

(a) mad or eccentric (person). Originally an Americanism derived from Looney Tunes, the name of a series of cinema cartoon comedies in the 1940s, the term has become fashionable in the 1980s in Britain and Australia.

● 'I've been hit twice in the face this morning and now some loony tune is breaking up my aircraft.'
(The Flying Doctors, Australian TV series, 1987).

● 'That is it, Mork! He's got to go, or I'll end up as loony-tunes as he is.'
(Mork and Mindy, US TV series, 1979).

looped adj American

drunk. A campus expression of the 1970s which may derive from **loopy** or be an invention (perhaps influenced by lubricate and **pooped**). It is probably unconnected with the British **loop-legged**.

loop-legged adj British

drunk. An inoffensive euphemism referring to an inebriated gait.

● 'As a whiskey salesman ... I'm often lit up by elevenses, loop-legged by luncheon and totally schnockered by 6.'
(Cartoon by Posy Simmonds, Guardian, 1979).

loop-the-loop n British

1 soup. An example of London working-class rhyming slang heard since the 1970s. It was used in a TV commercial for Heinz in 1988.

2 soixante-neuf or 69, in the professional jargon of prostitution and pornography.

loopy adj

a crazy, eccentric, silly.

b illogical, out of control.

A fairly mild pejorative, often said in bemusement or disbelief rather than disapproval. The word has been in use since the early years of the 20th century, but its origin is obscure.

loose adj

relaxed, nonchalant, unhurried, **cool**. A word from the jargon of jazz musicians to describe a free, unstructured style of play or mood evoked. This notion provided the late 1950s **beatnik** catchphrases **hang loose** and **stay loose**. In modern parlance the word is most often heard in connection with performances, whether of music or drama.

loose cannon n American

a dangerously uncontrolled ally or associate; a member of one's team who is liable to run amok or cause havoc. This piece of political and journalistic jargon has become fashionable in the late 1980s. It continues the nautical image evoked by such vogue clichés as 'take on board'. In this case the person in question is seen as an unsecured cannon careering unpredictably and dangerously across a deck with the pitching of a ship. The phrase was used of General Haig during the Nixon administration and of Colonel Oliver North under the Reagan administration.

● 'Danko is the perfect weapon Charlie – a loose cannon. If he helps us find Victor Rosla, great. If he screws up, breaks rules . . . he's a Russian.'
(Red Heat, US film, 1988).

loot n

money. A predictable extension of the standard English sense of booty. The word is an Anglicized spelling of the Hindi word lut which sounds and means the same as the English derivation.

● 'I tell you what though, Zackerman can recruit the very best because he's got the loot.'
(Serious Money, play by Caryl Churchill, 1987).

Lord Muck n British

a man thought to be 'putting on airs' or behaving high-handedly. This expression from the turn of the century is now probably less prevalent than the female equivalent, **Lady Muck**.

● 'Well, won't you just look at them Lord and Lady Muck.'

lose one's bottle vb British

to lose one's nerve, have one's courage desert one. A vogue term of the late 1970s, when it crossed from the jargon of marginals, criminals and the lower working-class into general currency. (For the origins of the expression see **bottle**.)

lose one's cool vb

to lose one's composure or one's temper. A phrase from the 1950s American **hip** vocabulary, usually heard in the form of an admonition. It was adopted in British, first by jazz fans and **beatniks** in the late 1950s.

● 'Try not to lose your cool even if the guy provokes you.'

lose one's lunch/ doughnuts/pizza vb American

to vomit. Hearty, jocular high school and college terms.

lose one's marbles vb

to become deranged or feeble-minded, go crazy. **Marbles** when referring to male faculties usually refers to testicles, but in this case one's wits or intelligence are in question. The origin of this phrase is uncertain, in spite of many attempts to clarify the choice of words (marbles have been seen as a synonym for the bearings which allow a machine to operate or as part of a catchphrase based on a story in which a monkey steals a boy's marbles). What is undisputed is that the expression originated in the USA.

lose one's rag vb British

to lose one's temper, lose control of oneself. This mainly working-class expression is of obscure origin; the word rag has meant variously one's tongue, a flag, to tease, to bluster or rage, but none of these senses can be definitively linked to the modern phrase.

- *'Don't you go losing your rag – stay cool.'*
  (*Eastenders*, British TV series, July 1988).

lotion n British

an alcoholic drink. A now dated middle-class term with the implications of the soothing medicinal effects of (strong) liquor. The word can be countable ('a lotion') or uncountable ('some lotion').

louie, louis n

1 British one-sixteenth of an ounce (of cannabis). This is the smallest quantity of the drug that can normally be bought by weight in Britain. The term was first heard in the late 1980s and is derived from Louis XVI, the king overthrown in the French revolution, in the same way as **Henry** for an eighth of an ounce.

- *'OK, make it a louie.'*

2 American a left-hand turn. The term is usually part of the phrase **hang a louie**. (The alternative is **hang a ralph**.)

lounge lizard n

an idle habitué of hotel cocktail bars, dances, etc., who seeks out the company of women. This now dated jazz-age phrase with its many overtones (seducer, reptile, cold-bloodedness, languor, etc.) is occasionally resurrected today, usually for humorous purposes.

love blobs n pl British

testicles. A jocular schoolboy or armed-forces coinage briefly popular in the early 1980s and broadcast in the BBC alternative comedy series *The Young Ones*. Similar phrases such as **love bumps** or **love handles** are also in use. 'Love bubbles' is an archaic euphemism for breasts.

love bumps n pl British

breasts. A 'schoolboyish' euphemism of the 1970s. 'Love bubbles' was a pre-World War II synonym. **Love lumps** is an alternative form.

love handles n pl

folds of flesh at the waist or paunch. An affectionate, joky, reassuring or polite euphemism usually applied to the male body by women or by the person himself.

- *'Little love handles sticking out like fishing piers/ Covered with shingles, bladder's getting weak.'*
  ('I'm a Wreck', song by Mojo Nixon, 1989).
- *'The love handles of Jonathan Ross are no strangers to this column, but news reaches us that they are shrinking by the hour.'*
  (*Time Out* magazine, July 1989).

love-in n

a gathering involving displays of mutual affection and/or ecstatic 'oneness'. An ephemeral phenomenon and term from the early **hippy** era, seized upon by the press.

love-in-a-punt n British

weak beer or watered-down alcohol. The expression is a pun playing pseudo-romantically on the plant love-in-a-mist and on the notion that the drink in question is 'fucking near water'. Paul Beale in Eric Partridge's *Dictionary of Slang and Unconventional English* (1984) specifies 'a brew sold in the Portsmouth area in the 1950s'.

love lumps n pl British

breasts. A jocular term used by university students and teenagers in the mid- to late 1980s in keeping with the trend to coin childishly coy expressions as alternatives to established or taboo terms. **Love bumps** is an alternative form.

love muscle n

the penis. A euphemism used particularly in black American slang and facetiously in Australian speech.

lover's nuts/balls n pl

alternative terms for **blue balls**.

low budget adj British

sleazy, sordid, shabby, poor. This phrase, inspired by its earlier application to feature films, has been adopted in the 1980s, typically by **yuppies** or **Sloane Rangers**, as a British version of the American **low rent**.

● 'She lives in an awfully low budget sort of place.'

low-heel, low-wheel n
Australian

a prostitute. The term refers to someone who is literally down at heel from walking the streets. The second form of the expression is based on a mis-hearing of the true phrase.

lowie n Australian

a prostitute. A shortened form of low heel.

lowlife n American

a disreputable and/or contemptible person. A fashionable term of the 1970s which was adopted by some British speakers to refer to those considered socially unacceptable.

● 'Jesus, Katy, what are you doing with this lowlife?'

low rent adj American

shabby, sordid, inferior. A phrase referring to lodgings, extended first to denote a poor district, then to signify anything or anyone considered dis-

tasteful or third-rate. **Low budget** is a near-synonym in British English.

low rider n American

a a devotee of customized cars with lowered suspension characteristic of Chicano or Hispanic youth gangs in Los Angeles and elsewhere during the 1970s. The term low rider (the fashion was still in evidence at the end of the 1980s) can also be applied to the car itself. Low riding involves (contrary to raising suspension for road racing or rallying) driving very slowly in convoys for display.

b an obnoxious or disreputable youth. This pejorative use of the word is an extension of the original sense, probably influenced also by standard terms such as low.

lube n

a shortening of lubrication in the context of car mechanics. A lube job (originally American) refers to a servicing of grease points.

lubra n Australian

an Aborigine woman. This racist pejorative term, first recorded in 1834, has as its origin a native Tasmanian name. It is a rarer alternative to the abbreviations gin or abo.

lubricated adj

drunk. A politely jocular euphemism on the same lines as **well-oiled**.

luck out vb American

a to 'strike it lucky'.
b to have bad luck. This term with its contrary senses is occasionally used by British speakers.

Lucy locket n British

a pocket. A piece of London rhyming slang inspired by a nursery rhyme character. **Sky-rocket** and **Davy Crockett** are alternative versions.

'lude n American

a Quaalude (pronounced 'kway-lood') tablet. A widely prescribed and misused methaqualone (hypnotic sleeping pill), equivalent to the British Mandrax or **mandy**. The drug was taken, particularly in the 1970s, for its relaxing and disinhibiting effects and to mitigate the after- and side-effects of other drugs.

lughole, lug'ole n British

ear. A common term of the 1950s and 1960s which now sounds folksy or dated, although the comedian Frankie Howerd still employs 'pin back your lugholes' as one of his catchphrases. Lug has been the commonest colloquialism for 'ear' outside London since the 16th century. It originated in Middle English meaning flap or ear-cover, from an older Scandinavian word *lugga*, to pull.

lulu n

1 something spectacular, impressive, exceptional. This word was originally an Americanism, in use since the mid-19th century: many attempts have been made to explain its etymology, which remains obscure. (It is almost certainly unconnected with the female nickname.)

2 British an elaboration of **loo**.

lumber n British

a trouble, burdensome difficulties. This sense of the word is usually expressed by the 'cockney' phrases '*in lumber*' or '*in dead lumber*'.

b a fight or struggle. A word which in working-class, particularly northern, usage is often in the form of an exclamation to signal the start of a street or playground brawl, and is another sense of lumber as 'trouble'.

● '*Tables flew, bottles broke, the bouncers shouted lumber/the dummy got too chummy in a Bing Crosby number.*'
(*Salome Maloney the Sweetheart of the Ritz*, poem by John Cooper Clarke, 1980).

lumme!

a now dated working-class expression of alarm, surprise, etc., which was popular until the early 1960s. It is a contraction of 'Lord love me'.

lummock, lummox n

a large, clumsy and/or stupid person. The word is used in the USA and Australia as well as in Britain, but is originally a rural British dialect form of 'lump', in the same way as hummock is a diminutive form of hump.

● '*The awkward lummox of a kid who, though only ten years old, was almost as big as his fifth grade teacher.*'
(*Wild Town*, Jim Thompson, 1957).

the lump n British

the casual work system in the British building trade, or the casual non-union work force, exploited by employers in the 1960s and 1970s.

lump it vb British

to put up with something, accept something unpleasant. A slang term of the 1950s which became widespread in the early 1960s, especially in the catchphrase '*like it or lump it*'. The expression is surprisingly old; it was first recorded in the early 18th century.

lumps n pl

breasts. A mock-childish word used facetiously, particularly by teenagers and adults.

lunatic soup n

alcoholic drink. A humorous expression on the lines of **electric soup**, **giggle water** and **laughing soup**.

lunchbox n

the stomach, belly or abdomen. A jocular euphemism, used particularly in the context of fighting.

- 'A kick/punch in the lunchbox.'

See also **open one's lunchbox**.

lunching at the Lazy Y n

phrase

engaging in oral sex, particularly cunnilingus. A humorous expression playing on the shape of a reclining person with their legs spread and a famous cattle brand from the American Wild West. (A 'lazy' letter in a brand was one lying on its side.) An alternative form is 'dining at the Y'.

lundy n British

a collaborator, traitor. A Northern Irish term derived from the name of the governor of Londonderry in the 18th century, Lieutenant Colonel Robert Lundy, who was suspected of Catholic sympathies by the Protestant community.

lungs n pl

breasts. A vulgarism heard in the USA and in Britain where it is now confined in use to older speakers, invariably male.

- 'She may not have much of a voice but she's got a fine pair of lungs on her.'

lunk, lunkhead n American

a slow-witted person, dullard. The term originated in the USA in the 19th century. It usually evokes a large, clumsy, ungainly person of low intelligence and/or slow reactions. It is a blend of lump and hunk.

lurgi, lurghi n

alternative spellings of **lerg(h)i**.

lurk n Australian

a dodge, shady scheme, clever and/or disreputable trick. The word is now used in these senses mainly by middle-aged and elderly speakers.

lurker n

1 British a a disreputable, suspicious, unwholesome person. A word often used by disaffected youth ironically of themselves, it was adopted as a name by a suburban London **punk-rock** group in 1977.

b a fly-by-night or unlicensed street trader.

2 Australian a petty criminal, fraudster or cardsharp.

All these senses are variations on the standard English meaning of lurk which comes from the Middle English lurken, to lie in wait.

lush n

an alcoholic, habitual drunkard or heavy drinker. This is an American term, adopted by British speakers in the 1960s, which derived from an earlier British usage which had fallen into desuetude; from at least the 18th century until the early 20th century lush had been used to mean alcoholic drink.

lush adj British

a very attractive and/or desirable.

- 'A lush bird.'
- 'I love your ski pants, Tray Nice aren't they! £12.99. You want to get some. You'll look lush.'
(The Fat Slags, cartoon in Viz magazine, 1989).

b delicious.

- 'Well, how was it?' 'Lush'

This British colloquialism, heard especially in the 1960s among schoolchildren, young people and unsophisticated adults, is a short form of luscious rather than the standard adjective (as in 'lush vegetation', for example).

lushed *adj*

drunk. This is probably a recent coinage inspired by **lush** meaning a heavy drinker. In fact lush as a verb, and lushed as a past participle, had existed in English slang and dialect since the early 19th century, but had fallen out of use in most areas before World War II. The renewed use of the term is mainly confined to teenagers and students.

M

M n

morphine. A drug users' abbreviation.

Ma Bell n American

the nickname of the Bell Telephone Corporation.

mac n

1 American a term of address to a male stranger. The word often conveys a hint of provocation rather than straightforward friendliness.

2 British a mackintosh, raincoat.

See **the dirty mac brigade**.

macaroni n

an Italian. In the 18th century the word meant an Italianate fop. It has survived as a less common synonym than eye-tie or **wop**.

machine gun n

a hypodermic syringe, in the language of drug addicts and prison inmates of the late 1950s and 1960s. This is one of many self-dramatizing terms (**shooting gallery**, **harpoon**, etc.) in the vocabulary of hard-drug users.

machismo n

assertive maleness, overt masculinity. The word evokes virility, supremacism, etc. It is not strictly speaking slang but a direct borrowing from the Spanish (and as such should be pronounced as in 'match' not 'mack').

macho adj

assertively male, aggressively masculine. The word is a direct borrowing from Spanish in which it means male, particularly in an animal context, hence virile.

- 'I mean I work, and when I say work, I mean I really do work. It's not inverted vanity, it's not macho don't-give-a-damn posturing.' (Cartoon by Michael Heath in The Sunday Times Men's Fashion Extra, October 1989).
- 'Her experience among women rappers trying to cut it in the macho world of Hip Hop, led Charlotte to look again at the girl groups from the Seventies she'd always loved.' (Ms London magazine, 4 September 1989).

macho up vb

an alternative form of **butch up** (to behave more assertively, courageously or to show more masculine characteristics). **Macho** is Spanish for male in the assertive or dominant sense of the word.

made-in n British

a 'two-one' honours degree. A students' jocularism based on 'made-in-Taiwan'. An alternative form is a **draw**; 'two won'.

mad money n American

a money set aside by a girl or woman in case she is abandoned or offended by her date. In this sense of the word mad signifies anger (on the part of the girl or her escort).

b money set aside for frivolous, impulsive or self-indulgent purposes. In this version the sense of mad is the British 'crazy'. Both uses of the phrase date from before World War II. They are now dated but not quite obsolete.

maggot n

1 a despicable, dirty and/or insignificant person. In British use, the predominant idea is usually 'beneath contempt', whereas in Australia maggot is a generalized term of abuse.

2 British money. A rare usage, heard among petty criminals or their imitators among others. Like many obscure synonyms for money it has been rehabilitated in the late 1980s.

- 'I've got to get hold of some maggot in a hurry.'

magic adj British

superlative, excellent. An over-used colloquialism since the late 1970s which is characteristic of garrulous or over-enthusiastic lower-middle-class and working-class speech. It is often heard in the context of sports such as football or darts.

- 'Belfast is "magic" – local demotic for "super" or "marvellous" or whatever high superlative leaps instinctively off the tongue.'
  (The Crack: a Belfast Year, Sally Belfrage, 1987).

magic, magic dust/mist n
American

the drug **PCP** (also known as **angel dust**).

magic mushrooms n pl

any hallucinogenic mushrooms such as psilocybin or the native British 'liberty caps'.

the magic word n Australian

fuck; a word which is ironically supposed when uttered to bring about either instant sexual compliance or speechless shock. An item from Australian male folklore.

make babies vb

to have sex, make love. A coy or jocular euphemism used by adults.

main drag n

the main or central street. An American phrase from the early years of the century, heard elsewhere since the 1970s. (**Drag** was also used to mean street in Victorian Cockney speech.)

main line n

a vein. A term in use among those injecting narcotics, **mainliners**.

mainline vb

to inject (an illicit drug) directly into a vein. The term is one of the most persistent pieces of addicts' jargon, contrasted with **skin-popping** (injecting subcutaneously or intramuscularly). The meaning is sometimes extended to denote the regular ingestion of anything in large quantities.

mainliners n pl

those who inject narcotics.

main man n American

a a boss, leader.
- 'He's the main man around here.'

b (a woman's) partner, boyfriend, husband or protector.
- 'He's my main man.'

c one's best friend, **buddy**, bosom pal.
- 'Yo, Billy, my main man! How're they hanging?'

main squeeze n American

a (one's) boyfriend or girlfriend, sweetheart.

b most important person, boss, leader.

make n American

1 a an identification or instance of recognition (of a suspect).

b a check in official records on the identity of a suspect or on another piece of evidence.

● *'Run a make on this guy, will you?'*

● *'Can we have a make on the license number?'*

2 a sex partner. The term is a back-formation from the sexual sense of the verb **make**, on the same principle as **lay**.

make vb American

1 to identify, recognize (a suspect or adversary). A piece of police and criminal jargon well-known from its use in fiction, TV and films.

● *'Can you make him?'*
(*The French Connection*, US film, 1971).

2 to have sex with, seduce. This turn-of-the-century euphemism, although understood, has never caught on in Britain or Australia. It has occasionally been adopted by individuals, including the philosopher Bertrand Russell.

make a connection vb

to establish a source for illicit drugs or to succeed in buying some narcotics. A euphemistic expression originally from the jargon of heroin addicts.

make out vb American

a to indulge in **necking** or heavy petting.

b to succeed in having sex.

Both are teenagers' extensions of the colloquial sense of the phrase; to be successful. The usage is probably influenced by the verb **make** as a euphemism for seduce or have sex with.

See also **make-out artist**.

make-out artist n American

a successful seducer, **stud**. The term is invariably applied to males. It is from the verb **make out**, meaning achieve sexual satisfaction or success.

make the scene vb

to be present (in a particular milieu), to arrive, in the literal sense or in the sense of achieving a desired position or level of recognition. The phrase is from the talk of jazz musicians, **hipsters** and **beatniks** of the late 1950s. It was briefly and self-consciously adopted in the same circles in Britain but did not survive the derision its use often occasioned.

mallie, mall rat n American

a (usually female) teenager who hangs around shopping malls in order to meet friends, misbehave and/or otherwise have a 'good time'. A phenomenon, and expression, in existence since the early 1980s.

mammy rammer n

a milder form of **motherfucker**, heard for example among British schoolchildren in the late 1980s. The phrase was probably adopted from Caribbean usage.

the Man n American

1 a the police, the government, the (white) establishment or any other authority, or person in authority. A usage coined by underdogs which was taken up by the black power and **hippy** movements of the late 1960s.

● *'Looking for a job in the city/ Working for the Man ev'ry night and day.'*
('Proud Mary' by John Fogerty,

recorded by Creedence Clearwater Revival, 1969).

- 'Dealers use them to carry drugs, because the man ain't gonna bother them. They're kids.'
(The Sunday Times, 10 September 1989).

b a sports champion, pop singer, etc. considered by the speaker to be the top practitioner of his craft.

- 'There were a lot of good heavyweights around in the '60s, but Ali was the Man.'

2 a supplier of illicit drugs, a **pusher**, **dealer** or **connection**.

- 'I'm waiting for the man/ Twenty-six dollars in my hand.'
('I'm Waiting for the Man' written by Lou Reed, recorded by The Velvet Underground, 1967).

mandie, mandy n British

a tablet of Mandrax (the British trademark name of methaqualone, a potentially addictive 'hypnotic' sleeping preparation). These drugs, like their American counterparts, Quaaludes or **'ludes**, were taken by drug abusers for their relaxant, dis-inhibiting and supposedly aphrodisiac effects (mandies were, according to users' slogans, certain to make one **bandy** or **randy**), particularly in the 1970s.

- 'She dropped a couple of mandies and started falling over in the Seven Stars.'
(Recorded, London, 1987).

- 'The staff and editors of Oz wish to protest against the flippant attitude of our art director towards Mandrax in the caption above ['Mandies make you randy']. Mandies are both addictive and dangerous.'
(Oz magazine, July 1972).

mangoes n pl American

breasts. One of many terms employing the metaphor of round fruit.

manicure vb American

to remove the stalks and seeds from herbal marihuana in order to purify it before selling or smoking.

man in the boat n

See **little man in the boat**.

manky adj British

grotty, disgusting or distasteful. A 1960s vogue word, mainly in middle-class usage. The word had existed previously in working-class speech: it may be an invention influenced by mangy, cranky, 'wonky', etc., or a corruption of the French manqué (lacking, failed). It is still used in northern England where its usual sense is naughty or spoilt.

manners n pl West Indian

situation, moral ambience. Usually heard in the phrase **under heavy manners**, meaning oppressed, behaving under the threat of discipline. The term was employed in the context of the Rastafarian and reggae subculture in the early 1970s and was briefly adopted by young whites, especially in the world of rock music.

manor n British

one's own district or area of jurisdiction. A word used by both police and criminals since before World War II.

man up! exclamation American

a cry of alarm, signalling the arrival of the police. A 1980s street-slang usage based either on **the Man**, meaning authority, or from military jargon meaning 'target identified and moving'.

- '"Man up!" the lookouts shout as plainclothes officers Jeff Ziernicki and Harold Braxton creep up Susquehanna Avenue in their boxy blue Plymouth.'

(*The Sunday Times*, 10 September 1989).

the man upstairs n
a humorous euphemism for God.

map of France/Ireland/ America/etc. n
a a stain on a sheet.
b a patch of vomit.
The use of the phrase map of Ireland to describe semen stains on bedsheets is said to originate among chambermaids, many of whom were themselves Irish.

map of Tasmania n Australian
female pubic hair. A male expression based on a fancied resemblance between the shape of the female pubic area and the Australian island state.

maracas n pl
a breasts. A mainly American usage.
b testicles. In British speech the (rare) term is reinforced by the rhyme with **knackers**.

marble orchard n
a cemetery, graveyard. A synonym for **bone orchard** or **boneyard** or **skull orchard**.

marbles n pl
1 testicles. A predictable drawing of a literal parallel (rather than, as some have claimed, an example of rhyming slang on 'marble halls'). **Pills**, **balls**, **stones** and **nuts** are similar metaphors.
2 common sense, sanity, mental faculties. This use of the word was originally American, perhaps deriving from a folk tale.
See also **lose one's marbles**.
3 money, wealth. This sense of the word, which exists principally in British and Australian usages probably derives from the children's wish to amass

a collection of marbles, influenced by the luxury implied by the use of the substance marble.

mardarse, mardie n British
a 'softie', a weak person. A schoolchildren's word heard from the 1930s onwards, particularly in the north of England. It is now rare, but not quite archaic, and comes from a dialect form of 'marred' which has the specific sense of spoilt or sulky. Anthony Burgess mentions that the word was used of him by tormentors during his childhood. Mardie has also been heard in use as an adjective.
● '*Go out with your Dad. Don't be such a bloody mardie.*'
(Recorded, Leicester, 1990).

mare n British
a woman. A derogatory working-class usage on the lines of **cow**, **bitch** or **sow**. Mare usually has overtones of 'nag' in both its senses and hence denotes a drab, wearisome woman. The word was given a wider currency by its use as a strong but acceptable term of abuse in TV comedies.

mark n
a dupe or target chosen by a conman, pickpocket, etc. An old term, recorded as long ago as 1885 and still in use all over the English-speaking world.
● '*[She] is drawn into an underworld of cons, scams, "marks" (suckers) and "tells" (their involuntary giveaway gestures).*'
(Review of David Mamet's US film, *House of Games, Independent*, 19 November 1987).

mark someone's card vb
British
to tip someone off, give someone a warning. This phrase from the jargon of horse-racing has been adopted by London working-class speakers, in

particular in police and underworld circles. The usual implication is a firm but gentle (or menacing) taking aside and 'putting in the picture'.

- *'You can leave it to me, I'll mark his card for him.'*

marmalize, marmelise *vb* *British*

to destroy, utterly defeat. This invented word, suggesting like **spifflicate** some unspecified but comprehensive punishment, is probably a children's invention, perhaps based on marmalade. It has been used by adults for comic effect, particularly on radio and television (by Ken Dodd's 'Diddymen' and the scriptwriters of *Coronation Street* among others).

- *'I'll marmalize you!'*

marps *n pl British*

marbles or the game of marbles. A children's term heard in various parts of the UK (but not apparently London).

marvie *adj American*

marvellous. A teenagers' term typically used either with gushing enthusiasm or irony.

mary ann *n British*

a male homosexual, effeminate man. One of several usages of common Victorian or Edwardian female forenames (Nancy, as part of **nancy boy**, and **jessie** are others which have survived) to refer derisively to effeminate men.

Mary Jane, Mary Warner, Mary Jane Warner *n*

marihuana. These are English puns or **hobson-jobson** versions of the Spanish name for cannabis. One spelling of the word, *marijuana*, is a literal translation of Mary-Jane, although the original Mexican form, *marihuana*, is a familiarizing prefix (from 'Maria') added to a native Amerindian word meaning something like 'herbal substance'.

the Marzipan set *n British*

a probably ephemeral **yuppie** coinage from 1987, defined by George Pitcher in the *Observer* as 'Those city flyers who are above the rich cake but below the icing'.

mash *n, vb British*

(to make) tea. From the use of the term in the beer-brewing process.

mataby *n British*

high-quality herbal cannabis originating in the Belgian Congo, now Zaire. This presumably native word, used particularly in the 1960s, is a rare alternative to the more usual congo grass. (Perhaps coincidentally the Zulu term *matabele*, known in Britain as the name of a Rhodesian tribe, means 'hidden'.)

matelot *n British*

a a sailor, referred to patronisingly by soldiers, policemen, etc.

b a member of the river police, as referred to by other sections of the police force. The word *matelot* is French for sailor.

mattress-muncher *n* *Australian*

a (passive) male homosexual. A rarer and probably later version of **pillow-biter**.

maulers *n pl British*

hands. A mainly middle-class schoolchildren's usage, popular in the 1950s and early 1960s.

- *'Keep your maulers off my things, will you.'*

mau-mau *vb American*

to harass, bully or coerce. The

phrase was briefly in vogue, mainly in literary and journalistic circles, in the early 1970s. It was the name of a Kenyan guerilla group which fought for independence in the 1950s and gained a reputation in the west for carrying out atrocities.

- 'Radical Chic and mau-mauing the flak-catchers and other stories.' (Title of book, Tom Wolfe, 1970).

mau-mau n

a American a 'black power' supporter or black activist.

b American a black street-gang member.

c British a black person.

The first two senses are not necessarily pejorative, the British usage invariably is.

maven n American

a nightclub host. The word, which means an expert or someone 'in the know', is from Hebrew (in which it means understanding) via Yiddish. It was given its specific sense in the 1970s (it had previously meant something like the later **huff** or connoisseur) by New York journalists and nightclub habitués.

max adv

at most, to the maximum extent. See also **to the max**.

- 'I swear he only earns £25k, max.'

mazooma, mazuma n

money. An American term heard since the early years of the 20th century. Like many other picturesque but dated synonyms it was revived in British speech in the late 1980s. The word is originally Hebrew, entering American slang via Yiddish.

mezoomas n pl

breasts. One of many similar invent-

ed terms probably based on the archaic **bazumas**, a corruption of bosom.

McAlpine's fusiliers n pl British

building labourers. A nickname inspired by the name of Britain's largest building and civil-engineering company and applied affectionately or ironically to casual labourers or **navvies**.

MCP n

a sexist man. An abbreviation of 'male chauvinist pig', a feminist vogue term which appeared in 1970. It was often used in this shortened form both in writing and, less often, in speech. If used, the expression is now usually truncated to chauvinist or even chauvo.

- 'He'd ordered a Heineken from a waitress who was a real throwback, an MCP's delight.' (The Serial, Cyra McFadden, 1976).

MDA n

methyldiamphetamine, a synthetic drug which is chemically related to the stimulant amphetamines, but which in some users elicits hallucinogenic experiences supposedly similar to those associated with LSD. The drug was first popular in the early 1970s in the USA, and came once again into vogue in the late 1980s in the UK, where it was known as **adam** or, more usually, **ecstasy**, and became the drug of choice among young club-goers and dancers. MDA has also been designated by the initials MDMA and MMDA.

mean adj

wonderful, impressive, excellent. A typical reversal of the standard (American) meaning in black code and later teenage usage, like the more recent **bad** and **wicked**.

mean machine n

any (supposedly) impressive, spectacular contraption such as a motorcycle or car, or figuratively a male or the male sex organ. A black American all-purpose euphemism of the late 1960s.

meat and two veg n British

the male genitals. A working-class vulgarism dating from the days when these components constituted the standard British meal, as advertised in cafés, boarding houses, etc. (Veg is short for vegetables and is spoken with a soft 'g'.) Meat has been a slang synonym for penis, as well as for human sexuality in general, since at least the 16th century.

meatball n

a clod or fool; a brawny but unintelligent male. The word may be used as a variation of **meathead**, or less pejoratively to denote an attractive male, **hunk** (albeit patronizingly).
- '*My Swedish Meatball.*'
  (Title of an American softcore movie).

meatball surgery n American

clumsy or incompetent surgery; operations carried out under difficult or primitive conditions, especially by armed-service doctors under field conditions. Originally a piece of armed-forces slang, its more general use was popularized by the long-running American TV comedy series *M*A*S*H*. It derives more from the imagery of butchery than from **meatball** meaning stupid.

meathead, meat head n

a stupid person, dullard. This word was first popularized in the USA. The image evoked is either based on meat signifying solid muscle (instead of brains) or perhaps on the sexual sense of **meat** as penis, in which case the expression is a precursor of the popular term **dickhead**.

- '*What I don't need is some meathead coming in and screwing everything up.*'
  (Recorded, journalist, London, 1986).
- '*A man of patient indulgence, apparently capable of putting up with every bozo and meathead who comes his way.*'
  (Jonathan Keates reviewing Malcolm Bradbury's *Unsent Letter*, *Observer*, 5 June 1988).

meathooks n pl

hands. **Hooks** has been a slang synonym for hands since the early 19th century; this embellishment came into use slightly later.

meat injection n British

an act of sexual intercourse. The vulgar euphemism is invariably used by male speakers.

meat market n

a place where people congregate in the search for sexual partners; a singles bar. The phrase is usually used dismissively of dance halls, clubs, etc. by non-participants or ex-participants.

meat puppet n American

a prostitute. A short-lived black Los Angeles term, adopted as the name of a **hardcore** group of the 1980s.

meat rack n

a place where, or occasion when available sexual partners are on display. The phrase is specifically used in a **gay** context to describe public places and events such as bars, discos, parties, etc. at which homosexuals gather.

meat wagon n

a a police van, **black maria**.
b an ambulance.
c a hearse.

All the senses of the phrase were first heard between the World Wars.

mega *adj*

enormous, hugely successful, great, wonderful. A popular teenage buzzword since the mid 1980s, by the end of the decade mega had penetrated adult speech, in particular journalese. In origin it was an adaptation by black American youth of the fashionable late-1970s prefix 'mega' into an independent adjective.

- 'This band is going to be mega, mark my words!'
- 'We had this real mega thrash.'

megabucks *n*

an enormous amount of money. An Americanism of the 1970s which is now heard elsewhere, including Britain, where 'bucks' remains the suffix although not strictly appropriate. (Mega was a fashionable prefix of the late 1970s.)

- 'He's making megabucks in the City.'

mellow *adj*

relaxed, unaggressive, free of unhealthy tensions and inhibitions. This specialized sense of the standard English adjective was originated by jazz and rock musicians and promoted by the **hippy** counterculture, for whom it encapsulated key ideals.

mellow out *vb*

to become relaxed, serene; to free oneself from tension and inhibition. The phrase is a cliché of the **hippy** era, taken from the jargon of jazz and, later, rock musicians. It is still heard, largely in American speech.

melons *n pl*

breasts. An obvious metaphor which exists in other languages, notably Spanish. The word was employed as a nickname by the British tabloid press in 1986 to refer to the supposedly buxom figure of Lady Helen Windsor.

Melvin *n American*

a boring person, nonentity. The Christian name was thought in the 1950s to be quintessentially mundane, personifying a suburban dullard. More recently it has been a term of abuse among college students.

memsahib *n British*

a one's wife.

b a dignified, domineering or redoubtable woman.

The word, now usually employed facetiously, is a form of madame-sahib (*sahib* is Hindi for master or lord), a form of address used by Indian servants in the colonial era. (The usual pronunciation is 'memsaab'.)

mensch, mensh *n*

a a reputable, admirable or dependable person (usually, but not invariably, a male). An approving term from Yiddish and German in which its literal meaning is man, woman, person or humankind.

b an exclamation of surprise or alarm from Yiddish or German.

mental *n*

See **throw a mental**.

mental *adj British*

mentally ill, subnormal or deranged, crazy. A widespread colloquialism which showed signs of losing popularity in the 1970s, perhaps due to increased sensitivity; this tendency was reversed by **punks**, fans of heavy-metal and others who enthusiastically adopted the term to refer to their characteristic frenzies, **headbanging**, etc. In these circles the word may be used to express admiration.

See also **radio rentals**.

me 'n' you n

a menu. A time-honoured pun heard in all English-speaking areas.

merch n American

'merchandise', stolen goods. A police and underworld term, in limited use since the 1960s and like similar shortenings (**nabe, perp**) undergoing a revival since around 1989.

merchant banker n British

a contemptible person, a **wanker**. This rhyming slang, coined in the late 1980s like its synonym **Kuwaiti tanker**, highlights a contemporary concern (in this case the spectacular mid-1980s developments in the financial centres of the City of London) to revitalize a familiar epithet.

merkin n

a the female pubic area or female sex organs.

b an artificial vagina, used as a sex aid.

Merkin is a late medieval word for a wig designed to be worn on the female pubis, usually in order to disguise the effects of syphilis. It probably originates as an affectionate diminutive form of Mary. In the 1960s the word was better known in the USA than Britain. A well-known Californian **groupie** of the late 1960s adopted the pseudonym, Trixie Merkin, and Anthony Newley used the fictitious names 'Hieronymous Merkin' and 'Mercy Humppe' in the title of a semi-autobiographical fantasy film.

merries n pl British

fairground rides. The word is a shortening of merry-go-round extended by children and teenagers to refer to funfair attractions in general.

mersh adj

commercial. A word used in the 1980s in fashionable youth circles and rock journalism, usually at least slightly pejoratively.

● 'Mersh tendencies.'

the Met n British

the London Metropolitan Police force. The abbreviation by which they refer both to themselves and their district or area of jurisdiction (which covers most of central and suburban London but excludes the City).

meth n

Methedrine (the trademark name for methamphetamine). A drug user's abbreviation for the powerful amphetamine-based stimulant (**speed**), which has been widely abused, particularly in the mid and late 1960s.

meths n British

methylated spirits, as drunk for its intoxicating effects by alcoholics, vagrants, etc.

Mexican breakfast n

a cigarette and a glass of water. A witticism originating in the USA, where the Mexican reference is supposed to evoke poverty and lack of sophistication or competence. There have been other, probably later, variations on this pattern, among which are **dingo's breakfast** and pelican's breakfast.

Mexican mud n American

a highly-refined, dark-coloured form of heroin imported to the USA from Mexico.

mick n

a an Irish person. This shortening of one of the most common Irish Christian names (along with Patrick or **Paddy**) was first used in the USA and Australia to personify the Irishman or person of Irish descent. The usage had spread to Britain by the early years of this century.

b a Roman Catholic, by extension from the first sense. In both senses, the word is usually used unaffectionately or pejoratively.

mickey, mokey n Australian
the female genitals.

Mickey (Bliss)
See **take the mickey**.

mickey (finn) n
a soporific or stupefying drug administered to a person without their knowledge. The word was first recorded in the USA in the early 20th century. It may derive from the name of a real individual or from a generic (probably seafarers') term for a cudgel or thug.

Mickey Mouse adj
amateurish, unworthy of consideration or respect. A contemptuous description beloved of the business world in the 1970s and 1980s, Mickey Mouse has in fact been used in this way since before World War II when the phrase was applied for instance to childish or simplistic music or the bands which played it. It subsequently denoted any institution or venture which did not deserve to be taken seriously.

● *'It's strictly a Mickey Mouse operation they're running there.'*

microdot n
a dose of the drug LSD sold in a tiny film of gelatin or as a blot on paper. The practice of buying LSD in this form began in the late 1960s.

middle leg n
the penis. **Third leg** is an alternative form of the euphemism.

middy n
1 *Australian* a medium-sized beer glass.

2 *British* a toilet. A form of the archaic standard English 'midden'.

milkbar cowboy n Australian
the Australian version of the American **drugstore cowboy**.

milko n
a milkman. The Australian abbreviation is now in use in Britain, too, largely replacing the dated milkie.

the milk round n British
a the annual tour of British institutions of higher education by prospective employers.

b the round of interviews followed by recent graduates seeking employment.

milk run n
1 something easy or safe, a **doddle**. American bomber pilots used the term in World War II to describe a raid where no anti-aircraft fire was expected, by analogy with a trip to the store to get some milk. The term was given wider currency by its use in Joseph Heller's best-seller *Catch-22*.

2 *British* a regular scheduled journey or process. The phrase is sometimes used as a synonym for **the milk round**.

milquetoast, milktoast n
American

an un-macho, meek man, a **wimp**. Reminiscent of the food given to invalids, Milquetoast derives from the name of the fictional character Caspar Milquetoast, created by the American cartoonist H. T. Webster. Zsa Zsa Gabor used the term, to the puzzlement of many British viewers, when interviewed during her trial for assault in California in 1989.

● 'Asked why she resisted, she said: "I'm a Hungarian woman . . . not a milquetoast".'
(Agency report on Zsa Zsa Gabor during trial).

minces n pl British

eyes. From the Cockney rhyming phrase, **mince pies**. The expression is still used today by working-class Londoners; it is now invariably heard in the shortened, one-word form.

● 'OK then, feast your minces on this!'

minder n

a bodyguard. A word which emerged from the obscurity of working-class and criminal slang into general usage in the early 1970s, mainly due to the fashion for quasi-realist crime drama on British television. This trend culminated in the later, gentler television series of the same name, starring Dennis Waterman and George Cole.

mindfuck n

a disorienting experience, a manipulation of or interference with one's mind, a staggering idea or event. A **hippy** expression which has lingered on into post-hippy usage. It has been used approvingly to describe a particularly strong drug.

minge n British

the female pudenda. A taboo word which was particularly prevalent in working-class speech of the 1950s. It originated in late 19th-century country dialect and may be from Romany.

● 'Minge is one of the assortment of words for the sexual bits that people think should keep him [Chubby Brown] off television because some viewers would not understand him anyway.'
(Independent, 31 July 1989).

mingy adj British

a term of childish criticism or abuse which is a blend of mean and stingy rather than an adaptation of the taboo word **minge**.

mink n American

a a woman, particularly a provocative, spirited and/or sexually attractive or active woman.
b the female sex organs, female sexuality.

● 'We gotta get us some mink.'

misery-guts n British

a depressive, morose or complaining person. A common British colloquialism.

● 'Here comes old misery-guts again.'

Mister Nice-guy n

a paragon of kindness, friendliness, tolerance, etc. This American expression has become international mainly in the form of the catchphrase 'No more Mr Nice-guy!', expressing exasperation.

mither vb British

to complain, nag, bother or prevaricate. A northern English dialect word which is now widely known due to its use by comics such as Jasper Carrot and in the soap opera Coronation Street. It is a variant form of 'moither' or 'moider', words first recorded in the 17th century and meaning both to babble and to baffle or bewilder.

● 'His endless mithering about what he's going to do and how he's going to afford it.'

mitt, mit n

hand. A shortening of mitten, first used to mean glove (particularly in boxing and baseball) and later hand. This American slang term, popular among pugilists and underworld 'tough guys', crossed the Atlantic in the early 20th century. Mitten itself is from an old French word (*mitain(e)*) which was either a pet name for a cat or a corruption of the Latin *media*; half (-fingered).

- 'He started with a cartwheel/
  finished in the splits/leaving
  Salome with his toupee in her mits.'
  (*Salome Maloney, the Sweetheart
  of the Ritz*, poem by John Cooper
  Clarke, 1980).

mo n

a moment, an instant. In British and Australian speech 'hang on a mo' and 'half a mo' have become popular colloquialisms.

mo vb, n American

(to behave like) a homosexual, particularly in over-familiar or over-affectionate behaviour or inadvertent toucher, etc. A high-school and college shortening of **homo**.

the mob n American

organized crime, the mafia. Mob was used to refer to gangster syndicates from the 1930s onwards, in underworld and police jargon and subsequently in journalese. The term is now standard. It has produced derivatives such as mobster and mobbed-up (involved with the mob).

mockers n British

misfortune, curse, frustration. An expression which is used by schoolchildren as an exclamation, sometimes of defiance, more usually in an attempt to put off or jinx an opponent in sports or games. The word mocker or mockers, meaning jinx or curse, has been widespread in Australian and British working-class slang since around the 1920s. Mockers probably derives via the Yiddish *makch* from Hebrew *makah*, meaning plague or wound, reinforced by the English words mock

and muck (up). In adult usage the word normally appears in the phrase **put the mockers on**, meaning to ruin, thwart or jinx.

mockie n American

a Jew. A pejorative term of uncertain etymology; it may be related to the British **mockers**, but this cannot be demonstrated conclusively.

mod n British

a member of a 1960s youth cult characterized by an obsessive interest in fashionable clothing, in the riding of motor-scooters and in listening and dancing to soul and ska music. The first mods, who began to gain prominence in 1962, referred to themselves as modernists, whence the more lasting epithet. The intention behind the word at this time was to distinguish these style-conscious, mainly working-class young people from the parochial or traditional appearance and attitudes then prevalent in Britain. The mods were influenced sartorially by Italy, France and the American 'Ivy League' look. Musical influences included American rhythm-and-blues and soul and Jamaican blue beat and ska, as well as native rock music represented by such groups as the Who and the Small Faces. The mod culture later expanded to encompass a much larger group of fashion-conscious young, in opposition to the **teddy boys**, **beats** and **rockers** of the time. So-called mod fashions were revived self-consciously in the late 1970s, one of the first attempts to find an 'acceptable' youth culture to replace **punk**.

- 'When we found out that mods were
  just as conformist and reactionary
  as anyone else, we moved on from
  that phase too.'
  (Pete Townshend, *Rave* magazine,
  February 1966).

mode *adj British*

affectedly fashionable, pretentious. A deliberate mispronunciation of **mod**, heard in the 1960s and used to express derision.

● *'Oh yes, get a load of that gear, very mode!'*

mog *n British*

a shorter form of **moggy**.

moggy, moggie *n British*

a cat. Moggy was originally a term of endearment/familiarity for any animal. In northern English dialect it was used to designate mouse, calf or cat for example. The exact etymology of the word is uncertain; it may be from the Norse *magi*, meaning stomach or from the use of 'Maggie' as a name for a pet.

mojo *n*

a a magic charm, spell or influence. A black American concept, popularized elsewhere by its use in blues and rhythm-and-blues records of the 1950s and early 1960s. The word's origin is though to be West African, but no specific source has been identified.

b any un-named object; thingummy. The word can be used as a euphemism for anything, but is characteristically employed for sex organs or drugs.

moke *n British*

a donkey. The term probably comes from the language of gypsies and other travellers; it was recorded in various forms (such as 'moak' or 'moxia') in the early 19th century. These almost certainly originated in a dialect pet name similar to 'Maggie' and **moggy**.

moll *n*

a *Australian* a prostitute. Moll, a short form of Molly (itself a familiar version of Mary) has been used to denote a woman of 'easy virtue' since at least the time of *Moll Flanders* by Daniel Defoe, published in 1722. This sense has survived in Australia, where a band moll, for instance, is a **groupie**.

b *American* a woman, specifically a female companion. This sense of the word, familiar from its use in crime fiction as gun moll or gangster's moll, is now outdated.

momma *n*

a female adherent to a Hell's Angels chapter. The momma is a sort of unattached member of the entourage; steady girlfriends are usually known as 'old ladies'.

● *'We've got a few mommas so they get passed around.'*
(London Hell's Angel, Oz magazine, April 1969).

momser, momzer *n*

a a contemptible person, particularly a cadger or sponger.

b a cheeky, enterprising or self-willed person.

The term, which is most often heard in American speech and applied to males, is the Hebrew word for 'bastard'.

mondo- *n American*

an all-purpose combining word which in Italian and Spanish means world (of) and in American English means 'a situation of . . . or 'a state of affairs characterized by . . . ' The word is then followed by the defining word, usually with a mock-Latin 'o' ending as in mondo-sleazo, mondo-bozo or mondo-cheapo. This pattern derives from the 1963 Italian documentary film *Mondo Cane* (translated as 'A Dog's Life') which acquired cult status and inspired first intellectual wits and later college students and **Valley Girls** to coin similar phrases. (The affixing of pseudo-Italian or Hispanic endings is

342

paralleled in the suffix '-ola'; an anglo-saxon equivalent is '-city'.)

money run/walk/parade n
British

a teenagers' promenade, a ritual parade of courting couples or hopeful 'singles'. This dated term was used particularly before World War II to describe both the location and the practice. The expression continued to be used by older speakers until the 1960s.

mong n *British*

an idiot, clumsy fool. A shortened form of 'mongol', itself a term (for those suffering from Downs' syndrome) now considered offensive. Mong was a vogue term of abuse among London schoolchildren in the early 1970s.

mongie, mongy adj *British*

(of a person) stupid, dull-witted, slow and clumsy. A 1970s derivation from **mong**, itself short for the pejorative mongol. Both spellings of the word are pronounced with a hard 'g'. Like the noun, the adjective was mainly heard among schoolchildren.

mongrel n

a a despicable person. This use of the standard word dates from the 1700s. It is now particularly prevalent in Australia and New Zealand.

- 'When they bring that mongrel back we'll make sure he gets what he deserves.'
  (*Home and Away*, Australian TV series, 1987).

b *Australian* a person of mixed race. A racist term of abuse since the 18th century.

moniker, monniker, monicker n

a name, nickname or alias. No definitive history of this word has been established. What is known is that it has existed in various spellings since the mid 19th century and that it was first used by tramps, vagrants and other 'marginals'. The three most likely derivations are from monarch, monk or monogram, but none of these is provable nor is there any clear connection with the (Saint's) name Monica.

- '*Christened by his father – a heavy duty John Wayne and Cowboy fan – with the name WAYNE WANG. Would this split-cultural, cartoon moniker destine the baby to grow up, leave Hong Kong and end up in California directing an all-American film . . . and a violent one at that?*'
  (*I-D* magazine, November 1987).
- '*Elvis Costello's latest album, Spike [has an] inscription proclaiming his new alter-ego as "the beloved entertainer". Judging by his performance at the London Palladium last week, it is a moniker he obviously relishes.*'
  (Concert review, *Observer*, 14 May 1989).

monkey n *British*

1 £500. A raffish term in use among gamblers, street traders, **spivs**, etc. The origin of the term is obscure; it has been in use since at least the early 19th century and, confusingly, is also used to refer to sums of £50 or on occasion, £50,000.

- '*My client is not the kind of man to be satisfied with a mere monkey for his services.*'
  ('Arthur Daley' in *Minder*, British TV series, 1987).
- '*When I said I was collecting for Hennessy's defence he said that was a good idea, he'd like to cough up a monkey. Then he took round a collecting tray and raised another £573 on top of his monkey. The Bollomsballs fund now stands at £3,897 which happens to be*

*precisely what I owe Access, which
is another coincidence, come to
think of it.'*
(William Donaldson, *Independent*,
26 August 1989).
2 an inferior or menial. Inspired by
such images as the organ grinder and
his monkey, the word is used to refer
dismissively or contemptuously to un-
derlings or errand-runners, etc.
● *'I'll deal with this myself; the
monkeys downstairs can take care
of the calculations.'*
(Recorded, accountant, London,
1986).

monkey's n British
a damn. A word invariably heard as
part of the dismissive or defiant expressions 'don't give/care a monkey's'.
The term is an abbreviated form of an
undefined but presumably offensive
phrase such as monkey's **fart, fuck** or
balls.
● *'What do they* [the police] *think of
us? I haven't got a clue . . . and I
couldn't give a monkey's.'*
(Actor from TV series *The Bill, One
Day in the Life of Television*,
November 1989).

monkey suit n
a uniform, particularly one which is
thought to demean the wearer. Typically applied to bellboys, doormen etc.
dressed in absurd or confining outfits,
the term derives from the practice of
dressing monkeys in such clothing for
carnival displays.

monniker n
an alternative spelling of **moniker**.

Montezuma's revenge n
diarrhoea. Heard all over the English-speaking world, this jocular expression is the American equivalent of
Delhi belly or **gyppy tummy**. In Mexico Montezuma (spelled Moctezuma lo-

cally and by many academics), the
16th-century Aztec emperor, is a national hero. Facetious references such
as this are not appreciated. However,
American Presidents Carter and Reagan both referred to this condition in
the presence of Mexican dignitaries
during their terms of office.

monthlies n pl
menstruation, a period. A woman's
euphemism in the form 'the monthlies'
or 'my monthlies'; this translation of
the Latin *menses* has been substituted,
like **(the) curse**, for medical terms. (Because of ancient taboos, a native Anglo-Saxon equivalent does not exist.)

moo n British
a woman, particularly a stupid or
unpleasant woman. It has been
claimed that the comedy script-writer
Johnny Speight invented this abusive
term for his 1960s television series *Till
Death do us Part* to avoid the BBC ban,
in force at that time, on the use of the
word **cow**. In fact the word already existed in London working-class vocabulary from at least the 1950s.

mooch vb
a to hang around, linger aimlessly,
idle.
b to 'sponge', cadge, take advantage
of (one's friends). The word has been in
use since the 19th century in both
senses and has formed part of the lexicons of tramps, criminals, **beatniks**
and the fashionable young of the 1980s
in both Britain and the USA. Its origin
is uncertain.

moody n British
a a sulk, fit of bad temper or sullen-
ness. A popular working-class expression of the late 1970s, usually in the
form 'throw a moody'. Moody was a
popular all-purpose Cockney term for
negative, fake or false in the earlier

20th century and 'doing a moody' used to mean acting suspiciously. Later, a moody signified a simulated fight or quarrel.

b a lie. A word which usually occurs in criminal or police usage, sometimes in the form old moody.

- 'Listen we don't need old moody, give us the names.'

moody adj British

illegal, counterfeit, of dubious value, quality or provenance. A London working-class term which in 1989 showed signs of spreading into fashionable youth parlance.

- 'They accused him of selling moody gear off his stall in the market.'
- 'This stupid bloke called me a freak, and kept asking why I was wearing "fucking moody strides".'
  (Caron Geary, Time Out, 26 July 1989).

mooey adj British

rotten. A word used by market traders, greengrocers and others in the 1980s to describe over-ripe fruit and vegetables. It is presumably a blend of mushy and gooey.

mook n American

a term of abuse of uncertain meaning and unknown origin. It may be a varient form of **mooch** or even **mug**.

- 'It's very nasty to call a person a honky mook.'
  (Steve Martin, All of me, US film, 1984).

moolah, moola n

money. A humorous word imported into Britain from the USA before World War II. It is an invented term, probably in imitation of Amerindian, African or other foreign languages as is the more recent British synonym, **womba**. Like most slang terms for

money, moolah underwent something of a revival in the late 1980s.

- 'Many congressmen arrive in Washington expecting to get rich – if not quick, at least before they leave. The art is in finding ways to get the moolah without contravening the various laws and rules of ethics.'
  (Observer, 12 June 1989).

moon vb

to exhibit the buttocks publically, typically from the window of a moving car. A term and practice popular with American teenagers since the 1950s. It has been a common practice among young male students in Britain from at least the late 1970s. (Moon refers to the white globes on display.)

- 'And it's hard not to warm to Panic's bare-faced nerve – mooning in discos, lifting a wallet and rifling through it insolently in full view of the impotent owner.'
  (Independent, 12 January 1988).

moonrock n

crack laced with heroin. A preparation which appeared (in **rock** form) in 1989.

mop-top n

a person with long and/or untidy hair. This fairly affectionate expression was applied to the Beatles and thus popularized in the mid 1960s.

moreish, morish adj British

appetizing, tempting. This predominantly middle-class colloquialism, applied to anything edible, is a pun on moorish (as in architecture), dating surprisingly from the 18th century.

moriarty n British

a party. A fairly rare item of rhyming slang employing the name of the arch enemy of Sherlock Holmes, later reinvented as a dastardly villain in the BBC radio comedy show *The Goons* in the 1950s, from when this usage dates.

morph n

morphine. The drug users' shortened form.

moshing n British

dancing in a packed scrimmage to heavy metal, **hardcore** or any other fast, loud rock music. This activity, which is more a form of energetic communal writhing than dancing, was adopted by fans of hard rock during the late 1980s as a successor to **slam dancing**, **headbanging** or the characteristic playing of imaginary guitars (air guitar). Often, part of the experience is for members of the audience to climb on to the stage then hurl themselves bodily into the crush at the front, a practice known as 'stage-diving'. The word mosh is an invention influenced by such words as jostle, mash, mass, squash, crush and thrust.

the most n

something superlative, the very best. A well-known item from the vocabulary of **hipsters**, **beatniks**, etc. of the 1950s. (A later jocular coinage by analogy is **the least**.)

mother n American

1 an abbreviated and euphemistic version of **motherfucker**. This version, more commonly than the full form, is often used appreciatively rather than pejoratively. In imitation of black or Southern pronunciation it is sometimes spelled **muthah**. The word is probably used to refer to objects and animals as often as humans.
- 'Man, that was some big mother.'
- 'Did you get a look at that mother?'

2 a male homosexual, particularly a man in a dominant, protective or influential relation to younger males.

motherfucker n American

a a despicable person. The most common term of strong abuse in the American vocabulary. (Euphemistic forms such as mother-raper, mother-jumper or just **mother** are sometimes substituted.) The expression, naming the ultimate in degeneracy, originated among poor blacks.
- 'Oedipus was a motherfucker.' (Graffito, Euston station, London, 1972).
- 'Up against the wall, motherfucker.' (Lyric from 'We can be together' by Paul Kantner, recorded by Jefferson Airplane, 1969, when this was a common slogan of the revolutionary left).

b an awesome or appalling thing, situation, etc.
- 'One motherfucker of a mess.'

mother's ruin n

gin. A late 19th-century nickname which refers to the widespread effects of cheap gin on the working class (of both sexes); to the later supposed predilection of women for the drink; and to its long-lived reputation as an abortifacient.

motor n British

a car. A word which has moved between working-class and middle-class colloquial speech, becoming prevalent since the early 1970s in working-class circles. It is characteristic of London speech, usually pronounced 'mo'or', that is, with a glottal stop in place of the 't'.
- ''Ello John, got a new motor?' (Song title, Alexei Sayle, 1984).
- 'Reggie Kray decided that Dickson should have a new motor and so took him to a car showroom in Walthamstow.' (Evening Standard, 9 May 1988).

346

motorhead n

a an afficionado of motorbikes or fast cars.

b an amphetamine user, a **speed-freak**.

An obscure, late 1960s American term, taken up by the pioneering British heavy-metal rock group of the same name who combined both attitudes.

motoring n British

making good progress, performing well. A driver's expression of the 1970s (meaning moving at speed) which has become generalized in the 1980s to mean roughly the same as the American **cooking**.

● 'OK, great, now we're motoring!'

motormouth n American

a person who talks excessively, a 'fast-talker'. A popular term from the mid-1970s, it originated in black ghetto slang. The word was later applied to amphetamine users, disc jockeys, comics and **rap** artists.

mott n British

the female sex organs. A vulgarism still widely used (by men) in the 1960s, but now rare. It is from the French *motte*, meaning mound, used by 19th century pornographers among others.

mouth-breather n

a primitive, brutish person. The phrase is used contemptuously for those considered thuggish and/or moronic, evoking the image of a shambling, open-mouthed, slack-jawed creature, invariably male.

mouthpiece n

a lawyer, specifically one's defence counsel or legal representative. A term used, particularly by the underworld, since the mid 19th century. The word is sometimes extended to refer to any spokesperson.

● 'A deliberate slip of the tongue gets a laugh. A sergeant begins a question: "When a defendant has got a mouthpiece—sorry, I mean solicitor ...".'
(*Inside the British Police*, Simon Holdaway, 1983).

mouthy adj British

talkative, boastful or verbose. A pejorative working-class term.

mover n

a a sexually enthusiastic person.

● 'Well, she's a right little mover.'

b anyone or anything considered dynamic, successful, extrovert or fast.

moxie n American

spirit, vim, courage, enterprise. Moxie was the trade name of a soft drink on sale in the USA in the 19th century (probably based on a local Amerindian place name). The drinks company used the advertising slogan: 'What this country needs is plenty of Moxie!'

Mozart adj Australian

drunk. The word is one half of the rhyming-slang phrase 'Mozart and Liszt'; **pissed**. The British equivalent is **Brahms (and Liszt)**.

mozzer, mozza n British

luck, good fortune. This seems to be the main surviving variant among many words (mozz, mozzle, mozzy) deriving from the Yiddish mazel; good luck. The words have existed in working-class speech since at least the 1880s.

● 'That was a bit of mozzer – all six at one stall.'
(Recorded, Newbury, 1989).

mozzie, mozzy n

a mosquito. A short form of the word in use in Britain and Australia.

347

Mr Sausage, Mister n

the penis. An adults' imitation nursery-word of the sort which has enjoyed a vogue since the mid 1980s, particularly in middle-class British usage. The playwright Mike Leigh used the term in dialogue ascribed to a **yuppie** couple in his 1988 feature film, *High Hopes*.

Mr Whippy, Mister n British

flagellation. A code term from the argot and repertoire of prostitutes. The light hearted euphemism is from the name of a brand of ice cream displayed on vans.

MTF n British

a sexually importunate male. The initials stand for 'must touch flesh'. An ephemeral early 1980s **Sloane Ranger** term of feminine disapproval.

muckamuck, (high) mucky-muck n American

a person in authority or a VIP, especially a self-important one. The term originated in the 19th century and apparently derives from an Amerindian phrase meaning plenty-to-eat.

- *'Fuck you. It* [a concealed gun]*'s in Mr Chancellor's name. He got it okayed by the muckamucks.'*

  (Jonathan Kellerman, *Over the Edge*, 1987).

mucker n

a friend, mate, pal. The term is said to have originated in armed-service usage as a longer expression; 'mucking-in pal' or 'mucking-in spud' soon shortened to mucker. The word survives mainly in the speech of hearty males.

- *'There you are, Keith, me old mucker.'*

mud n

opium. An early 20th-century nickname which is occasionally revived. It refers to the brown colour and soft consistency of raw opium.

mudsucker n American

an unpleasant or despicable person. A term of abuse coined to echo the syllables of the more offensive **motherfucker**.

muff n

the female sex organs and/or the female pubic hair. This euphemistic use of the standard word for an enveloping hand- or ear-warmer made of fur (deriving ultimately from the mediaeval Latin for mitten, *muffula*) originated in the 17th century and is still current, although less common than in the 1950s and early 1960s.

muff diver n

someone who indulges in cunnilingus. A vulgarism which is heard in all anglophone communities, but which is identified particularly with Australian speech.

muff-diving n

cunnilingus. A jocular coinage based on the long established use of **muff** to denote the female genitals.

muffin n

the female genitals. An elaboration on the older muff, used singularly or generically. The term is heard in Britain and Australia. In the USA the plural form is occasionally used to denote breasts.

mug vb

1 to pull faces, grimace. This is a 19th-century adaptation of the noun mug, meaning face. It originated in theatrical usage and is now a colloquialism rather than true slang.

2 to assault someone with intent to rob, demand money with menaces. Before the early 1970s the phenomenon and the term were considered peculiarly American. In fact similar expressions were in use in Victorian Britain (including 'mug-hunting' describing the search for victims or hitting on the head or in the face) and became obsolete.

mug n

1 face. The word has had this meaning since the early 1700s; it derived from the practice of making china drinking-mugs decorated with grotesque human faces.

2 a fool, dupe. This use of the word was inspired by the image of the victim as an open-mouthed receptacle.

muggins n British

a victim, dupe or 'loser', especially when referring to oneself. The word is an embellishment of **mug** (and is also an authentic, if comic sounding, surname). It is now so common as to be an innocent colloquialism rather than true slang.

● 'And muggins here was left holding the bill.'

muggles n American

marihuana. An archaic word of unknown origin, probably deriving from black slang, which was used by Raymond Chandler in the novel *Playback* and, more recently, by the crime thriller writer, Ed McBain.

mugshot n

a photographic portrait of a prisoner or suspect. An American slang term of the 1950s which has become standard throughout the English-speaking world. It is also heard as a description of any full-facial photograph.

● 'Come downtown and take a look at the mugshots.'

mugwump n American

an important, powerful person. This now rather dated word is invariably used facetiously or pejoratively and is especially applied to someone who has power and influence but is a maverick or unreliable. It is from the Algonquin Indian *mugquamp*, a chief.

mule n

a carrier of illicit drugs across frontiers and/or through customs, a transporter of contraband; someone hired to do this rather than the owner of the drugs. The term was first used by smugglers, later by law enforcers.

● 'He used to go over and buy the stuff, then pack it, but it was always brought in by mules.'
(Recorded, London, 1989).

mulled adj British

drunk. An inoffensive term heard predominantly outside the London area.

mumblefucker n British

an irritatingly clumsy, inept or fastidious person. A term heard in the early 1970s. There have been other invented terms, with a similar lack of meaning, playing on the comical overtones of the syllables employed; **fucknuckle** is an example.

mummerset n British

the (often grotesque and usually inaccurate) imitation of rustic West-Country speech used by actors. The theatrical term is a blend of mumble and Somerset.

● 'And what about that Mummerset accent? Even them Archers-folk don't speak like that no more.'
(Charles Catchpole, *News of the World*, 26 June 1988).

mump-hole n British

an unofficial place of refreshment for patrolling police officers. These places (hospitals, cafés, shops, caretakers' offices, etc.) offer temporary shelter for an implicit reciprocal exchange. The phenomenon is described in *Inside the British Police* by Simon Holdaway (1983).

mumping n British

scrounging, soliciting favours, begging. A word dating from the 17th century which survives in police and underworld argot. It used to refer to the activities of beggars and vagabonds; it is now often applied to the reciprocal favours encouraged by police officers in contact with local people. The word is descended from the Dutch *mompen*, to cheat.

(the) munchies n

hunger, especially a craving for food brought on by the lowering of blood-sugar levels that is a well-known side-effect of smoking cannabis. The word was a children's synonym for snacks which was adopted by **hippy**-era smokers of hashish and marihuana.

- *'Those smug, stupid hippies, who thought it so cool to be comatose called that post-smoke famished feeling "the munchies", and for once they were right.'*
(*Platinum Logic*, Tony Parsons, 1981).

munchkin n

a cute small child, dwarf, underling. An American expression taken from the name of the little people in the musical, *The Wizard of Oz*; the word is used affectionately or condescendingly. (A low-level munchkin is an employee near or at the bottom of a hierarchy.)

mung n

dirt, muck. A term that encompasses everything filthy or distasteful, used particularly by teenagers or students since the late 1970s.

munt n South African

a black person. A highly offensive term used by white racists. The word is Afrikaans slang deriving from the Bantu *umuntu*, a person.

muppet n British

a retarded, incapacitated or grotesque person. A word usually used with none of the affection or humour that its innocent source (the American TV puppet show of the 1970s) might suggest. The term has been applied to hospital inmates, mentally deranged prisoners or simply to unattractive teenagers by their peers.

murderate vb

to murder, defeat. A childish deformation of the word murder which was popularized by the *Popeye* cartoons.

murphy, the murphy n

1 British a potato. The Irish surname has been used as a joky synonym since the early 19th century.

2 the murphy American a confidence trick whereby valuables lodged for safekeeping are stolen or substituted by worthless goods.

murphy vb American

to subject (someone) to **the murphy** (a term denoting various forms of a simple confidence trick).

mush, moosh n British

1 face. A word which has been in use since the 19th century, when it often referred specifically to the mouth. Mush is nearly always used in connection with fisticuffs and may have originated as pugilists' slang. The precise etymology of the word is uncertain, but it has obvious connotations of softness and mastication.

2 a an all-purpose term of address to a stranger (invariably used by men to other men). A working-class, mainly London, usage which was common in the 1950s and 1960s but is now rarely used. The word is not particularly friendly and is quite often used provocatively. It comes from the Romany word for man, *moosh*.

● '*I suggest you buy better shirts in future.*'

● '*Are you asking for a punch up the faghole, mush?*'
(*Hancock's Half Hour*, BBC TV comedy, 6 November 1959).

b a man, unnamed person. The derivation for this usage is as for the previous sense. The word has rarely been used thus (rather than as a term of address) since the 1950s.

mushy adj

sentimental, cloying. A figurative extension of the standard sense of the word.

muso n

a a musician, player of rock music with real technical expertise.

b a rock or progressive music fan who displays a pedantic or obsessive interest in his or her favourite music and/or musicians.

The term, coined by musicians and used by journalists and fans, is sometimes pejorative (implying that the technical expertise does not compensate for or hide a basic lack of something to express) but can also be applied neutrally or appreciatively.

● '*Melody Maker was at last shaking off the "muso" tag that it had been lumbered with during the punk period.*'
(*Independent*, 1 December 1989).

mutant n

a clumsy, foolish or otherwise unpopular individual. A term used by adolescents to refer to unpopular or despised fellow-students or other contemporaries. The same word is used with the opposite connotations in the form **mutie**.

muthah n

an alternative spelling of **mother** (in its slang or euphemistic sense), particularly used by fans of heavy-metal music to refer appreciatively to each other or their heroes.

mutie n British

a daring exponent, devotee. A word used by skateboarders and some surfers and rock-music fans to refer to themselves and their fellows. The word is a diminutive form of **mutant** which itself is usually employed with negative connotations. Mutant has been used to evoke a science-fiction sense of extremism, exoticism and unpredictability when referring to designs, insignia or performance in the subcultures in question.

mutton, Mutt 'n' Jeff adj British

deaf. Rhyming slang, from the cartoon figures created by Bud Fischer, which were popular before World War II. The slang expression has been heard in London from the late 1940s to the present day. It was spread further afield by its use by the character of Albert in the popular 1960s television comedy series *Steptoe and Son*.

● '*I'm sorry, love, you'll have to speak up. I'm a bit mutton in my old age.*'
(Recorded, London, 1988).

mutton dagger n

the penis. A joky euphemism on the lines of **pork sword** and **beef bayonet**.

muttonhead n

a variation of **meathead**.

myrtle n Australian

sexual intercourse. The word is either a version of **nurtle** or is inspired by the eponymous heroine of a limerick involving a turtle.

mystery bags n pl Australian

sausages. The term is influenced by the name of a children's lucky dip sweet packet and is both a rhyming slang term for **snags** (another slang term for sausages) and an ironical comment on the dubious contents of some sausages. Often thought to be a native Australian coinage, mystery bags is another example of British slang of the 19th century which seems to have died out in the country of origin but has survived among the emigrant population; it was recorded in 1889 in this form; previously occurring simply as 'mystery' or 'bag of mystery'.

- 'What's for dinner?'
- 'Mystery bags ... snags ... sausages.'
  (Razorback, Australian film, 1984).

N

nab n British

the dole. A now obsolete acronym for National Assistance Board that was still heard in the 1950s and 1960s. The Board was sometimes jocularly personified as **Uncle Nab**.

● 'Even people wanting to be in on the love commune thing seem to be sitting around on their arses, drawing the NAB and waiting.'
(Letter to Oz magazine, June 1968).

● 'Oh, that was the day the nab was fab, The day we danced at the dole.'
(Chorus of a song by The Liverpool Scene, 1969).

nabe n American

a neighbourhood.

● 'A now guy in the nabe.'
b neighbour.

● 'The nabes are acting up again.'

A shortening of the sort popularized by Variety magazine and perpetuated in teenage speech. (**Merch**, **mersh** and **burbs** are other examples of this trend which enjoyed a particular vogue in 1988 and 1989.)

nadgers, the nadgers n pl British

1 the nadgers signified a state of nervous agitation, irritation, distress or unhealthiness in such phrases as 'he's got the nadgers' or 'it gives me the nadgers'. The word could also be used to describe a curse or jinx in the same way as **mockers**. This humorous nonsense term of the 1950s (popularized in broadcast comedies such as Hancock's Half Hour) is now virtually obsolete.

2 testicles. The word was probably used in this sense merely due to the resemblance to **knackers**. It has not been widely used since the 1900s.

● 'A kick in the nadgers.'

nads n pl American

testicles. An abbreviated form of gonads used jocularly by teenagers in the 1980s.

naff adj

tasteless, inferior, shoddy and unappealing. Naff had existed in working-class slang for at least 40 years by the time it became a vogue word in the later 1970s. It had been used in the jargon of prostitutes to mean nothing or negligible. In the theatrical, criminal and street-trading milieus it meant third-rate or poor quality. The word's sudden popularity occurred probably because it was seized upon by TV scriptwriters (particularly Dick Clement and Ian La Frenais in the comedy series Porridge) as an acceptable euphemism for **fuck** in such forms as 'naff-all' (meaning **fuck-all**), **naffing** and **naff off**. Naff's ultimate origin, which seems to be 19th century, is nonetheless obscure. It has been claimed that it is a backslang form of **fan(ny)** (in the sense of female sex organs) or an acronym or alteration of a phrase involving the word **fuck** (such as 'not a fucking fart' or similar). Neither etymology is attested (or particularly convincing), and the similarity to NAAFI is probably coincidental.

- 'To be naff is to be unstylish, whatever that may mean.'
  (The Complete Naff Guide, Bryson et al., 1983).
- 'Lancing is a healthy, wealthy school. So why do the boys look so naff? The school photo could be an advert for Top Man's summer collection.'
  (Tatler, March 1987).
- 'The Noddy backlash condemned the little chap as racist and thoroughly naff. Perhaps he's due for a reassessment.'
  (Observer, 3 April 1989).

naffing adj British

an all-purpose intensifying adjective used as a euphemism for **fucking**.

naff off vb British

to leave, go away. The expression is usually in the form of a dismissive exclamation or instruction synonymous with **fuck off**. First used in the TV series Porridge in the mid-1970s, the phrase was given great prominence in 1982 when Princess Anne told reporters who were pestering her to naff off.

naffed-off adj British

a politer version of **pissed-off**.

nag n

a horse. The well-known term is used particularly by horse-racing enthusiasts. It was first recorded in 1400 when it was paralleled by the Dutch negge, meaning a small horse.

nail (someone) vb

to identify, catch, punish or defeat (or any combination of these). This common term, which can now also by extension (and by analogy with **screw**) refer to the sexual conquest of a woman

by a male, has been heard since at least the 18th century.

'Nam n American

Vietnam.

- 'He was in 'Nam with me in '68.'

namby n British

1 a weak, cowardly person, a **wimp**. A schoolchildren's word of the late 1980s which is a shortening of the standard English adjective 'namby-pamby'.

- 'Him? He's a fucking namby.'
  (Recorded, teenage schoolgirl, London, 1988).

2 a committed opponent of a controversial environmental policy (such as nuclear power). This journalistic quasi-acronym of 'not in anyone's backyard' was coined in imitation of the more common **nimby** ('not in my backyard') in the USA in the mid-1980s.

nana n British

a silly fool. This word was very popular among children from the 1950s to the early 1970s and is still sometimes revived; adults, too, used the term in the late 1950s and early 1960s. It is a nursery shortening of banana, a meaning it still retains in post-colonial nurseries in areas such as India and the Caribbean.

nancy boy, nance n British

an effeminate man, a male homosexual. This term seems to have originated in the late 19th century, when the name Nancy, a diminutive form of Ann or Agnes, was applied indiscriminately to women as a term of affection and familiarity. The echoes of 'nice' and 'mince' in the rather prissy sound of the word probably went toward reinforcing its derogatory use for men. There was a vogue in the East End of London in the 1930s for male street-dancers in women's clothing who were known as nancy boys. The phrase was widespread in all social classes throughout Britain in the 1950s and 1960s, but is now somewhat dated.

- 'See the nancy boys do their dance.' (Poster in satirical illustration of decadent England, *Private Eye* magazine, 1963)

nanty, nanti, nants adj British

no, none, nothing. The word was in use in London working-class and theatrical slang from the early 19th century until the 1960s; this is an example of **parlyaree**, the Italian-inspired patois of actors, showmen and circus workers. Nanty originates in the Italian *niente*, meaning nothing. The last recorded instance of its use was in the radio comedy *Round the Horne*, in which the effeminate characters Julian and Sandy referred to Kenneth Horne's having nanty **riah** (no hair).

napper n British

head. This word has been used, especially by working-class speakers, since the 18th century. It is now virtually obsolete, except among the elderly. Napper's origin is obscure, although it is probably related to the archaic dialect and colloquial words 'nap' and 'noh'.

- 'You look dapper/ From your napper/ To your feet.' (Lyrics to the cockney song, 'Any Old Iron').

nappy hair n

pubic hair. Nappy denotes kinked (hair) in the terminology of grooms, whence it has also been adopted in black American speech. In Britain the term is reinforced in humorous adult speech by nappy as applied to babies' sanitary wrappings.

narc, narco n American

a narcotics investigator or member of a police drug-squad. The word is particularly heard among drug users referring to undercover agents. It may be influenced by, but is not directly related to the British **nark**.

nards n pl American

testicles. A distorted pronunciation of **nads**, itself an abbreviation of gonads. The word is heard among pubescent and adolescent males.

nark vb British

1 to inform on, betray. From the noun, **nark**.

2 to stop, or to keep quiet. This cockney usage invariably occurred in the command 'nark it!'.

3 to annoy or affront, **needle**. This expression, which was particularly popular in the 1950s and which is also heard in Australia, is derived ultimately from the Romany word *nak*, meaning nose. Nark in its modern sense is semantically related to such expressions as 'to have one's nose put out of joint', 'to get up one's nose', or 'poke one's nose in'. It is often heard in the form of its past participle, **narked**, meaning annoyed or affronted.

- 'The trouble is, many people today they won't do anything. I got a very poor opinion of my fellow creatures, a very poor opinion. So I nark them whenever I can. I like narking people.' (82-year-old Ted Bosley, quoted in the *Independent*, 18 May 1989).

nark n British

a an informer. The expression originated in the 19th century as 'copper's nark', meaning a police spy or **grass**, nark being an alteration of the Romany (gypsy) word *nak*, nose.

b a spoilsport, teacher's pet, nuisance or toady. This more generalized usage, deriving from the previous sense, was fairly widespread in the

1950s in working-class circles and is still heard among schoolchildren.

c a policeman. In underworld, prison and tramp's jargon.

narked adj British

irritated, annoyed, affronted. For the derivation of the word see the verb **nark**.

narky adj British

irritable, upset. A working-class term used principally in the North of England.

- 'She's been a bit narky all morning.'
- 'He's feeling narky.'

narly adj American

an alternative spelling of **gnarly**.

nasties n pl British

nursery slang for (old and dirty) underwear or swimming trunks. A narrowing of a general notion of 'offensive objects'.

- 'Don't forget to pack some nasties if we're going anywhere near a beach.'

(Recorded, social worker, London, 1986).

nasty n

1 a sex organ, genitals. A childish word used humorously by adults in phrases such as 'as dry as a nun's nasty'; thirsty.

2 a sexual act. A synonym of the coy or euphemistic **naughty**.

natch adv

naturally. A shortening used in **hip** talk.

natch n British

'Natural Dry Cider'. A drink manufactured by the Taunton Cider company which is popular among pub habitués and itinerants in the West of England.

nattum n Australian

sex. It has been suggested that this obscure term is an alteration of **naughty** or **nasty**, or backslang for mutton.

natty adj

impressive, admirable, **cool**. A vogue term in Jamaican youth patois, particularly in the phrase 'natty dread', but usable as an all-purpose term of approval. It derives from a shortening of 'natural', referring in Rastafarian terms to someone following the laws of God and nature, perhaps influenced by the standard English adjective meaning trim or smartly-dressed (which itself is probably a variation of neat).

naughty n

an illicit act, usually referring to sex and typically occurring in phrases such as 'have a (quick) naughty'. The coy expression, which sometimes also refers to a crime, is heard in both British and Australian speech.

naughty adj British

a criminal, corrupt. A typical piece of understatement from the argot of police and the underworld. This tendency is characteristic of London working-class speech, (**spanking**, meaning a (severe) beating-up, would be another instance).

b impressive, daring. A fashionable usage in working-class speech, generally among adults, in the late 1980s; the word is used to indicate admiration or approval as in 'That's a well-naughty looking bird'.

nause n British

a a nauseatingly unpleasant person. A middle-class term popular in the mid-1960s and now very rarely heard.

It has been suggested that this word is in fact a variation of **Noah's**, short for 'Noah's Ark', 1950s underworld rhyming slang for **nark**. As nauseate and nauseous were both fashionable terms in middle-class British and American use in the early 1960s, they would seem more likely origins.

- 'She was going out with a policeman; God, he was a real nause.'
(Recorded, student teacher, London, 1965).

b a nuisance, unpleasant situation or task. Nauseate had a (now obsolete) slang sense of bother, irritate or infuriate in the 1950s, whence this usage. The concept is rendered in modern speech by the colloquial expression to **get up one's nose**.

nauticals n pl British

haemorrhoids, piles. An item of jocular rhyming slang (on 'nautical miles').

navvy n British

a manual labourer, unskilled construction worker or road digger. Navvy is a shortening of navigator, which was a nickname given to open-air construction workers engaged in building roads, canals and railways in the late 18th and early 19th centuries. Canals in England were often built by navigation companies, hence the nickname of their employees.

neat adj American

an all-purpose term of approval which became popular among teenagers in the mid-1960s and has survived. It is often ridiculed by sophisticates as evidence of naïve or gushing enthusiasm. The word occurred with this sense in the slang of jazz musicians, the 'smart set' and adolescents as long ago as the early 1920s.

- 'You're a neat girl.'

- 'So are you – I mean . . . you're a neat guy.'
(Blue Velvet, US film, 1986).

neato-keeno adj American

exceptionally good. An elaborate version of **neat** and **keen** with the combined force of both these teenage terms of approval. Neato-keeno was a catchphrase of the mid-1960s.

- 'Wow, that's neato-keeno – I know I shouldn't say that!'
(Recorded, American high-school girl, London, 1969).

nebbish, nebesh, nebech n

a fool, an ineffectual, clumsy or pathetic person. The word entered English speech from Yiddish in which one of its meanings is a pitiful nonentity or 'loser'. The ultimate origin of the word is the Czech adjective nebohy, meaning unhappy, unfortunate or diseased.

- 'A nebech is more to be pitied than a shlemiel. You feel sorry for a nebech; you can dislike a shlemiel.'
(The Joys of Yiddish, Leo Rosten, 1970).

neck n

cheek, impudence, daring, **chutzpah**. This sense of the word is at least 100 years old, originating in rustic Northern English speech. It survives principally in the form **brass neck**, a synonym for bare-faced cheek.

- 'I tell you, she's got plenty of neck: she walked out [on her husband] and then told him to move out.'
(Recorded, housewife, London, 1988).

neck vb

to kiss, embrace and pet. An American euphemism dating from the early years of the century.

neck-oil n

alcohol. Drink thought of as a physical and social lubricant by (usually hearty) drinkers.

necktie-party n American

a lynching or hanging. A macabre pun (on the notion of a formal gathering where ties are de rigueur). The phrase originated in the later 19th century and survives principally in fiction and western movies.

neddy n British

a horse, gee-gee. A children's pet name appropriated by adults, particularly in the context of betting and horse-racing.

Ned Kelly n Australian

the belly. This piece of native rhyming slang takes the name of the 19th-century outlaw.

needle vb British

to tease, irritate, taunt, provoke. The image is of continually pricking at someone to goad them into a response. See the needle.

the needle n

1 British irritation, resentment, provocation. The word has been used in expressions such as 'take the needle', (take offence), 'give someone the needle' and get the (dead) needle since the late 19th century.

2 See on the needle.

needle-dick n

(someone with) a small penis. This expression (usually heard in the USA in conjunction with the synonymous bug-fucker) is also sometimes used as a non-specific term of abuse.

needle park n American

a nickname given to a public place which narcotics users frequent in order to inject themselves.

nellie, nelly n British

1 an ineffectual, weak, effete or sentimental person. Often given more emphasis by phrases like 'big soft nellie' or 'great wet nellie'. Nellie was used until the late 1940s in the USA and Britain as a humorous or contemptuous appellation for a male homosexual.

2 in 'not on your nellie', the word was originally Nelly Duff, an invented name providing a rhyme for puff in the sense of breath, hence life.

nerd n

a gormless, vacuous, tedious and/or ineffectual person. Since the later 1970s this has been a vogue term, particularly among adolescents. It was coined in the USA in the late 1960s or early 1970s by members of surfing and hot-rodding cliques to refer to outsiders considered feeble or conformist. The word was then taken up on student campuses and by hippies. (An underground cartoon strip of the early 1970s portrayed nerds as a sub-species of suburban dullards.) The word nerd itself (nurd was an earlier alternative spelling) is of uncertain origin, but may be influenced by turd.

- 'And the jock shall dwell with the nerd and the cheerleader lie down with the wimp and there will be peace upon the campus.'
  (Observer, 29 May 1988).
- 'Simon Templar is a nerd. What sensible human being, on the run from the police, continues to drive around at 100 mph in a car bearing his initials (ST 1) on the registration plate?'
  (TV review by Jaci Stephen, Evening Standard, 4 September 1989).

nerd pack n

a a set of coloured pens (normally held together with an elastic band and worn ostentatiously in a breast pocket). The item in question is held to characterize an eager but vacuous office employee. This item of business slang was quoted in the column 'Business Buzzwords' in *International Management Magazine*, March 1989.

b the same term was also used in the USA by high-school and college students to describe a plastic shield worn on a shirt breastpocket to prevent ink stains from pens.

nerdy *adj*
gormless, ineffectual, characteristic of a **nerd**. The adjective post-dates the noun.
- 'He favoured dark business suits, dark ties that hung straight down against his white shirts, and a short nerdy Afro.'
(Nelson George, *Where Did Our Love Go?*, 1985).

nerk *n British*
a fool. An invented, mainly middle-class term which predates the (probably unrelated) American **nerd**. Fred Nerk was a fictitious personification of idiocy or small mindedness in the 1950s.

nerts *n American*
a polite alteration of **nuts**.

never-never *n British*
See **on the never-never**.

The News of the Screws *n*
British
the nickname of the British tabloid Sunday newspaper, the *News of the World*. The paper specializes in sexual scandal and exposé.

newted *adj British*
drunk. A term based on the vulgar expression 'as **pissed** as a newt'.

niagaras *n pl*
testicles, **balls**. Rhyming slang from 'Niagara Falls'. A word heard in Britain and Australia, where it has been adopted especially by students, rock journalists, etc., from the original 1950s working-class usage.
- 'She kicked him in the niagaras.'

nibhead *n British*
a gormless or comical young person, especially a young man with the characteristic short hair and baggy trousers of the later 1980s (hence the supposed resemblance to a pen). The word was often used as a synonym for **pinhead** in London club-going circles.

nice guy *n*
See **Mister Nice-guy**.

nick *vb British*
1 to steal. The word has been used in this sense since at least the 1820s. The word is rare in the USA, but has been recorded in the sense of rob.
- 'The doctor's had his bike nicked and his place turned over, and the only time we see the Old Bill is when they're in here getting legless.'
(*Biff* cartoon, 1986).
2 to arrest. Nick was a colloquial term for catch from the 16th century. By the early 19th century it had also acquired this specific meaning.

nick, the *n British*
a prison or police station. This common expression dates from before World War II and post-dates the verb form **nick**, meaning to arrest.
- 'I think you'd better come down the nick and explain yourself.'
- 'He's been in nick on and off all his life.'
See also **nick-bent**.

nick-bent adj British

temporarily or expediently homosexual because incarcerated. A prisoners' term mentioned by the upper-middle-class former prisoner Rosie Johnston in 1989. **Nick** is a well established slang synonym for prison, **bent** for homosexual.

nickel-and-dime adj American

trifling, cheap, petty. Nickels and dimes (five and ten cent coins) constitute small change.

nickel bag n American

a portion of marihuana or another illicit drug worth five dollars (a nickel is five cents). One of the standard measures used by street dealers.

nicker n British

£1, one pound (sterling). This common term has been in use since about the turn of the century (when it also denoted a sovereign). Nicker was the name given to pieces of metal thrown down in a game and later applied, in racing, to flinging down a sovereign bet on a horse.

● 'I made about fifty nicker on the deal, didn't I?'

nick off vb British

to play truant. A synonym of **bunk off**, **wag it** or **wag off**.

niff vb, n British

(to give off) a bad smell. Originally an Eastern English dialect version of sniff.

● 'There's a terrible niff in here.'
● 'I wouldn't get too near to that dog; he niffs a bit.'
(Recorded, editor, London, 1988).

niffy adj British

noisome, stinking, pungent. The word was a colloquial or dialect version of smelly in 19th-century speech.

nifty n British

a fifty-pound note.

Nigel n British

an upper-middle-class or upper-class male. A pejorative term since the 1960s, Nigel is thought to epitomize ostentatious young men who drive sports cars and wear flat caps and tweed jackets.

● 'Naff causes of death: . . . racing a right Nigel from Oxford to Cambridge in a silly sports car.' (The Complete Naff Guide, Bryson et al., 1983).
● 'Each writer discusses sex and alcohol, scorns anyone "bespectacled" and uses the name Nigel for further derision.' (Laura Cumming reviewing The Oxford Myth, edited by Rachel Johnson, in the Evening Standard, 16 June 1988).

Nigerian lager n British

Guinness beer, stout. A witticism inspired by the black colour of the brew. **African lager** is a synonym.

nigger n

a black person. This word has been in use since the late 18th century. It is now a term of racist abuse when used by white speakers, although it can be used affectionately or sardonically between black speakers. The word is derived from niger, the Latin word for the colour black, via Spanish (negro), French (nègre) and the archaic English neger.

nig-nog n

1 a a fool, dunce. This sense of the word, dating from the 19th century and often applied to a novice at work or in the armed services, has now largely disappeared due to the preponderance of the racist sense.

b a contrary, tendentious or irritating person. A second sub-sense of the term, which survives but is rarely heard. (Many archaic dialect terms for simpleton or fool employ the letters nid- or nog-.)

2 a black person. An offensive term formed by a reduplication of a short form of **nigger**. The term is used rarely to refer to any foreigner, regardless of colour.

nigra n American

a representation of a southern American pronunciation of negro or **nigger**.

nimby n

1 an opponent of controversial legislation (typically on environmental issues) only so long as he or she is directly affected. The word is an acronym for the slogan or catchphrase 'not in my back yard', coined in the United States (where 'yard' is garden) in the 1980s to describe a syndrome whereby a person supports a potentially harmful move or policy in principle but opposes it for selfish reasons. The American expression entered common currency in Britain around 1986. (An unqualified opponent to the same issues is a **namby**.)

• 'He thinks working motherhood is a jolly good thing, but he's also a nimby ("by all means let mothers work, so long as it's not in my office").'
(Sarah Jane Evans, Sunday Times, 18 March 1989).

2 American nembutal. This is a much-abused barbiturate.

nine-bob note n British

a a homosexual, sexual deviant.

b something false, obviously counterfeit or crooked.

Both senses are usually expressed in the phrase 'bent as a nine-bob note', a surviving example of many expressions using comparisons beginning 'queer as –' or 'bent as –'.

ning-nong n Australian

a fool. A now-dated but not altogether obsolete word inspired by **nig-nog** (in the earlier non-racist sense) and nincompoop. It may be unrelated to the synonymous **nong**.

nip, Nip n

a Japanese person. (Nippon is the Japanese word for Japan.) **Jap** has been the preferred term among British speakers, but nip has made headway since the mid-1970s. This term is largely pejorative.

nit n

1 British a foolish person. A contraction of **nitwit** which was popular in the 1950s, especially among radio comedians, but is now almost obsolete.

2 American nothing. A variant form of **nix**.

nit! nitnit! exclamation British

warnings to keep silent or beware, these expressions (now obsolescent) were used in the speech of tramps, prisoners, street traders and schoolchildren until the mid-1950s. 'Nit' is a deformation of the Yiddish or German nix, nothing.

See also **nitso**, **nitto**.

nitso, nitto n British

nothing. British alternative forms of **nix**, in working-class London usage.

nitto! exclamation British

keep quiet!, don't do it! Variant forms of **nit!** or **nitnit!** used in cockney speech until the 1950s, these words are derivations of **nix**.

nitty *adj British*

silly, foolish. A rare adjectival derivation from **nit**.

the nitty-gritty *n*

the essentials, small details. This now common phrase was adopted in Britain from American speech in the second half of the 1960s. The expression originated in black slang in which nitty-gritty referred to the scalp in the context of grooming.

nitwit *n British*

a foolish and stupid person. Literally, someone with the brains of a head louse. An inoffensive colloquialism in modern speech, nitwit entered the language in the 1920s.

nix *n*

no, nothing, none. One of very few German words to enter the thieves' and low-life cant of the early 19th century and remain in occasional use. *Nichts* is the standard German for nothing or not, *nix* being a colloquial version.

nix *vb*

to forbid, veto. This form of the word is predominantly American, its brevity recommending it to journalese usage.
- '*The governor nixed the proposals.*'

nix!, nixes, nixies *exclamation*

don't do that! be quiet! These terms were in use among 'marginals' in Victorian society, surviving particularly in the speech of schoolchildren until the early 1960s.

nixon, Nixon *n American*

a spurious or fraudulent deal, especially one involving illicit drugs. An Americanism inspired by the reputation of the former president.
- '*They pulled a nixon on me.*'
- '*He got stuck with a nixon.*'

Noah, Noah's *n*

a *Australian* a shark.
b *British* a park.
c *British* a **nark** (informer).

All the senses of the word are examples of rhyming slang, from 'Noah's ark'. The two British instances are now rare if not obsolete.

nob *vb British*

to copulate. A working-class usage which became fashionable in the 1970s and early 1980s. It derives from the use of **(k)nob** to mean penis, and as such is usually, but not invariably used by and about men.
- '*We ate your food and nobbed your tarts.*'
(Jools Holland, of the pop group Squeeze, at the end of a tour of Venezuela, 1980).

nob *n British*

1 head. This now old-fashioned usage dates from the 17th century or earlier and is a form of archaic words which survive as napper, nape and knob.
2 an aristocrat or VIP. Nob in this sense may derive from sense **1** (by way of the notion of a famous, prominent or swollen-headed personage) from the use of nob to designate the head on the Jack card in cribbage or, more straightforwardly, as a shortening of noble or nobility.
- '*A second battle between the nobs and the yobs was a slice of real life, as filmed by BBC2's new documentary series, "Enterprise Culture". A builder named Ken King has bought Avebury Manor.*'
(Kate Saunders, TV review, Evening Standard, 17 May 1989).
3 penis. In this sense the spelling **knob** is usually preferred.

nobble *n British*

1 an act of dishonestly interfering

with a process, such as by bribing a member of a jury or drugging a racehorse. From the verb.

2 a trick, a devious scheme or clever way of doing things.

● *'I said, look, the nobble is to give me some money and I'll get you some [drugs]. It's just a bit of a nobble really.'*
(Rockstars' **minder**, *Guardian*, August 1987).

nobble *vb British*

to incapacitate or subvert. The term applies specifically to drugging or otherwise distressing a racehorse in order to adversely affect its performance, or to suborning or threatening members of a jury. The word probably originated in rustic use with the meaning 'knock on the head', perhaps influenced by **nob**, and hobble.

the nod *n*

assent, agreement. An extension of the literal sense of the term. It is usually heard in the phrase 'to give (someone) the nod'.

noddle *n*

one's head, intelligence, common sense. A light-hearted word dating from the 16th century. Nodle was a standard Middle English term for the back of the head and nape of the neck. The word is often used in the admonitory phrase 'use your noddle'. In the USA the form **noodle** is more common.

noddy *n British*

a buffoon, simpleton, clumsy or ungainly person. In modern usage the term has been specifically applied to low-ranking police officers by members of the CID and public. Noddy is an archaic rustic term for a simple-minded or cloddish individual, inspired by such a person's inadvertent head movements. The use of the word for the famous children's storybook character created by Enid Blyton reinforced the image evoked.

noddy bike *n British*

a Velocette motor cycle, as used by police patrolmen until the end of the 1960s. The ungainly, inelegant motorbikes were derided by professional police motorcyclists, motorbike enthusiasts, **rockers**, etc. **Noddy** is a nickname applied to low-ranking police officers reinforced by identification with the children's storybook character created by Enid Blyton.

nod out *vb*

to become unconscious or fall asleep. This racier version of the standard 'nod off' is used especially in connection with drug-induced somnolence or stupor.

noggin *n British*

a a drink. The word of unknown origin may designate a measure of a quarter pint or simply an alcoholic drink of any size or type.
b one's head.

nonce, nonse *n British*

a prisoner found guilty of sexual offences against children or other acts against the pale of prison morality. Short for 'nonsense boy', 'nonsense case'.

● *'Nonce meaning nothing, a nonsense, a no one, a non-thing, a phenomenon existing somewhere between noun and verb, between the most terrible acts and the dreadful word for them: pervert, child molester, sex offender, monster, beast . . . The nonce is the game in an open season.'*
(Ken Smith, *Inside Time*, 1988).

● *'I was very happy to note a black face hunched up in the corner of the van, but when I saw who it was, a*

nonce *who had raped several girls,
the happiness soon subsided and I
sunk down into my seat.'*
(Trevor Hercules, *Labelled a Black
Villain*, 1989).

nong *n Australian*
a fool. The word is of obscure origin;
it may originate in an Aboriginal word
or as a corruption of *non compos men-
tis* (meaning 'not of sound mind'). It is
probably unrelated to the synonymous
ning-nong.

no-no *n*
something forbidden, impossible,
unwelcome, inadvisable, etc. An
American slang term which, since the
early 1970s, has become a common
colloquialism in all English-speaking
countries.

noodle *n*
1 head. In this sense the word is a
variant form of **noddle**.
2 a fool or simpleton. This sense of
the word is probably inspired by the
notion of softness.

noodnik *n American*
an alternative spelling of **nudnik**.

noogie, nuggy *n American*
a a kiss or hug.
b petting or other sexual activity.
This Americanism, which may possibly be distantly related to the British
nookie, is a survival of an archaic British dialect term nug, which is itself related to the verb nudge, and which
meant to fondle.

nookie *n British*
sexual intercourse or sex in general.
This coy term became popular in the
late 1970s and 1980s, probably due to
its use in the media in place of more offensive synonyms. (Nookie also occurs, albeit rarely, in American usage.)

The etymology of the word is uncertain. It may be a form of the archaic
British dialect verb nug (which has
survived in American speech in the
form **noogie**: kiss or hug), or it may alternatively be an alteration of an older
euphemism for the female pudenda as
a 'shady nook'.

nooner *n*
a a drink at lunchtime.
b *American* a sexual act in the middle of the day. The usual implication is
of a snatched opportunity, perhaps a
lunchtime tryst between adulterous
lovers.

noov, noovo *n, adj British*
(a) nouveau riche (person). A dismissive term employed by upper-class
and public-school speakers and
pseudo-intellectuals. Etonian schoolboys applied the term to Harrovians in
the late 1980s.

noplaceville *n American*
a version of **nowheresville**.

norks *n pl Australian*
breasts. This word is said to be inspired by the wrapper design for butter
produced in the 1950s by the Norco
Co-operative Dairy Company, which
showed a cow with a full udder. The
word was introduced to British speakers by the *Barry McKenzie* cartoon series, running in *Private Eye* magazine
in the 1960s. 'Norkers' and 'norgs'
were earlier forms.

norm *n British*
a a heterosexual. A derogatory term
employed by homosexuals in the
1960s. In the era of **gay** liberation
straight supplanted this abbreviation
of 'normal'.
● *'We went to Malaga. Not a hotel
room to be had. All these old norms
darling. All norming about.'*

(Kenneth Williams, quoted in Joe Orton's diaries, 11 March 1967).

b an abbreviated form of **Norman Normal**.

Norman Normal n British

a very conventional, conformist person. The mythical Norman (supposedly an especially dull, typically bourgeois, or petit bourgeois, Christian name as well as resembling 'normal') was invoked by the last **beatniks** and, after them, the **hippies** as a term of light-hearted contempt.

north and south n British

mouth. A piece of Victorian London working-class rhyming slang that is still heard, always in the full form.

- 'What a mouth, what a mouth/
  What a north and south/ Blimey
  what a mouth he's got!'
  (Lyrics to 'What a Mouth', recorded by Tommy Steele, 1960).

nose candy n American

cocaine. Another euphemistic use of **candy** in particular and sweet imagery in general to describe drugs. This term was widespread among users following the adoption of cocaine as a middle-class fashion in the late 1970s.

nosh n British

food. In Yiddish, the noun (deriving from the verb form, itself from German naschen) signifies a snack or tidbit eaten between meals. In English usage it has been generalized to encompass all sizes of meal.

- 'Hey look at all that lovely nosh
  going to waste.'
  (Biff cartoon, 1986).

nosh vb

to eat. The word is a later alteration of nashn, a Yiddish version of the German word naschen, to snack or eat surreptitiously.

- 'After he'd noshed everything on
  the table, he started in on the
  fridge.'

nosh (someone) off vb British

to have oral sex with someone, perform fellatio or cunnilingus. A 1980s invention in self-conscious imitation of cockney forms of the 1950s.

not on your nellie

See **nellie**.

nouve, nouveau n, adj British

alternative renderings of **noov, noovo**.

nowhere adj

worthless, inferior, hopeless, uninteresting. A dismissive term which formed part of the **beatnik** vocabulary in the USA in the 1950s and later in Britain. When the Beatles recorded Nowhere Man in 1965, the word was in vogue in very limited circles; it was subsequently heard among **hippies**, particularly in the USA.

nowheresville n

an uninteresting, unimportant place or a worthless or inferior notion. A **hip** term using the situation suffix **-ville**, which was briefly adopted by British **beatniks**.

nowt n British

nothing. A Northern English dialect version of the archaic or literary naught. The word is sometimes appropriated by southern speakers for emphasis, irony or familiarity.

nozzer n British

a new naval recruit. This nickname, which has been used for some time in naval training establishments, was given wider currency in a TV documentary broadcast in 1987.

N.T.D. adj British

an abbreviation of 'not top-drawer'; a code term of snobbish disapproval sometimes used in all seriousness by **Sloane Rangers** or would-be members of the upper classes.

nuddy, nuddie adj British

nude, naked. A schoolchildren's humorous or coy mispronunciation of the standard English term, usually in the phrase **in the nuddie.**

nuddy, nuddie n British

a film containing scenes of nudity. An adult or adolescent jocularism heard since the 1960s. It is a deformation of 'nudie'.
- 'They're showing a couple of nuddies down the Essoldo.'

nudnik, noodnik n American

an irritating, boring or stupid person. This Yiddish word is derived from the Czech adjective nudny, meaning tiresome, boring.

'nuff n

a humorous rendering of enough reflecting its pronunciation in rapid or childish speech. The word is usually seen in this form in the cliché "nuff said'. Vogue expressions also employing the word were 'nuff-tuff', meaning bold or daring and 'nuff earn', enough money, both used by teenagers in the late 1980s.

nuggy n American

an alternative spelling of **noogie.**

nuke vb

a to attack with nuclear weapons. The verb was coined by 'hawks' in the USA in the early 1970s. During the Falklands War of 1981 T-shirts and car stickers were produced in Britain with the exhortation 'Nuke Buenos Aires!'.

b to devastate, defeat, overwhelm. By extension the verb is now used with this general meaning, particularly by teenagers and students.
- 'We nuked them in the inter-college playoff.'

nukes n pl

nuclear weapons. An abbreviated form first seen in the USA in the 1970s, especially in the disarmament slogan 'no nukes!'.

number n

1 a marihuana cigarette, **joint.** A vogue term of the late 1960s originating in the USA and deriving from the use of number to mean item, piece or unit. The word remains in use among cannabis smokers.
- 'Roll another number for the road.' (Song title, the Holy Modal Rounders, 1969).
- 'You've got the guns but we got the numbers.' (Lyrics to 'Five to One', written by Jim Morrison and recorded by the Doors, 1968).

2 an act of betrayal, a confidence trick, a scam. Most often heard in the phrase **do a number on (someone):** make a dupe of someone. Related is the phrase 'to get someone's number': to see through someone's deception.

3 a sexual partner. An unromantic term of the 1970s and 1980s denoting a casual or anonymous pick-up. (American author John Rechy published a novel with the title Numbers, dealing with gay liaisons, in 1970.)
- 'She goes to singles bars to pick up what she calls "numbers".' (Recorded, London, 1986).

number (someone) vb

to identify, single out, denounce.
- 'They numbered him as a prime suspect.'
- 'I got numbered.'

number-cruncher n

a (human or mechanical) calculator, handler or manipulator of (usually large) numbers. This light-hearted phrase evoking a mill or grinding mechanism fed with figures has become a standard item of business jargon.

number-crunching n

the activity or practice of handling complex calculations and large quantities (see **number-cruncher**).

number one(s) n, vb

urination. A nursery term dating from the Victorian concept of personal hygiene as a drill. The idea is usually expressed in the form 'do number ones'. In the USA it is occasionally a verb, 'to number one'.
See also **number two(s)**.

number thirteen n American

marihuana. A teen gang code-word of the 1960s and 1970s. M (for marihuana) is the thirteenth letter of the alphabet.

number two(s) n

defecation. A children's term often used humorously by adults. It occurs in both British and American speech.
See also **number one(s)**.

numb-nuts n

an ineffectual, stupid or contemptible person, invariably male. A term of abuse popular for instance with college students in the USA; since the mid-1980s it has been heard in other English-speaking areas. (Nuts refers to testicles, although the epithet has no sexual connotations.)

numero uno n, adj American

(something or someone considered) superlative or supreme. A borrowing, from Hispanic American speech, of the Spanish for 'number one'.

nunnie, noonie n American

backside, **butt**, **ass**. An invented inoffensive euphemism.

● 'You're gonna freeze your nunnie.' (M*A*S*H, US TV comedy series, 1981).

nurd n

an alternative spelling of **nerd**.

nurk n

an alternative spelling of **nerk**.

nurtle n Australian

sex. Like **nattum**, this word of obscure origin is largely used by males in phrases such as 'a bit of nurtle' or 'get some nurtle'. Suggestions have been made that the term originated in a limerick, proving a rhyme with Myrtle and turtle, but the evidence is scanty.

nut n

1 head. A predictable metaphor which had become established slang by the mid-19th century (see the verb form).

2 a a crazy, eccentric person. The word was used in this sense in the USA for about thirty years before its adoption by British speakers in the late 1940s, from **nut-case**.

b a devotee, fan(atic) or buff. The word is used, particularly in American English, as a combining form or suffix, as in 'health-nut'.

nut vb British

to butt someone with one's head, usually in the face, a common form of assault among street fighters and practised brawlers. The concept is also expressed by phrases such as **stick the nut on someone** or 'give someone the nut'; 'Gorbals kiss' and **Glasgow kiss/handshake** are colourful alternatives.

367

• '*Millions of TV viewers . . . saw the Wimbledon wildman nut Everton skipper Kevin Ratcliffe.*'
(*News of the World*, 12 February 1989).

nut-case n

a crazy person. A slang version of 'mental case' which spread from American speech into British usage at the end of the 1950s. It is now a fairly mild term, usually denoting harmless eccentricity. A racier, more modern version is **headcase**.

nut-house n

a psychiatric hospital, mental home. The phrase has been in use since the 1920s.

nut out/up vb

to go crazy, lose control of oneself, run amok. A recent teenagers' and college students' term.

nuts adj

1a crazy, absurd, insane. An Americanism of the turn of the century, adopted elsewhere before World War II, it derives ultimately from the 19th-century notion of '*off one's nut*', a slang version of the colloquial '*off one's head*'.
b extremely enthusiastic or enamoured.
• '*He's nuts about her!*'

nuts n pl

testicles. A metaphorical use of the word which serves as a more acceptable euphemism for **balls**.

nuts! exclamation

an exclamation of defiance which may be used without offence unlike the synonymous **balls**. The most famous instance of this (typically American) expression was General McAuliffe's one-word riposte to the German army's request for surrender at Bastogne in World War II.

nutter n British

a maniacal, unrestrained, unpredictable person. Often said in awe or grudging admiration of the subject's energy and capabilities.
• '*He then began saying I would get into trouble. "That boy of yours looks a nutter to me!"*'
(Joe Orton's diary, 12 May 1967).

nuttiness n

1 craziness, eccentricity.
2 *Jamaican* a quality of smartness, alertness.

nutty adj

1 crazy, absurd, eccentric. A usage which slightly pre-dates the almost synonymous **nuts**. By the 1960s it was considered a well-established colloquialism.
2 *Jamaican* **natty** (in the standard and patois senses), smart and spirited. Caribbean English has retained the 19th-century British sense of dandified. The word was applied by the white British pop group, Madness to themselves in a punning reference to their 'craziness' and the inspiration they gained from black music.

nympho n

a promiscuous woman. The word is a shortening of nymphomaniac. The word has often been used by schoolchildren since the 1950s.

O

O n

1 opium, in the jargon of drug users.
2 See **the big O.**

oater n American

a western film. This humorous categorization is a synonym for 'horse opera' in the jargon of actors, producers and critics.

oats n pl

See **feel one's oats** and **get one's oats.**

oatsy adj

spirited, assertive, restive or **feisty.** A coinage derived from the earlier phrase to **feel one's oats.**

ocker n Australian

a working-class male, especially one epitomizing the more boorish Australian attributes. This word, which seems to be related to the British **oik** by an unrecorded process, has a resonance beyond its simple definition. It has overtones of the American 'good ole boy'. 'Ockerism' and 'ockerdom' describe the cult or syndrome of male comradeship, beer-drinking and lack of refinement embodied in such cultural icons as the comedian Paul Hogan's 'Hoag' character and the Test cricketer Merv Hughes. (**Alf** is a less well-known synonym for ocker.)

● 'Paul Hogan . . . the archetypal
  Aussie Ocker.'
  (Photo caption, Southern Cross
  magazine, July 1989).

ockerina, ocarina n Australian

a female **ocker.** A play on words heard occasionally.

octopus n British

a sexually importunate male. A word used by women and girls of a male who is 'all hands'.

O.D., o.d. n, vb

(to) overdose. The abbreviation replaced the full form in the 1960s among 'counterculture' and street drug users. It is still in use and is sometimes extended to refer to a surfeit of something innocuous.

● 'Billy O.D'd on Drano on the night
  that he was wed.'
  ('People Who Died', written and
  recorded by Jim Carroll, 1981).
● 'Oh God, I've completely o.d.'d on
  those chocolates.'

oddball n, adj

(an) eccentric (person), nonconformist or outsider. An Americanism which has been established in British and American speech since the 1950s. The origin of the expression probably lies in pool playing or another sport.

● 'She's a bit of an oddball.'
● 'That's thoroughly oddball
  behaviour.'

odds vb British

to risk, take a chance on. A gamblers' term which occurred in working-class London speech from the 1950s to the late 1970s. The phrase **odds it** is the more durable alternative form.

odds and sods *n pl British*

a rhyming vulgarization of 'odds and ends'.

odds it *vb British*

to 'play the odds', take a risk or chance. A piece of London working-class terminology, used particularly by police officers and members of the underworld.

- 'You're oddsin' it a bit, aren't you?'
- 'I can't be sure, we'll just have to odds it.'

ofay *n American*

a white person. The word is said to be a **backslang** version of 'foe' in black American slang of the late 1960s. Another proposed etymology is the Yoruba word *ofé*, meaning a ju-ju or charm. The word probably originated earlier in the century in the immigrant underworld as a code reference to the police and other authority figures. It is sometimes encountered in the phrase 'ixnay ofay(s)', meaning 'no whites'.

- 'Nice integrated neighbourhood, ofays, Arabs, Chaldeans, a few colored folks. Ethnic, man.'
  (Elmore Leonard, The Switch, 1978).

off *vb American*

to kill. A word popular at the time of the Vietnam War when 'off the pigs' was a slogan much chanted by militant protesters. The term, possibly derived from **bump off**, was picked up by British speakers and enjoyed a brief vogue in the early 1970s. It is still heard occasionally, especially in the verb form 'off oneself' (to commit suicide).

- 'Isn't he the dude on trial for offing the undercover cop?'
  (The Last Innocent Man, US film, 1987).

- 'His wife committed suicide.'
  'The word around here was, he offed her.'
  (Hunter, US TV series, 1985).

offie *n British*

an off-licence. An abbreviated form of the word which has become increasingly popular through the 1980s.

off one's block/chump/ crust/head/nut/onion *adj*

mad, crazy. These phrases are all elaborations of the well established colloquialism, 'off one's head' (heard since the mid-19th century). The terms are sometimes extended to mean intoxicated by drugs or drink, more usually denoted by phrases beginning with 'out of', such as out of one's head.

off one's face *adj Australian*

completely drunk or under the influence of drugs. A variant of 'off one's head'.

- '"I went high at university!" he said reasonably. "Used to really get on my face in fact . . . "'
  ' "Off! Off! Dad, it's off your face," Mouche screeched from the bed.'
  (Girls' Night Out, Kathy Lette, 1989).

off one's trolley *adj British*

deranged, unstable, crazy. A variation on the **off one's block** theme, which has been popular in British speech since the 1970s. The original image evoked may be of a child losing control of a cart or scooter, or of a patient falling from a mobile stretcher or frame.

off-side *adj British*

unfair, improper behaviour. An upper- and middle-class term of disapproval, deriving from various field sports.

off-sider n Australian

an assistant, 'right-hand man' or companion.

off the wall adj American

eccentric, unusual, **way-out**. A phrase (possibly inspired by the unpredictable trajectory of a ball or an ice-hockey puck rebounding from a wall) which has been adopted outside the USA, usually in connection with zany and/or creatively original ideas or behaviour.

O.G. n American

'original gangster'; an older and respected gang member. A term from the code of the Los Angeles street gangs of the 1980s.

oggie, oggy n British

a Cornish pasty. A term of uncertain origin heard in the West of England. It more usually occurs in the form **tiddy oggie**.

oggle vb British

a humorous, or simply mispronounced version of the verb to ogle, usually in the sense of 'eye lasciviously'. A middle-class colloquialism.

-oid suffix

the suffix, seen in slang since the late 1960s, confers a sense of the pseudo-scientific or pathological on the preceding word or part of a word. It is invariably also pejorative, and as such performs as a negative version of the neutral '-ish' or '-esque'. Examples are **Ramboid**, 'bozoid' (from **bozo**), **trendoid** and **zomboid**.

oik n British

1 a vulgar, coarse, boorish or socially inferior person. This term was, and still is, applied by public schoolboys (rarely by girls) to local children or those attending state schools. It is also sometimes used self-effacingly or ironically by working-class males to refer to themselves. The word's origin is obscure, (one suggestion is that it was an imitation of the sound of unsophisticated speech), but seems to lie in the 19th century; it is almost certainly cognate with the 20th-century Australian **ocker**, also denoting a working-class male. Evelyn Waugh used the word, referring in his diary entry of 7 January 1920, to his host as a 'wizened, pleasant little oik'.

- 'I'm constantly amazed that a couple of oiks like me and Gray have managed to make it.'
  (Recorded, advertising executive, London, 1986).
- 'One Hooray Henry even came up to Mike and demanded: "Have you been invited here, you horrible little oik?".'
  (News of the World, 29 May 1988).
- 'A glum screening of the American comedy Ernest Saves Christmas In it, an oik with a mouth big enough to hold half a dozen candy bars all at once ... helps Santa through his yuletide round.'
  (Sheila Johnston, Independent, 16 November 1989).

2 a person with 'one income and kids'. An acronym in **yuppie** use in the late 1980s. Similar coinages are **dinky** and **oink**.

oiled adj

drunk. A less common version of the colloquial 'well-oiled'.

oily n British

a stupid, unsophisticated or unfortunate person. This derogatory term heard among black teenagers in 1989, is probably a blend of **oik** and **wally**, rather than a specialized use of the standard English adjective.

- 'I don't want to walk down the

street and have them shout, "Hey, oily" because of how I look.'
(Recorded, black youth, London, 1989).

oily rag n British

1 this disparaging term is applied to inexperienced or incompetent motor mechanics who are assigned menial jobs such as wiping away grease.
2 a cigarette. This piece of rhyming slang, from **fag**, was common in the 1950s but is now rarely heard.

oink n

a person with 'one income and no kids'. An acronym characterizing one type of worker in the **yuppie** milieu of the late 1980s. Similar coinages are **dinky** and **oik**.

oinker n American

a vulgar, obnoxious or greedy person. A young person's euphemism for 'pig'. The term was and is, predictably, applied to police officers.

OK, O.K., okay interjection

all right, correct. The term is no longer thought to be slang, but its origins are frequently debated by amateur and professional etymologists. The first recorded use was in the Boston *Morning Post* of 23 March 1839 by C. G. Greene, who used OK as a facetious abbreviation of a mis-spelled 'Orl Korrect'. This novelty, possibly reinforced by the Scottish phrase 'Och, aye', which has the same meaning and an almost identical pronunciation, was imitated by other comic writers and taken as the title of a Democratic political club in 1840; this last example was also probably a pun on 'Old Kinderhook', the nickname of the politician Martin van Buren. The several other proposed sources for the word, including a posited cry in French, *au quai!* ('to or on the quayside') are probably spurious. By the end of the 19th century OK was in use in Britain.

-ola suffix

this word ending has been appropriated from Spanish where it signifies large and negative. It is added to standard terms and slang terms (as in **payola** and **boffola**) to convey the notion of outrageous, excessive or 'super-'. The usage arose in the USA in the 1950s.

Old Bill, the Old Bill n British

See **the Bill**.

old boiled egg n British

the OBE (the 'Order of the British Empire' public service medal). A jocular nickname used by civil servants, diplomats, etc. since the 1930s.

old Dutch, my old Dutch n British

wife. This cockney phrase has been in use since the late 19th century. There is disagreement about its origin, which may be in the rhyming slang 'Dutch plate'; mate, or the use of 'duchess' as a term of endearment or affection. Old Dutch, usually preceded by 'my', is now rarely heard except among elderly Londoners.

old fellow n

penis. An affectionate euphemism used by hearty males.

oldie n

a an old person, parent.
b a pop record released more than a year ago.

old lady n

one's mother, wife or sweetheart. The term was notably adopted by **hippies** in Britain in the late 1960s, not from local working-class usage, but in imitation of American **bikers**, etc.

old lag n British

a recidivist, habitual offender or former prisoner. **Lag** is an elastic term which since the early 19th century has encompassed imprisonment, sentencing, a notion of transportation, or simply convict.

old man n

one's father, husband or sweetheart. See also **old lady**.

old moody n British

See **moody**.

old trout n British

a middle-aged or elderly woman, especially one who is frumpish or short-tempered. This expression has been used as a mild pejorative (very occasionally even affectionately) since the 19th century.

- 'Here's what's coming up for you; two old trouts and a man who should be in the army.'
  (Victoria Wood, As Seen on TV, BBC comedy series, April 1988).

Oliver (Reed), Olly n British

amphetamine, **speed**. A rhyming-slang term coined by middle class drug users in the 1970s, ironically taking the name of a film actor notorious for his liking for alcohol.

ollie n British

a marble, in the literal sense of the children's plaything (which is probably a variant form of **allie**), and in the figurative sense, as in the expression to **lose one's marbles**.

- 'Another few days with those dozy gob-shites and I'd have lost me ollies.'
  (Alexei Sayle, Great Bus Journeys of the World, 1988).

olly n

See **Oliver(Reed)**.

omi, omee n British

a man. A **parlyaree** word which survived into the modern era, omi is a corruption of the Italian uomo, man. The term featured in the language of the theatre and among street traders and vagrants among others.

omipolone, omipoloni n British

a male homosexual. This now dated form has survived in theatrical and film usage from more widespread earlier currency in the argot of the underworld, tramps, tinkers, etc. It is a portmanteau comprizing **omi** (man) and **polone** (woman). The word was used as a euphemism in the radio comedy series Round the Horne during the 1960s.

on canvas adj, adv British

in solitary confinement, in prison. The phrase derives from the fact that prisoners in solitary confinement are issued with canvas mattresses and nightshirts.

oncer n British

an alternative spelling of **oneser**.

one-eyed trouser snake n

penis. A colourful metaphor which probably originated in Australia in the 1950s. The word has spread to Britain and the United States and is nowadays generally truncated to **trouser snake**, which has developed further connotations.

oneser n British

a one-pound note or pound coin.

- 'All I got on me is a oneser.'

one under n British

a suicide on a railway or underground line. A piece of police jargon.

one-up someone vb

to (try to) out-do, better or snub someone. The common adjectival form is occasionally employed as a verb in all English-speaking areas.

● 'She tries one-upping me at every chance she gets.'

on holiday adj British

in prison (temporarily), in the argot of tramps and the homeless.

on one adj British

a under the influence of (a tablet of) **MDA** or **ecstasy**. An expression from the jargon of **acid house** club habitués.

● 'Are you on one, matey?'

b in the know, au fait or au courant.

In both senses, this is an adolescent vogue phrase of the late 1980s.

on one's Jack, Jack Jones
adj, adv, British

alone, on one's own. Rhyming slang from the name of the American singer.

on one's tod adj, adv British

alone, on one's own. The phrase is rhyming slang from 'Tod Sloan', the name of an American jockey active at the turn of the century.

on the blink adj British

malfunctioning, out of order, intermittently breaking down. The expression probably refers to the 'blinking' of worn-out light fittings or warning lights (later of TV sets).

on the brew adj phrase British

on the dole, unemployed. The sense of 'brew' in this phrase, which was heard in the 1980s, especially in the North of England, is unclear.

on the bum adj, adv

1 a on the road. Leading the life of a hobo or tramp.

● 'Just about a year ago I took off on the bum.'

(Lyrics from 'Lodi', written by John Fogerty and recorded by Creedence Clearwater Revival, 1968).

b engaged in cadging or begging. From the verb to **bum**.

2 malfunctioning, out of order. A less common synonym of **on the blink**, **bum** here meaning dud or useless.

on the drip adv, adj British

on hire purchase, by instalments. One of many synonyms (including **on the knock, on the never-never,** and **on the strap, on the lay-by**) in use since the 1950s.

on the earhole/ear'ole adj, adv British

cadging, trying to borrow money. An old London working-class expression still heard in the 1980s. For the etymology, see **ear'ole**.

on the elbow adv British

engaged in cadging, borrowing money or scrounging. A London working-class expression. The elbow reference may evoke literal nudging or figurative barging, pushing.

on the floor adj British

rhyming slang for poor.

on the fritz adj, adv American

malfunctioning, out of order. A synonym of **on the blink**. Fritz here may be the German nickname, probably alluding to imported German goods, thought by Americans in the 1930s to be shoddy. It may alternatively echo the sound of a short circuit, a buzzing in electrical equipment.

● 'We're thinking about getting a

doberman since the alarm system went on the fritz.'
(*Hart to Hart*, US TV series, 1981).

on the (h)orn n British

having an erection. A very common working-class and schoolboy vulgarism of the 1950s and early 1960s, now somewhat dated. 'Horn' has been a synonym for penis since at least the 18th century.

on the hurry-up adv British

at full speed. An item of London police jargon.

on the job adj, adv British

engaged in sexual intercourse. An unromantic euphemistic phrase which has been used increasingly in 'polite' company in Britain and Australia since the 1960s.

on the knock adj, adv British

1 on credit or hire purchase, by instalments.
See **knock**.
2 engaged in selling or canvassing door to door. An alternative form of **on the knocker**.

on the knocker adj, adv British

going from door to door. Typically to sell something of dubious worth or to persuade the gullible to part with items such as antiques for less than their true value. A non-regional working-class term.

on the lay-by adj, adv Australian

on hire purchase, (bought) by instalments.

on the needle adj

habitually injecting heroin or another narcotic.
• '*She finally admitted she was back on the needle.*'

on the never-never adj, adv British

on hire purchase, on credit, by instalments. One of many such phrases originating in the 1950s; this one ruefully reflects on the impossibility of ever getting out of debt once enmeshed.

on the nose adj Australian

stinking, smelly, rank. The expression is either a shortening of a phrase such as '*heavy on the nose*' or an inversion of an earlier expression '*to have a nose on (someone or something)*', meaning to dislike.

on the 'orn

See **on the (h)orn**.

on the piss adj, adv British

engaged in a drinking bout or habitual heavy drinking.

on the pull adv, adj British

looking for a sexual partner, hoping to pick up a member of the opposite sex. A working-class term in use since the late 1960s from **pull**; its predatory overtones mean that it is usually applied to males.
• '*Don't bother asking – those two are out on the pull again.*'
(Recorded, adolescent girl, London, 1987).

on the q.t. adv

discreetly, secretly. A version of 'on the quiet', first recorded in 1870.

on the rag adj British

menstruating. **Rag** is a common slang-synonym for sanitary towel.

on the square adj British

belonging to a Masonic lodge. A term from the code of freemasons themselves. (The square is a Masonic symbol.)

● *'Three Crown witnesses were themselves "on the square".'* (Former detective quoted in *Inside the Brotherhood*, Martin Short, 1989).

on the strap *adj, adv British*

on credit or hire purchase, by paying instalments. A less common alternative form of **on the drip**, **on the never-never**, etc. The exact significance of the strap in question is unknown, but there may be a connection with the colloquial *'strapped for cash'*. The phrase is old; strap has been used to mean credit since the 1830s.

● *'Don't buy a second-hand car, buy a new one. Get it on the strap.'* (Recorded, publisher, London, 1989).

on the thumb *adj, adv British*

hitch-hiking.

on the up-and-up *adj, adv*

above board, bona fide. Originally an Americanism of uncertain derivation (perhaps an intensification of upright), the term is now widely used in Britain, especially in London working-class speech.

● *'No it's OK: he finally convinced me that the deal was on the up-and-up.'*

on tilt *adj, adv American*

unsteady, unbalanced. The phrase comes from the light flashed on a pintable to say that the game has been curtailed because the machine has been forced out of alignment by overenthusiastic play. It often refers to a person who is behaving uncharacteristically or eccentrically.

on top *adj, adv British*

(caught) in the act, (caught) red-handed. A criminal and police expression evoking the image of, for example, a burglar on a roof, i.e. exposed.

oojamaflip *n British*

an unspecified or unnameable thing. A nonsense word used particularly by middle-class speakers in the same way as thingummybob, thingy, etc.

op *n*

a (surgical) operation.

o.p. *n British*

an observation post or point. An abbreviation from the jargon of the police, particularly the Flying Squad in the 1980s.

open one's lunch/lunchbox *vb Australian*

to **fart**. A vulgarism introduced to a British readership by the 1960s *Adventures of Barry McKenzie* (Barry Humphries' and Nicholas Garland's cartoon strip in *Private Eye* magazine).

oppo *n British*

1 opposite number, partner. A military abbreviation used in police, underworld and more general contexts. Most users assume understandably (and probably correctly) that this is based on 'opposite'. A more fanciful suggestion is that it is in fact a corruption of *'hop o' my thumb'*, rhyming slang for chum.

2 an operation, particularly a military operation (a surgical operation is simply an **op**).

oracle *n*

See **work the oracle**.

orange, orange sunshine *n*

LSD. These American terms of the late 1960s referred to the colour of home-made tablets – originally to a particular pure and powerful form of the drug supposedly originating from a laboratory in California.

orbital, orbital rave n British

an **acid house** party. In 1989 there was a vogue for large-scale gatherings of adolescent party goers, usually paying to attend clandestine dance celebrations which often ended in confrontations with the police. The practice was part of the **acid-house** cult in which the drug **ecstasy** played an integral part. The parties in question revived the dated term **rave** and were held within reach of the London orbital motorway, the M25, hence the names.

orchestras n pl British

testicles. The word is late 19th- or early 20th- century rhyming slang from 'orchestra stalls' (a category of theatre seating); **balls**. It is invariably used literally rather than figuratively.

the order of the boot n British

(notice of) rejection, dismissal or refusal. The humorous expression, based on the more exalted Order of the Bath, Order of the Garter, etc., is normally employed in the context of a sacking or a rejection by a lover. This form of words has largely supplanted the earlier 'order of the push'.

original gangster n American

See **O.G.**

O.S. adv Australian

overseas.
● 'Charlene's gone O.S.'

oscar adj British

unrestrained, out of control, wild. This pun on the name of the writer Oscar Wilde was in use among commune dwellers and **hippies** in the late 1970s in such phrases as to 'go completely

Oscar'. (In archaic slang in both Britain and Australia an oscar was a male homosexual.)

ossifer n

a police officer. A facetious and/or provocative deformation of the standard word, often said in imitation of the slurred speech of a drunk. It occurs all over the English-speaking world.

oswald n British

an ounce. A drug dealer and user's elaboration of the humorous pronunciation of the common abbreviation oz.

the other n

sexual intercourse or other sexual misbehaviour. A common euphemism probably deriving from the phrase 'this, that and the other', coyly referring, like 'hanky-panky' to unnameable activities. Until the late 1950s the other often signified homosexual activity as opposed to orthodox sex. Nowadays phrases such as 'a bit of the other' are usually heard in a heterosexual context.
● 'He asked me if I fancied a bit of the other, so I told him yes, but only if the bit belonged to some other bloke.'
(Recorded, London, 1965).

O.T.T. adj British

outrageous, wild and uncontrolled. A shortening of the late 1970s catchphrase **over the top**, given wider currency by its adoption as the title of an anarchic TV comedy show in the early 1980s. It often occurs in phrases such as 'go (completely) O.T.T.'.

out adj

living or behaving openly as a homosexual. The result of having **come out** (of the **closet**). A term from the gay lexicon.
● 'Bruce is out.'

377

• *'She's been out for some time now.'*

outasight *adj*

superlative, excellent, sensational. The phrase 'out of sight' was probably used first in this sense by jazz musicians and their **beatnik** imitators in the late 1950s in the USA. Outasight, like the earlier **way-out** and the coeval **far-out**, used the image of something far from the ordinary or far outdistancing its rivals. The expression was popular among the **hippies** of the late 1960s and in the jargon of soul music. It is now rarely heard outside the USA and is mainly confined there to black American speech.

outfront *adj American*

open, frank, honest and straightforward. A less common synonym for **upfront**.

outlaw *n*

a gang member. The word has been adopted by gangs in many different milieus, including the American **biker** gangs of the 1950s and more recently the black street-gangs of the USA and urban Britain.

outlaw *adj American*

exceptional, outstanding. A teenage expression, originally a term of approbation from the street, where outlaw is a term used of gang members by themselves.

• *'Outlaw dress'*
(*Broadcast News*, US film, 1987).

out of it *adj*

euphoric and/or semi-conscious after ingesting drink or drugs. A fashionable shortened version of **out of one's head/skull/box** which spread from the USA to other English-speaking areas around 1971.

• *'Her main hobby these days seems*

to be getting out of it as often as possible.'
(Recorded, female rock singer, Devon, 1986).

• *'1969 . . . got really out of it last night at the roundhouse.'*
(*Biff* cartoon, 1986).

out of one's head/skull/box *adj*

a mentally deranged.
b intoxicated by drugs or drink.

These terms became widespread in the mid-1960s, before which synonymous phrases (with the exception of *'out of one's mind'*) usually began with 'off'. When the Rolling Stones called their 1965 album *Out of Our Heads* the phrase was still a little-known Americanism. The 'box' version has been fashionable in Britain since the mid-1970s.

out of one's pram *adj British*

out of control, crazy. An alternative form of **off one's trolley**, the term has overtones of a childish tantrum or loss of temper rather than true insanity.

out of one's tree *adj*

a crazy, deranged.
b intoxicated with drugs or drink.

A colourful variation on **out of one's head** that is typically American and Australian. The implication is of someone volubly or energetically crazy or **high** and chattering like a monkey.

out of order *adj British*

1 transgressing, beyond the pale.

• *'"I think you're well out of order,"
he said. Apparently he had been waiting for seven years to see Grace [Jones] again, and was peeved about the extra four hours standing around.'*
(*Independent*, 30 March 1990).

2 incapacitated, particularly by

drink or illicit drugs. These extensions of the standard sense of the phrase became fashionable in raffish speech in the early 1970s. The first sense is more often heard in working-class speech, the second, predictably, in the drug-using subcultures.

out to lunch adj

a crazy, deranged.

- 'The second most out-to-lunch politburo in the north of England.' (Private Eye magazine, 27 October 1989).

b unconscious, incapacitated by drink or drugs. A usage which was particularly popular in Britain around 1975.

over the top adj, adv British

outrageous, bizarre, beyond the bounds of normal behaviour or decorum. The expression equally describes fury, extraordinary generosity or simple bad taste. It derives from the general idea of going 'off the scale', of being beyond measurable or acceptable limits, reinforced perhaps by the use of the phrase in World War I to describe troops climbing out of the trenches to go into battle, hence throwing caution to the winds. Often abbreviated to O.T.T., the phrase was a vogue term in 1979.

- 'There's no point in going over the top about someone like that '
- 'Wearing that dress with those shoes is really over the top.'

own goal n British

a suicide. An unsentimental item of police jargon since the 1970s.

Owsley acid n

(something purporting to be) a high-quality type of LSD manufactured in San Francisco in 1965 by the amateur chemist Augustus Owsley III.

oyster n

1 a gob of phlegm.

2 an unusually taciturn person. This usage is fairly common in American speech.

- 'They call me the human oyster.' (Newspaper advertisement for mail-order public-speaking course, Britain and USA, 1987).

Oz n

Australia.

Ozzie and Harriet n pl

American

a particularly stuffy, middle-class, middle-aged couple. The term is taken from the title of a long-running American TV show of the 1950s and 1960s, in which Ozzie and Harriet Nelson (incidentally the parents of the singer Ricky Nelson) played just such a couple. The names have become a by-word for respectability and domesticity.

P

packet n

the male genitals. A term from the **gay** lexicon, usually referring to the crotch as it appears clothed.

pad n

a home. The word now invariably refers to a room, apartment or house. In 17th-century Britain pad was used by peasants and poor travellers to designate a bed made of straw or rags, while in American slang before 1950 it designated a pallet or couch on which opium smokers or other drug takers reclined; this sense was later extended to encompass any room or place in which drug users gathered, or the beds on which they slept. The dissemination of **beatnik**-related jargon introduced the word to a wider audience, as did its adoption by the **hippy** generation. In Britain the word pad now tends to be identified negatively with the outdated hippy subculture and native slang terms such as **gaff** and **drum** are often preferred, although the term is still in use, often in a jocular context.

- 'Drop-out pads for the large numbers of people hitting London at the moment looking for the mythical beautiful dreamboat.' (International Times, April 1968).
- 'I strolled around to her pad, the light was off and that's ba-a-a-d.' (Lyrics to Here I Go, Syd Barrett, 1970).

paddle vb

to hit, beat, thrash. This synonym of wallop probably derives from the archaic use of the noun paddle to mean both hand, and more rarely, foot. Long before signifying a bat, paddle also denoted a small spade.

Paddy n

an Irish person. A nickname derived from the short form of Patrick, the most common male Christian name in Ireland. It has been used since at least the 18th century. Although the term can be used as an epithet, it may be used descriptively and is also heard among the Irish themselves, where it is usually a personification of a typical rustic Irishman. An alternative, usually with a slightly more pejorative emphasis, is **mick**.

- 'We Import More Paddies Every Year.' (Joke acronym for Wimpey, British construction and civil engineering firm).

paddywaggon n

a secure police van, a **black maria** or a police car. This term was introduced into Britain and Australia from the United States at the end of the 19th century. The reference to paddy reflects the importance of the Irish population of New York and other Northern cities in providing police officers at the time, rather than to the number of Irishmen arrested. **Meat wagon** is a racier, more modern alternative.

pafghani n British

black hashish. The term refers specifically to a type of hashish available in the West during the civil war in Afghanistan in the 1980s. It was widely rumoured to be the result of raw materials grown in Afghanistan being processed in, and shipped from, Pakistan.

pain in the arse/ass n

a nuisance, irritation or source of problems. A vulgar version of 'pain in the neck'; an expression in use since the early 20th century. (**Arse** may be substituted by any synonym or **balls**, etc.)

- '*A few drinks and respectable family men, dads, became lecherous pains in the ass.*'
  (Elmore Leonard, The Switch, 1978).

painters n pl

See **have the decorators/painters in**.

paki n British

a a Pakistani. The abbreviation, invariably in a racist context, began to be heard in the later 1960s.

- '*Paki scum go home.*'
  (Racist graffito, Whitechapel, London, 1980).

b a shop, usually a supermarket or general store, operated by a Pakistani or other South Asian.

- '*I'm just off down the paki for a can of beans.*'
  (Recorded, housewife, London, 1987).

The simple shortening is used, in the first sense, as an offensive racial epithet and in the second sense as a simple descriptive term for the many independent corner stores owned and run by immigrant families. In both senses the word is often applied, loosely, to any immigrant from the subcontinent, including those of Bengali, Indian or Sri Lankan origin.

paki, paki black n British

black hashish. The term is loosely applied in the West as a catch-all to commercial or low-grade hashish from all over the subcontinent, as opposed to premium products from Afghanistan, Kashmir, Nepal, etc. It is typically impure, being mixed with ghee, a form of clarified butter.

paki-bashing n British

the attacking, intimidation and harassment of Asians by white thugs or racists. The phenomenon began on a large scale in the **skinhead** era (around 1969) and has not abated.

paladic, palatic adj British

drunk, a light-hearted term of uncertain origin; it may be a corruption of **paralytic**.

palari n British

speech, talk, particularly in **camp** and theatrical circles. It is a corruption of the Italian *parlare* or of **parlyaree**.

palatic adj

See **paladic**.

palooka n American

a large, clumsy and/or slow-witted male. Before World War II the word was usually employed to describe a third-rate prizefighter. It was apparently coined by Jack Conway, an ex-baseball player and sports writer. The resemblance to *peluca*, Spanish for wig, may be coincidental.

- '*This big palooka has been trying to get me pregnant every which way but lop-sided.*'
  (The Boss's Wife, US film, 1986).

palookaville n American

a an out-of-the-way, slow, rustic town, **the boondocks**. The expression describes the kind of town popularly supposed to be inhabited by **palookas**.

b oblivion, ignominy. A metaphorical use, describing the state of mind characteristic of washed-up, punch-drunk prizefighters.

- *'You keep on fighting out of your class, you're buying a one-way ticket to palookaville.'*

pan n British

face, head. A now obsolete usage, still heard in the 1950s usually in the context of aggression as in *'a punch in the pan'* or *'shut your pan!'*.

pan out vb

to turn out, result. Originating in the language of those who searched for gold in America during the 19th century, the term soon spread to British and Australian English in which it has moved since the early 1970s from slang to colloquialism. It refers to the technique of panning, in which river silt is washed in a large flat pan in order to find gold dust.

- *'Let's just wait and see how it pans out.'*

pansy n

a male homosexual or an effeminate, effete or weak male. A word first used in this context in the 1920s and well-established until the late 1960s. It survives mainly in the speech of the middle-aged and elderly.

pants man n Australian

a promiscuous male, seducer or **stud**.

pantywaist adj American

an effete person, sissy or weakling. The term comes from the image of a male wearing women's underwear or a type of toddler's one-piece garment of the same name.

paper bag job n

an ugly or unattractive person. The image is of a person who could only be considered as a sexual partner if his or her face were covered. The expression, first heard in the 1960s, probably originated in US high-school or campus usage; it enjoyed a vogue among schoolboys in Britain in 1968–9.

Compare **bag one's face**.

para n

a paratrooper.

parallel parking n American

sexual intercourse. A popular euphemism since the 1970s among high-school students and **preppies**. (The phrase is displayed on car park notices to remind drivers of parking discipline.)

paralytic, paralyzed adj

(extremely) drunk. A very common expression in Britain (but less so in the USA, where **paralyzed** is probably more prevalent) since the first decade of the twentieth century.

paraphernalia n

the apparatus and equipment (pipes, cigarette papers, scales, etc.) accompanying the taking of illicit drugs. A euphemism popularized by its use in 'head shops' from the late 1960s, paraphernalia there refers to the soft-drug culture of cannabis and hallucinogens. The same term is used, especially by law enforcers, to describe the equipment used by hard-drug addicts and users.

park a custard/tiger vb British

to vomit. The chosen words are intended to suggest consistency or colour. The first version was said by Eric

Partridge to be in use in the Royal Navy in the 1930s.

● *'People . . . were actually trying to park a custard after eating something they had only identified after swallowing and didn't want to digest.'*
(*Love it or Shove it*, Julie Burchill, 1985).

parkie n British

a park-keeper. A children's term, popular in the 1950s, for a feared authority figure.

● *'If you don't come down out of that tree, the parkie will come and get you.'*

parking n American

necking and petting in cars. A teenage euphemism of the 1950s which is still in limited use. (In the early 1960s this activity – especially, though not exclusively, when done on the coast was known as 'watching the submarine races'.)

park one's arse/bum/carcass vb

to seat oneself, position oneself.

parky adj British

cold. A word of obscure origin dating from at least before World War II and still in use. Among middle- and upper-class speakers the term is occasionally altered to parquet (as in 'parquet flooring').

● *'It's a bit parky in here – mind if I close this window?'*
(Recorded, teacher, London, 1987).
See also **parkie**.

parlyaree, parliari n British

The strong Italian influence on the theatre, dance, music and the humbler entertainments of the streets from the late 17th to the late 19th centuries gave rise to an Italianate jargon. This termi-nology was adopted by English speakers (including vagabonds, street traders and the like), with resulting deformation of the original Italian words. This code, later known as par-lyaree or parliari (itself a corruption of the Italian, *parlare*, to speak) has died out slowly during the 20th century. Certain terms remain in limited use, among them **nanty**, **omi**, **khazi** and **bona**.

parni n

See **pawnee**.

paro, parro adj British

paranoid, in the popular sense of nervous or suspicious. These short forms were in use among schoolchildren at the end of the 1980s.

parquet adj British

See **parky**.

party vb American

to enjoy oneself. This verbal use of the noun was first used in a slang or colloquial context, often as a euphemism for illicit or excessive activities.

party down vb American

to let oneself go, to enjoy oneself to the full. A later embellishment of the verb **party**, with overtones of dedicated involvement or application.

party pooper n

a spoilsport, 'wet blanket'. This expression (see **poop** for the probable origin) was introduced to Britain from the United States in the early 1960s. It originally referred to adults interfering in teenagers' activities, but was later generalized to describe any morose or unconvivial person.

pash n British

a teenage 'crush', an infatuation; es-

pecially a young girl's feelings towards an older girl or teacher. A shortening of 'passion' still heard in public schools.
● '*Amanda has a pash on Miss.*'

passion fruit(s) n pl British
testicles. A pun from the 1950s.

passion killers n pl
clothing, particularly underwear, which discourages, inhibits or prevents sexual attraction or activity. The expression was originally applied to standard-issue clothing forming part of military or school uniform.

passion pit n American
a cinema (not necessarily a **fleapit**) or other location as a venue for seduction.

passion wagon n
a car or van used for purposes of dating and/or seduction. The word was probably first used in armed-services slang during World War II, describing buses used to transport female personnel. **Draggin' wagon** and **shaggin' wagon** are later, racier alternatives.

paste n American
semen.

paste (someone), paste one on (someone) vb British
to hit, beat up, 'thrash' or defeat. This use of the word paste, perhaps inspired by the slapping of paste on walls, posters, etc., or from baste or lambaste, arose in the 19th century and was popular in colloquial speech until the late 1950s. Paste one on (someone) was then an alternative version; 'give someone a (good) pasting' survives.

pasting n
a beating or resounding defeat. From the verb to **paste (someone)**.

patch n
one's territory, area of jurisdiction. A designation used by street-gangs, drug dealers and law enforcers.

patootie n American
1 backside, buttocks. An inoffensive term which may be an invention or a deformation of 'potato'.
● '*She fell flat on her patootie.*'
● '*You can bet your sweet patootie I will!*'
2 a girlfriend or boyfriend, sweetheart. In this (now obsolescent) sense the word is almost certainly a jocular alteration of (sweet) potato.

patsy n
a dupe. The term dates from the early years of the century but its original significance is lost. (Robert L Chapman's *New Dictionary of American Slang* tentatively derives it from *pasqualino*, Italian for scapegoat or loser.)

pattie n British
a 'first' (first-class degree). A student pun (rhyming slang on Pattie Hearst) on the pattern of **Desmond**, etc. A set of nicknames of this sort was coined in 1987 and 1988.

pavement pizza n
a patch of vomit in the street. A drinkers' term from the 1980s which forms part of a set of terms such as **road pizza**, **road apple** etc. as supposedly humorous euphemisms for distasteful discoveries.

paw n
hand.

pawnee n British
a a body of water; lake, pond, sea.
● '*Two ducks on the pawnee.*'
(Bingo callers' code for the number 22).

b water in any form (such as rain, tears, etc.). The word, now very rarely heard but not extinct, is a corruption of the Hindi *pani*, entering English through colonial slang, Romany, or both.

pax *exclamation British*
a request for a truce, usually heard in the course of children's games. The word is Latin for peace and was formerly used by public-school masters as well as boys to appeal for calm or silence. Non-public-school children usually employed the word **faynits**.

paydirt *n*
profit, reward, success. A mining metaphor originating in the USA.

payola *n*
bribery or extortion. This underworld term achieved prominence in the 1960s in the USA when it was applied to a scandal involving illicit payment to disc jockeys in return for airplays. It is the word pay with the Spanish suffix **-ola** (big, grandiose or outrageous).

P.C.P. *n*
angel dust. The initials are from phencyclidine, an animal tranquillizer that was abused (and manufactured in home laboratories), particularly in the USA in the 1970s, for its disorienting effects.

P.D.A. *n American*
a 'public display of affection'. A **preppie** code term for overt kissing, hugging, etc., usually said in a disapproving tone.

P.D.Q. *adj, adv*
'pretty damn quick'. A middle-class adults' expression often used in issuing commands or instructions. The

term was recorded in Britain in 1900 and may be earlier.

pea-brain(ed) *n, adj*
(someone who is) stupid.

peachy *adj American*
wonderful, excellent. The term, now often used ironically, is based on the earlier noun peach, meaning someone or something delectable. Peachy-keen is an intensive form of the word.

peanut butter *n American*
a powerful, dark-coloured form of the drug, heroin. A drug users' term from the 1980s.

pearl-diver *n*
a washer-up. A humorous glamorization of the menial work that was often the lot of itinerants, vagrants and later **beatniks** on both sides of the Atlantic, who first used the word. The activity was known as pearl-diving.

pears *n pl Australian*
breasts. Another example of the tendency for any vaguely rounded fruit to be used to symbolize breasts. Compare **apples, melons**, etc.

pecker *n American*
penis. The term may originate as a rural shortening of woodpecker, or as a euphemism for **cock**, or simply as a metaphor for an importunate member.
● 'When I told him to get a-hold of himself I didn't mean for him to get his pecker out.'
(Recorded, US oilman, Norway, 1982).

peckerhead *n American*
a fool, slow-witted or clumsy person. Originally used by country people, now a favourite term of abuse among college students and others.

The British and Australian equivalent is **dickhead**.

pecs n pl American

pectoral muscles. A word used particularly by body builders and by women admiring (or disparaging) the male physique. The shortening became widespread in the 1970s.

● 'The guys there [California] all have great pecs, but I guess that's not the only thing.'
(Recorded, American female executive, London, 1986).

pedigree chum n British

an upper-class girl's escort or boyfriend. A witticism inspired by **debs' delight** punning on the brand name of a dogfood. The phrase arose in the 1980s.

pee, pee-pee n

urine or an act of urination. The word is probably in origin a euphemistic form of the more onomatopoeic **piss**, but is reinforced by being the initial sound of **piddle** and a cognate of other European forms (such as the French pipi). It was not recorded before the 18th century.

pee, pee-pee vb

to urinate.
(For the origins of the word see the noun form.)

pee'd adj British

a more polite version of **pissed**.

pee'd off adj

a less offensive version of **pissed-off**.

peeler n British

a policeman. From Robert Peel, the 19th-century statesman responsible for Britain's first coherently organized police force. The term is now archaic in most parts of the British Isles but is still used by Republicans and their sympathizers in Northern Ireland to refer disparagingly to the British security forces.

peeper n American

a private eye. A term which has been in use since at least the 1940s and is not yet obsolete.

peepers n pl

eyes. A humorous euphemism.

peg it, peg out vb

to die. The first version of the phrase is currently more fashionable than the earlier peg out, which appeared in the USA in the mid-19th century, inspired by the use of pegs in the game of cribbage ('pegging-out' was finishing the game). The form peg out may also mean to collapse exhausted or fail in one's efforts.

pelf n British

money. An old term, like many others (**rhino**, **spondulicks**, etc.) revived in the money-conscious environment of the later 1980s. Pelf is from the Middle English pelfre, related to 'pilfer' and meaning loot.

● 'Miss Smith . . . Cold as the Ice itself; She admires nought but Pelf.'
(List of Covent Garden Ladies, or the New Atlantis, pamphlet, 1773).

pellets n American

Ritalin (a prescribed preparation often abused by addicts and drug users). Ritalin is related to amphetamines (**speed**) and was also known in street parlance as **fast one**.

pen-and-ink n, vb British

(a) stink. An early 20th-century Cockney rhyming-slang term which has survived to the present. It can be used as a noun phrase, as in 'there's a *real pen-and-ink in here!'* or as a verb, normally in a form such as *'it don't half pen-and-ink in here!'*.

pencil geek n American

a tediously studious person, **swot**. One of many high-school and campus categorizations of fellow students; **grind** and **conch** are synonymous.

See **geek**.

penguin suit n

formal male evening dress; a dinner suit.

the people n American

one's peer group, fellow gang-members and specifically one of the two main street-gang groupings in Chicago in the 1980s.

pep pill n

a tablet of amphetamine or a similar drug. This term was used in the 1940s when stimulant drugs such as caffeine and benzedrine were taken to combat fatigue and sleep. The expression was used by illicit drug takers until the early 1960s when it was appropriated by spokesmen for the anti-drug establishment and the media. **Speed** and **uppers** became the generic slang terms for this class of drugs from the mid-1960s.

percy n

the penis. One of a number of personifications of the male member which include **peter, dick, willie, John Thomas**, etc. The word principally functions as part of the phrase **point percy at the porcelain**.

perk vb Australian

to vomit. A variant of **puke**, perhaps influenced by the phrase 'to perk up' or the word 'percolate'.

perp n American

a wrongdoer, felon. An abbreviation of 'perpetrator' used by law enforcers.

- *'All three bridges raise and the perp can't get off the island.'*
  (*The Dancer's Touch*, US film, 1989).

personal n British

a small quantity of cannabis or another drug, one's 'personal **stash**'. The implication is that the amount in question is sufficient only to the immediate needs of the user and is not to be shared or sold.

- *'I'd like to help you out, man, but I've only got some personal.'*

personals n Australian

lingerie, (ladies') underwear. An adult euphemism used both facetiously and seriously.

- *'I wouldn't hang your personals out here in full view.'*

Peruvian flake n American

high quality cocaine, purportedly, but in actuality not necessarily, from Peru.

See **flake**.

Peruvian marching powder n

cocaine. A jocular middle-class American euphemism of the mid-to late 1970s which was probably too long and unwieldy to gain a wider currency.

perve, perv n

a lascivious or perverted person, a 'dirty old man'. A shortening of pervert heard since the 1960s.

perve, perv vb Australian

to behave lasciviously. From the noun form.

pervy adj

perverted or lascivious.

peter n

1 penis. A personification and predictable euphemism dating from the 19th century (if not earlier) and mainly used by adults.

- *'Absence makes the peter fonda.'*
  (Caption to nude photograph of Peter Fonda, OZ magazine, 1969).

2 a safe. In the jargon of the underworld peter originally meant a trunk or strongbox, later a safe. The word was being used with this sense as early as the 17th century, perhaps inspired by some sort of biblical pun, now lost.

peter-man n British

a safecracker. An underworld and police term in use for the last few decades or so. Peter is an old word for safe or strongbox.

pew n British

a chair. A colloquialism usually heard in the verb form 'take a pew'; sit down. This humorously elevated version of chair arose around the turn of the century.

P.I. n

a private investigator, private detective, private eye.

piano adj British

faint, delicate, 'under the weather' or indisposed. This upper-class expression derives from the Italian musical term *piano*, which is an instruction to play or sing softly. The British speaker's pronunciation, in imitation of the original Italian, is 'pee-aah-no'.

- *'Please don't disturb her, she seems to be feeling a little piano today.'*
  (Recorded, hostess, Dorset, 1974).

pickled adj

drunk. A fairly inoffensive term, usually heard in the speech of the middle-aged or elderly.

- *'I sat next to Pat Collins who is a very intelligent and delightful woman. I felt sorry that she had George Brown, completely pickled, on the other side of her.'*
  (Tony Benn's Diaries, 14 October 1969).

picky adj

choosy, particular, fastidious. An American term adopted in the UK in the early 1980s.

- *'Stop being so bloody picky – it's your filth.'*
  (*The Young Ones*, British TV comedy series, 1984).

piddle vb British

to urinate. A childish or humorous-sounding word, this is nonetheless one of Britain's oldest 'non-respectable' words in current use.

(*See also* the noun form **piddle**.)

piddle n British

urine or an act of urination. Piddle is etymologically related to puddle and to piddling meaning insignificant or trifling. It has been used as the name of small rivers in county districts and seems to have had a colloquial meaning of 'small water' or 'insignificant scrap' before its narrowing to the modern sense during the 18th and 19th centuries.

- *'Piddles were done out of the back window last night, standing on the bed.'*
  (Spike Milligan, *Adolf Hitler; My Part in His Downfall*, 1971).

piece n

1 American a gun. An underworld euphemism.

2 a graffiti artist's *oeuvre*. A shortening of 'piece of work' or 'masterpiece' and forming part of the graffiti sub-culture lexicon of the 1980s.

● 'Kids do it mainly for the clothes – jeans or trainers, or to buy cans of spray paint to do pieces (graffiti).' (Teenage mugger, Observer, 22 May 1988).

piece (of ass) n American

a woman (or, less often, a man) considered as a sexual object. Piece has been employed in a similar sexual context, invariably referring unromantically to a woman, since the 15th century. The various phrases such as piece of ass, **piece of tail**, etc. are probably more recent, arising, like **bit of fluff**, in the 19th century.

piece of piss/pudding n
British

something easy to accomplish, presenting no problems, a 'pushover'. Both terms are variants on the common colloquialism 'a piece of cake'.

piece of tail n

an alternative form of **piece of ass**.

pieces n pl British

See **do one's nut/pieces**.

pie-eater n Australian

a poor, unimpressive or unfortunate person. Meat pies are supposedly the staple diet of the poor working class.

pie 'n' liquor n British

a vicar. This piece of working-class London rhyming slang invokes a favourite dish of Victorian cockneys. (The liquor was the liquid formed from mashed peas, used as gravy.)

piff n British

nonsense. A 1980s shortening of the colloquial 'piffle', heard among adolescents.

● 'A load of piff.'

piffy adj British

dubious, doubtful, suspect. A middle-class usage, often said disdainfully or superciliously. Its origin is obscure; it does not appear to be related to piffling, in the sense of insignificant, but may be influenced by 'iffy' or 'piffle'.

pig n

1 a policeman or -woman. An offensive term that gained its greatest currency in the 1960s in the USA whence it was reimported into Britain. (It was used in the same sense in the late Victorian underworld.)

● 'Today's pig is tomorrow's bacon.' (Anti-war protestors' and demonstrators' slogan of the 1960s).

2 a a girl. A usage from the argot of street-gangs, **beatniks**, etc. since the 1950s. Surprisingly in these contexts the word is not necessarily pejorative.

b American an ugly, repellent girl. A term current in the late 1980s at US colleges, where 'Pig of the Year (or Week)' contests took place and the unwitting winner presented with a prize.

3 a sexist male, as characterized by feminists. A shortening of the catchphrase 'male chauvinist pig' (also rendered as **MCP**).

4 a segment of an orange.

These sub-senses evoke the familiar images of the pig as gluttonous and disgusting or round and chubby.

pigfucker n

a despicable, disgusting and/or unpleasant person. An all-purpose term of strong abuse, usually applied to males. This version of the insult is probably more prevalent in the USA; **fuckpig** is a British synonym.

pigging adj British
an intensifying adjective used as a milder substitute for **fucking**. Pigging has the merit of being able to be broadcast. It is used, often with vehemence, by both men and, particularly, women.
• *'I told him to take his pigging "peace offering" and get lost.'*

pig it vb British
to behave in a disgusting manner. The expression may apply to living in filthy surroundings, acting in a slovenly way or 'slumming'.

pig Latin n
a synonym for **backslang**, or a means of coining slang terms by the rearranging of syllables. **Ixnay** is an example.

piglet n Australian
an unattractive teenage girl. See **pig**.

pigmobile n
a police car. A term used by adolescents and **hippies** since the early 1970s.

pig off vb
to leave, go away. A euphemism for more offensive terms such as **piss off**, etc., usually heard in the form of an imperative. It is often used by women who wish to express themselves forcefully without obscenity.
• *'I finally got fed up and told him to pig off.'*
(Recorded, female teacher, London, 1989).

pig out vb
to eat excessively and/or messily, to behave in an outrageous or obsessive way. This racier version of the colloquial 'pig (oneself)', meaning to over-indulge, probably originated in the

USA, and was established in Britain during the later 1960s.

pig's, pig's ear n British
1 beer. A London rhyming-slang term that is still heard. (The dismissive exclamatory phrase 'in a pig's ear!' is unconnected, being a euphemism for 'in a pig's arse!'.)
• *'I'll have a pint of pig's.'*
2 another version of **pig's breakfast**.

pig's breakfast/arse/ear n British
a mess, an outrageous failure, a complete disaster. Most often heard in forms such as *'you've made a right pig's breakfast of that!'*.

pigskin bus n Australian
the penis. An authentic item of Australian slang introduced to a British readership by way of the comic strip *The Wonderful World of Barry McKenzie*, written by humourist Barry Humphries and drawn by Nicholas Garland, which ran in the satirical magazine *Private Eye* from 1965 to 1970. 'To drive the pigskin bus' is to engage in sexual intercourse or to masturbate.

piker n American
a mean, 'tightfisted' person; a welsher on a bet or a shirker. A now obsolescent word, related distantly to the British **pikey**, or from an abbreviation of 'turnpike', piker occurred in the writings of Raymond Chandler in the 1940s. It originally referred to the unreliability of vagrants or itinerants.

pikey, pikie n British
a gypsy or vagrant. The term now properly denotes one of the travelling people who lives in a settlement, such as a member of a family of hop-pickers. It is now fairly rare, but was still common in the 1950s. The precise origins

of these terms (and the American **pik-er**) is unclear because of the convergence of two similar senses of pike; the first is a toll road as in turnpike, the second is an archaic British verb meaning to depart or travel.

pill n British
1 a ball. A schoolboy term of the 1950s.
● *'If I pla there is dead silence becos i never hit the pill at all they are all air shots chiz.'*
(Geoffrey Willans and Ronald Searle, *Back in the Jug Agane*, 1959).
2 **pills** testicles; by extension from the above.
3 a foolish or stupid, annoying person. A shortening of **pillock**.

pill-head n
an amphetamine user or addict.

pillock n British
a foolish or stupid, annoying person. A vulgar but not taboo term of abuse which had existed in British slang usage since the 1950s (its exact date of origin is undetermined), coming into vogue in the mid-1970s; various etymologies have been proposed for the word: 'pillicock' was a late medieval term for penis, sometimes used as an expression of endearment or affectionate abuse; pillocks has also been explained as a rural term for rabbit droppings, or as a synonym for testicles (**pills**) employing the diminutive or affectionate suffix '-ocks' (as in the case of **balls** and **bollocks**).

pillow-biter n
a male homosexual, particularly a passive partner in sodomy. This expression probably originated in Australia, where it is common. It was introduced to the British public during the trial of Jeremy Thorpe (accused of plot-

ting the murder of a male model, Norman Scott, in 1974) by the satirical magazine *Private Eye*.

pill-popper n
a user of amphetamines or tranquillizers.

pimps n, adj British
(something) very easy, a 'pushover'. A word used by young schoolchildren in the late 1980s, particularly when showing off or boasting. The word is usually used in an exclamation such as 'that's pimps!' or 'it's pimps!', meaning 'there's nothing to it'. There seems to be no relation between this term and the standard English word for a procurer or the archaic use of pimp to mean sneak or inform upon.

pimpsy, pipsy adj British
easily accomplished, no trouble. A variant of **pimps** used typically by middle-class schoolchildren.

pinch vb, n
(to make) an arrest. An underworld and police term on both sides of the Atlantic.

pineapple n
a hand grenade. From the resemblance of the knobbed surface of a grenade to the skin of the fruit. This colourful term came to prominence with American gangster fiction of the 1930s, but originated in World War I.

pineapple n Australian
See **rough end of the pineapple**.

ping n, vb British
urination, urinate. An echoic nursery word.

pinhead n
a a fool, idiot.

b a person with a small head and a (proportionately) large body.
See **nibhead**.

pink *adj*

a code or facetious term for **gay** adopted from the heterosexual lexicon by the male homosexual community for ironic or semi-ironic self-reference. (The Nazis affixed pink triangles to homosexuals.) **Lavender** is a similar usage.

pinkie *n*

1 a white person. A term of mild racist abuse used by black speakers in London in the mid-1970s. A more accurate and less flattering version of **whitey**.

2 the little finger. An American term now generally understood in Britain and Australia. (In his autobiography, Tom Driberg notes that the ecclesiastical representatives at W.H. Auden's funeral (in 1973) had to be reassured that the word's meaning was not 'impure'. It occurred in one of Auden's own poems recited during the service.) Some lesbians in Britain and the USA wear so-called 'pinkie-finger rings' as a covert self-identification.

pinko *n, adj American*

someone with liberal or left-of-centre politics or ideas. The image is of a watered-down 'red' (someone with extreme left-wing beliefs).

pinko *adj, n Australian*

(intoxicated by) methylated spirits, which are often dyed pink.

Pink Panther country *n British*

Durham, the city or the county. It is humorously suggested that the local pronunciation of the name is reminiscent of the rhythm of the introduction of Henry Mancini's signature tune for the film and TV cartoon series 'The Pink Panther'. A playground witticism of the 1980s.

pinned-up *adj British*

under the influence of heroin. An addicts' or users' term of the 1980s referring to the way the pupils of the eye contract to pinpoints after an injection of the narcotic.

pipe *vb British*

to look at, watch. The origin of this use of the word is obscure, it seems to have come to Britain at the end of the 19th century from the United States, where it was used in underworld circles to mean spy on or keep an eye on. The word now sounds dated in British slang speech, but is still occasionally heard.

- *'Pipe the widow ginger!'*
(Recorded, bookie's runner, London, 1958).

the Pipe *n British*

the London underground railway system. A workman's slang variation (which is now almost obsolete) on the common colloquialism, the Tube.

pipe one's eye *vb*

to weep. This phrase is now almost obsolete, except in self-consciously fanciful speech. Although 'pipe your eye' has been interpreted as Cockney rhyming slang for cry, the expression had been recorded as early as the beginning of the 19th century (before either Cockney rhyming slang or the use of the word cry to mean weep were widespread). Connections have been drawn with plaintive, tear-provoking pipe music or the more prosaic image of waterworks, but the precise origins of the term remain uncertain.

piper *n American*

a **crack** smoker. A term of the late 1980s.

• 'Clocking means getting a pack of cocaine from somebody like Felix, then standing on a street corner to hand off caps of crack to the pipers and users who drift by.'
(Sunday Times, 10 September 1989).

piss, the piss n

1 urine or urination. An echoic word with cognates in other European languages (piss*er* is the French verb), which has been in use since the Middle English period. Its level of respectability has varied; originally it was a generally acceptable term, by the 18th century a vulgarism, and by the mid-19th century virtually taboo. Since the 1960s it has been possible to use the word in public although **pee** is preferred in polite company.
2 British **the piss**. Alcoholic drink. In this sense the term usually occurs in the phrase **on the piss**.
3 weak beer.
4 nonsense.
See **take the piss**.

piss about/around vb

a vulgar version of 'mess about'.

piss all over (someone) vb

to thoroughly defeat, humiliate or overwhelm. The image is taken from the literal behaviour of animals or humans ritually signalling victory.

piss and wind n

See **all piss and wind**.

piss-ant, pissant adj American

trifling, paltry, insignificant. Although a fairly strong indicator of contempt or dismissal, this word is not treated as a taboo item in the same way as other compounds containing **piss**. The word is originally a rustic noun (also rendered 'piss-mire') meaning an ant. The piss element refers to formic acid.

piss-artist n British

an habitual or accomplished heavy drinker, drunkard. A term used sometimes with contempt, sometimes with admiration.

pissed adj

1 British drunk. This usage came into the language at some unrecorded date early in the 20th century. It presumably originally referred to the incontinence of a helpless inebriate, or else to the equation of alcohol itself with urine. This sense of the word is rare in American English, but is encountered for example in the 1980s parlance of East coast sophisticates.
• 'He served in Northern Ireland, but mainly he played sport and got pissed. Then he was sent off to the Falklands, where he found himself at the centre of the biggest British cock-up of the war, the bombing of the Sir Galahad, which killed 48 men.'
(Observer, 9 April 1989).
2 American upset, angry, **pissed-off**.
• 'When I told him to go he got really pissed.'
• 'I was pissed at her for making me go through all that grief.'

pissed-off adj

angry, irritated, disappointed, upset. Like the verb to **piss (someone) off**, this usage emerged at the time of World War II.
• 'Well . . . people who bought from our competitors are probably pretty pissed off. The plastic should be worn through just about now!'
(Record bootlegger, Oz magazine, February 1970).

piss-elegant adj American

smart, refined or fashionable. This

(fairly mild) vulgarism implies either that the elegance in question is excessive or pretentious or simply that the speaker is envious or disapproving.

pisser n

1 something annoying or disappointing. Originally an Americanism the term spread to Britain in the mid-1970s.
2 a toilet.

pisshead n

1 British a habitual drunkard, **piss-artist**.
2 American an unpleasant person, **shithead**.

pisshole n British

a toilet, particularly a public lavatory. This working-class expression of the 1950s is now rarely heard.

pissing adj British

an intensifying adjective in the same way as **bloody**, **fucking**, etc.

piss in the wind vb

to do something futile, make a doomed attempt. A vulgar version of such colloquialisms as 'whistle in the wind/dark'.

piss it vb British

to succeed effortlessly. A term probably deriving from **piece of piss**; a ridiculously easy task. The expression piss it was widespread in the 1980s throughout all social classes.
● 'They told Sophie the entrance exam would be a bugger, but she absolutely pissed it.'
(Recorded, personal assistant, London, 1989).

piss off vb

to leave, go away. This vulgarism has been in use throughout the 20th

century, particularly in British speech. The word piss has no specific significance, but adds intensity and often overtones of exasperation both where used descriptively and as an instruction.
● 'I feel like pissing off and spending the night in some Arab doss house.'
(Joe Orton's Diary, 14 May 1967).

piss (someone) off vb

to irritate, anger, annoy or provoke. This phrase entered the English slang lexicon around the time of World War II and was probably more prevalent in American speech than British until the 1970s.
● 'It really pisses me off the way she just assumes I'm going to pick up the pieces.'

pissoir n

a public toilet. The word is a borrowing from French, in which it denoted, among other amenities, the famous circular street urinals seen in France until the early 1970s.

piss-poor adj

dreadfully bad. Piss is used here as an intensifying addition. The phrase was earlier used to mean destitute; since the late 1970s it has enjoyed something of a vogue, particularly in journalistic circles to denote 'of miserable quality', pitiful.

piss pot n

a chamber-pot, potty.

piss-take n British

an act of mockery, parody. A common back formation from the phrase to **take the piss (out of)**.

piss-up n British

a drinking bout, drunken celebration. A vulgarism generally used neutrally or with cheerful overtones rather than disapprovingly.

- 'Bob Bee, for Hawkhead Productions, has secured the ultimate television commission: to organise a piss-up in a brewery.' (Independent on Sunday, 1 April 1990).

pissy adj

insignificant, trivial, inferior.

pistol n American

an attractive, active or powerful person. Used of and by both sexes as a term of admiration, the word need not have sexual connotations, but in modern usage often does.

- 'Isn't she a pistol?'

pit n

1 a bed. A popular word in the armed services since before World War II, now in general use.

2 any dirty, sordid or unpleasant place. A more recent alternative to dump, a synonym for **tip**.

See also **the pits, throttle pit**.

the pits n

an unpleasant, disgusting and/or unbearable place, situation or person; the worst place, situation or state of affairs imaginable. This Americanism has become widely used throughout the English-speaking world. It is in origin said to be a shortening of armpits.

- 'You are the pits of the world!' (John McEnroe characterizing an umpire, Wimbledon Lawn Tennis Championship, 1981).
- 'This review has nothing to do with the world of mountaineering and in a sport where there is a wealth of first-rate literature, this "offering" can only be regarded as the pits.' (Reader's letter, Sunday Times Books supplement, October 1989).

pit stop n

a a pause in a drinking bout in order to visit the toilet.

b a pause in a journey or other activity for alcoholic refreshment.

Both senses are humorous adaptations of the pit stops made by racing drivers in order to undergo refuelling, a change of tyres or running repairs.

pizzle n

penis. A term which is virtually standard English when used in connection with animals. The word is cognate with or descended from the Flemish pezel or Low German pesel.

P.Js. n pl American

pyjamas.

- 'He was wearing his overcoat and overshoes over his p.js.'

plank n

1 British a dull-witted person, someone who is as 'thick as two short planks'.

2 a solid-bodied electric guitar. A musician's term of the 1980s; playing such a guitar is known as **spanking the plank**.

plank vb American

to have sex (with). A fairly rare usage inspired by the image of laying flat.

plastic adj

(usually of a person) artificial, shallow, insincere. A **hippy** buzzword of the 1960s, borrowed from **beatnik** usage to castigate the conformist and materialist world of the **straights** as well as the legions of 'weekend' **hippy** imitators. The word submerged during the 1970s, but by 1990 was back in use in British playground slang.

plat n Australian

a stupid person. The word's origin is

uncertain (Eric Partridge derives it from the French *plat*; flat), but the resemblance to **prat** may not be fortuitous.

plate *vb*

to perform fellatio. A term from the 1960s, now dated, which was part of the jargon of rock-music **groupies**. Conflicting etymologies cite the rhyming slang 'plate of ham' for **gam** (a synonym for fellatio), or simply the image of licking a plate.

plate-captain *n American*

a busboy. A humorously grand title for someone who works clearing tables.

plate-face *n Australian*

someone of oriental origin. A derogatory racist term referring to the supposedly wide, flat, round faces of the Mongoloid racial type.

plates (of meat) *n pl British*

feet. A well-known example of Cockney rhyming slang which is actually still used, although almost always in the shortened form, by working-class Londoners.

● *'I've got to sit down – I've been on me plates all day.'*

plating *n*

fellatio. A term from the jargon of prostitutes and pornographers which was adopted by **groupies** in the late 1960s.

See **plate**.

players *n pl British*

a persons involved in terrorist activities. A British army form used in Northern Ireland since the early 1970s.

b speculators, **punters** or fellow conspirators. A financiers' jargon term of the late 1980s influenced by 'playing

the stock exchange'. Both senses are specializations of the standard meaning of participants in a game.

play footsie *vb*

a to indulge in amorous or flirtatious caresses with the feet, typically covertly under a table.

b to flirt with or toy with in a general sense; often in the context of business and commercial relationships.

play gooseberry *vb British*

to be the unwanted third person present at a romantic assignation, as a chaperone, uninvited guest or unwitting intruder. The expression dates from the 19th century: in the language of parents and children 'gooseberry' then as now denoted a buffoon or figure of fun, possibly from the supposedly comic appearance of the fruit or its sour taste.

play hardball *vb American*

to behave in a tough, unrelenting or uncompromising way. A phrase used for instance among business people, politicians, sportsmen, etc. from the 1960s, and now heard outside the United States. A metaphor taken from baseball, where a hard ball is used by professionals and a soft one by juniors and amateurs.

play hooky *vb American*

to play truant. Hooky (or 'hookey') is related to the Cockney **hook it**; 'to take to one's heels', escape.

play hospitals/doctor/doctors and nurses *vb*

to engage in sexual play or activity. The reference can refer literally to children's exploratory play or, coyly, to adult sexual activity. **Doctors and nurses** is a variant.

396

play the whale vb Australian

to vomit. The image is of a whale spouting. This vulgarism was introduced to a British readership by the comic strip *The Wonderful World of Barry McKenzie*, written by humourist Barry Humphries and drawn by Nicholas Garland, which ran in the satirical magazine *Private Eye* from 1965 to 1970.

pleb n

a plebeian, member of the lower classes. A fashionable term in Britain in the early 1960s when class-consciousness preceded 'consciousness-expanding' among the educated young.

plod, the plod n British

the police force or a uniformed policeman. From 'P.C. Plod', a character from the popular children's stories featuring Noddy, written by Enid Blyton in the 1950s. The term additionally evokes a slow-witted, literal and figurative plodder in a civilian context.

plonk n British

wine, especially cheap wine. The word usually refers to red wine, although it was originally a corruption of vin blanc coined by British soldiers in France during World War I.

plonker n British

1 penis. A term probably influenced by 'plonk (down)' in the sense of place down heavily or present defiantly. The word has been in use since early in the 20th century. It was rarely heard during the 1960s and 1970s but was revived during the 1980s vogue for 'schoolboy' vulgarity.

● '*If she's game and wants your plonker wear a Jiffi so you can bonk her.*'
(Promotion slogan for Jiffi condoms, 1988).

2 a **dickhead**. Inspired by the previous sense of the word and by the suggestion in 'plonk' of ponderous or clumsy movement, this usage has become a vogue term of the late 1980s. Unlike its synonym **dickhead**, it can be broadcast, and has gained popular appeal, particularly when applied to the character 'Rodney' in the British TV comedy series *Only Fools and Horses*.

● '*You end up shouting at the people who care about yer, not to the plonkers who treat you like dirt.*'
(*EastEnders*, British TV drama series, 1989).

3 a gaffe or blunder.

4 a kiss, particularly a heavy **smacker**.

ploughed, plowed adj
American

drunk. One of many terms evoking an image of laid low, crushed or destroyed. **Blitzed**, **smashed**, **legless**, etc. are others on this theme.

p.l.u. n, adj British

'people like us'. An upper-class code term of approbation and social discrimination.

● '*I'm afraid they're not really quite p.l.u.*'

plums n pl

testicles. One of many examples of fruit as a sexual metaphor.

P.N.G. vb, n British

(to declare someone) persona non grata. A foreign office and diplomatic term.

● '*They P.N.G.'d old Fry only a month or two after he arrived.*'

po n British

a chamber-pot, potty, toilet. Now a dated nursery word, po was used by adults until the 1960s. The word is an imitation of the French pronunciation of *pot (de chambre)*.

pocket billiards/pool n

(of a man) manipulation of one's genitals through the trouser pockets. The first phrase is British, the second the American version.

pod n American

marihuana. A dated term derived from the seedheads found in herbal cannabis.

point percy at the porcelain vb

to urinate. An expression invented by Barry Humphries, which via the comic strip *The Wonderful World of Barry McKenzie* has passed into common currency in Britain as well as Australia. **Percy** is one of many common personifications of the male member.

pointy-head n American

an intellectual or person of excessive refinement. The expression has been used in the USA since the late 1960s by the self-consciously philistine or genuinely uncultured in expressing contempt for political or social pundits, artists, academics, etc.

poison dwarf n British

an obnoxious small person, brutish individual. The epithet was coined by Germans referring to Scottish members of the British Rhine army. The phrase lodged itself in the British lexicon of abuse (whence it was borrowed by Terry Wogan to refer to the character of 'Lucy Ewing' in the US TV series *Dallas*, for instance).

poke n

1 an act of sexual intercourse. Poke shares this sexual sense with **bang**, **boff**, **knock**, etc., which are all synonyms for strike.

2 a punch, blow. A specialized sense of the standard English word poke meaning to prod (having the same meaning as the Middle Dutch poken).

3 a (paper) bag. In modern colloquial Scottish English this usage is fairly common; it is from the same source as the following.

4 a wallet. This item from the jargon of criminals, tramps, etc. on both sides of the Atlantic, derives either directly from the Old English *pocca* (bag) or via a shortening of Middle English *poket* (pocket).

polack n

a Polish person. The slang term, often pejorative in American usage, is the word for Pole in the Polish language.

polisher n

a toady, ingratiating person, obsequious flatterer. A London working-class term also briefly in vogue in the media in the early 1980s. It is a truncated form of the (originally American) **apple-polisher** (from the image of a schoolchild presenting an apple to a teacher in order to curry favour).

poll adj British

an archaic upper-class term meaning roughly 'non-u' or **naff**. The word is of obscure origin, but may be derived from the Greek *polloi* (common people). Poll was recorded as a verb, meaning to snub, in late Victorian speech.

polluted adj American

drunk. A probably ephemeral campus and **preppie** term which (probably as a separate coinage) seems to have existed prior to the environmental concerns that have gained popularity since the 1970s.

pollywog, pollywag n

1 a tadpole. This old word is still heard in North America and in Britain, where it is a dialect or nursery word. It derives from the Middle English 'pol', head, and 'wigeln', to wiggle.

2 a novice or inexperienced sailor. Its counterpart in nautical slang is **shellback**.

polone, poloni n British

a woman, female. A near-obsolete term of theatrical and showman's slang, dating from the 19th century. The word is an example of non-Italian **parlyaree**, ultimately derived from beluñi, a Spanish gypsy term for an (immoral) woman.

See **omipolone**.

pom n Australian

a native of Britain, especially an Englishman. The word is a shortening of the earlier **pommy**.

pomgolia n

an alternative form of **pongolia**.

pommy, pommie n, adj Australian

(a) British (person). The standard and usually derogatory slang term for natives of or immigrants from the British Isles, pommy is probably a corruption of 'pomegranate', chanted as a humorous semi-rhyme for 'immigrant'. The epithet has been in use since the first decade of the 20th century. The noun is now probably more common in the form **pom**.

ponce n British

1 a pimp, procurer. This sense of the word was first recorded in the late 19th century.

2 a an ostentatious, effeminate male.
b a parasite, 'sponger', idler.

Ponce derives either from the standard English pounce, or possibly from the French pensionnaire, in the sense of non-paying guest. In its first and literal sense, ponce is virtually standard English (used by the police force among others). The following senses are terms of contempt directed at individuals thought to be showy, smugly idle or parasitic.

ponce (off someone) vb British

to take advantage (of), borrow or cadge (from). A widespread usage derived from the noun.

● 'Can I ponce a fag off you?'

ponce around/about vb British

to behave in a showy and/or irresponsible manner. A usage based on the noun, **ponce**.

ponced-up adj British

smartly dressed or overdressed. From the noun **ponce** (pimp, idler or show-off).

pong vb, n British

(to) stink. The word is of uncertain origin but may derive from a similar Romany (gypsy) verb.

pong n Australian

an oriental. A racist epithet, either based on **pongo**, or imitating the sound of oriental speech.

pongo n

1 a black man, a coloured person, a foreigner. A patronizingly derogatory middle-class term used, for example, in public-school and army speech.

2 a soldier. A pre-World-War I term still in use. It probably derives from the pet name of a monkey or dog to whom soldiers or their uniforms were likened.

3 an English person; an Australian

and New Zealand slang term derived from the previous sense of the word.

pongolia, pomgolia n
Australia and New Zealand

the UK, Britain. Jocular terms based on **pom** and **pongo** and punning on Mongolia (evoking the notion of a distant and barbaric country).

poo n British

a nursery term for excrement that has passed into standard colloquial English.

2 champagne. A **yuppie** and **Sloane Ranger** abbreviation of **shampoo**.

• '*You're getting good at this. Extra poo tonight.*'
(*Serious Money*, play by Caryl Churchill, 1987).

pooch n

a dog. This well-known term, particularly well-established in the USA, is of mysterious origin. Possible etymologies are from a dialect version of pouch (alluding to a dog's insatiable desire to 'tuck away' food) or from a term of endearment, possibly the German *putzi*.

• '*Podgy Chas Clark, son of ex-Chancellor Nigel Lawson's financial guru Sir William Clark, called his pooch Charlie – a nickname for cocaine.*'
(*News of the World*, 29 October 1989).

poodle-faker

an effete, over-refined or offensively genteel young man, specifically a young man in attendance on older ladies. Faker here implies insincerity and poodle the attitude or appearance of a lapdog. The word appeared in Britain in the second decade of the 20th century.

poof, pouff, poove, poofter, pooftah, puff n

a male homosexual. The most common slang term in Britain and Australia. The variations of the word go in and out of fashion. Poof and poove were popular in the 1960s, poofter in the 1970s. The origin of the epithet is obscure and the subject of argument. Possibilities include 'pouff!' as a supposedly affected exclamation of disdain, or a Northern English pronunciation of 'puff', which itself could be a dialect exclamation of disgust, a reference to puffed-up with pride, or a Victorian term for a sodomite. It might equally be inspired by the 'puff' of 'powder puff', or the French words *pouffe*; a stuffed seat and *pouffer (de rire)*; giggle.

poofy, puffy adj British

(of men) effeminate, homosexual. From the noun form **poof**.

poon, poontang n American

1 the female pudenda.

2 women in general, seen as sexual objects. The word is from Louisiana French in which it is a corruption of *putain* (the standard French term for **whore**), first applied to black women.

• '*I guess this means my poon days are over.*'
(Remark widely attributed to John F Kennedy following his inauguration as US president, 1960).

poop n, vb

excrement, **crap**. A nursery word used humorously by adults and in the phrases poop-scoop, a small lidded shovel used to clear up dog-droppings, and **hot poop**, the latest news or gossip, the newest fashion. Poop is heard all over the anglophone community but is particularly prevalent in the USA. It has existed since the time of Middle English and the same word has been used with the same meaning in Dutch. Poo-poo is a synonym.

poop catchers n pl

See cack-catchers.

pooped, pooped out adj

exhausted, out of breath. The word is probably an imitation of the sound of puffing and blowing, although there is a theory that it derives from British sailors' slang for a ship being swamped by a 'poop' wave. In its current sense originally a North American term, it spread to Australia and Britain in the 1960s.

- 'Too pooped to pop.'
- 'Can't I stop [skating] now, I'm pooped.'

(For Your Eyes Only, British film, 1981).

pooper n

See party pooper.

poo-poo

See poop.

poot n, vb

(to) fart. Originally an echoic nursery word, probably originating in the USA, poot has achieved prominence in the vogue for references to flatulence in adolescent humour of the late 1980s (epitomized by Viz magazine). In American usage poot may also mean excrement.

- 'Ronnie helping Kenny helping burn his poots away!'

('Let's Make the Water Turn Black', written by Frank Zappa and recorded by the Mothers of Invention, 1967).

poove n British

a version of poof which was current in the early 1960s.

poovy adj

a version of poofy which was current in the early 1960s.

pop vb

1 British to pawn. The word has had this meaning since the 18th century.

See pop one's clogs, popshop.

2 a to take (an illicit drug) orally. The expression refers particularly to amphetamines or barbiturates rather than hallucinogenics such as LSD or hard drugs such as heroin.

b to inject a narcotic. The word is used more often in connection with intramuscular than intravenous injection, often in the specific forms skin-pop and joy pop.

3 to hit, punch.

- 'He popped him one in the eye.'

4 to give birth.

- 'Has she popped yet?'

5 to have sex with or to achieve orgasm. This usage of the word is long-established, pre-dating for instance pop one's rocks.

6 to kill. An underworld euphemism.

pop a vein vb American

to become apoplectic with anger. A children's equivalent of 'burst a blood vessel', applied to and about furious adults.

pop it vb

to die. The phrase is heard in Britain and Australia.

pop one's clogs vb British

to die. A humorous, sometimes incongruously light-hearted phrase popular for example with TV presenters, disc jockeys and other entertainers. 'Pop' here is probably the old slang word for pawn, the suggestion being that when the family member dies, his or her clogs are sold.

pop one's rocks vb

to achieve orgasm, ejaculate. A version of **get one's rocks off** which was briefly a vogue expression in the early 1970s. Pop has been used in a sexual sense at least since the 19th century. (An American synonym is 'pop one's cookies'.)

poppers n pl

amyl nitrite capsules. This strong stimulant drug, prescribed to relieve angina pectoris, comes in glass phials which are broken under the nose and sniffed. The drug was taken for pleasure in the 1960s and 1970s and later specifically for its supposed effects as an enhancer of sexual pleasure by the **gay** community in the 1970s and 1980s.

poppy n British

money. A word from the working-class speech of London. It may refer either to the 'gaudy' attractiveness of cash or banknotes or to **pop** in the sense of pawn. The term is in only limited circulation and has not as yet featured in the revival of archaic synonyms for money which began in the late 1980s.

popshop n British

a pawnshop, pawnbrokers. This old London term, first recorded in the 18th century, was almost obsolete when revived as the name of a television programme in 1988.

porcelain n

See **point percy at the porcelain, pray to the porcelain god**.

pork vb American

to have sexual intercourse (with someone). A college students' word that has been widely used in films in the 1980s. It probably derives from the earlier **pork sword** and **dork**.

• 'He claims to be porking her.'

porker n

1 a fat person. From the use of **pig** to mean glutton.

2 a police officer. This is a later development from **pig**, used for instance by anarchists, squatters and late-1980s **hippies**.

pork pie, porky pie, porky n British

a lie, untruth. A piece of rhyming slang from London working-class speech that surfaced suddenly in the playground and the media and became widely popular at the end of the 1970s.

• 'I think you'll be finding that William's been telling porky-pies again.'
(Recorded, secretary, London, 1986).

• 'You wouldn't be tellin' me porkies would you, son?'
(Minder, British TV series, 1987).

pork sword n

penis. A term used particularly by American college students on the same lines as **mutton dagger** or **beef bayonet**.

porridge n British

a term of imprisonment. Leaden, grey, institutional porridge is evoked as an image of the general deprivations of prison life, but is probably in origin a pun on **stir**. This underworld term was given wider currency by its use as the title of a BBC TV comedy series, starring Ronnie Barker.

posse n

a Jamaican a criminal gang or secret society. The self-dramatizing term, from western movies, was adopted in the 1970s to describe **yardies**. It became known through their overseas activities in Britain and the USA in the 1980s.

b a youth gang. The word was adopted in urban Britain by teenagers in the late 1980s.

postie n

a postman, mailman. A shortening that is heard in Britain and Australia.

pot n

1 cannabis. This 1950s term was considered old-fashioned by drug users by the early 1960s, but was adopted by critics and commentators in the press to refer to hashish and marihuana. This use of the word originated in North America in the early years of the 20th century but its etymology is unknown. Some authorities claim a derivation from an obscure Mexican term for the drug (*potiguaya* or *potaguaya*), others that there is a connection with the use of **tea** as a nickname for marihuana, or that it is a deformation of **pod**, an attested synonym.

- '*I do not advocate legislation of pot, merely because I dread the inevitable hassle of commercialism.*'
  (Letter to *Oz* magazine, June 1969).
- '*But it didn't stop singer Barry Gibb smoking pot at his baby brother's funeral.*'
  (*News of the World*, 15 May 1988).

2 a pot belly.

- '*He's got a bit of a pot on him.*'

potato-head n

a a person with coarse or indistinct features.

b a stupid person. 'Mr Potato-head' was a children's toy popular during the 1970s. It consisted of a set of plastic parts to stick into a potato.

potato peeler n Australian

a woman. The term, usually used in full, is rhyming slang for **sheila**.

pothead n

an habitual smoker of cannabis (hashish or marihuana). An early 1960s term which was out of fashion by the late 1960s, save in whimsical or ironical usage.

potter n British

a Jew. A piece of London rhyming slang from 'pot o' glue', rarely heard, but always occurring in the shortened form.

potty adj British

eccentric, slightly mad, impractical. A (usually) affectionate epithet deriving from crackpot (which itself derives from 'crack-pate'), typically used by middle-class schoolchildren in the 1950s and 1960s and now a rather dated colloquialism.

pouff n

an alternative spelling of **poof**.

pound, the pound n Australian

a solitary-confinement cell or wing in a prison. A term employed in the Australian television cult drama series, *Prisoner: Cell Block H*.

pound one's pork/pudding/meat/weenie, etc. vb

(of a male) to masturbate.

pox, the pox n

venereal disease. Originally referring to syphilis, pox is a variant form of 'pocks' (as in pock-marks) meaning pustules and itself related to pocket.

poxy adj British

very bad, worthless, inferior. Originally signifying diseased, from the use of **pox** to mean syphilis, poxy is now a fairly strong (mainly working-class) term of contempt.

P.R. n American

a Puerto Rican. The abbreviation is usually heard in a derogatory context.

pram n

See **out of one's pram**.

prang vb, n British

(to) crash. A word, used in the context of motoring, which has moved from echoic air-force slang of the 1940s to become a common colloquialism of the 1970s and 1980s.

prannet n British

a fool. A term which enjoyed a vogue in the late 1970s. Prannet looks like a blend of **prat** and **gannet**, both widespread terms of mild abuse. However, it is probably a form of a much earlier word (also seen in the form **pranny**) denoting buttocks and the female pudenda.

pranny, prannie n British

a fool. Variant (and possibly earlier) forms of **prannet**.

prat, pratt n British

1 a backside, buttocks. A word dating from the 16th century or earlier which is currently an inoffensive if rare synonym for **bum**, etc. (encountered in the compound 'pratfall').

b the vagina. This sense of the term is an extension of the preceding, it has been rare since the 1960s.

2 a fool, idiot, buffoon. A sharp, but not obscene term of criticism or abuse, in vogue in the 1980s. The word denotes extreme foolishness and is derived in the same way as the synonymous **arse** or **twat** from the previous senses of the term.

● 'Anyone who bought a futon from the Nagasaki Futon Company should return this to the shop immediately as a serious design fault could result in the owner looking like a stupid prat.'
(Great Bus Journeys of the World, Alexei Sayle, 1988).

prat about vb British

to behave stupidly or irresponsibly, to do things in a disorganized, messy way. From the noun, **prat**.

prawn n

See **come the raw prawn**.

pray to the porcelain god vb

to vomit.

preggers adj

pregnant. Originally an upper- or middle-class expression using the Oxbridge and public school termination '-ers'.

preppie, preppy n American

a a student or ex-student of an American preparatory school. The term was popularized by Erich Segal in his bestselling novel Love Story. American prep schools (as opposed to the British version which educates boys from 8 to 13) prepare teenage boys for higher education.

b a young person embodying the values, manners and dress of upper-class America. The preppy is roughly the equivalent of the British **Sloane Ranger**.

● 'He is variously described as "Ivy League" or "preppy" and he is instantly recognizable by his blue button-down Oxford cloth shirt, navy blazer, club tie and penny loafers. He might be viewed as an American Hooray Henry, except that he is quietly-spoken, excessively polite and never throws muffins.'
(Independent, 12 March 1988).

previous *adj British*

premature, impetuous, presumptuous. A term of mild disapproval favoured by London working-class speakers and members of the police force, usually in the phrase '*a bit previous*'.

previous *n British*

a criminal record, previous convictions. A shortening adopted by police officers and the underworld, usually in the phrase '*has he/she got any previous?*'.

prick *n*

1 penis. The Oxford English Dictionary records the first use of the term in 1592; it was probably extant in the spoken language for some time before. Prick was probably coined with the image of a thorn in mind, from the shape and the image of penetration evoked. In the 20th century while it is in 'polite company' the least acceptable of the many terms (**cock**, **tool**, etc.) for the male member, it is nevertheless commonly used, together with **dick**, by women in preference to those alternatives.

2 a fool, obnoxious or contemptible male.

● '"He's a rude prick who's suing Val Hennessy for libel," I said. "That's a bloody scandal," he said, and told everyone to shut up. "Do any of you layabouts know a rude prick called Bolloms?" he shouted. No one did.'
(William Donaldson writing in the Independent, 26 August 1989).

● 'Freddie isn't exactly Mr Popular down at the HQ ("Some of my chaps think you're a bit of a prick," admits his Commander).'
(*Today*, 19 March 1988).

prick-tease, prick-teaser *n*

a potential sex partner who excites sexual arousal without allowing consummation. This phenomenon, usually in the context of male-female encounters, is paralleled by the French *chauffe-cul* and the synonymous **cock-tease, cock-teaser** in English.

primo *adj*

first class. (From the Spanish for first.) **El primo** is an alternative version.

Pringle *n British*

a young male working-class member of a late 1970s and early 1980s social sub-group characterized by wearing designer-label sports clothing and including so-called 'football hooligans' and **casuals**. (Pringle is the brand name of a variety of expensive and typically pastel-coloured woollen sweaters.)

privates *n pl*

genitals, 'private parts'. A euphemistic or humorous term.

prod *n British*

a Protestant. Prot is an Australian alternative version.

prole *n British*

a proletarian, member of the 'lower' classes. A contemptuous term employed by overt snobs or, ironically or self-deprecatingly, by the 'proles' themselves.

prong *n*

penis.

prot

See **prod**.

prune *n British*

a foolish person. A mild term of childish abuse, employing one of the less appetizing elements on the typical family and/or school-dinner menus of the 1950s and 1960s.

pseud n British

a pseudo-intellectual, pretentious or 'bogus' individual. A buzzword of 1962 and 1963, largely because of its frequent use in *Private Eye* magazine. The word, originating among public-school (it was current at Shrewsbury around 1960, where some of the founders of *Private Eye* were educated) and Oxbridge speakers, epitomized the focus of contempt of hearty sportsmen, 'establishment' conformists and genuine intellectuals alike. *Pseud's Corner* in *Private Eye* is a long-running column, reprinting instances of pretentiousness.

psych (oneself) up vb

to work oneself into a state of mental alertness, aggression, intensity. The phrase originated in the USA (probably in the context of self-expression or therapy groups) in the early 1970s.

● *'In fact his [the footballer Vinny Jones] disturbing habit of psyching himself up before a game by screaming, kicking doors and head-butting dressing-room walls is causing team-mates increasing concern.'*
(*News of the World*, 12 February 1989).

psych (someone) out vb

to unnerve, outmanoeuvre or overwhelm. An Americanism which has spread to other areas, psych out originally meant to use psychology to gauge an opponent's weakness.

psychedelic adj

mind-expanding, hallucinatory. A scientific term invented to describe the effect of hallucinogenic drugs such as LSD, mescaline, psilocybin, etc., and

subsequently applied to music, illustration, design, etc., evoking these effects. The term (from the Greek *psyche*, soul, and *udeloun*, to show) was parodied by American schoolchildren as psy-cadillac.

P.T. n British

1 prick-tease. A pun on the school subject physical-training.
2 See **Egyptian PT**.

pudding

See **pull one's pud/pudding**.

pudding club n

See **in the club**.

puff n

1 an alternative spelling of **poof**.
2 *British* life. In humorous working-class speech the notion of 'breath of life' has given rise to this usage. It is probably most prevalent in Northern English conversation.
● *'Budgie never had a winner in his puff.'*
(*Budgie*, British TV series, 1971).
● *'Never in all my born puff.'*
(*Coronation Street*, British TV series, 1989).

puff-bucket n American

a braggart or 'wind-bag'. A mild term of abuse denoting a loquacious or pompous individual.

puffy n British

cannabis. This innocent-sounding nursery term, playing upon puffs of smoke, is used typically as a code word by users and dealers.
● *'There's no news on the puffy front – my friend's friend is still out in Morocco.'*
(Recorded, drug dealer, London, 1987).

puke vb

to vomit. An echoic expression pre-dating Shakespeare's reference to 'an infant mewling and puking'.

pukka adj British

authentic, first-rate. A word adopted from the Hindi pakka (meaning sub stantial) for use in the Anglo-Indian speech of the colonial era.

puky, pukey adj

disgusting, sickening, awful. An ad-olescent usage based on the ancient verb to **puke**.

pull vb British

1 to 'pick up' a member of the oppo-site sex. A common term applied to males searching for sexual partners, since the late 1960s when it was usual-ly part of a phrase such as 'pull a bird' or 'pull a chick'. In current working-class usage predatory males are said to be **on the pull**. (Pull is now part of the homosexual as well as heterosexual lexicon and women also use the ex-pression.)

2 to arrest or take into custody. A po-lice jargon usage.

pull a stroke vb British

to succeed in a clever manoeuvre, ef-fect a trick or deception. 'Stroke' is a common colloquialism for move, ploy or action.

pullet n British

a young male who is a passive homo-sexual partner or victim of an older man. A version of **chicken**, the more widespread term for an underage sexu-al partner.

- 'Tricker calls them pullets – young chickens – which is gay slang for boys game for sex. He said: "Through the job, I can meet loads of pullets and pick up their phone numbers".'

(News of the World, 7 May 1989).

pull finger vb New Zealand

to get a move on, stop dawdling, in-crease efficiency. A brusque shorten-ing of **pull one's finger out**.

- 'OK, it's time to pull finger and get moving.'

pulling power n British

sexual attraction, the ability to at-tract and/or 'pick up' members of the opposite sex. The term, from the verb **pull**, is usually applied to males.

pull (oneself/someone) off vb

to masturbate oneself or someone else. A term used invariably of men, now dated.

pull one's finger out vb

to stop dawdling, get a move on, in-crease efficiency. Often heard as an im-perative addressed by an authority fig-ure to an idling or incompetent subordinate, this is now a relatively re-spectable term, used by the middle classes and middle-aged. It was in ori gin a vulgarism, the location of the of-fending digit being variously ascribed to one's own anus or another's sexual parts.

pull one's pud/pudding vb British

(of a man) to masturbate. The word pudding has been used with various connotations in a sexual context (pe-nis, semen, pregnancy, etc.) since the 16th century.

pull someone's jacket vb American

1 to **feel someone's collar**.

2 to withdraw someone's file or dos-sier (**jacket** in office jargon) in order to consult, amend or destroy it. Both

407

senses of the word occur in law enforcement jargon.

pull the plug *vb*

to commit suicide. An unsentimental euphemism, from the colloquial sense of the phrase meaning to abort (a venture).

- '*Kathy was eleven when she pulled the plug, on 26 reds and a bottle of wine.*'
  (Lyrics to 'People who died', Jim Carrol, 1981).

pump *vb*

1 *British* to **fart**. A children's term adopted by adults and now appearing in print in such publications as Viz magazine.

2 *American* to have sex (with). A vulgarism usually heard in the catchphrase '*pump 'em and dump 'em*', a male expression of the late 1980s.

pumps *n pl British*

tennis shoes, trainers. Like **daps** and **bumpers**, this is typically a schoolchildren's term.

punctured *adj British*

drunk. A light-hearted term.

punk *n*

1 a bumptious but insignificant or contemptible person. This sense of the word has been well-established in American English since the 19th century referring typically to a youth, particularly a presumptuous or irritating one, or to a petty criminal or gangster. The word originated in British slang around the end of the 17th century when it was used to denote a **whore** and later a precursor of the modern **rent boy**. In the 20th century the term punk fell out of use in Britain, being reintroduced via the American media and later by way of the punk phenomenon of 1976 and 1977.

- '*The play-house Puncks, who in a loose undress*
  Each night receive some Cullie's soft address . . . '
  (*Poor Pensive Punck*, poem by John Dryden, 1691).
- '*At midnight when each Buck was drunk*
  And each had got his roving punk . . . '
  (*Buck's Midnight Ramble*, a London pamphlet published in 1774).

2 an adherent of a youth sub-culture first coalescing in 1976 around punk rock music. Punk rock was so called because of the callow, defiant poses and amateurish musicianship of its proponents. Led by American groups such as the Ramones and the British band the Sex Pistols, punk rock became the musical vogue of 1977, accompanied by a self-consciously nihilistic and pessimist attitude and imagery, spikey and mohican hairstyles, safety pins and chains, etc. While the first wave of the phenomenon metamorphosed into other subcults (neo-**mods**, **goths** and **grebos**, etc.), later imitators perpetuated punk in a frozen iconography. It now forms part of modern British folklore, much in the same way as the **teddy boy** image persists.

punkette *n*

a young female **punk** (rocker).

punter *n British*

a a gambler, speculator. Coming from the terminology of card games, punt was transferred to the context of horseracing, then to betting in general in the 19th century. In the late 1980s it was used for example of small investors or share purchasers. The term enjoys continuing popularity.

b a customer or client. The sense of punter as gambler was extended to refer to anyone paying money for a service or item. First specifically applied to prostitutes, and street-trader's customers, punter became a key word in the market-oriented 1980s.

purple hearts n pl

amphetamine tablets. The phrase referred to purple or blue coloured tablets of amphetamines, barbiturate or a mixture of the two as prescribed and abused in the USA in the late 1950s. (The 'purple heart' was a medal awarded for bravery.) In Britain the word was adopted in the early 1960s as a generic term for **pep pills**, **speed**.

push n Australian

a gang of **larrikins**. The word was recorded in the 1880s and evokes the image of a band of street toughs shouldering people out of the way as they walk down the street.

push vb

to sell illegal drugs, especially when the sale involves coercion.

pusher n

a supplier of illicit drugs, especially addictive drugs. The word implies that the seller uses coercion or tries to lead people into addiction in order to profit from them (if this is not the case, **dealer** is the alternative). The term is now used by police, journalists, parents, etc. and only rarely by drug users or sellers.

puss n

1 American face, mouth. A word often used in compounds such as 'sour puss' and 'glamour-puss', puss was a favourite word of pugilists and 'tough guys' in the earlier 20th century. It derives from the Irish Gaelic pus, mouth.

- 'He told her if she didn't shut up he'd give her a sock in the puss.'

2 **pussy** (in all its senses).

pussy, pussycat n

1 the female genitals. A cause of many double entendres and minor embarrassments, this usage of the word derives from the resemblance of pubic hair to fur, perhaps reinforced by male notions of affection. (The French equivalent is chatte, virtually a literal translation.) Pussy or **puss** was first recorded in the sexual sense in the 16th century.

2 women viewed as sex objects. An unromantic male term used in the same indiscriminate manner as **tail**, **ass**, etc. In this generic sense, the term may be expressed as pussy, 'some pussy' or occasionally 'a piece of pussy'.

- 'He did not think he had ever been "in love" ... You fancied a bit of pussy ... and you tried your luck.'
- 'I hate to say it but I understand in London there's a lot of pussy over there.'
  (US police officer, Sunday Times colour supplement, 1 January 1967).

3 also **pussycat** a weak, harmless male, a timid person. A word which probably originated in the boxers' lexicon to describe the feeble, patting punches of a loser.

- 'He's a pussy, Frank.'
  'Yeah, but he's our pussy.'
  (Blue Velvet, US film, 1986).

4 fur(s). In underworld argot.

5 a coquettish or 'kittenish' female, in lesbian parlance.

pussy-whipped adj

'hen-pecked'. An American vulgarism probably inspired by the western cliché 'pistol-whipped'. **Pussy** is a long-established term for the female genitals or women in general.

put (someone) down vb

to snub, humiliate or belittle. A vogue term among British **beatniks** in the early 1960s, adopted from American street slang.

- 'Evil hearted you, you always try to put me down, with the things you do and the words you spread around . . .'
  (Lyrics to 'Evil-hearted You', the Yardbirds, 1965).
- 'Why are we American teenagers hated so much? Every time we pick up an English magazine the teens are putting us down.'
  (Reader's letter, Rave magazine, February 1965).

putdown n

a snub or humiliation. A back-formation from the verb to **put (someone) down**.

- 'Being left off the guest list was the ultimate putdown.'

put-on n

a deception, fraud, cheat. A back-formation (with slightly changed emphasis) from the verb to **put someone on** (although Partridge cites instances of the expression in Victorian use).

put one on someone vb

to hit, punch. An aggressive euphemism which is also rendered by **lay**, or **hang one on** someone.

- 'One of my colleagues said that he felt like "putting one on" the attendant for the way he treated the child.'
  (Inside the British Police, Simon Holdaway, 1983).

put one's hands up vb

to surrender, give in, confess. A euphemism popular among the British police and underworld.

- 'It was brilliant. He couldn't believe it. He had to put his hands up. Yes I did that one by subterfuge.'
  (Police officer quoted in Inside the British Police, Simon Holdaway, 1983).

put someone away vb British

to kill. A euphemism employed by underworld or would-be underworld figures.

- 'When I told him he went spare – he threatened to put the guy away.'

put someone on vb

to tease, mock or deceive (someone). This American usage spread to Britain in the later 1960s as a synonym for kid, fool or **con**. It is now usually heard in the phrase 'you're putting me on!'.

put the bite on vb

to pressurize someone, especially for a loan or repayment of money owed, or as part of a campaign of intimidation. This expression seems to have originated in North American usage early in the 20th century.

put the boot in vb British

a to kick (someone). An expression used by **skinheads** of the late 1960s as part of their repertoire (along with **aggro**, **bother** and **put the nut on**).

b to attack someone figuratively, particularly when they are already under attack, vulnerable or incapacitated.

put the frighteners on (someone) vb British

to menace, threaten or intimidate. An underworld and police expression employing a familiar form of words (as in **put the bite/kybosh/mockers on**).

put the kybosh/kibosh on vb

to frustrate, ruin, prevent, jeopardize. Many conflicting and often far-fetched etymologies have been suggested for this phrase, first recorded in the 1830s meaning to defeat. Its ultimate origin remains obscure.

put the mockers on vb British

to frustrate or jeopardize (someone's plans), to curse with bad luck. This old phrase was last popular in the 1960s, but is still heard occasionally. It almost certainly originates in the Yiddish mockers, curse or bad luck, from the Hebrew maches, plague.

put the nut on vb British

to butt (someone) with the head. A form of the verb to **nut**, used, like the tactic, by brawlers, **skinheads**, etc. **Stick the nut on (someone)** is an alternative rendering.

putz n American

a foolish, clumsy or unfortunate person. The word is the Yiddish for 'ornament' used as a synonym for the male member, hence **prick**. Despite its (little-known) origin, putz is a relatively mild term of abuse in English; in Yiddish it still carries more pejorative overtones.

Q

Q.T., q.t. n

See **on the q.t.**

quack n, adj

a doctor. This usually lightheartedly pejorative term originated in the 17th century when it referred to a peddler of spurious cures. It is a shortening of 'quacksalver' which is composed of quack (give one's verbal 'patter'), and salve (save, soothe or cure), and is a pun on quicksilver.

quackers n British

(a) duck. A generic nickname used by **green welly** or **Sloane Ranger** hunters.

● 'Going in search of quackers.'

quail n

a girl, young woman, or females viewed as sex objects. This equating of the female with the game bird is approximately three hundred years old, surviving in the language of American high-school and college students, where predatory males also talk of going out 'loaded for quail' (ready or equipped for seduction).

quandong n Australian

a woman. The quandong fruit (*santalum acuminatus*) is fleshy with a hard seed centre; the word has thus been appropriated to refer to women with supposedly similar qualities – either prostitutes or friendly females who refuse to be seduced.

quarter-to-two n British

a Jew. A less common rhyming-slang alternative to **four-by-two**.

quean n British

the earlier spelling of **queen**, meaning an effeminate homosexual. This spelling coexisted with queen until the early 1960s when it virtually disappeared. Quean was a descendant of Old and Middle English words related to (but not derived from) queen, stemming ultimately from an Indo-European ancestor, *gwena*, meaning woman. Over 1,000 years the senses of quean shifted from 'woman' to 'wanton', before being transferred to a male context.

queen n, vb

an (effeminate) homosexual. The word **quean** signified a **whore** in early 19th-century slang. This appellation was transferred to male prostitutes (often transvestite) and thence to male homosexuals in general. The use of the word is obviously reinforced by its colloquial use to mean an imperious or ostentatious (older) woman. In the **gay** environment of the 1970s and 1980s queen has been used to refer specifically to individuals who are affected in manner, elderly and/or consciously effeminate.

● 'And he's just a go-getting queen. He's interested in you purely because of your plays.'
(Kenneth Halliwell, quoted in Joe Orton's Diary, 2 May 1967, 1986).

queer n, adj

(a) homosexual. Until the 19th century queer denoted odd or curious, as it still does in standard English. Its use as first a euphemism, then a slang synonym for homosexual arose between the World Wars, probably first in the USA. Since the advent of the neutral term **gay** and pejorative terms such as **bent**, queer has been relegated to the role of a somewhat dated term of disapproval. (The 1980 pop song 'Johnny are you queer?' by Josie Cotton was banned by several US radio stations under pressure from gay groups.) Queer ultimately derives from quer, a German word meaning crooked or awry.

● 'You can't expect to pick up a young post-office worker and his middle-aged keeper, and burst into tears because the keeper is queer.' (Joe Orton's Diary, 2 May 1967, 1986).

queer-basher n

a hooligan or thug who preys on male homosexuals; by extension, anyone who is violently critical of homosexuals. A term from the late 1960s still in use at present.

● 'There is a chilling Hampstead dinner-party, where one of the guests reveals himself to be a full blooded queer-basher, to the embarrassment of his hostess.' (Book review, Independent, 12 May 1988).

queer-bashing n British

the attacking, intimidation or **mugging** of male homosexuals. A practice indulged in by **teddy boys** and later **skinheads**, among others. The term has more recently been extended to denote verbal aggression or prejudice against **gays**.

queer-rolling n British

the robbing of homosexual males. A practice which was particularly prevalent in the late 1950s and early 1960s when homosexuality itself was illegal and **gay** victims rarely dared to report the crime.

queer street n British

bankruptcy, financial difficulties or ruin. The term is a corruption or nickname of Carey Street (location of the bankruptcy courts in London) influenced by queer in the sense of awry.

● 'The way things are going we'll end up in queer street.'

quiche out vb British

to eat very greedily or to excess. A probably ephemeral **Sloane Ranger** or **yuppie** version of **pig out**.

quickie n

a hurried or short-lived sex act.

quid n

a pound sterling. The word was first used to refer to a guinea, then a sovereign, later to the sum of one pound. The origin of the word (it arose in the 17th century) is obscure. Partridge suggests 'what' (quid in Latin) as a synonym for 'wherewithal'. An equally plausible derivation is from quid pro quo, alluding to the words on older banknotes, 'I promise to pay the bearer the sum of . . . '

quidlet n British

a pound (sterling). A jocular diminutive form of **quid**, used particularly by middle- and upper-class speakers. The word was first heard in the early 1970s, but did not become established until the mid 1980s.

quidlets n pl British

money, pounds sterling. A humorous version of **quid** using the diminutive suffix -let.

413

quiff n

1 *British* a pompadour hairstyle, kiss-curl or backcombed fringe. The quiff was fashionable among **teddy boys** and **rockers** among others.

2 *British* a male homosexual or effeminate male. The usage is probably influenced by the words **queer** and **poof**.

3 a **fart**.

4 *American* a prostitute or promiscuous woman.

quill n American

the cover of a book of matches folded to hold cocaine, heroin, methedrine, etc. for sniffing. A term from the drug users' lexicon.

quim n British

the female sex organs. A taboo term featuring in 19th-century pornography and the 20th-century lexicon of obscenity. The word has probably lost popularity since the 1950s, although it remains in use, invariably among males, particularly outside the southeast of the country. The exact origin of quim is unclear. It may be related to the Chaucerian queynte (vagina) or the Welsh *cwm* (valley or crevice).

quince n Australian

a male homosexual or effeminate male. The word is probably a blend of **queen** and 'mince'. It may also be derived from the Asian fruit of the same name.

quoit n Australian

anus. A coinage inspired by the earlier **ring**.

R

raas n Jamaican

an all-purpose term of abuse or exclamation of anger or contempt. A version of (up) (your) **arse** or a short form of **raasclat**.

Compare **yass**.

raasclat, rassclaat n Jamaican

a term of strong abuse used as an insult or as an exclamation. The word literally means a rag for wiping the backside, the equivalent of the later American insult **ass-wipe**, **raas** being a patois version of (your) **arse** and clat, cloth.

Compare **bloodclat**.

rabbit vb, n

(to) talk, gossip, (have a) conversation. The term is cockney rhyming slang, from 'rabbit and pork': talk. The word gained widespread currency through TV comedies of the 1970s and the soundtrack to a 1980s advertisement for Courage Best beer. Rabbit (or 'rabbit on') is now often used by middle-class speakers unaware of its rhyming provenance. Genuine cockneys often prefer the derivation **bunny**.

rabbit hutch n British

the groin area, rhyming slang for crotch (generally pronounced as 'crutch' in working-class London speech, of which this is an example).

race off, race vb American

to seduce. A common term in the 1960s. The original image evoked is that of sweeping a victim off her feet and away.

rack n American

a bed. This use of the word is probably of armed-service origin.

rack attack n American

a bout of extreme laziness, a period spent in bed. A campus witticism (other rhyming compounds are **snack attack** and **tack attack**) based on the use of **rack** to mean bed.

racked-off adj Australian

irritated, disgruntled. An expression ranking in vehemence somewhere between 'cheesed-off' and **pissed-off**.

racked-up adj American

tense, stressed, **strung up**. An expression heard occasionally since the 1970s.

• 'I remember my first shoot. You know I was really racked-up but the lieutenant was there for me.'
(Miami Vice, US TV series, 1988).

rack off vb Australian

to go away, leave. A brusque, but less offensive alternative to **piss off**, **fuck off**, etc. The phrase, usually in the form of an admonition, has been introduced to a British audience via Australian soap operas of the late 1980s, such as Neighbours.

rack (out) vb American

to lie down and/or go to sleep. An expression now used principally by teenagers and college students, but which originates in the armed-service slang noun **rack**, meaning bed.

rad adj American

excellent, outstanding, admirable. A shortening of **radical**, used as a term of great approbation by school and college children in the late 1970s. It is also heard in the UK and Australia in the 1980s where it has become a vogue term especially among the subcultures of surfers and skateboarders.

- '*But the really rad word is still to be had from the skater/authors themselves . . . '*
  (*Mail on Sunday 'Biz' magazine*, June 1987).

radical adj

excellent. The word has moved from its political sense, via 'radical chic' to a generalized meaning in adolescent speech of admirable. It is sometimes shortened to **rad**.

- '*The word "radical", which no longer has rebellious or left-wing connotations but means simply wonderful or remarkable.*'
  (*Independent* magazine, 24 December 1988).

radio rentals adj British

crazy, deranged, **mental**. A humorous expression recorded in 1988, employing an approximate rhyme using the name of a television hire chain.

- '*If you ask me, she's completely radio rentals.*'

rag n

1 a newspaper. Generally a pejorative term.

2 a sanitary towel. Rags were literally used for this purpose until the 20th century.

See also **lose one's rag**, **on the rag**.

rage n Australian

a wild party or celebration. A 1960s expression which is the equivalent of the British **rave-up** and, like that term, undergoing a revival in the late 1980s.

ragged out/up adj American

1 dressed or dressed up. Since the 19th century this term has been used colloquially like 'dolled up' or 'in one's glad rags'. **Ragged up** is an alternative version.

2 distasteful, unpleasant. A teenage and **Valley Girl** expression of the late 1970s.

raggedy-ass, ragged-ass adj American

unkempt, uncouth, disorganized. An elaboration of ragged.

rag-head n

an arab. A pejorative term inspired by the headdress worn particularly by gulf arab males. The term is occasionally applied to turban-wearers, too. An alternative is **towel head**.

raging n British

a 'first'(-class honours degree). Students' rhyming slang of the late 1980s, on 'raging thirst'. **James** and **Pattie** are alternative versions.

- '*He was tipped for a raging, but he ended up with a Desmond.*'

See also **Douglas**, **Hawaii**, **Made-in**, **Richard**, **Taiwan**.

rag-top n

a convertible car. The Americanism has also occasionally been heard in Britain as an alternative for soft-top or the earlier drop-head.

rainbows n pl

any multi-coloured spansules or pills taken by drug abusers.

rainy day woman n American

a **reefer** or **joint**. This colourful phrase, which probably pre-dates Bob Dylan's 1965 song of the same name, is based on the notion of the marihuana providing solace to a lone, housebound male.

rally vb American

to behave outrageously, indulge in wild activity. A **preppie** term, used invariably by and about males.

- 'Come on, let's rally!'
- 'They were really rallying.'

ralph vb

1 to vomit. One of many echoic terms for the activity, ralph is typically heard among students in all English-speaking areas. 'Call (for) Ralph' is another version.

2 also **hang a ralph** American to take a right turn.

ralph n

a right turn. The word is usually part of the phrase **hang a ralph** (as opposed to **hang a louie**).

ram n

a sexually promiscuous or successful male. A rare synonym for **stud**.

ram vb

to have sex (with). A term normally used by or of males with the implication of animal forcefulness or brutish assertiveness.

Ramboid adj

brutally excessive, aggressive and mindlessly **gung-ho**. A pejorative term inspired by the character 'Rambo' interpreted by Sylvester Stallone in the films of the same name.

rambunctious adj

lively, troublesome, loud. A facetious invention elaborated from rumbustious. The term has been in use since the early 19th century and is probably Irish or American in origin, although the invention of such jocularities (as in the 19th-century 'obstrepalous' and the recent 'spondicious') was paralleled in Britain.

- 'This is a lullaby my mother used to play when I'd get rambunctious. It always seemed to calm me down.' (Kindred, US film, 1987).

ramp up vb British

to organize or arrange. The phrase presumably comes from the terminology of car mechanics whence it has been extended in working-class usage (by police officers among others) to mean mounting any sort of operation.

ramrod n

penis.

R and R n

1 relaxation. A piece of armed-services shorthand (for 'rest and recreation') now used by civilians.

2 rock 'n' roll. A short term used by aficionados and the record industry

randy adj British

sexually aroused, lecherous. A word which was formerly considered unsuitable for normal use, but which since the 1960s has been used in the media and in 'respectable' conversation. (Mickey Dolenz of the pop group The Monkees heard the phrase 'randy Scouse git' on the British TV comedy series 'Till death us do part' and used it as the title of a single in 1967. This was deemed too offensive for radio and in Britain the song title was changed). Randy is of uncertain origin. It was first recorded at the end of the 18th century. Two suggested etymologies for the word are: a dialect verb meaning to behave in a wild or wanton manner, and a

Hindi word meaning lustful. Of these, the first (the rarely-recorded word was related to 'rant' and 'random') is the more likely. The use of randy is rare in American English except as a short form of Randolph.

- 'Girls . . . showing their arms in thin, thin frocks (good luck to randy grandfathers).'
  (About Town magazine, June 1962).
- 'Brandy makes you randy but gin makes you sin.'
  (Lyrics to traditional song, interpreted by the Gymslips on the album Rocking with the Renes, 1980).
- 'Randy banker's wife Marilyn Divall revealed last night how an evil conman turned her into his sex slave. The bonking brunette admitted to having an orgy with EIGHT men.'
  (News of the World, 7 May 1989).

rank, rank out vb American

to insult, taunt or provoke. A rather dated usage among adolescents.

ranking adj Jamaican

pre-eminent, powerful, impressive. A code word in Jamaican patois.

ranting n British

a style of stand-up poetry recital which became popular in the post-**punk** milieu of the late 1970s. The poems were characterized in content and delivery by anger and aggression: the principal exponents of the style were Steven 'Seething' Wells and Attila the Stockbroker. The word ranting accurately describes the performance style as well as recalling the name of the sect of 17th-century dissident preachers.

rap n

1 a a conversation, especially an earnest and/or lengthy discussion. A word which became an important part of the counterculture lexicon at the end of the 1960s, rap was originally used by blacks and **beatniks**, deriving from the verb form.

b a rhythmic spoken chant, often to a musical background. This form of (originally) improvized delivery became a vogue first among young blacks in New York and other eastern American cities (inspired by Jamaican **toasting**), and then a worldwide pop phenomenon in the 1980s.

2 an accusation or charge, blame or punishment. An 18th-century British use of the verb rap was to denote swearing an oath against, accusing of, or charging (with a crime). This sense survives, via American English, in the phrase 'take the rap' and 'beat the rap' and the term **rap sheet**.

rap vb

a to talk, converse or discuss. A key term from the **hippy** era which usually denoted an earnest or communal exchange of ideas. The word was first heard in this sense in black American speech; it was subsequently adopted by white **hipsters**, **beatniks** and **hippies** in turn. (Rap was in use in Britain in the late 1960s but in its original sense is now confined to the remnants of **hippy** culture.)

The exact origin of this use of the word is not at all clear; possible etymologies include a shortening of rapid (speech), rapport or repartee. The term might come simply from the similarity between talking and tapping ('rapping') on a drum or other surface; this might fit an origin among jazz musicians. Alternatively, in archaic slang a rapper was someone who 'talked' to the authorities (see the noun form) and this notion may have become generalized in black argot into 'talk'.

b to deliver an (originally improvized) monologue to a musical backing; to perform **rap** music. This musical form of the 1980s originated as a street phenomenon among black youth in American cities in the 1970s.

rapper n

a practitioner or devotee of **rap** music.

rap session n American

a conversation or discussion. A phrase first used in the 1950s by black Americans, **hipsters** and **beatniks**, later taken up by **hippies**, alternative therapists and teenagers.

rap sheet n American

(documentary evidence of) a person's criminal record. The expression has been in use since World War II and derives from the underworld slang noun-form **rap**, meaning arrest or arraignment.

rapt adj

delighted. A vogue term of the late 1980s which seems to have spread from Australia to both Britain and the USA in the **hip** parlance of adolescents. The word is the standard (literary) English term meaning enraptured.
- 'She wasn't exactly rapt when I told her, I can tell you.'

rare adj British

an all-purpose term of approbation, often employed as an exclamation by schoolchildren in the late 1980s. This sense of the word probably originated among black youth-culture in the USA and was transmitted via **rap**, skateboarding terminology, etc. Rare was previously used as a generalized vogue term in this way by **mods** briefly in 1966. It was used as long ago as the 16th century, with sporadic examples in between.

rash adj

wonderful. A term of high apprecia-

tion among American teenagers and aficionados of hip-hop in the 1980s. It is nearly always expressed as 'totally rash' and was coined on the lines of **wild, bad, wicked,** etc.

raspberry n

a farting sound made by blowing through the lips, a **Bronx cheer**. Now an innocent colloquialism heard all over the English-speaking world, it derives from the late 19th-century London rhyming-slang, 'raspberry tart'; **fart**.

raspberry charlotte vb, n
British

(to) vomit. An ephemeral term among middle- and upper-class adolescents in the 1970s, from the name of a cream, custard and fruit dessert.

raspberry (ripple) n British

a cripple. A piece of London rhyming-slang playing on the name of a type of ice cream.

rasta n

a Rastafarian. The word is a shortening of the name of the devotees of Ras Tafari (one of the titles of the late emperor of Ethiopia, Haile Selassie) whose sacrament is **ganja** and who wear **dreadlocks**. The language of the Jamaican movement has influenced English slang mainly via reggae music.

rasta box n

another name for a **ghettoblaster**.

rat-arsed adj

drunk. The terms rat-arsed, **ratfaced** and the milder **ratted** enjoyed a vogue among adolescents and young adults (particularly those from middle- and upper-class backgrounds) from the mid-1980s. Terms employing rat- as a prefix evoking disgust were heard throughout the English-speaking community in the 1980s (see **rat-boy**, **rathole**, **ratshit**, etc.) particularly in Australia and the USA.

ratbag n Australian

a despicable, disreputable or obnoxious person. This term of abuse originated in Australia where it derived either literally from a bag used by a rat-catcher or from the notion of a bag full of rats as the epitome of obnoxiousness. The word became popular in Britain in the early 1960s (helped in no small part by its frequent use in the popular radio comedy-series *Hancock's Half Hour*) and is now often used with a degree of affection. In Australia it often denotes an eccentric.

- '*She's a total ratbag – I don't want to have anything more to do with her.*'
  (*Neighbours*, Australian TV soap opera, 1987).

rat-boy n American

a male 'cop-killer'. An item of police slang inspired by the 1986 horror film of the same name. Rat-boy denotes a supposedly degenerate criminal, typically a delinquent killer of a police officer.

rat-faced adj

drunk. A vogue term of the late 1980s among all social classes in Britain, (particularly heard among **Sloane Rangers** and **yuppies**).

ratfink n American

a treacherous, despicable person. The word is a combination of rat (traitor) and **fink** (informer) and was first used to refer to union blacklegs or **scabs**. It enjoyed a vogue in the 1960s in its more generalized sense and is still used, albeit less widely.

See also **fink**.

rathole, rat-hole n

a disgusting, squalid place. A fashionable expression of distaste in the later 1980s. In 1987 the college lecturers' union NATFHE condemned 'Thatcher's rathole Britain' in a press handout.

rat (on) vb

to inform on or betray (someone). An Americanism employing the familiar identification of a rat with treachery or spite. The phrase was imported into Britain and Australia before World War II.

- '*Rule number one is you don't rat on your friends.*'

rat out vb

to abandon, betray, cravenly withdraw. An Americanism which is also heard in Australia and, to a lesser extent, in Britain. Usages involving the 'rat' components have been in vogue during the 1980s.

- '*She ratted out at the last minute.*'
- '*They ratted out on us.*'

rat-run n British

a side street used for fast commuter traffic. A phrase and phenomenon of the late 1980s.

ratshit adj Australian

worthless, inferior, utterly disappointing. The word (pronounced like 'ratchet') usually expresses bitter disapproval or disillusion.

ratted adj British

drunk. A more polite version of **rat-faced** or **rat-arsed**. All three terms have been in vogue in the second half of the 1980s.

- '*When we were looking for the personification of the Kentucky face, we got so ratted, so drunk . . . for an entire week.*'

(Ralph Steadman, *I-D* magazine, November 1987).

rattlehead n British

someone listening to a personal stereo in a public place, or on public transport. The term refers to the noise leaking from the headphones to the discomfort of fellow passengers. Rattlehead has been heard among adolescents in the later 1980s.

rattler n

1 a surface or underground train. The word has been used in Britain and the USA (where travelling hobos referred to 'hopping a rattler') since the 19th century. Until the late 1950s the London underground system was sometimes known to workmen as the Rattler.

2 British a womanizer, seducer. It derives from the verb form **rattle (someone)**, meaning to have sex with, and like that term is heard mainly in Scotland.

rattle (someone) vb British

to have sex (with someone). The term, which originates in Scotland, has overtones of dry impersonality about the act and is typically used by unsentimental young 'womanizers' and their emulators.

rattle someone's cage vb

to provoke, disturb, rouse. A phrase in mainly working-class usage, like others ('drop off the perch', 'sick as a parrot') using the imagery of a caged bird or animal. The expression usually forms part of a provocative rhetorical question 'who rattled your cage?' addressed to someone suddenly roused to anger or indignation. **Yank (someone around/someone's chain)** is an American alternative.

raunch n

earthiness, eroticism, lust. A less widespread back-formation from the adjective **raunchy**.

raunchy adj

a sexually provocative, earthy, risqué; lustful or lust inducing. The word probably took one of its original meanings, 'ripe' or over-ripe in the metaphorical sense, from the Italian *rancio*, rank or rotten, although a British dialect origin has also been posited. Until the late 1960s raunchy was mainly in American usage. It is now a fairly common colloquialism in all English-speaking areas.

b cheap or slovenly. This exclusively American sense of the word is now old-fashioned. Its origin is the same as the more popular connotation.

rave, rave-up n British

a wild party, dance or occasion of abandoned behaviour. A usage originating in bohemian circles in the late 1950s. In the early 1960s the word was taken up by **mods** and shortly thereafter by the media and the older generation, who still employ the term. More recently still the **acid** youth cult has adopted the word to refer to their (typically large-scale and movable) celebrations, sometimes specified as **orbital raves**, (those within reach of the M25 motorway). By 1990 school children were also using the word as a synonym for party.

raver n British

an unrestrained, hedonistic person. An archetypal 1960s term which originated in the 1950s among bohemians and **beatniks**, when it was applied to frequent attenders of all-night parties and jazz clubs, etc. In the later 1960s the already slightly dated word epitomized **hippy** abandonment to euphoria. Subsequently the word has survived mainly in working-class male usage to refer, rather like **goer**, to wild or promiscuous (usually young) women in expressions such as '*right little raver*'.

- '*Wouldn't it be nice/To get on with me neighbours?/But they make it very clear/They've got no room for ravers.*'
  ('Lazy Sunday', Steve Marriot and Ronnie Lane, recorded by The Small Faces, 1968).

raw meat n

a euphemism for sex organs or sexual activity, heard in the late 1960s and 1970s.

razoo n Australian

a very small sum of money, 'a brass farthing'. A word said to be of Maori origin, used in negative phrases such as '*I haven't got a brass razoo*' or '*without a razoo*'.

razorblade n British

a black person. An unaffectionate rhyming-slang term (based on **spade**) used by police officers among others in the 1970s and 1980s.

razz vb

to tease or deride. A word which is currently more popular in Australia and the USA than Britain (although it features in British public-school argot). Razz was originally a theatrical shortening of **raspberry** and the verb is still used in theatrical parlance to mean jeer. In modern usage it often appears to have overtones common to 'rag', rouse and **roust**.

readies n

cash, banknotes, money. A shorter and racier version of the phrases 'ready cash' or 'ready money'.

- '*It was always the same old story. "I've no money on me. Have you*

any readies, Al?" They must think we're a bit daft up North.'
(*Guardian*, 12 December 1987).

ready, the ready n

money, cash. This is currently a less common form (except in the USA) of the plural **readies**. Ready or the ready was in fact probably the original form of the term, first recorded in the 17th century.

ready-wash n British

crack. A probably ephemeral youth term. It is a native coinage inspired by a jargon term relating to detergent and washing instructions and to the fact that cocaine requires chemical 'washing' in order to produce the more potent **crack**.

- '*In other areas "ready-wash", one of the several British terms for manufactured crack, was less common.*'
(*Guardian*, 5 September 1989).

rear-admiral n American

a proctologist, in nursing slang.

rec n British

a local recreation ground. A significant term among children and teenagers in the 1950s who often congregated in these small urban or suburban gardens or other open spaces for want of organized entertainment.

recce n British

a reconnaissance or reconnoitring. An armed-service shortening (pronounced 'reckie'), which has been generalized in civilian usage to mean a preliminary check or look around.

recco n Australian

recognition, peer-group respect. An abbreviation heard among young adults and adolescents.

record changer n American

a lackey, minion, unskilled menial. A probably ephemeral expression.

● *'How did a record changer like you get a car like that?'*
(*The A Team*, US TV series, 1987).

red biddy n British

cheap red wine or methylated spirits as drunk by tramps or derelicts. Biddy, originally a diminutive of Bridget, was an affectionate name for a woman, preserved in the colloquial term 'old biddy'.

the red-eye n

an early-morning or overnight flight or train service. The expression, which refers to the tired appearance of the passengers, originated in the USA where it was a nickname given to coast-to-coast flights.

red-inker n British

a recorded arrest. A 'score' in the tally of arrests for a particular officer or police station, in the jargon of the police force.

redneck n American

a rustic bigot or boor. This now familiar expression became well known in the late 1960s when it was extended from the original sense of a rural white Southern farmer (with a neck red from being bent to the sun, or from anger) to include all opponents of liberation or the counterculture.

red Ned n Australian

cheap red wine. The Australian version of **red biddy**.

reds, red devils n pl American

capsules of Seconal, a barbiturate used by drug abusers, from the colour of the capsules.

● *'The use of "reds" or barbiturates*

for highs (lows would be more descriptive) seems to be increasing again.'
(Dr Hip Pocrates (Eugene Schoenfeld), 1969).

red sails in the sunset adj

menstruating. A phrase, taken from the title of a popular song, which has been used (almost invariably by men) since the 1960s.

● *'Looks as if she's red sails in the sunset.'*

Red Sea Pedestrian n

a Jew. A jocular euphemistic phrase invented by the Australian comic and writer, Barry Humphries.

reeb n British

beer in **backslang**. A word which was heard in the 1950s and which survives in limited use (among young market-workers for instance).

reef n

a short form of **reefer** still used by American teenagers.

reefer n

a a marihuana cigarette, an earlier term for **joint**. A word which fell out of favour with cannabis smokers in the late 1950s but which was perpetuated by the media and law enforcement agencies.
b marihuana. A famous and risible American anti-drug film of 1936 was entitled *Reefer Madness*. In origin the word is a corruption of *grifa*; the Spanish slang for marihuana.

reen n British

an alternative spelling of **rene**.

re-entry n American

in the parlance of LSD users, the return to normality after the effects of an

LSD **trip** have worn off. A term briefly popular in the mid- and late 1960s, derived from the jargon of space exploration.

reffo n Australian

a refugee. An unaffectionate term for an immigrant (typically a European fleeing Nazi or Soviet repression).

reggies n pl British

aircraft spotters. This term is an abbreviation of registration number or registration mark.

rego n Australian

a (car) registration. A typical Australian diminutive or familiar form (pronounced 'redge-oh').

reject n

a term of abuse popular among British schoolchildren in the 1980s.

rello n Australian

a relative, relation.
- 'We're having the rellos over.'

rene, reen, renee n British

a young female working-class Londoner. The term was used (and perhaps coined) by the South London female group the Gymslips to epitomize people like themselves. Rene is the christian name Renée in its anglicized form and pronunciation. According to the group, renes characteristically wear monkey boots and have short cropped hair, drink beer and enjoy pie and mash.
- 'Rocking with the Renes.'
(LP title, the Gymslips, 1980).

rentacop n

a hired security guard. A term generally used disapprovingly or derisively, particularly in the era of student unrest when US campus authorities frequent-

ly called on such personnel for assistance.

rent boy n British

a young male prostitute. A **gay** slang term of the later 1960s that moved into common currency following press revelations of scandals in the 1980s. Young, sometimes homeless (and often heterosexual) rent boys frequented the Piccadilly area of London from at least the 1970s.

repo man, reepo, reep n American

a repossessor of cars on which credit repayments have lapsed. The term was made known outside the USA by its use as the title of a film made by the British director Alex Cox in 1984.

reptiles n pl

1 shoes or boots, particularly those made of alligator, lizard or snakeskin. This footwear, favoured by American pimps, for instance, is also referred to as **lizards** or **alligator shoes** (which also ironically denotes old, open-toed shoes).
- 'I wanted to wear the silk suits, wear the reptiles on my feet.'
(Washington DC drug dealer, World in Action, British TV documentary, 10 April 1989).
2 journalists, reporters, the press in general, especially those from the gutter press. A usage popularized by its use in the Dear Bill letters featured in Private Eye magazine.

result, a result n British

a an outcome in one's favour, what is due, a good result. The term originated in football jargon where to 'get a result' means not to lose.
- 'He owes me money. He's not ill – it's just a ploy to stop me getting a result!'
(Minder, British TV series, 1982).

b an arrest and/or conviction. A specialized use of the above among members of the police force.

retard n

a term of abuse among schoolchildren in the UK and the USA (where it is more fashionably shortened to **tard**) since the 1970s.

rettes n pl American

cigarettes. A shortening fashionable among **preppies** in the late 1970s.

rhino n British

money. A raffish term which seemed obsolescent until its revival along with synonyms such as **pelf**, **dosh**, **moolah**, etc. during the glamorizing of finance and commerce in the mid-1980s. The word has had this meaning since the end of the 17th century, perhaps because of the value of the (supposedly aphrodisiac) rhinoceros horn or simply because the animal was at that time a fabulous symbol of wealth and exoticism.

rhubarb n British

meaningless babble, nonsense, empty talk. The theatrical term for background mumbling or hubbub has been adopted by London working-class users as a contemptuous or dismissive term for rubbish of all sorts.
- 'He gave me a load of old rhubarb.'

riah, riach n British

hair, head of hair. One of the few instances of **backslang** to escape from a very restricted milieu. The word, usually pronounced to rhyme with 'fire', was used in the 1950s and early 1960s by actors, dressmakers, hairdressers, etc.

rice-burner n American

a Japanese motorcycle. A contemptuous term used by US **bikers** and particularly by police motorcyclists who were forced to exchange their Harley Davidsons for Japanese motorcycles in the 1970s.

Richard n British

a third-class university degree. Like **Desmond**, **Pattie**, **Taiwan** and **made-in**, it is a student witticism, based on 'Richard the Third'. A **Douglas** (Hurd) is a more recent and fashionable version.

Richard the Third n British

1 a bird (in the literal sense or as slang for a woman)
2 a turd.
The phrase has two senses in cockney rhyming slang; the first is now dated whereas the second has achieved limited currency among non-cockneys in the 1970s and 1980s.
3 the longer (rarely used) form of a **Richard**.

riddle n

See **Jimmy Riddle**.

ride vb

to copulate (with). A metaphorical usage which has been in evidence since at least the 16th century, when it was a standard synonym or euphemism in the same way as mount. Ride is still heard in this sexual sense, albeit rarely, whereas the noun form is still fairly widespread.

ride n

an act of sexual intercourse or a sex partner. This is a later derivation of the (now less common) verb form of the word.
- 'She tried to take me upstairs for a ride.'
  ('Honky Tonk Woman', written by Mick Jagger and Keith Richard, recorded by The Rolling Stones, 1970).

ride someone's ass vb
American

to nag, harass. The phrase is a pun on 'ass' as donkey, as well as evoking an image of driving or urging from behind.

- *'Quit riding his ass over this, will you?'*

ride the porcelain Honda/bus vb American

to suffer from diarrhoea, sit on the toilet. A **preppie** witticism on the pattern of **kiss the porcelain god**, (to vomit).

riff n, vb

(to play) a short, repeated sequence of musical notes, usually on a guitar. By extension, the phrase can be applied to any repetitive, over-used phrase, slogan or argument. This jazz musicians' jargon term was picked up by rock musicians and their fans in the mid-1960s.

rift n

See **get a rift on**.

rig n American

1 the male sex organs. A word used, especially by women, in the **hippy** era, although the word is older.

- *'I got this cute little pendant in the form of a flying rig.'*
  (Groupies, US film, 1973).

2 a truck, large van or bus.

righteous adj American

a good, admirable.

- *'A righteous dude.'*
  b large or excessive.
- *'A righteous mess.'*

Both senses are originally black adaptations of the standard English term, influenced by religious jargon. The terms are now also used, sometimes ironically, by white speakers.

right-on adj American

admirable, thoroughgoing, authentic. A term of approval from the late 1970s which derives from 'right on!', the 1960s exclamation of enthusiasm, support, agreement or solidarity (itself originally from black American speech). The phrase is increasingly used ironically to mean **gung-ho** or self-righteous.

- *'A right-on guy.'*
- *'She was right-on.'*

the right stuff n American

sterling qualities, the requisite grit and heroism. An armed-service phrase popularized by Tom Wolfe's book of the same name telling the story of the first US astronauts.

rigid adj

drunk. The term often (but not necessarily) refers to someone helplessly drunk.

rim vb

a to lick the anus as part of sexual stimulation.

b to sodomize.

ring n

the anus. A common vulgarism in all English-speaking communities. The word has also occasionally been used for the vagina.

ringburner n British

a hot curry, or the condition following its digestion and excretion. An expression used typically among males for whom a hot curry is a test of **machismo** and/or a natural adjunct to drinking. (The ring in question is the anus and the word is a pun on a designation of a stove or cooking hob.)

ringer n

1 a something, such as a stolen or de-

fective car, a racehorse or greyhound, which has been tampered with or doctored in order to deceive.

b a person who alters the appearance of a car, racehorse, antique, etc., in order to deceive.

2 American a substitute introduced by subterfuge into a game or race to gain an unfair advantage.

ring someone's bell vb

to bring to a sexual climax. A euphemistic phrase which appears in the lyrics of several soul and disco records of the 1970s, also sometimes meaning simply 'catch someone's eye' or 'strike a chord'.

rinky-dink adj British

1 cute, neat, smart.

This fairly rare sense of the phrase may be based on a misunderstanding of the American usage, or a separate coinage influenced by **dinky**.

2 American shoddy, makeshift, meretricious. The phrase probably originated as an imitation of the sound of fairground music, evoking gaudiness and kitsch.

ripcord n American

an alternative term for **fag tag**, used by **preppies**, among others.

rip off vb

to cheat, steal (from) or take advantage (of). A raffish black street euphemism for steal or rob, in the mid-1960s rip off passed quickly via **hippy** jargon into popular currency all over the English-speaking world.

● 'Well, just about everyone in the music business has been ripped off, financially speaking. That's Entertainment!'
(Ms London magazine, 4 September 1989).

● '"Why shouldn't we [the Jamaicans] make money out of you? You treat us like shit so we'll just rip you off." They assumed that because I had enough money to stay there, I was going to as well.'
(Lenny Henry, Time Out, 26 July 1989).

rip-off n

an instance of theft, deception or unfair appropriation. It is now used in fairly mundane contexts, such as overcharging or plagiarism. The noun, like the verb, is from 1960s black argot in which it meant a robbery or a fraud.

rip-off adj

(of goods) overpriced; (of people) grasping; and (of financial arrangements) crooked.

ripoff artist n

a practitioner of **rip-offs**, fraudster or thief. The late 1960s -**artist** suffix does not denote expertise, but merely habitual involvement.

ripped adj

1 stoned on marihuana or a similar drug. The word is occasionally also used to mean drunk and is often elaborated into 'ripped to the gills' or 'ripped to the tits'.

● 'We're just sitting around getting ripped and listening to records.'
(IT magazine, July 1972).

2 American killed. A 'tough guy' euphemism of the 1970s and 1980s.

● 'He just got ripped.'

ripper adj Australian

excellent, first-rate. A word which goes in and out of vogue, ripper was a British term of admiration, probably originating in the sports world (it has denoted a well-bowled cricket ball or a devastating punch in boxing) in the mid-19th century.

ripple n British

See **raspberry (ripple)**.

rippy adj British

excellent, thrilling. A late 1980s version of the archaic 'ripping' (Australian **ripper**), heard among middle-class teenagers, for instance.

ripstitch n British

an unruly, wild and/or reckless person. This homely and old-fashioned word is still used in parts of England, usually by adults of teenagers or children.

Rit n

Ritalin. A prescribed drug taken illicitly for its stimulant effects (similar to amphetamines or **speed**). Other slang nicknames for the preparation are **fast one** and **pellets**.

rizzer n British

a candidate for student office whose chances are 'risible'. A probably ephemeral term employed by Oxford University students in 1988.

roach n

1 a the butt of a **joint** (marihuana cigarette). An American term adopted elsewhere in the late 1960s; this use of the word arose before World War II and is probably simply a borrowing of cockroach. (Some authorities have suggested a connection with 'to roach', i.e. to clip a horse's mane.) In Britain roach may apply to the cardboard filter inserted into joints made of hashish mixed with tobacco. In the USA the lack of these necessitates the use of roach clips; metal tweezers that allow the stub of a marihuana cigarette to be held and smoked to the end without burning the fingers.

b a marihuana cigarette, **joint**. A US teenage usage, probably derived from the first, more widespread sense of the word.

2 American **a** a despicable or contemptible person.

b an unattached girl.

road apple n

a piece of horse manure on the highway. In the USA where the term probably originated the synonym **alley apple** also exists.

road brew, road sauce n
American

beer. A college-students' term. The significance of the 'road' component is unclear; **brew** and **sauce** are both slang terms for alcohol in their own rights.

roadie n

1 a rock group's assistant, responsible for handling equipment and general tasks. The word is a short form of the portentous official title 'road manager'.

2 American beer. A shortened version of **road brew** or **road sauce** in **preppie** jargon. It is usually in the plural form.

● 'Let's grab some roadies.'

road pizza n American

any small creature that has been run over and flattened by a car. The sardonic witticism of the late 1980s.

Compare **pavement pizza** and **street pizza**.

roarer n British

a male homosexual, especially one who is actually or supposedly flagrant. This alternative form of 'roaring **pouff/queen**', etc., is a heterosexual term of abuse of the 1970s and 1980s.

rock, the Rock n

1 a gem, diamond.

2 crack, cocaine. The term has been used for many years by dealers and users to denote any crystalline preparation of a narcotic. In the USA in the late 1980s, rock is the most widespread generic term for crack among law-enforcers and breakers.

- 'Mr Wardle said the [black British] girls didn't call it crack. "They'd heard of crack from the media, knew it was a very bad thing and some of them thought that crack and heroin are the same drug." However, they were alarmingly familiar with "rock".'
(Guardian, 5 September 1989).
- 'A $15 "rock" – costing about the same as two cinema tickets – contains six "hits", enough to keep two people high for 90 minutes.'
(Independent, 24 July 1989).

3 the Rock.

a Gibraltar.

b Alcatraz, the escape-proof island prison (now closed) in San Francisco Bay, USA.

rocker n British

a member of a youth cult of the early 1960s, characterized by the wearing of black leather jackets and enthusiasm for motorcycles and 1950s rock 'n' roll music. These mainly working-class teenagers and young adults were the successors to the ton-up boys and coevals of the self-consciously 'progressive' **mods**, who despised them for their adherence to 1950s American fashions and music. Mods and rockers fought each other sporadically until the late 1960s, when each group metamorphosed; rockers into **greasers** and subsequent anonymity, or into **bikers**.

- 'Rockers' hard-wearing clothes were of the type worn out of doors. Mods on the other hand were recruited in the main from the forum of office juniors and shop assistants.'
(Johnny Stuart, Rockers, 1987).

rockets n pl

breasts, particularly when prominent or 'jutting'.

rock-head n American

a stupid person. Like its later derivative **rubblehead**, rock-head is based on the uniquely North American notion of having rocks in one's head instead of brains.

rock house n American

premises where **crack** (also known as **rock**) is processed and/or sold.

- 'In the depressed inner-city areas of Los Angeles or New York, crack is frequently consumed in "crack houses" or "rock houses" – derelict buildings, often occupied by squatters, where addicts can buy and consume the drug.'
(Sunday Times, 10 September 1989).

the rock 'n' roll n British

the dole, or a dole office (the term is extended to cover Social Security payments and offices). A piece of recent rhyming slang.

- 'On the rock 'n' roll again.'
- 'I'm going down the rock 'n' roll.'
See also **rocky**.

rocks n pl

testicles. An American version of the archaic British 'stones', rocks is now in limited use elsewhere in the English-speaking world.
See **get one's rocks off**.

rockwash n British

crack. A term heard among drug abusers in 1989 which is probably a native invention, unlike most of the vocabulary associated with crack which is imported from the USA. For the derivation, see the component parts, **rock** and **wash**.

429

rocky, rock 'n' roll n British

Moroccan hashish. Both terms are code-words from the lexicon of drug users themselves, in use since the early 1970s.

rod n

1 *American* a gun, particularly a pistol or revolver.

2 the penis.

3 a short form of hot rod.

Rods n British

the **Sloane Ranger** nickname for the department store Harrods.

rod-walloper n

a male masturbator. **Rod** is an occasional slang synonym for penis.

roger vb British

to copulate with (a woman). First recorded in 1711, the term is probably older. Roger, like **dick**, **peter**, **willie**, etc., has been used in the past as a nickname for the penis. It was also frequently given as a name to bulls and rams. In modern British middle-class use it is often employed as an 'acceptable' alternative to taboo synonyms. Roger has also been employed to denote buggery (in a homosexual context).

● '*Should not a Half-pay Officer roger for sixpence?*'
(James Boswell, writing in his *London Journal*, 1762).

roll vb

1 to rob or mug (someone). Originally the term referred to robbing someone who was dead drunk or asleep, hence literally rolling over an inert body in order to rifle pockets.

2 to have sex with. The verb form is much rarer than the noun in this sense.

roll n

1 an act of sexual intercourse. Usually heard in a fairly light-hearted context, particularly in the cliché 'a roll in the hay'.

2 a wad of banknotes, a bankroll.

3 an act of mugging or robbing, particularly of an already unconscious person. A rare noun form of the verb sense.

roller n British

a Rolls-Royce car. A working-class and underworld nickname that entered general colloquial use in the later 1970s.

rollick, rollock vb British

to dress (someone) down, upbraid or chastise. A mainly middle-and upper-class euphemism for **bollock** which has been heard since before World War II. Its use is probably reinforced by the jocular use of 'rowlocks' as a noun synonym for **bollocks**.

See also **rollocking**.

rolling adj British

rich. A middle-class colloquial shortening of 'rolling in it', which is itself based on the image of a pig, horse or other animal rolling in manure.

● '*She's absolutely rolling.*'

rollocking n British

a severe dressing-down, an angry and pointed tirade. The word is a euphemism for **bollocking**.

● '*Though Dad gave me a real rollocking, in the end I won. I just fluttered my eyelids at him and promised I wouldn't be seeing Josh again.*'
(Jade Jagger, quoted in the *News of the World*, 29 March 1989).

roman candle n British

(a death caused by) parachute failure, in the jargon of the armed services.

ronk vb British

to stink. An invented word probably combining 'stink' and 'rotten'. **Honk** is a synonym. Ronk is a popular word in Liverpool and elsewhere in the North of England, though its use is not restricted to this area.

● 'God, it doesn't half ronk in here.'

ronk n British

a foul smell, a stink. A term heard mainly in the North of England.

'roo n

a kangaroo.

rookie n

a learner, neophyte or newcomer, particularly to a job or a sports team. The term originated in Britain in the armed forces of the late 19th century, but more recently rookie has been in more widespread use in the USA. The word is said to be a deformation of 're-cruit', perhaps influenced by the noisy chattering of rooks.

● 'Are you crazy? You're just a rookie. I've been on night patrol for years.' (Night Patrol, US film, 1984).

rooster n

a male homosexual, particularly a predatory prison inmate who dominates or victimizes younger fellow prisoners. In **gay** and prison jargon, roosters or **chickenhawks** prey upon **chickens**. Rooster is American for cock in the sense of male chicken.

root vb

to have sex (with). A vulgar euphemism which occurs in working-class English speech and which is common in Australia. It derives from the archaic use of root to mean penis and from 'root/rootle around', in the sense of searching in crevices. The term, first recorded in the 19th century but prob-

ably older, is hardly ever used in a homosexual context or by women.

root n

1 a an act of sexual intercourse.
b a sexual partner or available 'sex object'.
The noun senses post-date the verb, and are widespread in British and Australian usage.
2 American a cigarette or **joint**. A rare term which may originate in 'cheroot'.

rooted adj Australian

ruined, destroyed, broken. Used in the same way as the more offensive **fucked** and **buggered**, this expression derives from the verb **to root**.

● 'Christ, now the engine's rooted!'

rooter n

1 British an energetic, willing or promiscuous seducer or sex partner.
2 American a fan or supporter; someone who roots for a team, etc..

root-faced adj Australian

humourless-looking, having a morose expression. A phrase known in Britain mainly through the writing and performances of the Melbourne satirist, Barry Humphries, it is inspired by the wooden, knotted appearance of an old root.

roots n, adj Jamaican

authentic, culturally and ethnically sound, a term of approbation (and later often irony) from the Alex Haley book and TV series Roots (1974) which focused on black American origins. The term was satirized in the hit song 'Uptown Top Ranking', recorded by Althia and Donna in 1977.

rope n

a American a cigar.
b tobacco.

c marihuana. The connection and resemblance between tobacco, hemp and rope has given rise to these usages.

ropeable adj Australian

furious or berserk. A slang interpretation of the notion contained in the colloquial expression 'fit to be tied'.

• *'Well when we broke the news to her – I tell you, she was ropeable.'*

rort n Australian

1 a swindle, a small-time confidence trick. This term of uncertain origin, until recently used mainly by people over 40 years of age, is undergoing something of a revival in media circles.

2 a noisy, riotous and wild party or celebration. In this sense the noun is probably a back-formation from the adjective **rorty**.

See **rorter**.

rort vb Australian

to cheat, manipulate or bamboozle.

• *'The Federal Government is to crack down on abuse of English language courses to rort the migrant selection system following examination of an inter-departmental submission to Cabinet.'*
(LAW [London Australasian Weekly] magazine, 4 September 1989).

rorter n Australian

a swindler, small-time confidence trickster or cheat. The origin of the Australian terms based on the word **rort** is unclear; one suggestion is that they are in fact based on 'wrought(er)', an archaic British term for trick(ster).

rorty adj Australian

riotous, wild, usually drunken. The word was used in Britain in the late 19th century, but has been obsolete for many years. Its original meaning was spirited, lively or enjoyable. The etymology of the term is obscure; there seems to be no logical connection with other Australian slang words containing **rort** in the sense of cheat, which suggests that there may be a relation to roar or riot.

rory n British

1 the floor.

2 a door.

Both senses are examples of rhyming slang which still belongs to a restricted working-class London milieu. The rhyme is 'Rory O'Moore', a fictional personage invoked since the 19th century.

rory adj

flat broke. The word is from the rhyming slang for '(on) the floor'; 'Rory O'Moore'. 'On the floor' is itself rhyming slang for poor. The Rory O'Moore in question is a probably fictional Scots/Irish personification of the 19th century.

roscoe n American

a pistol or revolver. An obsolete underworld term occasionally resurrected for literary or humorous use. It derives from the use of the male Christian name as an affectionate nickname for one's handgun.

rosie, Rosie Lee n British

tea. A genuine example of cockney rhyming slang which has been adopted for light-hearted use by non-cockneys. The term seems to have originated at the turn of the century, from a common proper name, and was reinforced by the later fame of the American striptease artist Gypsy Rose Lee.

• *'A nice cup of rosie should do the trick.'*

rot-gut adj, n

low quality alcoholic drink. A four

hundred year-old term which was applied formerly to weak beer, but which more recently has usually denoted inferior spirits or wine.

rotten *adj*

very drunk. A euphemism in British and Australian usage.

the rough end of the pineapple *n Australian*

a disadvantageous position, the worst of a deal. A colourful alternative to such phrases as 'the sharp end of the stick' or 'the shitty end of the stick'.

rough stuff *n*

in the jargon of prostitution and pornography, rough stuff encompasses all sexual activities involving sado-masochism or mutilation, etc.

rough trade *n British*

a a homosexual lover (usually a casual pick-up) considered to be lower class, uncouth and/or violent. From the homosexual underground slang of the 1950s, used for instance by male prostitutes about their customers. The phrase was later used to characterize a stereotypical homosexual icon, i.e. the muscular, aggressively masculine 'working man'

b an uncouth or violent client of a heterosexual prostitute.

● '*Behind the throat-level peep-holes eyes took in the body swathed in Ralph Lauren finery trailing after her piece of rough trade.*'
(*Platinum Logic*, Tony Parsons, 1981).

roundeye *n*

1 a white person. The term, used originally by orientals as an opposite of 'slit-eyed', is also used by blacks.

2 *American* the anus, especially as a focus of sexual attention.

● '*All night long that last night . . . he walked the floor of his cell, singing a pornographic little song that he had composed himself . . . the principal theme was "Oh, how I love my roundeye!"*'
(Robert Stroud, the Birdman of Alcatraz, recalling the homosexual serial killer Carl Panzram, *Killer; a Journal of Murder*, T E Gaddis and J O Long, 1970).

roundhead *n British*

(a male with) a circumcized penis. A schoolboy counterpart to cavalier.

round the houses *adv British*

a on a (long and) futile mission.

b all over the body. The phrase is prostitutes' and pornographers' code for all-over sexual stimulation.

round the twist *adj, adv British*

a racier version of the colloquial 'round the bend', this phrase moved from limited working-class usage to general currency in the 1960s.

roust *vb American*

to disturb, harass and/or arrest. The word is usually used to describe the actions of police against suspects. Roust was first used by criminals or street-frequenters in the early 20th century, later by the law-enforcers themselves; it is from the noun 'rouster', a version of 'roustabout', employing a strong form of rouse.

rozzer *n British*

a police officer. This word originated in the 19th century and is still in limited use. The standard derivations offered by reference sources (Romany *roozlo*, meaning strong, or 'roosher', a supposed corruption of 'rusher') are not entirely convincing.

rub-a-dub, rubbidy *n*

a public house. These rhyming-

433

slang phrases (with pub) are heard in both Britain and Australia. Rub-a-dub(dub) has also been used in Britain, especially in underworld circles, as rhyming slang for club.

rubber, rubber johnny n

a condom. The first version is international English, the second British. **Johnnie**, **Johnny** and Johnny-bag are synonyms.

rubbish vb

to deride, condemn, tease. Originally Australian, the expression has established itself in British English since the early 1970s.

rubbishing n

a thorough denigration, condemnation or dismissal. An Australianism, from the verb **to rubbish**, which has spread to British speech during the 1970s.

rubblehead n American

an idiot. A term, like **rock-head**, which evokes the notion of having rocks rather than brains in one's head. This version was popular among teenagers and college students in the late 1980s.

rube n American

a yokel or rustic simpleton. A short form of the male Christian name Reuben.

rub off vb

(of a female) to masturbate.

rub out vb

to kill, murder. A euphemism from the language of the American underworld of the 1920s and 1930s, enthusiastically adopted by crime novelists. In modern street parlance the phrase is often shortened to rub.

Ruby (Murray) n British

a curry. This item of rhyming slang comes from the name of an Irish-born popular singer of the 1950s. The word or phrase is perpetuated by some speakers too young to be familiar with its inspiration.

ruck n British

an undisciplined brawl, gang fight. A characteristic London working-class use of a mild-sounding term (from 'ruckus') to denote something often involving extreme violence. (**Bother** and **aggro** are examples of the same tendency.) The word is an important element in the football hooligan and **skinhead** vocabulary.

- 'He [a hooligan] brags about his "rucks" with Millwall's notorious F troop.'
(News of the World, 17 July 1988).

rucking, ruck-up n British

a brawl, row or dressing-down. These are variant forms of **ruck**.

ruddy adj British

an inoffensive intensifying adjective, now dated, but used extensively from the turn of the century until the mid-1960s as a milder euphemism for **bloody**.

rude bits n pl British

the breasts and/or genitals. A coy quasi-nursery term in middle-class use.

rude boy n Jamaican

a gangster, gang member.

- 'Interestingly, there is a theory that the word "reggae" was originally derived from its Kingston rude boy exponents being derided as "ragamuffin men".'
(Independent, 1 September 1989).

rudie n

1 a sex act. A euphemism on the lines of **naughty** or **nasty**.

2 *Jamaican* a **rude boy**.

rug n

1 a toupee, wig. A predictable pre-World-War-II jocularism which probably originated in theatrical slang.

2 see **cut a rug**.

rug bug n

an alternative form of **rug rat**.

rugger bugger n British

a hearty (usually boorish) sportsman. The expression became popular from the 1960s primarily to denote the stereotypical rugby-club mentality.

rug rat n

a child. A phrase which, like the synonymous **ankle-biter**, has become popular, especially in young middle-class families, in the 1980s. **Rug bug** and **carpet rat** are alternative forms.

ruined adj British

drunk. A fairly rare term.

rum adj British

strange, puzzling, mysterious. The term, which is a rather obsolescent colloquialism, usually has an added sense of 'disreputable' or 'suspicious' implied by its origin in the Romany word for a man, *rom*, used by and about gypsies, the traditional outsiders or nonconformists.

- 'Protheroe is a rum cove who used to be a colonel in the Territorial Army while running the Beeb.'
(*Private Eye* magazine, April 1989).

rumble n

a fight, especially a planned street-fight or brawl involving gangs. An American expression used by teenage neighbourhood gangs since the 1950s, the word has subsequently been picked up in other English-speaking areas.

rumble vb

1 to fight. The word like the noun form originated in the slang of American urban gangs of the 1950s. It has since been appropriated and generalized by other adolescents in the USA, UK and Australia.

- 'If you wanna stop us then you'll have to come and rumble us.'
(*The Firm*, British TV play, 1989).

2 *British* to uncover (a deception), to be disabused. Now a fairly widespread colloquialism, rumble, like tumble, in this sense originated in the 19th century. Rumble probably derives from the archaic 'romboyle', to search for a wanted fugitive or suspect (a 17th-century term of unknown origin).

- 'We better get out of here – we've been rumbled.'

rum bum n

a drunkard, dissolute individual. A phrase encountered in Britain and Australia.

rumpo n British

sex. A 'smutty' euphemism first popularized by the fictitious folk-singer and specialist in innuendo, 'Rambling Sid Rumpo', played by Kenneth Williams in the Kenneth Horne radio comedies of the 1960s. In the 1980s the term is seen as an acceptable suggestive euphemism. It derives from rump as an archaic verb meaning to copulate and from the noun as a synonym for **tail**, **arse**, etc. **Rumpty-tumpty** and **rumpy-pumpy** are elaborated forms.

- 'Susannah Hoffs is writing a "steamy" romance novel. Packed with intrigue and rumpo, it will, she claims "put Jackie Collins in the shade".'

435

(*Smash Hits* magazine, November 1989).

rumpty-tumpty, rumpy-pumpy n British

sex, or sexually-related 'naughtiness'. Quasi-nursery elaborations of **rumpo**, used typically by disc jockeys, TV comedians and tabloid journalists in the 1980s.

● '*And if they were to temporarily stray from marital fidelity, where would they turn for a bit of royal rumpy pumpy?*'
(Viz magazine, May 1989).

run n

1 American a rally by Hell's Angels, usually involving a lengthy mobile debauch.

2 an initial euphoric sensation following the ingestion or injection of a narcotic, particularly heroin; a **rush**.

● '*When I'm rushing, on my run/And I feel just like Jesus's son.*'
('Heroin', the Velvet Underground, 1967).

runaround n

an evasion or obstructive and/or confusing response. Usually heard in phrases such as 'to get the runaround' or 'be given the runaround', this American expression has become an international colloquialism.

runner n British

a an escapee. The word is thus used in police jargon.

b an escape, disappearance, unauthorized departure. A usage well known in the form **do a runner**.

run off at the mouth vb

American

to talk excessively, to say more than one should. Usually used in an accusatory way, for instance to someone who betrays secrets.

the runs n British

an attack of diarrhoea. The expression is based on both the notion of runniness and running to a place of relief. A more sedate alternative is **the trots**.

rush n

the initial heady or euphoric sensation consequent on taking a mind-altering drug. The word is used especially, and most literally, of stimulant drugs such as cocaine and amphetamines; it generally refers to the sudden effects of a drug injected intravenously or taken through the mucous membranes rather than the more gradual onset attendant upon smoking or swallowing. The term is sometimes extended to refer to any exciting or stimulating action or situation.

● '*There's nothing like stepping off a cliff and shooting straight up in the air. What a rush!*'
(Recorded, hang-gliding enthusiast, Wales, 1984).

● '*When you inhale real hard, even before you exhale you're starting to feel the rush. It just goes straight to your head quicker than any other drug, and a better rush than any other drug.*'
(crack smoker, *Independent*, 24 July 1989).

rust-bucket n

an old dilapidated or shoddily manufactured car. The term was earlier applied to ships and aeroplanes.

S

S.A. n American

sex appeal. A coy abbreviation used typically by female high-school and college students.

sab vb British

to sabotage. A shortening used by animal-rights activists and hunt saboteurs in the 1980s.

sabbing n British

an act of sabotage. A word used by animal-rights activists and hunt saboteurs in the 1980s.

- 'Meeting to discuss sabbing tactics.' (Campus announcement, Essex University, 1986).

sack n

bed. The word was probably first used of hammocks in the 19th century. See also sad sack.

sack artist n

a womanizer, seducer, lothario. In the Literary Review, June 1987, in a review of Intercourse by Andrea Dworkin, Jane Ellison attributes this to Martin Amis. She is wrong. It is North American in origin, in common with other formulations such as 'con artist', spreading to Britain in the 1980s. Sack artist started life with the quite different meaning of a lazy person or idler (who spent most of their time in the sack).

sack out vb American

to go to bed, (lie down and) sleep. A colloquialism based on the long-established use of sack to mean bed.

sack time n

a bed time. An armed forces and prison usage, carried over into civilian colloquialism.

- 'Lift that weight drag that
  woodbine/ lights out mate
  sackarooni time/ lights out sack
  time.'
  ('36 Hours', poem by John Cooper Clarke, 1980).

b time spent sleeping.

sad sack n American

an unfortunate or characteristically depressed or confused individual. This term originated before World War II and was subsequently widespread in armed service slang to discribe a misfit or pitiable person (normally male). The name was given to a popular cartoon character of the 1950s.

safe adj British

good, fine. The standard meaning was extended in schoolchildren's slang at the end of the 1980s to encompass anything positive. The word is thus used as an all-purpose term of approbation, often as an exclamation. 'Safe' in this generalized sense probably derives from its over-use by petty criminals and gang members.

salad n British

a member or supporter of the Social and Liberal Democrat party (SLD). The term was used mockingly in the press in 1988 and 1989.

See also **scuba**.

salam' n American

a campus version of **salami**.

salami n American

1 penis. A teenagers' term almost always heard in the phrase **hide the salami** (a euphemism for sexual intercourse).

2 a fool. A high-school and campus term.

the Sally-Ann n

the Salvation Army, or a hostel or kitchen run by that organisation. The nickname is used, especially by tramps and vagrants, in Britain and the USA.

salt n

1 British a girl. A term used by London **mods** in the 1960s. They adopted the usage from the argot of working-class and marginal milieus where it had been heard since at least the 19th century. Since the 16th century 'salt' had been used as an adjective meaning lecherous or lewd, and as a noun meaning a sex act or (female) sexual partner. These now archaic terms are derived from the French *assaut* (whence 'assault') in its literal sense of 'on the jump'. Salt meaning girl is pronounced in London speech as 'sort' for which it is often mistaken.

- '*I had a game of soccer this afternoon and afterwards popped a bit into my salt – she don't take none of your tablets either.*'
  (Letter to *Oz* magazine, June 1969).

2 American heroin. From the resemblance.

sambo n

a black person (usually male). This derogatory racist term comes from *zambo*, the Spanish American designation of those (slaves) with three-quarters negro and one-quarter Amerindian or European blood. The word was picked up by English speakers in the early 18th century and its use was reinforced by the 19th-century children's storybook character, 'Little Black Sambo'. The term has fallen out of use in the USA since the 1950s but is heard in Britain and Australia.

sandbag vb American

1 a to attack unexpectedly, stop (someone) dead, incapacitate or thwart. A sand-filled bag was formerly used as an improvised cosh or blackjack. The word has been taken up into business jargon in the 1980s. (**Handbag** has been coined as a feminine counterpart.)

- '*You sandbagged me on Blue Star!*'
  (*Wall Street*, US film, 1987).

b to obstruct or outmanoeuvre, especially by feigning weakness. The word is a gambling term now extended to other contexts.

2 to drive at full speed, in the jargon of 'hotrodders'.

S. and M. n

sado-masochistic practices, in the code of pornographers and prostitutes.

sap n American

1 a fool, simpleton or dupe. Originally a British term, the word is now more often heard in the USA. It was in origin a shortening of the word 'sapskull', meaning wooden-head, dating from the late 17th century. In the 19th century schoolboy **swots** were known as 'saps' from the Latin *sapiens* (wise or knowledgeable) and this meaning applied ironically may have converged with the older sense of the word.

2 a blackjack, cosh. This sense of the word is probably based on sap meaning hoe or shovel in archaic speech.

saphead n American

a fool, simpleton or dupe. A version of **sap**.

sarnie n British

a sandwich. A diminutive form which has spread from the north of England.

sashay vb

to walk proudly, stride, flounce or 'mince'. Sashay originated as an Americanization of the French *chassé* (in this case a rapid, gliding movement; a term used in square dancing).

● 'She sashayed up to the bar and ordered a daiquiri.'

sass vb American

to speak or behave irreverently or insolently (towards), to cheek (someone). The verb is from the earlier, but now rarer, noun form.

● 'Don't you sass me, boy.'

sass n American

impudence, insolence. Sass is a folksy or dialect form of 'sauce', in the sense of sauciness. It is now rare in the noun form although the verb is still used.

● 'I don't need none of your sass.'

sauce n

alcoholic drink. In Britain this is a mainly middle class euphemism employed particularly by heavy drinkers; the implication is that alcohol is liberally dispensed. There may also be a subconscious identification with **soused**.

● 'I couldn't stop – I got on the sauce real good.'
(*The Dancer's Touch*, US film 1989)

sauce vb British

to have sex with. A middle class euphemism.

● 'Have you sauced her yet?'
(*The New Statesman*, British TV comedy series, 1989).

sauced (out) adj

drunk. A usage based on **sauce** as a slang term for alcoholic drink (and influenced by **soused**). The '-out' version is a racier modern variant.

sausage grappler n Australian

a male masturbator. One of many synonymous vulgarisms (**rod-walloper**, etc.) heard since the 1960s.

sawbuck n American

a ten dollar bill. The Latin X for ten was thought to recall the wooden cross-struts of a saw horse.

say uncle vb American

See **uncle**.

scab n

a strike breaker, a worker who defies a union picket. This usage arose in the USA early in the 19th century, but by then the word had been used to signify a worthless or contemptible individual for about two hundred years. Scab, at least in the speech of union members, is now so well established as to be a standard term rather than slang.

scads, scad n American

a great deal, large quantity (particularly of money). This colloquialism is of uncertain origin; it probably derives from a British dialect form of 'shed(full)' or from a dialect word 'scald', meaning multitude.

scag, skag n

heroin. This word entered American usage in the later 1960s, probably from black street slang in which skag and **skank** were used to refer to anything inferior or unpleasant. The word presumably first referred to low-quality narcotics.

- *'The ladies kept a couple of grams [of cocaine] in the refrigerator. Ordell said he would not tolerate any scag, though.'*
  (Elmore Leonard, *The Switch*, 1978).

scag jones n American

an addiction to heroin. See **jones**.

scag nod n American

a state of stupor or drowsiness from taking heroin.

- *'He told them if he saw any lady in a scag nod he'd throw her ass out the window.'*
  (Elmore Leonard, *The Switch*, 1978).

scally n British

a a young man, lad.

b a criminal, delinquent or hooligan.

c a male inhabitant of the Liverpool area.

The word has overtones of 'cheeky', 'smart' and 'one of the boys'; it is a regional shortening of 'scallywag', a word meaning reprobate or rascal first used abusively in the USA before the Civil War. Scallywag itself is probably a form of an older expression from English or Scottish dialect meaning something like 'scurvy wretch'.

scalper n

a ticket tout or other form of ruthless (though small-scale) profiteer. The term comes from the verb to scalp which was 19th-century stock-exchange jargon for buying cheap and selling at an exaggerated price (from the notion of 'taking a cut off the top').

scalping n

profiteering, particularly by re-selling tickets at an inflated price.

- *'This is a shrewd and practised*

Londoner trading in what the Americans call "scalping". We call the business "touting", and this summer ticket touts are set for a final beano'.
(*Evening Standard*, 9 May 1988).

scam n

a deception, fraud, swindle or confidence trick. This Americanism entered fashionable British usage around 1977, subsequently becoming fairly widespread, particularly in business parlance. 'Scampery' was British slang for highway robbery in the 18th century, a word lated used by vagrants, showmen etc. This, via American adoption, may explain the modern term (the similarity with 'scheme' is probably fortuitous). By the late 1980s scam had come sometimes to be used to mean merely 'dubious scheme or display'.

- *'I'm always glad to hear of my friends coming up with new scams.'*
  (Recorded, expatriate British businessman, London, 1985).
- *'"You know, I think there are a million people running scams out there," said Suzanne McGuire, the tournament's director of corporate marketing. "But what can you do? This is New York."'*
  (*Sunday Times*, 10 September 1989).

scam vb American

to perpetrate a fraud, deception or devious scheme. The verb is derived from the noun.

scarf (up/down) vb

devour greedily and completely, eat and/or drink voraciously. Perhaps a humorous alternative, tinged with onomatopoeia, of **scoff**, the term originated in the USA where it was adopted by adolescents from 'low-life' milieus in the 1960s. ('Scarf out' is another derivative; a synonym of 'pig-out'.)

- *'Harvey watched Joan scarfing down Milanos, biting them in half with her even teeth.'*
  (*The Serial*, Cyra McFadden, 1976)

scarper *vb*

to leave hurriedly, run away. The word was adopted by cockneys at the turn of the century, from **parlyaree**, the Italianate pidgin used by peddlars, showmen, actors, etc. *Scappare* (to escape) is the original Italian. Since World War I many have assumed that the word is rhyming slang: 'Scapa flow'; go.

scene, the scene *n*

1 the fashionable, **hip** or currently favoured milieu. A favourite word from the **beatnik** and later **hippy** vocabularies, often used in such phrases as **make the scene** (to be present or active in the currently hip environment) and 'on the scene'. 'It's not my scene' was a common dismissal of an undesirable activity or place. In colloquial usage the word simply means environment or 'world', as in 'the music scene'. The word is now dated but is still used by some journalists and, self-consciously or ironically, by the fashionable young.

2 a state of affairs, situation. In this generalized sense the word is now dated.

- *'"It was a very emotional time, a lot of yelling and screaming, a really bad scene," Bolker remembered.'*
  (*Sunday Times*, 24 September 1989).

3 *See* **have a scene (with)**.

scene-chaser *n British*

a person who seeks new forms of excitement by assiduously cultivating different groups of people. A derogatory term used typically by the fashionably bohemian in the 1960s.

sch- *prefix*

Many slang words of Yiddish origin may be spelled with these initial letters, but 'Sch' is the standard German form and, as such, is not employed in this dictionary, except for words which have been specifically recorded in this form. The alternative spelling **sh-**is used in writing by most Yiddish speakers and writers in English-speaking countries and is therefore preferred here.

schizo *adj, n*

(behaving like) a schizophrenic, crazy. A popular Americanism of the 1960s and thereafter. It almost invariably refers to a generalized notion of craziness, rather than 'true' schizophrenia.

schizzed-out *adj American*

a deranged, uncontrolled.

b drunk. The term is an elaboration of 'schizophrenic' or 'schizoid'. In fashionable slang of the early 1970s, schizzed out was used in the same way as the more common **flipped out** or **freaked out**. The sense of drunk was an adaptation by high-school and **preppie** speakers.

schlemiel *n*

a fool, clumsy unfortunate, loser. A Yiddish word (pronounced 'shlermeal') used with a mixture of pity and contempt. In 1813 von Chamisso wrote *Peter Schlemihl's Wunderbare Geschlichte*; a parable describing a man selling his shadow and his soul. The author probably took the name from Schlumiel, a biblical general notorious for losing battles.

- *'I've never been able to stand Woody Allen – he's such a schlemiel.'*

(Recorded, antiquarist, London, 1986).

schlong n American

penis. A Yiddish word (meaning 'snake') which has entered the mainstream of American slang since the 1960s. It has been used in the novels of Elmore Leonard, Philip Roth's *Portnoy's Complaint* and the film *Sophie's Choice*, among other instances. In the late 1980s wits coined an alternative form; 'schlort'.

schlub, schlob n American

alternative or earlier forms of **slob**.

schmaltz n

sickly sentimentality. The word is Yiddish, from the German for cooking fat or dripping. The word was used in the New York Jewish community to describe what Leo Rosten in *The Joys of Yiddish* (1970) defines as 'corn, pathos, maudlin and mawkish substance; excessive sentimentality, overly emotional mush, sugary banality'.

● *'With chapter headings such as "I'm in love with a dishwasher", "I love you too, Mommy", "I love you, Michael", and "We all love each other", On the Outside Looking In has more schmaltz than a New York deli.'*
(Book review by Nigella Lawson, *Sunday Times*, April 1989).

schmeck n American

1 a sniff or taste (in Yiddish from German).
2 heroin. It is this second sense which is the origin of the more recent **smack**.

schmeet n American

heroin. The word is a corruption of shmek or **schmeck**, the Yiddish forerunner of the now common term **smack**.

schmendrick, shmendrik n

American

a foolish or clumsy nonentity. A Yiddish word which is used by Jews and non-Jews alike in American speech. Shmendrik was a character in an operetta by Abraham Goldfaden.

schmock, schmuck n

heroin. A variant form of **schmeck** and an earlier form of **smack** used by addicts and prisoners in the USA and Britain until the early 1960s.

schmuck n American

a pitiful, foolish or obnoxious person, usually male. Schmuck is from the Yiddish word *shmok*, itself from the German *Schmuck*, meaning ornament. In Yiddish usage the word was used first as a euphemism for the male member, then becoming a synonym for the English **prick**, figuratively as well as literally. As employed especially by non-Jewish speakers today schmuck is a fairly mild term of abuse, often used ruefully, despairingly or affectionately. It was perceived as an obscenity in the USA for many years with the result that the euphemism **shmo** was invented in the 1940s.

● *'He gave his small son a gun and taught him how to shoot all God's little creatures . . . and called him "his little schmuck", giving Mike a nice warm glow, until he finds out what it means.'*
(Nigella Lawson, *Sunday Times*, April 1989).

schmutter n

clothing. The word is Yiddish, deriving from the Polish *szmata*, meaning rag. Schmutter was popularized in Britain by its use in the tailoring trade.

● *'A nice bit of schmutter if you ask me.'*
● *'They used to be in the schmutter business.'*

schnockered adj

drunk. The word is probably not Yiddish or German, despite its most usual spelling, but may derive from an archaic dialect term 'snock', to hit. Schnockered, also spelled **snockered**, is encountered more often in American speech than British.

- '*As a whiskey salesman ... I'm often lit up by elevenses, loop-legged by luncheon and totally schnockered by 6.*'
  (Posy Simmonds cartoon, Guardian, 1979).

schnook n American

an unfortunate, timid or pathetic person. The word is Yiddish, but apparently coined in the USA. It is probably related to the German *Schnucki*; darling, or *Schnuck*; a small sheep.

schnozzle, schnozz n

nose. The word is Yiddish, from German, in which *Schnauze* is the translation of 'snout'. The comedian Jimmy 'Schnozzle' Durante (named for his large nose) introduced the word to non-Americans.

school n

a group of drinkers, particularly hard drinkers, who congregate regularly for drinking bouts. This specific sense of the standard word (as in shoal, card school) is predominantly an Australianism although not unknown in middle-aged or elderly circles in Britain.

scoff n British

food. A noun formed from the colloquial verb (itself probably from an imitative dialect word) and used, particularly by young people, as a more fashionable synonym for **grub**. In fact this use of scoff dates from the 19th century.

- '*What I've got my eye on is all that lovely scoff.*'
  (Recorded, student, London 1987).

scoot exclamation American

a mild exclamation inspired by **shoot**, itself a euphemism for **shit**.

scoots n pl American

dollars. A word of unknown origin used mainly by adolescent speakers.

score n

1 British £20. The word has been particularly popular in underworld and police usage since before World War II.

- '*I thought it was worth at least a hundred, but I only got a score for it.*'

2 a success or coup, especially a successful crime, seduction or arrest.

- '*Shaft's Big Score!*'
  (Title of US film, 1972).

3 a drug purchase. From the verb form.

- '*They set up a score downtown.*'

score vb

1 a to buy (illicit drugs). An Americanism that became the standard term world-wide in the late 1960s.

- '*Addicts devote all their money to feeding their habit, not their body. They spend their time "scoring", and become unhealthy, malnutritioned.*'
  (Tam Stewart, Independent, 4 April 1988).

b to obtain. This is a young person's generalization of the previous raffish usage.

- '*Look on the bright side – you may not have got the job, but at least you scored a free lunch.*'

2 to succeed in gaining sexual satisfaction.

- '*I saw you leaving the pub with that redhead – did you score?*'

scorf n, vb British
  a a variant form of **scoff**.
  b a variant form of to **scarf**.

Scotch egg n British
  leg. A rhyming-slang expression using the name of the uniquely British preparation of a hard-boiled egg cooked in a case of sausage-meat covered with breadcrumbs.
  • '*He's a bit unsteady on his Scotch eggs.*'

Scotch mist n British
  1 a phantom, mirage, will o' the wisp, something insubstantial or totally non-existent. The expression almost always forms part of a contemptuous or ironic phrase used to upbraid someone who is being obtuse or dismissive.
  • '*Nothing here to drink? What's this, then, Scotch mist?*'
  2 teeming rain, a downpour. A humorous appropriation of the standard sense of the phrase (which means 'fine drizzle') by those acquainted both with the climate of Scotland and its people's propensity for taciturn understatement.

scouse adj British
  of or from Liverpool. The word is derived from 'lobscouse', a stew traditionally containing vegetables, hardtack or ship's biscuit, and sometimes meat. Lobscouse was eaten by sailors and was popular in the Liverpool area.

scouse n British
  the accent and speech of the Liverpool area.

scouser n British
  a Liverpudlian. From **scouse**.

scrag vb
  1 British to torment, tease, attack, beat up. A schoolboy term dating from the 19th century, inspired by the earlier use of the word to mean hang, strangle or grab by the neck. ('Scrag', meaning neck, is from Scottish dialect 'crag', 'craig'.)
  2 American **a** to kill, destroy.
  b to copulate (with). Both usages derive from the senses recorded above and are now fairly rare.

scram vb
  to leave quickly, go away. Nearly always heard in the form of a brusque dismissal, the word is a shortening of 'scramble', first used in the USA at the turn of the century. (The **pig Latin** version of the term is **amscray**.)

scratch n
  cash, ready money. This sense of the word has been in use since the end of the 19th century. It is either derived from the notion of 'scratching a living' or of banknotes which are 'up to scratch', i.e. genuine.
  • '*What about you Charlie; why don't you try to come up with some scratch for a change.*'
  (*The Late Show*, US film, 1977).

scratchy adj
  irritable or bad-tempered and oversensitive. Predominantly American with rustic overtones, the word is a synonym for prickly or tetchy.

scream n American
  ice cream. A conflated form heard among adolescents.

screamer n
  a flagrant homosexual. A derogatory term used typically by flagrant heterosexuals, derived from 'screaming queen/nancy,' etc. The word is heard in Britain and Australia.

screaming (h)abdabs n pl
  British

444

a state of mental agitation bordering on hysteria. Usually heard in the phrase 'It gives me (a case of) the screaming abdabs'; it makes me extremely irritated, agitated.

See **'abdabs**.

screw vb

1 to have sex (with). This use of the word was recorded in Grose's *Dictionary of the Vulgar Tongue* in 1785. It may be a direct metaphor or may be influenced by the archaic use of screw to mean a key (turning in a lock). Since the late 1960s the verb can refer to the sexual act from the woman's point of view as well as the man's. The word owed much of its popularity to the fact that it is a synonym for **fuck** which is nevertheless acceptable in the media and what used to be referred to as 'mixed company'.

2 a to take advantage of, defraud, cheat or treat unfairly.

b to ruin or spoil. An extension of the previous sense paralleled by **fuck, bugger** etc.

3 British to stare (at). In working class London speech, especially among skinheads of the late 1960s, the question 'Who're you screwin'?' was often the prelude to violence. It has been suggested that this use of the word is in origin a shortening of scrutinize, but this seems hard to credit. Screwing up one's eyes or metaphorically boring a hole into someone are other possibilities.

● 'Villains call it clocking in Leeds, eyeballing in Manchester and screwing in London's East End . . . It came as a shock: juries can be intimidated by a stare.'
(*Sunday Times*, 5 June 1988).

4 British to rob, in the argot of the underworld.

screw n

1 a an act of sexual intercourse.

b a sexual partner. Both usages derive from the verb form.

2 British a prison guard. This is the standard term applied to prison officers by inmates since the 19th century. It derives from the archaic use of the same word to mean key. Thus 'turnscrew', later shortened to screw, was a synonym for turnkey.

● 'A banner was draped from the cell windows reading: Support the screws – Old Bill out.'
(*Guardian*, 31 January 1989).

3 an income, wage or salary. In this sense, first recorded in the mid-19th century, the word almost invariably occurs as part of the common phrase '(on) a good screw'.

screw around vb

1 to 'mess about', behave clumsily, irresponsibly or irresolutely. The phrase, which is particularly popular in the USA, is a milder form of **fuck around/about**.

2 to behave in a sexually promiscuous way. A brusquer version of 'sleep around'.

● 'The strongest possible piece of advice I would give to any young woman is: Don't screw around, and don't smoke.'
(Edwina Currie, government minister, *Observer*, 3 April 1988).

screw (someone) around vb

to cause inconvenience, especially by indecisive action.

screw the pooch vb American

to waste time. A phrase heard typically in the slang of the armed services, it is a slightly politer version of 'fuck the dog', meaning to engage in idle or futile activity.

screw up vb

a to make a mess, or mistake, perform ineptly, fail, ruin. This phrase was in predominantly American currency until the late 1960s.

b to traumatize, render maladjusted.

• 'She claims she's been screwed up by her upbringing.'.

screwy adj

crazy, eccentric. Pre-World War II slang which has become a popular colloquialism, deriving from the notion of having a 'screw loose'.

scrote n British

a non-specific term of abuse used, and perhaps invented by Clement and la Frenais in their 1970s TV comedy Porridge (set in a prison). It is presumably inspired by scrotum.

scrubber n British

a coarse, vulgar and/or promiscuous female. This now common term was first heard in the 1920s. 'Scrub' had been used to mean a shabby or seedy person, or prostitute since the 18th century. Scrubber, like scrub, derives from the notion of having to scrape and forage for food or money, rather than to scrub floors, etc.

scuba n British

an adherent to the SLD Social and Liberal Democrat party (thought of by some as a 'sinking ship'). An ephemeral term of stereotyping contempt among Oxford University students in 1988. Salad was a politer synonym.

scuffer n British

a police officer. This word (more often heard in the plural) originated in the Liverpool area. It derives from dialect terms associated with 'shuffle', 'scuff' and 'cuff' (in the sense of a blow).

scumbag n American

a despicable person. This term of abuse is now widespread and is per-

mitted in the broadcast media, in spite of the fact that its origin, unknown to many of its users, is as an obscene euphemism for condom, 'scum' being an obsolescent American term for semen. The word was adopted by British speakers around 1985.

• 'Even scumbags have rights here in the USA.'
(Red Heat, US film, 1988).

scum-sucker n American

a despicable, contemptible or degenerate person. This word, originally synonymous with cocksucker, in that 'scum' is an obsolescent American slang term for semen, is now often used as if it were a milder, euphemistic epithet.

scum-sucking adj American

disgusting, contemptible. The word is usually employed as a meaningless intensifier in longer terms of abuse. (For the original sense see scum-sucker).

• 'This scum-sucking low-life deserves to die!'

scumwad n American

an alternative version of scumbag, heard in the late 1980s. (Wad is a common component of vulgar compounds, having as it does several sexual connotations.)

scungy adj Australian

dirty, messy, unkempt or sordid. The word is probably a coinage blending the sounds and connotations of such words as 'scurvy', 'mangy' and gunge. It may alternatively be influenced by scunner.

scunner n British

a despicable, traitorous, or devious person. This unusual word has spread beyond its origins in Scottish dialect and is occasionally heard throughout the north and Midlands of England.

scuttlebutt n American

gossip or rumour. The scuttlebutt was a cask or fountain of drinking water on board naval ships, around which news was exchanged.

- 'I hear some scuttlebutt says he likes to kick the ladies around.' (*Night Game*, US film, 1988).

scuzz n American

a dirt, seediness, anything distasteful. The word has been widely used since the late 1960s and probably postdates the adjective form **scuzzy**. The word had been picked up by some British speakers by the 1980s.

- 'Foul-mouthed critics and their lairs – Old Compton St, the Coach and Horses, Private Eye, The Spectator, Fleet Street Freelancer – the whole scuzz world of journalism is here in black and white (albeit seen through the bottom of a glass).' (*I-D* magazine, November 1987).

b also **scuzzball, scuzzbag, scuzzo**; a disreputable, unpleasant, unattractive or worthless person. A derivative of **scuzzy** which has been popular since the early 1970s.

- 'He's upstairs smoking dope with some scuzz.' (*The Last Innocent Man*, US film, 1987).

scuzzed out adj

disgusted. A more recent synonym of **grossed out**, based on **scuzzy** and **scuzz**.

scuzzy adj American

dirty, unpleasant, distasteful, shabby and disreputable. This word, which is used particularly by young people, may be a nursery version of 'disgusting' or an invention influenced by

'scum' and 'fuzz'. Scuzzy has been heard in North America since the late 1960s but to date has not been adopted elsewhere, except by a handful of journalists.

second storey work n American

gaining illegal entry to private homes, especially by breaking into apartments (seeking information). This term belongs to reporters' jargon.

seeing-to n British

a a beating-up, an assault. A typically understated, hence menacing euphemism in working class, police and criminal usage.

- 'He's asking for a seeing-to.'

b a sexual act; specifically the sexual 'possession' of a woman by a man. The word has simultaneous and revealing overtones of brusque, no-nonsense domination, of a duty accomplished and of an unaffectionate resolution.

- 'Well, I gave her a good seeing-to, didn't I.'

semi n American

a large truck. The word usually pronounced 'sem-aye' is short for 'semi-trailer, or 'semi-truck' and denotes what in Britain would be called an articulated.

- 'I remember hearing those semi's gearing down My Mom and me we lived right on the highgrade into town.' (Lyrics to 'Mama Hated Diesels' by Commander Cody and his Lost Planet Airmen, 1972).

send vb

to transport emotionally or intellectually. This supposed **beatnik** term of the late 1950s (originating among US jazz musicians in the 1940s) was used to characterize **hip** youth in various unhip media.

447

● *'I just love Elvis. He sends me!'*

sender *n*

See **solid sender**.

sent down *adj British*

sentenced to imprisonment, imprisoned. This euphemism, also used to mean expelled from university, has been in currency since the 19th century. The phrase may originate in the image of the convict descending the steps from the dock.

sent up *adj American*

imprisoned. The American version of **sent down**. Sent up has been in use since the late 19th century; it may be derived from **upriver**. In Britain, to be 'sent up' is to be imitated in a parodic manner.

septic *n Australian*

an American. A piece of native Australian rhyming slang, from septic tank; **Yank**. The word was first recorded being applied to visiting American servicemen during World War II. It is still in use among older speakers and shows signs of being in continued currency among the younger generation. (**Sherman (tank)** is a British equivalent.)

sesh *n British*

a drinking bout. A shortening of '(drinking) session' used typically by middle class youths in Britain in the late 1980s.

● *'We had a good sesh last night.'*

set *n*

the latest word for gang in the 1990 argot of the Los Angeles **rap** and street-gang subcultures.

severe *adj*

impressive, excellent. An all-pur-

pose vogue term of approval used first by British **mods** in 1963 and 1964 and later by American teenagers and their British imitators in the 1970s and 1980s.

● *'That's a really severe shirt.'*
● *'How did she look? – severe, man!'*

sex bomb, sexpot *n*

a very attractive person. The first term is a journalese coinage, usually applied to female stars or starlets; the second a semi-jocular colloquialism. The expressions first became popular around 1960.

● *'Silvana Mangano was the first of the European sex-bombs.'*
(Obituary in the *Independent*, 18 December 1989).

sexing *vb British*

having sex. A term used by young children.

● *'Fraser said he saw someone in a car sexing.'*
(Recorded, 8-year-old, London, 1988).

sexy *adj*

attractive or enticing, particularly in commercial or financial terms. A jargon use of the common colloquialism, heard sporadically from the late 1970s. The usage became well established in **Yuppie** parlance of the 1980s.

sh- *prefix*

This form is generally preferred in this dictionary for the many words of Yiddish origin which exist in modern English slang. Certain terms are recorded under the alternative (German) **sch-** when there is evidence of their prevalence in that form.

shackerette *n Australian*

a female live-in lover. A humorous, sometimes condescending and fairly rare coinage from **shack up**.

shack up vb

to live with someone in a sexual relationship outside marriage. Such a relationship is sometimes known as a 'shack-up'. The term was an Americanism first used by itinerants and marginals between the World Wars; it was adopted into World English during the 1960s.

shade n American

a receiver of stolen goods, **fence**. The word may be derived from 'shady' (dealing).

shades n pl

sunglasses. The word was first used in this sense in the USA in the 1940s. (Shades are blinds in American English.)

shaft n

1 penis. A predictable but rare use of the standard term.

2 a an act of sexual intercourse.
● 'A quick shaft.'
b a sex partner.
● 'A good shaft.'
These usages are back-formations from the verb.

3 the shaft an alternative form of a **shafting**. It usually occurs in the form 'get the shaft'.

shaft vb

1 to have sex with, to penetrate. From **shaft**: penis.

2 to ruin, damage, destroy (someone). Most often heard in the form of the past participle 'shafted', this term is another example of a slang word literally meaning to have sex with someone used metaphorically to mean humiliate or abase.

Compare **fuck, bugger, roger, screw**.
● 'I tell you, we were well and truly shafted over that Abco deal.'

shafting n.

an instance of extremely harsh, ruinous and/or unfair treatment. The term derives from the sexual senses of the verb to **shaft**.

shag vb

to have sex (with). A common vulgarism in Britain and Australia which is unknown in this sense in the USA. The word is an archaic relative of 'shake', which was used in a sexual sense from at least the 16th century. In Britain shag took over the taboo role in the 18th century, while in the USA it took on the (now obsolete) meaning of 'run off' or 'run after'. In modern usage the word is considered less offensive than **fuck** in male company, but more vulgar than other synonyms. Like fuck it occurs in other forms, such as the noun **shag**, the intensifying adjective 'shagging' and phrases such as 'shag off'.
● 'When I was 17 I was obsessively in love with a girl who only liked me. It blighted my adolescence. I would have given anything to shag her.'
(Ben Elton, quoted in NME, March 1989).

shag n

1 British a sexual act or a sexual partner. See the verb form for origins.

2 American **a** a boyfriend, girlfriend or escort. This now obsolete term has none of the overtly sexual and vulgar overtones of the British and Australian usages.

b the Shag a teenage dance craze of the 1960s. When a film of this name was released in Britain in 1988, press hand-outs were necessary in order to reassure the public as to the innocence of the term.

shagged out, shagged adj
British

exhausted, worn out. The vulgar ori-

449

gin of the phrase (tired out from sexual activity) is partially forgotten in the modern usage wherein the expression serves as a more robust version of **knackered**.

- *'Listen. I really can't make it, I'm feeling absolutely shagged.'*

shaggin' wagon, shag-wagon n

a more vulgar term for **passion wagon** or **draggin' wagon**. This form of the expression is heard in Britain and Australia.

- *'Old Gregory turned up in a brand new shaggin' wagon.'*

shake vb

1 *British* to alert, rouse, summon. This use of the word, obviously deriving from the literal shaking of someone to wake them, is now employed as part of police, underworld and working class jargon.

- *'The solicitors . . . We'll shake them for you.'*
  (*Flying Squad*, British TV documentary, March 1989)

2 *American* to search, or stop and harass (a suspect). The word, used by police and criminals, is a shortening of the more familiar **shake down**.

shake down vb American

1 to extort money from (someone) either face-to-face (usually by threats), or by blackmail.

2 to search a person or premises. The phrase usually refers to an official search by police officers which may involve a degree of harassment or force.

shakedown n American

1 an act of extortion or blackmail.

2 a search of a person or place, usually by police.

shamed-up adj British

humiliated, shamed. A 'buzz-term'

among teenagers in the 1980s, from the admonitory catchphrase 'take the shame!'. This playground phrase is from black slang.

shampoo n

champagne. A **Sloane Ranger** and **yuppie** witticism of the 1980s. The word is often abbreviated to **poo**. In the USA **preppies** and others also use the terms.

shamus n American

a private detective. This word has been popular in crime fiction from Raymond Chandler onwards. In the USA it was formerly sometimes applied to police officers and other law enforcers. The suggested origins of the word are *shamos* (Yiddish) or *shamash* (Hebrew), meaning guardian (of a synagogue), or Seamus, the Irish version of the Christian name James, applied generically to uniformed policemen. Of the two, the former seems more plausible. The word may be pronounced either as 'sharm-us' or 'shame-us'.

shank n American

a homemade knife. A term used in prisons and by the members of street gangs since the 1950s. In standard English shank denotes the shaft or connecting rod of a tool or instrument.

Sharon n British

the female equivalent of a **Kevin** or **Wayne**. The name is used to designate a supposedly typical (and by implication uncultured) working class young woman. These generic epithets were coined in the 1970s for the purpose of social stereotyping. (In 1965 Sharon was the tenth most popular Christian name for new-born girls in Britain.)

- *'A thousand slavish Sharons copied Diana's wedding look, as*

they did her flicked 'n' sprayed hairstyle.'
(Judy Rumbold, *Guardian*, 11 December 1989).

- *'The male models in leopard-skin-print Gaultier jackets getting eyeballed by Sharons with Bucks Fizz haircuts and pound signs in their eyes at the Limelight.'*
(*Observer*, section 5, 7 May 1989).

sharpies *n pl Australian*

members of a short-lived teenage youth movement of the 1950s who were contemporaries of the **bodgies** and **widgies**. Sharpies were short-haired, aggressive and less flamboyant than the **teddy boy**-like bodgies.

shat upon *adj*

humiliated, slighted, victimized or punished. Shat is a past tense of the verb to **shit**.

sheeny *n*

a Jew. The term appeared in Britain in the early 19th century when it did not necessarily have the offensive racist overtones it has acquired in the 20th century. Many possible etymologies have been proposed for sheeny: the three most plausible are the German word schön (beautiful) as applied either to their children or to merchandise by Jews, the 'sheen' of dark hair or skin as perceived by Anglo-Saxons, or the Yiddish phrase *a miesse meshina* ('an ugly fate or death'), a phrase supposedly common among Jews. There is no reason to prefer one or other of these suggestions. The word is now rare in both Britain and the USA, but not yet obsolete.

sheep-dip *n*

low-quality alcoholic drink.

sheepshagger *n British*

a rustic, bumpkin or primitive. A

vulgarism heard since the 19th century.

sheila *n Australian*

a woman. This well-known Australianism, although old-fashioned, is still heard. It is an alteration of an earlier word 'shaler' (meaning 'young woman'), of Gaelic origin, which was used by Irish immigrants. The word became a generic term for females, the feminine counterpart of **paddy**, and was altered to coincide with the female Christian name.

- *'Cripes! I was nearly up shit creek that time. Now I'm stuck with this po-faced Sheila!'*
(Barry Humphries and Nicholas Garland, *The Wonderful World of Barry McKenzie*, 1988).

shekels *n*

money, coins. Sheqel or shekel is a Hebrew word, used since Biblical times to denote a unit of weight or a silver coin based upon that unit. The word is currently applied to the currency unit of Israel.

- *'I'm sorely in need of a few shekels.'*

shelf *vb Australian*

to inform on (someone). A now obsolescent underworld term. To be 'on the shelf' meant among other things to be under arrest or in prison, hence this derivation.

shell *n American*

1 a dollar. This usage may recall the use of cowries and other sea shells as currency, or come from the verb 'shell out' (in which shell refers to the shell or pod containing seeds). **Clams** is a synonym.

2 a beer, beercan. This rare sense of the word may conceivably draw a comparison between empty beer cans and discarded (ammunition) shell cases.

shellacked *adj*

drunk. A term originating in the USA in the 1920s; shellack (its standard meaning being to apply varnish) first meant to beat or punish; this was then extended to denote the effects of alcohol.

shellacking *n*

a beating, defeat. A humorous borrowing of the standard term meaning to slap on shellac, a resin used for varnishing and insulation. The slang sense arose in the USA where it is still heard; it is not unknown in British speech.

shellback *n*

a sailor who has crossed the equator; the opposite of **pollywog**. A 19th century term of uncertain origin which is still occasionally heard, usually meaning an experienced seaman.

Sherman (tank) *n British*

an act of masturbation, a **wank**. A probably ephemeral piece of rhyming slang of the late 1980s, quoted for instance in Steve Bell's *If* comic strip in the *Guardian* newspaper, it replaces the 1950s use of the same phrase for **yank**.

shickered, shikkered, shicker *adj*

drunk. The word is used primarily in the USA and Australia. It is from *shikker*, the Yiddish word for inebriated, which itself is from Hebrew *shikor*.

- *'You're stoned, Bazza!'*
  Come off it – just a bit shicker.'
  (*Bazza Comes into His Own*, cartoon by Barry Humphries and Nicholas Garland, 1988).

shikse, shiksa *n American*

a non-jewish female. A Yiddish term used by Jews of gentiles often, but nowadays not always, pejoratively.

shill *n*

a con-man's accomplice. The word has been used since the 19th century to denote a decoy or agent planted in a crowd to stimulate trade or encourage spending. Nowadays it usually refers to a participant in a rigged card game or other fraud. The origin of the term is unclear; it is said to be based either on a proper name such as Shillibeer or on an archaic dialect form of 'skill'.

shine *n American*

a black person. This now dated, usually pejorative term from the early 20th century (used by Raymond Chandler among others when describing the Los Angeles low-life of the 1940s) is still occasionally heard. The origin of this usage is obscure; it may be inspired by the appearance of black skin or contrasting white teeth, or may even be a shortening of shoe-shine.

shined-on *adj American*

ignored, disregarded. Its origin may be by analogy with **mooning** (showing one's buttocks as a gesture of contempt) or connected with **shine** meaning black person, hence social inferior; or more poetically may derive from the image of the moon shining down with cold indifference.

- *'I'm not going to be shined on! I think I deserve some attention.'*

shiner *n*

a black eye. The word has long been used to signify something prominent or noticeable; it acquired this specific sense around the early 1920s.

shirt-lifter *n*

a male homosexual. An Australian euphemism used pejoratively but usually humorously. The phrase originated in the 1960s and had been adopted by some British speakers by the late 1970s. (The Melbourne satirist Barry Humphries has frequently used the term, and has coined 'chemise-lifter' as a lesbian counterpart.)

shit n

a excrement. This word of Anglo-Saxon origin has parallels in other Germanic languages (in modern German *Scheisse*, for example). It derives from an ancient common verb, imitative of the sound of defecation. In English shit is now a mild vulgarism, although in rustic speech it has been the standard term for centuries.

b an act of defecation, usually in phrases such as have or take a shit.

c a contemptible person. This usage conveys real dislike or disapproval and has been common, particularly in upper and middle class speech in Britain since the 1920s.

● 'I've never known a fisherman to be a complete shit.'
(Recorded, fisherman, London 1986).

● 'Tiny 19-year-old Mark Aldrich beat up two youths who called him "a little shit" – but the comment "could be appropriate" a judge said yesterday.'
(Daily Mirror, 10 September 1988).

● 'He [Sir Anthony Meyer] was very disloyal over the Falklands and I think he's a shit.'
(Anonymous Tory minister, Guardian, 5 December 1989).

d an illicit drug, especially hashish. In the 1950s heroin users referred to their drug as shit; by the mid 1960s the word usually designated hashish (which is characteristically brown) or marihuana. When used in this context the word is synonymous with 'stuff' and carries virtually no pejorative overtones.

● 'Hey, this is excellent shit, man.'

● 'P.S. I cannot get any shit, my friends have split to other lands, they are free.'
(Reader's letter in Oz magazine, February 1970).

e rubbish, something worthless or inferior.

f nonsense, lies or deceitful talk. This is a specific use of shit as something worthless, or simply a shortening of **bullshit**.

● 'Come on, don't give me that shit, I wasn't born yesterday.'

g unnecessarily hostile behaviour or ill-treatment.

● 'I've put up with a lot of shit from them over the years.'
(Recorded, disgruntled employee, London, 1987).

shit vb

1 to defecate. The verb probably predates the noun form. Both seem to have existed in Old English, deriving from a common Germanic ancestor, itself cognate with the Greek *skat-* (later giving 'scatological'). Used intransitively the verb is now probably rarer than phrases such as have a shit. (The usual past form in British English is shat, in American shit.)

2 a to deceive, bamboozle, confuse (someone).

b to browbeat or annoy (someone). These transitive usages may originate as short forms of the verb **bullshit**, but have taken on separate identities as a designation, usually in American speech, of time-wasting or harrassment by lies or deceit.

3 'shit oneself' to be overcome with fear or panic.

shit adj

1 awful, inferior. A simple transference of the noun form, popular especially in British youth parlance of the 1980s.

● 'a shit record.'

453

2 *American* excellent, admirable. In the **hip** language of the street, of **rap** and hip-hop practitioners and their teenage imitators, shit has been used with this unexpected sense. The probably explanation is that it is a shortening of **shit-hot**.

shit a brick, shit bricks *vb*

to panic, be in a state of nervous apprehension. '*Shit a brick!*' is sometimes used as an exclamation of surprise or irritation.

shit and derision *n British*

a terrible state of affairs, confusion, mess. A mainly middle-class term typically used ruefully or humorously.

shit-ass *adj American*

very unpleasant, worthless, contemptible. Used especially in Canadian English, in much the same was as **shithouse** in Australia.

shitbag *n British*

an obnoxious or unpleasant person. A term which was widespread in the 1960s but is now less common.

shitcan *vb*

a *Australian* to denigrate, to **rubbish**. The word is used to signify the upbraiding or insulting of someone who deserves to be humiliated.
b *American* to throw away, reject.
Both senses derive from the noun shitcan as a toilet receptacle or rubbish bin.

shite *n British*

a variant form of **shit**, heard particularly in Northern English speech.

shitfaced *adj American*

drunk, helplessly or squalidly intoxicated. The term was particularly in vogue in the mid 1970s.

- '*She was totally shitfaced.*'
- '*Let's get shitfaced.*'

shit-for-brains *n*

a very stupid person. This term of abuse, deriving from an earlier rustic expression on the line of *he/she must have shit for brains*, has been widespread in the USA and Australia since the 1970s. It is now sometimes used adjectivally as in *a shit-for-brains idea*.

shithead *n*

1 a a despicably unpleasant or unfriendly person. This sense of the word has been predominant since the 1970s.
b a stupid or foolish person.
2 a hashish smoker. This sense of the word was briefly current from the mid 1960s, before being replaced by synonyms such as **doper**, etc. (**Pothead** was a less contentious or ambiguous synonym.)

shitheel *n American*

an unpleasant or obnoxious person. An embellished form of the milder and more common 'heel'.

shit-hot *adj*

a first-rate, excellent, powerful or dynamic.
b very keen, enthusiastic or punctilious. Shit here is used as an intensifier rather than a metaphor.

shithouse *n*

a a toilet.
- '*I like to think that in the shut up shit-house boxes respectable persons are behaving in a way of which they are slightly ashamed.*' (J. R. Ackerley, diary entry, 28 July 1953).
b a dirty or untidy place.

shithouse *adj*

terrible, inferior, worthless. This

elaboration of **shit** or **shitty** is particularly common in Australian speech.

shit-kicker n

a lowly menial, humble worker or rustic. An alternative to 'shit-shoveller' heard particularly in the USA and Australia.

shit-kicking adj

wild, earthy, primitive. The word is used especially in the context of country or rock music and signals approval rather than criticism.

- 'Some stomping, howling, shit-kicking rhythm 'n' blues'.

shit-list n American

a real or imaginary black list: either as kept by organizations or individuals.

- 'Jerry's top of my shit-list this week.'
- 'I think I'm on the shit list of every bar in town.'

shit on one's own doorstep
vb British

to do something damaging or un pardonable which will rebound upon oneself or one's friends; ruin one's own environment. This expression, like the politer 'foul the nest' has equivalents in most European languages (normally involving beds rather than doorsteps).

the shits n

a diarrhoea.

b a feeling of annoyance, disgust or bitter resentment. This figurative sense of the preceding vulgarism seems to be acquiring a separate identity, usually in the form it/he/she gives me the shits.

shit-scared adj British

terrified. An intensive form of the standard adjective.

the shitter n

a toilet.

shitty adj

a unpleasant, unfair. The word may mean merely bad or nasty, but usually carries overtones of resentment on the part of the speaker

- 'That was a really shitty thing to do.'

b inferior, poor quality.

- 'That cassette machine's got shitty sound.'

shiv n

a knife. An alternative rendering of **chiv**, a Romany word used in British underworld and low-life milieus since the 17th century. In the 20th century the word has been used (also in the USA) to mean any bladed weapon, including homemade knives and razors. **Shiv** was also used as a verb, particularly in the argot of street gangs of the 1950s and early 1980s.

shlemiel n

See **schlemiel**.

shlep, schlepp vb

a to drag, haul pull or carry.

b to drag oneself, move or travel with difficulty. This is the Yiddish version of the German verb *schleppen*, to drag. It has entered English slang via the American underworld and entertainment industry.

- 'I don't want to shlep all the way down there.'
(Budgie, British TV series, 1971).

shlep, schlepp n

1 a long, tedious, or tiring journey or burdensome task. The noun form is based on the verb.

- 'I hate having to go there – it's a real shlep up that hill.'

2 American a tedious, feeble or irritating person. This sense of the term is

inspired by the notion of burden and drag (literally and metaphorically) in the verb to **shlep**.

shlepper, schlepper n

1 a clumsy, inept and/or irritating person.

2 *American* a cadger, scrounger or hustler.

3 a sluttish, slovenly and/or immoral person. All the sub-senses of shlepper, which encompass a number of nuances and connotations, derive ultimately from the verb **shlep** with its suggestions of burdensome activity. In British English sense 3 has been extended to denote a prostitute in London slang.

shleppy, schleppy adj

American

irritating, tedious or awkward. The adjective derives from the verb **shlep** and the nouns **shlep** and **shlepper**.

shlock n

anything shoddy, inferior or meretricious. The word is Yiddish from German (either *schlacke*; dregs, or *schlagen*; slap or knock, in the sense of jacking up prices or damaged goods). The main application of shlock in American and later British slang has been to the products of the entertainment industry, particularly films and television.

shlockmeister n American

a a purveyor of shoddy or inferior merchandise.

b a TV quizmaster or master of ceremonies. The word is American Yiddish, based on **shlock**.

shlong n

See **schlong**.

shlub n

See **schlub**.

shm- prefix

this is the spelling representing the initial sound of many slang terms of Yiddish origin (see also **sch-** and **sh-**). Jewish wits and their emulators substitute these letters for the standard beginnings of English words to indicate mockery or negation.

- 'Revolution; Shmevolution.'
  (Headline in *Wall Street Journal*, January 1968).
- 'It's not the season for beagling.'
  'Season shmeason!'
  (*Ticket to Ride*, British TV series, 1988).

shmarmy adj British

smarmy, offensively ingratiating or smug. This new pronunciation of the common colloquialism represents a late 1980s phenomenon in fashionable and youth circles whereby certain words are altered to resemble the many words of Yiddish origin beginning with **sh-**.

- 'That shmarmy man in the coffee advert.'
  (Interview, *Making the Break*, British TV documentary about advertising, 1989).

shmeg n British

an idiot. A schoolchildren's term, fashionable in the 1980s, which is a variant form of **smeg** or **smeggy** (from smegma), a word popular among young males in the **punk** era. The altered pronunciation is influenced by Yiddish words such as **schmock**, **schmuck**, **schmendrick**, etc.

shmegegge, shmegeggy n

American

a contemptible or foolish person. The word is Yiddish, but seems to have been an American coinage, often heard in showbusiness circles. It does not appear to derive from any older term.

shmek n

an alternative spelling of **schmeck**.

Shmendrik n

See **Schmendrick**.

shmo, shmoe n

a fool, 'sucker' or **jerk**. The word was invented in the USA as an acceptable euphemism for the Yiddish **shmuck** in the late 1940s when the latter term was understood in its literal and obscene sense. Shmo, like shmuck, has been heard in Britain in Jewish and non-Jewish circles since the 1950s.

- 'She seems to like him but the guy's a bit of a shmo if you ask me.'

shmooze, shmoose vb

American

to chat or gossip at length, to have a heart-to-heart talk. This American Yiddish word comes from the Hebrew shmous, meaning 'things heard'. The word with a hard or soft final 's', has overtones of intimacy and affection rather than malicious gossip.

shmuck n

an alternative spelling of **schmuck**.

shmutter

See **schmutter**.

shnide adj British

snide (in both its standard sense of sneering and its slang sense of counterfeit). This quasi-Yiddish pronunciation has been popular with the **hip** young and some working class speakers since the 1950s; other words are having their pronunciation altered in similar fashion, (see **shmarmy** and **shmeg**, for instance). In this case the speakers may be reproducing the original pronunciation (see **snide** for the origins of the word).

shnorrer n

a cadger, scrounger or hustler. This is a Yiddish word occasionally used by non-Jewish speakers, particularly in the USA, to refer to a sponger or parasite. It derives from the German verb schnorren, to beg (itself from schnurren, purr or whirr – the sound of a beggar's entreaties or their musical accompaniment).

shoe adj American

excellent, admirable, fashionable or acceptable. A **preppie** term of approval, of uncertain derivation.

shoefly n

See **shoo-fly**.

shonk, shonker n British

1 a nose, especially a large and prominent one. A synonym of **conk**, this is derived from the following sense.

2 a Jew. An offensive, racist term dating from the 19th century, when shonniker was a Yiddish word denoting a small-time trader or pedlar.

shonkie, shonky n, adj

1 (a) Jew(ish). Like **shonk** and **shonker**, these words derive from shonniker an archaic Yiddish term for a pedlar or small-time tradesperson.

2 (a) mean, grasping (person).

shoo-fly n American

a detective, particularly an undercover agent investigating police corruption. Both shoe (or **gumshoe**) and fly are archaic terms for a plain clothes police officer. But that is not the only derivation on offer; 'shoo, fly, don't you bother me!' was the chorus to a song of the 1860s and 'shoo fly pie' was a delicacy so-called because it attracted flies.

shoo-in n American

a certainty; a candidate or contestant who is certain to win. The term is inspired by the idea of a horse which merely has to be ushered across the finishing line. The phrase is a common colloquialism in the USA which was picked up by some British journalists in the second half of the 1980s.

shoomers n pl British

patrons of clubs playing **acid house** music. *Shoom* was the name of one such club in London in 1988 when the cult was at its height (and before the **orbital raves** of 1989 became established). The word probably evokes the rush of euphoria experienced by users of the drug **ecstasy**.

shoot n American

an inoffensive euphemism for **shit** used as an exclamation since the 19th century.

shoot vb

1 also **shoot off** to ejaculate. The word has been used in this sense since the 19th century.

2 also **shoot up** to inject. A drug user's term, widespread since the late 1950s.

3 to leave hurriedly. A word used in Britain mainly by young people since the 1970s. It is probably a shortening of 'shoot off'.

● *'I've got to shoot, I'll see you later.'*

shoot a cat vb British

to vomit. A mainly middle and upper class phrase, since the 1970s largely replacing 'shoot the cat' which has been heard since the early 19th century. 'Cat' itself is an archaic verb for vomit, either from the sound of the word or from the cat's habit of deliberate regurgitating.

shooter n British

a gun. Neither a colourful nor particularly imaginative piece of slang, but the only term with any real currency, as opposed to the inventions of crime fiction.

● *'Standing over two corpses with a hot shooter in your hand.'*
(Len Deighton, *Twinkle, Twinkle Little Spy*, 1976)).

shooting gallery n

a place where drug users gather to inject themselves. The word has been applied to open spaces, pubs and communal flats for instance. It is an addict's pun which the police have also adopted both in Britain and the USA.

● *'Sam got his leg broken recently in some mysterious street-corner dispute – heading for the shooting gallery they call the Chateau Luzerne.'*
(*Sunday Times*, 10 September 1989).

shoot one's bolt/load/wad vb

to ejaculate. These terms for the male orgasm have been in use since the 19th century.

shoot one's cookies vb

American

an alternative form of **toss one's cookies/tacos**.

shoot the breeze/bull vb

to chat inconsequentially.

● *'[Stephen King] A regular guy who just happens to have 70 million copies of his books in print; a literary mechanic who has stepped off the production line to shoot the breeze for an hour or two.'*
(*Sunday Times* magazine, 15 October 1989).

shoot the shit vb American

to talk, gossip. A vulgarization of **shoot the breeze**.

shoot through vb Australian

a to die. An expression probably first introduced to an English audience via the lyrics of Rolf Harris's hit record 'Tie Me Kangaroo Down, Sport'.

b to leave, depart. The phrase has been in use in Australia since before World War II and is still heard.

shoot up vb

to inject (a narcotic).

shop vb British

to inform on (someone). The noun shop meant prison in 16th-century British underworld parlance. The verb form was first used to mean imprison, then (since the first decades of the 19th century) to cause to be imprisoned. The word has become a well-known colloquialism since the 1960s; in school and prison slang it has largely been overtaken by the synonymous **grass**.

the-short-and-curlies n pl British

pubic hair(s). The expressions 'got/grabbed/caught by the short-and-curlies', meaning rendered helpless or vulnerable, is a common vulgarism.

short arm n

the penis. A euphemism heard especially in the armed services; short arm is an archaic variation of 'small arm' in the sense of handgun. 'Arm' also reflects the common notion of the penis as a limb. 'Short-arm inspection' was the medical examination for symptoms of venereal disease.

shortarse n

a small person. A contemptuous term heard particularly in London working class speech and in Australia since the early years of the century.

short dog n American

a bottle of (cheap) wine or spirits. The phrase originated among hobos and winos. It may originally have specifed a small or half-bottle.

short-eyes n American

the underworld and prisoners' term for a child molester. The equivalent of the British **nonce**. The exact significance of the words is unclear; the phrase may be related to 'shut-eyes' an archaic term for sex offender.

short hairs n pl

pubic hair(s). A euphemism in use since the 19th century. It is most often heard figuratively in phrases such as 'they've got us by the short hairs' (i.e. at their mercy, rendered helpless).

short-house n British

a now obsolescent polite version of **shortarse**, mainly used in working class speech.

short out vb American

to lose control of oneself, lose one's temper, 'blow a fuse'. The image is of an electrical system developing a short circuit.

● 'He tries to keep his cool, but every now and again he shorts out.'

short-stuff n American

a small person. An affectionate or condescending form of address almost invariably said to a child by an adult.

shot n

an injection.
See **hotshot**.

shotgun n

a manoeuvre involving blowing the smoke from a **chillum** or **joint** containing cannabis into another person's mouth. The term dates from the **hippy** era. (It is also known as a 'blowback'.)

shout n British

1 a round of drinks or the ordering thereof.

● 'It's my shout.'

2 a message indicating an emergency, request for help, etc. (usually by radio). A piece of jargon used by police and emergency services.

shout vb Australian

1 also 'shout at the floor' to vomit.

2 to buy (someone) (a drink), to treat someone to something.

● 'Real generous . . . like giving me a job when I was stoney and shouting me all them chilled stubbies the other day.'
(The Adventures of Barry McKenzie, cartoon strip by Barry Humphries and Nicholas Garland, 1988).

show n British

an accidental display of a woman's underwear or naked body. A schoolboy word used especially in the later 1960s when 'revealing' skirts, blouses, etc. were in fashion.

shreddies n British

revolting, tattered, (shredded) underwear. A mainly middle class usage among students and schoolchildren, punning on the name of a popular breakfast cereal. The term has been heard since the 1960s. The term may possibly derive from the British rugby players' practice of 'shredding'. This involves an attempt to remove a pair of underpants from a male victim by pulling them upwards rather than downwards.

shrimper n American

a foot-fetishist. The term draws an analogy between the small pink crustaceans and the toes.

● 'I feed hamburger meat to the ants and roaches and a shrimper just happens to wander by and we have a love scene.'
(Mary Vivian Pearce, describing a scene from John Waters' film Mondo Trasho in The Incredibly Strange Film Show, British TV documentary series, 1988).

shrimping n American

sucking someone's toes for the purposes of sexual gratification, a jargon term among pornographers, prostitutes, etc.

shrink n

a psychiatrist, psychoanalyst. Shrink is a shortening of the earlier **headshrinker**, which was imported from America to Britain and Australia in the 1960s.

● 'We called in a consultant, a psychiatrist.'
'A shrink?'
'A highly respected doctor.'
(The Dancer's Touch, US film, 1989).

shtick n

a a performance, term, act or routine, in the context of the entertainment business.

b a piece of (repeated) behaviour characteristic of a particular person.

c a gimmick, trick or ruse.

The Yiddish word shtik from Middle German stücke; piece, was passed via American showbiz slang into fashionable speech and journalese in the 1980s.

shtum adj

silent, unspeaking. Most often heard in the phrase 'keep' or 'stay shtum'; be quiet. A Yiddish term from the German *stumm*; dumb, which entered London working-class slang via Jewish influence in the East End.

shtup *vb*

to have sex (with). This Yiddish word meaning press or push (oneself) is from the German *stupsen* (push). In American slang it has come to mean copulate in which sense it was occasionally heard in fashionable British speech in the 1980s.

- 'As any regular reader of Marie Claire magazine knows, some four out of five young French women would rather shop than shtup.' (Julie Burchill, *Elle* magazine, December 1987).

shudder, a (quick) shudder *n British*

a sex act. A rare expression (recalling the more common **knee-trembler**) used invariably by males.

shufti *n British*

a look, glance. The word is Arabic and was imported by armed service personnel before World War II.

shyster *n*

a dishonest, avaricious, contemptible person. The term is usually applied to unscrupulous professionals, particularly lawyers, who were the original subjects of the epithet in the USA in the mid-19th century. The etymology of shyster is open to several interpretations; 'shicer' was a 19th century anglicization of the German *scheisser* (literally 'shitter'); 'shy' was used in the 19th century colloquially to mean disreputable. In addition there is a historical record of a lawyer named Scheuster who was officially reprimanded in New York courtrooms for obstructive and unprofessional behaviour.

sickie *n Australian*

a day off work sick. The expression is used in cases of genuine illness, but usually has overtones of malingering.

- 'The people without whom planes cannot take off from Sydney airport strategically use the sickie to ruin the ambitions of thousands of tourists.' (Michael Parkinson, *Daily Mirror*, 17 April 1989).

sicko *n*

a pervert or mentally disturbed person. The word generally denotes a sexual deviant and is now heard in Britain as well as the USA, where it originated.

sidley, siddly *adj British*

stealthy, furtive, but in an elegant, even arrogant way. This rare word could possibly be a variant of 'sidity', an Edwardian word meaning affectedly insincere, which itself may be related to the notion of 'side', meaning duplicity or hypocrisy

- 'You've got to admire those sidley spades.' (Recorded, art student, London, 1986).

(the) siff *n*

an alternative spelling of **(the) syph**

simoleons *n American*

coins, cash, dollars, money. This archaic term (a blend of 'Simon'; obsolete slang for dollar and 'Napoleon'; a 20 franc gold coin) is occasionally revived in the same way as similar British words such as **rhino** or **pelf**.

simp *n*

a dim-witted individual. The word, originating in the USA early in the 20th century, was a shortening of 'simpleton'. More recently it has sometimes acquired connotations suggested by 'simper' and **wimp**.

- 'Some guest and some employer –
  the simp and the blimp.'
  (Honeymooners, US TV comedy
  series, 1951).

simpatico adj

agreeable, pleasant, friendly. The
Spanish and Italian word has been
adopted by certain English speakers.

sin bin n British

a place to which difficult or 'hopeless' cases are consigned. The term is
applied particularly to schools or other
educational or correctional institutions. It is derived from ice hockey,
where the sin bin is the rinkside area
where transgressing players serve out
time penalties.

sing vb

to inform, confess, give information
to the authorities. This underworld
term, originating in the USA before
World War II is often embellished as
'sing like a bird' or 'sing like a canary'.

- 'Last month the alleged cocaine
  importer from America was driven
  north to a secure house where he is
  said by detectives to be 'singing like
  a bird'.'
  (Observer, 16 August 1987).
- 'Suppose he got a bit of summary
  justice, then, did he?'
  'I don't know about that but I know
  the one who was caught was singing
  like mad.'
  (Police officers quoted in Inside the
  British Police, Simon Holdaway,
  1983).

sink vb

to drink, down (alcohol). This drinkers' euphemism usually occurs in such
phrases as the invitation to 'sink a few
(jars)'.

sink the sausage vb Australian

a version of hide the sausage.

siphon/syphon the python
vb

to urinate. A humorous vulgarism
introduced to a British audience via
the Australian character Barry McKenzie in Barry Humphries' and Nicholas
Garland's cartoon strip in Private Eye
magazine in the late 1960s. Drain the
lizard/dragon/snake is an alternative.

- 'Hang on a jiff, though, will you?
  I've just got to nip into the dunnee
  to syphon the python.'
  (Bazza Pulls It Off, cartoon strip by
  Barry Humphries and Nicholas
  Garland, 1988).

sit down vb

to acquiesce, submit or suffer in silence. The opposite to 'standing up for
oneself', sit down is a synonym for the
(probably more widespread) lie down.
The phrase has become a vogue term
and a business-jargon expression rather than a mere metaphor.

- 'There's no way I'm going to sit
  down for this one. We've taken
  enough!'

sit-down n

an act of defecation, a squat. A euphemism which can be used on the
broadcast media (occurring in the US
TV series Hill Street Blues, for instance).

sixty-nine n

simultaneous and mutual oral sex.
The term, originating in the French
soixante-neuf (suggested by the shape
of bodies engaged in cunnilingus and
fellatio) is from the jargon of pornography and prostitution. The expression
also occurs as a verb.

size queen n

a male homosexual who favours sexual partners according to the size of
their genitals. The expression is part of
the post-1960s gay lexicon and is gen-

erally used to indicate disapproval. The term is occasionally applied to women adopting the same criterion.

skag n

another spelling of **scag**.

skank n, adj American

something or someone unpleasant or disgusting. The word seems to have arisen in black speech, but its etymology is uncertain. Skank is sometimes used specifically to denote an immoral woman or prostitute.

skanking n

a swinging and jerking style of dancing characteristic of reggae and the 'two-tone' music of 1977 to 1980. The word originally means stealing, and hence behaving disreputably, moving stealthily, in Jamaican patois.

skat adj

fashionable. A short-lived vogue word from 1985 and 1986, of unknown origin. The word was used by adolescents in the fashion, music and club milieus of New York and London.

skate n American

a pushover, easy task, a 'smooth ride'. A 1980s usage, from the image of skating across a surface or between obstacles.
- 'Relax, it's going to be a skate.'

skedaddle vb

to flee, leave quickly. The term is often heard as an imperative. It was first recorded during the American Civil War and several suggestions have been made as to the word's derivation; it is probably a form of a dialect version of 'scatter' or 'scuttle'.

-ski, -sky suffix American

a humorous ending added, usually to slang terms, by teenagers and students. Examples are **brewski**, **finski**, **buttinsky**. The suffix occurs in Slavonic languages and in many Yiddish surnames.

skid vb

1 to leave, go away. A usage which was fashionable among adolescents in Britain in the late 1980s.

2 British to 'slum', make do with little money, secondhand clothes, etc. This student term of the 1980s is probably inspired by 'skid row'.

skid-lid n British

a crash helmet.

skid-marks n pl

traces of excrement on underwear.
- 'Hand-me downs – me first nappy had your skid-marks on it!' (Birds of a Feather, British TV comedy series, October 1989).

skidoo, skiddoo vb

a version of **skedaddle**.

skids n pl Australian

the fortunes of fate, hard luck, the 'breaks'. An encapsulation of the philosophy of the young and callously indifferent, most often heard in the shrug-off sentence 'them's the skids': 'that's the breaks'.
- '"Them's the skids", as the young fry say.' (Peter Corris, The Greenwich Apartments, 1986).

skied adj American

a **psyched up** or **psyched out**.
b **spaced out**. A fairly rare American adolescents' term.

skill n British

a younger schoolchildren's exclamation of admiration, appreciation or approval, heard in the late 1980s. The word has been extended from its original literal sense to become an all purpose vogue word, sometimes in the phrase 'skill and brill'.

skimming n

taking money illegally (for example before declaring it for tax purposes, or to defraud the eventual recipients) from income or profits, especially in casinos. The word is part of underworld jargon as used by organized crime in the USA. 'Skim' was used to mean money or profit in both Britain and the USA in the 19th century, the image being evoked being that of taking the cream off the top of the milk.

skin n

1 *British* a **skinhead**.

2 *British* a cigarette rolling paper, as part of the makings of a **joint**. A word from the lexicon of drug users since the 1960s, now occasionally heard to describe cigarette papers put to more legitimate use.

See also **skin up**.

3 *American* a dollar bill.

skin vb

to rob or defraud, **rip off** or 'fleece' someone. The word implies comprehensive and efficient removal of wealth.

● '*He thought he was pretty smart but those guys skinned him.*'
● '*We got skinned in that deal.*'

skin and blister n British

sister. A cockney rhyming-slang phrase which is still known if not used by many Londoners.

skinflick n

a pornographic or semi-pornographic film. The skin element of the phrase refers to nudity; **flick** has been a slang

term for film since the days of the silent movie. Skinflick is an Americanism which has been understood albeit not widely used in other English-speaking areas since the early 1970s.

skinful n

an excess of alcohol. The word dates from the 18th century and evokes a distended belly or bladder.

● '*We'd better get him home, he's had a skinful.*'

skinhead n

1 a bald person or someone with close-cropped hair. (**Chrome-dome** is a more recent synonym.)

2 a member of a working class youth cult originating in the late 1960s. the skinheads (the term was applied scornfully by longer-haired contemporaries, particularly **hippies**) mutated from the **mods** and **tickets** of the mid-1960s. They dressed in a functional uniform of American shirts, jeans and, often, **bovver boots** and espoused soul music and gang violence. The style survived with only minor changes into the 1980s and 90s; in the 1970s skinheads became firmly identified with racism, right-wing extremism and football hooliganism.

skinny-dipping n

bathing in the nude. An Americanism which established itself in world English in the early 1970s.

● '*Once every summer teenagers are caught skinny-dipping after dark, causing a scandal.*'
(*The Official Preppie Handbook*, Lisa Birnbach, 1980).

skin-pop vb

to inject (an illicit drug) intramuscularly or into flesh, rather than into a vein. An addicts' term.

skins n pl

1 drums, in the jargon of jazz and rock musicians.

2 car or motorcycle tyres in the jargon of racers, bikers, etc.

3 British **skinheads**.

skin up vb

to roll a **joint**. From **skin**; a cigarette rolling paper.

skip n

1 British an escape or an instance of jumping bail. This specialized use of the common colloquialism for 'avoid' is part of underworld jargon.

2 American a person who fails to answer a bail bond, an escapee.

3 British boss, **guvnor**. A shortening of **skipper**, used typically by police officers in familiar address to a superior, or, in sports, by team-members to their captain.

4 British a place to sleep or shelter. A shortened form of the tramps' **skipper**.

5 British a dilapidated, old or cheap vehicle, particularly a car. The name of the common large metal refuse containers has been appropriated as a vogue term among schoolchildren since around 1988. (One of a series of popular jokes at the expense of Skoda, likening the Czechoslovak car to a rubbish skip.)

skipper n British

1 a captain of a ship or a team. Skipper in this sense is not, strictly speaking, slang, although it is considered to be so by some. The word has been in use since it was anglicized from the Middle Dutch schipper (from schip, ship).

2 British a rough shelter, place to sleep for the night, typically in a derelict building. The word, which may describe no more than a patch of rough ground, is now a near-synonym for **doss house** or **derry**. It is part of the vocabulary of tramps, **dossers** and other down-and-outs, and originated in Celtic words for barn (rendered as ysgubor in Welsh, sciber in Old Cornish).

● 'When you're drunk and face-down in some skipper you just don't think there's much future in it.'
(Recorded, vagrant, Waterloo, London 1987).

3 British friend, **mate**. A friendly term of address between males, now rarely used except by vagrants.

skipper vb British

to sleep rough, be homeless. From the noun.

● 'I tell you, I was forced to skipper. I never had any choice.'
(Recorded, vagrant, Waterloo, London, 1987).

skippering n British

sleeping rough, living in derelict buildings or improvized or makeshift shelters. From the second sense of the noun **skipper**.

skippy n American

a male homosexual, particularly an effeminate or affected one. the word was previously used to refer to female prostitutes by the US army in the Pacific. 'Skibby' was an earlier form of the word, the derivation of which is obscure: some relation to 'skivvy' looks possible, but there is no proof of this.

skip-tracer n American

a (latter-day) bounty-hunter, in the updated jargon of law enforcers. The meaning of **skip** in this example is someone who has jumped bail or escaped from custody.

skirt n

a woman or girl, or females in general. A depersonalizing term as used by males in the 20th century. The usage is

465

much older, probably originating in the 1500s.

skive n British

a dodge or ruse. From the verb form.
- *'Bill's got a good skive for getting off games.'*

skive, skive off vb British

to avoid work or duty, malinger. Skive is either from the obscure verb in standard English meaning to shave off (pieces of leather), from Old Norse *skifa*, to slice, or from another unrecorded dialect term. It has been heard in the sense of shirk since the early 20th century.

skiver n British

an idler, malingerer, avoider of work.
- *'That bastard's hardly done a day's work since he's been here. He's a right little skiver.'*

skivvies n pl American

men's underwear. The origin of the word is not known.
- *'Ordell looked over at Louis Gara having his morning coffee in his skivvies, his bare feet up on the coffee table.'*
(Elmore Leonard, *The Switch*, 1978).

skull n American

1 a synonym for 'head' in racy speech or **hip** talk. The word most usually occurs in the phrase **out of one's skull** (intoxicated or crazy) or in the following extended specialized sense.
2 oral sex, especially fellatio. This term, popular among college students since the late 1970s, is either derived from, or an imitation of black street slang; a racier version of **head**, in its sexual context. It is usually used as part of the parodic exhortation 'whip some skull on me baby!'.

skull vb Australian

to drink (alcohol).

skulled adj

drunk or **stoned** on drugs. the term is a shorter form of **out of one's skull** (although when used by Australian speakers the verb skull meaning to drink may also come into play).

skull orchard n

a cemetery. An alternative form of **bone orchard**, heard especially in the USA.

sky pilot n

a priest, particularly a naval or military chaplain. The phrase dates from the later 19th century.

sky rocket n British

a pocket. A piece of London rhyming slang which is still used unselfconsciously by some older speakers. **Davy Crockett** and **Lucy Locket** are alternative forms.

slack n

See **cut (someone) a little/slack**.

slack adj Caribbean

immoral, particularly in a sexual context. This use of the word is archaic in Britain (although it was probably the origin of **slag**) but survives in **Jamaica talk**.
- *'The spurned wife of Tessa Sanderson's lover called the Olympic athlete "slack" – Jamaican slang for promiscuous.'*
(*Guardian*, February 1990).

slag n British

a a (supposedly) promiscuous woman. A derogatory word used mainly by working-class men and women which often carries overtones of slovenliness and coarseness.

• 'Self-conscious and self-adoring parodists of slagdom, such as Madonna and Samantha Fox, understand this; that a man who calls a woman a slag isn't saying anything about her, but a lot about his condom size.'
(Julie Burchill, Elle magazine, December 1987).

• 'I had an argument with this other girl over a boy. Her mates wrote "Donna is a slag" in the school toilet.'
(Observer, February 1988).

b a despicable male. The word conveys real contempt and distaste; it is now generally heard in London working-class or criminal usage. Slag has been used since the 18th century to convey notions of moral laxity and worthlessness. The ultimate source of the word is probably in 'slack' rather than 'slag' meaning mining or smelting residue.

slag vb
See **slag off**.

a slagging n British
a bout of criticism, denigration or abuse, a serious dressing-down. The noun comes from the verb to **slag** or **slag off**.

• 'This time at The Marquee, they provoked a review in Melody Maker – "a slagging, but still worth it".'
(Independent, 27 January 1989).

slaggy adj British
criminal, reprehensible, coarse and drab. An adjective applied to individuals, derived from the noun **slag**.

slag off, slag vb British
to denigrate, criticize bitterly or insult. This working class term probably derives from the dialect slag, meaning to smear, or from the standard English

noun slag, meaning refuse or waste material. In the form 'slag' the modern expression occurs in American speech. US authorities cite the German verb schlagen (to beat or lash), but this is an unlikely source for the British usage.

• 'We get slagged off something chronic by a lot of people.'
(Recorded, telephone engineer, London, May 1989).

• 'The announcement this week that Turkey and Bulgaria have signed an agreement to bury hatchets startled not only outside observers – used to the two countries slugging each other off since time immemorial – but also many officials from the countries concerned.'
(Independent, 26 February 1988).

slaister n British
a messy eater, dribbler, a dirty, slovenly person. A Scottish dialect term used especially of children and occasionally heard south of the border.

slam dancing n
a form of dancing associated with **hardcore** music in which devotees literally hurl themselves bodily at each other (and at walls, stages or other fixtures).

slammed adj British
drunk. A mainly middle- and upper-class term of the 1980s. (Certain cocktails are known as 'slammers'; both words evoke the sudden and stunning effect of strong alcohol.)

slammer n
prison. An Americanism used in Britain and Australia since the early 1960s, it was originally a 1930s slang word for door, hence cell door and, since World War II, jail.

• 'You're consortin' with a criminal,

*so when he goes to the slammer,
you go, too!'*
(*Smokey and the Bandit III,* US
film, 1983).

slant *n*

an oriental person. A shortening of
'slant-eyed', used in the United States
and Australia since the 1960s and now
heard among young Londoners; for example, young city businessmen referring disparagingly to the Japanese.

slap *n British*

1 make-up, face-paint. A piece of
theatrical slang which Partridge's *Dictionary of Slang and Unconventional
English* dates to 1860 and claims to be
obsolete by 1930. In fact the term is still
in common currency in the theatre in
the late 1980s.
● *'We're going to need some more
slap on here.'*
2 a meal, feast. Derived from 'slap-
up' (meal), the term was recorded
among bohemians and students in the
late 1950s and early 1960s.
● *'A good slap.'*

slap-and-tickle *n British*

petting, kissing and caressing. A
joky and innocuous euphemism for
love-play of various degrees of intensity. The phrase dates from the Edwardian era but was most popular in the late
1950s, usually in the form 'a bit of slap-
and-tickle'.

slapper *n British*

a prostitute or slut. This working
class term from East London and Essex
is probably a corruption of **shlepper** or
schlepper, a word of Yiddish origin,
one of whose meanings is a slovenly or
immoral woman.

slash *n British*

an act of urination. A vulgar term,
used generally by males. The word
came into use in this sense sometime
before the 1950s, but was not recorded
in writing until recently. The word
usually occurs in phrases such as 'have
a slash' or 'take a slash'. Slash may be
echoic (as 'slosh' or 'slush') or may be
inspired by the standard use of the
word to refer to rain driving obliquely.

slash *vb British*

to urinate. The verb form is less common than the noun.

slats *n pl*

1 ribs. A now obsolete slang term
from the argot of boxers, bruisers,
brawlers, etc., usually in the form of 'a
punch/kick in the slats'.
2 *Australian* the vulval labia.

sleaze *n*

1 shabbiness, sordidness, immorality. This term is a back formation from
the earlier **sleazy**. Like the adjective,
the noun form was adopted from
American slang in the early 1970s.
2 a squalid, disreputable or reprehensible person. A term indicating
great distaste and disapproval, based
on the earlier adjective, **sleazy**.
See *also* **sleazo**.

sleazeball, sleaze-bag, sleaze-bucket *n American*

a very unpleasant person. A socially
acceptable alternative to terms such as
shit-bag, etc., popular in the late 1970s
and 1980s.

sleazo, sleazoid *n*

a **sleazy** person; a disreputable, immoral or otherwise repellant individual. These Americanisms are now heard
elsewhere.

sleazy *adj*

sordid, squalid, shabby and/or disreputable. This word existed in Ameri-

can speech for many years, but remained obscure until the late 1960s. By the early 1970s it had started to establish itself in British and Australian usage. Sleazy is said by some to be a corruption of 'Silesia', used first in Britain to denote low quality linen from that region. Eric Partridge demurs, deriving it from slimy and greasy.

sleeping policeman n British

a ridge across a road or driveway in order to slow down traffic. These were known as speed-bumps or speed-ramps in official jargon and as sleeping policemen in popular speech since the 1970s when they were introduced. The phrase is said to come from Caribbean English.

sleighride n American

2 a smooth or easy passage, the easy achievement of a task.

2 a bout of cocaine intoxication. A witticism inspired by the exhilaration resulting from ingestion of **snow**.

slewed adj

drunk. The word (formerly sometimes spelled 'slued') has been used in this sense since the mid-19th century.

slice-and-dice n American

another term for **splatter movie**. (The phrase was originally used in advertising kitchen food processors.)

slime vb

1 to behave in a devious, sycophantic or ingratiating way. A usage popular among adolescents and young adults in the 1980s.

2 Australian to ejaculate.

slime, slimeball, slimebucket, slimebag

a despicable person; popular terms of abuse or distaste in the 1980s.

Slim Jim n

a bootlace tie as worn by cowboys, **teddy boys**, etc.

sling one's hook vb British

to leave, go away. This term which originated and largely survives in working-class speech is either of nautical or mining origin. It dates from the second half of the 19th century. **Hook it** is a racier alternative.

● 'We don't want you here. Go on, sling your 'ook!'

slip it to someone vb British

to have sex with someone. A version of the more common vulgar euphemism, **slip someone a length**. The phrase is generally employed by men and usually implies a casual and surreptitious coupling.

slip someone a length vb

to have sex with someone (from the male point of view). A euphemism originating in the 19th century.

slit n

a the vagina.

● 'A vagina indeed! Admittedly, some people did call it a slit sometimes.'
(Nice Work by David Lodge, 1988).

b a female. The word in the plural was adopted as the name of a British all-girl **punk** group in 1977.

Sloane Ranger, sloane n
British

a young upper-middle or upper-class person, educated at a public school and affecting certain well defined modes of dress and behaviour. The phrase was applied to a recognizable sub-category of British youth displaying characteristics of what used to be known as the 'county set'. The equivalent of the American **preppies** and the French 'B.C.B.G.'s, (for 'bon chic, bon genre'), Sloane Rangers were defined and described by the journalists Peter York and later Ann Barr in articles in Harpers and Queen magazine and publications such as The Official Sloane Ranger's Handbook (1982). The first time the words appeared in print was in October 1975, but Peter York was not the originator of the expression. It was used by bar-room wits of the early 1970s to refer to would-be 'men about town' frequenting Chelsea pubs, only some of whom were the upper-class youths (then known solely as **Hooray Henrys**) later so described. The source of the pun, the Lone Ranger was the dashing cowboy hero of a 1950s TV series; Sloane Square is in Chelsea.

● 'The appalling Sloane Ranger look. Worn by strapping, horsey girls aged 20 going on 53. Other components: striped shirts, a tame string of pearls, impenetrable pleated skirt, blue tights and prissy shoes. Printed headscarves optional. Thick ankles mandatory.' (Description of female Sloane Ranger, Judy Rumbold, Guardian, 11 December 1989).

slob n

a coarse, slovenly and/or lazy individual. This word had existed for many years in Anglo-Irish speech where it denoted a fat, slow child (probably from slab, Irish Gaelic for mud). Coincidentally a similar word, apparently of Slavonic origin and rendered as zhlub or shlub, exists in Yiddish. It means an uncouth person, but is probably derived from a root form related to the Czech zlobit, to get angry.

slope n

an oriental person, especially a Vietnamese. This derogatory term, deriving from 'slope-eyed', moved from the US to Australia in the 1970s.

● 'The newest "new Australians", as anyone who looks foreign is called, are the Lebanese and the Vietnamese, the "slopes".' (Observer magazine, 13 December 1987). Compare **slant**.

slope off vb

to leave, depart surreptitiously. This colloquialism derives from the 19th century slang use of 'slope' alone to mean decamp or sneak away. The term originated in the USA. It is either from the Dutch sloop, to steal away or from the standard verb.

sloppy joe n

a large baggy sweater as worn by students, **bobby-soxers** and especially **beatniks**. The term originated in the USA in the 1940s.

slosh vb British

to hit. This word was very widespread in the 1950s and early 1960s among working-class speakers and in school playgrounds. The word often referred to serious violence.

● 'Say that again and I'll slosh you.'

sloshed adj

drunk. One of the most common and least offensive terms in British usage since the late 19th century. It is also heard in the USA.

slot n

a the anus. In **gay** parlance.
b the vagina.

smack n

heroin. Originally an American term, the word spread to Britain and Australia at the time of the Vietnam War. It is derived from the Yiddish *shmek*, meaning a sniff, whiff or taste, reinforced by the English word's suggestion of a sudden, violent effect.

- 'I don't think Jimmy Hendrix was on smack 'cos I was with him last Saturday night and I know when a man's on smack and he wasn't.' (Murray Roman, quoted in Oz magazine, June 1969).
- 'Two days later I was in All Saints Road, Notting Hill, with a knife being held against my neck after I tried to score some smack.' (Former addict quoted in the Observer Magazine, December 1987).
- 'While Liverpool's council estates regularly hit the headlines with their tales of smack use among the high rises, Tam's acquaintances avoided publicity.' (Independent, 4 April 1988).

smacked-out adj

addicted to, or under the influence of heroin (**smack**).

- 'Nathan had staked everything he had ever worked for on this loser who was too smacked out to worry about taking MOM Records into the bankruptcy court.' (Platinum Logic, Tony Parsons, 1981).

smacker n

a noisy or explosive kiss. This common term is often elaborated into 'smackeroo' or 'smackeroony'.

- 'She gave him a big smacker and sent him on his way.'

smackers n pl

pounds or dollars. Like **smacker** in the sense of kiss, this lighthearted term is often embellished to give 'smackeroos' or 'smackeroonies'. The original word probably refers to the slapping of coins or notes onto a table or counter or into the palm of an outstretched hand.

- 'Do you wanna take the thousand smackers or try for the sensational bathroom suite?' (Biff cartoon, 1986).

smack-head n adj

a heroin addict, a junkie. A combining of **smack** with the '-head' suffix meaning habitué. ('Smack-freak' was a synonymous term of the late 1960s and early 1970s, subsequently yielding to smack-head in popularity.)

- 'If a smack-head tries to chat you up, what's he really after?' (UK Government anti-heroin advertisement, 1986).

smartarse, smartass n, adj

(a) know-all, smug or insolent (person). The word describes someone whose display of real or supposed cleverness renders them obnoxious. 'Smart alec' or 'wise-guy' are politer synonyms.

- 'If she felt like giving them a smartass answer, why didn't she? Because she couldn't think of a smartass answer fast enough.' (Elmore Leonard, The Switch, 1978).

smartmouth n American

a cheeky, insolent or disrespectful person.

smartmouth vb American

to cheek, speak disrespectfully or insolently (of someone).

smarts n

intelligence, wits. A coinage inspired by the word wits itself and/or 'brains'. The word is American, but is occasionally heard in Britain.

- 'She's got more than her share of smarts.'

smashed adj

drunk or intoxicated by drugs.

● 'Having discovered that it is
possible to be smashed, keep on the
stereo headphones AND read, I
have managed to . . . get through
. . . several books.'
(Jim Anderson in Oz magazine,
February 1970).

● 'Her husband Russ added: "She
[Joan Kennedy] looked smashed
and I do mean smashed. She was
goo-goo-eyed."'
(News of the World, 10 July 1988).

smash mouth vb American

to kiss. A humorous equivalent to
the better known 'chew face' among
adolescents.

smeg, smeggy n British

a foolish and/or dirty person. These
terms, deriving from smegma, are vulgarisms which have been popular with
schoolboys, students, **punks** and other
youths since the mid 1970s. Despite
their origin the words do not usually
indicate great distaste but rather mild
contempt or even affection. Smeg and
various derivatives such as 'smeg-
head' were used in the cult British TV
comedy series of the late 1980s Red
Dwarf as an all-purpose swearword, a
euphemism for **fuck**.

smidgin, smidgeon, smidgen, smidge n

a small amount, soupçon, touch.
The word is a mid-19th century American variant form of 'smitch', an English
dialect word (for stain or smut), itself a
form of 'smudge'. Smidgin is now common throughout the anglophone
world.

● 'If the House is sitting, I tend to
smuggle a smidgin of High Tea –
perhaps a toasted cheese and baked
bean sandwich, or some of Mr
Matthews's excellent Turkey
Drumsticks – into the Chamber in a
trouser pocket.'

(Private Eye, 27 October 1989).

smoke vb American

a to kill. A euphemism in underworld and police usage since the
1940s, this unsentimental term was
fashionable in teenage speech and
crime fiction in the 1980s.

b also 'smoke out', 'smoke off' to defeat or to better (someone) in the **hip**
jargon of the rock music business since
the 1970s.

● 'Out-playing the headliner is
known in the trade as "smoking"
. . . Thin Lizzy were notorious for
smoking their superiors – and
consequently for being
mysteriously removed from bills.'
(Independent, 27 January 1989).

smoke n

a tobacco.
b hashish or marihuana.

the smoke, the big smoke n

London or any large town or city (in
British and Australian usage). The
word was first recorded in this sense in
1864 referring to London. It usually
evokes the city as seen by those who
are not native to it or are in temporary
exile from it.

● 'This is one of the things they have
come for – an escape from the
Smoke and a whiff of the sea.'
(Town magazine, September 1963).

● 'Physical action . . . football and
walking or even climbing up
scafolding [sic] don't tell that
there's much of that in the smoke.'
(Letter to Oz magazine, June 1969).

smoke-o, smoko, smoke-ho
n Australian

a break from work for tea, coffee and/
or a cigarette.

smoker n British

1 an old, worn-out or mechanically

472

unsound motor-car. A piece of jargon from the vocabulary of second-hand car dealers and enthusiasts.

2 a cannabis smoker.

smokey, smoky n American

a police officer. The term derives from 'Smokey the Bear', a cartoon character wearing the hat of a Forest Ranger, who issued warnings against careless behaviour that could cause forest fires; it was then applied, jocularly at first, to any uniformed authority figure. Smokey became the CB (Citizens' Band) radio code word for highway patrol officer in the 1970s.

the smother game n British

pickpocketing. An underworld term of the 1950s. ('Smother' is an even older word for overcoat.)

smudger n British

1 a friend, 'mate'.
- 'All right me old smudger?'

2 a photographer. A jocular reference to inept developing and printing.

3 a flatulent person. All three sense of the word are from working class speech; the first and third specific to the London area. All are now dated but not obsolete.

snack attack n

a bout of compulsive eating, (the) munchies. A late 1980s vogue term, in limited circulation (as is its contemporary, tack attack).
- 'I'm afraid in the middle of the night I had a snack attack.'

snafu n

an impossible situation, a foul-up, a labyrinth of incompetence. The expression, from 'Situation Normal, All Fucked Up' was developed in the US army in World War II (in imitation of that institution's passion for acro-

nyms) to describe the quotidian effects of bureaucratic stupidity.
- 'I tell you, its been snafu after bloody snafu here.'
(Recorded, businessman, London, 1987).

snags n pl Australian

sausages. A word in use since the 1940s and still heard, particularly at barbies.

snakes n Australian

a urine or an act of urination. The word is native Australian rhyming slang from 'snake's hiss'; piss.

b a toilet.

snap n British

1 a snack, packed lunch. A Northern English dialect version of snack often heard in the phrase 'snap tin'; lunch box.
- 'My senior managers go to the local pub and the men prefer to bring their own snap.'
(Nice Work, David Lodge, 1988).

2 a glass ampoule of amyl nitrite. The stimulant drug, which has been widely abused, is inhaled after the ampoule has been broken open. Popper is a more modern term.

snart vb, n British

a (to) snigger or snort (with derision).

b (to) sniff or inhale. (In the latter sense, 'snart up' is an alternative form.)

c to sneeze.

A rare expression heard among students and others since the early 1970s. It is a humorous corruption of snort in both its standard and slang senses.

snatch n

1 a the vagina.

b women in general. In the 16th century this word was used to denote an impromptu and/or hasty ('snatched') sexual encounter. The meaning was transferred to the female pudenda, and in the 20th century extended to refer to females as sex objects. The use of snatch in these senses has never been common but enjoyed a brief vogue in the late 1960s and early 1970s, first in the US and Canada, subsequently in Britain.

2 British an instance of bag-snatching, in the argot of teenage muggers.

● 'The child muggers told with chilling frankness how and why they resorted to muggings or "snatches" as they are sometimes called.'
(Observer, 22 May 1988).

3 a kidnap or abduction, in underworld jargon.

snazz n

elegance, smart showiness, élan. The noun, most commonly encountered in American speech, is a back-formation from the adjective **snazzy**.

snazzed-up adj

smart, elegant, dressed-up, embellished or enhanced. A more recent derivation of **snazzy**.

snazzy adj

smart, elegant, stylishly impressive. The word (and its connotations) are a blend of 'snappy' and 'jazzy'. It originated in the USA in the 1940s.

● 'They'd toy with their goddamn transistor radios, and admire their snazzy new clothes in front of a full-length mirror.'
(Len Deighton, Twinkle, Twinkle Little Spy, 1976).

sneaky Pete n American

very cheap, low quality alcohol, especially wine or the dregs thereof. The phrase is used by hobos, among others, and is probably inspired by the notion of a surreptitious nip of a 'familiar companion' or of the effects 'sneaking up' on the drinker.

sneeze n

cocaine. A term used by **yuppies** in the late 1980s.

snide adj British

illegal, counterfeit, dishonest or unacceptable. The word's exact origins are obscure but it is related to the German schneiden (or its Dutch or Yiddish equivalent), meaning clip, and was used in the context both of coin-cutting and of cutting remarks. The former sense gives rise to the modern slang usage and the latter to the standard English meaning. Snide was first heard in Britain in the mid-19th century. Interestingly, young speakers have begun to revert to a Yiddish or Germanic pronunciation of the word as **shnide**.

● 'Are you accusing me of selling snide gear?'
(Recorded, street trader, Portobello Road, London, 1986).

snip n

a small, insignificant and/or irritating person. The word usually implies aggression and pettiness. It is derived from the notion of snip meaning to cut.

● 'Some little snip throwing her weight around.'

snippy adj

irritatingly critical, brusque or presumptuous. Snippy is a dialect word for 'cutting' in origin.

● 'She struck me as a little snippy snitch.'

snit n

1 a a small, obnoxious or devious person. The term is typically used of a smug or devious child.

b an insignificant person. The word

is an invention influenced by **snip**, **snitch** and possibly **snot**.

2 a fit of irritation, tantrum.

snitch *vb*

to inform (on someone). Snitch was originally a slang term for nose which was itself used to signify a police spy or grass in the 18th century (as was **nark**). Snitch began to be used in the verb form in the 19th century and is still in use in the USA, although in Britain it survives mainly in children's speech, meaning 'tell tales'.

snitch *n*

an informer. the word (like **nark** originally meaning 'nose') was first used in this sense in the 18th century. It is still used in the USA to mean a paid police informer, whereas in Britain it is largely confined to the language of children, in which it denotes a 'tell-tale'.

snockered *adj*

1 an alternative form of **schnockered**.

2 American completed, finalized, solved. A term heard particularly among schoolchildren, students and parents.

snog *vb*

to kiss ('snog up', used transitively, is a racier late 1900s version). This lighthearted word, used typically by children and adolescents, first appeared in Britain before World War II. It is probably a variant of 'snug' and 'snuggle (up)'. In the 1950s particularly in the USA, snog took on a more general sense of flirt. It retains its specific sense in Britain.

● 'And I expect she's seen you
walking out with Dolly Clackett,
and snogging on the front porch.'
(*Hancock's Half-hour*, BBC radio
comedy, May 1960).

snog *n British*

a kissing session. (For the origin of the term, see the verb form.)

● 'They were having a quick snog
while the lights were out.'

snoot *n*

1 nose. A humorous variant form of 'snout'. (In Middle English snout was written snute and pronounced 'snooter'.)

● 'A punch on the snoot.'

2 a snooty person.

snooze *n*

something boring or tedious. A synonym of **yawn**.

● 'I must admit that last Tuesday's
board meeting was a bit of a
snooze.'
(*Maid to Order*, US film, 1987).

snore *n*

a boring experience. A synonym of **snooze** and **yawn**, typically used by adolescents.

● 'A three hour talk on the EEC; God
what a snore!'

snork *n Australian*

1 a baby or immature person. The word is said to be a distortion of 'stork', but may also be influenced by such words as 'snort', 'snicker', 'snit', 'snot' and the following sense of the word.

2 a sausage. This rare use of the word may be related to the synonymous **snag**.

snorker *n Australian*

a a sausage.

b penis.

The words are obviously related to the Australian **snork**, and perhaps to **snag**, but the exact origin of all of these terms is obscure.

snort

snort vb

to sniff or inhale (illicit drugs such as heroin, cocaine, amphetamines, etc.). An Americanism which spread to Britain and Australia in the 1960s. The word supplanted the more sedate 'sniff', used previously.

- 'And am I dreary if I think that showing someone snorting coke on the telly is not such a great idea?' (Janet Street-Porter, Today, 19 March 1988).

snort n

1 a drink of alcohol, typically of spirits. A colloquialism which imitates the sharp exhalation accompanying a gulp of liquor.

2 a single dose of a drug usually inhaled, such as cocaine.

- 'We're down to our last couple of snorts – I'd better phone the Man.'

snot n

1 mucus from the nose. The word is from Middle English snotte, itself from old English gesnot, variant forms of which existed in all Germanic languages. These terms are related either to 'snout' or to an Indo-European root meaning to flow. Snot is a widespread term but because of its distasteful context is considered a vulgarism.

- 'Wipe the snot off your face and cheer up.'

2 an obnoxious person, usually a young or diminutive and self-important individual.

- 'That little snot.'

snot-nosed, snotty-nose(d) adj

obnoxious and immature; young and over-confident.

- 'I'm not letting some snot-nosed kid tell me what to do!'

snot-rag n British

a handkerchief.

snotty adj

1 suffering from catarrh, afflicted with a runny nose.

2 obnoxious, self-important, snooty.

snout n British

1 nose.

2 a paid police informer. 'Nose' was used to denote a police spy or informer and so were slang synonyms such as **nark**, **snitch** and snout. Snout is of more recent origin than the other terms, dating from between the World Wars.

3 tobacco, a cigarette. The use of snout to mean tobacco dates from the end of the 19th century when it originated among prison inmates. It was inspired by convicts touching their noses, either while cupping a surreptitious smoke or as a silent sign requesting tobacco. (The explanations are not mutually exclusive, one may have given rise to the other.) In the 1950s the use of 'a snout' for a cigarette became widespread in working-class speech.

snout vb British

to inform, especially regularly in return for pay. The verb is derived from the earlier noun form.

- 'Naff ways of making money – snouting for a gossip columnist (esp. Nigel Dempster).' (The Complete Naff Guide, Bryson et al, 1983).

snow n

1 cocaine. The white crystalline drug resembles snow and its anaesthetic effect numbs like cold. The slang term dates from the turn of the century. ('Snowbird' and 'snowball' were elaborations used in some circles.)

- 'A little snow at Christmas never did anyone any harm.' (Legend on a 1969 Christmas card sent out by the record producer Phil

Spector, featuring a still from the film *Easy Rider*, in which he had a cameo role as a cocaine dealer).

2 a **snow job**.

3 *Australian* a nickname for a blond male, usually used pejoratively.

snow vb

to fool, cheat, bamboozle, especially by overloading someone with information. This Americanism (now occasionally heard in Britain) is based on the notion of 'snowing someone under' in order to deceive or manipulate them. It may also have originally evoked a 'snowstorm' of documentation.

- *'When you go into town on a false pass who do you think you're snowing?'*
(*Battle Cry*, US film, 1954).

snowdrop vb

to steal clothes, typically underwear, from a clothes line. The underworld and police term may refer to a fetishistic practice or the actions of vagrants.

- *'We busked on street corners and snowdropped clothes from the backyard Hills Hoists of trendy Paddington.'*
(*Girls' Night Out*, Kathy Lette, 1989).

snowdropper n British

someone who steals clothing, usually lingerie from washing lines, in the language of vagrants, police and prisoners. The term first referred (in the early 19th century) to the theft of clothes due to poverty; it now often denotes the act of a fetishist.

snow job n American

a case of deceit, browbeating or manipulation, particularly by means of glib or overwhelming persuasion or flattery. The phrase has been common since World War II.

snow out vb

to lose one's bearings or consciousness, 'blank out'. The term evokes the sensation of being lost in a snowstorm or the 'snowstorm effect' of a blank TV screen. Snow out has been heard, typically but not exclusively among drug users in the 1980s.

snuff vb

1 to kill. An old term, derived from the notion of extinguishing a candle. The curt 'tough guy' use of the word remains popular in street slang and crime fiction, particularly in the USA.

See **snuff movie**.

2 to sniff cocaine. An item from the drug user's vocabulary.

snuff n

cocaine.

snuff dipping n

chewing tobacco. In 1985 and 1986 the fashion among young people, especially in rural America, for chewing small bags of tobacco received publicity when the practice was revealed to involve a high risk of cancer.

snuff it vb British

to die. Inspired by the snuffing out of a candle, this expression has been heard in British English, particularly in working class usage, since the turn of the century.

- *'If geology has taught me one thing, Stuart, it's that we are on the earth for only a short time. I am 50 next week. In 10 years I could snuff it. I have to get out there and make things happen.'*
(Professional fossil-hunter Stanley Wood, quoted in the *Sunday Times*, 17 December 1989).

snuff movie n

a violent, **hardcore** pornographic film supposedly featuring the actual death of one of the actors. Rumoured to have been made in the early 1970s, the actual existence of such a movie has never been proved. In the 1980s the term began to be applied to **splatter movies**, where the death and mayhem is indisputably faked.

snuffy n British

an individual who derives sexual excitement from sniffing (clothing, bicycle saddles, etc.).

soap-dodger n British

a dirty, unkempt or smelly person, a 'scruffbag' or **dosser**. **Bath-dodger** is a synonym. An expression of disapproval among adults.

S.O.B., s.o.b. n American

son of a bitch. The initial letters are often used in order to moderate the strength of the phrase, which is highly offensive in American usage.

● *'Some S.O.B. walked off with her purse.'*

sod n British

1 a an unpleasant person (of either sex, but more often male). The word often implies unfair or cruel behaviour on the part of the person described.

● *'I'm sorry I was such a sod to you.'*

b an individual. Like **bugger**, the term is used when referring to someone with pity, irony or mild contempt.

● *'And that was another coincidence because he was the bloke I'd met earlier in the boozer, so I gave him my last £20 note because I thought, poor sod, he'll soon be dead.'*
(William Donaldson, Independent, 26 August 1989).

c a nuisance or annoyance.

● *'That lid's a real sod to get off.'*
● *'I'm a lazy sod.'*

('Pretty Vacant,' Sex Pistols, 1977).

2 a sodomite. The original sense of the word is almost never heard in current English, it was last used in this way in the early 1960s. (The inhabitants of Sodom were according to the book of Genesis guilty of unnatural sexual practices.)

sod vb British

the verb usually occurs as part of expletives such as 'sod you!' (indicating indifference, rejection, etc.) or 'sod it!' (indicating irritation or anger). Unlike its synonym **bugger**, the word is not used to mean sodomize.

soda n American

cocaine or **crack**. A term current among police and drug users in the late 1980s. From the resemblance and volatile effects of the drug(s).

sod-all n British

nothing, **bugger-all**.

● *'He got the profit and I got sod-all.'*

sodding adj British

an intensifying adjective like **bloody**, bleeding, etc. Sodding usually carries overtones of extreme irritation, impatience, etc.

sod off vb British

to leave, go away. The phrase is almost always an imperative, sometimes conveying only mild annoyance or aggression.

● *'I told them to sod off and leave me alone.'*

soft boy n Jamaican

a male homosexual or an effete or effeminate man. This phrase from Jamaican patois was adopted ironically as a name by the Soft Boys, a London rock group of the 1970s.

softshoe vb

to move or behave surreptitiously or in a manner both cautious and devious. Like **tap-dance** the metaphor is applied in raffish or **hip** talk to someone manoeuvring cleverly in social or professional situations. The expression is of course from the 'softshoe shuffle' dance step.

● *'The guy managed to softshoe his way out of trouble again.'*

soggies n British

breakfast cereal. A middle and upper class term of the late 1970s and early 1980s inspired by the trademark names of cereals such as *Shreddies* and *Frosties* and their eventual consistency.

soixante-neuf n

See **sixty-nine**.

soldier

See **dead soldier**.

solid adj

admirable, impressive. The specific slang extension of the colloquial sense of 'dependable' originated among 1930s jazz musicians and was adopted by **hipsters**, **beatniks** and teenagers.

● *'He blew some real solid sax.'*

solid n British

hashish (which is sold in blocks) as opposed to marihuana (herbal cannabis), in the jargon of drug dealers and users of the 1980s.

solid sender n American

an exciting musician. The expression originated among pre-World War II American jazz musicians; solid is a surviving **hip** term for excellent, 'sender' implies generating and communicating excitement. The phrase has been adopted as the name of at least two rock groups of the 1970s.

something else n

(something or someone) outstanding, excellent, exceptional. An enduring phrase from the **hip** lexicon of the 1950s.

● *'She goes with all the guys from out of my class*
But that can't stop me from thinking to myself,
"She's sure fine looking, man, she's something else."'
('Something Else', written by Sharon Sheeley and Eddie Cochran, recorded by Eddie Cochran, 1959).

son of a bitch, sonofabitch n American

an unpleasant, obnoxious or despicable person. The expression is roughly the equivalent of the British **bastard** or **sod**, and often implies active nastiness, although it may be used with pity ('poor son of a bitch') or annoyance ('that engine's a son of a bitch!'). The epithet fell out of use in British speech around the middle of the 19th century. (The British Reverend Benjamin Newton records in his diary for 1818, a wealthy fellow clergyman who had two sons, calling the one born out of wedlock 'son of a whore' and the one born within 'son of a bitch'.) In American speech the phrase son of a bitch was until recently considered too offensive for 'polite company' or broadcasting and would often be reduced to **S.O.B.**

● *'Wherever he went, Andy would have to be the nice guy and I had to be the sonofabitch.'*
(Fred Hughes on Andy Warhol, *Observer* magazine, March 1988).
● *'He [Patrick McGoohan] has been called everything from a difficult son of a bitch to a genius.'*

(*Evening Standard*, 17 March 1988).

sook, sooky n Australian

a 'cry-baby'. The noun probably post-dates the adjective **sooky**, but the origins of both forms are uncertain.

sooky adj Australian

a sulky, sullen.

b sentimental, 'soft' or 'unmanly'. The word may be a corruption or nursery version of 'sulky' itself, but the etymology is obscure. It has been suggested that it may derive from an archaic diminutive of Susan.

sooty n British

a black or coloured person, an arab. The racist epithet is derived from the colour of soot and the name of a glove puppet of a yellow bear, a popular figure in children's entertainment, especially television, since the 1950s. Although sooty does not sound unaffectionate, in actuality it is often used highly offensively. (In 1745 Henry Fielding referred to Jews as 'the Sooty Tribe' in his *Covent Garden Tragedy*.)

- 'We're pretty liberal really, we've only got one rule: no sooties.' (Recorded, proprietor of **Sloane Rangers'** nightclub, 1986).

sort n

a girl or woman. This specific sense of the word as used in working-class British and Australian speech is probably a version of **salt**.

sorted adj British

in a satisfactory situation, comfortable and content. This contraction of 'sorted-out' was heard in working-class London speech of the 1980s. The expression enjoyed a vogue among adolescents in 1988 and 1989, sometimes in the form 'well-sorted'.

- 'I reckon if you've got a girl, a car and a few bob, you're sorted.'

sort (out) vb British

1 to beat up. An innocuous euphemism describing a brutal reality, in keeping with a tendency of London working-class slang toward menacing understatement (see **bother**, **seeing-to**, etc.).

- 'I'll go and sort this Daley geezer.' (*Minder*, British TV series, 1987).

2 to have sex with. A masculine vulgarism with overtones of de-personalization and brusqueness.

soul kiss n American

a late 1960s synonym for **French kiss**, now dated.

sounds n

music. A **hippy** term from the 1960s, now dated.

- 'Got any new sounds, man?'

souped-up adj

(of engines or vehicles) made more powerful, faster. An Americanism which was adopted by British speakers in the 1950s, souped-up is a version of the word 'supercharged', reinforced by the 1940s use of 'soup' to mean petrol, oil or engine additives and nitroglycerine.

soused adj

drunk, from the standard use of the word to mean soaked or drenched.

sov n British

one pound. The word is a shortening of 'sovereign' and was used to designate that gold coin (worth one pound) until its discontinuance in 1914. Sov has been popularized by its copious use in the popular TV series *Minder*, set among the working-class and criminal population of London.

- '[Eric] *Idle sounds as though he*

might just have relieved a punter of 500 sovs for a second-hand motor.' (*Independent*, 17 March 1989).

sow n British

an unpleasant woman. The (fairly rare) term of abuse usually implies real distaste or bitter recrimination.

S.P. n British

starting price, the odds on a horse. Hence essential information, a basis for judgement, the known form. A term fashionable in working-class and raffish circles in the later 1980s. It has been in underworld and gambling use since the 1950s.

● *'What's the S.P. on Murphy? Dead from the neck up!'*
('Arthur Daley' in *Minder*, British TV series, 1984).

space vb American

to daydream, lose concentration or enter a euphoric state. An adolescents' expression based on the earlier **spaced out** and **spacy**.

● *'She puts on the headphones and just starts to space.'*

space cadet n American

an eccentric, mad or **spaced-out** person. A popular expression since the later 1970s, which has entered British and Australian usage. The term is inspired by the expression **spaced out** and the 1950s science fiction TV series, *Tom Corbett, Space Cadet*. 'Space-case' is a synonymous term.

space-case n American
See **space cadet**.

spaced out adj

under the influence of drugs or behaving in an eccentric or insane fashion. A term that originated in America and spread to Britain with the drug-

culture of the 1960s. The term is based on the notion of being extremely **high** and disconnected from earthly realities.

spack adj Australian

an all-purpose term of disapproval or doubt, in use among schoolchildren in the late 1980s. The word, of uncertain origin, is used as an adjective or exclamation.

spacy, spacey adj

a producing euphoria or evoking a dream-like state.
● *'Spacy music.'*
● *'This is spacy dope.'*
b behaving in a distracted, euphoric or **spaced out** way.

spade n

a black person. The term comes from the expression 'as black as the ace of spades' and originated sometime before the 1920s. Spade has almost never been used with racist connotations; it was the word used by white devotees of West Indian culture and music in Britain in the 1950s and 1960s, notably in the title of Colin Wilson's landmark novel, *City of Spades*, published in 1959.

● *'The spades have taken over the city dump.'*
(Caption to Robert Crumb cartoon in *Head Comix*, 1968).
● *'A constable said to me, as he left the canteen, "I'm going to get a spade now, sarge". He punched a fist in the palm of his hand.'*
(Simon Holdaway, *Inside the British Police*, 1983).

spag n British

spaghetti. The abbreviation form was particularly popular among students, for whom 'spag bol' (spaghetti bolognaise) was a cheap staple dish.

spaghetti-eater, spaghetti-bender, spag n

an Italian. These are derogatory terms heard predominantly in Australia, referring to immigrants. The equivalent American term is usually simply 'spaghetti'.

the Spanish archer n British

a rejection (by an actual or potential lover). The phrase, heard among university students in 1989, is a strained pun on 'the elbow' ('el bow' being the mock Spanish).
- 'She gave him the Spanish archer.'

spank, spanking n British

a beating, usually a severe one. An example of menacing understatement in working-class slang, as used by police and criminals. The term is used only slightly more lightheartedly as a euphemism for sadistic games or flagellation.
- 'D'you want your spankin' now?' (The Firm, British TV play, 1989).
- 'Taking part in spanking sessions.'

spank the plank vb

to play the guitar. A piece of musicians' jargon.

spare n British

an unattached, and presumably available female or females. A condescending, slightly archaic term, usually forming part of a phrase such as 'a bit of spare'.
- 'What's it like down the dancehall? Plenty of spare?'

spare adj British

out of control, furious. The word usually in the form 'go spare' has been in use since before World War II. It derives from the notion of excess.

sparkler n British

a lie, especially a welcome or helpful lie. A working-class Londoner's expression.
- 'So he wouldn't say the old sparkler?' (Simon Holdaway, Inside the British Police, 1983).

sparklers n pl

jewels, gems. A long established term from the lexicon of thieves, counterfeiters, **spivs**, etc.

spark out, sparko adj, adv British

fast asleep or completely unconscious. The expression is now a mainly working-class colloquialism; it was formerly a rustic expression evoking a dead fire or extinguished candle. Sparko is a variant form heard in the 1980s.
- 'He had three or four drinks and went spark out.'
- 'She's been sparko for the last hour or so.'

sparks n

a a radio operator in the armed services. The term has been popular since the first decade of the 20th century.
b an electrician.

sparrowfart n

dawn. A jokey euphemism inspired by 'cock-crow'. The phrase became obsolete in Britain in the 1930s but remained in use in Australia, and was revived in Britain in the late 1960s by the cartoon strip The Adventures of Barry McKenzie, published in the satirical magazine Private Eye. The term originally may have been a vulgarization of 'sparrow-cough', an ironic comment on the air pollution of industrial cities.

spastic adj, n

(behaving like or reminiscent of) a

clumsy, unfortunate, feeble, foolish or unpopular individual. A schoolchildren's vogue word in Britain from the early 1960s onwards, prompted by the publicity given to charities and other schemes to aid spastic children. The same word was used in the 1950s by adults, particularly in the armed services, and in the 1960s by schoolchildren and adolescents in the USA. The noun form is frequently shortened to 'spas' or **spazz**; the adjective altered to 'spazzy'.

● 'That's an utterly spastic idea.'
'You can't fancy him! He looks an utter spastic.'

spazz, spaz n, adj

(a) foolish, clumsy, incapable (person). A version of **spastic** used by schoolchildren in Britain and the USA.

spazzmobile n British

a an invalid car.

b an old, decrepit or (supposedly) ludicrous vehicle.

The word has been used by schoolchildren since the 1960s.

spazz out vb American

to lose control of oneself; become hysterical or agitated, go berserk. A teenage phrase of the 1970s and 1980s from **spastic**.

spearchucker n

1 a savage, wild person. The expression (often heard among soldiers, sailors, etc.) is usually used as a term of abuse to or of black people.

2 a javelin thrower.

spear the bearded clam vb

Australian

to have sex with a woman. A colourful vulgarism dating from the 1960s, possibly originating in **surfie** parlance. Like many similar expressions it was introduced to a British audience via the cartoon strip The Adventures of Barry McKenzie, by Barry Humphries and Nicholas Garland running in Private Eye magazine in the late 1960s and early 1970s.

spcc n British

a friend, comrade. In an article in the New Statesman and Society, Maria Manning reports this word, of unknown origin, as being used in school playgrounds in the UK in February 1990.

speed n

an amphetamine drug. The word was first applied in the 1960s to methedrine, a powerful stimulant. By 1968 it was becoming the generic term for all amphetamines (which literally 'speed up' the nervous system).

● 'Someone suffering (and they do!) from speed hang-ups and come-downs really drags the whole scene down.'
(Letter to Oz magazine, June 1968).

speedball n

a combination of stimulant and depressant (for example heroin and cocaine) for injection. The word arose among hard-drug users of the 1940s in the USA. By the 1980s it was also used to designate various other concoctions including those taken orally or by inhalation.

● 'Cocaine hydrochloride is water soluble and a few have always injected it, sometimes as a "speedball" – a cocaine/heroin cocktail.'
(Guardian, 5 September 1989).

speedfreak n

a a user of **speed** (amphetamines).

b by extension, a person who behaves as if over-stimulated.

speeding *adj*

under the influence of **speed**.

spick, spic *n, adj*

a person of Latin origin, an Italian or Hispanic. This highly offensive racist term parodies the speech of such people in the catchphrase 'no spick da Inglish'.

spiel *vb, n*

(to give) a speech or talk, particularly a glib or persuasive patter. The expression may also encompass hard luck stories or lengthy excuses. The word originated in the 19th century, deriving from the German *Spieler* (player) or *spielen* (to play) as applied to card-sharps, hence hucksters, fast-talkers, etc.

- *'He gave me this long spiel about how he was so overworked he wouldn't have time to help.'*

spiffed, spiffed-up, spiffed out *adj*

dressed smartly. These expressions, now popular among American teenagers, are like the British **spiffy**, **spiffing** and **spiv**, a derivation of the early-19th century British dialect term 'spiff', meaning dandy. Spiffed itself was heard in British speech until the 1930s and spiffed-up until the 1960s.

spiffing *adj British*

excellent, first rate. This adjective, often used as an exclamation of delight or approval, is now invariably used mockingly in imitation of the dated upper-class speech of the earlier 20th century. Like **spiffy** it comes from the archaic dialect term 'spiff' meaning smart.

- *'Oh, I say, jolly spiffing old boy!'*

spifflicate *vb British*

to beat up, thoroughly defeat. A nursery word of the 1950s, spifflicate was coined in the 18th century (the first recorded use was in 1785 meaning to confound). It does not derive directly from any standard or dialect term, but is an invention imitating latinate multisyllabics.

spiffy *adj*

smart, dapper, impressive. A word which, since it is in mainly middle- and upper-class use, is generally considered colloquial rather than slang. It derives from the archaic 19th century dialect word 'spiff' (noun and adjective) meaning a dandy or smartly dressed, which is also the origin of **spiffing** and **spiv**.

- *'That's a spiffy little car you've got.'* (Recorded, **Sloane Ranger**, London, 1982).
- *'You're the best looking cop in the place.'* *'Well, you look pretty spiffy yourself.'* (Legwork, US TV series, 1987).

spike *n*

a hypodermic syringe. An item of drug addicts' jargon dating from the 1950s. The word was used to denote an ordinary needle for many years before that.

- *'When I put a spike into my vein, Then I tell you things aren't quite the same.'* (Lyrics to 'Heroin', written by Lou Reed and recorded by the Velvet Underground, 1967).

spike up *vb*

to inject onself (with a narcotic).

spill *vb*

to confess, own up or reveal a secret. A racier version of the colloquial 'spill the beans', the term is typically used in an underworld context, often involving informing on associates or otherwise betraying a confidence.

- 'I couldn't get him to spill.'

spill one's guts vb

to confess or reveal information. An elaboration of **spill** or 'spill the beans' used particularly by or about criminals.

- 'They put a little pressure on him and the creep spilled his guts.'

spin n British

a search (of a home or other premises), typically by police. A derivation of **spin (someone's) drum**.

- 'I think we'd better give their gaff a spin.'
- 'He's about due for a spin.'

spin (someone's) drum vb
British

to make an official search of someone's house, in the jargon of the police force. **Drum** is one's home, spin provides the play on words, referring to the spinning of a drum in a fairground lottery. In 1990 spin has been heard as an expression synonymous with 'up yours', and is accompanied by a one-fingered gesture.

spit n American

a rubbish, nonsense, **shit**.

b nothing at all, **zip**, **zilch**. In both cases spit is a euphemism for **shit**, usable in fairly polite company or in the mass media.

- 'What did he tell me? – he told me spit.'
(Macgruder and Loud, US film, 1985).

spit n

See **the big spit**.

spitball vb, n American

(to make) a halfhearted accusation or criticism, a spiteful but feeble attack.

Spitballs are saliva-soaked wads of paper thrown in the classroom (and also a controversial illegal delivery in baseball, when the pitcher smears saliva on the ball in the belief that it makes the pitch more unpredictable in its flight).

- 'I wouldn't get upset as long as they're just spitballing.'

spit-spot adj

fine, excellent, as it should be. A euphemistic version of **shit-hot**. (The expression is used by the fictional Mary Poppins in the film of the same name, as a synonym for 'chop-chop'.)

spiv n British

a disreputable, flashy male, typically one who lives by shady dealing rather than orthodox work. This word had existed in the jargon of race-track habitués and petty criminals since the late 19th century, but came into its own after World War II, when it was adopted by the press and public to designate the touts, black marketeers and 'wide boys' who flourished in the late 1940s and early 1950s. Spiv is an alteration of 'spiff', an archaic dialect word for dandy which also gave rise to the adjectives **spiffy** and **spiffing**.

- 'He [the marketing manager] may be a little spiv but he certainly brings in the customers.'
(Recorded, language-school owner, York, 1981).
- 'Max Kidd was an ex-plumber made good; a total spiv down to the last camel hair in his coat.'
(TV review by Kate Saunders, Evening Standard, 17 May 1989).

splash the boots vb

to urinate. A euphemism heard, particularly among drinkers, in Australia and Britain since the 1960s.

- 'Excuse I, but could you direct me to the bathroom. I've got to splash the boots.'

(*The Wonderful World of Barry McKenzie*, cartoon strip by Barry Humphries and Nicholas Garland, 1966).

splatter movie n

a film in which many characters are killed off graphically and bloodily for the entertainment of the audience rather than the furtherance of the plot. The first film to earn the title was *The Texas Chainsaw Massacre*, 1974. It is a journalistic generic term.

See also **snuff movie**.

splay n American

marihuana. A word of obscure origin used by schoolchildren and students.

splice vb British

to have sex with.

- 'I spliced his woman while he was on bar duty downstairs.'
  (*Harry's Kingdom*, British TV film, 1986).

spliced adj

married. Often in the form 'get spliced'. The verb to splice has had this colloquial sense since the 17th century.

spliff n

a cannabis cigarette, **joint**. The word which is of uncertain derivation, originated in Britain or the Caribbean in the 1960s. In the USA it designates a joint containing both cannabis and tobacco, in the 'English style'.

split vb

to leave. A piece of American slang that came to Britain in the **hippy** era, it is a shortening of the earlier **beatnik** term 'split the scene' (from the notion of separating oneself from a group or gathering).

splosh n British

1 a a woman, women in general.
b sex.

Both these related uses are vulgarisms popular in London working-class usage since the late 1970s, often in the form 'a bit of splosh'.

2 money. This sense of the word is now almost obsolete, but existed in the vocabularies of cockneys, **spivs** and their upper-class imitators in the 1950s.

spod n British

a clumsy, dimwitted or socially unacceptable person. The term is applied to school misfits by fellow pupils and was reported to be in current use at Eton in the September 1989 issue of the *Tatler*.

spon n British

1 money. A clipped form of **spondulicks**, fashionable in certain circles in the late 1980s.

- 'We're going to have to go round to Bill's to pick up some spon.'
  (Recorded, self-employed decorator, London, 1988).

2 a fool. This childish term of abuse or disparagement has been obsolete since the early 1960s. It was almost certainly a survival of the early 19th century use of **spoon** to mean simpleton (see the verb form of **spoon**).

spondulicks, spondoolicks n

money, wealth. A lighthearted term which was obsolescent by the 1960s (having originated in the USA in the 1850s), but which like other synonyms for money was revived in the 1980s (compare **rhino**, **pelf**, etc.). It originated as a learned witticism, borrowing the Greek term, *spondylikos*; pertaining to the *spondylos*, a seashell used as currency.

sponk adj British

infatuated, romantically obsessed or fixated. This middle and upper class schoolgirl term has disappeared since the end of the 1960s. It was probably inspired by the archaic 'spoony' (silly and sentimental) and **bonkers**. The word occurred in the phrase 'to be sponk on (someone)', meaning to have a crush on.

spook n American

1 a black person. The reference is either an ironic one to the subjects' black colour (as opposed to the white of spectres) or to their 'haunting' of certain locations.

2 a spy, secret agent. This usage may be a simple reference to unseen 'ghosts' or may derive from the fact that many World War II agents were recruited from the Yale secret society the 'Skull and Bones'.

● 'In 30 beautifully crafted novels during the past 16 years, he [Ted Allbeury] has revealed details from the real world of spooks that have been struck from others' memoirs.' (Sunday Times, 17 December 1989).

spoon vb

to kiss and cuddle. An archaic term occasionally revived, usually for humorous use. The noun spoon was used in Victorian times to denote a simpleton or doting lover. (It comes from the idea of a spoon as an open, shallow vessel.)

spot (someone) vb American

to pay for, lend or advance money to. This usage of spot probably derives from gambling or sports jargon in which it means to specify odds or conditions.

● 'Spot me a twenty will you?'

spout off vb British

to talk volubly, pompously or out of turn. A post-1970 version of the earlier 'spout' or the more literary 'spout forth', suggesting the outpouring of words. Spout off, like 'mouth off', is usually used intransitively and is more disparaging than the earlier forms.

spring (someone) vb

to obtain someone's release from captivity or prison, either as a result of a legal manoeuvre or, more commonly, by assisting their escape.

spring for vb British

to pay for. A raffish expression used typically by working-class speakers indicating willingness or alacrity.

● 'OK, keep your hand in your pocket, I'll spring for the grub.'

sprog n British

a a child, offspring.

b a novice, new recruit.

The first sense of the word has become widespread in colloquial speech since the mid 1970s, the second is limited to the context of institutions including the armed services. The exact origin of the word is obscure, but it is reasonable to assume that it is a blend of 'sprout' and 'sprig'. Sprog also means head in Australia.

spud n

a potato. This universal slang term has been recorded since the 1840s. A 'spud' was a small narrow spade (from Middle English spudde, dagger, itself from Italian spada, sword) of the sort used to dig up potatoes.

spud-bashing n British

potato-peeling, especially as a punishment.

spunk n

a spirit, vim. The word has been recorded in this sense since the 18th century. Most authorities derive it from *spong* a Gaelic word for tinder (itself from Latin *spongia*, sponge), hence 'spark'.

b semen. The idea of life-force, 'vital spark' or spirit in the male context led to spunk being used in this sense (as was 'mettle' in archaic speech) from the 19th century onwards.

2 *Australian* a **spunk rat**. The shorter form, usually referring to males only, has become increasingly widespread since about 1987.

spunk rat n Australian

a sexually attractive young person. The phrase is based on **spunky** in the sense of spirited, influenced also by **spunk** in the sexual sense.

● *'But it's all right for her, she's got a whole smorgasbord selection of classic spunk rats.'*
(Kathy Lette, *Girl's Night Out*, 1989).

spunky adj

spirited. The adjective is derived from the noun **spunk**.

sputnik n British

a potent form of hashish produced by mixing quantities of low or medium quality resins with small quantities of hashish oil. The term comes from the supposedly **spacy** effects of the combination (Sputnik was the name of the Russians' first space satellite, launched in 1957).

squaddie n British

an army private. The word is either from 'squad' or from the archaic 'swaddy', a bumpkin.

square adj, n

(a) conventional, conservative or un-fashionable (person). Since the 17th century square has been used to mean honest, reputable or straightforward. The modern sense of the word dates from the 1930s **jive talk** of black jazz musicians in Harlem, New York. (Cab Calloway's 1938 lexicon defines a square as an 'unhip person'.)

● *'To be square is to be dull, middle aged, old fashioned. To be square is to be not with it.'*
(*About Town* magazine, June 1962).

squarehead n

1 a German. The North and East Germanic peoples supposedly have squarer heads than Anglo-Saxons. This supposition was reinforced in the World Wars by German military hairstyles (and in World War II by helmets).

2 a **square**.

squashed adj American

drunk. A rare **preppie** term, in the tradition of employing synonyms for 'destroyed' (**smashed**, **wrecked**, etc.) to mean intoxicated.

squat n American

(a) **shit**. From the action of squatting down to defecate. By extension, squat, a word used typically in country areas of the USA, is also used to mean nothing, or a worthless thing. **Doodly squat** is an elaboration.

● *'It ain't worth squat.'*

squawk vb

1 to complain noisily or raucously.

2 to inform (on someone). A rarer synonym of **squeal**.

squawk n

a radio message. A term used especially by police or military personnel for a short burst of information coming into a walkie-talkie radio or field telephone.

squeak n British

a young naive teenager. A term applied by older adolescents to would-be members of the fashionable circles of London in the late 1980s. The term usually refers to a girl of the sort previously designated as a teenybopper.

- 'The bouncer gets a bit heavy demanding ID from a group of squeaks who look like they have given their babysitter the slip.'
  (Evening Standard magazine, May 1989).

squeal vb

to inform (on someone). The usage arose in early 19th century dialect, spreading to underworld argot first in Britain and subsequently in the USA.

squealer, squeal n

an informer. In the USA the words are also applied to an individual lodging a complaint against the police.

squeeze n

1 American a girlfriend or boyfriend, sweetheart. The word is inspired by the squeeze of an embrace and is often heard in the form main squeeze (which has the added meaning of 'most important person').

2 British money, cash. The word often has overtones of hard-earned or reluctantly paid.

squeezebox n

an accordion, concertina or harmonium. A musician's term from before World War II which, like the instruments themselves, is heard less often today.

squid n American

a swot. A high school and campus term, perhaps suggesting 'oiliness'.

squiff n Australian

a a drunkard.
b a drinking bout. Both terms are back formations from the adjective squiffy.

squiffy adj

(slightly) drunk, merry or inebriated. An inoffensive, lighthearted word suggesting slight disorientation, squiffy has been in use since the 19th century.

squiffy doo adj British

dubious, doubtful, suspect. A middle class expression heard in the 1980s. It derives from the notion of 'askew', 'out of true' expressed by the adjective squiffy.

squillion n British

a hyperbolically huge number. A pseudo-nursery word, typically used by condescending or ingratiating journalists in teenage magazines, that became a teenage vogue term of the 1980s.

- 'Last week we got thirteen squillion letters asking which video company brought out Star Trek IV, our fab giveaway. Well it was CIC. So there.'
  (Just Seventeen, teenage girls' magazine, December 1987).

squirly adj American

restless. A word with rustic overtones which is probably a form of 'squirrely' (which itself was not only a metaphor, but formerly a punning synonym for nuts).

- 'Come on, don't be so squirly.'
  (The Hunter, US film, 1980).
- 'He [Richard Ford] tends to throw plenty of relish onto his words, especially ones like "squirly" which you do not often hear, even in Bath (it means "restless").'
  (Independent, 8 July 1989).

squirt n

an insignificant, diminutive and/or impudent and annoying individual (usually male). This figurative use of the standard word dates from the mid 19th century. It is not certain whether it originated in British of American speech.

squit n British

an insignificant, small and/or irritating person. The word is a variant form of the synonymous **squirt** and has been heard since the 1880s.

- 'There are 5 squits, 9 snekes, 19 cribbers, 2 maniaks, 4 swots.'
  (Geoffrey Willans and Ronald Searle, Back in the Jug Agane, 1959).

(the) squits, squitters n

a case of diarrhoea. Both words are onomatopoeic.

- 'No thanks, love, olive oil doesn't agree with me.'
  'Gives you the squits, does it, Grandad?'
  (David Lodge, Nice Work, 1988).

stack adj

1 excellent, fantastic. An ephemeral teenage vogue word of 1987, used as an exclamation of approval or delight. The term spread from the language of hip-hop in New York to London afficionados.

- 'Just forget about using the word mega to express your delight. The latest expression is stack!'
  (Daily Mirror, September 1987).

2 the word like many similar vogue terms is also used to mean its virtual opposite: inferior, negative, 'no way', etc.

- 'Stack (meaning: not at all, i.e. Samantha Fox is immensely talented ... STACK!) is now the only logo to be seen with (we know, we invented it).'

(Advertisement in I-D magazine, November 1987).

stacked adj

having large breasts (of a woman), 'well-endowed'. A male term of approbation which is now offensive to most women. The expression, first popular in the USA, is a shortening of 'well-stacked'.

- 'When one person is important and the other person is stacked and/or well-hung.'
  (Sub-heading in P. J. O'Rourke's Modern Manner, 1983).

stage-door Johnny n

a male admirer of a female performer. The phrase, which dates from the 1890s, is surprisingly not yet obsolete. John and Johnny have been generic terms for a male **punter**, customer or sweetheart for more than 100 years. The more modern and less romantic **groupie** is rarely applied to males.

stains n pl British

unfashionable, tedious individuals or **swots**. The term of contempt was in use among university students in the late 1980s. It is usually a synonym of **anorak**; unbeknown to most users it is short for 'wank-stain' i.e. a despicable nonentity.

- '"Stains" are "replete with acne and anoraks".'
  (Evening Standard, 16 June 1988).

stalk n

a an erection or penis. This British and Australian sense of the word principally survives in the phrases **stalk fever** and **stalk-on**.

b effrontery (in a male), cheek, **bottle**. A rare working-class usage (recorded in The Signs of Crime, A Field Manual for Police by Deputy Assistant Commissioner David Powis, 1977).

stalk fever n Australian

lust (experience by a male), priapism. The expression was in use until the late 1960s but is now rare. It derives from the slang sense of **stalk** as erection or penis.

stalk-on n

an erection. A vulgarism heard since the 1950s.

stallion n

a **stud**. the term has been used figuratively in this way since the 14th century.

stand, stand-on n

an erection.

stand-up adj American

honourable, reliable, steadfast. A term of (mainly male) approbation or admiration in such clichés as 'a stand-up guy'. It derives from the notion of 'standing up for someone' or being willing to 'stand up and be counted'.

● 'It's funny that priest going AWOL. I always thought he was a real standup guy.'
(V, US TV film, 1983).

star-fucker n

a **groupie**. The word was used as the title of a song by the Rolling Stones.

starkers adj British

naked. A characteristic public school or Oxbridge version of 'stark naked' which has become a common colloquialism. (It is sometimes elaborated into **harry-starkers**.)

stash vb

to hide, put (away). The word, which spread from America to the rest of the English-speaking world at the turn of the century, was probably originally a blend of 'stow', 'store' and 'cache'. It was formerly often spelled 'stache'.

state n British

a mess, disaster. This word became an all-purpose vogue term in London working-class speech of the early 1970s. The original notion of 'to be in a (bit of a) state' was transformed so that state (**two-and-eight** in rhyming slang) came to refer to the individual rather than the situation.

● 'He looks a right old state, doesn't he?'

static n American

criticism or hostile interference. A respectable slang term inspired by the standard sense of electrical disturbance or interference. The suggestion is typically of opposition from various quarters that threatens to frustrate a scheme.

● 'We're getting a lot of static from higher up now that the powers that be have been informed.'

stay loose vb American

an alternative version of **hang loose**.

steal n

a bargain, something easily accomplished, a pushover. This common use of the word derives from the dialect or non-standard colloquial use of 'steal' in Britain and the USA as a noun meaning something stolen.

steamboats adj British

drunk. A lighthearted term of uncertain derivation. It may have something to do with the use of a name such as 'Steamboat Bill', possibly in a lost rhyming-slang expression.

● 'He was completely steamboats by midday.'

steamed adj American

furious. A 1980s variation on the more generalized 'steamed-up'.

steamers n pl British

gangs of muggers who enter a shop, train compartment, etc. en masse and overwhelm their victims with some force. From the colloquial 'steam (in)'; move forcefully and quickly. The term arose in London in 1985 among black street gangs.

steamie n British

a laundry. The term referred to the steam laundries of the 1950s.

steaming n British

the activity of **steamers**.

- 'Steaming is very modern, a term for mob-handed theft often by joeys, young criminals.'

(James Morten, Independent, 23 December 1988).

steaming adj British

an otherwise meaningless intensifying adjective, almost invariably used in the now dated expression '(a) steaming nit' which was briefly popular in the early 1960s.

step on adj

to adulterate, cut (a drug). The term has been used by drug users and dealers since the end of the 1960s, particularly in reference to cocaine or heroin; occasionally it is used of amphetamines, but not of cannabis or other organic substances.

- 'You expect a cut at this level, but this stuff has been stepped on by a gang of navvies in hob-nailed boots.'

(Recorded, cocaine user, London, 1982).

stewed adj

drunk. The word has been used in this sense since the 18th century.

stick n

1 a **joint**, **reefer** (cannabis cigarette). A term which was fairly widespread among smokers of the drug (**beatniks**, prisoners, etc.) until the mid 1960s, when joint and **spliff** largely supplanted it.

2 British chastisement, physical or verbal punishment. Originally implying a literal thrashing with a stick or cane, then generalized to any violent assault, the expression is now used, especially by middle-class speakers, to encompass verbal abuse, denigration or nagging.

- 'You've done nothing but snipe at me since I got home – what have I done to deserve all this stick?'

3 British a police truncheon.

- 'His trousers weren't done up and his shirt tails were flapping and he had a stick in his hand.'

(Police officer, Inside the British Police, Simon Holdaway, 1983).

4 an excessively serious, dull or repressed person.

From the notions of rigidity, woodeness and chastisement.

5 a pickpocket's associate or decoy. See **sticksing**.

the sticks n

the countryside, a rural or provincial place, the 'backwoods'. Originally in the USA and Canada a humorous reference to trees, the term had spread to other English-speaking areas by the 1950s.

- 'He lives way out in the sticks somewhere – Ongar I believe.'

sticksing n British

pickpocketing. A term used in black criminal circles.

stick the nut on (someone)

vb British

See to **nut**.

sticky adj Irish

connected with or frequented by the official, as opposed to Provisional, IRA. The word is used in the London Irish community, as well as in Ireland, to designate certain pubs.

sticky n British

a liqueur. The word (like the object in middle-class and 'society' usage) is occasionally extended to refer to sweet wines.

sticky beak n Australian

a 'nosy parker', an interfering or inquisitive person. The common phrase evokes a bird poking its bill into something viscous.

- 'If he hasn't told you . . . it's certainly not my place.'
- 'And what is your place? Head chook in the sticky beak brigade?' (Neighbours, Australian TV series, 1988).

sticky-beak vb Australian

to poke one's nose into other people's affairs. A back-formation from the noun.

stiff vb

1 to kill. An Americanism based on the noun form of the word (meaning corpse). Since the 1960s the term has been heard in raffish or underworld parlance in Britain.

2 to take financial advantage of (someone); cheat, rob or extort from.

- 'She tried to stiff me for the fare.'

3 to 'stand someone up', snub (someone).

- 'I don't like getting stiffed like this.'

4 to flop, fail. A term used typically in the context of the entertainment business or sports.

- 'Their last single stiffed.'

The first four senses of stiff are related to the noun form denoting a corpse.

5 American to aggress, treat harshly. The term is from 'stiff-arm', a version of 'strong-arm'.

6 British to have sex with. A working-class vulgarism.

stiff n

a a corpse. An unsentimental term inspired by rigor mortis and originating in American slang in the 19th century.

b a rigidly conventional, dull or serious person.

c an individual, particularly one to be pitied.

- 'I'm just a poor working stiff.'

d American a hobo, vagrant.

e a drunk.

f a flop or failure.

Most of the many sub-senses of stiff are related to the idea of corpse-like rigidity or absence of life. The notion of 'stiff-necked' also plays a part in the case of sense **b**.

stiffie n British

1 an erection. A jocular term heard principally among middle class males, although women also employ the word.

- 'Got a stiffie? Wear a Jiffi!' (Promotional T-shirt logo for Jiffi condoms, 1985).

2 an invitation card. The term describes the engraved social missives exchanged in traditional, **Sloane Ranger** and **yuppie** circles.

sting n American

a a confidence trick, fraud or act of extortion.

b a scheme devised in order to trap or entrap criminals.

Both senses of the word (popularized by the film of the same name released in 1973) imply an elaborate arrangement with a sudden 'pay-off'.

stinking adj British

1 a short form of 'stinking rich'.
2 extremely drunk, **stinko**.

stinko adj

drunk. This word (abbreviation from 'stinking drunk', with the addition of the lighthearted adjectival suffix -o) is almost obsolete in British speech except in upper-class usage.

stinky finger, stink-finger, stinky pinky n

manual stimulation of a woman's genitals. The phrases are typically used by adolescent males.

stir n

prison. Various Romany (gypsy) words such as *stardo, steripen,* dealing with the concept of imprisonment gave rise to 'start', an 18th-century-British slang term for prison, and later, in the mid-19th century to stir, which has remained one of the most widespread words for jail or imprisonment in all English-speaking areas, particularly in the phrase **in stir**.

stir crazy/happy adj

psychologically disturbed as a result of confinement in prison (**stir**). The notion is sometimes extended to encompass a sense of frustration or hysteria felt in any institutional surroundings. (The less common form **stir happy** is now dated.)

stirrer n British

a troublemaker, particularly someone who foments trouble or provokes a confrontation by spreading malicious gossip. The expression is originally a shortening of shit-stirrer, although it may be used without awareness of the fact.

- '"She might have got away with it if a couple of stirrers on the cast [of EastEnders] hadn't made a fuss," said her pal.'
  (*News of the World,* 5 February 1989).

stitch n American

something funny, a source of hilarity. A typically middle-class and **preppie** term derived from the expression 'to be in stitches'.

- 'Oh Jean-Marie, you're a stitch!'
  (*Planes, Trains and Automobiles,* US film, 1987).

stitch (someone) up vb British

a to concoct false evidence against someone, to **frame**. A piece of underworld and police jargon from the 1950s which penetrated popular speech in the 1980s.

- 'Openshaw, 41, allegedly said on his arrest: "I'm being stitched up." The trial goes on.'
  (Court report, *Daily Mirror,* 14 July 1989).

b to outmanoeuvre comprehensively, defeat by devious means, render helpless. This extension of the previous sense of the phrase became a vogue term of the early 1980s.

- 'Leched over by managers, stitched up by agents, girls in the music biz have traditionally paid a high price for succumbing to the lure of lurex.'
  (*Ms London* magazine, 4 September 1989).

stitch this! exclamation British

an exclamation of defiance said while hitting someone, particularly when butting them in the face. The phrase is used by 'toughs'.

stodge n British

suet pudding or dumplings as

served (and often loathed) in school canteens. A children's term heard since the 1950s.

stogie n American

a cigar. An old but surviving nickname which is from Conestoga, Pennsylvania, where covered wagons were manufactured. The driver of the wagons smoked cheap cigars which became known as stogies.

stoked adj

excited, thrilled, stimulated. An adolescents' vogue word in the late 1980s; it occurs in British, Australian and American speech. It derives from the idea of 'stoked up' or perhaps from the words 'stunned' and 'choked'.

stomp vb

to beat up, attack and/or defeat. A usage which was part of the Hells Angels' lexicon, referring to the ritual punishing of enemies. The word was adopted by hippies in the USA and Britain in about 1968.

stompers n pl American

a the American term for brothel creepers, thick-soled shoes as worn by teenagers in the 1950s.

b heavy workboots or cowboy boots.

stone n

a period under the influence of cannabis; the effects of the drug. A back-formation from the adjective stoned.

● 'He said he got an amazing stone off that Afghani.'

stoned adj

intoxicated by narcotics or alcohol. In the 1960s stoned proved the most popular of a number of synonyms employing the metaphor of punishment or damage (**wrecked**, **destroyed**, **blitzed**, etc.). It became the standard term to describe the effects of cannabis

in particular. This use of the word originated in the argot of jazz musicians and bohemians in the USA in the 1940s.

● '[Richard Neville] suggesting making love when stoned with stereo headphones on both partners, playing the first Blind Faith album.'
(Oz magazine, February 1970).

stone ginger n, adj. British

(something) absolutely certain, (a) 'dead cert'. A London working-class expression, now obsolete. 'Stone-' is a combining form meaning complete(ly); stone ginger, apart from being a spice, was the name of a racehorse, famous in the first decade of the 20th century.

stone me! exclamation British

an exclamation of surprised realization or astonishment. The working-class expression has been heard less often since the late 1960s. It enjoyed a vogue in the late 1950s and early 1960s especially in TV comedy dialogue.

stone the crows! exclamation British

an exclamation of astonishment, heard particularly in working class speech in the 1950s.

stonewall bonker n British

a certainty. This raffish phrase has been in use since the 1930s and is still heard in certain underworld and working class circles. Unbeknown to most speakers, the 'bonk' or 'bonker' in question was originally the blow of an auctioneer's gavel in closing a deal. 'Stonewall' is an elaboration of 'stone' in the colloquial sense of absolute(ly).

stonker n British

a something stunning, devastating or powerful. This invented word should logically be derived from a verb 'to stonk' which is however unrecorded in modern slang although **stonkered** and **stonking** are. In origin the term is probably influenced by words such as 'stun', 'clunk', 'bonk'.

b See **stonkers**.

stonkered adj

a drunk.

b destroyed, out of action, devastated or exhausted. (For the probable derivation see **stonker**.)

stonkers n pl British

breasts. A vulgarism heard among males which is either a specific use of the previous sense or perhaps an elaboration of 'stunner'.

stonking adj British

extremely. The word is an all-purpose intensifying adjective, usually in place of more offensive terms. Mainly in working class and armed service usage, stonking was in vogue in the late 1980s. It probably post-dates **stonker** and **stonkered**.

stony, stoney adj

penniless. A shortened form of 'stony broke', heard especially in Australia.

stooge n British

an innocent stand-in at an identity parade. A term from the jargon of police, from the standard colloquial senses of menial, dupe, etc. (The word stooge, which appeared in the USA in the 19th century, is said to be a corruption of 'studious' or 'students').

● 'They don't think they can get the I.D. parade off the ground. I don't know if there are problems with the stooges, or what.'
(Flying Squad, British TV documentary, March 1985).

stoolie n

an informer. A shortening of **stool pigeon**.

stool pigeon n

an informer. In North America in the 19th century pigeons were tied to wooden frames (known as stools) as decoys to lure game birds. The expression was later applied to a cardsharp's human decoy and later still to a police informer or spy. By World War I the use of the phrase had spread to Britain where it was adopted by crime fiction and the real underworld. The term is commonly shortened to **stoolie**.

stoshious, stotious, stocious, stoshers adj British

a drunk.

b silent, tight-lipped, discreet. This mysterious word can be traced to the 19th century and was thought by some authorities to be extinct by the 1930s. It survives however in jocular usage. The term is either a mock-latinate invention or a corruption of a dialect word for waterlogged or muddy.

stoush n Australian

a brawl. The word is probably a descendant of lost dialect terms for 'uproar' or 'strike'.

S.T.P. n

a hallucinogenic drug claimed to be much more powerful than L.S.D. which it resembled in its effects. It originated in **hippy** circles in the USA in about 1970 and was named after a well-known engine oil additive.

straight n

1 a heterosexual, particularly heard in the language of homosexuals.

2 a conventional person, someone who does not take drugs or ascribe to 'counterculture' values. A term from

496

the language of drug abusers and counterculture members which was a 'buzz word' of the later 1960s.

- 'Would you say Hunter Thompson was afraid of anything in particular? "Ah ... Straights".' (Ralph Steadman, I-D magazine, November 1987).

3 a cigarette (as opposed to a **joint**). A now dated cannabis users' term in wide currency in the 1960s.

- 'If you give me a straight I'll roll us something for the journey.'

straight adj

1 a honest, not criminal or corrupt.

- 'You couldn't bribe or compromise him because he was straight. However, he was also naive.' (Former detective, Inside the Brotherhood, Martin Short, 1989).

b heterosexual. (In the first two subsenses, the slang alternative in British English is **bent**.)

c not under the influence of drugs, not a drug-user.

- 'I've been straight for three days.'
- 'Don't offer her any, she's straight.'

The word has been used to mean 'upright' or honest, fair, scrupulous, etc. for more than a century. The sub-senses above, not always used approvingly, have been established in the 1950s and 1960s. The following sense is in ironic contrast.

2 restored to one's desired state of drunkenness or drugged euphoria.

- 'Just one shot and I'll be straight again.'

straight arrow, straight-shooter n American

an honest, trustworthy straightforward person. Terms of approbation inspired by the language of western fiction. They are often heard in a business context.

straightened-out adj

bribed, suborned or otherwise corrupted. A euphemism in underworld and police usage.

- 'Their tip-off was supported by a tape recording of a bugged conversation involving an American criminal, referring to "a top man" who had been "straightened out in Scotland Yard".' (Observer, 16 August 1987).

strain the potatoes vb

Australian

to urinate. The phrase is a survival of a 19th century British euphemism inspired by the resulting colour of water. In Britain, the phrase 'strain the greens' was heard before the 1950s.

strangle a darkie vb Australian

to defecate. A fanciful vulgarism used by Barry Humphries in his cartoon strip The Wonderful World of Barry McKenzie in the satirical magazine Private Eye. Other versions are **choke a darkie** or **throttle a darkie**.

strangler n British

an enviably lucky person. A shortening of 'jam-strangler' (which gives **jammy**). The term is rare, occurring in armed-service slang in particular.

strapped adj

short of money, broke. A short version of the phrase 'strapped for cash'.

strawberry n American

a prostitute who sells sex for drugs.

- 'All the vice girl victims [of a Los Angeles serial killer] were known as strawberries – American slang for hookers who trade sex for drugs.' (Sunday Mirror, 3 March 1989).

streak *vb*

to run naked in a public place. The term came to prominence along with the fad in the early 1970s. It began as a form of mass or individual protest and was quickly taken up for the purposes of fun and/or exhibitionism.

● *'She streaked across the campus for a £5 bet.'*

streak *n*

1 a run through a public place while naked. From the verb.

● *'Some guy did a streak at the Test Match.'*

2 British a person of ectomorphic build. A mildy pejorative term, sometimes expressed more brutally as **long streak of piss**, invariably said of males. **Long streak of misery** denotes a tall, thin and morose or excessively serious individual.

streaker *n*

someone who performs a **streak**.

● *'That's the second streaker we've had today.'*

street *adj American*

'streetwise' or having 'street credibility'. A term of approbation originating in black argot of the 1970s.

● *'She's OK, she's street.'*

street apple *n*

See **road apple**.

street pizza *n*

See **road pizza**.

stretch *n*

1 American a tall, thin person. A term of cheerful mockery. The equivalent of the British **streak**, or rather, the nickname 'Lofty', since stretch is often a term of address.

● *'How're y' keeping, Stretch?'*

2 a period of imprisonment. This underworld term originally referred specifically to one year's incarceration; it is now generalized to mean a term of whatever length.

● *'He did a four-year stretch.'*

strides *n*

trousers. The word has existed in raffish usage since the turn of the century; it is now heard in Britain and Australia.

● *'Fair crack of the whip! Lady, I'm not taking me strides off for anyone.'*
(*Bazza Pulls it Off*, cartoon by Barry Humphries and Nicholas Garland, *Private Eye*, 1970).

● *'This stupid bloke called me a freak, and kept asking why I was wearing "fucking moody strides". I went home really annoyed and thought right, I'm not having this.'*
(Caron Geary, *Time Out*, 26 July 1989).

strine *adj, n*

Australian or Australian speech. The word imitates the pronunciation of the word 'Australian' in the nasal accent of that country. The term strine was popularized in Britain in the 1960s following the publication of *Let Stalk Strine* by Alistair Morrison in 1965.

stripe *n*

a scar, especially as the result of a knife or razor slash.

stroke book *n American*

a pornographic or semi-pornographic publication. 'Stroke' in this context refers to male masturbation.

stroll on! *exclamation British*

a cry of dismissal or disbelief. The phrase usually conveys indignation.

the strongbox n British

a prison cell in which people are kept in solitary confinement.

strong it vb British

to behave aggressively, presumptuously or excessively. A working class expression heard particularly in the London area in the 1980s. It is a variation on the colloquial phrases 'come on strong', 'come it strong', 'go it strong'.

- 'You been strongin' it again down our boozer?'

stroppy adj British

obstreperous, aggressive, uncooperative. The word is an alteration of obstreperous, perhaps via a fanciful deformation of the word such as 'obstropalous'. Stroppy appeared in the 1940s. Various deformations of obstreperous have been recorded since the 18th century.

strop the mulligan vb

Australian

(of a male) to masturbate. The significance of the surname is unclear (it may be a trademark of some sort).

strung out adj

a tense, nervous and upset.

- 'She was strung-out inside, nibbling there on her lower lip and smoking one cigarette after another.'

b suffering from the effects of an illicit drug, or from withdrawal.

- 'Strung out on morphine'.

The first, now widespread, usage derives from the second which is a drug user's slang expression dating from the 1950s.

strung up adj

a less common variant of strung out.

stubby, stubbie n Australian

a small bottle of lager.

stud n

a sexually active, powerful, potent male. Only slang when applied to men as opposed to (real) animals, the term often indicates a degree of approval or admiration, even if grudgingly. In black American street parlance the word was sometimes used in the 1960s and 1970s simply to mean 'guy'. There seems to be no female equivalent that stresses sexual power rather than degeneracy.

- 'The eternal teenage sexual paradox is that boys who "put it about" are called "studs" by their admiring friends but girls who do the same are "slags".'

(17-year-old public-school pupil, Harpers and Queen magazine, August 1970).

studsley n American

a smart, dapper or sophisticated male. A term of address between males which seems to have originated as a black elaboration of stud in the sense of fine fellow'.

stuff vb

1 to have sex with. The verb has very seldom been used in the active or transitive form since the 19th century (and it was never common). The abusive exclamation 'get stuffed' is its main legacy.

2 to dismiss, throw away, destroy. This adaptation of the sexual sense of the word, or of the expression 'stuff it up your arse!' has proved useful as a non-taboo means of conveying strong rejection, impatience, etc. It often occurs in the all-purpose exclamation 'stuff it!'

- 'Stuff the wedding!'

(Anti-royal-wedding slogan written

499

on walls and reproduced on badges in Britain 1981).

Stuff is currently fashionable in media, sporting and raffish circles with the sense of defeat or humiliate.

- '*I once stuffed a member of our Davis Cup team. No great achievement you may think, and I'm lying anyway!*' (William Donaldson, Independent, 31 March 1990).

stuff n

1 a euphemism for an illicit drug.
- '*Got any stuff?*'
2 See **short-stuff, the right stuff**.

stuffed adj British

ruined, abandoned, 'kaput'. A brusque but fairly inoffensive derivation of the verb **stuff**.

stumblebum n American

a vagrant or derelict, literally a stumbling, helpless tramp. The word is now usually generalized to denote an inept, incompetent or clumsy person.

substance n British

cannabis; hashish or marihuana. A euphemism adopted by users of the drug from the legalistic description (employed particularly in sentences such as '*Certain substances were taken away for analysis*').
- '*Got any substance?*'

suck vb American

to be repellent, inferior or worthless. An extremely common term of strong disparagement or denigration in American English, suck is both a euphemism for **fuck** and an amalgam of notions contained in words such as 'sucker', **cocksucker**, etc.
- '*To say something or someone "sucks" is to use America's most common term of disparagement ...*

The term suck originally had as its prefix the word for a male hen.' (Simon Hoggart, Observer magazine, 1989).

sucker-punch vb American

to attack from behind or without warning, to land an unfair or surprise blow. From the colloquialism 'sucker'; a dupe or easy victim.
- '*You're a witness, Alex. I just came here to talk to you and Fruitfly sucker-punched me.*' (Jonathon Kellerman, Over the Edge, 1987).

suck face vb American

to kiss. An adolescent euphemism on the lines of **swap spit**.

suck-hole, suck-holer n Australian

a sycophant, toady or other contemptible person. A more recent variant on the ancient notion expressed by 'bumsucker', **arse-licker**, etc.

suck off vb

to perform fellatio (on someone).

suds n American

beer; a 'college-boy' word.

sudser n

a soap opera. A piece of journalese from the 1970s.

suedehead n British

a member of the youth subculture of the later 1970s who resembled **skinheads**, but wore their hair slightly longer, hence this epithet.

suffer! exclamation Australian

a cry of defiance, challenge or contempt as used by schoolchildren and adolescents from at least the late 1970s.

sugar daddy n

a wealthy older protector and lover of a young woman. Judith S Neaman and Carole G Silver in their *Dictionary of Euphemisms* (1983) date this expression to the 1920s and derive it from American rhyming slang 'sugar and honey'; money. While this is possible, sugar had been a term of endearment or a metaphor for affection or luxury for many years before.

• *'I see Natalie's managed to find herself another sugar daddy.'*
(Recorded, magazine editor, London, 1986).

suit n

a bureaucratic functionary, *apparatchik*, corporation man. The term appeared in the 1980s and is used contemptuously or dismissively by working people and, especially, the fashionable young. In 1989 and 1990 the elaboration, 'empty suit' was heard, underlining the notion of anonymity. In the jargon of advertising agencies in Britain in the late 1980s the word is applied (neutrally rather than pejoratively) to the account executives who deal face to face with clients as opposed to the creative staff who dress casually.

• *'What the hell is that?'*
'Some suit from the mayor's office.'
'Just in time for the evening news.'
(*Cagney and Lacey*, US TV series, 1982).

sunnies n pl Australian

breasts.

sunshine n

1 British a term of address. The word is used teasingly or provocatively, usually between males. It originated as an ironic reference to a morose person.

2 a type of LSD. Several home-made varieties of the drug bore nicknames containing the word. **Orange sunshine**

(sold in the late 1960s and early 1970s) was probably the best-known.

supercharge n American

one of many nicknames for **crack**.

surfboard n

1 a flat chested girl. An expression popular among pubescent schoolgirls.

2 a promiscuous girl or woman. From the image of supine acquiescence and the sexual connotations of **ride**.

surfie n Australian

a member of a 1960s sub-culture based only partly on surfing. They were the contemporaries of British **mods** and contributed (like their American surfer counterparts) many colourful expressions to modern Australian slang.

suss adj British

suspect or suspicious.

• *'I thought it was a bit suss when they offered it to me for nothing.'*

suss n British

1 'knowhow', 'savvy'. A usage in currency since the 1970s, based on **suss (out)**.

• *'I wouldn't worry about her, she's got a lot of suss.'*

2 also **sus** suspicion. The much criticized Vagrancy Act under whose provisions (young) people could be arrested for 'loitering with intent (to commit an arrestable offence)', was known as 'the sus law'. 'On sus(s)' refers to being taken into custody on suspicion.

suss (out) vb British

to discern, discover, deduce or realize. A vogue expression among **beatniks** of the early 1960s (in the longer form); it had probably been in sporadic use before that. At first the phrase usually meant to perceive someone's true

501

nature or intentions, it is now a fairly common colloquialism, often meaning no more than 'work out'.

- *'I think I've managed to suss out a way round this.'*
- *'She sussed him out in five minutes.'*
- *'It took me half an hour to suss that video. Useless machine!'*
(Recorded, London, May 1990).

sussed, sussed out *adj British*

(of a person) well-adjusted, adapted to the circumstances, self-aware or self-reliant. This more recent derivation of the verb **suss out** is based on the notion of **suss** in the sense of 'know-how'. In the 1980s it is often in the form 'well-sussed'.

- *'This time, man, we've got it all sussed ... all the albums gonna be made here, first class jobs.'*
(Record bootlegger, Oz magazine, February 1970).
- *'A post punk skatezine that's aggressive, sussed and caustic about skating UK.'*
(*Mail on Sunday*, 'Biz' magazine, June 1987).

swag *n*

loot, booty, stolen goods. In this sense the word originated among itinerants and thieves in the early 19th century. It had earlier denoted goods or possessions when carried. The word is ultimately related, via dialect, to 'sway' and 'swing'. In modern usage swag is usually used humorously.

swallow *n British*

a drink of alcohol.

- *'Shall we go for a quick swallow?'*

swap spit *vb American*

to kiss, particularly referring to **French kissing**, in the jargon of teenagers and students.

sweat *vb American*

to put pressure on (someone).

- *'No-one's sweating you to join a gang.'*
(Los Angeles policeman to street-gang member, ITV documentary, August 1989).

sweat-hog *n American*

a physically repugnant person. A term of contempt or abuse typically applied by males such as college students to females.

the Sweeney *n British*

the Flying Squad, the elite criminal investigation division of London's Metropolitan police. The term is rhyming slang from the mythical Sweeney Todd, 'demon barber of Fleet Street'.

sweep (clean) *vb*

to remove listening devices (from a place); 'de-bug'. A piece of police and security-services jargon.

sweet F.A./Fanny Adams *n British*

a nothing at all, **fuck-all**.

b a pitifully small amount. In 19th century naval slang, 'Fanny Adams' was tinned or cooked meat, a sardonic reference to a girl of the same name who was murdered and dismembered in 1867. The name was later matched with the initials of **fuck-all** and used euphemistically in its place.

sweet lucy *n American*

wine, particularly cheap, sweet wine. A term used by **hobos** and **winos**.

swell *n British*

a well-off single woman in **yuppie** argot of the late 1980s. An acronym ('single woman earning lots of lolly') also recalling the dated description of a fashionable 'person-about-town'.

swift vb British

to give false evidence, 'bend' the evidence. A piece of police slang. A police officer who is adept at this practice is known as 'a (bit of a) swifter'. 'Swift it' is another form of the verb.

swing vb

a to behave in an uninhibitedly hedonistic way. This use of the word, originating in jazz and rock music circles, was popular in the 1960s; by the early 1970s it had been narrowed to its current sense (see sense **b**).

b to engage in 'liberated' and/or sophisticated sexual practices, particularly wife-swapping and group sex. The word is a catch-all euphemism for promiscuity, originating and still mainly heard in the USA.

swing both ways vb

to engage in sexual relations with both men and women. A euphemism heard in the USA since the later 1960s.

swinger n

a a sophisticated hedonist, fashionable pleasure lover. This quintessential 1960s term evolved quickly into sense **b** (see below).

b a euphemism for a practitioner of wife-swapping or other types of sexual adventure. This American term was adopted by 'adult' magazines, contact agencies, etc. in the 1970s as an acceptable designation for adultery and/or promiscuity, etc.

swipe vb

to steal. The word was first used in this sense in the USA, appearing in British speech at the turn of the century.

swish n American

a **gay** or effeminate male. A mildly pejorative term, inspired by the actual or supposed flouncing of the individuals in question. It is used by **gay** as well as heterosexual commentators.

switched-on adj British

a fashionable, alert. A vogue term of the 1960s equating with **turned-on**.

b excited either sexually or by drugs. A short-lived sense of the phrase, current in the mid to late 1960s.

switch-hitter n

a bisexual person. the phrase is used in the USA and Australia; it is from baseball jargon in which it denotes an ambidextrous batter.

sword n

See **pork sword**.

swot n

a diligent, hard-working student. A pejorative term which has survived from the mid-19th century into modern usage. It is an alteration of 'sweat' and like that word may be used as noun or verb. In the USA there are many terms used enviously or contemptuously of conscientious fellow-students, among them **grind**, **pencil-geek**, **squid** and **wonk**.

● 'But finally armed with a baseball bat, he intervenes when a bullying sports-star humiliates a kindly swot, preaching a sermon that converts the whole institution.'
(Observer, 29 May 1988).

(the) syph, siff n

syphilis.

syphon the python vb

See **siphon the python**.

syrup (of figs) n British

a wig. A piece of approximate rhyming slang invoking a laxative remedy.

● 'Got a groovy syrup of figs, Oliver Cromwell make.'

('Surgery' written and recorded by the Gymslips, 1981).

- *'That is* **not** *a syrup.'*

- *'I've got a tenner here says that's a syrup.'*
(*Only Fools and Horses*, British TV comedy series, 1989).

T

T n

marihuana. An alternative form of **tea**.

tab n

a tablet, specifically a tablet or dose of the drug LSD, from the jargon of users in the late 1960s and 1970s.

- '*A tab a day keeps reality at bay.*' (Graffito, Canterbury, 1970).
- '*Well, the one that stopped me from doing acid forever was when I dropped seven tabs. I completely lost my mind and went to Muppetland – the whole trip lasted for about six months.*' (Zodiac Mindwarp, I-D magazine, November 1987).

tache, tash n British

a moustache.

tack n

squalor, shabbiness, seediness, bad taste. A back-formation from the earlier Americanism, **tacky**. 'Tackiness' is an alternative noun form. (Very often tackiness refers to the quality, tack to the evidence thereof.)

tack attack n British

a fit or bout of bad taste. A witticism based on **tack** and **tacky** heard among fashionable 'young professionals' and media circles in London in 1988 and 1989. (**Rack attack** and **snack attack** are other rhyming phrases.)

- '*Judging by the décor of his flat, I'd say he'd had a tack attack.*'

tacker n British

a child. A northern English dialect word of obscure origin but possibly related to thumb(tack). It is occasionally heard in other parts of Britain.

tackiness n

seediness, bad taste, vulgarity. **Tack** is an alternative, also derived from the earlier adjective **tacky**.

tackle n British

a short form of the humorous euphemism **wedding tackle** (male genitals). Tackle alone was used in this sense from the 18th century, if not earlier.

tacky adj

shabby, seedy, inferior, vulgar. An American term which had existed in Southern speech in the USA since the late 19th century, before being understood (in the early 1970s) and partially adopted (in the late 1970s) in Britain. The origin is not in 'tacky'; sticky or viscous, but in a dialect word for an inferior horse, hence a shabby yokel. '*Tack-e-e-e*' is the last word and final verdict in the main text of Kenneth Anger's *Hollywood Babylon* (1975), an exposé of showbusiness scandal.

- '*That's just not me. I tried to avoid the papers the next day but I saw a couple of the tacky ones.*' (*Sunday Times*, 26 November 1989).

taco-bender n American

a Mexican or other person of Hispanic origin. A derogatory term coined on the lines of **spaghetti-bender** or **bagel-bender**. (A taco is a Mexican fried bread pancake.)

tacos n pl American

See **toss one's cookies/tacos**.

tad n, adj, adv

a small or slight amount, a little, slightly. An American expression now fairly widespread in British use, especially in phrases such as 'a tad hungry'. In American English tad has been used to mean a small boy since the late 19th century. It is probably from earlier British dialect, in which it is related to 'toad' or 'tadpole'.

tadger n British

penis. A vulgarism of unknown origin (probably from a lost dialect verb) used for many years in the North of England and revived by students, alternative comedians, etc. in the 1980s. **Todger** is an alternative modern version.

Taff, Taffy n British

a Welshman. The word is a nickname or epithet which can be used derogatively or affectionately. It is an anglicization of Dafydd, the Welsh form of the common Christian name, David, and has been in use since the late 17th century.

taffia n British

the 'Welsh mafia'. A humorous coinage also applied to the entourage of Neil Kinnock, the Welsh-born leader of the Labour party in the 1980s.

tag vb, n

(to spray) a graffiti artist's personalized signature or motif. The word has been a colloquialism for a person's name for many years. It was adopted by teenage graffiti artists in the 1970s in the USA, whence it spread with the craze.

● *'If you go to one of the big guys of hip hop art and they have not heard of your tag, you are nothing. But if they've seen it and like it then you are bad.'*
(15-year-old graffiti artist, *Evening Standard*, 11 November 1987).

tagger n

a graffiti 'artist'. From the use of **tag** to mean one's name or pictorial signature.

taig, teague n British

a Roman Catholic. A derogatory term used by Protestants. The nickname used to denote an Irishman in general and derives from an English rendering of the Gaelic proper name *Tadhg*. (It is sometimes further anglicized to **tyke**.)

tail n

a a woman, or women, seen as sexual objects. The word usually occurs in phrases such as 'a bit/piece of tail', tail being a euphemism dating from the 14th century for the less polite **arse** or **ass**.

b (particularly in Caribbean or **gay** usage) a man or men as sex objects.

● *'She spend all her time chasin' tail!'*
(Recorded, Trinidadian student, London, 1988).

tailpipe n American

the anus. A US teenagers' term. This predictable use of the word ('exhaust-pipe' in British English) is possibly influenced by the car driver's experience of having another driver 'up one's tailpipe', i.e. driving too close.

Taiwan n British

an upper second or 2.1 ('two-one') university degree. A student nickname on the lines of **Desmond**, **Pattie**, **Doug-**

las, etc. coined in the mid-1980s. A **made-in** is a synonym from the same source.

take a bath vb
to suffer a financial loss or commercial setback. A piece of business jargon that has become fairly widespread. The image evoked seems to be of drenching rather than washing.

take a dive/tumble/fall vb
to deliberately lose a boxing match or other contest. Expressions in use since the inter-war years, originating in the USA.

take a dump vb
See **dump**.

take a leak vb
See **leak**.

take a pop (at) vb
to attack, hit, lash out at. A phrase popular in working-class London speech in the late 1980s.
- 'Now you're taking a pop at my business partners.'
(EastEnders, British TV drama series, 1988).

take a powder vb
to leave (quickly), go away. A now dated expression originating in the USA in the 1920s. The powder in question refers to a laxative or stimulant medicine.

take a raincheck vb
to accept a postponement, put something off to a future date. An Americanism which has entered international English since the mid-1970s. The raincheck in question was originally a ticket stub entitling the holder to entry to a ball game at some future date if the fixture is rained off.

take down vb American
to kill or immobilize. A 'tough-guy' euphemism.

take names vb American
act resolutely and/or primitively, chastise. The image evoked is that of an authority figure noting the names of miscreants. The phrase is often placed after **kick ass**.
- 'Listen you're going to have to go in there and kick ass and take names!'

take one's lumps vb American
to suffer misfortune or harsh treatment.

take out vb
to kill or destroy. A military euphemism which came to public notice in the USA during the Vietnam War. The term was subsequently appropriated for use in the context of crime and law enforcement.

take the huff vb British
to take offence, to lose one's temper or 'go off in a huff'. An expression mainly heard in the North of England and Scotland. 'Huff' here means to snort or utter threats.

take the mick/mickey/michael vb British
to mock, deride, poke fun at. These expressions are milder versions of **take the piss**. Unbeknownst to most users, they employ rhyming slang; Mickey is short for a mythical 'Mickey Bliss', providing the rhyme for **piss**. 'Michael' is a humorous variant. The phrases, like their more vulgar counterpart, have been in use since the 1940s.

take the piss (out of someone) vb British
to mock, deride, poke fun (at). This vulgarism has been in widespread use

since the late 1940s. The original idea evoked by the expression was that of deflating someone, recalling the description of a self-important blusterer as **all piss and wind**.

take the shame vb British

to accept the blame (publicly and/or wholeheartedly) or face the criticism of one's peers. A key phrase in the playground vocabulary of London teenagers since the later 1970s. The concept is from black speech; 'shamed-up' is another derivation from the same source.

talent n British

attractive potential sexual partners. A generic term first applied before World War II to women and men. Since the mid-1960s female speakers have also applied the word (sometimes ironically) to desirable males.
● 'Let's check out the local talent.'

talk on the big white telephone vb

to vomit in a toilet. This colourful expression probably originated among US college students, like the synonymous 'kneel' or **pray to the porcelain god**.

talk turkey vb

to perform oral sex. A 1980s pun on the slang usage **gobble** and the well-known colloquial American expression meaning to discuss openly (also perhaps influenced in US usage by **turkey-neck**; penis).

tall poppies n pl Australian

'over-achievers', persons of prominence. The expression originates in the 1930s when the Lang government threatened to enforce tax laws which would 'cut off the heads of the tall poppies'.

tamale n American

See **hot tamale**.

tampi n

cannabis. An outdated drug users' and prisoners' term of the late 1950s and early 1960s. Its origin is obscure; it may derive from a native African or oriental word, or alternatively from the standard verb to tamp, which could describe the construction of a **reefer** or **joint** by analogy with the filling of a pipe.

tam rag n British

a sanitary towel or tampon. A variant of **jam rag** influenced by 'tampon' and the trademark 'Tampax'.

T and A n American

'**tits** and **ass**'. The American equivalent of the British **B and T**, a phrase describing a visual or tactile experience of a naked woman or women. The abbreviation and the expression in full probably originated in the jargon of journalists and/or showmen.

T and E adj British

'tired and emotional', i.e. drunk. An upper- and middle-class euphemism.

tank n

1 American a firearm, handgun. A hyperbolic term occasionally used by criminals and law enforcers.
2 British a police car or van. The word is used in this way by ironic or self-dramatizing police officers.
Compare **gunship**.

tank vb British

a to crush, overwhelm.
● 'They'd all tank Tyson.'
(Headline in the Sun, 28 February 1989).
b to move forcefully and powerfully.
● 'Tanking up and down the

motorway all holiday . . . but
Christmas itself was very quiet . . .
very pleasant . . . .'
(Biff cartoon, Guardian, December
1987).
Both senses of the word became popular in the later 1980s.

tanked, tanked-up adj

drunk. A common term since the
turn of the century; the shorter form is
more recent. Tank up evokes the filling
of a container or fuelling of a vehicle
and parallels such expressions as **loaded** and **canned**.

● 'I'll do the washing-up tomorrow if I
don't get too tanked-up tonight.'
(Biff cartoon, Guardian, 1986).

tanner n British

six pence, in pre-decimal coinage, or
the coin worth that amount. The small
silver coin continued to circulate after
decimalization, when it was worth 2½
new pence, but was eventually withdrawn. The origin of the word as used
in this sense is unknown, although it is
said by some authorities to derive from
the Romany tawno, meaning small.

tap, tap up vb

to borrow, or seek to borrow, from
(someone). To tap meant to spend liberally in archaic slang; by the early
20th century it had acquired the second sense of solicit, borrow or obtain.
The origin of the term is in the tapping
of liquid from a container, reinforced
by tapping someone on the shoulder to
gain their attention and the later slang
sense of 'hitting' someone for a loan.
Tap is international English, while the
form tap up is in British usage.

tap city n, adj American

(the condition of being) penniless,
broke. A humorous version of **tapped-
out**.

● 'It's no good asking me. I'm in tap
city.'
● 'It's tap city the rest of this month.'

tap-dance n

a clever evasion, devious manoeuvre. The term, which is used all over
the English-speaking world recalls a
dancer either **busking** or improvizing
in a difficult situation or merely exe-
cuting an elegant sequence of steps.

● 'That was not an opinion – that
was a tap-dance worthy of Fred
Astaire.'
(Hooperman, US TV series, 1987).
● 'On occasions he [Harvey
Goldsmith] has done as much tap-
dancing, financially speaking, as
Low Grade in his Lordship's first
business career.'
(Sunday Times magazine, June
1989).

tap-dancer n

a person who can avoid danger by a
combination of clever, if devious or
dishonest actions and luck; someone
able to talk themselves out of difficult
situations

● 'That man's a born tap-dancer: he's
always out the back door five
minutes before the front door's
kicked in.'
(Recorded, drug dealer, London,
1988).

tapioca adj

broke, penniless (usually temporarily). A **preppie** witticism derived from
tapped-out.

tapped-out adj American

a without money, broke. A term
used especially by gamblers, and more
recently by adolescents. It is inspired
by the very old slang use of the word to
tap, meaning both to spend, and later
to obtain money from another person.

● 'I'm tapped-out, Mark. American

509

Express got a hitman out looking for me.'
(*Wall Street*, US film, 1987).

b exhausted. From the idea of being 'drained'.

tarbrush n

See **a touch of the tarbrush**.

tard n American

a fool, simpleton. A teenagers' shortening of the popular term of contempt, **retard**. The word has been adopted by British adolescents in the late 1980s.

tarmac vb

to 'jet-hop' from one airport to another, as in the case of campaigning politicians or shuttling diplomats. A piece of journalese from the late 1980s.

tart n

a promiscuous, vulgar or sexually provocative woman. This modern sense of the word has gradually supplanted the older meaning which was simply a woman or sweetheart. As a term of affection (inspired by the pastry sweetmeat and reinforced by 'sweetheart'), tart was applied to women of all ages from the mid-19th century. By the early years of the 20th century it was more often used of the flighty or immoral and by the inter-war years often referred to prostitutes. In modern theatrical, **gay** (where it is often used of men), cockney and Australian speech, tart is still used affectionately.

tart about vb British

a to flounce about, behave archly or flamboyantly.

b to mess about, behave in a disorganized or irresolute way.

Many derogatory or vulgar terms (**arse**, **dick**, **fanny**, etc.) have been converted to verbs on the same pattern.

tash n British

an alternative spelling of **tache**.

tassel, tassle n

a penis. An inoffensive term often used by parents and children and referring particularly to the member of an immature male. In older (pre-1950s) British usage, 'pencil-and-tassle' was a euphemism for a boy's genitals.

tasty adj British

attractive, desirable, smart. An all-purpose term of approbation, used in working-class London speech for many years and more specifically as a fashionable word among the young in the late 1970s and 1980s.

● *'A tasty geezer.'*
'Love the threads. Really tasty.'

tasty n British

an alcoholic drink. A specific application of the wider notion of something desirable, from the popular cockney adjective.

● *'I know a pub that does late tasties.'*
(*Only Fools and Horses*, British TV comedy series, 1989).

tat n British

shoddy, cheap or low-quality material. A colloquialism, originally meaning specifically rags or cloth remnants, which is derived from tatter(s) and tatty (themselves ultimately descended from an old Germanic term meaning tuft).

● *'Liverpool comprehensive pupils would not be seen dead in "second-hand tat", however grand the previous incumbent.'*
(*Sunday Times* magazine, 30 July 1989).

ta-tas, tatters, tats n British

a walk. A nursery term, usually used in the form 'go ta-tas', which was especially widespread in the 1950s. Pronounced 'tatters', the word probably, but not provably, derives from 'ta-ta!', meaning goodbye.

taters n British

1 potatoes. A short form most often heard in London and the south of England.

2 see **do one's nut/taters etc.**

taters (in the mould) adj
British

cold. This authentic cockney rhyming-slang expression has survived in its shortened form to the present day. It is now common in 'respectable' jocular speech and is usually thought by users to be merely a shortening of 'cold potatoes'.

● *'It's a bit taters out there, I can tell you.'*

taties n pl British

potatoes. A variant form of **taters** more often heard in Scotland and the North of England.

tats, tatts n pl

1 a Australian teeth, especially false teeth.

b British dice.

Both senses of the word are now rare; the first probably post-dating the second. The origin of the term is obscure but may imitate the clattering of the objects in question.

2 another form of **ta-tas.**

3 tattoos.

tatters n British

See **ta-tas.**

tax vb

to **mug** or steal from someone, leaving them with a proportion of their money. A miscreants' jargon term for partial robbery, recorded among street gangs in London and Liverpool since the late 1970s.

taxi-cabs n pl British

(a case of) **crabs**; an infestation of body lice. The rhyming-slang phrase has fallen from use since the mid-1960s.

T.B.A. n, adj American

to be avoided. An item of **preppie** code similar to the British **Sloane Ranger** term N.S.I.T. ('not safe in taxis') but extended to refer to things and situations as well as people.

tea n

marihuana. Tea has been a nickname for herbal cannabis since the early years of the 20th century. Originally an Americanism, the term derives from the close resemblance in all but colour between the two substances. By the mid-1960s tea was a dated word restricted to older speakers, having been supplanted by such synonyms as **pot**, **charge**, **shit**, etc. **Teaed-up**, in the sense of intoxicated by marihuana, survives in teenage use.

See also **T** and **vitamin T.**

teach n

a teacher. An affectionate or more often irreverent form of address by pupils.

teaed-up, tea'd-up adj
American

high on marihuana. A (mainly middle-class) teenagers' term which preserves the otherwise obsolescent **tea** as a euphemism for cannabis.

teague n British

an alternative spelling of **taig.**

teahead n

a marihuana smoker. An outdated and transitory term from the early 1960s, soon supplanted by **pothead.**

tea-leaf n British

a thief. A well-known item of rhyming slang in use since the end of the 19th century. It also occurs in Australian speech and is occasionally heard as a verb.

team n

a street gang. Like **firm** and **crew**, the usage evokes the notion of camaraderie and united effort.

tear-arse, tear-arse around/about vb British

to rush about or otherwise behave hastily and recklessly. The image evoked is of activity so violent that it would tear the bottom out of a vehicle or of one's clothing.

tearaway n British

a wild, reckless (usually young) person. This previously obscure term, which had referred to a 'tough-guy' or **mugger** since the turn of the 19th century, was popularized as a useful epithet for unruly youths or 'juvenile delinquents' in the early 1960s. It is still heard in colloquial usage.

tear off a piece vb

to have sex. A phrase denoting seduction or sexual achievement from the male point of view. The expression is American or Australian and dates from the end of the 19th century. (The use of 'tear off a strip' with this sexual sense has been recorded in Britain.) The unromantic image evoked is that of tearing a piece of meat off a carcass for consumption.

tear one off vb

to succeed in seduction, have sex. A less common version of **tear off a piece**, and like that expression used mostly in the USA and Australia.

tease, teaser n

a sexually provocative person, one who entices sexually, but fails to satisfy. The word, popular in the 1960s and applied to females, is a less offensive version of **prick-tease(r)**.

- 'She's a big teaser/She took me half the way there.'
  ('Day Tripper', written by John Lennon and Paul McCartney, recorded by the Beatles, 1966).

technicolour yawn n

an act of vomiting. An Australian expression of the early 1960s, popularized in Britain by the *Barry McKenzie* comic strip by Barry Humphries and Nicholas Garland.

ted, teddy boy n British

a member of a youth cult of the 1950s characterized by a particular style of dress (a long drape or waisted jacket worn with **drainpipe** trousers and thick crepe-soled **brothel-creeper** shoes) and music (jitterbug from about 1948, rock 'n' roll from 1956). Teddy boys, mainly working class in origin, combined a rough simulacrum of Edwardian dress (hence their name: they were sometimes jocularly referred to as **Edwardians**) with the adoption of American teenage hairstyles and music. As a living subculture, the ted phenomenon was virtually over by about 1963, but many of the original adherents and younger imitators have perpetuated the style which greatly influenced later fashions.

teenybopper n

a lively, fashionable teenager or pre-teenager. The word, originating in the USA sometime in the mid-1960s, has often been used in a condescending or derogatory sense in the 1970s and 1980s. (When used approvingly or neutrally in the 1970s, the term was often shortened to **bopper**.) The expression is composed of a diminutive form of teen(ager) and **bop**, to dance or behave enthusiastically.

- 'The Doors are a chance for all the little teenyboppers in the States to think they're digging something avant garde.'
(Mike Ratledge of the Soft Machine, Oz magazine, February 1969).

telephone n

See **talk on the big white telephone**, **trombone** and **dog (and bone)**.

tell n American

a hint or clue, especially one picked up by a swindler. A word from the jargon of gamblers and confidence tricksters.

- 'Margaret . . . is drawn into an underworld of cons, scams, "marks" (suckers) and "tells" (their involuntary give-away gestures).'
(Review of US film House of Games, Independent, 19 November 1987).

Thai sticks n pl

herbal marihuana (of Thai origin) wrapped in small cylindrical bundles for sale. A dealer and users' term.

thang n

an imitated southern or black American pronunciation of thing.

thicko, thickie n British

an unintelligent, slow witted person. Common terms, especially among children and adolescents, derived from the colloquial use of 'thick' to denote cloddish, 'dense'.

- 'I'm not some blinkin' thickie, I'm Billericay Dickie and I'm doin' very well.'
('Billericay Dickie', recorded by Ian Dury, 1977).

thing n

a synonym for **scene**, **kick**, **vibe** or

trip in the sense of main activity, preferred ambience. This item of raffish or **hip** usage (originating in the USA, probably in the 1940s) has become a well established colloquialism in such phrases as 'it's not really my thing'.

third leg n

the penis. A variant of **middle leg**.

thrash n

1 a wild celebration, dance or party. In this sense the word has been used since before World War II.

2 a variety of very fast 'heavy metal' music of the late 1980s, in the jargon of rock journalists and aficionados.

threads n

clothes. A usage which originated in the black-influenced **jive talk** of the 1930s in the USA. Like many similar Americanisms, it was imported into Britain and Australia with the youth culture of the 1960s. If used today the term is generally self consciously **hip**, humorous or ironic.

- 'Wide-boy or spiv, personified in Oliver Schmitz' film by Panic, an unprivileged South African black in loud threads and two-tone shoes.'
(Independent, 12 January 1988).

the threepenny bits n

diarrhoea. A rhyming expression for **the shits**. **Tray-bits** and **tom tits** are alternative versions; all are especially popular in Australian speech.

throat n American

a **swot**, in **preppie** jargon. This is one of many synonyms used by US adolescents for a tedious, conscientious and/or unpopular fellow-student; **grind**, **squid** and **pencil geek** are others.

throne n

a lavatory, toilet pedestal. A humorous synonym widely heard since before World War II and still in use. (A 'potty throne' was a device formerly used for toilet training.)

● 'He can't come to the phone right now – he's on the throne.'

throne room n

a lavatory, toilet. A humorous pun playing on the euphemism **throne** for toilet pedestal and the room used by a sovereign for giving formal audiences.

throttle a darkie, throttle one vb Australian

to defecate. Synonymous expressions substitute **choke** or **strangle** for throttle.

throttle pit n Australian

a toilet. A vulgarism inspired by several expressions using the verb **throttle** as a synonym for defecate.

throw, throw up n, vb

(to) vomit. Throw is a short form of synonyms such as throw up, **throw one's voice**, etc.

throw a mental vb American

to lose control of oneself, lose one's temper. A teenage and **Valley Girl** term of the early 1980s.

● 'I totalled the car and Mom threw a mental.'

throw a wobbly/wobbler vb British

to suddenly behave irrationally or to have a temper tantrum. This phrase has become popular in Britain since the end of the 1970s, but dates from the 1950s. Its exact derivation is unclear, but may reflect simply an attack of shaking or quivering, or alternatively refer to throwing or bowling a ball in an erratic and confusing arc, or to the loss of control when a wobbling wheel

comes off a wagon or a bicycle for example.

● 'She's been very up and down lately. She threw another wobbly a couple of days ago.'
(Recorded, London, 1988).
See also **wobbler, wobbly**.

throw one's voice vb

Australian

to vomit. One of many colourful synonyms originating in Australia in the late 1950s. Since the 1970s the expression is often shortened simply to **throw**.

thumb n

See **on the thumb**.

thumbsucker n British

an immature weakling, baby.

● 'I ain't followin' a bunch of thumbsuckers – you want to run a national firm, friend, you put your arse in gear behind us.'
(The Firm, British TV play, 1989).

thumping, thump-up n British

a beating, physical attack. Since the 1950s these have been terms in use in the school playground and among street gangs and thugs: the second version is a more recent and racier alternative.

● 'Bar-room fights, a thump-up in a dance hall, a vicious war like Vietnam.'
(Pete Townshend of the Who, Rave magazine, February 1966).

thunder-bags n pl Australian

male underpants. A jocularism drawing the analogy with explosive flatulence or defecation, more often encountered in the expression **thunderbox**.

thunder-bowl n British

a toilet. A variant of **thunderbox**

514

used by predominantly middle-class speakers.

thunderbox n

1 *British* a toilet. The word was originally applied particularly to a commode, in the colonial period. It was later extended, especially in middle- and upper-class usage, to a small privy and later any lavatory.

2 *American* a **ghettoblaster**.

thunder-thighs n

a heavily-built, overweight or intimidating female. A term of derision or fearful respect commonly, but not exclusively, used by males. The nickname was applied, for example, to the heiress Christina Onassis, in 'society' circles and the media.

tick n *British*

1 a smaller, and often younger, school pupil, usually one considered insignificant and irritating. A traditional public-school term which is still heard today, it likens the person to the parasitic insect.

2 hire purchase, short-term credit. Tick meant 'credit' in post-17th-century slang. It has survived mainly in the phrase 'on tick'.

ticked off adj

annoyed, irritated, angry or resentful. A politer form or euphemism for **pissed-off**, heard especially in the USA.

- '*Thank you guys, but Mork's not here and I'm too ticked off to go anywhere.*'
  (*Mork and Mindy*, US TV comedy series, 1981).

ticker n

one's heart. Ticker was first slang for a clock or fob-watch then, by analogy, the heart.

- '*Oh my dicky ticker!*'

(Catchphrase from the British TV comedy, '*Allo 'Allo!*).

ticket n *British*

a would-be **mod**. Ticket, like **face**, first denoted a singular person or individual, hence one of the fashionable crowd. In 1964 the term began to be applied derisively to less sophisticated emulators of the mod elite; tickets typically wore parkas, garish T-shirts and cheap sports shoes. The word was last heard in 1966.

tickle n *British*

a a hint.

b an inkling.

c a minor success or sign of future success.

d a mild expression of interest.

All these closely-related sub-senses of the word are well established in working-class speech and commercial jargon. They derive from the use of tickle to denote the sensation felt when a fish nibbles at a bait.

tickle the ivories vb

to play the piano.

tickle the pickle vb

(of a male) to masturbate. A humorous coinage in imitation of the more widespread **jerkin' the gherkin**, mainly heard in Britain and Australia.

ticky-tacky n *American*

shoddy, inferior material(s). This light-hearted expression (related to **tacky**, which has survived and flourished), was popularized by its use in the song 'Little Boxes', written by Malvina Reynolds and sung by Pete Seeger in 1960.

tiddler n *British*

a anything very small; an affectionate term for a small child, small or young fish, etc.

b a (new) half-penny coin. The tiny post-1971 ½p coin was withdrawn from circulation in 1986.

tiddly, tiddlywink n British

1 a drink. A piece of rhyming slang dating from the 19th century and still heard in the early 1960s referring invariably to alcohol. The well known adjective tiddly is derived from this.

2 a Chinese person. London rhyming slang for **chink**.

tiddly-dum adj British

tedious, dull, boring. An imitation of bored humming, synonymous with but rarer than **ho-hum**.

tiddy oggie, tiddie oggy n
British

a Cornish pastie. The etymology of the phrase is unclear: 'tiddy' may be a form of **taters** or **taties** (potato) or a word meaning small; oggie is even more obscure, but could be descended from a dialect word ('hogail') for berry, or an altered form of egg.

tie off vb

to bind one's limb in order to raise a vein in which to inject narcotics. An addicts' term.

tie one on vb

to get drunk. Like its synonym **hang one on**, this phrase was a 1930s Americanism, now heard in other English-speaking areas. The precise etymology of these expressions is not clear, but probably conveys the image of attacking a quantity of liquor or the burden resulting from its ingestion.

tiger n

1 a forceful, formidable or *farouche* individual. The word is often used as a teasing or ironic term of address to a supposedly sexually attractive male.

2 *see* **park a custard/tiger**.

tiger's milk/sweat n

very strong alcoholic drink. These terms date from the colonial era and are not yet quite obsolete. 'Tiger's milk' is also the brand name of a type of white wine.

tight adj

1 mean, stingy, miserly. Now a common colloquialism rather than slang, this usage originated in the USA in the early 19th century. The image evoked is of someone who is 'tight-fisted'. A modern elaboration is **tight-arsed**.

2 tipsy or drunk. The word was first used in this sense in the USA in 1843, being adopted almost immediately in Britain. The word evokes someone full of or bulging with alcoholic liquid.

3 *American* very friendly, close.

● *'Me and Harry been tight since we were kids.'*

tight-arse, tight-ass n

1 a mean, miserly person. This sense of the word is more common in British usage than the following sense. The term has existed, mainly in working-class speech, since the early part of the 20th century. Tight alone has had this meaning since the mid-19th century.

2 a repressed, prudish or **uptight** person, an 'anal retentive'. This use of the expression is probably more widespread in American speech. In the 19th century it usually meant specifically sexually repressed, puritanical or chaste.

tight-arsed adj British

miserly, mean, stingy. This is an elaboration of **tight** (itself used to mean stingy since the 1820s), heard since the early years of the 20th century.

tighten one's face vb American

to shut up, keep quiet. A teenagers' and **Valley Girl** expression, usually heard in the form of an instruction.

● '*Aw, come on, you, like tighten your face!*'

tight little unit n
See **t.l.u.**

tightwad n
a miserly, ungenerous person. A pre-World-War I Americanism later adopted elsewhere. The **wad** in question is a role of banknotes.

Tijuana bible n American
a pornographic magazine or book. Just across the US-Mexico border, the town of Tijuana has long been a centre of uncontrolled sexual amenities for visitors from the north.

time n
a term of imprisonment. This well-known expression, usually in the phrase 'do time', originated in underworld argot in the mid-19th century.

time-bomb n
an illicit drug taken orally, wrapped in paper, pastry etc. The drug (usually cannabis or amphetamine) enters the bloodstream through the stomach wall.
● '*Then my nose couldn't absorb it any more. So I started swallowing speed in tiny paper parcels known as "time bombs".*'
(Sun, 10 August 1988).

tin n
money, cash coins. A fairly rare expression.

tin-arse(d) adj, n
a lucky, privileged. The expression which is now dated in British usage, but well established in Australia, is a humorous parallel to 'copper-bottomed' in the sense of well protected, solidly based or invulnerable.

b smug. A less common sense of the phrase.
● '*We knew you were homo and therefore we expected none of that conventional tin-arse filth which one finds in the hetero about man and woman relationships.*'
(Robert Graves in an (undated) letter to Tom Driberg, quoted in Driberg's autobiography).

tincture n British
1 an alcoholic drink. An adult male middle-class term, popularized by the fictional Denis Thatcher in the satirical 'Dear Bill' letters in *Private Eye* magazine in the 1980s.
2 tincture of cannabis; hashish in liquid form as legally prescribed to some drug users for a period in the 1960s.

tin-cupping n
cadging or begging for money. The phrase has become part of business jargon where it refers to approaching a series of companies for loans.

tinker n British
1 a nursery term of endearment, used usually by women to little boys in the form 'little tinker'. (Tinkers were formerly thought to be archetypally mischievous.) The expression is often applied ironically to older males.
2 penis. In this sense the word may be a version of or a confusion for **tinkler**, or an extension of the preceding usage.

Tinkerbelle n British
an effeminate, effete or fey male. A term of derision typically employed by 'tough guys' derived from the famous female fairy in *Peter Pan*.

tinkle n British
1 an act of urination. A coy, humor-

ous or childish expression, in common use since the 1920s.
- *'I'm just off upstairs for a tinkle.'*

2 a telephone call. This colloquial usage was inspired by the thin, slow ringing of early telephones.

3 money, cash, wealth. A working-class term heard especially in the late 1950s and early 1960s.
- *'Got any tinkle for me?'*

tinkle vb

to urinate. A childish, coy or humorous euphemism which has been in widespread use since the 1920s, although it probably originated earlier as an echoic nursery term.

tinkler n British

penis. A nursery term from **tinkle**, also applied ironically or derisively in reference to older males.

tinkle the ivories vb

an alternative, less common version of **tickle the ivories** (play the piano).

tinnie, tinny n Australian

a can of beer. There has been recent argument in Australia as to whether this term is now archaic or not, but as late as 1988 it was recorded in London among young expatriate Australians.

Tin Pan Alley n

the area (7th Avenue in New York City and Denmark Street in London) where the popular-music business is based.

tinsel town n

Hollywood, its showbusiness milieu and the values thereof. An often derogatory nickname which has become established in journalese.

tiny n British

a small child, younger fellow-pupil.

'The tinies' is the (usually dismissive or condescending) standard middle-class, prep or public-school designation of children 'lower down' the school.

tio taco n American

the Hispanic American (**Chicano**) version of **Uncle Tom**, i.e. a collaborator with the **anglo** establishment. *Tio* is Spanish for uncle, *taco* is a Mexican fried bread pancake.

tip n British

a dirty, messy or squalid place. The term has become a popular colloquialism in the 1980s, often describing an untidy bedroom. It is a shortening of 'rubbish tip'.

tiswas, tizwoz n British

a state of confusion and/or flustered excitement. Usually found in the expressions 'all of a tiswas' or 'in a (bit of a) tiswas'. This folksy, light-hearted term probably comes from 'it is – it was', that is, expressing a disorientation in time; or else is an elaborated form of the colloquial 'tizz' and 'tizzy'.

tit n

1 a a breast. Various Old Germanic languages and late Latin dialects contained related words formed on the root *tet-* or *tit-* (*teta* in Spanish and *téton* in French are modern cognates). Teat was for many centuries the standard English form; in the 17th century the alternative spelling and pronunciation tit began to be used. It is only in the 20th century that the variant spellings and pronunciation have clearly differentiated vulgar and standard usages.

b any button, knob, nipple or small protuberance.
- *'You have to attach it to the tit on the end.'*

c the sight or touch of a woman's

breast(s). An exclusively male vulgarism.

● '*I got some tit.*'

d women in general, seen as sexual partners. An exclusively male vulgarism.

● '*There's loads of tit around.*'

2 a fool, buffoon. The word has been heard in this sense since the early 20th century in British usage.

● '*There were two outstanding things about Q.E.D.'s "The Battle Of The Sexes" – Faith Brown. Stuart Hall merely made a right tit of himself.*' (Charles Catchpole, News of the World, 5 February 1989).

tit about/around vb British

to mess about or behave in a disorganized or ineffectual manner. One of many synonyms such as **arse about, fanny about, fart about,** etc.

titfer n British

a hat. One of the best-known examples of rhyming slang (from the cliché 'tit-for-tat'), the term probably dates from the end of the 19th century and is still heard.

tit-man n

a male whose preferred part of the female anatomy is the breasts: **arse-man** and **leg-man** are alternatives.

tittie, titty n

1 a breast. An affectionate or diminutive form of **tit,** in use since the 18th century when it was considered less vulgar than it is today.

2 see **tough titty.**

t.l.u. n American

a **tight little unit,** i.e. an attractive compact girl. An item of **Valley Girl** slang from earlier surfers' jargon.

toadsucker n American

a teenage term of abuse which while

offensive has the advantage of not being obscene.

toasted adj American

drunk or tipsy.

● '*It's not much [money], just enough to go out and get toasted some time you need it.*' (Working Girl, US film, 1988).

toasting n

a form of music in which a rhythmic narrative is chanted over a reggae backing. Toasting was the 1970s forerunner of **rap** music.

● '*Imagine a female Eek-A-Mouse toasting over a Yello track, the lyrics written by Morrissey with a spliff in his mouth, and you'll have a very close approximation.*' (Time Out magazine, 26 July 1989).

tod n

See **on one's tod.**

Tod (Sloan) n British

See **on one's tod.**

todger n British

penis. A version of the more common **tadger.**

● '*Orange Y-fronts with a slogan like "my todger is in here".*' (Alternative-comedy act, Jo Brand, ('the Sea-Monster'), Montreal Comedy Festival, 1988).

to die adj American

utterly excellent, wonderful. A **preppie** term, used typically by female speakers in thrilled approval or admiration. The expression refers to the notion of dying for something or of love for someone and is probably influenced by a usage such as **killer.**

● '*Did you see that boy in the cut-off chinos? My god, he was to die!*'

● '*It was just to die.*'

toe-jam n

an accretion of dirt between the toes.

toerag n British

a contemptible person, a scrounger, ne'er-do-well, tramp or thief. Toe-rags were the bindings wound around the feet of convicts or tramps in the 19th century. The word had taken on its present meaning by early in the 20th century in both Britain and Australia. During the 1950s and 1960s toerag was an obscure cockney term; it was given wider currency in the 1970s by TV programmes such as *The Sweeney* and the pop songs of Ian Dury. From the mid-1980s it has been revived by working-class Londoners. In Britain toerag is often used facetiously or slightly dismissively, in Australia it can sometimes indicate approval of one who acts like a (natural, rather than social) gentleman.

toes n pl

See **have it (away) on one's toes.**

toff n British

a socially superior and/or wealthy person. The word dates from the middle of the 19th century and probably derives from 'tuft' (used of a titled undergraduate at Oxford or Cambridge who wore a decoration on his cap) rather than the later **toffee-nosed**. The word had an archaic ring in the 1960s and early 1970s but like other working-class terms relating to money and status has been revived by modern cockneys and their 'upwardly-mobile' emulators.

- '*Max was trying to build a high-tech laboratory complex, but all kinds of posh people were blocking his path. Basically, nobody loves you if you're common and you presume to take liberties with toffs.*' (Kate Saunders, *Evening Standard*, 17 May 1989).

toffee n British

1 nonsense, empty talk or flattery. This is predominantly a working-class usage, particularly popular in the armed forces and in London. The origin of the image is probably in the idea of something sweet, sticky and attractively wrapped.

- '*She gave me a load of old toffee as usual about what a reputable organisation they are and how they enjoy doing business with us.*' (Recorded, advertising executive, London, 1988).

2 gelignite. A term used by criminals and terrorists since the 1950s, from the explosive's appearance.

toffee-nosed adj British

'snooty', snobbish, 'stuck up'. A fairly common colloquialism which is inspired by the screwing up of the nose into a supercilious expression. It arose sometime before World War II.

together adj

in control of oneself, well organized, adjusted, collected. Derived from the phrase **get it together**, this became a catchword of the late 1960s and early 1970s, designating an approved state of self-possession, inner harmony, etc.; the antonym was **untogether**. The usage is now dated.

togs n pl

clothes. Now a well established informal term which has given rise to expressions such as 'togged up' and 'togged out' (dressed) and 'toggery' (clothes shop or wardrobe); togs originated in the early 19th century from a verb to 'tog', ultimately related to 'toga'.

toilet n

a disgusting, squalid or depressing place. A usage which has been in vogue during the 1980s.

toilet-talk n

'smutty', coarse or obscene conversation. An American euphemism of the 1950s which has since been adopted for ironic or jocular use in Britain and Australia.

● *'OK I'll go next door and you two can get on with your toilet-talk.'* (Recorded, Devon, 1986).

toke vb, n

(to take) an inhalation of a **joint** or pipe of cannabis. This has been a standard term in the marihuana and hashish smokers' vocabulary since the late 1960s. Toke probably comes from the Spanish *tocar* meaning to touch, although, perhaps coincidentally, the word existed for many years in British underworld slang meaning prison bread or a small piece or slice, becoming archaic by the 1930s.

tokus n American

See **tush**.

tole n

a street fight, brawl. A now archaic working-class term of the 1950s. Its origin is obscure; a relation to toll (in the sense of strike) seems plausible but cannot be demonstrated.

tom n British

1 jewellery. A piece of underworld rhyming slang, from 'tomfoolery'.

2 a prostitute. In police jargon and in the slang of the underworld and prison this has been a standard term since the 1940s. It derives from a 19th-century use of the nickname Tom to denote a masculine, assertive or aggressive streetwalker.

● *'... and he says that the tom couldn't have been where the police officer said she was because she was in bed with him. He was transferred the same day.'*

(Police sergeant, *Inside the British Police*, Simon Holdaway, 1989).

3 an act of defecation. Rhyming slang from 'tom-tit' (the bird); **shit**.

4 an injection of a narcotic. A shortened form of the rhyming slang **Tom Mix** (the Hollywood cowboy hero of silent films); **fix**.

tom vb British

to work as a prostitute. A fairly rare extension of the noun sense.

tombstones n pl

teeth. A jocular simile often applied to gapped, uneven or partly discoloured teeth.

tomcat, tomcat around vb

American

to prowl, usually at night, in search of sexual activity. A term used disapprovingly, usually by women of men.

tomfoolery n British

jewellery. A piece of rhyming slang more often heard in the short form **tom**.

Tom Mix n British

1 an injection of a narcotic. A piece of drug abusers' terminology from the 1960s, rhyming on **fix**. (Tom Mix was the star of silent western movies.)

2 a predicament, difficult situation, rhyming on the colloquial meaning of 'fix'.

tommy-gun n

a hypodermic syringe. Like **machine gun** and other words such as **artillery**, this is an item from the self-dramatizing vocabulary of hard-drug addicts of the late 1950s and 1960s. ('Tommy-gun' is the Thompson sub-machine gun favoured by US gangsters of the 1920s and 1930s.)

the toms, the tom-tits n

Australian

an attack of diarrhoea, or feelings of intense discomfort or dislike. A vulgarism based on the rhyme tom-tits; **shits**. The singular form is more prevalent in British rhyming slang.

ton, a ton, the ton n

a the ton (or less commonly **a ton**), 100 miles per hour. A term, used typically by British motorcyclists, which has been in use since the early 1950s. It was popularized by the press describing the activities of **ton-up kids**. The word was adopted by American hotrodders in the 1960s.

b a ton £100, in working-class and underworld parlance.

tongue-job, tongue-bath n

a a French kiss.

b an act of cunnilingus.

Both uses of both terms are from the late 1960s lexicon of **hippies** and pornographers. In the sense of kiss the expression has been supplanted in US teenage and **preppie** usage by **tongue sushi**.

tongue sushi n American

'French' kissing. A **preppie** term inspired by the Japanese raw fish delicacy fashionable from the late 1970s and 1980s.

tonk n British

an act of copulation. A back-formation from **tonking** heard increasingly from the 1980s. 'Tonk' is a now rare term for hit, as is the synonym **bonk**.

tonk, tonker n Australian

a a fool.

b an effeminate or homosexual male. Both usages date from before the 1950s and are of unknown origin. ('Tong' is an archaic term for penis but may be quite unrelated.)

tonking adj British

a euphemism for **fucking** in its literal sense, used especially in the armed forces in the late 1970s and 1980s. The noun **tonk** is also increasingly in evidence, although **tonk** as a verb is rare.

ton-up kid/boy n British

a teenage or young adult motorcyclist, precursor of the **rocker**. Ton-up boys were the bugbears of the popular press in the late 1950s. **A ton** or **the ton** was 100 mph, the goal of the leather-jacketed groups who gathered near suburban by-passes and main roads to stage informal speed trials and races or to go for a 'burn-up' (to drive as quickly as possible, simply for the enjoyment of speed).

- 'The BBC broadcast of "Morning Service" from Keele University, Staffs, yesterday was interrupted when a record about "ton-up" boys was heard above the hymn singing. A loudspeaker was found hidden behind a stage in the chapel.'
  (Daily Telegraph, 25 January 1965).

tool n

1 the penis. The notion of the male member as an implement is very ancient. The word tool itself appeared in Middle English and by the 16th century had been recorded as a sexual metaphor. It was at first an acceptable colloquialism, but since the beginning of the 19th century has been considered vulgar.

- 'Play it safe
  Play it cool
  Wear a Jiffi
  On your tool'
- (Promotion slogan for Jiffi condoms, 1988).
- 'He had a thing about his penis. When he was away from me, he was always referring to it as "my noble tool".'
  (Anna Kashfi referring to ex-

husband Marlon Brando, *Sunday Mirror*, 3 September 1989).

2 a fool. Like many other words designating the male member, tool has the secondary meaning of a stupid (male) person.

3 a weapon. This usage is now rare, but has given rise to the standard underworld and police jargon expression **tooled-up** (armed with firearms) in British English.

tool *vb British*

to attack with a razor. A slang term used by streetgang members in the 1950s, particularly in London and Glasgow.

tool along *vb*

to move smoothly and or casually. Tool has been used in the sense of steer, drive or ride since the early 19th century.

- '*I was tooling along at 45 in the inside lane, minding my own business.*'

tool around/about *vb*

to idle or loaf, mess around at trivial tasks. Originally an upper-class Edwardian phrase, (probably from the sense of tool as meaning to drive (a coach) skilfully and smoothly, hence to perform without effort). In modern speech there may also be a convergence with the sense of **tool** as male member, paralleled in the synonymous usage **dick around**.

tooled-up *adj British*

a armed, issued with firearms. A term used by the underworld and the police since the early 1950s. The noun **tool**, denoting a firearm, is now archaic. The expression tooled-up has become more widely known in the later 1970s and 1980s after reference in the media; it is sometimes extended to de-

note armed with knives, coshes or other weapons.

- '*Some of the briefing scenes could have come straight from a movie thriller as the elite Squad members get "tooled up" – issued with snubnosed revolvers and pump-action shotguns.*'
(*News of the World*, 5 February 1989).

b equipped with housebreaking implements. A piece of police and underworld jargon.

tools *n pl*

cutlery.

tool up *vb British*

to arm oneself.

- '*We're going to have to tool up if we take that lot on.*'

too much *exclamation*

excellent, exceptional, outstanding. A now dated usage which originated in the **jive talk** of pre-World-War II jazz musicians in the USA and became a (sometimes derided) cliché expression of **hippy** enthusiasm.

toot *vb*

to take any inhaled drug, but especially cocaine or amphetamine crystals (**speed**). This word had existed in the drug users' lexicon since the mid-1960s, but became widespread in the late 1970s with the increased popularity of cocaine among otherwise 'respectable' people. It employs the predictable simile (as in **bugle**, **hooter**) of the nose as a musical instrument.

toot *n*

1 a an inhalation or sniff of a crystalline drug.

- '*D'you want a toot of this?*'

b a drug normally inhaled, particularly cocaine.

- '*This is grade A toot.*'

2 *Australian* a toilet.

tootie-fruitie *n*

See **tutti-frutti**.

tootin' *adv, adj American*

absolutely (right). An adjective used to intensify, as in the cliché expression 'damn' or 'darn tootin' right', whence the shortened version 'darned tootin'' or simply 'tootin'', meaning correct. The word is ultimately derived from 'rootin'-tootin'', meaning originally cheering and whistling.

tootsie roll *n American*

a dark-coloured, powerful form of heroin originating in Mexico, as sold by street peddlers in the late 1980s.

tootsies *n pl*

feet. A nursery term which is formed of 'toot', an imitation of a baby's attempt at pronouncing foot, with the diminutive or familiarizing suffix '-sy'.

top *vb*

to kill or execute (someone). The term, which is part of underworld jargon, has existed since the late 18th century when it referred to hanging.

top bollocks *n pl*

female breasts. A vulgarism used by males in Britain and Australia since the early 1960s.

top man *n British*

a vulgarly or unfashionably dressed male. The ironic term, heard among adolescents and young adults, particularly students and **yuppies** in the late 1980s, refers to the Top Man stores which sell low-price fashion clothing.

torch *vb*

to set fire to something, usually to get rid of incriminating evidence or as part of an insurance fraud.

● *'But torching the building made little difference to the neighbourhood. There are three other crack houses within easy walking distance.'*
(*Sunday Times*, 10 September 1989).

torch *n*

an arsonist, especially one who is paid to burn down buildings in order to collect fire insurance. The word, which is part of police and underworld jargon, is also used as a verb.

torch job *n*

an act or case of arson.

torpedo *n American*

a hired gunman, thug or **hit-man**.

● *'What is there to worry about? I have the protection of Chicago's top torpedo.'*
(*Murderer's Row*, US film, 1966).

tosh *n British*

1 a term of address to a stranger, invariably used by a man to another man. This working-class word, now obsolescent, was a favourite with **spivs** and young toughs in the 1950s and early 1960s. It can be used with bravado, in rough comradeship, or provokingly. In this sense it possibly derives from Scottish or Cornish dialect, in which it meant smart or well-dressed.

2 nonsense. A 19th-century public-school and university term that was obsolescent, except in affected usage, during the 1960s and 1970s but was revived in the 1980s, it often forms part of phrases such as 'tosh and tarradiddle' or 'tosh and twaddle', equating with 'stuff and nonsense'. The origin of this sense of the word is obscure: it

may be an imitation of a snort of derision (as in 'tish' or 'bosh') or derive from 'toshy' meaning over-dressed (see preceding sense).

- 'He gave me some sort of explanation, but it was basically a load of old tosh.'
  (Recorded, film producer, London, 1986).
- 'Instead of owning up to being fantastic tosh, it [a TV drama]tries to be incredibly realistic.'
  (Charles Catchpole, News of the World, 26 June 1988).

toss n British

something futile, worthless or useless. A word usually found in the phrase 'a load of old toss'. It denotes the semen ejaculated in masturbation, influenced also by **tosh**, meaning nonsense.

toss vb

1 to deliberately lose a match, game or contest (usually as part of a gambling conspiracy). A racier version of 'throw'.

2 to search and/or ransack premises in pursuit of evidence of crime or of booty. An underworld and law enforcers' term.

3 Australian to defeat. A term used particularly in sport; it probably derives from the image of a wrestler or bull tossing an opponent, or simply from the standard sense of 'toss aside'.

tossed adj American

searched and/or ransacked. A law-enforcers' and underworld term meaning the same as the colloquial 'turned-over', as applied to a room, apartment, etc.

tosser n British

an idle, worthless or foolish person. A mainly working-class term of contempt which enjoyed a particular

vogue in the later 1970s. It is a synonym of a **wanker**, from the verb **toss off**.

- 'Yis wan to be different, isn't tha' it? Yis don't want to end like these tossers here. Amn't I righ'?'
  (The Commitments, Roddy Doyle, 1988).

tossle n British

penis. An alternative (and much rarer) form of **tassel**.

toss off vb

to masturbate. This verb, used transitively or intransitively, has been in use since before its first recording in 1735 to refer to male masturbation. In modern English slang the word is restricted to British and Australian speech.

toss one's cookies/tacos vb
American

to vomit. Jocularisms popular among college students in particular.

toss-pot n

1 a drunkard or habitual heavy drinker. This term of disapproval or affectionate abuse has been a British colloquialism for hundreds of years. The pot in question is a jar of ale, which is tossed down the throat. In the 1980s the expression has undergone a revival in jocular middle-class usage.

2 a foolish, weak, unpleasant or incompetent person. Users of the term in this sense probably confuse it with **tosser**, falsely identifying the verb with the sense of masturbate. In Australia the expression toss-pot is sometimes used as a meaningless term of hearty address.

total vb

to destroy completely. A widespread term, especially among teenagers, since the 1960s; it derives from the notion of a 'total wreck' or a 'total loss' in official accident reports. Originally an Americanism, it is now heard elsewhere.

- *'I was so out of control I totaled the car, crashed it somehow into the side of the road.'*
(John Philips, *Papa John*, 1986).

to the max *adv American*

to the greatest extent, utterly. A **Valley Girl** term typically occurring in exclamations such as 'grody to the max' (utterly awful), but sometimes used on its own to mean absolutely or completely.

- *'Was it really awful?'*
'To the max!'

totsie *n British*

a girl. A now dated version of **tottie**.

totter *n British*

a rag and bone man: the merchant who tours the streets, traditionally with a horse and cart, asking for old iron, other scrap or salvage. The term has been used in London since the 19th century; 'totting', meaning scavenging, may derive from 'tot', a variation of 'tat', meaning rag or scrap. The word totter was brought to the notice of the public by the 1960s TV comedy series *Steptoe and Son*.

tottie, totty, totsie *n British*

a girl, or women in general, seen as potential sexual partners. The word meant prostitute or woman of easy virtue in the 19th century and is probably an affectionate diminutive of Dorothy. It is still a fairly common term all over Britain particularly among working-class males and servicemen.

- *'A nice little tottie.'*

touch (someone) for (something) *vb*

to solicit, cadge. This colloquialism, used almost invariably in connection with a loan, has been recorded since 1760. **Touch up** is a less common alternative form, particularly in the USA.

a touch of the tarbrush *n*

(having) a skin colour which suggests a trace of black or coloured ancestry. This euphemism, often heard in a discriminatory context, originated in the mid-19th century, when it was also used to refer to sailors (the tarbrush being used on board ship).

touch up *vb*

1 *British* to caress sexually, grope. A phrase (often used derogatively) prevalent among adolescents.

2 touch (in the sense of solicit a loan from).

tough bounce/buns *n*

hard luck. These are rueful or, alternatively unsympathetic versions of the colloquial 'tough luck'. The expressions originated in American speech.

tough titty *n*

hard luck, a raw deal. The phrase is most often heard as an unsympathetic dismissal of another's complaint.

touristas *n pl American*

an alternative spelling of **turistas**.

tout *n British*

an informer. A Northern Irish expression, used typically by the IRA or its supporters of a turncoat or **grass**. In mainland British English, the sense of tout as a **spiv** or lookout, from which this usage derives, is now archaic, having been replaced by the sense of cheapjack (ticket) salesman or tipster. All these derive ultimately from the Middle English verb tuten; to peer or peep.

towel head n

an arab. A predictable pejorative term. **Rag-head** is a more widespread synonym.

- 'Some towel-head from Hizbullah marched up and down the street twice.'
(Republican Party Reptile, P. J. O'Rourke, 1987).

town bike/pump n

a local woman supposedly available for sex with all and sundry. A form of this masculine term of contempt occurs in all English-speaking countries: the first variant employs **ride** as a sexual metaphor; the second is American.

toyboy n

a young male lover of an older woman. A vogue word from 1987 which started as a code term among sophisticates and was eventually popularized by the press. The expression filled a 'lexical gap' in the English language, coinciding with the perceived trend whereby many celebrities of the 1960s were taking up with younger lovers. (The female counterpart was often provided by **bimbo**.)

tracks, trackmarks n pl

needle marks or scars on the limbs of addicts of hard drugs resulting from regular injections into the veins.

- 'You got more tracks on you baby than the tracks of this train.'
(Lyric from 'Been on a Train', Laura Nyro, 1970).

trad n

traditional jazz. A nickname for a style of jazz originally played in New Orleans in the early 1900s. It enjoyed a vogue in Britain during the early 1960s, (just before the 'beat boom').

trade n

a sexual partner or partners, particularly a paying customer of a prostitute. A generic term for custom or customers in the jargon of male and female streetwalkers, the word has sometimes been extended since the late 1960s in the **gay** lexicon to refer to any sex partner.

- 'He'd been having the trade back and finally his landlady said "You've been bringing people back, haven't you?". She looked disapproving.'
(Kenneth Williams, quoted in Joe Orton's Diary, 25 April 1967).

traf, traff vb, n British

(to) **fart**. An instance of **backslang** heard in working-class speech in the late 1950s and occasionally since.

train n

an act of serial sexual intercourse. The word is usually used as part of a phrase such as **do a train (on someone)**.

train surfing n

joy-riding on the top or outside of mainline or underground trains. A lethal teenage prank of the 1980s in the USA and, more recently, Britain.

tranks, tranqs, trancs, tranx n pl

tranquillizers. The abbreviations are employed by drug abusers rather than the estimated three million people in Britain suffering from dependency on prescribed drugs.

tranny, trannie n British

1 a transistor radio. An abbreviated form which has survived beyond the dated full phrase from the 1960s.

- 'Now lean closer to your trannie'
(Recorded, DJ, Radio London, 1987).
- 'Records were less affordable in those days (a "trannie" and Radio

Caroline being the nearest thing to free music).'
(Maureen Nolan and Roma Singleton, *Very Heaven*, 1988).
2 a a transexual.
b a transvestite.
Both shortenings were part of the **gay** lexicon of the 1980s.
3 a (photographic) transparency. This is particularly popular in the parlance of designers and publishers.
4 a transport café.
5 a Ford Transit van. The means of transport for many (humbler) pop groups.

traps *n pl*

drums, a drum kit. A musicians' term from the 1940s, still occasionally heard.

trashed *adj American*

drunk. A teenage and **preppie** term on the familiar lines of **destroyed**, **smashed**, etc.

trashed out *adj American*

exhausted. A popular phrase among teenagers and students since the 1970s. The term recalls synonyms such as 'shattered' or **wrecked**.

the trays, tray-bits *n Australian*

an attack of diarrhoea. A 'tray-bit' is a turn-of-the-century British term for a threepenny piece (from **parlyaree**; '-tray' is from the Italian for three, tre). The phrase was adopted in Australia as rhyming slang for **the shits**. Widespread in the 1950s, the expression is now obsolescent.

treach *adj*

a hip hop term of approbation. It is probably, but not certainly, a shortening of 'treacherous', by analogy with **wicked** and **bad**.
• *'This month's music selections are*

frightfully def, totally treach and all those other hip hop clichés.'
(*I-D* magazine, November 1987).

trendoid *n*

a (self-conscious) fashionable individual, someone with up-to-date ideas, dress, appurtenances. A more recent British and Australian version of the colloquial 'trendy' (or 'trendie'), usually used disparagingly or enviously.
See **-oid**.

trey, trey-bits *n Australian*

an alternative spelling of **the trays, tray-bits**.

trich, trick *n*

trichomoniasis, a mild sexually transmitted infection.

trick *n*

1 a a prostitute's client.
• *'Sandy had invited two girlfriends to live with them who gave Ordell "rent money", twenty per cent of what they made entertaining tricks, so it wasn't like Ordell was pimping.'*
(Elmore Leonard, *The Switch*, 1978).
b a session or transaction between a prostitute and client. These senses of the word have been current in the USA since the first decade of the 20th century. They derive from the notion of an entertainer's 'turn' or stratagem. Trick has appeared in British English since World War II, often in the phrases 'on a trick' or **turn a trick**.
2 see **trich**.

trick *vb American*

to sell sexual favours for money. This derivation from the noun form has not crossed the Atlantic.
• *'Whenever she runs out of dope she goes out tricking.'*

trick adj

fancy, attractive and sophisticated. A 1980s term used by enthusiasts in fields where high technology is admired.

- 'A legendary homemade speed machine dominated the bike park last summer: a Kawasaki-powered, Harris-framed, turbo-charged, nitrous oxide-assisted rocket. To bikers, this bike is "trick", very trick.'
  (Independent, 6 April 1988).

trick cyclist n

a psychiatrist. A humorous alteration of the standard word, evoking like **shrink** a suspicious contempt for the profession. The phrase was first heard in the 1930s.

- 'They are suspicious of the "trick cyclist" (nearly every policeman I have met uses the phrase to describe psychiatrists).'
  (Town magazine, March 1964).

triff adj British

terrific, wonderful, exciting. This shortening like the more widespread **brill** became a vogue term among teenagers in the 1980s.

trimmed adj

cheated, swindled, in the parlance of gamblers. The word implies the neat removal of a dupe's (excess) money or winnings.

trimmer n British

a prevaricator, hypocrite, an individual who adapts his or her behaviour to expediency. This term is arguably not slang, but a colloquialism which is fairly well-established in the vocabulary of older upper-and middle-class speakers. Among the younger generation it may often be perceived as slang. The expression derives from the nautical practice of 'trimming one's sails' to the wind.

trip n

1 a an experience of a **psychedelic** drug such as LSD. A typical LSD trip would last around 6–8 hours, during which time the user would undergo profound sensory and psychological changes. The image evoked is that of an 'inward journey'.

- 'Leary himself has been on over 300 trips although he has abstained for nearly a year.'
  (Sunday Times colour supplement, 1 January 1967).

- 'There follows much discussion of the Floyd and Peel's one and only acid trip – "I hired a boat on The Serpentine in Hyde Park with Marc Bolan and floated about to the strains of 'Interstellar Overdrive''.'
  (New Musical Express, 7 February 1987).

- 'It may not be the last trip I ever take, but it was probably the last time for Billy and me in this flat.'
  (Recorded, middle-aged drug user, London, 1989).

b a single dose, tablet, or capsule of LSD.

- 'I bought 20 trips from Paul, but by the time I had sorted out all my mates I only had five left.'
  (Recorded, middle aged drug user, London, 1989).

2 a state of mind, state of affairs or personal experience. The original 1960s counterculture sense of LSD experience was soon broadened to encompass these meanings. The word was used in a variety of sub-senses, in expressions such as a guilt trip (a bout of remorse), 'lay a trip on someone' (subject someone to one's own preoccupation, obsession or problem), a heavy trip (a devastating or oppressive experience), or 'on one's own trip' (preoccupied with oneself, introverted).

trip (out) vb

to experience the effects of LSD or a similar hallucinogenic drug. The term was coined in California in the early 1960s to describe the period (often around 8 hours) under the influence of the drug wherein one is 'transported on an inner voyage'.

tripehound n British

a term of abuse, now often used affectionately but formerly with real venom, particularly in the North and Midlands of England. The image is that of an offal-eating dog.

tripped-out adj

a under the influence of LSD or a similar hallucinogenic drug.

b exhibiting signs of euphoria or eccentricity caused by, or typical of, the use of LSD.

trippy adj

exhibiting or suggesting the euphoric, surrealistic effects of **psychedelic** drugs such as LSD. The word, based on **trip**, was heard from about 1967.

- 'Listen to this – it's got a really trippy guitar solo.'

trog vb British

to trek, walk energetically or wearily. An armed-services' term which passed into civilian usage in the 1970s. It is probably a blend of trek and slog.

trog, trogg n British

a simplistic, (literally or figuratively) low-browed person, someone of restricted intelligence or no social graces, a 'Philistine' or 'Neanderthal'. This shortening of 'troglodyte' (cavedweller) was used in the armed forces in the early 1950s and particularly by jazz enthusiasts, **beatniks** and students in the late 1950s and early 1960s to describe those who were dull, boorish or out of touch. The word had virtually died out in fashionable teenage use by the mid-1960s, when a pop group from Andover self-deprecatingly called themselves the Troggs. Trog continues to be periodically resurrected, usually in middle-class speech.

Trojan n American

a condom. The word is a trademark name used generically in the USA in the same way as **Durex** in the UK.

troll vb, n British

(to take a) prowl, wander or **cruise**. This alternative form of 'trawl' has existed since the 15th century. It acquired the sexual sense in the 1930s and was a vogue **gay** term of the 1960s.

- 'Orton insisted the trolling fed his work; but it also fed Halliwell's rage.'
  (John Lahr, preface to Joe Orton's Diaries, published 1986).
- 'I don't just get married because I enjoy trolling down the aisle.'
  (Joan Collins, TV talk show, 1988).

trolleys, trollies n pl British

underpants. A fairly rare public-school expression. It is of uncertain origin but may be related to the archaic 'trolleybobs', a nursery version of trousers. (In her diary entry for 8 January 1934, Barbara Pym mentions buying trollies at Marks and Spencers.)

trombone n British

a telephone. A rhyming alternative to **dog (and bone)**.

tronk n British

a foolish, clumsy or contemptible person. A rare schoolchildren's and student's term, possibly related to the Australian synonym **tonk**.

troops n pl British

personnel, police officers (in police jargon). The use of the word extends the lexicon of militaristic self-dramatizing language adopted by the police since the 1970s. **Gunship** and **tank** are other examples.

troppo adj Australian

unhinged, deranged, crazy. The word is an abbreviation of 'tropical' and is usually heard in the phrase **to go troppo**, originally referring to someone overcome by tropical heat but now generalized to mean something like **over the top**. The word originated among armed-service personnel in World War II.

trot n British

a Trotskyite. A popular abbreviation from the late 1960s until the early 1980s, when Trotskyite activists were a significant element in student politics and within the Labour party.

the trots n British

an attack of diarrhoea. The expression, heard since World War I, evokes swift but controlled movement to the lavatory.

trotters n pl

feet A humorous colloquial usage.

troub, troubs n British

See **trub**.

trouble (and strife) n British

wife. A piece of 'cockney' rhyming slang which is still in (mainly jocular, ironic or self-conscious) use; it is now generally shortened simply to trouble by Londoners.

trough vb British

to eat. A humorous middle- and up-per-class verb evoking (but not necessarily involving) gluttony.

trouser vb British

to pocket. A humorous alternative term from the 1980s.

● 'Strobes then insisted on accompanying Chancellor to the prize-giving in Milan, and trousered the cheque himself.'
(Private Eye magazine, 17 March 1989).

trouser n British

a generic term for males as sex objects. A 1980s women's version of '(a bit of) **skirt**', satirizing the 'predatory' male expression.

trouser bandit n British

a male homosexual. A humorous though pejorative euphemism, evoking the image of a predatory or promiscuous **gay**. 'Bum bandit' and **arse bandit** are alternative versions.

trouser chuff n British

a fart. A mock-childish term used by adolescents in the 1980s and popularized in the best-selling Viz magazine.

● 'Johnny Fartpants' "trouser chuffs" always get him into meddlesome scrapes – losing his pocket money or causing the San Francisco earthquake of 1906 . . . '
(Time Out magazine, December 1988).

trouser snake n

1 a penis. A young person's joke euphemism adopted by adults; the full version is **one-eyed trouser snake**.

2 a disreputable or reprehensible person. This sense of the expression is typically used in the 1980s by American girls as a term of disapproval applied to males, emphasizing the treachery inspired by 'snake' rather than the sexual aspect of the image.

trout n

See **old trout**.

trub, troub(s) n British

trouble. A shortening used typically in middle-class badinage.
- 'We've been in a spot of trub recently.'

trucking n

a an exaggerated way of walking (with the body leaning back and taking long strides). This comic gait, adopted by **hippies** in 1969 and 1970, was an imitation of rural American farmers, cowboys or urban pimps. The name is from a jitterbug dance step adopted by (mainly) black marathon dancers between the world wars.

b persevering, continuing in one's efforts. This use of the word stems from the exhortation **keep on trucking!**, shouted in the marathon dances mentioned above. It was revived as a catchphrase in the hippy era.

trumpet n British

1 a **fart**. A children's word which enjoyed a vogue in the late 1980s.
- 'Lucy did a trumpet.'
  (Recorded, 10-year-old boy, Devon, 1986).

2 the telephone. A rare synonym of **trombone**, **blower**, etc.

tub n

1 a a boat.
- 'Can't this tub go any faster?'
  (Friday 13th part VI, US film, 1986).
b a car, truck, bus etc.

2 a 'tub of lard', a fat person. A widespread colloquialism.
- 'She used to call you buttercup?'
  'What's so funny about that, Norton?'
  'You were a little cup of butter, now you're a whole tub of lard.'
  (The Honeymooners, US TV comedy series, 1950).

tube, the tube n

1 the tube television, from the cathode ray tube.

2 the tube the London underground railway system, from the tubular construction of the tunnels. This nickname dates from the turn of the century.

3 British a person. A vogue word among teenagers in the late 1980s; it is a synonym for **dude** although it sometimes has the added sense of foolish or gormless.

4 Australian a can of beer. (**Tinny** is a slightly later synonym.)
- 'Alex Buzo, who is minder of the Australian language among his other activities, records that it is 20 years since he last heard beers referred to as tubes.'
  (Observer magazine, 13 December 1987).

5 the hollow formed by a breaking wave. A surfer's term from which the term of approbation **tubular** is derived.

tube steak n American

penis. A euphemism heard in **hip** circles in the 1980s, from black street-usage of the 1970s. It was originally a jocular term for a frankfurter sausage.

tubular adj

an all-purpose term of teenage approbation, deriving from riding the **tube** as being the highest form of surfing experience. Like many 1960s surfing terms this expression (often intensified as 'totally tubular') was adopted by **Valley Girls** in the later 1970s and subsequently became a vogue usage in international English in the 1980s.

tuchis n American

See **tush**.

tuck, tucker n

food. The first version of the word is typical of British public-school vocabulary, the second Australian. Both date from the 19th century and probably derive from the verb to tuck in(to), which originally implied the humorous notion of tucking food surreptitiously into oneself or behind one's clothing.

tucked up adj British

1 imprisoned, incarcerated. A homely euphemism for a grim reality in the tradition of London working-class usages.

● 'Adjusting back to normal society is not easy when you've been tucked up for a bit.'
(Recorded, ex-prisoner, London, 1986).

2 cheated, duped. A London working-class usage paralleling the more widespread stitch (someone) up.

tuckered (out) adj

exhausted. This is originally an American term deriving from an archaic sense of the verb tuck, signifying rebuke or reproach. (In Old English tuck also had the sense of ill-treat.) Now heard in such phrases as 'plumb tuckered out', the word has folksy overtones.

tude n American

(bad) attitude, a surly defiant or negative disposition. A short form of the type (burbs, nabe, perp, tard) fashionable in adolescent circles in the late 1970s and 1980s.

tuft hunter n

a sycophant, toady or 'crawler'. (Titled undergraduates at Oxford and Cambridge were known as 'tufts' after the tassels they were entitled to wear.) This expression is now virtually obsolete.

● 'He met Kenneth Williams by writing a fan letter to the theatre at Oxford where Kenneth was playing. He's a tuft hunter.'

(Joe Orton's Diary, 2 May 1967).

tug n British

an arrest or detention of a suspect (in the jargon of the underworld or police), a collar.

● ''E won't be expecting a tug at that time of night.'

tukus n American

a version of tush, tushie.

tumble n

1 an act of sexual intercourse. This fairly inoffensive expression is often elaborated to 'tumble in the hay'.

2 British an attempt, try. In working-class usage 'give it a tumble' is the equivalent of 'give it a whirl' (the Australian give it a burl).

3 arrest, capture or detention. In criminal and police parlance in both Britain and the USA the word is used in these senses by analogy with a fall suffered by a racehorse or sports contender.

tumble (to) vb

to become aware (of a fact or a situation). This usage, which is probably a form of stumble across, has been in colloquial use since the 1850s.

tummy banana n

the penis. A nursery expression adopted, or perhaps invented for jocular use, by adults. The phrase was first heard in middle-class circles in the early 1970s.

tuna n American

1 a a girl or woman. Users of the term, who include teenagers and preppies, are often unaware of its origins in the senses which follow.

b sexual activity.

c the female sex organs.

The expressions use the seafood (popular in the USA long before it was readily available in Britain) as a euphemism for femininity or femaleness inspired by the piscine quality of the female sexual odour.

2 marihuana. The reason for this usage is unclear; it may simply be a transference of the idea of tuna as a delicacy or staple food.

tune in vb

to attune to one's environment, achieve harmony with one's peer group, the counterculture and/or the cosmos. This **hipster** and **beatnik** term became part of the catchphrase slogan of the **hippy** movement; 'turn on, tune in, drop out': unlike the other two verbs tune in was not itself adopted into mainstream colloquial speech.

tup vb British

to have sex (with). The country persons' term for the copulation of a ram with a ewe (from the Middle English word for ram, tupe) is by extension used vulgarly of humans.

turd n

1 a piece of excrement. A descendant of the Anglo-Saxon word 'tord', the term was freely used until about the 17th century, by which time it was being avoided in polite speech and writing. It is still considered vulgar by many speakers, although when referring for example to dog droppings, it is sometimes now used even in broadcasts.

● *'He said one ancient stool excavated in York, known as the "Lloyd's Bank turd" came from a forbearer who was infested by several hundred whipworms . . . '*
(*Independent*, 16 September 1989).

2 an unpleasant and/or despicable person. In this sense the word has the same connotation of obnoxiousness as the literal and figurative synonym, **shit**.

turd burglar n British

a male homosexual. One of several jocular but hostile phrases of the 1980s (such as **fudgepacker** and **browniehound**), used by heterosexuals to suggest the faecal aspects of sodomy.

turf n

a streetgang or street drug dealer's territory.

● *'In fact he's a lookout, a lookout for cops and strangers, for other dealers stealing "turf".'*
(*Guardian*, 5 September 1989).

turistas, the turistas, touristas n American

an attack of diarrhoea. *Turista* is Spanish (or Mexican) for tourist.

turkey n American

a a fool or dupe. This expression, used to describe someone dull-witted, gullible or simply stupid, is rarely heard outside the USA.

b a flop, failure or embarrassment. A sub-sense of the word applied for example to a show-business disaster.

turkey-neck n American

penis. From the supposed resemblance.

● *'When your mother's crying at the funeral, I'm gonna goose her with my turkey-neck.'*
(*Barfly*, US film, 1987).

turn a trick vb

to service a (prostitute's) client. The phrase, evoking a neat execution of a deception, stratagem or performance, has been in use since the early years of the 20th century.
See also **trick**.

turned-on adj

1 aware, **hip** or liberated. A term of approbation of the 1960s, deriving from the notion of being 'turned on' by a mood-altering drug. **Switched-on** was a British alternative form.

2 a sexually aroused. A slang phrase of the 1950s which has become a common colloquialism.

b stimulated, fascinated. A generalization of the previous sense of the term.

turn-off n

a depressing, deflating, disappointing or unexciting experience. The phrase was coined by analogy with its opposite, turn-on.

- 'It's really nice that you want to be well groomed, but you get hair in the food. Hair in the food is a turn-off, Joan, sweetie.'
  (The Serial, Cyra McFadden, 1976).
- 'I find all that sort of thing [male body-building] a complete turn-off.'
  (Recorded, female social worker, London, 1987).

turn on vb

a to take a drug. The term first referred to hard narcotics, but was later applied to cannabis and LSD. It was originally based on the notion of stimulus at the throw of a switch.

b to allow oneself to experience a heightened or more liberated reality. One of the three 'commandments' of the alternative society of the late 1960s; 'turn on, tune in, drop out'.

- 'Within a year the league [for Spiritual Discovery] will have a million members who will turn on with LSD every seven days.'
  (Timothy Leary, Sunday Times colour supplement, 1 January 1967).

turn-on n

a a drug, specifically a user's drug of choice.

- 'What's your turn-on?'
  b anything arousing or exciting, a

sexual stimulus. A back-formation from **turned-on**.

- 'I love shoes – patent leather stilettos are a real turn-on.'

turn (someone) over vb British

a to cheat, rob.

- 'I never thought my best mate would turn me over.'
  b to attack, beat up.
  c to raid and/or search premises.

All three sub-senses are in working-class use, particularly in London. The first two have been heard since the 1950s, the third from the mid-19th century.

turps n Australian

alcoholic drink. A joky 1950s euphemism, still in use, which is inspired by the handyman or workman's turpentine.

tush, tushie n American

buttocks, backside. These are inoffensive terms used in the family and elsewhere. They derive from Yiddish toochis, also written tokus, tukus, or tuchis, which in turn derives from the Hebrew tokheth.

tutti-frutti, tootie-fruitie n

an effeminate, frivolous or ridiculous male. This slang use of the name of the Italian ice cream dish (vanilla with pieces of glacé fruit) originated in the USA where **fruit** denotes a **gay** male. (Tutti frutti is Italian for 'all fruits'.)

tux n American

a tuxedo. The American word for a dinner jacket comes from Tuxedo Park, a resort in New York State.

- 'He showed up in a rented tux.'

T.V. n

transvestism or a transvestite.

535

twang (the wire) vb

to masturbate. This word, used only of men, was originally an Australianism with rural overtones.

twat, twot n British

1 the vagina. A word first recorded in the 17th century. The etymology is obscure but it probably derives from a rural dialect term.

2 a foolish or obnoxious person. The word has had this sense (firstly in London slang) since the late 19th century. Until the early to mid-1960s the word was in widespread use in this context, often by schoolchildren and some adults who were unaware of its provenance (and probably thought it an intensive form of **twit**).

● *'What kind of creature bore you/ was it some kind of bat?/they can't find a good word for you/but I can/ twat.'*
(*A love story in reverse*, poem by John Cooper Clarke, 1978).

● *'"We hate tense people," says guitarist John Squire. "The tense people are the twats who are only interested in making money and who ruin things for everybody else."'*
(The Stone Roses, *The Observer*, August 1989).

tweak vb American

1 to suffer physical symptoms of drug withdrawal. This 1980s term evokes the irritation and spasmodic nature of drug-induced distress, as well as recalling words such as twitch and weak.

2 to adjust or fine-tune. A piece of jargon applied to motor mechanics and computers, for instance.

twenty-five n American

LSD (lysergic acid diethylamide), the hallucinogenic drug. This rare term from the mid-1960s recalls the isomer number of the most powerful and effective form of the drug.

twerp, twirp n

an insignificant, silly and/or obnoxious person. An invented word which appeared in the 1930s and gained widespread currency in the 1950s.

● *'My stuff is outrageously conceived and devastatingly realised.'*
'Oh do shut up you boring little twerp!'
(*Biff* cartoon, 1986).

twig vb British

to understand, 'catch on'. A formerly raffish term which since the late 1960s has become a fairly common colloquialism. This usage has been recorded since the 18th century and derives either from 'tweak' in the sense of snatch or grasp, or from a Gaelic verb meaning comprehend.

twig n

See **drop off the twig**.

twigs n pl British

matches. A now obsolete term from the 1950s, then used typically in the armed services, scouting and among prisoners.

twillie, twilly n British

a foolish, clumsy or stupid person. An adolescent term in use since the early 1970s. It is a blend of **twit** and silly.

● *'A complete twillie.'*

twimp n American

a foolish and/or insignificant individual. A high-school term of mild abuse from the late 1980s, blending **twit**, **twerp** and **wimp**.

twinkie, twinky, twink n

American

a a male homosexual or effete, fey or eccentric man.

b a cute, attractive person.

Both senses of the words derive from the trademark 'Twinkies', a sort of cupcake. The word has echoes of 'twinkletoes', twinkling and **Tinkerbelle**. Twink is sometimes used as a (usually male) nickname in Britain for someone with sparkle or vim.

twirp n

an alternative spelling of **twerp**.

twist n American

a girl or young attractive woman. This term, used typically by underworld or working-class speakers is a rare example of American rhyming slang, from 'twist and twirl'; girl.

● 'M-m-m – goodlooking twist!'
(Panic on the 5.22, US film, 1974).

twit n British

a foolish or absurd person. A common colloquialism, particularly in the 1950s or 1960s, the word was probably coined in the 1920s under the influence of nitwit, **twat** and **tit**. In the 1970s the word has gained currency in the USA via British TV comedies.

twitcher n British

a bird watcher, ornithologist. A word of unknown origin, although a blend of 'tit' and 'watcher' has been half-seriously posited, as has the twitch of excitement on first spotting a rare specimen.

two and eight n British

a a fit of agitation.

● 'What with coming home to find the place burgled, then all these bills arriving, I was in a right two and eight.'

(Recorded, middle-aged woman, London, 1988).

b a dishevelled, disorganized or grotesque person.

● 'Look at 'er, she's a right two-and-eight.'

Both senses of the term are London working-class rhyming slang for a 'state'. The rhyming-slang versions were in vogue in the early 1970s.

two-bit adj American

cheap, penny-pinching, worthless. This Americanism of the mid-19th century is now occasionally used even in countries where 'two bits' does not signify 25 cents (a 'bit' is one-eighth of a dollar).

two-pot screamer n Australian

a person more than usually unable to cope with the effects of strong drink. A term of disapproval used by hearty males in particular.

● 'Hi! my husband's pissed again – he's always been a two pot screamer.'

(The Wonderful World of Barry McKenzie, Barry Humphries and Nicholas Garland, cartoon strip in Private Eye magazine, 1968).

twot n British

an alternative spelling of **twat**.

tyke n

a Roman Catholic. A word heard in this sense particularly in Australian speech, but not unknown in Britain. It is probably a corruption of **taig**. Tyke is commonly heard in expressions such as 'You little tyke!' (meaning 'you little rascal').

U

Uganda n

See **discuss Uganda**.

ugly pills n

an imagined source of repellent physical characteristics, manners or behaviour. The words usually form part of a sardonic speculation that the person in question has been **taking ugly pills**.

u-ie n

a U-turn. The expression is used by skateboarders as well as drivers, usually in the form '*do a u-ie*' or '*hang a u-ie*'.

See **hang a louie, hang a ralph**.

umbrella n British

penis. A fairly rare euphemism mainly used by women and usually occurring in the expression **the umbrella's up**, meaning that an erection has been achieved.

uncle n

1 British a pawnbroker. A use of the word which arose in the 18th century, referring (probably ironically) to the moneylender's avuncular assistance. The term was still heard in London in the 1950s and may survive. From the 1980s it was heard in the British TV series 'Eastenders'.

2 American a cry of concession. To **say uncle** or **cry uncle** is to surrender or admit defeat, in playground games for instance. The reason for this choice of word is obscure.

3 American the law-enforcement establishment seen as benevolent, protective or rewarding by crooks.

All three main senses of the word derive from the notion of uncle as a potential protector or provider of funds (in the third case perhaps reinforced by **Uncle Sam**). There are many other instances of this, for instance in theatrical jargon where the word equates with **angel**.

uncle, Uncle Dick adj British

sick. One of many rhyming-slang expressions using 'uncle' and a convenient rhyming Christian name.

● '*You look a bit uncle to me.*'
(Minder, British TV series, 1984).

Uncle Bill, Uncle Bob n British

the police force. These irreverent nicknames are versions of **the Old Bill** and **bobby**, respectively.

Uncle Dick adj

See **uncle** (in the adjectival form)

Uncle Mac n British

heroin. London drug-users' rhyming slang for **smack**. 'Uncle Mac' was a presenter of children's radio programmes from the 1930s to the 1960s. This sinister borrowing dates from the late 1970s.

Uncle Nab n

See **nab**.

Uncle Ned adj, n British
1 dead.
2 bed.
3 head.

All these senses have been recorded in London rhyming-slang usage; the first is possibly the least dated.

Uncle Sam n

the personification of the United States, or the US government in particular, as an avuncular male, taken from the letters US. The nickname is not recorded before the War of 1812.

Uncle Tom n

a black person who collaborates with, or kow-tows to, an oppressive white community. This term of contempt takes the name of the hero of Harriet Beecher Stowe's *Uncle Tom's Cabin* (published in 1852) as a symbol for blacks who ape white manners or abase themselves before whites (the rarer female counterpart is **Aunt Jemima**). Originating in the USA, and particularly widespread during the Black Power era in the 1960s, the phrase is now in use all over the English-speaking world.

Compare **tio taco**.

uncool adj

unacceptably or unfashionably intrusive, assertive, dull, reckless, conventional, etc. An all-purpose negative complement to the all-purpose term of approbation, **cool**. In late 1980s usage uncool perhaps retains unfashionable overtones of the **hippy** era, whereas cool has been enthusiastically adopted by the younger generation.

● 'Weekend hippies and the like who think "what a groovy joy-ride" and are very, very uncool.'
(*International Times*, April 1968).

under n British

sexual activity. A 1960s expression in mainly working-class use, primarily in the phrase **a bit of under**. It is probably a shortening of 'undercover work', used as a euphemism for covert and scandalous behaviour.

underarm adj British

a underhand, **dodgy**
b illegal, illicit.

The use of underarm in these senses stems from the literal sense of passing or carrying something concealed under the arm, reinforced by the supposed offensive nature of the armpit. ('Under the arm' is an archaic expression, once used by vagrants and marginals and meaning bad or inferior.)

underchunders n pl Australian

underpants (male or female). A humorous vulgarism which employs **chunder** (vomit) as a rhyme, rather than for sense (unless the original image was of a sickening item of clothing).

underdaks n pl Australian

(men's) underpants. The Australian equivalent of the North of England expression **underkocks**, from **daks**, the trade name of a popular brand of casual trousers.

underground n, adj, adv

(belonging to) the 'alternative society' or counterculture, opposed to bourgeois society. A term from the 1960s adopted from the wartime usage applied to clandestine resistance movements. (The term 'underground railroad' was earlier used for the system of sympathizers/safe houses by which escaped slaves were taken from the Southern States to the North before emancipation.)

under heavy manners adj, adv

in a state of oppression. A phrase from the counterculture patois of Jamaica which became known in Britain and elsewhere due to its use by reggae musicians in the early 1970s.

underkecks n pl British

underpants. An extension of the (mainly northern English) use of **kecks** to mean trousers.

underwhelmed adj

disappointed, unimpressed. A humorous counterpart to the standard English overwhelmed. The coinage began to be heard in the early 1970s and is now in fairly widespread use.

● *'I must tell you I was distinctly underwhelmed by what I saw.'*

unglued adj

another version of **untied**.

unhip adj

unaware, culturally and/or socially out-of-touch, unfashionable. The opposite of **hip**. The word has rarely been heard since the early 1970s, except among the remnants of the 'counterculture'.

unit n

a the genitals. An unromantic 1970s and 1980s term used by the self-consciously liberated or promiscuous to refer to (usually male) sex organs.

b a potential or actual sexual partner or conquest. A cold-blooded piece of singles-bar jargon from the mid- to late 1970s, similar in usage and connotation to the more common **item**.

● *'Would ya look at that li'l unit in hotpants, though!'*
(R Crumb cartoon, *Head Comix*, 1970).

unload vb

a to defecate.
b to **fart**.

A vulgarism which is heard all over the English-speaking world but which is particularly popular in Australia.

unmentionables n pl

a underwear.
b genitals.

A mock-Victorian euphemism for taboo personal items. The expression was used fairly seriously in the early 1900s; since at least World War II, the usage has invariably been facetious.

unravelled adj

an alternative version of **untied**.

unreal adj

a unbelievably good, excellent.
b outrageous, excessive or unreasonable in behaviour.

Both usages are from the jargon of teenagers, firstly (since the 1960s) in the USA and later elsewhere in the English-speaking world. The expression in fact originated in the **beatnik** era when unreal was an exclamation of hallucinated delight or admiration.

unstrung, unstuck adj

alternative versions of **untied**, **unglued**.

unthinkables n pl British

a underwear.
b genitals.

A students' facetious mock-Victorian euphemism coined in imitation of **unmentionables**.

● *'She left her door open and I got a glimpse of her unthinkables.'*
(Recorded, male university student, London, 1988).

untied, unglued, unravelled, unstuck, unstrung, unwrapped adj

in a state of nervous crisis, upset, helpless, out of control. These expressions (mainly in American usage) are probably inspired by 'unstuck' in the expression 'come unstuck', but here give the sense of someone 'held together' by self-control or the rules and conventions of normality. The terms are normally part of the phrase **come untied**, etc.

- *'I'm afraid she's going to come untied if she goes on like this.'*
- *'He seems kind of unglued.'*

untogether *adj*

disorganized, confused, diffuse. This popular **hippy**-era term more often than not refers to the personality or mood of someone who is not in equilibrium emotionally, intellectually or psychically. It postdates its opposite, **together**. Untogether is now rarely heard, but survives in the sociolect of those reaching adolescence in the late 1960s.

unwrapped *adj*

another version of **untied, unglued**.

up *adj*

1 American 'dried', having forgotten one's lines. A theatrical term of uncertain origin.

2 exhilarated or intoxicated, high

up against the wall

exclamation

a shout of rage, defiance or menace. This americanism, chanted on anti-war or Black Power demonstrations in the late 1960s and early 1970s, and invariably followed by the epithet **motherfucker**, was intended to evoke the righteous rage of a revolutionary mob about to summarily execute their oppressors, and to parody the police instruction when 'spreading' a suspect or captive.

upchuck *vb*

to vomit. A humorous reversal of

chuck up (itself based on 'throw up'), this expression surfaced in the USA in the 1920s and, having spread to British and Australian speech, has enjoyed a limited currency ever since.

up each other/one another

adj, adv Australian

engaged in mutual flattery, 'in cahoots'. The image is that of mutual sodomy, colourfully suggesting an unhealthy or illegally close relationship (often in a political or business context).

upfront *adj*

bold, assertive, open, straightforward, trustworthy. The word is usually used approvingly of someone acting honestly or without guile.

up oneself *adj Australian*

self-satisfied, smug, high-handed. A vulgar version of 'full of oneself', evoking auto-sodomy.

- *'They're all up themselves, that lot.'* (Referring to members of a University Department, teacher, Melbourne, 1988).

uppers *n pl*

stimulant drugs such as amphetamines (**pep pills, speed**), cocaine, as opposed to **downers** (barbiturates and sedatives).

- *'He acts as if he's on uppers.'*

upriver *adj, adv*

in prison. Sing Sing penitentiary was upriver from New York City, hence this expression, now also heard outside the USA, usually in the phrase 'sent upriver'.

up shit creek *adj*

in serious trouble. Shit creek was a 19th-century nickname (probably coined by British or American sailors) for any stagnant or dangerous backwater or river. The expression is often embellished as '*up shit creek without a paddle*', sometimes adding '*in a barbed wire canoe*'. '*Up the creek*' is a less offensive version.

upstairs *adj, adv*

a (in) the brain, head, mental or cerebral faculties. Used in such expressions as '*nobody home upstairs*' (i.e. a person is stupid), or '*she's got a lot upstairs*' (i.e. she is intelligent).

b the breast area (referring to women). Used in phrases such as '*there's plenty upstairs*' (of a well-endowed woman).

c (in) heaven. Reference may be made to '*the man upstairs*' (God).

A widely-used colloquial euphemism.

upstate *adj, adv American*

in prison. A euphemism (synonymous with **upriver**), based on the fact that New York's major prisons are upstate.

up the duff *adj British*

pregnant. A working-class synonym of **up the pole/spout/stick**, here employing the long-established British metaphor of pudding. Duff is an old-fashioned boiled or steamed pudding; the word is a dialect version of 'dough'. It has an all-purpose sexual sense (encompassing gratification, penis, semen, woman and baby).

up the poke/pole/spout/stick *adj British*

pregnant. These expressions are in mainly working-class use. They are all vulgar, simultaneously evoking the male and female sex organs and the idea of a baby being lodged or jammed. They can describe either the act of conception, as in '*he's put her up the stick*' or the condition, as in '*she's up the stick again*'.

uptight *adj*

1 tense, repressed, humourless, unrelaxed. A black slang term which is probably in origin a short-form of 'wound-up tight' or 'screwed-up tight'. The term was adopted into the **hippy** vocabulary to express the unliberated, repressed characteristics of **straight** society, particularly the authority figures thereof. Since the early 1970s uptight has passed into (mainly middle-class) colloquial usage, although by the late 1980s it had begun to sound rather dated.

● '*The cops? Oh, just about as uptight and corrupt as in Britain.*'
(Terry Reid interviewed in *Oz* magazine, February 1979).

2 *American* satisfactory, in good order. In black American street-talk the expression retains a second, rare and positive connotation, possibly deriving from 'locked-up tight', meaning fixed, settled, under control, or, alternatively and more probably, from a sexual sense of being 'coupled' or 'snuggled-up tight'.

● '*It's uptight, everything is all right/ Uptight, it's out of sight.*'
(Chorus lyric from 'Uptight' by Stevie Wonder, 1963).

urban surfing *n*

riding on the outside of a moving car, bus, train, etc. A dangerous fad of the later 1980s among adolescents, first in the USA and later elsewhere.

u.s. *adj British*

useless. Mainly used by middle- and upper-class speakers, the term can apply to objects or people.

● '*This female razor thing is absolutely u.s.*'
(Recorded, female, Bath, 1986).

user *adj*

a habitual drug user, especially referring to a heroin addict.

using *adj*

addicted to heroin or habituated to another hard drug. A euphemism employed by law enforcers and drug abusers.

● *'Looks like she's using again.'*

ute *n Australian*

a 'utility vehicle', i.e. a light truck or van. A word introduced to British audiences by Australian TV soap-operas from *A Country Practice* (1986) on.

u.vs *n pl American*

ultra-violet rays, sunshine. A **preppie** and **Valley Girl** usage in phrases such as 'catch/cop/grab/soak up some u.vs'.

V

V *adj British*

very. Often heard in middle-class speech as in 'v. good', 'v. difficult', etc.

vac *n British*

a (university or other institute of higher education) vacation. The summer recess is sometimes known as the long vac(s).

vag *n American*

a vagrant. Pronounced 'vagg', the word is mainly heard in middle-class families, used disapprovingly.

Vals, Valley Girls *n pl American*

a Californian (and later more widespread) youth culture of the early 1980s, based on the habits, mannerisms, and distinctive vocabulary of teenage girls from the San Fernando Valley region of outer Los Angeles. The **Vals**, daughters of affluent parents working typically in the media, music industry or professions, had developed a sybaritic lifestyle in which consumerism ('recreational shopping') and leisure activities were elevated to a social code. The phenomenon was articulated in the US press by Moon Unit Zappa, daughter of the rock musician Frank Zappa, subsequently by *The Valley Girl's Guide to Life* (by Mimi Pond, published 1982) and in Britain by an article in *Harpers and Queen* magazine in 1983. Vals employed a colourful hyperbolic repertoire of slang, typically expressed in a high-pitched, breathless drawl. Their lexicon was partly invented and partly adopted or adapted from the argot of surfers, college and high-school students and other sources. (**Grody**, **gnarly** and **to the max** are examples). Many of these terms became teenage vogue expressions on a wider scale in the mid-1980s.

- *'The greatest creative work that any Val does is trying to think of a good slogan for her [car number] plate.'*
(*Harpers and Queen* magazine, 1983).

Valspeak *n American*

the jargon of Valley Girls, as spoken in California in the early 1980s, and subsequently elsewhere.

- *'Valspeak is an almost impossible farrago of surfer expressions, Midwesternisms and irrational neologisms, delivered in nasal lockjawed whining tones.'*
(*Harpers and Queen* magazine, 1983).

vamoose *vb American*

to leave, go away, get moving. The word, familiar since its use in cowboy-era fiction and subsequent film and TV drama, is a corruption of the Spanish *vamos* ('we're going') or ¡*vamonos*! ('let's go!').

- *'OK I think it's time we vamoosed.'*

vamp *vb, n*

(to behave as) a seductress. The word is usually employed only semiseriously to denote an individual (usually but not invariably female), affecting a languid, mysterious and predatory air. The term arose in 1918, inspired by the vampire legend as interpreted by such film stars as Theda Bara.

vamp up vb British

a to intensify, make more effective, improve or renovate.

b to improvise, ad-lib.

These colloquial usages are from the standard informal musical sense of 'vamp' (an improvised accompaniment, ultimately from the archaic French avantpied) not, as is often assumed, from the verb **vamp** (to pose as a temptress).

V and T n British

See **V.A.T.**

varder, va(h)da(h), vardy, vardo vb British

to see, look (at). These are forms of the Romany verb to watch (originally rendered as varter), used especially in the 1950s and 1960s in the slang of the street market, fairground and theatre. The word was briefly exposed to a wider audience by its use by the **camp** characters 'Julian' and 'Sandy' in the Kenneth Horne radio comedy shows of the 1960s.

V.A.T. n British

(a) vodka and tonic. This abbreviation, popular in London in the 1980s, puns on that for Value Added Tax. The American usage 'V and T' is the more usual form.

va-va-voom exclamation, n American

this imitation of a revving engine or explosive takeoff is used to suggest overwhelming sexual potential or allure. The word was particularly popular (among males) in the 1960s and of-

ten featured in *Mad* magazine, usually as the name of a starlet.

V.C. n American

a (member of the) Viet Cong, a North Vietnamese combatant. This designation, from the time of the Vietnam War was first expressed as 'Victor Charlie', the code words for the initial letters, subsequently by the initials alone.

veep n American

a V.I.P., 'very important person'.

veggie, vedgie n, adj

(a) vegetarian.

veg/vedge-out vb

to vegetate, idle or loaf. A predominantly adolescent usage, heard in the 1980s, first recorded almost simultaneously in the USA and Australia.

• 'I think we'll spend next week just vegging out in front of the TV.'

velcro n

a lesbian. The use of the trademark term dates from the late 1980s and is derived from the supposed similarity between the lesbian practice of pressing pubic areas together and Velcro fasteners, consisting of two pieces of rough fabric.

velcro-head n

a negro. A phrase from the 1980s, deriving from the supposed likeness between Velcro (a trademark name for a fabric fastening material) and a black person's hair. Like **rag-head** and **towelhead** as applied to Arabs, the term is invariably pejorative.

ventilate vb

to shoot (someone) full of holes. A usage largely confined to crime or western fiction.

ventilate someone's shorts

vb American

to give someone a severe telling-off or dressing-down. A colourful campus phrase of the 1980s invoking the image of a miscreant with backside (and underwear) shredded by a blast of buckshot.

verbal *vb British*

to incriminate a suspect by inventing or embroidering a verbal confession. Before the very recent advent of video- and audio-taped interviews, the transcript of a supposed confession in a police officer's notebook was (and is) often sufficient evidence for a conviction. An item of police jargon also expressed as 'put the verbal in' or 'put the verbals on'.

See also the noun form of **verbal(s)**.

verbal(s) *n British*

'a verbal is an oral statement of admission or incrimination which is invented by the arresting or interviewing officer and attributed to a suspect' (wrote Deputy Assistant Commissioner David Powis in his *Field Manual for Police* published in 1977). A verbal is in other words a lie. The word can also be used in the phrases 'work the verbal' (synonymous with **work the oracle**) or 'put the verbal in', 'put the verbals on', or as a verb, to **verbal**. These are all items of police jargon in current use.

verboten *adj*

forbidden, prohibited. The German term has been used, usually facetiously, in English since World War II as an intensive form of its literal translation.

• *'Talking to his girlfriend is absolutely verboten.'*

vet *n American*

a veteran (soldier). A term best-known in the context of the post-Vietnam war era.

'vette *n American*

a Chevrolet Corvette (the archetypal American sports car).

vibe *n*

ambience, atmosphere, mood, the latest news. A shortening of **vibrations**, popular in the **hippy** era, vibe was applied catholically to anything that was 'in the air' from an intuitive empathy (*'I like it here. There's a really good vibe about the place'*) to an item of hot gossip (*'Hey man, what's the vibe about Mary?'*). The plural **vibes** was a more widespread near-synonym.

vibe on *vb American*

to be sympathetic toward, understand, appreciate. A **hippy** term deriving from the notion of having good vibes about someone.

• *'Some people would say things like, "Oh, that boy's gonna really be great. You don't know how talented that boy is." And the others would say, "Yeah, yeah, yeah, uh-uh, sure." They didn't really vibe on me.'*
(Stevie Wonder, *Musician* magazine, 1984).

vibes *n pl*

feeling, atmosphere, mood. A key term and concept in the **hippy** psychic repertoire, vibes denotes the unseen and unheard but nonetheless experienced **vibrations** linking individuals with each other and with the cosmos. The word originated among jazz devotees and **beatniks** and survives in the post-hippy era in limited and usually facetious usage. (James Taylor was ridiculed by British rock journalists when he claimed that he 'grooved to the vibes' at a 1973 Albert Hall concert.)

• *'Besides, nobody there gave off vibes that heavy. I'd say the*

heaviest vibes on the premises were on the order of $100,000 a week.'
(Drug dealer, *IT* magazine, July 1972).

vibrations *n pl*

invisible emanations or forces, experienced as psychological sensations; feelings, ambience. A word (and notion) in evidence since its use by 19th-century spiritualists, but in very limited currency until it became part of the vocabulary of jazz musicians, **beatniks** and, most significantly, **hippies**. The word was generally shortened to **vibes**.

vicious *adj*

impressive, powerful, exciting. A teenage term of approval, admiration or satisfaction on the lines of the more widespread **bad** and **wicked**.

victim *n*

a combining word enjoying a vogue in the 1980s in such phrases as style victim, fashion victim. The usage evokes the notion of someone helplessly infected or attacked by a pernicious force.

villain *n British*

a criminal. The standard police slang designation of a lawbreaker, villain has been used in this way since the inter-war years.
- *'Labelled a Black Villain.'*
(Title of autobiography of Trevor Hercules, 1989).
- *'He found two villains in possession of stolen goods. They offered him a substantial bribe and he devised a way to get them out of trouble.'*
(Former detective, *Inside the Brotherhood*, Martin Short, 1989).

-ville *suffix*

a termination used in **hip** talk, beat-

nik slang and later teenage usage. It denotes place, situation or state of affairs. **Endsville** (the ultimate in either boredom or pleasure) and 'Dullsville' (boredom only) are typical examples. The French form *ville* (town, from Latin *villa*) was used by early American settlers, like '-city' or '-burg' to create placenames.

vino *n*

wine. This is the Italian and Spanish translation of the English word.

vitamin A *n*

LSD, **acid** or **ecstasy**.

vitamin C *n*

cocaine.

vitamin E *n*

ecstasy.

vitamins *n pl*

capsules or tablets of illicit drugs. The word has been used by drug abusers as a euphemism for various kinds of **upper**, **downer** or **psychedelic** drug.

Vitamin T *n*

marihuana. This rare usage is based on the otherwise archaic use of **tea** as a synonym for cannabis.
- *'Vitamin T, it's good for me.'*
('Making it Natural', Dr. Hook and the Medicine Show, 1974).

vitamin X *n*

ecstasy.

voice *n*

See **throw one's voice**.

vom *vb, n*

(to) vomit. A shortening typically used by teenagers and students.

W

wabblefats n American
an alternative spelling of **wob-blefats**.

wack, wacker n British
a term of address between males in working-class speech of the Liverpool area. The word may be connected with **whack** meaning share or portion (as in 'pay one's whack').
See also **whacker**.

wacko n
See **whacko**.

wacky adj
See **whacky**.

wacky baccy n British
See **whacky baccy**.

wad n
a a bundle of banknotes, a large quantity of money. Wad had been used in this sense all over the English-speaking world since the end of the 19th century. In Britain the word was heard principally in working-class speech before being adopted as a vogue term in 1988 following its use by the alternative comedian Harry Enfield. One of his **Loadsamoney** character's catchphrases was 'wanna see my wad?' shouted before brandishing a roll of notes.
b the male genitals. A vulgarism in both homo- and heterosexual use. (Wad had previously signified semen; a metaphor based on the plugs used in

loading muskets and cannon. That sense of the word survives in such expressions as **jerkwad**.)
c British a bun or (thick) slice of bread.

wadge n British
a variant spelling of **wodge**.

wag vb Australian
to play truant. A variant of the older British form 'hop the wag', in which the wag in question is a shortening of waggon.
● 'And don't you go wagging school this afternoon either – I might be bringing Frank round.'
(Richmond Hill, Australian TV series, 1988).

wag it vb British
to play truant. A modern version of the phrase 'hop the wag', in which the wag is a shortening of waggon. The Australian **wag** and **wag off** are other modern derivations.
● '"All these kids", says Marjorie disapprovingly. "Wagging it, I suppose".'
(David Lodge, Nice Work, 1988).

wag off vb
to bunk off, play truant. This 1980s variant on the old phrases 'hop the wag' and 'on the wag', used by schoolchildren, is heard in Britain and Australia. (The word was defined for viewers in a report on Newsround, a BBC

TV children's programme, in June 1988.) Compare **wag** and **wag it**.

waldo n American

a fool. An American personification, similar to the British **wally**, in use among teenagers and college students.

walk vb

1 to go free. A term popularized by its use in US TV crime dramas and the like.
- *'Just give us the names we want and we'll let you walk.'*

2 to escape, leave, disappear.
- *'And the guy walked. (He walked with twenty million dollars but he walked.)'*
(Serious Money, play by Caryl Churchill, 1987).

walkabout n, adv

See **go walkabout**.

walk on! exclamation American

the US equivalent of the British **stroll on!**

wallah n British

a fellow, person. A well-known Anglo-Indian word, surviving into the modern era. The term, often used as a combining form meaning 'person in charge of' as in the obsolescent 'box-wallah' (a peddler or salesman) and modern coinages like 'office-wallah', is from the Hindi *wala* meaning inhabitant (of) or protector (of).

wallop n

strong alcoholic drink. A light-hearted term inspired by the supposed effect of alcohol (although until recently, the word more often denoted beer than spirits).
- *'A pint of wallop.'*

wallopers n pl British

police officers. A nickname from the 1950s, now obsolete in Britain but occasionally heard in Australia.
- *'Please, please Sid. You'll have the wallopers in here in a minute.'*
(Hancock's Half Hour, British comedy series, October 1060).

wally, wallie n British

1 a pickled gherkin. This old working-class name for a bottled delicacy is still heard in London. It may be a variation of 'olly', a corruption of olives, to which the gherkins were likened by earlier unsophisticated eaters.
- *'Want a gherkin, Doll? . . . Charlie calls them Wallys I call them gherkins.'*
(East Ender, Sunday Times colour supplement, 2 June 1968).

2 a foolish, ridiculous, clumsy and/or unsophisticated person. This word emerged from obscurity into great popularity between 1976 and 1978 and many theories as to its origin have since been advanced. What seems certain is that the word originated in working-class London usage. In the early 1970s it was recorded in two specific senses: used by police officers, particularly members of the CID, it referred to low-ranking supposedly unintelligent uniformed officers; in the terminology of rock groups and their entourages at the same time, wally denoted a gormless or annoying fan or concert-goer. The word began to be used in the school playground and in the media from about 1978 (with a meaning very similar to its almost contemporary American counterpart, **nerd**). The term may derive from the earlier sense of a pickled gherkin (**dill** is a synonym in both senses) or from an obscure dialect origin (the archaic Scottish dialect *waly draigle*, meaning weakling has been proposed). **Punks**, who helped to popularize the expression, cited an eponymous Wally, friend and fan of the Sex Pistols and other coevals; it also seems possible that the usage simply arose because of what was felt to be the inherent comicality of the Christian name.

- 'All the jolly wallies on day-time Radio 1 hate Morrissey's guts. He must be doing something right.' (Independent, 26 February 1988).
- 'The George Formby Appreciation Society in plenary session. Until you have seen this herd of wallies, all long past their sell-by dates and playing their ukeleles in time to a film of their diminutive hero, you haven't lived.' (John Naughton, Observer, 15 January 1989).

3 a cry or chant, heard for example at rock concerts (particularly of the **punk**, post-punk, **hardcore** variety). This phenomenon recalls the street and playground cry 'ollie, ollie, ollie!' heard in London in the 1950s and 1960s and recorded in cockney use as long ago as the 1870s as a shout of recognition or derision.

wallybasher n British

a a person employed by a rock group to remove or intimidate intrusive fans (the latter known as **wallies** before the term became widespread).

b a stupid, clumsy or unfortunate person, **wally**. This usage is probably due to a misunderstanding of the first: both arose in the mid-1970s in the jargon of rock musicians and their entourages.

wallyhumper n British

an assistant or menial in charge of moving equipment and/or dealing with troublesome intruders or customers (**wallies**). A variant form of **wallybasher**, like that term originating in the jargon of itinerant rock groups in the mid-1970s.

wamba, womba n British

money. A vogue word in 1988 and 1989, emerging from London working-class argot into more general usage (to the extent that it was included in the dialogue in a TV advertisement in summer 1989). Wamba like many other obscure or dated synonyms (**rhino**, **moolah**, **spondulicks**, etc.) has come into use in the financially oriented atmosphere of the later 1980s. It is presumably an imitation of exotic 'tribal-sounding' words influenced by the Amerindian 'wampum'.

wang, wanger n

penis. More recent spellings of **whang**, **whanger**; words which emerged around the turn of the century. They probably derive from an echoic British dialect word meaning beat, hit or slap, with a secondary meaning of strike in the figurative sense of impress or surprise. Although a vulgarism, wang is often considered less offensive than **prick** (but probably more offensive than synonyms such as **dong**, **willie**, etc.). Unlike many similar terms, wang is not also used to denote a fool.

wanger, wanga n

1 British a schoolchildren's euphemism for **wanker**. This expression from the late 1980s is apparently sufficiently disguised to allow its use in the presence of adults or even on broadcasts such as the British children's TV series Grange Hill.

2 an alternative spelling of **whanger**.

wank vb British

1 to masturbate. This very widespread vulgarism (with some recent exceptions still taboo in the printed and broadcast media) is, perhaps surprisingly, of obscure origin. It seems to have entered the spoken language in the late 19th century, significantly at a time when the word **whang** was emerging as a vulgar term for penis. Wank (earlier spelled 'whank') is probably derived from the same source; 'whang' as a dialect word first meaning hit, beat or slap. Wank may be simply a variant pronunciation, or a development of the earlier word influenced by 'whack' and 'yank'. Since the 1960s the word has been used of and by women as well as men.

2 to behave in an ostentatious, self-indulgent and/or futile manner. A usage deriving from the interpretation of masturbation as purposeless and/or offensive.

wanker n British
1 a masturbator. For the probable etymology of the word see **wank**.
2 an inconsequential, feeble, self-indulgent or otherwise offensive person. The term of abuse or disapproval (most frequently applied to males) has been in use since the early 20th century, but became extremely common in the 1970s. In the USA the word is known, but its force as a taboo term in Britain is often underestimated by American speakers.

wank off vb British
to masturbate. A longer version of the more widespread term **wank**.

wank stain n British
a tedious, insignificant and/or obnoxious person. This vulgarism seems to have arisen in the 1970s among adolescents; in the 1980s it became a popular term of abuse, particularly among students. The less offensive shortening, **stains**, was a vogue term of the late 1980s.

wannabe n
an aspirant or imitator. A fashionable Americanism of 1986 and 1987 which was quickly adopted in the UK.

The wannabe, typically a teenager or young adult, exhibits an envious or ambitious desire, characterized by phrases such as 'I wannabe like Madonna', 'I wannabe thin', 'I wannabe in the Seychelles', etc.

● '*There are two types of Wannabee. The first kind are the clones – the stagedoor Georges, the Cindy Lauperettes, the Apple scruffs, the Madonna Wannabees (aka Wannabes) – the devoted fans who ape their idols as closely as possible. The other kind are the young urban upstarts with a desperate lust for fame.*'
(*I-D* magazine, November 1987).

● '*The film [School Daze] is set on an all-black campus in the Deep South divided into the politically active "Jigaboos" who want the college to divest itself of South African holdings and the lighter-skinned "Wannabes" (as in "Wanna be white") who are all for partying, parading, pledging to fraternities and raising hell generally.*'
(*Evening Standard*, July 1988).

warby n, adj Australian
(something or someone) filthy, inferior or defective, coarse. This Australianism is a survival of a Scottish dialect term for maggot, archaic in Britain since the 19th century.

warehouse vb British
to hold or attend an **acid house** party.
See **warehousing**.
● '*The philologically inclined will note that in Tony's world the word "warehouse" has turned into a verb. "Yea," says Tony, "I warehouse, you warehouse . . . we was warehoused . . . " Essentially what it means is this: to overwhelmingly swamp with people.*'

(*Evening Standard*, 9 October 1989).

warehousing n British
the practice of arranging or attending **acid house** parties, also known as **orbital raves**; a youth sub-culture phenomenon of 1988 and 1989. The large gatherings in question require meticulous planning, being held in such venues as hangars or warehouses and publicized through semi-underground networks in order to foil police seeking to stop them. (Revellers usually pay to attend.)

warm fuzzies n American
affection, comfort, friendliness, compliments. A light-hearted phrase from the 1970s, adopted by the business community to denote praise applied deliberately as a motivator. The notion is that of something warm, and perhaps furry, to be nuzzled as a reward or consolation.

war-paint n
make-up, female (earlier, theatrical) cosmetics. A humorous usage heard all over the English-speaking world since the mid-19th century.
• 'She's next door putting on her war-paint.'

wart n
an irritating, bumptious or unpleasant person. A term often applied by schoolchildren to younger pupils.

wash n British
crack. Washing refers to the chemical purifying of cocaine (with ether for instance) in order to produce freebase (*see* **freebasing**) or the more potent crack. Wash or the more common **ready-wash** are British slang terms of 1989; **rockwash**, **rock** and **base** are other synonyms.

washing n
the purification or chemical treatment of a drug such as cocaine in order to render it more potent, (thus producing **crack**).

WASP n
a 'white anglo-saxon protestant', a member of the traditionally dominant ethnic group in the US establishment. This was probably the first of many acronyms, first denoting ethnic subgroups (*see* **Jap**), later social sub-cultures (**yuppie** etc.). WASP originated in the 1960s.
• 'That's the thing you gotta understand about WASPs – they love animals. They can't stand people.'
(*Wall Street*, US film, 1987).
• 'When I hear "Yo, cab!" now and turn around to see a WASP debutante hailing a limo, I tell myself that in a polyglot city like New York a lingua franca helps to break down barriers.'
(*Evening Standard*, 22 January 1987).
• 'Brooks Brothers is the natural habitat of the W.A.S.P. The image of the store is synonymous with the white, Anglo-Saxon Protestant male – a virile but wholesome species flourishing in middle America.'
(*Independent*, 12 March 1988).

waste (someone) vb
to kill. A euphemism inspired by 'lay waste'. In the 1950s, US street-gangs used the word to mean defeat, criminals to mean kill. In the Vietnam War era the term first signified devastate and then annihilate and kill.

wasted adj
a exhausted, drained of energy.
b intoxicated by drugs (or occasionally alcohol), **stoned**. This is an exten-

552

sion of the sense of devastate, annihilate (arising in the late 1960s) on the pattern of **wrecked, smashed, blitzed,** etc.

c *American* penniless, broke. A now obsolescent sense of the term, heard in the 1950s.

water sports *n pl*

urination as part of sex play. A euphemism from the repertoire of pornographers and prostitutes.

wave the woodbine (in the Mersey Tunnel) *vb British*

to have sexual intercourse in which the size of the female sex organ dwarfs the male. A jocular vulgarism evoking masculine fears of inadequacy, real or unfounded. A woodbine is a brand of small untipped cigarette particularly popular in the 1950s and 1960s.

Wayne *n British*

an alternative personification to **Kevin**. Wayne and his female counterpart, usually **Sharon**, are embodiments of crassness, bad taste, etc. from the late 1970s and 1980s. The names are thought to epitomize working-class adolescents or young adults and are used derisively by those considering themselves socially superior or more sophisticated.

way-out *adj*

extreme, excessive, exotic, eccentric. A vogue term first among pre-World-War II jazz aficionados, later among **beatniks**. The phrase was picked up by more conventional speakers to refer to unorthodox behaviour and has become a fairly common, if dated expression.

weasel *n*

1 a sly, devious, unprincipled and/or vicious person.

2 *British* **a** a dodge, stratagem or half-truth.

b a tip, reward achieved by trickery.

The weasel is a by-word for deviousness in all English-speaking areas. Historically, even its name embodies this; Old English weosule is related to the Latin virus and originally meant slimy liquid or poison.

weasel *vb British*

a to behave in a devious, sly or underhand way.

b to carry luggage in order to earn or extract a tip.

The second sense is a specific instance of the more prevalent notion of untrustworthiness and unscrupulousness associated with the animal.

weasel words *n*

insincere, devious or unscrupulous talk. This well-established usage probably derives from the weasel's claimed ability to suck the contents from an egg without shattering the shell, hence the notion of evasion.

weather *n*

bad weather, turbulence. A term from the jargon of pilots and air-crews.
● 'We ran into a spot of weather.'

wedding tackle *n British*

the male genitals. A humorous phrase which is an elaboration of the earlier 'tackle', (heard in this context since the 18th century). Wedding tackle is a euphemism which is considered inoffensive enough to be broadcast and printed, as well as used in conversational contexts. It was popular during the 1980s but probably dates from much earlier. (Partridge dates the synonym 'wedding kit' to 1918.)

wedge *n*

money, wealth. In the 18th century wedge specifically referred to silver, which criminals melted down and reconstituted as 'wedges' (ingots or bars). The term has been used throughout the 20th century by working-class speakers including street traders and criminals. Perhaps unconsciously influenced by **wad** and 'edge' the word has enjoyed renewed popularity like most of its synonyms in the money-conscious environment of the 1980s.

● *'I've come into a bit of wedge.'*
(*Budgie*, British TV series, 1971).

wedged *adj British*
financially well-endowed, wealthy or 'flush'. A racy working-class back-formation from **wedge** meaning money. Wedged or 'well-wedged' were adopted in the **yuppie** era by middle-class speakers.

wee, wee-wee *n*
urine, an act of urination. A nursery term in use for the last 90 or so years. The word is an invention probably influenced by **pee**, wet, the word wee meaning small (as opposed to **big jobs**) and the sound of urination.

● *'One Way Out (BBC1) began unpromisingly for all but doting parents, with talk of wee-wees and poo-poos in the Wendy house, before getting down to the adult business of anatomising Bernard, the Glaswegian psycho-sexual incompetent whose ultimate disposal in a refuse sack we deem reasonable.'*
(Howard Jacobson, *Sunday Correspondent*, 17 September 1989).

wee, wee-wee *vb*
to urinate. An inoffensive nursery term, often used facetiously by adults.

weed, the weed *n*
1 marihuana. The plant, *cannabis sativa*, which yields marihuana leaves

grows like a weed in warm dry climates, and somewhat resembles nettles.

2 a also **the weed**, tobacco. In this form the word is often used when referring to the harmful nature of the plant and its derivatives.

● *'Back on the weed again?'*

b a cigarette. A usage popular among American teenagers.

3 *British* a weak, ineffectual person. This usage, beloved of schoolboys in the 1950s and 1960s, is inspired by the visual comparison with a thin etiolated plant.

4 *British* **the weed** a system of extra, unofficial work or a scheme yielding unofficial or illicit income. The sense of the word, used by workers and fairground employees among others is probably now obsolete. It is related to the following verb form.

weed *vb British*
to steal, pilfer or embezzle. A piece of criminal jargon dating from the 19th century. Inspired by the removal of garden weeds, the term usually denotes the gradual and surreptitious removal of small sums or objects.

weedhead *n*
a marihuana smoker. A term which has been unfashionable since the mid-1960s, but which survives, like its synonym **pothead** mainly in teenage parlance.

weedy *adj British*
weak and ineffectual.

weenie *n American*
another spelling of **wienie**.

weenie-wagger *n American*
See **wienie-wagger**.

weensy *adj*
tiny, minuscule. An altered form of

'teeny-weeny', (sometimes heard as 'teensy-weensy'), itself an elaboration of 'tiny'.

weepie n
a maudlin, sentimental film, story, etc.

weight n
1 British one pound of hashish or marihuana. The drug dealers' and users' jargon term since the early 1960s; it is a shortening of 'pound weight'.
- 'He sold them a weight of black.'

2 American narcotics. The word in this context originally had the sense of a necessary or measured amount, but is often generalized to mean heroin or more recently marihuana, cocaine, etc.
- 'I need some weight.'

weirdie, weirdo n
a non-conformist, eccentric, a beatnik or hippy. The terms have been used, typically by disapproving adults, since the end of the 1950s; weirdie was the standard British version ('bearded weirdie' was an elaboration) until about 1966 when the American weirdo became more prevalent. The standard English word 'weird', (from old English wyrd; fate) not only describes the appearance and behaviour of 'deviants' but was a vogue word among beatniks themselves, meaning impressive and acceptable as well as bizarre.

weird out vb American
to behave eccentrically, undergo a disturbing change of mood. An extension of the use of 'weird' in hipster, beatnik, hippy and later teenage parlance originally frequently used in a drug context, the phrase is currently more often referring to unpredictable or temperamental displays by chil-

dren, parents etc. To weird someone out is to disorientate or confuse them.

weisenheimer n American
a know-all, 'wise-guy', wiseacre or wiseass. The word, dating from the first decade of the 20th century, is an elaboration of the standard term 'wise' into a quasi-German or Yiddish surname (on the lines of Oppenheimer, etc.).

welch, welsh vb
to fail to repay a loan or wager or to evade another obligation. Now virtually standard English, this term originated as 19th-century racecourse slang inspired by the archaic belief of the dishonesty or meanness of the inhabitants of Wales.
- 'I knew he'd welch on the deal.'

welcher, welsher n
someone who fails to (re)pay money owed or otherwise evades responsibility or obligations. The words date from the 19th century and are derived like the verb from the notion of the Welsh as financially unscrupulous.

well adv British
very. A vogue usage among adolescents and younger schoolchildren since about 1987, from the slang of the streets (used by black youth and some white working-class adults) of the earlier 1980s. Typical instances of the word as intensifier are 'well good' and 'well hard'.

well-hung adj
having large genitals. A vulgarism applied to males, (only very rarely used of large female breasts), for at least two hundred years.
See also hung.
- 'No male streakers are naff, least of all stupendously well-hung men

who invade the pitch at a Test Match and upset Richie Benaud.' (*The Complete Naff Guide,* Bryson et al., 1983).

wellie, welly *n British*
1 a force, impetus, power. The word often occurs in the phrase **give it some wellie**.
b brute strength, brawn as opposed to brain.
● *'It was just welly, welly, welly. The ball must have been screaming for mercy.'*
(Ron Yates characterizing Wimbledon FC's style, *Independent,* May 1989).
2 a dismissal, the sack, as in get the wellie, the order of the wellie.
3 a condom. A term from the late 1980s using the name of one piece of protective rubberwear for another. Also known as a **willie-wellie**.
4 a **green welly**.
Wellie as a diminutive of wellington (boot) became a household word in the 1970s. It was quickly applied to figurative or metaphorical uses of the word or notion of 'boot', both as a noun and, later, a verb. The first instances of the use of the word have not been definitively identified, although the Scottish comedian Billy Conoolly popularized the term, closely followed by several radio disc-jockeys.

wellie *vb British*
1 to kick out, dismiss, sack.
2 to defeat, bully or attack. These are back-formations from the noun form of the word, heard since the end of the 1970s.

wellie-wanging *n British*
a sport in which competitors vie to throw a wellington boot the furthest. The pastime enjoyed a vogue at village fêtes, fund-raising events, etc. from the end of the 1970s. The 'wanging' com-

ponent probably echoes the sound of the boot rebounding against turf or concrete, or else is influenced by 'fling' and 'wing'.

well-oiled *adj*
drunk. A colloquial synonym for **lubricated**.

welsh *vb British*
an alternative spelling of **welch**.

welsher *n British*
an alternative spelling of **welcher**.

wench *n*
a girl or woman. The archaic or literary term (from Anglo Saxon wencel; child) is used with condescending or offensive overtones in hearty male speech.

Wendy *n British*
a feeble, ineffectual or contemptible person, a **weed, swot** or misfit among schoolchildren. The word is typically applied to schoolboys by their contemporaries in the 1980s. The name is supposed to epitomize 'girlishness' and, like **Tinkerbelle**, probably owes its resonance to a character in *Peter Pan* by J. M. Barrie.

wenwies, wenwe's *n pl*
tedious boasters, self-proclaimed sophisticates or cosmopolitans. This rare term of derision, heard from about 1985, is, like **wannabe**, based on the repeated reference to '*when we . . .* ' (' . . . *were in L.A.*', ' . . . *met Madonna*', etc.).

wet *adj British*
1 a ineffectual, irresolute, feeble or foolish. A characterization common in service and public-school usage since the early 20th century.
b (of a Tory) having liberal views as opposed to being resolutely 'Thatcher-

ite'. The schoolboy term began to be applied in 1980 as a term of disapproval to MPs with reservations about the style and substance of the current cabinet policies.

2 (of a woman) sexually aroused. Also expressed as **damp**.

wet n British

1 a a weak irresolute or foolish person.

• *'Oh Nigel, you're such a wet!'*

b a Tory who is not a wholehearted supporter of the policies of Margaret Thatcher. The word was used by the Prime Minister herself in 1980.

2 the wet Australian the rainy season in North Australia.

wetback n American

an illegal immigrant from Latin America. The term refers specifically to those swimming the Rio Grande, the river which forms the Mexican–US border. It dates from the 1940s.

wet scene n American

a gory killing. An item of police and secret-service jargon of the 1970s.

• *'hellacious wet scene.'*

(Jonathon Kellerman, *Over the Edge*, 1987).

the wet season n Australian

a woman's menstrual period. A supposedly humorous male euphemism.

wet weekend n British

a miserable, depressive or morose person.

whack n

1 British a quantity or portion. The word is imitative of a slapping or smacking (down); here in the sense of dumping or depositing spoils onto a table or other surface.

• *'He insisted on his full whack.'*

2 American a contract killing. A variant of **hit**.

3 heroin. A later variant form of **smack**.

4 American a **whacky** person.

See also **wack**.

whack vb American

to kill. A racier and more recent coinage based on the well established use of **hit** in this sense.

whacked adj British

exhausted. This colloquialism, from the echoic verb meaning to beat, has been in use since the late 19th century.

• *'Gorblimey! You two look whacked! Been burning the yuletide candle at both ends I expect!'*

(*Biff* cartoon, *Guardian*, December 1987).

whacker n

1 a **whacky** person, an irresponsible or eccentric individual.

2 an alternative spelling of **wack** or **wacker**.

whacko, wacko n, adj

(someone who is) crazed, eccentric, insane. This racier version of the colloquial **whacky** has been heard since the mid-1970s.

• *'We got enough to handle without her going whacko on us.'*

whack off vb

to masturbate. A vulgarism heard all over the anglophone world. Like many synonymous terms it employs the notion of striking or slapping.

whacko-the-diddle-o!

exclamation Australian

an expression of joy or triumph. This hearty cry, brought to the attention of a British readership via *The Adventures of Barry McKenzie*, the 1960s cartoon strip by Barry Humphries and

557

Nicholas Garland, may be expressed by the shorter 'whacko!' or the equally colourful 'whacko the chooks!' (a **chook** is a chicken).

whacky, wacky *adj*

crazed, eccentric, insane. This now widespread colloquialism seems to have originated in northern English dialect meaning a fool (either by analogy with 'slap-happy' or as an imitation of 'quacking' speech). The word was particularly popular in the 1980s.

- '*Let's face it, Lady Sylvia is so wacky there are no boundaries of taste.*'

(Amanda Donohoe, *Time Out* magazine, March 1989).

whacky baccy *n*

marihuana. A humorous nickname from **whacky** (eccentric or crazy) and **baccy** (tobacco).

whale *n*

See **play the whale**.

wham-bam-thank-you-ma'am *n*

a catchphrase used to characterize a brusque, cursory sexual act. The expression was heard among American servicemen in World War II (probably adopted from cowboy parlance). Currently the phrase is most often employed disapprovingly by feminists and others to describe a selfish or boorish male attitude to sex.

- '*I was hoping for something interesting or exciting, but it was just wham-bam-thank-you-ma'am.*'

whammers, wammers *n pl*
British

breasts. An adolescent vulgarism heard in the late 1980s.

whammy, the whammie *n*
American

a supernatural power, spirit or curse, responsible for punishment or retribution. A fanciful evocation, adapting the colloquial term 'wham', imitative of a heavy blow. The word is sometimes part of the phrase 'to put the whammy on someone or something'.

- '*Sarge, you got the whammy on me!*'

(*Bilko*, US TV series, 1957).

whang, whanger *n*

penis. These are earlier (and still current) spellings of **wang, wanger**.

whatchamacallit *n*

an unnamed or unnameable object.

whatsit, wotsit, whatsitsname *n*

an unnamed or unnameable object.

wheelie *n*

a manoeuvre in which a vehicle is driven at speed on its back wheel(s) only. The term may apply to bicycles, motorcycles or cars: (in the case of cars the term may apply only to the spinning of the rear wheels).

- '*Stealing and nicking gives you lots of pleasure and money for everything. And it's easy . . . you just get an old lady in your sights and do a 360-degree wheelie on her moustache.*'

(Teenage mugger, *Observer*, 22 May 1988).

- '*Felt raffish, so I did a "wheelie" outside Caz's flat, and my arm is in a sling.*'

(*Observer*, Section 5, 30 April 1989).

wheelman, wheels-man *n*

a getaway driver. A piece of criminal

and police jargon in use in all English-speaking environments.

wheels n

a car or means of transportation.

whiff vb

1 to sniff (cocaine).
2 British to smell bad. A synonym of **niff**.

whiffy adj British

having an unpleasant smell. **Niffy** is a synonym.

● 'It's a bit whiffy in here, isn't it?'

whinge n

a complaint, bout of self-pity.

● 'His "memoirs" are really an extended whinge at how terribly he's been treated by the corporation – seldom offered any work, never appreciated enough, sneered at by pinkoes, and so on.'
(Private Eye magazine, 27 October 1989).

whinge, winge vb

to complain or make excuses, especially in a wheedling tone. A blend of 'whine' and 'cringe' which existed for some time in Australian usage before becoming established in Britain in the second half of the 1970s. The word was originally often found in the phrase 'whingeing pom', describing the perpetually complaining British immigrant.

● 'English people love a good queue, and they love a good disaster; they seem to love a good moan. I think the notion of the "whingeing Pom" is true. But I've become a whinger too, since I've been here.'
(Australian nurse, NOW magazine, March 1988).

whiplash hustler n American

a pedestrian who stages a traffic ac-cident in order to claim insurance damages. These pseudo victims are also known as **fender-benders**. 'The whiplash effect' is medical jargon for a characteristic – and easily fakeable – injury in car crashes, collisions, etc.

whipper-snipper n Australian

a lawn trimmer. A suburban pun on 'whippersnapper' (meaning a diminutive or insignificant person), heard in the 1980s.

whip some skull on (someone) vb American

to perform fellatio. A phrase (using **skull** as a substitute for **head** in a similar context), which was often used as a ribald exclamation by college boys and **hippies** among others in the late 1960s and early 1970s.

the whirling pits n British

a feeling of giddiness and/or nausea, tinged with hallucination, brought on, for instance, by the combination of alcohol and a drug such as hashish. The expression describes a condition characterized by lying on one's back, unable to move, while one's stomach heaves and the room whirls about one's head.

whirly-bird n

a helicopter. A nickname which was fairly widespread in the 1950s and 1960s. (The word was taken as the title of a US TV series of the late 1950s.) **Chopper** and **Huey** are synonyms from the 1960s and 1970s respectively.

whistle n British

a suit (of clothes). From the rhyming-slang phrase 'whistle and flute'. This term dates back to before World War II and has survived into the late 1980s. It was used by London **mods**, for instance, and is now heard among students as well as working-class

Londoners. Since the 1950s the phrase has almost invariably been abbreviated to the one word.

whistle bait n

an attractive girl. A now obsolete phrase from the vocabulary of **teds** and **rockers**, also heard in the USA. **Bait** alone and **jailbait** have also been used in the same way.

white bread n, adj American

(someone) virtuous, well bred, but dull and insipid. A dismissive term, usually applied to straitlaced or ingenuous people, from the **preppie** lexicon. The word is also used in marketing jargon, meaning bland or inoffensive.

white-knuckle adj

terrifying. The phrase is often applied to funfair rides.

● '*I tell you it was a white-knuckle experience.*'

white lady, the white lady n

a cocaine.

b heroin. Often used to denote a spectre in folklore, the phrase is employed here to romanticize or dramatize the white powders or crystals in question.

● '"*I've been through pot, white lady and blue lady (forms of synthetic heroin) and I can't go through this much more,*" says Jean Hobson.'

(Sunday Times, 10 September 1989).

white lightning n

1 raw spirit, illicitly distilled grain alcohol. The phrase evokes the sudden, devastating effects (and perhaps the accompanying visual disturbance) of the substance in question.

2 a generic nickname given to white tablets or **microdots** of LSD in the late 1960s and early 1970s, in the same

fashion as **orange sunshine** or **blue cheer**.

whitener n British

cocaine. A **yuppie** term.

● '*There are guys who blow out, sure, stick too much whitener up their nose.*'

(Serious Money, play by Caryl Churchill, 1987).

white space n

free time. **Yuppie** jargon of the late 1980s inspired by blank spaces in an appointment book, but deriving from the jargon of graphic designers, printers, typographers etc. in which white space refers to areas deliberately left blank in a layout.

● '*I think I have some white space towards the end of the week.*'

white telephone, big white telephone n

the toilet bowl or pedestal. The term occurs in phrases such as 'making a call on the big white telephone', evoking the image of someone being noisily, and usually drunkenly, sick. The phrases probably originated in US campus slang of the early 1970s, which also gave synonyms such as **pray to the porcelain god**. One phrase combining both notions is 'call God on the big white phone'.

white trash n

a poor whites living in the southern states of the USA. A term coined by black speakers in the mid-19th century to refer to their neighbours, either pejoratively or ruefully. The term was also used by whites and survives into the late 20th century; it is often used with connotations of degeneracy and squalor.

b decadent rich or sophisticated individuals, the 'jet set' or their hangers-on and imitators. The phrase has been extended to refer contemptuously to cosmopolitan socialites (often in the phrase 'International White Trash'). **Eurotrash** is a derivative.

- 'She came from South Los Angeles, near Watts, every day and her parents had saved all their lives to buy her in among this rich white trash.'
(Julie Burchill, The Face magazine, March 1984).

whitey n American

a white person. A predictable term used by black speakers to or of individuals and of the white community in general. It is usually, but not invariably, pejorative or condescending. **Pinkie** is a less common Caribbean and British form.

whizz n

See **wizz**.

whoopsy, whoopsie, whopsy, woopsie n British

an act of defecation, excrement. A nursery term sometimes used facetiously among adults, usually in the phrase 'do a whoopsie'.

whop vb

a to hit. An echoic term which is over 200 years old.
b to defeat.

whore n

a prostitute. The word has been used in this sense since about the 12th century; before that time it denoted an adulteress and, earlier still, a sweetheart. The ultimate derivation of whore is the Latin carus; dear or beloved. In Germanic languages this became horr or hora (old Norse) and hore (old English).

- 'Thugs, whores, cabbies, street arabs, gin jockeys — these are by nature conservative folk.'

(Republican Party Reptile, P. J. O'Rourke, 1987).

whorehouse n

a brothel.

- 'Pundits summarize [the history of Manila] as "four hundred years in a convent, fifty years in a whorehouse".'
(Republican Party Reptile, P. J. O'Rourke, 1987).

whoresucker n American

a contemptible person, a parasite or degenerate. A compound term of abuse.

wick n British

penis. This sense of the word combines the candle-wick as phallic image and the London rhyming slang phrase **Hampton Wick** (for **prick**). Hampton Wick is a small community in the southwest London suburbs, familiar to cockneys of the past hundred years as being on their route to the nearby riverside, Hampton Court or Bushy Park. Wick is rarely found alone but rather in the phrases **dip one's wick** or **get on one's wick**.

wicked adj

good, excellent. A US term of approbation adopted by UK teenagers. First in black and streetgang use, the word is now employed by analogy with **bad** but in this sense is probably much older, dating from the turn of the century. By 1989 wicked had become a vogue term even among primary-school children, (sometimes in the emphatic form 'well wicked', meaning extremely good, and may sometimes be spelled **wikkid**).

- 'I know it's a bit sexist, oh alright, misogynistic but the scratching is wicked man, wicked.'
(I-D magazine, November 1987).
- '[Oxford University] aristocrats

561

disguise themselves with lingo like: "It's wicked, guy".'
(Evening Standard, 16 June 1988).
- 'And within minutes, thousands, repeat thousands of cars, people, music, din have descended on some quiet little farmstead. "Wick-ed!" Tasha looks moved.'
(Evening Standard, 9 October 1989).

widdle n British
an act of urination. This middle- and upper-class nursery vulgarism is a blend of **wee** and **piddle**.

widdle vb British
to urinate. A combination of **wee** and **piddle**. This nursery term was given prominence when employed by Prince Philip to describe the actions of an ape during a visit to London Zoo.
- 'Now sneak pictures of Prince William, apparently widdling into a hedge, are published in colour on the front page of the unsavoury Sunday People.'
(Victoria Mather, Evening Standard, 22 November 1989).

wide-on n
a feminine, feminist or jocular female version of **hard-on**.

widget n
a device, small contraption or product. This synonym for, and adaptation of the word 'gadget' has been in use since before World War II in the USA. In Britain it has been widely used since the 1970s to denote a hypothetical otherwise unnamed product in business simulations, calculations, planning etc.

widgie n Australian
a female equivalent/counterpart of a **bodgie** (**teddy boy**). The widgie was a less respectable Australian version of

the **bobby soxer**, characterized by the wearing of hair tied into a ponytail, a long skirt or blue jeans, often accompanied by 'delinquent' behaviour. The name is said to be a diminutive of 'widgeon', as used as a term of endearment.

widow n, adj British
(an) American. A piece of now almost obsolete London rhyming slang from around World War II, playing on Widow Twankey (a character in the pantomime Aladdin); Yankee.
- 'Pipe the widow ginger!'
(Recorded, bookie's runner, London, 1958).

the Widow n British
Veuve Clicquot champagne in the 'society' and **Sloane Ranger** lexicon. (Veuve is the French for widow.) The nickname is sometimes facetiously applied to Veuve du Vernay, a cheaper champagne-style drink.

(the) widows' and orphans' fund n American
money given as bribes. A police euphemism. In Britain the 'policeman's ball' has been employed in a similar euphemistic role.

wienie, weenie, wiener n American
1 a frankfurter type sausage. The word is a contracted form of wienerwurst (Vienna-sausage).
2 penis. A term which is usually derisive, inspired by the small size and flaccidity of the sausage of the same name.
3 an ineffectual, foolish or tedious person. This sense applies particularly to **swots** in the argot of students.

wienie-wagger, weenie-wagger n American

a a male masturbator.
b a male sexual exhibitionist, a **flasher**.

- *'He's just a wienie-wagger . . . that's what the cops call them.'*
  (*Lady Beware*, US film, 1987)

wiggy *adj*

crazy, eccentric, irresponsible. The word, from the **beatnik** lexicon, was often used approvingly as a synonym for **wild**. It derives from the use of wig to mean head or brain and the notion of 'flipping one's lid'. (**Liddy** is a less common synonym.)

wig out *vb*

to go crazy, 'lose one's cool', 'flip one's lid'. A term from the argot of the **beatnik** era, based on wig used as a jocular term for head or brain in pre-World-War II **jive** talk.

wikkid *adj*

an alternative spelling of **wicked** (in its vogue youth sense of admirable).

wild *adj*

exciting, impressive, excellent. This was a vogue term among jazz aficionados, hipsters and beatniks of the 1950s in the USA. It is inspired by the use of wild to mean enthusiastic in the phrase 'wild about something'. The transferred use of wild as a term of approbation mainly survives in adolescent and pre-teenage speech.

wilding *n*

running amok. A black youth vogue term, seemingly first published in the *New York Times* on 22 April 1989.

- *'A beautiful woman jogger viciously gang-raped and left in a coma by a mob of "wilding" youths in New York's Central Park has woken from the dead.'*
  (*People*, 14 May 1989).

wilf *n British*

a fool. A mild term of (usually) jocular or affectionate abuse from London working-class speech. The word, typically heard in a school context, is either based on the supposedly inherent comic nature of the name Wilfred, or on the use of that name for a character in the cartoon strip *The Bash Street Kids* appearing in the *Beano* children's comic since the 1950s.

- *'Come on, don't be such a wilf!'*

William *n British*

the police, a police officer. A personification based on **(the) old Bill** and usually used facetiously or ironically.

willie *n British*

penis. A schoolchildren's word which is used, usually coyly or facetiously by adults. It is a personification like many similar terms (**Peter, John Thomas**, etc.), in this case first recorded in 1905.

- *'"genital cold injury" . . . is described as "Arctic Willy" in the current edition of* The British Medical Journal.'
  (*Independent*, 22 December 1989)
- *'We asked Lenny Henry to write about good and bad comedy; instead, he proved more keen on revealing why Michael Jackson touches his willy, who the real Theophilus P Wildebeeste is, and what Prince needs for a picnic.'*
  (*Time Out* magazine, 26 July 1989).

willie-wellie *n British*

a condom. A humorous expression (**wellie** is a wellington boot), playing on the notion of protective rubberwear.

wiltshire *n British*

impotence. A middle- or upper-class embellishment of 'wilt', heard since the early 1970s.

- '*It was a case of wiltshire, I'm afraid.*'

wimp n

a feeble, weak or timid person. This now well-established term first appeared as a term of derision employed by US high-school and college students in the mid-1970s. Its exact origins are obscure: suggested derivations are from 'whimper'; from a British undergraduate term for a girl (which was however in very limited use and was obsolete by 1930); from the name Wimpy, given to a character in the Popeye cartoons; or from a blend of weak, simple or **simp**, and limp or **gimp**. By the late 1970s the word had spread to adult speech and beyond the USA.

- '*Well, goodnight Ralph. It was nice meeting someone so sensitive, aware and vulnerable. Too bad you're such a wimp.*'
  (*Real Men Don't Eat Quiche*, Bruce Feirstein, 1982).
- '*Lunch? You gotta be kiddin'. Lunch is for wimps.*'
  (*Wall Street*, US film, 1987).
- '*It's official, George Bush is a wimp. He admitted it himself last week – to David Frost, of all people. "We Bushes cry easily," he told the veteran broadcaster.*'
  (*Sunday Times*, 10 September 1989).

wimp-bod n British

a tedious, unfashionable or unsophisticated person. This elaboration of **wimp** was heard in the 1980s particularly in London disco and media society, where it was used to refer disparagingly to those refused entry to exclusive clubs, for instance.
See also **bod**.

wimp out vb

to act in a feeble or cowardly man-

ner. A later coinage based on **wimp**, by analogy with the many phrasal verbs employing 'out' (**freak out**, **weird out**, etc.).

- '*Listen, just pull yourself together; this is no time to wimp out.*'

wimpy, wimpish, wimpo, wimpoid adj

feeble, weak or cowardly. Formed from the noun **wimp**.

windbag n

someone who is garrulous, loquacious or full of empty rhetoric. An old and well-established colloquial expression.

- '*Mr Kinnock appears to be sinking under a barrage of criticism to the effect that he is an ill-educated Welsh windbag carried high by chippy class hatred.*'
  (*Evening Standard*, 25 July 1989).

wind-bonker, wind-wanker n British

the phrases are dismissive nicknames applied to windsurfers by wave surfers and others in the 1980s.

window n

a an opportunity.

b a period available for meetings, appointments or other tasks. This fashionable jargon term of the **yuppie** era derives from the use of window in space engineering to denote a set of parameters in time and space. The term was carried over into data processing and other semi-technical usage.

wind someone up vb British

to provoke, tease, deceive. A London working-class usage which became fashionable at the end of the 1970s in raffish circles. It described the sort of straightfaced manipulation of a victim which discomfits increasingly; the image is probably that of winding up a clockwork toy, or tightening a winch. By the early 1980s the phrase was in widespread colloquial use and was generalized to encompass mockery, deliberate irritation, etc.

- *'It took me a few minutes to realize that she was winding me up.'*

wind-up *n British*

a provocation, teasing or deception. A London working-class back-formation from the verb **wind someone up** which became a fashionable term in the late 1970s, spreading into general colloquial usage around 1979. (An expert at this kind of deliberate irritation is a 'wind-up artist'.)

windy *adj British*

cowardly, nervous, timid, frightened. A colloquialism dating from the turn of the century, becoming common, unsurprisingly, during World War I. This use of the word is probably based on the phrase 'to get the wind up' which itself may refer to intestinal 'wind' as a result of nerves (Eric Partridge's Dictionary cites a ribald marching song which referred ambiguously to 'wind up the trousers' having a disconcerting effect.) The word is now dated, but survives in armed-service and public-school speech.

- *'I could see he was getting windy, so I tried to reassure him.'*

wing it *vb*

1 to improvize, ad lib. Rather than being inspired, as is sometimes thought by the phrase 'on a wing and a prayer', this usage almost certainly comes from a 19th-century theatrical term 'to wing', meaning to learn one's lines at the last moment (while standing in the wings, literally or metaphorically).

2 to leave, go away.

wing-wong *n British*

an object or contraption the name of which is unknown or forgotten. The expression is probably a nursery term, also used among some adults.

winkie, winky *n*

1 British penis. A nursery term which is probably a diminutive of **winkle**.

2 American the backside, buttocks.

winkle *n British*

penis. This nursery term is based on the supposed resemblance between a (peri)winkle (a seafood delicacy traditionally associated with working-class outings) and a child's member.

winkle-pickers *n pl British*

shoes with pointed toes. The term was first applied to male footwear in fashion from 1959 to about 1961. (Winkles, a traditional working-class seafood delicacy, were extracted from their shells by pins or toothpicks.)

winnet *n British*

an alternative word for **dingleberry**.

wino *n*

an alcoholic or habitual drunk. A term particularly applied to vagrants. (In the USA cheap domestic wine is the standard means of intoxication for tramps and poor alcoholics.)

wipe *vb*

1 to kill or destroy. A racier version of the standard phrase wipe out.

2 Australian to snub, ignore or **blank** someone. This usage was prevalent in the 1950s.

wiped out *adj*

1 a exhausted.

b intoxicated by drink or drugs.

2 devastated, ruined, defeated.

These senses of the phrase are all based on the standard meaning of annihilate or massacre.

wipe out vb

a to fall off or be capsized by a wave. A surfer's term.

b to fail, particularly in a decisive and/or spectacular way. The second sense is a transference of the first, which came to prominence during the surfing craze of the early 1960s.

wipe-out n

a failure, particularly a sudden and/ or spectacular one.

wired adj

1 tense, edgy, manic. The word combines the notion of highly strung with that of electrified. It arose among amphetamine (and later cocaine) users in the 1970s, first in American speech. The word was subsequently adopted in the USA in a non-drug context to denote overstimulated or anxious.

● 'Frankie man you're all wired, you're all pumped up – you know you're not thinking straight.'
(Satisfaction, US film, 1988).

2 American well-connected, integrated in a social or information network.

wiseacre n American

a know-all, insolent or smug person. The word is an anglicization of the Dutch wijssegger (literally 'wise-sayer', originally meaning soothsayer).

wiseass vb, n American

(to behave as) a know-all, an irritatingly smug or insolent person. This vulgar version of 'wise-guy' has been heard since the early 20th century. (The word wise has flourished in American speech because of reinforcement from the synonymous Dutch wijs and German weise.)

wisenheimer n American

an alternative spelling of **weisenheimer**.

witchy adj

mysterious, uncanny, fey. This term probably originated in black American speech; it became fairly widespread in the **hippy** era, describing a bewitching or other-worldly quality or atmosphere.

with-it adj

fashionable. A vogue term of the early to mid-1960s which in its sense of stylish or up-to-date is still used by the middle aged in particular, but now sounds dated. It derived from the phrase 'get with it', an essential item of pre-World-War II **jive talk** and postwar **beatnik** parlance. In its sub-sense of 'on the ball' or in touch with events the phrase may be used by speakers of all ages.

● 'The "Galerie 55" . . . has a madly with-it cabaret of saucy "chansons paillardes".'
(About Town magazine, September 1961).

witten n British

an alternative word for **dingleberry**.

witter vb British

to prattle, talk tediously or inconsequentially, fuss. An adapted form of 'twitter' used since World War II and particularly widespread since the 1970s, often in the form 'witter on'.

● 'He went wittering on about his marvellous contribution and how much they all owed him.'
(Recorded, University administrator, London, 1988).

wizz, whizz n British

amphetamine sulphate, **speed**. The term, which dates from the later 1970s, is used by the drug abusers themselves.

wob n British
a piece, chunk, lump. A term in mainly middle-class usage in the 1980s. It is a coinage presumably inspired by **wodge**, 'gob(bet)', 'knob' etc.

wobblefats, wabblefats n American
an obese person. A term of abuse heard mainly among adolescents.

wobbler, wobbly n British
a bout of erratic, neurotic or extreme behaviour. The term usually occurs in the phrase **throw a wobbly/wobbler**. The wobbling in question is probably the unsteadiness or trembling of a disturbed or uncontrolled subject and the usage may have arisen among medical or psychiatric personnel. The word has been widespread since about 1980.

wodge, wadge n British
a lump or slice. The word is a blend of **wad** and **wedge** and has been in use since at least the mid-19th century.

wog n British
1 a foreigner. The word was first used to refer to dark-skinned inhabitants of other countries, and is still usually employed in this sense. First recorded in the late 19th century, the term is derived by some from the initials for 'Westernized Wily Oriental Gentleman', a condescending euphemism supposedly applied to Indians or Arabs working for the British colonial authorities. An equally plausible source is the word 'golliwog' (originally 'golliwogg') denoting a black doll with curly hair; a character invented by the children's writer Bertha Upton in the late Victorian era. The later extension of the term (epitomized in the phrase '*wogs begin at Calais*') encompasses everyone beyond the chauvinist or racist's own homeland. The word is common in Australia and not unknown in the USA.

- '*The only reason I was opposed to them calling me a wog was because I realise that in this country the word is used adversely against dark-skinned people.*'
(Marsha Hunt, Oz magazine, July 1969).
2 the wog Australian another version of **wog gut**.

wog box n British
one of many terms for a **ghettoblaster**. (This is probably the only overtly racist expression, others include **Brixton briefcase, boogie box, rasta box**.)

wog gut n
an upset stomach, diarrhoea, **gyppy tummy**. A World War II armed-services term surviving mainly in Australian usage, also in the form **the wog**.

wolf n
a predatory male. This word has been used since the early 1900s in the USA to denote an aggressive womanizer and in the **gay** and criminal subculture, an aggressive, promiscuous and/or violent male homosexual. Since the 1960s the heterosexual sense has been adopted in other English-speaking areas.

- '*A self confessed wolf, with the morals of a tom-cat.*'
(The judge in the Argyll divorce case, speaking in March 1963).

wolly n British
an alternative spelling of **wally**, sometimes used in the late 1970s before the word became firmly established in colloquial speech.

womba n British

an alternative spelling of **wamba**.

womble n British

a foolish, clumsy or unfortunate person. Since the appearance of the books and television puppets of the same name in the early 1970s, the word has been appropriated, particularly by schoolchildren, to refer to someone considered feeble, contemptible or a misfit. **Gonk** and **muppet**, both names of grotesque creatures, have been used with the same connotations.

- 'She hangs around with wombles.' (Recorded, schoolgirl, London, 1986).

wonk n American

a **swot**, in **preppie** and high-school jargon. The word is probably an arbitrary coinage, although it may possibly derive from the British **wanker**.

wonky adj American

excessively studious, tediously conscientious. An Ivy League term of disapproval applied to fellow students (known as **wonks**).

woodentop n British

a uniformed police officer. A term of mild derision used by plain-clothes detectives and disseminated through TV police shows. The Woodentops were a family of puppets featured on British children's television in the 1950s. There is also an obvious parallel with 'woodenhead' meaning fool.

- 'You'd better get your uniform cleaned – you'll be down among the woodentops next week.' (Rockcliffe's Babies, British TV police series, 1989).

woodie n American

a an American estate car or station wagon. Wooden exterior trim was a feature of the models manufactured in the 1930s, 40s and 50s.

b any vehicle used by a surfer for transporting people and boards to the beach. Old or customized estate cars were originally favoured for this purpose.

- 'I've got a 34 wagon, and we call it a woodie/ You know, it's not very cherry, it's an oldie but a goodie/ Well it ain't got a back seat or a rear window/ But it still gets me where I want to go.' ('Surf City' written by Jan Berry and Brian Wilson, recorded by Jan and Dean, 1963).

woof, woofter n British

variant forms of **poof** and **poofter** heard since the mid-1970s.

woof (one's custard) vb

to vomit. The woof is echoic, (in colloquial usage it may also describe 'wolfing down' food).

Woolies n British

the nickname for Woolworths (the chain store).

Woolloomooloo Yank n Australian

an Australian who imitates American speech and/or manners, in order to impress or to sell something, etc. This term of contempt applied to hucksters is noted by Barry Humphries the Melbourne satirist in A Nice Nights Entertainment (1981). The term dates from the 1940s and Eric Partridge also records Woolloomooloo Frenchman. (Woolloomooloo is located on the outskirts of Sydney.)

woopsie n British

an alternative spelling of **whoopsy**.

wooz, wooze n American
  alternative forms of the more common **wuss**.

wop n
  an Italian. This derogatory term originating in the USA is now common in all English speaking areas. The word was first applied to young dandified ne'er-do-wells, thugs or pimps in New York's Little Italy in the first decade of the century. It derives from the Sicilian dialect *guappo*, itself from Spanish *guapo*; handsome.

  ● '"At our last New Year's Eve party, we had 65 wops, and five Brits", says Maro. "They behaved atrociously, all huddled up in a corner".'
  (Maro Gorky, *Harper's and Queen* magazine, November 1989).

word n, adj American
  a virtually meaningless interjection, used in black street-speech and subsequently by teenage imitators to indicate agreement, affirmation, approval or solidarity. The usage enjoyed a vogue, particularly in New York, in the early 1980s. Word is used arbitrarily in conversation as an affectation; it recalls expressions such as 'the good word', 'I give you my word' and 'the word on the street', but in this punctuating role it is borrowed from rap music, where it is a substitute lyric when no rhyming word can be found.

  ● 'Enjoying wide usage this winter is my favourite word "Word," which formerly had the sense of "listen" (as in "Word up, man, you be illin'").'
  (Charles Maclean, *Evening Standard*, 22 January 1987).

word up vb American
  to speak out, tell the truth, say something meaningful. A street slang expression in the early 1980s, originating in black speech and used as an interjection like **word**.

working girl n
  a prostitute. A euphemism in use among prostitutes themselves as well as police, **punters**, etc.

  ● 'I'm useful for introducing girls to the stars as well. I know most of the working girls in Sheffield, because I work part-time as a bouncer in a massage parlour.'
  (Rockstars' minder, *Guardian*, 12 December 1987).

work out vb American
  to be tough, redoubtable, intimidating. This adaptation of the notion of strenuous physical exercise is used in the phrases 'he works out!' or (more often) 'she works out!' as an expression of awe.

works n
  a hypodermic syringe, in the language of **junkies**. The term may also apply to the other paraphenalia of drug-taking but usually specifies the means of injection.

work the oracle vb British
  to invent an oral statement of guilt on the part of a suspect. A term from police jargon (synonymous with **verbal**).

  ● 'I wondered if his return was a consequence of his reluctance to verbal, to "work the oracle" as it is sometimes called . . . .'
  (*Inside the British Police*, Simon Holdaway, 1983).

the worst n
  1 something considered contemptible, pitiful, miserable, inferior. A straightforward application of the standard word in use among American teenagers and others.

  ● 'God, that movie – it's the worst!'

2 something excellent, admirable, superlative. This sense of the word is by analogy with **bad**, in its black street and youth culture sense of good. The worst was used in this sense by adolescents at least in the 1980s.

wotsit n
an alternative spelling of **whatsit**.

wowser, wowzer n Australian
a spoilsport, puritan or 'wet blanket.' A word which has been recorded in American usage, but not in Britain; wowser originated in the late 19th century and is of uncertain origin. Most suggested etymologies refer to 'wow' as a roar or bark of disapproval or exclamation of shocked surprise.

wrap n
a portion of **crack**. Measured amounts of the drug are wrapped in paper or tinfoil for sale to consumers. This term was in use in Britain in 1989.

wrecked adj
intoxicated by drink or drugs. A coinage which parallels such usages as **smashed, bombed, blitzed, destroyed**, etc.

wrinklie, wrinkly n, adj
(an) old (person). A popular term among adolescents since around 1980, synonyms are **dusty, crumbly** and **crinkly**. The word is often used of (middle-aged and elderly) parents.

write one's name on the lawn vb
to urinate (outdoors). The term is used by males, among whom 'writing one's name in the snow' in a similar way is an actual practice and the subject of several ribald stories.

writer n
a doctor who is prepared to write prescriptions for restricted drugs in exchange for money or favours. A term from the lexicon of drug users.

wrongo n American
the equivalent of the British **wrong'un**. A fairly rare term.

wrong 'un n British
1 a criminal, ne'er-do-well or other undesirable character.
2 something to be avoided, a nuisance. The term has been a common working-class colloquialism since the later 19th century.
● *'They're petrified that their journey to the western fringes of the Greater London area may result in what they [cab drivers] call a "wrong un" – a job, say, to Hillingdon, which takes them only a few miles.'*
(*Observer, Section 5, 9 April 1989*).

wuss n American
1 a weak, feeble person, and by extension a dupe. A word used by college students and young people from the 1960s and probably inspired by 'puss', 'pussy' or 'pussy-wussy', used as a term of endearment to a kitten.
● *'I'm such a wuss!'*
(Richard Dreyfuss, *The Statement*, US film, 1987).
2 in Swansea and other parts of Wales, the word wuss is commonly heard as a synonym for mate or buddy. This is a shortening and anglicization of the Welsh *gwas* meaning servant.
● *'Hiya wuss. How's it going?'*

wussy n American
a variation of (and probably the origin of) the more common **wuss**.
● *'Come on, toxic waste won't kill you. Don't be such a wussy.'*
(*Armed and Dangerous*, US film, 1986).

570

X

X *n*

1 a kiss. A teenagers' term, from the use of the letter x to symbolize a kiss at the end of a letter. The word is used in phrases such as 'give us an x' or, as an affectionate exclamation, 'x, x, x!'.

2 the drug **ecstasy**.

x-out *vb*

a cross out, cancel.

b kill, eliminate, **rub out**.

(The phrase is pronounced 'ecks-out'.)

x-rated *adj*

a salacious, taboo, extremely daring or pornographic. Often used nowadays with at least a degree of irony, the expression is an extension of the categorization applied to films deemed suitable only for those over 18.

● *'We had this real x-rated date!'*

b terrifying, horrifying, dreadful. A second sense inspired by the term's application to horror films.

● *'She's got this x-rated boyfriend.'*

xtc *n*

an alternative spelling of **ecstasy** (the amphetamine-based disinhibiting drug), in vogue in the late 1980s.

Y

Y, the Y *n American*
a the Y.M.C.A. (Young Men's Christian Association) hostel.
b YMCA, representing the male **gay** community. An ironic code (or **kode**) term originating in the American homosexual lexicon of the early 1970s. The implication is of a hearty, healthy association of young men.

yaas *exclamation*
See **yass**.

yack *vb, n*
an alternative spelling of **yak**.

yacka, yacker *n*
See **yakka**.

yackers *n British*
money. A variation on **ackers**, in mainly working-class usage.

yah, yaah *n British*
an ex-public school young person, a **hooray**. The term derives from the class's characteristic drawling of the word 'yes'.
('OK, yah' was a catchphrase featured in the Steve Wright radio show and elsewhere in the mid-1980s.)

yahoo *n*
a lout, oaf. The word, imitating a wild shout, was used by Jonathan Swift in *Gulliver's Travels* as the name of a race of brutish humans. The modern usage varies slightly in the English-speaking countries. In Britain the word often denotes a boisterous, inconsiderate youth, and is used of **hoorays**, students, etc.; in Australia the word generally equates with **yob**, while in the USA it may mean a stupid and/or coarse person.

yak, yack *n*
1 incessant talk, idle chatter. The word imitates the sound of monotonous, grating and/or inane speech. Nowadays variants of the verb form such as **yak away** or **yak on** are often preferred.
● *'How much longer are you going to be yakking into that damn phone? We're late.'*
(Recorded, middle-class woman, Bristol, 1989).
2 a laugh, joke or instance of humour. **Yok** is an alternative form, favoured in fashionable journalism.

yakka, yacka, yacker *n Australian*
work. The word is a native Aboriginal proper name.

yakkety-yak *vb, n*
an elaborated form of **yak** heard especially in the USA and enshrined in the pop song of the same name (written by Jerry Leiber and Mike Stoller and a worldwide hit for the Coasters in the late 1950s). The term often denotes gossip as well as chatter or talk.

yammer vb

a to wail, complain or jabber fearfully.

b to talk or shout insistently.

Yammer is probably a modern descendant of an Anglo-Saxon verb meaning to murmur or lament. Its use is reinforced by the influence of words like yell and stammer and, in the USA, by the similarity to the German and Dutch jammeren, which means whine or lament and derives from the same Old Germanic root as the English cognate.

yang n American

penis. This term may be an alteration of the more established **whang**, influenced by the verb to yank; or is perhaps a shortened form of the post-1970s expression **yinyang** (itself possibly containing the Chinese yang, meaning masculine principle).

- 'Hanging around toilets waiting for some poor guy to reach for a cop's yang by mistake.'
  (Elmore Leonard, The Switch, 1978).

yangyang n American

a variant form of **yinyang**.

yank, yankee n

an American, a native or inhabitant of the USA. Yankee is the older form of the word and seems to be connected with the early Dutch settlers in Connecticut and the rest of New England. It may be a familiar form (Jan-Kees) of the common forenames Jan and Cornelius, a diminutive Janke ('Johnny'), or an invented epithet Jan Kaas ('John Cheese'), all applied to Dutchmen in general. Other suggestions are that it is from a nickname given to English-speaking pirates and traders by the Dutch, or a deformation of the word 'English' by Amerindian speakers. It may possibly be connected with yon-

ker, Dutch for young (noble-)man. In the USA Yankee is used as an epithet by which old-school southerners damn northerners and also as a straightforward designation of an inhabitant of the northeastern states.

yank (off) v

(of a man) to masturbate. A fairly rare, but geographically widespread term.

yank (someone around/someone's chain) vb American

to mislead, deceive, harass or irritate. The image on which the expression is based is that of a chained or leashed animal or prisoner being thoughtlessly or maliciously jerked about or led in different directions. (Phrases commencing with **jerk** are used in the same way.)

yanking n British

consorting with American service personnel. The word was specifically used to describe British women fraternizing with Americans stationed in Britain during and since World War II.

yank someone's crank/weenie/zucchini vb American

to mock, mislead or irritate. These expressions are all vulgarizations of 'pull one's leg'.

yap vb

to talk incessantly and/or inanely. An echoic term also used to depict the persistent high-pitched barking of small dogs.

yap n

1 a talk, idle chatter.
b mouth.
This echoic term is often heard in the form of the working-class 'shut your yap!'.

2 *American* a country bumpkin. This sense of the word is from an archaic British rural dialect term for simpleton.

yard, the Yard n

1 penis. Said to be archaic by most authorities, but still revived from time to time by those in search of a robust or rustic-sounding euphemism.
2 *British* **the Yard** Scotland Yard, the headquarters of the London Metropolitan Police.
3 *American* one thousand. Also one hundred (dollars).
4 Jamaica. A nickname used by the local inhabitants, probably deriving from the notion of 'my own backyard'.

yardbird n American

a a military recruit or other person assigned to menial outdoor duties.
b a convict, prisoner.
c a hobo frequenting railyards.

yardie n Jamaican

a a member of a secret Jamaican crime-syndicate or gang, said to operate in Britain and the USA in the late 1980s.
b a person from Jamaica or the Caribbean. In Jamaica itself the term has had this more generalized meaning, it comes from the use of **yard** to denote Jamaica or home (probably from 'my own backyard').

yard (on) vb American

to cheat, be unfaithful to (one's spouse). A black American slang term, deriving from the notion of adulterous trespassing in the back yard; compare **backdoor man**.

yarra adj Australian

crazy, mad. There is a psychiatric hospital at Yarra Bend in the state of Victoria.

yass, yaas exclamation

an exclamation of derision, defiance or provocation in black Caribbean English. It is a conflation of '(up) your **ass**'. The expression was briefly adopted by some black Americans and white British speakers in the early 1970s. (The Rolling Stones' use of the term ya-yas in the title of their 1970 live album, *Get yer Ya-Yas out* was a misreading of this expression.)

yatter, yatter on vb

to talk incessantly, frivolously or inanely. This colloquialism is a blend of **yap**, **yak**, chatter and natter.

yawn n

something extremely boring, dull, uninspiring. A colloquial term, particularly prevalent in middle-class usage. It is either a noun, as in *'the film was a total yawn'* or an interjection as in *'they took us round the exhibition – yawn!'*. A racier alternative is **yawnsville**.

yawn vb, n

(to) vomit. Particularly popular in Australia, where it is often embellished as **technicolour yawn**, the usage also exists in Britain and the USA.

yawnsville n

a boring thing, person or situation. An American teenage expression adopted in Britain and Australia. It uses the common slang suffix **-ville** to denote place, situation or state of affairs.

year n American

one dollar. A teenage and **preppie** expression. The connection between the term and its more conventional meaning is obscure.

yecch *exclamation*
the usual American version of **yuk**.

yecchy *adj American*
a version of **yukky**.

yegg *n*
a safe-cracker or burglar. The word is of unknown origin, but is probably derived either from an archaic dialect verb or from the name of a famous thief. Yegg, but not its obsolete alternative form 'eggman' was introduced to Britain from the USA around the time of World War II, but is rarely heard.

yell *n British*
1 a a good joke or source of hilarity.
● *'That's a yell!'*
b a riotous party or good time.
● *'We had a real yell last night.'*
Both usages were heard among young people from the late 1970s. The first is also in use in upper-class and theatrical milieux.
2 an instance of vomiting.
● *'He's up in the bathroom having a yell.'*

yellow *n*
1 oriental women considered as sex partners; a more vulgar version of **yellow satin**.
● *'A bit of yellow/piece of yellow.'*
2 American LSD (lysergic acid diethylamide), the hallucinogenic drug. This ephemeral name referred to yellow-coloured home-made pills in which the drug was commonly sold in the 1960s.
● *'We scored some good yellow.'*

yellow *adj*
cowardly, afraid. This now common term is of obscure origin. It is an Americanism of the late 19th century which was quickly adopted into British and Australian English. (In English slang of the 18th and early 19th centuries, yel-

low meant jealous and/or deceitful.) Some authorities derive the modern sense from the activities of the sensationalist 'yellow press'; other suggestions include a racial slur on the supposedly docile Chinese population of the Western US or reference to a yellow-bellied submissive reptile or animal, but it seems more likely that it is an extension of the earlier pejorative British senses.

yellow-belly *n*
a coward. This phrase, learned by modern schoolchildren from the language of Western movies, was probably coined after the turn of the century. The use of **yellow** to denote cowardice is a 19th-century development.

yellow-jackets *n pl American*
barbiturate pills, specifically (in the USA) Nembutal (also known as **yellows**). Yellow-jacket is a name given to various types of wasp in the USA.

yellows *n pl*
barbiturate pills, specifically (in the USA) Nembutal. A drug abuser's nickname.

yellow satin, yellow silk, yellow velvet *n*
an oriental woman or women considered as a sexual partner. These quasi-romantic but offensive descriptions (probably influenced by **black velvet**), are typically used by predatory males such as those visiting Bangkok, Bali, Manila, etc., in search of sex.

yen shee *n*
opium. A term from the vocabulary of drug users in the 1950s and 1960s which is now rare. It derives from the Cantonese *yan* or Mandarin *yen*, meaning smoke and hence opium. Yen *shi* literally means opium user or addict.

575

yen sleep n

a waking trance state brought about by the smoking of opium, or, by extension, a drowsy, restless sleep resulting from opium or heroin withdrawal. An expression from the 1950s jargon of drug abusers. The Chinese word yen, meaning smoke or opium, is also the source of the English word for a yearning.

yenta, yentl n

a shrewish woman, gossip or crone. The word is a middle-European Jewish woman's name or title (probably related to forms of the word 'gentile'). The yenta became a comic figure in Jewish folklore, particularly in the American Yiddish theatre before World War II.

yeti n British

a primitive, repellent or stupid person. A term from the repertoire of schoolboys, army recruits, etc., since the 1970s. The word can be used both with facetious affection (e.g. as a nickname) or to express strong contempt.

yid n

1 a Jew. The word is the Yiddish term for a Yiddish-speaking Jew (Yiddish being a Germanic dialect influenced by Hebrew). When used in English the word is invariably racist and derogatory.

2 British a supporter of Tottenham Hotspurs ('Spurs') football team. Ever since the fictional racist TV character Alf Garnett, in his capacity as a West Ham supporter, characterized the average Spurs crowd/board, etc. as 'a bunch of Yids', the team/crowd, etc. have been taunted with the name and have adopted it as a badge of pride, replying with cries of 'Yiddo, Yiddo' when challenged.

● 'West Ham kill yids.'
(Graffito, Raynes Park, London, 1989).

yike n Australian

a brawl or violent quarrel.

yinyang, ying-yang n
American

1 a the anus.

b (a) sex organ(s).

Yang and w(h)ang are both common expressions for penis. Yinyang may be an embellished version of these; it may be a genuine nonsense nursery word for any unnameable thing or part (it was used in a pseudo-Chinese music-hall chorus in the earlier years of the century) or, alternatively, an adult imitation thereof influenced by 'yang' and 'yin' describing the Chinese masculine and feminine principles respectively (given currency in the early 1970s via the I Ching and subsequently in therapy and sex manuals).

2 a fool, dupe, inept person, yoyo. This use of the phrase probably postdates its other sense of anus or genital(s), by analogy with most other words of similar meaning.

● 'Well, if it's a yinyang you want, you've got three much better guys for this job.'
(Vice Versa, US film, 1988).

yippy, yippie n

a hippy activist, a member of the so-called 'Youth International Party' founded by Abbie Hoffman and Jerry Rubin in 1968, the date of the Chicago Democratic Convention where they put forward a pig as a presidential candidate. This short-lived movement was a loose coalition of radicals, anarchists, libertarians and left-wingers concerned with 'situationist' and confrontational political methods. The term was sometimes applied to other politically involved hippies and was one of the sources (a heavily ironical one) of the later word yuppie.

● 'Yippy politics, being made up as it goes along, are incomprehensible.'

(*Oz* magazine, 1970).

yob, yobbo n British

a thug, lout, brutish youth. This is one of the only pieces of **backslang** to enter the popular lexicon; it was heard occasionally in working-class and underworld milieux from the 19th century until the early 1960s, when it became a vogue word and was extensively used in the newly-liberalized entertainment media. Yobbishness, yobbery and even yobbocracy are more recent derivations, often used to refer to brutal behaviour in the social and political context as well as in connection with juvenile delinquency and hooliganism.

- 'The London International Financial Futures Exchange, terrible place, full of the most frightful yobs.'
  (*Serious Money*, play by Caryl Churchill, 1987).
- 'The Singhs are being threatened by a gang of racist yobs.'
  (*The Sunday Times*, 26 July 1987).

yock n

an alternative spelling of yok.

yodel vb, n

(to) vomit. An expression used particularly by teenagers and college students.

yodel in the canyon/valley vb

to perform cunnilingus. The first is a jocular expression originating with American college students in the 1960s and now heard elsewhere. The second version is Australian and British.

Compare **yodel**.

yok, yock n

a laugh, chortle or instance of humour. A racier version of **yak** or **yuk**,

popular for instance with rock-music journalists.

- 'There's lots of yoks in this new movie.'

yomp vb British

to tramp across rough country wearing or carrying heavy equipment. This item of arcane military slang became known to the general public at the time of the war between Britain and Argentina over the Falkland Islands in 1981. The word is now used by non-military hikers and others, more or less as a synonym for 'trek'. It is either an invented blend, influenced by words like tramp, hump, stomp and jump, or an imitation of the sound of boots slamming into muddy ground.

yoni n

the vagina. This Sanskrit word (meaning originally 'abode' or 'womb' and later the female equivalent of a religious phallic symbol), is sometimes used jocularly or by writers on sexual matters in place of a taboo or clinical-sounding alternative. It has been familiar to Western readers since the publication of the *Kama Sutra* and other Hindu texts in the early 1960s.

yonks n British

a very long time, ages. This now popular word began to be heard in the early 1960s, mainly in middle-class usage. Its exact etymology is obscure; it may be a children's deformation of 'years' or alteration of 'donkey's years'.

- 'God, I haven't seen her for yonks.'

Yorkshire n British

a a term of address to a person from that county, occasionally extended to an all-purpose term of address by vagrants, street traders etc.

b a quality of avarice and/or bumptiousness originally conceived of as typical of inhabitants of Yorkshire.

The usage has existed since the 17th century.

you-and-me n British

tea (the drink or the meal). A surviving example of London rhyming slang. You-and-me is more commonly used to refer to the meal in contrast to **Rosie Lee** for the drink. 'Glory-be' is a less well-known variant.

Compare **me 'n' you**.

you-know-what n

sexual 'misbehaviour'. A coy euphemism also used for other supposedly indelicate things, such as the lavatory, parts of the body, etc.

youngblood n American

a black youth. The term, inspired by its literary use referring to Amerindian braves, is used particularly of a junior member of a street gang. In the late 1980s the word was often shortened to **blood** (which also derives from 'blood brother').

young fogey/fogy n British

a youngish person of self-consciously traditional attitudes, manners and aesthetic ideals. Young fogey, by humorous analogy with the colloquial 'old fogey', characterizes another social sub-group of the 1980s. Personified by the fastidious and conservative novelist and critic, A. N. Wilson, these mainly male members of (or aspirers to) the upper-middle-class re-create in their lifestyle and outlook the more refined pre-1960 establishment values ([high] Anglicanism, literary dabbling, a liking for traditional cooking, clothing, etc.).

- 'These days a "party" is often a sedate à deux affair at the latest Young Fogy night-spot.'
(The Sunday Times, Men's Fashion Extra, October 1989).

your father's mustache!

exclamation American

a comical cry of contempt or defiance in imitation of the colourful imprecations in use in Latin and Arab cultures.

youth n Jamaican

a specialized usage of the standard English term, youth means young hero, young gangster or, still in the singular form, young people in general. It is often pronounced 'yoot'.

- 'There's nothin' round here for the youth. No wonder they out on the street looking for trouble.'
(Recorded, Jamaican woman, London, 1988).

yoyo n

a silly, eccentric or frivolous person. This use of the word, which may be said affectionately of a dizzy nonconformist or contemptuously with the straightforward meaning of fool, originally referred to someone who vacillated or behaved in an irresolute manner.

yuck

1 n something or someone disgusting.

2 exclamation repelled distaste or disapproval.

3 an alternative spelling of **yuk**.

4 adj an alternative spelling of **yucky**.

(in American English this echoic approximation of retching is often transcribed as **yecch**.)

yucky, yukky, yecchy adj

unpleasant, disgusting, sickly, cloying. A very popular word, particularly since the mid-1970s among children and teenagers, it derives from **yuck** as an exclamation of distaste.

yuk n

an alternative form of **yok** in the sense of laugh.

yumpie n American

a shortlived, alternative version of **yuppie**; it derives from an acronym of 'young upwardly-mobile person'.

yumyum(s) n

anything considered irresistible, such as a potential sexual partner, an illicit drug, or a sum of money. A less-respectable usage of the colloquial and childish, lipsmacking exclamation meaning 'delicious'.

yuppie n

an acronym for 'young urban professional' (later also interpreted as 'young upwardly-mobile professional') with an added -ie ending in imitation of **hippie**, **yippie**, **surfie**, etc. The word was coined sometime between 1978 and 1980 to denote a new social phenomenon which needed to be distinguished from the existing **preppies**. The yuppie, originally identifiable in New York City by a uniform of a business suit worn with running shoes, is an ambitious work-oriented materialist, usually highly paid and extremely receptive to consumer fashions. The term quickly became established all over the English-speaking world, epitomizing the 'aspirational' mood of the 1980s. The word is now often used with derogatory connotations and has given rise to such forms as **yuppify**, yuppification and yuppiegate (a 1986 financial scandal in New York).

- 'Yuppie scum fuck off/Kill a yuppie today.'
  (Graffiti protesting the gentrification of the East End, London, 1988).

yuppify vb

a to renovate and improve (a neighbourhood), specifically to create a residential or work environment which will attract wealthy 'young professionals'. The term was coined by analogy with the earlier 'gentrify'.

- 'Their "bashers" (shacks) will be forcibly removed by police to make way for developers who want to "yuppify" the Charing Cross area.'
  (Observer, 16 August 1987).

b to render less radical or more ambitious and/or materialistic. This sense of the word has been used in the specific context of changes in the image and identity of the Labour Party in the late 1980s.

the Y-word n

the **yuppie** name for yuppies. A humorous, self-deprecating euphemism on the lines of **the f-word** (**fuck**) or 'the S-word' (**son**).

- 'I have to warn you, they're the essence of the Y-word.'
  (Cheers, US TV comedy series, 1988).

Z

za n American

a pizza, in the jargon of **preppies**.

zaftig adj American

a version of **zoftig**.

zap vb

a to overwhelm, destroy, obliterate (literally or figuratively). The term derives from a comic-book sound effect applied to the action of ray-guns in the 1950s and 1960s.

● 'Director Elizabeth Esteve-Coll, zapping the cognoscenti.'

(Observer, 12 February 1989, photo caption referring to a leading figure in the staff dispute at London's Victoria and Albert Museum).

b to target an individual or organization for protests, picketing, situationist political action, etc. A word from the lexicon of radical **gays** in the 1970s.

● 'The Sisters of Perpetual Indulgence . . . used to go out and zap various things dressed as nuns.'

(Gay activist, Out on Tuesday, British TV documentary series, 1989).

zapper n

a TV remote control. This term established itself in some households in the 1980s. It was coined perhaps to convey the power and relish experienced by viewers now able to switch channels or turn off at a touch.

zappy adj

energetic, speedy, dynamic, decisive. A back-formation from **zap**.

zee n American

a Japanese sports car, in the argot of black street-gangs of the late 1980s.

● 'I saw a guy I knew, my age, had a Blazer [a Chevrolet Blazer − 4-wheel drive jeep]. Another guy got a "zee".'

(**Crack** dealer, Independent, 24 July 1989).

zeppelin n

a a large cannabis cigarette (**joint**).
b a large penis.

Both senses are inspired by the size and shape of the original Graf Zeppelin airship. The second sub-sense may be influenced by the use of the slang **joint** for both **reefer** and penis.

zero n

an insignificant individual, dull nonentity.

● 'The guy's just a total zero.'

zero-cool adj American

extremely, impressive, admirable, nonchalant etc. An intensive form of **cool** probably coined by **hipsters** or **beatniks**, now in use among adolescents.

zero out vb American

a to run out of money, to go broke or bankrupt.

● 'But, dad, I'm totally zeroed out.'

(*Maid to Order*, US film, 1987).
b to 'hit rock bottom', reach one's lowest point.
c to fail utterly.

zhlub n American
a version of **slob**.

zilch n
1 a nothing. The word became common in US speech in the later 1960s, spreading to Britain in the 1980s. It is either an invented alteration of 'zero' or from sense **b**.
b a nonentity. Zilsch or Zilch is a Yiddish/German family name borrowed for a comic character featuring in *Ballyhoo* magazine in the USA in the 1930s.
2 the name of a dice game.

zilch vb American
a to defeat (utterly).
b to fail (utterly).
Both usages, found in adolescent speech, are based on the earlier noun form.

zillion n
a very large number; a humorous coinage by analogy with million, billion and 'trillion'. (Squillion is a similar mythical number.)

zillionaire n
an immensely wealthy person. A jocular formation from **zillion**.

zing vb American
to deliver a sudden attack, retort, etc. This use of the word is derived from the colloquial sense of fly, spin, hum or perform zestfully.
● '"Did you hear him zing my lawyer?" Mr. Gotti asked reporters. "Bruce should hit him on the chin".'
(Mafia trial report, The Times, 7 February 1990).

zinger n
something or someone extremely impressive, spectacular, energizing, exciting, etc. The word comes from the use of 'zing' to mean a shrill, high-pitched sound and a lively zestful quality.

zip n
nothing. Originally often used for a score of zero, the sound of zip evokes brusque dismissal. It has become a fashionable term in racy speech, as have synonyms such as **zilch** and **zippo**. Originating in the USA, zip is now heard in the UK, particularly among **yuppies**.

zip it vb
shut up, keep quiet. A shortening of **zip one's lip**.
● 'Zip it, Fred!'
(All of Me, US film, 1984).

zip one's lip vb
to shut up, keep quiet. A racier update of **button one's lip**, typically used as a brusque instruction.

zippersniffer n
a a male homosexual, particularly one considered to be predatory or importunate. The phrase, (originating in the USA, where 'zipper' is used in preference to 'zip'), refers to someone giving attention to the trouser fly of another.
b a 'predatory' or sexually-importunate female.

zippo n
nothing. An embellished form of **zip** in the sense of zero. Zippo, originally an Americanism, is now found elsewhere (albeit less often than **zip**).
● 'I checked and re-checked and got zippo.'
(Hooperman, US TV series, 1986).

zit n

a spot or skin blemish. This Americanism has become well established in British usage in the later 1980s, featuring for instance in a TV commercial for anti-acne cream using the slogan 'blitz those zits!'. The etymology of the word is obscure.

zizz n, vb

(a period of) sleep or rest, nap. A British coinage dating from the 1920s. The word echoes the sound of light snoring or susurration associated with sleep.

zlub n American

a version of **slob**.

zod n American

a dullard, fool, nonentity. A 1980s teenage term of unknown provenance.

zoftig, zophtic, zaftig adj

American

pleasing, luxuriant, voluptuous, succulent. The words are Yiddish forms of **zaftig**; 'juicy' from the German *Saft*, juice. The expression was extended to refer admiringly or lasciviously to women, then to the general sense of pleasurable or satisfactory.

zoid n

a foolish, clumsy or despised person. This teenage expression is an invention probably influenced by such terms as **zomboid** and 'bozoid'. It originated in the USA, but by 1988 was heard in British schools, usually denoting a misfit.

zombie n

1 a dull, vacuous or inert person.
2 a UFO or rogue or unidentified object or signal. Both senses derive from the voodoo walking-dead of Haitian folklore.

zomboid adj

dull, stupid, inert or intoxicated. A coinage from **zombie** with the 'pathological' suffix **-oid**.

● *'I mean any man who more-or-less turns the American genocide squad into a bunch of nodding, scratching hepatitic zomboids can't be all bad.'*
(Hashish dealer quoted in IT magazine, July 1972).

zoned, zoned out adj

stoned, **spaced out**, semi-conscious. Originally a piece of US drug-users' jargon, the word may now be employed in a non-narcotic context to mean worn out.

zone out vb

to lose consciousness or concentration, become intoxicated. A drug users' expression related to the notion of **spaced out** and perhaps influenced by the mythical 'twilight zone'. The term has become generalized for use in more innocuous contexts.

● *'I didn't really notice – I guess I must have been zoning out.'*
(Recorded, American sub-editor, London, 1989).

zonked, zonko adj

intoxicated, overwhelmed, stunned. Zonked began as a term evoking the result of a blow to the head (a 'zonk', similar to **bonk**), applied to the effects of drink or drugs. The word is now in widespread use and may refer to more innocent sensations such as surprise or exhaustion.

● *'I was zonked on enormous quantities of drug cocktails. Once you're on those things it's almost impossible to get off them.'*
(Former patient in a psychiatric hospital referring to his treatment, Time Out, February 1988).

oob, zoobrick, zubrick n

penis. The several forms of the word are all derived from the Arabic slang (in which there are variant forms rendered usually as zob or zip).

zoom n

amphetamine (**speed**) or cocaine. A drug abuser's nickname. The term refers to the exhilarating **rush** experienced by those using these stimulants.

zoot suit n British

a zipped forensic-evidence bag or 'body bag'. A police term recorded in the 1980s. The phrase was first applied to the fashionable suits with exaggerated lapels and shoulders, drape jacket and wide trousers worn by American youths, pimps and jitterbuggers in the 1930s and 1940s.

zophtic adj American

an alternative spelling of **zoftig**.
- 'A pill and a cup of coffee and Im [sic] being already zophtic so who's complaining.'
(Hubert Selby Jr, Requiem for a Dream, 1979).

zowie n

'pep', force, energy. An American teenage usage (which is in fact surprisingly old; first recorded in the 1920s), deriving from exclamations such as 'wowie-zowie!' and the use of 'zow' in cartoons and comics to signify force or speed.

z's n American

sleep. From the use of 'z' to indicate the rasping sound of snores, hence sleep, in cartoons. The word pronounced in the American way, is usually part of a phrase such as 'grab/cop some z's'.

zucchini n American

penis. This Italian term for courgettes is also used throughout North America to refer to the vegetable in its singular form. In addition to its culinary usage, it is also a fairly widespread jocularism for the male member.

zulu n, adj British

a black person. A term of abuse current for instance in the army in the 1980s.